American Folk Music and Musicians Series

SERIES EDITOR: RALPH LEE SMITH
1. *Wasn't That a Time!: Firsthand Accounts of the Folk Music Revival*, edited by Ronald D. Cohen. 1995, paperback edition, 2002.
2. *Appalachian Dulcimer Traditions*, by Ralph Lee Smith. 1997, paperback edition, 2001.

SERIES EDITORS: RALPH LEE SMITH AND RONALD D. COHEN
3. *Ballad of an American: The Autobiography of Earl Robinson*, by Earl Robinson with Eric A. Gordon. 1998.
4. *American Folk Music and Left-Wing Politics, 1927–1957*, by Richard A. Reuss with JoAnne C. Reuss. 2000.
5. *The Hammered Dulcimer: A History*, by Paul M. Gifford. 2001.

SERIES EDITORS: RONALD D. COHEN AND ED KAHN
6. *The Unbroken Circle: Tradition and Innovation in the Music of Ry Cooder and Taj Majal*, by Fred Metting. 2001.
7. *The Formative Dylan: Transmission and Stylistic Influences, 1961–1963*, by Todd Harvey. 2001.

SERIES EDITOR: RONALD D. COHEN
8. *Exploring Roots Music: Twenty Years of the JEMF Quarterly*, edited by Nolan Porterfield. 2004.
9. *Revolutionizing Children's Records: The Young People's Records and Children's Record Guild Series, 1946–1977*, by David Bonner. 2007.
10. *Paul Clayton and the Folksong Revival*, by Bob Coltman. 2008.
11. *A History of Folk Music Festivals in the United States: Feasts of Musical Celebration*, by Ronald D. Cohen. 2008.
12. *Ramblin' Jack Elliott: The Never-Ending Highway*, by Hank Reineke. 2010.

D0982254

RAMBLIN' JACK ELLIOTT

The Never-Ending Highway

HANK REINEKE

American Folk Music and Musicians Series, No. 12

THE SCARECROW PRESS, INC.
Lanham • Toronto • Plymouth, UK
2010

Published by Scarecrow Press, Inc.
A wholly owned subsidiary of The Rowman & Littlefield Publishing Group, Inc.
4501 Forbes Boulevard, Suite 200, Lanham, Maryland 20706
http://www.scarecrowpress.com

Estover Road, Plymouth PL6 7PY, United Kingdom

British Library Cataloguing in Publication Information Available

Library of Congress Cataloging-in-Publication Data

Reineke, Hank, 1961-
  Ramblin' Jack Elliott : the never-ending highway / Hank Reineke.
    p. cm. — (American folk music and musicians series ; No. 12)
  Includes bibliographical references and index.
  ISBN 978-0-8108-7256-1 (pbk. : alk. paper) — ISBN 978-0-8108-7257-8 (ebook)
  1. Elliott, Jack, 1931- 2. Folk singers—United States—Biography I. Title.
  ML420.E435R45 2010
  782.42162'130092—dc22
  [B]
                                                                    2009032879

Printed in the United States of America

"There's More Pretty Girls than One," Jack Elliott sings on his Vanguard album of 1964, and he's absolutely correct in his assessment. With that in mind, I dedicate this book, with all my love, to the four "Pretty Girls" in my life…

To my mother, Janet Reineke, for a lifetime of wisdom and encouragement.

To my daughters, Emily and Sara, my two greatest treasures.

To my wife, Christa, in gratitude for her selfless love and support and kindness, and for being, in every sense of the word, my best friend in this world.

CONTENTS

Series Foreword

ANK REINEKE'S COLORFUL AND DETAILED biography of Jack Elliott is an excellent addition to the "American Folk Music and Musicians" book series. The author has mined a vast array of primary and secondary sources in tracing the career of a musician who rambled around for over half a century, while leaving little personal documentation. This is a fascinating story that makes it clear that the folk music revival was not just limited to the 1960s, but has had a long, continuous, and rich history. Although Jack Elliott is most known through his relationships with Woody Guthrie and Bob Dylan, whose musical lives and contributions are crucial to the story, his musical career has touched upon scores of other musicians, record companies, club and festival organizers, and so many more who have contributed to promoting folk music to a broad, developing audience into the 21st century. Of particular importance is the story of his role in bringing American folk music to an English (and European) audience beginning in the 1950s, part of a transatlantic musical exchange that had important repercussions for the development of popular music into the 1960s and after. This is a fitting companion to the other biographies and studies in the series, while focusing on a most fascinating and influential individual.

Ronald D. Cohen

Acknowledgments

THE SINGER-SONGWRITER STEVE FORBERT once wrote a song titled "It Takes a Whole Lotta Help (To Make It on Your Own)" and, I'm telling you, the man speaks the truth. When I first agreed to take on this assignment, I was hoping I would be able to write a serviceable *professional* biography of Ramblin' Jack Elliott from my collection of tattered LPs, a scrapbook or two of press clippings, and a boxful of old cassette tapes of radio broadcasts. That was the plan, anyway. By the end of the project, I found that steadfast old friends and near strangers had rescued me time and again. Here are some of their names.

To begin, I thank John Wraith and Mike Wyvill of *The Bridge* (P.O. Box 198, Gateshead, Tyne-and-Wear, NE10 8WE, England) for publishing my three-part article "Appearing Now: Son of Jack Elliott" between the winter of 2003 and the summer of 2004. It was the publication of that series that brought the offer to write this book. Special thanks to Tiffany Colannino, archivist at the Woody Guthrie Foundation and Archives (250 W. 57th Street, Suite #1218, New York, NY 10107), for expertly shepherding me through the paper treasures housed there in a series of file cabinets. As a lifelong Woody Guthrie fan, my visit to the Archives, and the opportunity to read through such material as Woody's original *Skybally* manuscript, was reward enough for taking on this project. Thanks to my friend Robert Wylie, Jack Elliott's biggest fan and the excavator of the already legendary *Lost Topic Tapes*, for years of correspondence and unflagging enthusiasm. I am especially happy to say that Robert's marathon length transatlantic telephone calls were always on his dime! Thanks to my friend Ian Woodward who proved time and time again that he is anything but a "Wicked Messenger." Ian selflessly shared information and press cuttings and images and tapes, and I was grateful for his assistance and generosity. As far as I can tell, Ian's encyclopedic knowledge of the folk music artists of American and British Isles is without peer. Cheers!

I sincerely thank all the photographers who generously shared the images found inside (and on the cover) of this book: Michael Crouser, Terry Cryer, Alain Fournier, Gordon McKerracher, and Robert Wylie. I only wish my words could be half as eloquent as their photographs. Thanks to Dee Brown, Bruce Bryant, Roger Sprung, and Israel G. ("Izzy") Young for graciously sharing their memories with me.

Thanks to Aiyana Elliott and Dick Dahl for allowing me to play a small behind-the-scenes role in the making of their wonderful documentary film *The Ballad of Ramblin' Jack*. The night of the film's premiere at the Loews AMC in Times Square was a night I will not soon forget. Though I did not realize it at the time, the rooftop concert that followed the screening would be the last opportunity I would ever have to see such folk music legends as Odetta and Dave Van Ronk, my old guitar teacher, perform. I miss you, Dave. Thanks to Richard Weize for the opportunity to contribute the notes to the Bear Family CD *Jack Elliott—The Lansdowne Sessions*.

Thanks to Beat Bopp, Chris Cooper, David Cox, Jeff Friedman, Jeff Johnson, Joe Kivak, Dan Mahoney, Dave Moore, Michael Paris, Tim Price, Chad Stuempges, Jeff Townsend, Tony Trischka, and Christian Williams for sharing information and materials over the years. Thanks to journalist John May for his kind words in regards to *The Bridge* series and for sending along a copy of his wonderful unedited London interview with Jack Elliott from February 12, 2005. A very special and heartfelt thanks to Mitch Blank for generously sharing information and materials and for taking the time to walk this disgruntled, neophyte author through the process (and travails) of photo licensing.

As a lifelong Luddite, I suppose I will forever be in the debt of those who helped me navigate the perils of the computer age. Thanks to Jim Phillips for his consultation and his expert photographic skills. You came through when I really needed you, Jim! I won't forget it. Thanks to my niece Amanda Phillips for spending nearly five hours scanning and cropping over 50 images for possible use in the book. All this for the promise of a ticket to a Bob Dylan concert (in the rain) and a plate of Chinese food! Thanks to Linda Thiel for graciously taking the time out of her own work to create a digital copy of the book that could be forwarded to the publisher. I really appreciate your kindness. Thanks to Michael Ustupski for uncomplainingly keeping the family's bank of computers up and running and the beer ice cold. Thanks to Marc Allen, Bob Moschella, Caryn Phillips, and Barbara Ustupski for your encouragement and friendship. Special thanks to my wife, Christa, and my mother, Janet Reineke, for their unflinching support and helping out with the indexing.

I am in the debt of all the writers and journalists who have come before and have written about Jack Elliott from 1955 through the present. As a lifelong bibliophile, I actually enjoyed visiting the dusty catacombs of university libraries in an attempt to uncover some long-buried item of information. I would suggest to future Jack Elliott scholars that they begin their research by studying the articles of Bill Yaryan. I am a fan of Bill Yaryan who wrote splendidly about Jack Elliott and Derroll Adams in the November 1965 and December 1967/January 1968 issues of Sing Out! Though Bill's research is more than 40 years old, it still holds up amazingly well, and both of his articles proved to be a helpful springboard in my own research. Randy Sue Coburn's essay "On the Trail of Ramblin' Jack Elliott" (published in the April 1984 issue of Esquire) is essential reading, my absolute favorite study of the musician in his middle years. Steven Stolder, writing for the National Academy of Recording Arts and Sciences, was able to accomplish what few journalists could do, that is, keep the notoriously nonlinear Jack Elliott "on topic." Stolder's interview with Elliott, published in 1996 around the time that Jack walked off with a Grammy for his South Coast album, is, without question, the finest interview of the artist.

Thanks to the staff and copy shop employees of the Library of the Performing Arts at Lincoln Center in New York City and at Rutgers University, New Brunswick, New Jersey, for all your assistance. Thanks to William LeFevre, the reference archivist at the Walther P. Reuther Library of Labor and Urban Affairs, Wayne State University, Detroit, Michigan. Special thanks to Ryan K. Lee, assistant archivist at the Office of University Archives and Records Management, Indiana University–Bloomington, who diligently combed through the papers of the late Richard A. Reuss in search of some particularly rare clippings. I would be remiss if I did not acknowledge Richard Reuss's book A Woody Guthrie Bibliography 1912–1967 as an invaluable tool in my research. Thanks too to Steve Weiss, Southern Folklore Collection, University of North Carolina at Chapel Hill, and Jeff Place, archivist at the Center for Folklife and Cultural Heritage, Smithsonian Institution, Washington, D.C., for your helpful replies.

Thanks to Mary Bearden for her careful copyediting, and to Andrew Yoder for guiding me through the final stages of the book's production.

A very special thanks (and apology) to Renée Camus at Scarecrow Press for her patience in dealing with a first-time author who did not read the submission guidelines all that carefully. Lastly, I send a special thank you to Dr. Ronald D. Cohen for his enthusiasm, skillful editing, and unwavering support for this project. This book would absolutely not have been written had it not been for his encouragement. Thanks, Ron, for making me believe I could do it . . . even when I was not so sure.

Preface

I WAS MADE AWARE OF THE MUSIC OF Woody Guthrie and Ramblin' Jack Elliott through the music of Bob Dylan. I was a second-generation Dylan fan, thirteen when first introduced to Dylan's music through FM radio play of "Tangled Up in Blue" from his seminal *Blood on the Tracks* album. It was a great time to discover Dylan. Excluding one live album and two "best of" collections, his back catalog in 1975 numbered only eleven titles. Among those were *The Freewheelin' Bob Dylan*, *The Times They Are A-Changin'*, *Another Side of Bob Dylan*, *Bringing It All Back Home*, *Highway 61 Revisited*, *Blonde on Blonde*, *John Wesley Harding*, and *Nashville Skyline*—each album a classic. I was hooked. Around the time I was busy catching up on what I had missed, I happened upon a not so gently used, dog-eared paperback of Anthony Scaduto's *Bob Dylan: An Intimate Biography*. I didn't simply read the Scaduto book, I devoured it. It was through Scaduto's study that I was first introduced to Woody, Ramblin' Jack Elliott, Pete Seeger, and Cisco Houston. It seems impossible to me today but, aside from the chorus of "This Land Is Your Land," I'd never heard of any of these songs or any of these people. I was no "red diaper" baby; my beloved grandparents were staunch Republicans who had twice voted for Nixon.

Scaduto made me aware that Dylan hadn't sprung from nothingness. I was particularly curious to hear the music of this Woody Guthrie fellow I had read about. I borrowed a cassette tape of Woody's *Dust Bowl Ballads* from a Jersey City library and, for better or worse—probably worse, but that's another book—my life has never been the same. Woody's lyrics and music, that stark guitar and harmonica accompanying his dusty, plain vocals, was unlike anything I had heard before. I wanted to learn as much as I could about Woody Guthrie, but aside from his novels *Bound for Glory* and the posthumously published *Seeds of Man*, there really wasn't anything out there that could be found easily. As for Guthrie's LPs, no department store in suburban New Jersey (where I purchased all my music at the time) carried that sort of thing, so I violated copyright law and duplicated the library cassette. From what I had read about Woody's socialist sympathies, I was confident he would have been OK with that. Though Woody had passed on when I was all of six years old, Scaduto mentioned that he had left behind a disciple, Ramblin' Jack Elliott, and I was determined to catch a performance if he ever played near my home.

It was sometime in the late 1970s that I first had the opportunity to catch Jack Elliott. He was scheduled to perform at Folk City on West 3rd Street in Greenwich Village, and I traveled into Manhattan with no ticket in hand. After paying six or seven dollars to an attendant at the door, I was led by a waitress through the darkened nightclub and, much to my surprise, situated front and center on a creaky wooden chair. I ordered a two-dollar beer and waited for the show to begin. I did not yet own a Ramblin' Jack album, and had no idea what to expect. I am pretty certain the first photograph I ever saw of Elliott was on that very night: a promotional black and white eight-by-ten glossy on display in the window of the club.

It was showtime. Following a perfunctory introduction, Elliott ambled onto the stage to warm applause. Cradling his trademark Martin D-28 guitar in his arms, Jack sat himself atop a bar stool and near-whispered into the microphone that he was suffering the effects of a cold and was feeling out of sorts. To be honest, my first impression of Jack Elliott was that he was sort of cranky and aloof, the brim of his cowboy hat pushed forward over his eyes, keeping his face in shadow most of the night. I was surprised to hear him announce from the stage that we should not expect much from him this evening, that, at best, we might get a few talking blues as these songs would not stress his vocal cords.

For whatever reason, Elliott rallied. He sang a number of songs in the high and dry, occasionally harsh bark that, I soon learned, was pretty much standard, coarsened this night by his malady. I loved all the songs and stories I heard that evening, but it was Elliott's reverent performance of Guthrie's "Talking Sailor (Talking Merchant Marine)" that stilled the room, cannily transporting all listening to another time and place. It was one of the greatest, if most understated, performances I had ever been privileged to witness, Elliott's matter-of-fact guitar playing and laconic drawl masterfully cool. I was determined to find a Jack Elliott recording of the song.

It would take a couple of years. Trying to find a Ramblin' Jack Elliott LP in the late 1970s was not terribly easy. Only Vanguard's *The Essential Jack Elliott* (1976) and a Fantasy Records reissue (1977) of two albums made for Prestige-International in the early 1960s remained in print, but even these titles were not easy to find outside of a big city. Luckily, I lived just across the Hudson River from Manhattan. "Talking Sailor," to my great disappointment, was not featured on either recording, but both collections brimmed with other wonderful songs and performances, cementing my admiration for his music. I was determined to search out all of his out-of-print albums, which, I soon learned, would be something of a challenge.

It took some 20 odd years to find some of the more elusive titles, particularly those of European and Japanese origin. But it was apparent that as great as many of those record albums were, none were nearly as memorable or sublime as the nightclub gigs I began to attend with as much regularity as geography and finance would allow. The problem with Jack Elliott's recording oeuvre is that there is no definitive recording in his scattered catalog, no touchstone to direct the new converts to, no *Dust Bowl Ballads* or *Highway 61 Revisited*. Some argue that Elliott's best albums were the ones he recorded in the 1950s for Topic Records of London. Others suggest his 1961 album of Guthrie songs for Prestige-International is his one true masterwork. Depending on my mood, I might agree with either assessment, though I am often drawn to the mid-career *Kerouac's Last Dream* (Germany 1981), which masterfully captures Elliott as elder statesman.

There's a general consensus among critics, fans, and colleagues that Elliott's record catalog, for all its charms, is hardly emblematic of his art. To truly appreciate the subtleties of his music, most concede that it is only onstage that Ramblin' Jack manifests greatness—and only then if he happens to be in the mood. Elliott's spiritual brother, Arlo Guthrie, wrote in 1969, "I've heard most of Jack's thirty albums or so and there are none . . . that mean anything real until you have heard him live—not once, but many times. I believe I've heard Jack at his most worst and his unbelievable best." In *The Folk Music Sourcebook*, authors Larry Sandberg and Dick Weissman share Arlo's estimate, arguing, quite convincingly, that no "studio recording . . . can capture the impact of Elliott performing on a good night. He improvises on melodies and twists them around, singing free of commonplace phrase structure and of his own guitar rhythms. Taking great, crazy risks and usually succeeding, he generates a tremendous excitement of which his recordings offer a small glimpse."[1]

Elliott, by his own admission, has not invested all that much energy in the making of records; he prefers the concert stage as it is only there that he gets "instantaneous reaction and paid the same day." He regards most of his records as little more than product and rarely listens to them. "I don't like to bask in reflected glory and the romance of what I did," he told the *Worcester Telegram & Gazette.* "Sometimes, I'll sit down and listen to a record I made. Usually, it's very embarrassing. Most of those have been recorded in studios. I've often wished that I could just record more of my shows."[2]

Elliott's honest self-assessment of his talents as recording artist are shared by several of his producers, most notably guitarist Bruce Langhorne, who ministered *Young Brigham* (1968), Jack's first foray into folk-rock. Langhorne told music writer Richie Unterberger that Elliott was a difficult client, as "he would not do the same song twice anything like the same way." Langhorne suggested the only way to produce an excellent Jack Elliott album was to "give Jack an audience and a mike, and just record and record and record and record and record and record and record," knitting his best performances into a cohesive whole.[3]

Perhaps it is not fair to dwell on his recordings, as the albums make up only a small part of his legacy. But the truth remains that it is only the records that will survive long after Elliott, and the rest of us, are no longer here. The chronology of this book is loosely built around the albums Jack Elliott has recorded between 1954 and 2009. No doubt, one could fill a book with outrageous Ramblin' Jack remembrances by fellow musicians, club owners, and cowboys. I hope to read such a tome someday, but as my interest in Elliott here lies primarily with his music, there is purposefully little gossip or retelling of famously tall tales, real and apocryphal, to be found in this book. For those interested in the more personal aspects of Elliott's affairs, I direct them to screen Aiyana Elliott's award-winning documentary film *The Ballad of Ramblin' Jack* (2000) or to read chapters 3 through 5 of June Shelley's memoir *Even When It Was Bad . . . It Was Good* (2000). Elliott's personal history is testament that the life of a freewheeling, ramblin' man is not without cost. For the record, Elliott has been married five times, the first four of those unions ending in divorce. (Janice Windsor Currie, his fifth wife, passed away in 2001.) Suffice to say, Elliott's legacy will not be that of preeminent family man. Woody Guthrie was, by Elliott's estimation, not only a musical role model. He told the *San Francisco Chronicle* that the composer of "So Long, It's Been Good to Know You" also gave him "several bad habits that caused me to have three divorces in a row. My wives always mentioned Woody Guthrie in the papers as a reason why they would divorce me." He earlier told Joe Ross of *Folk Roots* magazine that he had regrets he had not been a better father: "I let the mother[s] raise our two daughters, just because I don't know much about raising a girl child, and I couldn't make it go with marriage." Ultimately, I didn't feel it necessary to dwell on Elliott's private affairs to tell his story. This is fair, I believe, as evidence suggests that the music that he has made over the years has rarely been informed by the dynamics of his personal relationships. He has written few songs over a half-century of music making, admitting to an audience in Philadelphia that his career has not demonstrated much of an arc: "I started off with cowboy songs and ended up with cowboy songs."[4]

That may be so, but few artists can sing those old cowboy songs better, and the legacy of Woody Guthrie—and a handful of notable others—would have been far less reaching had it not been for Ramblin' Jack Elliott. It is true that his association to the legends of Guthrie and Dylan has been a double-edged sword. His relationship to both artists has helped keep him working for some 50-odd years, but their formidable legacies have obscured his own contribution to the tradition. It is a source of frustration, and those who know him best wish he might still get his full due. Arlo Guthrie has offered that most see Elliott "in the light of a legend or two" and, mistakenly, "assume that that's where he's at." Aiyana Elliott, Jack's filmmaker daughter, sighed that her father "can't do an interview without being asked about Bob and Woody and he's so much more than that." Dennis McNally, the Grateful Dead archivist and author, offered flatly, "It's not fair, but in the end, music historians will record him as an early influence on Dylan or as a sidekick to Woody Guthrie."[5]

McNally's prognostication is probably right. To most music fans, Ramblin' Jack will forever be known as the figure that bridged two American musical and cultural giants. Interestingly, Elliott seems content with that legacy, honored to play a transitive role in the passing of the torch. How Elliot Charles Adnopoz of Brooklyn, a middle-class son of a doctor and teacher with no intention of making music a career, improbably found himself the disciple of one American musical legend and an early mentor to another is but one facet of his story.

Simultaneous with the green-lighting of this book, it was announced in the trades that Jack Elliott had been signed to write an autobiography. This was great news, disappointing to me only in the sense that I had hoped I might get Elliott's assistance on this project. But as I have collected hundreds of published articles and interviews in research, I believe Elliott's voice is well represented here. Though the promised autobiography (originally slated for November 2006 publication) did, in fact, not appear, there have been reports that producer Roy Rogers has been taping Elliott for an oral history project, which should prove fascinating. Perhaps this book might serve as an appendix to Elliott's own memoir, should one appear. My original intent was to establish some sort of corroborative chronology that might help correct much of the misinformation that surrounds Elliott. Through the combing of library archives, listening through countless hours of rare tape, and collecting sentence-length mentions in half-century-old folk and jazz music magazines from England, I hope I have partly achieved this. There is, of course, the danger that I have only added to the misinformation, but I promise you that I have tried my best to sort it all out.

Notes

1. Arlo Guthrie liner notes to *Bull Durham Sacks & Railroad Tracks* (Reprise 6387, 1970); Larry Sandberg and Dick Weissman, *The Folk Music Sourcebook* (New York: Alfred A. Knopf, 1976), 104.

2. Tim Ryan, "Ramblin' through Town: Folk Legend Jack Elliott has a knack for takin' a good story and makin' it his own," *Honolulu Star-Bulletin*, http://star bulletin.com/.../06/features/story1.html (2 March 1997); Paul Jarvey, "Ramblin' Jack Elliott Wanted to be a Cowboy," *Worcester Telegram & Gazette*, 10 October 1993, Sec. Datebook, 9.

3. Richie Unterberger, *Turn! Turn! Turn!: The '60s Folk-Rock Revolution* (San Francisco: Backbeat Books, 2002), 247.

4. James Sullivan, "Ramblin' Jack's Friends Join Him on CD," *San Francisco Chronicle*, 15 March 1998, Datebook, 44; Joe Ross, "Ramblin' with Jack: Joe Ross Talks to an American Legend," *Folk Roots*, January/February 1993, 43; Jack Elliott, Tin Angel, Philadelphia, PA, 15 June 1996.

5. Arlo Guthrie liner notes to *Bull Durham Sacks & Railroad Tracks* (Reprise 6387, 1970); Mike McGonigal, "Film: Aiyana Elliott," *New York Press*, Vol. 13, No. 33, 16–22 August 2000, 36, 38; Paul Liberatore, "Ramblin on: Ramblin' Jack Elliott, a folk legend, turns 75—and has a new album," *Marin Independent Journal*, 3 September 2006.

Me and Billy the Kid   1

O N OCTOBER 9, 1940, THE FIFTEENTH ANNUAL World Championship Rodeo was to commence at Madison Square Garden in New York City. The gathering was the grandest affair of the professional rodeo circuit, the national finals of 105 competitions held throughout the United States since early January. Two hundred and thirty-five cowboys and cowgirls would compete for $45,000 in prize money in an exciting, and dangerous, "series of seven Western sports events." The contestants would be supported by a cast of 167 horses and some "six hundred and fifty-five head of wild-range stock." Everett Colborn, the rodeo's managing director, proudly announced he was bringing to Manhattan the last Texas longhorn steers to be found in the States. The rodeo was scheduled to run for a full nineteen days, with special matinees slated for weekend afternoons and on draft registration day. The Garden would host an exhausting 27 separate performances before the rodeo would end its Manhattan run on Sunday evening, October 27.[1]

Four days before the big event, an 18-car train pulled into Manhattan's Central yards near 40th Street and Eleventh Avenue, bringing in a lively crew of cowboys, cowgirls, livestock, and roustabouts. On October 7, rodeo staffer Emile Avery of Paris, Texas, confirmed to members of the press that Gene Autry, Hollywood's most famous singing cowboy, "would arrive by plane tomorrow afternoon to take a star role in the show." He would be bringing along two of his "wonder horses," including *Lindy Champion*, the gleaming gelding he favored for personal appearances. On the afternoon of October 8, a busload of wranglers and Everett Johnson's Cowboy Band traveled to LaGuardia Field in Queens to greet the plane that had flown Gene Autry to New York. The next day Stanley H. Howe, Mayor Fiorello LaGuardia's executive secretary, officially welcomed the rodeo to New York City. The *New York Times* reported Howe received some "200 colorfully clad cowboys and cowgirls at the downtown City Hall." He greeted nearly everyone assembled, from Gene Autry to the less celebrated Jasbo, the rodeo clown, who "led his mule up the front steps and through the corridors to Mr. Howe's office."[2]

Regardless of the show business trappings, the World Championship Rodeo was the real deal. The finest and toughest cowboys and cowgirls from across the nation had earned their tickets to compete in the national finals. The rodeo featured such contests as steer wrestling, calf roping, bareback riding, bulldogging, trick riding, and bronco busting. It was an exciting sport, but a dangerous one, and in two weeks' time, the beds of nearby Polyclinic Hospital had filled with some 50 casualties of the event, nearly one-quarter of the rodeo's participants.[3]

The promoters also scheduled a series of goodwill performances. The first, a benefit for "ill and crippled youngsters," was held on the grounds of Bellevue Hospital. The afternoon event featured Autry and a demonstration of western rope tricks by three of the sport's best: Vern Goodrich, Chester Byers, and Junior Eskew. The second performance was a benefit at the Garden itself for 17,000 underprivileged children. Every child polled agreed they had been thrilled, equally, by the bone breaking action of the bronco busting contest and the greatly anticipated introduction of Gene Autry and Champion. Most nights the Garden was filled to its capacity of 18,000, with hundreds of others turned away. Those able to score tickets could consider themselves fortunate.[4]

Among those able to manage tickets were Dr. Abraham Adnopoz and his wife Florence (Flossie, as she was casually referred to among family and friends). Dr. and Mrs. Adnopoz had brought their starry-eyed *greenhorn* son, Elliot Adnopoz, for a mere night's entertainment. Elliot, all of nine years of age, was not brought along unwillingly. He was completely fascinated by cowboys and horses, of rodeos and all things western. The floor of the Garden arena was a two-acre sea of dirt, eight inches deep, specially trucked in that week from Long Island. The audiences that filled the Garden each night rose to their feet and stood at rigid attention when Everett Johnson's cowboy ensemble kicked things off with a stirring, western flavored *Star Spangled Banner*, as "a cowboy in a green shirt, astride a white horse, stood in a pool of light, holding a gold-embroidered American flag." Elliot Adnopoz, later to be known as Ramblin' Jack Elliott, had not been a great fan of Gene Autry or western movie serials, but he was certainly familiar with them as Thomas Edison himself had been cranking out these so-called horse operas as early as 1898. But Gene Autry would have been a celebrity figure to any nine-year-old American child. In 1940, the Theater Exhibitors of America voted Autry the industry's fourth biggest box office attraction, losing out only to Hollywood heavyweights Clark Gable, Mickey Rooney, and Spencer Tracy.[5]

Near the end of the program the lights dimmed at the Garden until the entire arena fell dark. Suddenly, without warning, 22 Texan longhorn steers charged onto the midway, chased by a team of cowgirls on horse-back. Though the floor of the arena was completely enveloped in darkness, the audience could chart the course of the charging steers by their translu-cent horns. The steer's longhorns had been covered with a phosphorescent paint that left behind a ghostly trail in their charging wake. The cowgirls were outfitted in hats with six-inch-wide brims trimmed with the same lu-minous paint. Soon the entire floor of the arena swirled in ghostly circles as cowgirls and steers raced by. On cue, the western music of Curly Clements and his Rodeo Rangers began to play. Clements's band, a simple combo consisting of guitar, dog house bass, and accordion, struck up a familiar western melody and the crowd snapped to attention. A white spotlight swung to the far end of the arena where an unusually large paper circle had been erected. As the band played on and the steers charged, Gene Autry and Champion crashed through the circle and into the spotlight.[6]

The audience cheered wildly. Though Elliott wasn't the only nine-year-old enjoying the night out, he was, without doubt, one of few with the prescience to note that the resplendent, glittering Gene Autry appeared awfully well scrubbed in comparison to the genuine cowboys. The rodeo cowboys were bruised and beat up, covered from head to toe in dirt and mud and blood. Their spurs hung loosely from their boots, crudely affixed with rolled tape and baling wire. In contrast, Gene Autry's spurs were polished and ornate. They gleamed in the spotlight, the light ricochet-ing off them like shooting stars. Autry and Champion galloped around the floor of the arena a time or two and, holding the reins in his fisted left hand, acknowledged the applause by waving his cowboy hat with an outstretched right arm. As the applause echoed, Autry made his way to the center of the arena where a ribbon of microphone descended from the ceiling. Autry handed the reins of Champion to a handler, grabbed hold of his Martin D-45 guitar, and, moving his fingers over the resplendent mother-of-pearl inlay of its fingerboard, began to croon his signature song "Back in the Saddle Again." It was the sort of perfectly staged Hollywood entrance that could strip away the stone-canyon facade of even the most hardened city-dweller.[7]

"Gene Autry turned my head around, knocked me for a loop," Elliott later acknowledged. It was at that moment that Jack made the decision he *wasn't* going to follow in his father's footsteps. He wasn't interested in becoming a doctor or a professional of any sort. Nearly fifty-five years following the Madison Square Garden rodeo, Elliott recollected, "My parents brought me to the rodeo when I was little. I never got over it and they always regretted it."[8]

Jack Elliott was born Elliot Charles Adnopoz on August 1, 1931, in the borough of Brooklyn, in the city of New York. It could be argued that *Ramblin'* Jack Elliott was born nearly two decades after *that*, nearer the year 1951. It was actually Jack's alter-ego, Elliot Adnopoz, who had been born that first day of August when a cool wind from the north brought relief to a city suffering from heat and humidity. Elliott's paternal grandparents, Morris and Dora Adnopoz, were Russian émigrés who arrived in the United States around 1890 and settled in Connecticut before bringing the family to Kings County, Brooklyn. They had three children, Isodore, born 1892, Abraham, Elliott's father, born June 3, 1900, and Milton, born 1906. Jack Elliott's parents were wed circa 1930 and were known to all as respectable, educated people. Abraham had studied medicine and by 1924 had completed his medical residency at Long Island College Hospital. Dr. Adnopoz soon found a position on the staff of surgeons at Brooklyn's Cumberland Hospital, a 321-bed facility on Auburn Place and North Portland Avenue. Jack's mother, Florence Adnopoz, born July 25, 1901, was employed as an elementary schoolteacher. The Adnopoz family resided comfortably at 102 Linden Boulevard, between Bedford and Rogers Avenues, where his father maintained an office. Ebbetts Field, the home of the Brooklyn Dodgers, sat less than a mile away, and Jack could hear the fervent roar of the crowd every time Pee Wee Reese or Duke Snider scored a key single. But Elliott was not much of a fan of baseball or the Dodgers. As a youngster growing up in Brooklyn in the 1940s, it was wise to be careful who you admitted this to. This, in essence, was Jack's childhood dilemma. He felt he simply did not belong to Brooklyn, that his being there was the result of some sort of cruel, cosmic accident of which he had no control. He would ride his bicycle through the streets "in search of beautiful scenery," but the only beauty he could find was the sight of the tall ships sailing in and out of the harbor. He once rued, "the stork who brought me was supposed to drop me out west so I could be a cowboy." Instead, it was obvious to Elliott that the "stork got drunk and lost his bearings and dropped me in Brooklyn by mistake." The stork also brought Jack a brother, David, but as the first-born son, it was Jack who was expected to follow in his father's footsteps. But he never seemed to show any interest in the sciences or the study of medicine. In fact, he demonstrated an almost immediate aversion to the profession. "The smell of ether and babies crying was a real turn off," Jack explained.[9]

Some members of Dr. Adnopoz's family had chosen to stay behind at their farm in rural Connecticut. Jack recalled that whenever his father spoke of his own early life growing up on the family farm near Westport, it was "in a very romantic voice, wistful-like." He believed that his father missed the country life but, by most accounts, Dr. Adnopoz was a man of great reserve, and no one was ever quite sure what he was thinking. Two of Jack's uncles had farms in Connecticut, and it was there that he first learned how to groom and feed horses. On occasion, Dr. and Mrs. Adnopoz would discuss the merits of finding a small home in the country as a holiday retreat. Jack recalled he enthusiastically "encouraged" that scenario whenever the subject arose but, disappointingly, the idea was never followed through. The family stayed on in the urban sprawl of Flatbush.[10]

In nearly every way, Jack enjoyed a normal middle-class upbringing. Though space travel was still decades away, there were plenty of children's books on the subject, and he dreamed of outer space, rocket ships, and spacemen. He loved leafing through *National Geographic* magazine and imagined visiting all the exotic, faraway places that he had read about each month. Following his solo flight across the Atlantic Ocean from New York to Paris in May 1927, Charles Lindbergh was christened America's hero. Jack, caught up in the excitement and adventure of the Lindbergh flight, dreamed of flying his own airplane one day. He remembered looking skyward and yelling "at planes to come and land in my backyard," but none ever did.[11]

If there was anything memorable about Jack, it was probably his fascination with cowboys and the American West. It was an obsession that made him little different from a score of other children of elementary school age in the 1930s and 1940s. His interest in cowboy life was partly influenced by Gene Autry. Shortly after attending his first rodeo, he admitted he found himself "hung up" on Autry for nearly a year. He cut a section of clothesline and, in the privacy of his backyard, "started roping with it." But Jack's interest in Autry, interestingly, did not extend to his music. "I didn't care anything about the guitar then," he admitted. "I thought it was sissy when Gene Autry sang."[12]

Dr. Adnopoz's nurse, a Miss Malone, presented young Elliott the gift of the book *Lone Cowboy—My Life Story*. *Lone Cowboy* was a fanciful autobiography, one that would change Jack's life in ways that Miss Malone could never have imagined. *Lone Cowboy* had been written in the 1930s by Will James, the author and illustrator of such classic novels of the American West as *The Drifting Cowboy*, *Flint Spears: Cowboy Rodeo Contestant*, and *Smoky the Cowhorse*. *Smoky the Cowhorse* was so popular that the book had been published in several languages and made into a feature film on three separate occasions. By his own account, Jack read "three quarters of the books" penned by Will James and found himself more enthralled, one might say obsessed, with cowboys and horses and rodeos.[13]

But like so many legendary characters, Will James was not completely who he seemed. His true name, in fact, was not Will James at all. He was born Joseph Ernest Nephtali Dufault on June 6, 1892, in St. Nazaire de Acton, Quebec, Canada. In *Lone Cowboy*, James records he was born not in a province of Quebec at all but in a covered wagon in a Montana basin, and that is only the first of his many tall tales. According to biographer Anthony Amaral, "Will James, from a fertile imagination, had invented much of himself and his deeds." Such self-mythologizing would prove troublesome later. Amaral compared James's work to that of Rudyard Kipling in its ability to "attract the imagination of a child, and of the child in the adult who has not lost his ability to dream and imagine." Indeed, the west that James so romantically captured through his words and illustrations was so enchanting that he was held in some circles as the "old west" equivalent of William Shakespeare. The problem was that so much of what James wrote about was simply fabricated. Amaral describes James as having lived "under relentless emotional tension, caught between secrecy and fear of exposure." He was also, by many accounts, a difficult man to get close to. James was a brilliant artist and shared many of the traits assigned to those involved with creative work; he was described by friends as moody, arrogant, and fiercely independent. He was also something of a drunkard, and his drinking and temperament worsened with his paranoia. James feared he would someday be discovered as less authentic than he portrayed himself.[14]

James's books were not the only stories of adventure Jack enjoyed reading. He was also fond of Arthur T. Walden's classic *A Dog Puncher on the Yukon*, which told the story of the tough men and tougher sled dogs of the Klondike, racing to find riches in the snow and ice of the Alaskan gold rush of 1899. He also thrilled to Captain Joshua Solcum's *Sailing Alone Around the World*, the autobiography of the first sailor to circumnavigate the globe on his sloop *The Spray*. Another favorite was Alan Villiers's *By Way of Cape Horn*, which detailed the perilous voyage of the *Grace Harwar* around the southernmost tip of the Americas.[15]

Jack had "an old, wore-out wicker chair" that he sat in as he listened to the radio in his bedroom. He enjoyed Will Rogers, the Oklahoman whose folksy storytelling gifts were without peer. Occasionally, Rogers would be followed on the radio by *Tom Mix and the Straight Shooter's Club*. Mix was among the first and, without doubt, the most famous cowboy hero of the silent screen. In 1933, at the end of the silent film era, Mix had signed on with the Ralston-Purina Company, who used his name and image for a series of western-themed radio programs broadcast over a period of ten years. Mix's own vocal talents were never actually used. As most of the 370 films he made between 1909 and 1935 were silents, Ralston-Purina was confident that none of the children tuning in would notice the deception. Nearly seven decades after the last Tom Mix broadcast, Jack could still sing all the verses to Mix's Ralston Shredded Wheat commercial.[16]

Tom Mix never successfully made the transition from the silent to sound era. He died, tragically, in an automobile accident on October 12, 1940, eighteen miles south of Florence, Arizona, when the car he was driving overturned, crushing him and a female companion under the wreckage. That very same night at Madison Square Garden, Gene Autry paid tribute to his old friend, describing Mix as one who "contributed a great deal to the betterment of the American cowboy and cowboy sports." Jack was probably as startled as anyone by the tragic death of Tom Mix, but aside from the occasional Buck Jones serial, he hadn't shown all that much interest in the cinema. The first feature film that made an impression on him was William Wyler's *The Westerner*, featuring Gary Cooper, released in September 1940.[17]

In any event, there were plenty of heroes to be found closer to home. One of Jack's neighbors was a harbor pilot captain by the name of Robert Hinkley. To young Elliot Adnopoz, Captain Hinkley seemed a character out of a storybook. He was a rugged, virile gentleman whose face was permanently reddened from the winds of the harbor. Hinkley would have paid little attention to his young neighbor had Jack not approached him one morning as he exited a taxi in front of his home. The twelve-year-old approached the captain, telling him that he too hoped to become a sailor one day and, to that end, had been studying the *Bluejacket's Manual*. The Bluejackets were, essentially, the scout group of the U.S. Naval Academy, and the *Bluejacket's Manual* was the absolute bible of all things nautical. Jack wanted to sign on with the local chapter that met each week in the basement of a local church. He was impressed with the Bluejackets as they wore sharp, naval-styled uniforms and learned about boating and signaling and flags at each meeting. The group seemed to be the antithesis of the rather staid local Boy Scout troop he had joined for a short time. Jack became fast friends with Captain Hinkley and for the next two years visited him, two or three nights a week, at the apartment the old salt shared with his wife and two young daughters. "Cap'n" Hinkley, as Jack always respectfully called him, was impressed by the young boy's curiosity; he seemed determined to absorb everything he could of nautical terminology and procedures. The captain suggested that, when old enough, he might consider enrolling at the New York Public Nautical School at Fort Schuyler in the Bronx. Most nights the captain would regal his young friend with stories, some real and some apocryphal, of the sea and of ships and of sailing men. Once a whaler, he was now a harbor pilot who controlled all of Brooklyn's ship traffic. Jack enjoyed listening to Cap'n Hinkley spin his yarns, and would tell his friends that the Cap'n was informally schooling him to be an officer in the Merchant Marine. The Cap'n once made Jack "memorize the names of all the standing and running rigging on a Clipper ship, the 32 Compass points and knots and splicing." Jack treasured the friendship, recalling his meeting the captain as "the most exciting thing that had happened in my life."[18]

Another early friend was Ben Churchill. Jack remembered that Churchill looked a bit like the author Jack London, as he sported "a face like a St. Bernard dog." Ben was among the first of a long string of friends whom Jack admired, indeed, sought out, because they were adventurous, colorful, and unconventional. Jack and Ben shared an enthusiasm for the recordings of Burl Ives, the radio star and folksinger of pop music sensibility. Ben Churchill could play guitar and sing in the style of the balladeer, and it was mostly through Churchill's interest that Elliott had been "turned . . . on to this Burl Ives stuff." At nineteen, Churchill was much older than his young friend, smoked a pipe, and seemed to already have "been everywhere." He told young Elliott he had been in the navy, knew how to fire a six-shooter, once owned a Shetland pony, had run away from home, rode freight trains, and built a log cabin. It was not all completely true, but it was, importantly, through Ben Churchill's appreciation of Ives that Jack was first introduced to folk music.[19]

There was music in the Adnopoz home, but Jack had not yet developed any significant interest in the art. Flossie had a little background on the piano and could play through a short program of "classical tunes like Mozart and all that stuff." Jack recalled he "didn't like it much. And I disliked it all the more when she played it, 'cause she wasn't really very good." His uncle Leo also played the piano "enthusiastically" when he wasn't off publishing *Cordage* magazine for the rope industry. The family was well off enough to have their own piano in the family parlor for such occasions, but Jack had very little interest in the instrument or its repertoire. He preferred the cowboy and hillbilly songs that he had occasionally heard at night on his radio.[20]

Though Jack's parents were still expecting that their eldest son would grow out of his cowboy fantasy and study medicine, they certainly were not against a musical education. Having little interest in his mother's piano, Jack chose to take guitar lessons. But his first experiments with the guitar were less than satisfying. By his own admission he was only "fooling around" with the instrument. His parents found a competent guitar instructor who lived nearby, but the lessons did not last long, since Jack found the enterprise to be a bore. He quickly lost interest and did not follow through. Jack described his first guitar as a "crummy" instrument, a "Collegiate" model, but the real problem wasn't the instrument, it was the repertoire. "I wasn't playing cowboy music, and it wasn't country music," Jack recollected. "It was just to play the guitar."[21]

Brooklyn, of course, afforded few opportunities for a budding roots guitarist to see and hear genuine country music artists at work in their natural element. Most country and western performers did not even include New York City dates on their tour itineraries. A handful of motion picture cowboy singers visited semiregularly, but they were Hollywood cowboy acts and the music they made, while entertaining with their smooth yodels and ornate guitars, was hardly indicative of anything resembling traditional country music. In fact, the term "country music" or "country and western" had not yet come into vogue. The music was simply labeled "hillbilly," a term that could be considered derisive or endearing depending on one's sensibilities. More often than not, a listener's tolerance for "hillbilly music" depended less on one's musical palette than on which side of the Mason-Dixon line they had been born. As a resident of Linden Boulevard, Jack Elliott found himself completely on the "wrong" side of that border.

Jack attended Erasmus High School on Flatbush and Church Avenues in Brooklyn, but he was, at best, an unremarkable student and found little solace in secondary-school studies. Though he enjoyed running track his freshman year, Erasmus was ill remembered as an institution that attempted to cram "seven thousand students in a school built to hold two thousand people."[22]

One of Jack's rites was to awake each morning to the sound of the horse-drawn milk wagon as it made its way down Linden Boulevard. Near sunrise Jack would listen for the distinct clomp of the Belgian horse's hooves on the street, followed by the rickety clatter of the trailing wheels of the wagon. On the morning Jack was to start his sophomore year, he heard the familiar gait of a horse on cobblestone but, oddly, the distinct clomp was not followed by a rattling cycle. Jack remembered, "I wasn't even out of bed when I heard the horse comin' down the road." He jumped from his bed and quickly made his way to the window, where he spied a cowboy on horseback making his way slowly down Linden Boulevard. Jack quickly got dressed, ran outside, and found his bicycle. Pedaling hard, he caught up with the cowboy about two blocks from his home and bicycled alongside for the next four miles. The cowboy's name, Jack learned, was Tiny Westley, and his horse's name was Shorty. Westley, who was of somewhat short stature himself, told the wide-eyed kid that he had just arrived from Montana and was scheduled to compete in the saddle bronc riding competition at Madison Square Garden. This was all patently untrue, Jack would soon learn, but it made for a good story. Westley appeared to be very much the rugged cowboy ideal. "He looked just like those guys in the Will James' books," Jack remembered. "He had that lantern jaw and busted lip." Tiny explained he was riding to Long Island where he was boarding his horse. Jack listened with fascination but finally bade farewell to his new friend. Jack made it to his classes that day, but his thoughts, as usual, were far from his studies.[23]

Jack never made it to school the following day. That morning he hopped a subway train into Manhattan, transferred at Grand Central Station, and boarded a train for Flushing, Queens. He then rode a bus to the very end of the line, walked a few blocks, and found the stable where Westley was boarding his horse. Tiny was in the process of unsaddling Shorty when Jack arrived. Though surprised by the kid's unscheduled appearance, the two new friends chatted awkwardly, mostly about horses and then a little about music. Westley, who played some guitar, learned that Jack was fooling around with the instrument, so the two of them climbed into Tiny's car and drove to his brother's house. Tiny's brother was also a guitarist, and a pretty good one at that, and Jack's visit with the Westley brothers lasted through the night. Tiny owned an electrified Gibson guitar, and Jack listened as the brothers performed duets of Roy Acuff's "Wabash Cannonball" and "Pins and Needles." Jack was finally among his element, but as day turned into night and the night into early morning, the truth surfaced that Tiny Westley was not a genuine cowboy from Montana at all. He was a lifelong resident of Flushing, employed as the driver of a milk truck. Like Will James, Tiny had simply made up the story about being a cowboy from the west.[24]

The next morning Jack telephoned his father. This was the first time that he had gone off without a word to anyone. He had not actually skipped classes with the intent of "running away." The pilgrimage to Flushing was simply an adventure that, by accident rather than conspiracy, ran too long. But his parents had been terribly worried about their son's disappearance and were relieved to get the morning phone call. Jack's father remained remarkably calm and made arrangements to collect his son. Jack recalled his father tried "not to be too uptight about it, 'cause he was bereaved that I had disappeared." But Dr. Adnopoz decided that the time had come to send his errant son to a private boarding school in Connecticut.[25]

The Cherry Lawn School was founded in 1915 in Stamford, Connecticut, by Dr. Fred Goldfrank, who relocated the institution to the town of Darien in 1920. Dr. Goldfrank's mission was to establish an institution based on a "progressive and innovative approach to education that focused on the development of the whole person." Though still far from a model student, Jack felt more at ease in the bosom of Cherry Lawn's idyll setting. He was also excited to learn the school maintained its own stables and hosted horse shows each spring. The student body of the prestigious private school was also populated by interesting and erudite classmates, friends emotionally simpatico. Two of those friends were Carl Jay Margulis and Don Finkel.[26]

In May 1947, Elliott, Margulis, and Finkel, on recess from Cherry Lawn, met in a Greenwich Village tavern for drinks. Elliott recalled that he and his friends were "misfits" of a sort, and these tavern sessions were enjoyed each time Carl and Don returned to New York "to visit their families and psychiatrists." It was primarily through Finkel that Elliott broadened his musical interest beyond the country songs he had been listening to. Finkel introduced Jack to boogie-woogie and New Orleans jazz. Jack was immediately drawn to the sound of boogie-woogie piano, as performed by Albert Ammons, Pete Johnson, Meade Lux Lewis, and, particularly, Clarence "Pine Top" Smith. Smith's 1928 recording "Pine Top's Boogie" got everyone's feet tapping.[27]

Although Jack and his friends were not yet of the legal drinking age (Jack was only fifteen), each appeared older than their years and rarely had a problem getting served. Finkel and Margulis were self-proclaimed poets ("early beatnik-type writers," Jack would call them) who often talked of breaking free from their ennui and humdrum, middle-class existences.

Both wanted to set off on an adventure of some sort, but neither Carl nor Don had any idea where they would actually go. Elliott, too, was keen on the idea of hitting the road. Finkel had recently introduced him to the music of New Orleans's clarinetist Bunk Johnson. Jack had recently read that Johnson's New Orleans Jazz Band, with George Lewis on clarinet, was playing that week in Chicago. "Let's go there," he suggested. Though Don and Carl were "slumming" in a Manhattan tavern, both were wearing the suits and ties required by Cherry Lawn. They mulled over Jack's suggestion. "Why don't you guys go home to your parents' homes tonight," Jack prodded. "Change into some blue jeans and take off those neckties. You don't need those kinds of clothes when you're hitchhiking. Wear some comfortable clothes. We'll meet up tomorrow."[28]

Early the next morning, May 8, 1947, Jack hopped on the subway and met his friends near the Bronx entrance of the George Washington Bridge, the span that connects New York City to the western skies of New Jersey. The first order of business was to find a car willing to whisk the trio across the bridge. This was accomplished easily enough, but following the short shuttle across the span, they found few motorists or truck drivers with the cab space, or desire, to accommodate three hitchhikers. After some time, a truck finally pulled over and the passenger door swung open. The three young men explained that they were trying to get to Chicago, but the driver told the boys that he was en route to Winston-Salem, North Carolina. The truck driver also pointed out there was only room in the cab for one passenger. Continuing to act as the unofficial "group leader," Elliott hastened a decision to maintain the momentum of their wanderlust. If they could not get to Chicago to see Bunk Johnson, Jack decided they would do the next best thing. "Let's go right down to New Orleans. . . . I'll meet you guys in Winston-Salem, North Carolina. . . . Why don't you guys meet me at the Greyhound Bus Station?" Before Don or Carl could respond, Jack climbed into the cab of the truck, waved good-bye, and watched them disappear in the truck's rearview mirror. He'd never see them again.[29]

By nightfall Jack and his truck-driving friend had made it as far south as Wilmington, Delaware. They slept that first night at "a very cheap, smelly hotel," but Jack was happy to at least have managed a bed. In the morning, they climbed back into the rig and resumed the streaming banter that helped the miles pass by. At one point Jack mentioned that he had left home with only 25 dollars in his pocket. The driver winced, telling him he would be "sure to end up in jail or get in trouble" traveling so far from home with so little cash. Elliott recalled the driver's sage advice that if he was serious about traveling to New Orleans, "the best thing I could do was go home and not set forth again until I had some money."[30]

By the time the truck reached the outskirts of Washington, D.C., Jack decided his friend was right. This guy was a seasoned veteran of the road; he knew what he was talking about. So Jack bid farewell and "jumped truck." He had already decided he would use some of the money he had brought along to purchase a ticket for the train back to New York City. But as he made his way to the railroad terminal, Jack took note of a huge billboard sign heralding an appearance of the J. E. Ranch Rodeo at Washington's Uline Arena.[31]

Being a faithful reader of books and magazines on rodeos and rodeo life, Jack was familiar with the J. E. Ranch Rodeo. The J. E. Ranch Rodeo was the only rodeo company in all of the eastern United States that had the distinction of being sanctioned by the RCA (Rodeo Cowboy Association). Colonel Jim Eskew was the "J. E." of the J. E. Ranch Rodeo, the outfit's founder and paymaster. Born James William Eskew in Wilson County, Tennessee, in 1888, Eskew produced his first "Wild West Show" as early as 1918, and in 1933 formed the J. E. Ranch Rodeo, the only professional rodeo outfit operating east of the Mississippi River. In 1939, Eskew, who had been stabling his horses and bulls in Texas during the off season, was approached by a group of businessmen and asked to relocate his base of operations from Texas to a 300-acre spread in the small town of Waverly, nestled deep in the countryside of Tioga County in western New York. Eskew agreed after the town made generous allowances for the colonel to lease the old Loomis farm atop Talmadge Hill for the rodeo's off season. It was an arrangement that would benefit both parties. The Waverly Board of Trade agreed to purchase the farm for use by the J. E. Ranch Rodeo, and Eskew's lively payroll of cowboys, rodeo-hands, roustabouts, and Native Americans would provide the local merchants, feed companies, and saloon keepers with a small but guaranteed economic boom. Before long, Waverly was dubbed the "Rodeo Capital of the East," and the hamlet became a tourist attraction for fans of rodeos and devotees of western serial films. Colonel Jim maintained long-standing friendships with such western matinee heroes as Tom Mix, Gene Autry, Roy Rogers and Dale Evans, Hopalong Cassidy, and Lash LaRue. Every summer, Eskew would parade his Hollywood singing-cowboy friends at his rodeos, and these celebrity appearances would, unfailingly, draw faithful crowds to Waverly. Even when the outfit was touring on their grinding mid-Atlantic and New England rodeo circuit schedule, the J. E. Ranch Rodeo would always return to the Loomis farm every July 4 for the annual, and highly anticipated, Independence Day performance.[32]

Elliott wanted, desperately, to be a part of it. He took the train back to New York City and, undetected by his sleeping parents, quietly rummaged through the belongings in his room. He searched for an old wallet that held 40 dollars and collected several changes of clothing. He then slipped quietly out of his parents' house. It was "kind of a rotten thing to do," he admitted. "I must have really wanted my freedom pretty bad."[33]

Jack's second attempt at hitchhiking proved more difficult than the first. "It was a weekend," Jack remembered, "and hard to get a ride." There were few tractor trailers on the highway, but he slowly managed his way south by hitching a series of short rides in everything from garbage trucks to passenger cars driven by "crazy people." In subsequent years, Jack would learn the secrets of successful hitchhiking and would turn the practice into something of an art. He learned quickly that it was best to catch a ride with a truck. Truckers were, for the most part, friendlier, and the tractor trailers they commanded tended to go farther distances. Elliott thought of truck drivers as modern cowboys of a sort: "I liked the way they told stories and it seemed . . . they were more humble and happy in their lives." But it was also a lonely way of life, and most truckers seemed pleased to have company. Once they spied Jack's guitar, they often offered to trade a ride for a little music. The music helped keep them awake. Some of the more brave, or foolish, truckers were even willing to teach Jack how to operate their 18-wheelers so they could surrender the wheel for a spell when they tired. Hitchhiking in automobiles, on the other hand, was often not worth the effort.[34]

Though it took a number of relays, Jack finally made it back to Washington, D.C., and immediately set off for the Uline Arena. To his surprise, the rodeo had finished its run and was in a state of disassembly. He watched as the rodeo hands and roustabouts busily folded tarpaulins, stacked poles, and boarded the horses and livestock into the trailers. The rodeo, he learned, was to soon set off for Pittsburgh. Realizing he didn't have much time, Jack asked where he might find Colonel Jim. Though he did not have any *real* experience, Jack shyly explained to the colonel that he wanted a job badly and enjoyed working with horses. He told the colonel of his horse-grooming experience gleaned at his uncle's farm in Connecticut. Surprisingly, he was brought on board.

"OK. We'll hire you on as a groomer," Colonel Jim told him. Jack was expected to feed the horses and bulls and groom a string of six horses for two dollars a day. It was not a lot of money, but it was not too bad and the work sounded interesting. Besides, legend had it that Colonel Jim would pay five dollars for a full week of off season work on the Waverly Ranch, and that wage included free room and board and all the Bull Durham tobacco a cowboy could smoke. Jack excitedly accepted the colonel's terms and was sent out to meet the cowboys and hands with whom he would be working. It was only then that things began to get somewhat uncomfortable.[35]

"When the cowboys asked me my name I said 'Elliot Adnopoz,' kinda like I was ashamed," Jack told *Esquire* magazine in 1980. "I wanted to be a cowboy ever since I was nine and I wanted to be accepted as one of them—not discriminated against 'cause I was a Jew. I didn't know how to lie. They asked me where I was from and I said 'New York,' like I wasn't proud of that either. And the cowboys told me 'It ain't where you're from that counts, it's where you're going!' I sure liked that. It made me feel excused and at ease."[36]

The cowboys had difficulty pronouncing Jack's surname so they simply dubbed him Poncho, the name of a famous rodeo clown who "had this talent for getting bulls to hook the belt of his pants with their horns. He'd use the momentum to fly up in the air and do a back flip and land on his feet—or maybe not." Jack settled into his new life with enthusiasm. He was, to his honor, the personal groomer of Junior Eskew's horse Blue. Junior Eskew was one of the greatest trick ropers in the country. Jack had seen him at work at the Madison Square Garden rodeo in 1940 and now, seven years later, he was grooming Junior's horse. Jack was, at last, the cowboy he had long dreamed of being. That first night he attempted a difficult sleep on a truck bed laden with tent poles. As he tossed and turned uncomfortably, he overheard some cowboys talking of returning to the rooming house they had rented for the night. Jack asked if he might join them and they agreed, four "road apple" fragrant cowboys sleeping in a single bed. The next morning the four took a rare bath, with Jack, the lowest man on the roster, getting the "last bath in dirty, cold, scummy, soapy water." He dried off with a towel, equally cold and filthy. The rodeo left Washington, D.C., that morning for Pittsburgh, where they were next scheduled to perform. In Pittsburgh, Elliott opted out of another bleak rooming house scenario and chose to sleep in the Horse Top, the tent set aside to board the horses. Elliott recalled his new life as a cowboy was "very romantic, at first, until the malnutrition . . . set in."[37]

One of the performers who traveled with the J. E. Ranch outfit was the rodeo clown "Brahma" Rogers. Claude W. Rogers played the guitar and the five-string banjo and would spin stories, recite poems, and serenade the cowboys and roustabouts, for 25 cents each, in the intervals between the riding and roping events. "He would pass the hat between shows and we'd all put a quarter in it," Jack recalled. His early dalliance with Burl Ives not withstanding, Elliott remembered his first authentic "exposure to storytelling and folklore and folk music" was through Brahma. Rogers hailed from east Texas and sang and played five-string banjo in the bright, highly rhythmic, drop-thumb style of the Grand Ole Opry's Grandpa Jones. Rogers sang a lot of old cowboy and mountain songs such as "Mountain Dew" and "Stay All Night (Stay a Little Longer)." Rogers stood apart from most of the cowboys he traveled with as he never outfitted himself in a pair of blue jeans. Rogers favored the loose-fitting "Booger Reds" or "Alamos," a light brown heavy-duty set of stiff trousers made of canvas. Rogers remained extremely loyal to Colonel Jim over the years. He stayed in the employ of the J. E. Ranch Rodeo for 22 years and even named his son "James" in tribute to the colonel.[38]

Though Brahma Rogers survived two decades with the rodeo, Poncho Adnopoz's tenure lasted only three months. Jack's parents, distraught by their eldest son's disappearance, contacted local police who sent them to their missing persons bureau. The bureau, under Chief Inspector Martin J. Brown, immediately issued a missing persons handbill, offering a $500 reward for information leading to his return: *"Police Department—City of New York. Missing since May 8th, 1947. Elliott Adnopoz, 102 Linden Boulevard, Brooklyn. 5' 8"—120 lbs., age 16 (looks older), slim—light complexion, brown hair—brown eyes—gold rim glasses—wore Navy Blue sweater—blue dungarees—black and white checkered jacket—carrying small brown canvas bag—probable destination a ranch. (Parents not opposed to his staying on a ranch.) If located notify: Missing Persons Bureau, New York City or your local police."* Correctly suspecting their errant son's destination was a ranch or rodeo, Abraham and Flossie had meticulously compiled a mailing list of every active rodeo on the U.S. circuit, all of which received a copy of the handbill.[39]

The J. E. Rodeo had returned to its home base in Waverly following the end of the summer rodeo season. It was there in his office, beneath stacks of unattended summer mail, that Colonel Jim Eskew found the copy of the "Missing Persons" bulletin. He studied the enclosed photograph and realized that the bespectacled kid on the flyer was "Poncho." He summoned Jack to his office.

"Is this your picture, Poncho?"

"Yeah, that's my picture."

"Why didn't you tell me that you was a runaway?" the colonel drawled. "I wouldn't have hired you if you was a runaway."

"That's why I didn't tell you," Jack replied.[40]

"For a while I was known as the '500 Dollar Kid,'" Jack told the *Boston Herald*, "Very embarrassing." Colonel Jim contacted Jack's bereaved family, and Dr. and Mrs. Adnopoz found themselves in their car for the long road trip from Brooklyn to Waverly. Once again, his parents were forgiving, greatly relieved that their eldest child was alive and well and not involved in any sort of criminal activity. Jack recalled his parents telling him, "If I wanted to stay I could stay. If I'd like to come home, I could come home." He did not return home with his parents that same day, as he needed some time to think things over. In the end, Jack decided that "It wasn't the broncos and the bulls that tired me out, it was the food. Two dollars a day wasn't enough to feed a growing boy." Though Colonel Jim gentlemanly forfeited the $500 cash reward, Elliott's mother felt compelled to present the colonel with a gift. Flossie presented him with a table setting of fine silverware, long treasured by the family. The gift was a reward "for having taken such good care" of her son, but such generosity left Jack bewildered. In Jack's view, the colonel did his "best to starve me to death." More disappointingly, he rued, "I never got to ride a horse the whole time I was there."[41]

Just before he left Waverly, a rodeo clown by the name of Lost John Carruthers pulled Jack to the side. He recalled the clown as "a very philosophical old buzzard." Out behind the cook house, Carruthers handed Jack his very first cigar, a King Edward, and said, "If you go home and finish up high school, you can be anything you want, including a cowboy. But if you stay here, you'll be nothing but a cowboy. You think it's fun now, but it may not be so fun after awhile."[42]

Though Jack returned to the comfort, and regular meals, of his parents' home, he genuinely missed the excitement, freedom, and friends he had found with the rodeo. He soon became lonesome for the cowboy music he had heard while in Colonel Jim's employ. At night he would scan the radio in his bedroom in hopes of hearing some genuine cowboy music. There weren't many bona fide cowboy songs being broadcast, but there were a few reasonable facsimiles. Elliott remembered it was only following his return to Brooklyn that he started listening "to some New Jersey radio stations that featured country music on the air."[43]

Jack found solace in the radio. The country music chanteuse Rosalie Allen, originally from Bucks County, Pennsylvania, hosted the popular "Prairie Stars" program on New York City's WOV. Allen was also, importantly, the owner of a small, specialty record shop in Manhattan and something of a local celebrity, having waxed discs with the famed yodeling guitarist Elton Britt and New Jersey's own Shorty Warren & His Western Rangers. WAAT, a small station that broadcasted from Newark, regularly programmed country music with DJ Don Larkin spinning a mix of early bluegrass and mountain music. Newark was an unlikely candidate as the "Nashville of the North," but by the 1950s the city was home to nearly a half-dozen bars and nightclubs where one could hear genuine hillbilly music in the shadow of the Manhattan skyline. On Saturday nights, Jack would faithfully tune in to WSM and the Grand Ole Opry broadcasts from the Ryman Auditorium in Nashville.[44]

Radio signals beaming from Nashville and Newark introduced Jack to the music of many of the Opry's finest stars. His favorites were Roy Acuff and the Smoky Mountain Boys, Ernest Tubb and the Texas Troubadours, the Blue Sky Boys, Bill Monroe and the Bluegrass Boys, Homer & Jethro, and Johnnie & Jack. He was also fond of the songs of the Carter Family, taking special note of Maybelle and Sara Carter's distinctive guitar style. "Mother" Maybelle had developed a very distinctive guitar method, flat-picking melody lines on the bass strings while brushing down across the chords on the offbeat. Played right, this method produced a very bouncy, syncopated effect that worked equally well for solo accompaniments and ensemble playing.[45]

Jack rummaged through his closet and found the guitar that he had abandoned some three years earlier. "It was a terrible guitar, very painful to play," Jack would remember. "It had very high action." But his memories of Brahma Rogers and the inspiration of another cowboy and guitar-playing friend named Todd Fletcher had instilled a discipline not earlier present. Jack bought himself a copy of a cowboy songbook and set himself to work. The first song in the folio he set out to play was the old folk chestnut "Red River Valley." It took some time to learn to work out the chord figures, but once the lament had been mastered, Jack returned to the folio in search of a more interesting song. One song that intrigued him spun an exciting tale of cattle drives, wild storms, and of rough, frontier justice metered out by the cowboys betrayed by the unscrupulous drover who hired them. Jack studiously sketched out the melodic line of "Buffalo Skinners" on his guitar, but his instincts told him that the arrangement, as presented, was unsuitable for such a dark tale. This was potentially a great song, but one in need of a far more dramatic arrangement.[46]

Elliott was now totally inspired, practicing the guitar with unaccustomed discipline. While his parents slept, Jack situated himself at the kitchen table, the cowboy songbook flattened out before him, quietly playing the guitar for hours on end. His fingers ached from pushing down on the strings. It wasn't too long before Jack's bruised fingers developed calluses as thick as "elephant's feet." But his guitar playing improved markedly and, by his own estimation, he figured he had gotten "pretty good after about six months." Jack's aunt Mildred, a music teacher with a sunny disposition, thought likewise. Impressed with his progress, she suggested he take more formal guitar lessons at the home of a friend, a classically trained Cuban guitarist. Though Jack would not study long with Aunt Mildred's friend, it was this teacher who suggested he would make significant progress with a better instrument. He brought Jack to the Harry Newcorn & Sons Music Store at Third Avenue on Manhattan's Lower East Side. There he found a good deal on a Gretsch Rancher guitar. It was a beautiful instrument, worth nearly $300, but Elliott was able to purchase it for all of $75. It had sat too long in the shop's window, suffering cosmetic damage due to sunning. Part of the guitar's binding was starting to come loose, but the instrument sounded great and was offered at a bargain. Newcorn agreed to make the necessary repairs and Jack walked out of the store the proud owner of his first good guitar. Now he needed a place to play it.[47]

Notes

1. "Rodeo Opens Here Oct. 9," *New York Times*, 22 September 1940, 51; "Rodeo Show to Open at Garden Tomorrow," *New York Times*, 8 October 1940, 31; "Steer Herd Brings Portent of Rodeo," *New York Times*, 29 September 1940, 46; "Rodeo Will Open Tonight," *New York Times*, 9 October 1940, 20.

2. "Here for the World's Championship Rodeo," *New York Times*, 6 October 1940, 31; "Rodeo Riders Add Touch of West to 8th Ave.; World's Championship Will Open Wednesday," *New York Times*, 7 October 1940, 19; "Rodeo Show to Open at Garden Tomorrow," *New York Times*, 8 October 1940, 31; "Rodeo Spectacle Opens Season Here," *New York Times*, 10 October 1940, 31.

3. "2 Rodeo Riders Injured," *New York Times*, 14 October 1940, 27; "Injuries at Rodeo Reach Total of 49," *New York Times*, 20 October 1940, 46.

4. "Rodeo Entertains Bellevue Patients," *New York Times*, 16 October 1940, 20; "17,000 Child Guests Whoop It Up at Rodeo; Bronco-Busting Is a Hit and Autry Is 'Swell'," *New York Times*, 22 October 1940, 22.

5. "Rodeo Show to Open at Garden Tomorrow"; "Rodeo Spectacle Opens Season Here"; Allan Taylor interview with Jack Elliott, "*Shared Experience*," BBC Radio 2, broadcast 29 February 1996; Holly George-Warren, *Public Cowboy No. 1: The Life of Gene Autry* (Oxford, NY: Oxford University Press, 2007), 34–36.

6. Jack Elliott, *Live from Jorma Kaukonen's Fur Peace Ranch*, Meigs County, Ohio, 4 May 2002.

7. Elliott, *Live from Jorma Kaukonen's Fur Peace Ranch*.

8. Buddy Blue, "Ramblin' Jack Elliott: The Rodeo Made Him Do It," *San Diego Union Tribune*, 12 May 2005, Sec. Night & Day, 20; Jack Elliott, Bottom Line, New York City, 10 August 2000.

9. Ed Condran, "Weary Jack Elliott Not the Ramblin' Man He Used to Be," *Bucks County Courier Times*, 10 May 2001, www.phillyburbs.com/c...ertimes/news/news_archive/0510elliott.htm. (accessed 4 July 2001); j. poet, "A Ramblin' Kinda Guy," *San Francisco Chronicle*, 1 October 2006, PK-46; Seth Rogovy, "The Legend of Ramblin' Jack," *Berkshire Eagle*, 11 September 2003, www.berkshiresweek.com/091103/?id=article05 (accessed 29 January 2005); Colin Irwin, "Folk: Living Legend," *Melody Maker* 55, 16 August 1980, 39.

10. Steven Stolder, "Traveling Back with Ramblin' Jack Elliott," *NARAS Inforum*, www.grammy.com/features/jackelliot.html (accessed 22 May 1997); Lee Winfrey, "In Woody's Name . . . and Beyond," *Miami Herald Sunday Magazine*, 18 April 1965, 52.

11. Rogovy, "The Legend of Ramblin' Jack."

12. "All Hung Up," *Newsweek*, 14 August 1961, 47; Winfrey, "In Woody's Name . . . and Beyond," 52.

13. "Ramblin' Jack Elliott," in Denise Sullivan, *Rip It Up! Rock & Roll Rulebreakers* (San Francisco: Backbeat Books, 2001), 176.

14. Anthony Amaral, *Will James, The Last Cowboy Legend* (Reno, NV: University of Nevada Press, 1980); Anthony Amaral, *Will James, the Gilt Edged Cowboy* (Los Angeles: Westernlore Press, 1967).

15. John May interview with Jack Elliott, London, England, 12 February 2005; James Sullivan, "A Daughter's Devotion," *San Francisco Chronicle*, 29 August 2000, Sec. Daily Datebook C1.

16. Catherine Felty, "Jack of All Trades," *If Magazine*, No. 18.3, 25 August 2000, www.ifmagazine.ifctv.com/common/article.asp?articleID=788 (accessed 4 July 2001).

17. "Tom Mix, Rider, Dies Under Auto," *New York Times*, 13 October 1940, 1; Sullivan, "A Daughter's Devotion."

18. Tim Ryan, "Ramblin' through Town," *Honolulu Star-Bulletin*, 1997, http://starbulletin.com/.../06/features/story1.html (accessed 2 March 1997); Bob Atkinson, "Ramblin' with Jack Elliott," *Sing Out!* Vol. 19, No. 5, March/April 1970, 3; John May interview with Jack Elliott.

19. Rita Houston interview with Jack Elliott, broadcast on WFUV, Fordham University, New York City, 30 May 1995.

20. Jim Catalano, "Elliott Brings 50 Years on the Road to Ithaca," *Ithaca Journal*, 11 September 2003, www.theithacajournal.com/entertainment/stories/20030911/culturalevents/232881.html (accessed 29 January 2005); Meg McConahey, "Travelin' Troubadour's Tales," *Santa Rosa Press Democrat*, 7 February 1999, Q15; John May interview with Jack Elliott.

21. Stolder, "Traveling Back with Ramblin' Jack Elliott"; Tristam Lozaw, "Ramblin' Man: Woody Guthrie Lives On," Guitar.com, http://ramblinjack.com/sk_092001.html (accessed 15 May 2008).

22. Stolder, "Traveling Back with Ramblin' Jack Elliott."

23. Atkinson, "Ramblin' with Jack Elliott," 3.

24. Stolder, "Traveling Back with Ramblin' Jack Elliott"; Atkinson, "Ramblin' with Jack Elliott," 3.

25. Stolder, "Traveling Back with Ramblin' Jack Elliott."

26. "Cherry Lawn School History," www.cherrylawnschool.org/history/history.html (accessed 12 February 2009).

27. Randy Sue Coburn, "On the Trail of Ramblin' Jack," *Esquire*, April 1984, 82; Calvin Ahlgren, "'60s Folk Singer Ramblin' Jack Elliott Still Round and About," *San Francisco Chronicle*, 7 May 1989; John May interview with Jack Elliott.

28. Coburn, "On the Trail of Ramblin' Jack," 82; Edvins Beitiks, "Jack of Hearts," *San Francisco Examiner Magazine*, 4 August 1996, 10.

29. Randy Poe, "Ramblin' Jack Elliott: An American Minstrel," *Sing Out!* Vol. 45, No. 3, Fall 2001, 35; Chris Flisher, "Living Legend Ramblin' Jack Elliott Keeps Folk Standards High," *Worcester Phoenix*, 2–9 May 1997, www.worcester phoe.../05/02/JACK_ELLIOTT.html (accessed 18 July 1997).

30. Stolder, "Traveling Back with Ramblin' Jack Elliott."

31. Coburn, "On the Trail of Ramblin' Jack," 82; Stolder, "Traveling Back with Ramblin' Jack Elliott."

32. Gail Woerner, "Behind the Chutes and Elsewhere: Colonel Jim Eskew & the JR Rodeo," www.rodeoattitude.com/dir_hd/gail/ch_03_06.htm (accessed 29 October 2007); "J.E. Rodeo: Rodeo Capital of the East," *Evening Times*, Sayre, Tioga County, New York, 17 September 1979, www.rootsweb.com/~nytioga/rodeo.htm (accessed 27 October 2002).

33. Stolder, "Traveling Back with Ramblin' Jack Elliott."

34. Tristan Lozaw, "Travelin' Man: Ramblin' Jack," *Boston Phoenix*, 20–27 July 2000, www.bostonphoenix.com/archive/music/00/07/20/JACK_ELLIOTT .html (accessed 29 January 2005); Tim Ryan, "Ramblin' Through Town," *Honolulu Star-Bulletin*, http://starbulletin.com/.../06/features/story1.html (accessed 2 March 1997); John Bream, "Legends about Ramblin' Jack Elliott Amaze Him as Much as the Public," *Minneapolis Star Tribune*, 23 April 1989, 01F; Stolder, "Traveling Back with Ramblin' Jack Elliott."

35. Winfrey, "In Woody's Name . . . and Beyond", 52; Woerner, "Behind the Chutes and Elsewhere: Colonel Jim Eskew & the JR Rodeo;" Stolder, "Traveling Back with Ramblin' Jack Elliott."

36. Coburn, "On the Trail of Ramblin' Jack," 82.

37. j. Poet, "A Ramblin' Kinda Guy," *San Francisco Chronicle*, 1 October 2006, PK-46; Craig Harris, "A Mosaic of Stories," *Dirty Linen*, Vol. 63, April/May 1996, 16; Stolder, "Traveling Back with Ramblin' Jack Elliott."

38. Harris, "A Mosaic of Stories," 16. Rob Patterson, "Reason to Roam: At 67, Ramblin' Jack Elliott Reclaims—Temporarily—the Urge to Wander," *Houston Press*, 9 April 1998, www.houstonpress.com/issues/1998-04-09/music.html

(accessed 4 July 2001); John May interview with Jack Elliott; Gail Woerner, *Fearless Funnymen: The History of the Rodeo Clown* (Austin: Eakin Press, 1993).

39. Booklet to *The Ballad of Ramblin' Jack* (Vanguard 79575-2), 2000.

40. Jack Elliott in *The Ballad of Ramblin' Jack* (Winstar/Fox Lorber Centerstage), 2001.

41. Monica Collins, "Ramblin' Man: Emmy-Winning Cowboy Folk Singer Regales with Tales of Travels," *Boston Herald*, 14 July 1998, Sec. Arts, 33; Bruce Robinson, "Telling Tall Tales: Ramblin' Jack Elliott's Awfully Big Adventures," *Sonoma Independent*, 5–11 December 1996, www.metroactive.c...12.05.96/music 9649.html (accessed 2 May 1997); Patterson, "Reason to Roam."

42. Patterson, "Reason to Roam."

43. Stolder, "Traveling Back with Ramblin' Jack Elliott."

44. Peter Spencer, "Folk Legend Elliott Really Does Tend to Ramble," *Newark Star-Ledger*, 27 October 2000, 18.

45. Marianne Horner, "Ramblin' Jack Elliott: The Road Less Traveled," *Country Spotlight*, 23 October 1997, www.countryspotli...m/country/artist/971023 (accessed 11 November 1998).

46. Stolder, "Traveling Back with Ramblin' Jack Elliott."

47. Steve Boisson, "Hard Traveling: Is Ramblin' Jack Elliott, the Legendary Troubadour of American Folk, Finally Settling Down?" *Acoustic Guitar*, November 1995, 63, 66; Harris, "A Mosaic of Stories," 16; John May interview with Jack Elliott; Stolder, "Traveling Back with Ramblin' Jack Elliott."

The Great Historical Bum 2

I N THE SPRING OF 1946, folk song enthusiast George Margolin began
to sing to himself, and to everyone within earshot, on his Sunday afternoon stroll through Greenwich Village's Washington Square Park.
Earlier that year, Margolin, a commercial printer, had become a member
of People's Songs, a loose-knit collection of politically left-tilting singers
and songwriters. People's Songs had been founded on New Year's Eve
1945 in Pete Seeger's in-laws' Greenwich Village basement at a "meeting
. . . of songwriters, singers, union representatives, and workers in allied
cultural fields." The raison d'etre of People's Songs was to disseminate a
politically progressive agenda through the use of folk songs and popular
music. The organization encouraged sympathetic souls to sign on and,
here in the heart of the Village, George Margolin was contributing to the
revolution in his own small way. Initially, Margolin simply ambled around
the park and sang a cappella, but after a few weeks he carried his guitar
along for accompaniment. The regular bench sitters of Washington Square
enjoyed Margolin's tuneful eccentricity and began to look forward to his
appearance each Sunday. Before long, the singer found himself performing
to small crowds, his audience a mix of genuine folk song aficionados and
the merely curious.[1]

Margolin's ability to draw faithful crowds did not go unnoticed by
the other folksingers in the area, some politically simpatico, others merely
enamored of the do-it-yourself ethos of the music. It wasn't long until
guitarists, banjo pickers, fiddlers, dulcimer and autoharp players, and harmonica blowers of every stripe and level of ability began to congregate
around the center fountain of Washington Square. Jack Elliott would soon

find himself among the musicians who gathered each Sunday. In 1947, a guitar-playing friend introduced Elliott to Tom Paley, a supremely talented multi-instrumentalist who channeled the discipline of his classical music training into the study of old-time mountain music. He was not a displaced hillbilly; Paley had been born in New York City on March 19, 1928, and was a student at City College. One of the few established instrumental virtuosos of the scene, Tom was a regular attendee of the Sunday sessions at Washington Square and one of Jack's earliest, and most encouraging, musical friends. In Elliott's estimation, Paley "could pick some of the best guitar you ever heard," often in the complex finger style of country music legend Merle Travis. Paley not only encouraged Elliott as a guitarist, but also as a dedicated musician of the mountain music school. Decades after they had first met, Elliott continued to cite Paley as "one of my favorite guitar players ever. . . . I'd started to play in 1947, and I'd call Tom up on the telephone and we'd play guitars over the phone for hours."[2]

The Sunday afternoon sessions developed into something far more than a cheerful afternoon's entertainment. It became a place where musicians could meet people of similar interest and swap songs, share instrumental technique, form bands, exchange telephone numbers, and network. In Washington Square such "citybillies" as Tom Paley, Roger Sprung, Jack Elliott, John Cohen, Erik Darling, and Harry and Jeannie West would join hundreds of others to jam the afternoon away. They were, by and large, a youthful cadre romanced by the sound and ideals of folk music. Elliott recalled 1947 as the start of "a whole era in my life where I was playing constantly, every day and night practically, going to parties at different people's houses around Manhattan."[3]

There was a constant stream of parties. On occasion, the budding folk-singers would escape the concrete canyons of Manhattan and set off on a boat charter to more rural, and therefore more authentic, surroundings. The forested state parks off the Hudson River were a favorite destination. But, more often than not, such parties were held in the backyard of a parent's home in one of Manhattan's outer boroughs. Banjoist Roger Sprung recalled, with a wide smile, one party where Elliott, suspended upside down at the knees from a low hanging tree limb, strummed his guitar and sang for friends in a Queens backyard.[4]

Music also allowed Elliott to make friends outside the folksinging circle. One Sunday afternoon, following a session with Paley and Sprung and a "whole bunch of hillbilly musicians" in Washington Square, Jack was approached by a young woman wearing a peasant skirt. The skirt hung so low to the ground that it nearly covered her bare feet. "You talk a lot about boats," she said to Jack matter-of-factly. "You gotta meet my brother-in-law. He's a sailor and he likes boats too." Intrigued, Jack followed the barefoot girl to her sister's second-floor apartment off Sixth Avenue. Once inside, Jack was introduced to Lillian and her husband, George. Jack's jaw went slack when he surveyed the apartment and found the walls lined with bookcases housing a staggering collection of books on navigation, ships, and the sea. "I spent about a week" with George, Jack reminisced, the two new friends discussing all the fine points of sailing, but mostly "talking about knots." George loaned Jack his copy of *50 South to 50 South*, Warwick M. Tompkins's thrilling account of his adventures on the *Wanderbird*, an eight-five-foot pilot schooner that the author sailed from Tangier around Cape Horn to San Francisco. The reading of such true life adventure stories stoked Jack's desire to travel the world.[5]

Occasionally one of folk music's "old lions" would visit Washington Square to see what all the fuss was about. Sometimes Woody Guthrie, the legendary Oklahoma balladeer, or Pete Seeger, who resided only a few blocks from the park, would make an appearance and share in the music making, but such instances were few. Though Guthrie was an infrequent visitor to Washington Square, Sprung recalled he remained accessible. Though all of the young musicians held Guthrie in high regard, many were wary of his company. Sprung remembered Guthrie as a "nice guy," but was often unsettled by his presence. His wariness was triggered by the fact that Woody often appeared to be foggy and lost, that he did not seem to care in the slightest for his own well-being. He recalled Woody "used to walk across the street and not look at the cars," oblivious to the dangers posed by Manhattan's streaming traffic. Though no one at the time knew what exactly was wrong with Woody, everyone could tell there was something odd about him. Sprung admitted he only knew Guthrie when it was obvious to everyone that the "dustiest of the dust bowlers" was, in some manner of speaking, "afflicted." Most attributed Woody's baleful condition to his drinking, not realizing that he was manifesting the symptoms of Huntington's disease.[6]

In 1945, Nathan Rudich, a program director for New York's municipal radio station WNYC, offered a Canadian folksinger named Oscar Brand an opportunity to host his own radio program. WNYC had broadcast performances by folksingers in the past, including programs by Henrietta Yurchenco, Pete Seeger, and Huddie ("Lead Belly") Ledbetter (who, for a time, had a WNYC radio show of his own). But Brand's program was devoted exclusively to the art of folk song. On Sunday, December 11, 1945, Brand's *Folksong Festival* program made its debut appearance on WNYC.

Brand was very proud of his program, later boasting that the "show has been the only continuous folk song program in the country and, for that reason, has had a sizable influence."[7]

Jack Elliott was among those who tuned in each Sunday evening to listen to *Folksong Festival*. One night, Brand introduced Elliott to the music of a guest who sounded authentically *western*. The singer spoke and sang with a laconic drawl, the words tumbling from his mouth in an unhurried stream. He told Brand about a time he had been riding the rails, crossing the country hobo style, securing passage on a succession of rattling freight cars. He had been trying, without success, to avoid the attention of the "bulls," or railroad police. This was difficult as he had been carrying along a fiddle and, curiously, the instrument was bringing him a great amount of unwelcome attention. At every freight yard, the fiddle's case was seized and carefully inspected. Brand's guest explained that the police were searching for a fugitive reportedly carrying a concealed weapon in a similar violin case. The man the railroad bulls were looking for was an outlaw by the name of Pretty Boy Floyd. The man telling the story over WNYC that evening was Woody Guthrie.[8]

Following his adventure with the rodeo, Elliott had returned home to complete his studies, eventually earning a diploma from Brooklyn's Midwood High School. Though friends Don Finkel (class of 1947) and Carl Jay Margulis (class of 1950) would graduate from tony Cherry Lawn with honors, Elliott had no such option. He was, reportedly, perhaps apocryphally, expelled from the preparatory school for trying "to ride a Shetland pony as if it were a bronc." Following graduation, Elliott enrolled at the University of Connecticut at Storrs with the vague ambition of studying pre-veterinary medicine or animal husbandry, but he found "chemistry was beyond me. I couldn't hack it. I flunked out." He enrolled at Adelphi College on Long Island for all of six months, but that too did not work out. It was becoming clear that Elliott would need to look elsewhere for an education.[9]

One of Jack's classmates at Adelphi was Richmond Shephard. Shephard shared Elliott's interest in hillbilly music and loaned him a 78 rpm folio titled *Struggle: Asch Documentary #1*. The cover featured artist David Stone Martin's grim, charcoal portrait of haunted looking workingmen carrying a coffin to its final resting place. Inscribed in the bottom left-hand corner was the somber legend "Burial at Ludlow." The album had been issued by Asch Records, a New York City company owned and managed by Moses Asch, the son of famed Yiddish writer Sholem Asch. The name of the recording artist was curiously absent from the album's front cover. It was as if a statement was being made that the teller of the tale was not nearly as important as the tale to be told. Only on the label itself could you find the name of the artist: Woody Guthrie. *Struggle* featured some of Guthrie's greatest songs and performances: "Buffalo Skinners," "Pretty Boy Floyd," "Ludlow Massacre," "1913 Massacre," "Lost John" (with Cisco Houston and Sonny Terry), and "Union Burying Ground." The album was entirely comprised of grim ballads recounting tragic historical touchstones of America's past: labor struggles that ended in tragedy, the ballad of an unscrupulous cattle drover who meets a vengeful fate at the hands of the very cowboys he cheated "on the plains of the Buffalo," a graveyard filled with union men who died by violence in the course of organizing the workers, and of 73 children murdered by scabs and company hired gun thugs. The collection also included "Pretty Boy Floyd," the song that Elliott first heard on Brand's radio program, fancifully recounting the saga of the celebrated Robin Hood outlaw of Depression-era America.[10]

Jack recollected his very first Guthrie album "had songs on it like 'Hard Traveling' and 'Union Burying Ground' and a few others. I thought it was great [and] I listened to it avidly for a whole month." Though Jack's enthusiasm is evident, his memory seems to be in error; the original 1946 issue of *Struggle* did not contain "Hard Traveling." It is probable that after being bitten by the Guthrie bug, Jack sought out *Ballads from the Dust Bowl* (Disc 610). In any event, Guthrie's "Hard Traveling" would soon be appropriated by Elliott as not only a personal theme song but as a statement of being. It was the first song of Woody's that Elliott would glean from a record. Of the twelve songs offered on *Struggle* and *Ballads from the Dust Bowl*, two-thirds of them ("Buffalo Skinners," "1913 Massacre," "Ludlow Massacre," "Pretty Boy Floyd," "Hard Traveling," "Pastures of Plenty," "Rambling Blues," and "Talking Columbia") would be incorporated into Elliott's working repertoire. He would play all eight songs, tirelessly, for the next 60 years.[11]

The *Struggle* album would dramatically transform Jack Elliott's life. Woody Guthrie was obviously a country singer of some pedigree. But his laconic style and the songs he sang could not have been more foreign from that of a more commercial hillbilly singer such as Roy Acuff. Acuff was great; he would forever remain one of Jack's favorites. But the Opry star seemed to sing, almost exclusively, railroad and gospel songs. Guthrie sang many of the same songs, but the lyrics to the gospel tunes were blasphemously rewritten by Woody so they might reflect his own particular worldview. Guthrie's music was less tuneful than Acuff's, but Elliott, ultimately, found it more exotic. He was very impressed by the relaxed, easygoing facility in which Guthrie could deliver a song. The songs that Woody sang were mournful but, at the same time, stubbornly indignant. In Elliott's estimation, Woody was not a mere recording artist, he "sounded like somebody who'd actually been there." Jack was immediately attracted to Guthrie's rough, often dissonant style of singing and guitar playing; Woody coupled his dusty drawl to a basic, no frills flat-pick country guitar technique appropriated from the recordings of the Carter Family. It was a synergetic combination that produced a mournful prairie howl. John Steinbeck, author of *The Grapes of Wrath*, once described Guthrie as "harsh voiced and nasal, his guitar hanging like a tire iron on a rusty rim—there is nothing sweet about Woody, and there is nothing sweet about the songs he sings." But it was that voice and those songs that made Jack Elliott a disciple of Woody Guthrie.[12]

There was a strangely detached quality to Woody's singing. This was unusual as Woody routinely sang about tragedy and greed and suffering, but he did so without pathos. According to Elliott, Woody had the gift of telling "a terrible damn story about something that was real." Jack was certain that Woody's detachment from the incendiary and harrowing couplets of his own ballads were, in part, due to his Oklahoma/Texas upbringing and the circumstances of his own tragic life experiences.[13]

"I was fascinated by the way Woody sang," Jack would later recall to the *NARAS Inforum*, "without any fancy embellishments or histrionics like some of our pop singers. He was totally real and natural. Telling it like it is, not putting in a lot of false grunts and groans for the ladies in the balconies." Artistically, the content of Woody's songs seemed not only far removed from the norms of the pop music industry, but also from the self-pitying repertoires of the hillbilly artists Jack treasured. Elliott admitted to not initially being a big fan of 1950s country music legend Hank Williams, as Hank was always "sobbing and crying, all this singing about some girl ripping him off. Woody Guthrie . . . was singing about the working man getting ripped off. That meant more to me." Fred Hellerman, the guitar-playing singer of the Weavers, was another son of Brooklyn who could identify with Jack's Guthrie epiphany. Hellerman, only four years older than Elliott, was a student at Brooklyn College when he was first introduced to Woody's seminal *Dust Bowl Ballads*. Hellerman recalled hearing *Dust Bowl Ballads* in the early 1940s, when the country was just turning the corner on the Depression. Hellerman remembered being "really knocked out of my chair" upon hearing the album. "Being raised on the kind of musical diet I had been raised on," Hellerman recalled, "the subject matter for a song was always the 27 shades of love: requited, unrequited, self-inflicted and so on . . . but all of a sudden I was made aware that there was a whole other world that could be sung about."[14]

In February 1951, Tom Paley was invited to appear on Oscar Brand's WNYC program. Paley asked Elliott if he would be interested in attending the session as his guest. Jack was delighted to be invited and accompanied his friend to the studio. That night Jack learned from Paley that his friend had been invited to attend a party at the Coney Island home of Woody Guthrie. Jack, intrigued by the idea of meeting the balladeer whose records had moved him so, asked if he might tag along. But as Paley was not the host, he was in no position to offer an invitation. So he suggested another option. "I'll tell you what," Paley replied, "I'll give you the phone number. You call him, he's a friendly guy. Just tell him about yourself."[15]

Technically, Jack had met Guthrie two years earlier, but the moment was decidedly undramatic. Elliott told one journalist, if he had his way, "I'd like to say I bumped into [Woody] on a boxcar changing trains in Omaha, Nebraska, in a snowstorm with a guitar." But that scenario would be far from the truth. The first contact was the briefest of encounters at the WNYC studio in early 1949. Elliott and a few friends from Washington Square Park had trekked up to WNYC where Lead Belly was scheduled to perform as a guest of Oscar Brand's. Woody was also there, but Elliott remembered Lead Belly was the focus of everyone's attention. Lead Belly was a very formidable figure, powerful and commanding. Woody Guthrie, with his slow drawl and rudimentary guitar playing, was a very slight figure by comparison. Following the broadcast, Lead Belly packed away his Stella and gently pushed through the crowd of youngsters outside the control room. Lead Belly accidentally bumped into Elliott on his way out of the studio, turned, and politely said, "Excuse me." It was the only physical and verbal encounter that Elliott would ever have with Huddie Ledbetter, one of his, and Woody's, greatest heroes. Lead Belly passed away on December 6, 1949, and Elliott recalled that Guthrie was devastated by the loss: "Woody was drunk the whole year Lead Belly died."[16]

Though Lead Belly was gone, in 1951 Woody Guthrie was still very much alive. "I must have waited a week or more before I got the courage to call Woody," Elliott remembered. Jack finally telephoned Guthrie at his home in Coney Island, and Woody himself answered the call. He introduced himself to Woody as "Buck" Elliott, explaining he was a friend of Tom Paley's. He also told the 39-year-old balladeer, with no hint of understatement, "I've heard your records and I like your music." Guthrie was already thought of as an eccentric by the folks in the neighborhood. He was not unaccustomed to strangers telephoning him at odd hours or knocking on the door of his home to play guitars or just hang out. So his friendly reply was not at all that surprising. "Well, why don't you come over and visit me one of these days, Buck? Bring your guitar and we'll knock off a couple of tunes together. . . . But don't come today because I got a belly-ache and I'm not feeling good." Elliott was relieved that Woody had been very friendly on the telephone. He also recalled being "amazed and thrilled to hear the voice of the man I'd been hearing on the records singing."[17]

After that first contact, Jack waited two days before calling again. This time, Woody's wife, Marjorie Mazia Guthrie, answered the phone.

"Is Woody there, please?"

"No," Marjorie answered, "Woody is in the hospital. He has appendicitis."

"Oh, no. . . . I'm Buck Elliott. I called a few days ago. Can I visit him in the hospital?"

"Oh, no, he's ill," Marjorie replied firmly. She added Woody was bedridden and "dopey from all the pain pills." He simply could not entertain guests. Jack learned that Woody was convalescing at Coney Island Hospital, an institution that was across the street from the Guthrie household. Jack waited several days before his enthusiasm to meet the great Woody Guthrie finally got the better of him. Despite Marjorie's warning, Jack chose to make the pilgrimage to Coney Island Hospital to visit his ailing idol.[18]

He did not call ahead or let anyone from Guthrie's family in on his plans. But there was one problem. He really was not sure what Woody Guthrie looked like. The albums of Guthrie songs he had been studying featured no artist photograph, and the night he watched Lead Belly perform in a crowded control room at WNYC studios was, at best, remembered dimly. Elliott learned the room number where Guthrie and another patient were recuperating, but admitted he "went right past him, I didn't recognize him." Undaunted, Jack looked around the room and "saw this little guy who had black, curly hair, looking crazy."

"Woody?"

"That's my name," Guthrie weakly replied.

"I'm Buck Elliott. I called you on the telephone the other day."[19]

It was an awkward beginning to a long-lasting friendship. Woody, still ailing, was sedated and not in any condition to receive visitors, much less one from an absolute stranger, a guitar-toting, nineteen-year-old kid dressed head to toe in blue denim and wearing a cowboy hat. There was an awkward exchange of small talk, followed by a long interval of uneasy silence. The silence was finally broken by the clasps of Jack's guitar case being unhitched. Jack shouldered his guitar, readying to play for his bed-ridden musical hero. "You want to hear a little music? I'll play you some guitar." Woody winced and replied, "No, the guy in the next bed just came off the operating table. Better not make any noise." To his disappointment, Jack did not get the opportunity to serenade his hero that afternoon. Instead, he admitted to standing "stupidly by" Guthrie's bedside for some time. In an attempt to curtail the visit, Guthrie suggested to "Buck" that he go over to the window of the hospital room. Woody directed him to look across the road and described the back of his house that sat across the street. "You know I'm married?" Guthrie asked. "Go over and introduce yourself to Marjorie. . . . See my kids . . . go over to the house and visit them." Jack peered out the window and spied Woody's children, Arlo, age three and a half, Joady, age two, and Nora Lee, age one, playing on the family's back porch. Dutifully, he went across the street and introduced himself to Marjorie and the rest of the Guthrie family.[20]

It was February 1951. Following his first, genuine face-to-face encounter with Woody Guthrie, Jack thought it best that he allow Woody time to mend. With little else on his agenda, he decided to hitchhike to Westport, Connecticut, where he had friends. He found his first ride easily enough. A woman in a gleaming Cadillac pulled over and offered him passage, but she told him she was not heading to Connecticut, but to the christening of a new tugboat out on Long Island. Elliott was tempted to go along. Through Captain Hinkley, he had become fascinated with tugboats, but somehow managed to resist the temptation. He really wanted to get to Westport and see his friend Eric Von Schmidt.[21]

Von Schmidt was nearly the same age as Jack, born on May 28, 1931, in Westport, Connecticut. Eric's father, Harold, was a well-known artist whose western-themed work often graced the front covers of the *Saturday Evening Post, Collier's Weekly,* and *Cosmopolitan.* Eric inherited his father's talent and he would later study art in Florence, Italy. Much like Elliott, Von Schmidt had also developed an interest in American country music, religiously listening to the Grand Ole Opry on his shortwave radio. His life changed dramatically in 1948 when he chanced to hear Lead Belly perform "Goodnight, Irene" on radio station WQXR. He taught himself the song with the intent to impress his girlfriend, also named Irene. Eric soon found two Lead Belly 78 rpm record albums and had become totally enchanted by the sound of the artist's booming twelve-string guitar. He set forth to learn as much as he could and, along with New York City's Fred Gerlach, became one of the first notable disciples of Lead Belly's music and twelve-string guitar technique. It was also through the albums of Lead Belly that

Eric was first introduced to Guthrie's music. Elliott first met Eric in 1950, telling the *Boston Globe* he was immediately impressed with Von Schmidt's musical aptitude, that Eric "sang Lead Belly's songs with the same kind of spirit Lead Belly had. . . . And he was also the only person I ever heard sing Woody Guthrie songs really well. Eric's got that wild spirit, and he doesn't water the music down for polite society; he just roars it out."[22]

The fact that Jack Elliott had met Eric Von Schmidt at all bordered on the serendipitous. Elliott was no stranger to Westport. He had family there and had friends in the area as a result of his short-term enrollment at the University of Connecticut. Elliott had heard stories about Von Schmidt, but Eric never seemed to be around town the same time Elliott was visiting. Elliott had recently caught a glimpse of Von Schmidt when he found himself leafing through the February 1951 copy of *Argosy*, a popular men's adventure magazine. Elliott recollected that *Argosy* featured exciting stories "of terrific things . . . happening all over the world: mountain climbing and boats sailing hither and yon." One photograph depicted Von Schmidt, barefoot and sitting on some scaffolding suspended on the stern of a 75-foot Belgian pilot ketch. He was painting over the former name of the vessel, changing the original name of the ketch to the sponsor-friendly *Argosy*. Elliott learned that the magazine was planning an around the world cruise with Captain Dod Orsborne at the helm. Orsborne was a World War II–era British spy, made famous in the pages of *LIFE* magazine as code name "Laundry Mark 45." Elliott had breathlessly read of the captain's espionage activities, spying on the Germans while at sea in the Mediterranean. Orsborne had rigged his vessel with all types of "false accoutrements." There were smokestacks with hinges, a variety of interchangeable masts and sails and booms, and all types of maritime props, ranging from fishing gear to radio antennas to sea plane cranes. Orsborne was able to monitor German ship movements undetected, as his vessel could morph from a trawler to a schooner to a cargo vessel with the swapping out of nautical props. The whole affair seemed very exciting to Jack, and after carefully reading through the magazine, he learned the *Argosy* was being refitted at a Westport boatyard.[23]

It was in the dead of winter. Of Captain Orsborne, Elliott recollected, "It was a thrill to meet one of my childhood heroes," but it was his friendship with Von Schmidt that proved to be more enduring. Jack's friends had been right about Eric. He was a terrific musician who traded off easily between the twelve- and six-string guitars and five-string banjo, and his renditions of Lead Belly's songs brimmed with spirit and authenticity. Eric recalled playing a lot of guitar with Jack Elliott in the early days "when we were all just learning." Von Schmidt was present when Elliott first "figured out how to play a B7th chord," a moment he recalled as "magic." Eric and his friends in Connecticut knew Elliott by the nickname "Xerxes" rather than "Buck." Von Schmidt remembered Xerxes as a lost soul "casting about for a persona. He finally met Woody Guthrie and he didn't have to look any farther."[24]

Elliott was welcomed aboard the *Argosy* as an unpaid member of the crew. He would live on the ketch for a better part of a month, keeping warm under an old army blanket he had sensibly brought along. There was plenty of rehabilitation work to keep everyone busy, though Elliott and Von Schmidt spent most of their time "chopping ice off the deck with an axe." The smell of tar and whiskey and coal were ever present. There was a coal-burning stove down in the cabin to where they'd retreat when the winter weather turned brutal. Though there was no pay, Jack recalled, "there was a lot of entertainment what with the whiskey and the songs." Captain Orsborne was a character who sported "a face like a rat." He had a moustache and thin chin beard, always wore his coat collar up, and turned his hat down rakishly over one eye. He enjoyed the pleasures of a bottle of whiskey and an ever lit smoking pipe. Orsborne sang through a salty repertoire of sea chanteys and profane sailor songs, most bordering on the obscene.[25]

The month rushed by. Captain Orsborne enjoyed Elliott's company, appreciated his contributions, and hated to see him go. He told Elliott that he was welcome to come along on the around the world sail of the *Argosy*, provided he could come up with the $2,000 fee asked of all crew members. Disappointed, Jack said a reluctant good-bye and disembarked the *Argosy*, absentmindedly leaving behind his army blanket.

While in Westport, Eric told Elliott that a going away party had been planned for their mutual friend Cole Cooper. Cooper had joined the armed services and was expected to report for duty at Travis Air Force Base in Fairfield, California. At the party Elliott learned that Cole was not too enthused about making the drive to California alone. "Hey, Xerxes," Cooper asked, "do you want to help me drive this car out to California?" Elliott mulled over the offer and responded, "Oh, sure. Yeah. Why not? Let's go!" There was one problem. Having just hitchhiked from New York City, Elliott had brought along only his toothbrush and guitar, and little money. But he reasoned he could afford a razor and wear the same clothes. After all it was wintertime, and one "could get a lot of miles out of your clothes . . . if you didn't run around too much." Following the party, Elliott tossed his guitar into the backseat of Cooper's 1937

Plymouth Coupe and the two friends headed west. They pinned the speedometer at 50 miles per hour and, one potentially serious motor vehicle accident later, made it to California, "still fresh as a daisy" in a little more than eight days.[26]

Once in California, Jack and Cole went their separate ways. Cooper took his dented car, Jack's only source of transportation, to the air base. Elliott hitchhiked south to San Francisco, where he found work at the Merchant Marine Museum restoring old sailing ships. That temporary employment led to a welcome meeting with Warwick "Commodore" Tompkins, Jr. Commodore's father was Warwick Tompkins, Sr., who had sailed around Cape Horn on the motorless 1880s German pilot boat called the *Wanderbird*. Elliott learned the *Wanderbird* was moored in Sausalito, so he made the trip across the Golden Gate Bridge for an inspection. He introduced himself to Commodore as Buck Elliott and was graciously invited on board by the son of his childhood hero. Commodore mistakenly introduced Elliott to his mother, also on board, as "Jack" rather than "Buck," and Elliott, "too shy . . . to correct him," said nothing of Commodore's faux pas and the name stuck. The two men became fast friends. Elliott took up temporary residence on the *Wanderbird*, listening all day and night to Commodore's collection of Pete Seeger and Woody Guthrie records. For three months, Elliott carefully studied the Guthrie records and absorbed all the subtle nuances of Woody's vocal and guitar style.[27]

Elliott arrived back in New York City in May 1951 and immediately telephoned Guthrie. He shared with Woody the details of his three-month adventure out west, explaining that he had been singing "Hard Travelin'" in every bar along Route 40 as he hitchhiked his way east. It was easily Jack's favorite song of Woody's, and he had it down cold. "I knew the song upside down and inside out," Jack would proudly tell Woody's son Arlo some years later. It wasn't only Woody's songs that Elliott had committed to memory; he also perfectly, some might say disturbingly, appropriated nearly all of Woody's nuances on vocals and guitar as well.[28]

Woody vaguely remembered that Elliott had first introduced himself as Buck on their first meeting. But now it seemed he was no longer going by that name. Elliott told him, "My name has changed," as if there was no need of further explanation. It was all a bit confusing to Woody, but Jack recalled, "I went through a lot of names back then." He later remembered, "I was 'Buck' Elliott when I met [Woody] and I was Jack Elliott when I came back." Woody, for one, did not like the latest name change. "There's a thousand *Jacks'* for every *Buck*!," he scolded. But it was too late. He was now, and for all time, to be known as Jack Elliott.[29]

On the telephone, Guthrie told Elliott, "Come to a party. Got a pencil? 1-2-0 University Place." Jack agreed to meet Guthrie at the party in a fashionable apartment building nestled not far off the northeast corner of Washington Square Park. By the time Jack arrived he found Guthrie singing and playing his guitar, entertaining requests from guests at the rate of a nickel a song. As Elliott sat off to the side and listened, someone asked Guthrie to sing "Foggy, Foggy Dew," an old British broadside made popular by Burl Ives, not a song typical to the Guthrie canon. Without missing a beat, Guthrie turned toward the earnest Ives fan and coldly drawled, "I get fifteen cents *extry* for Burl Ives!" Jack eventually pulled out his own guitar and tuned to Guthrie's instrument. They played and sang a few songs together and, though the two men had never played together before, it just sounded *right*—so right, in fact, that Woody asked Jack that night, "How'd you like to sing with me in a group?" "Sure would," Jack enthusiastically replied, not quite believing this turn of events. "But wouldn't you rather use Tom Paley?" Paley was already an occasional accompanist of Guthrie's and could run rings around the playing of such relatively primitive guitarists as Woody and Jack. But Paley's talent was his musical Achilles' heel. He was simply *too* smooth and Guthrie preferred a more rough hewn, less adorned sound. "No," Woody told Jack flatly, "you can follow better." Indeed, Elliott's worshipful study of Guthrie's recordings had enabled him to follow Woody's unconventional guitar methodology more easily. Guthrie was always adding or subtracting beats at whim. He often held measures for several bars too long, and would, on occasion, hold a single chord for the duration of an entire song. Elliott recalled Woody, generously, as "a very erratic guitar player. He needed somebody to follow him and fill in the gaps."[30]

It was well past midnight when the party ended. As Jack was putting away his guitar Woody asked, "You need a ride back to Brooklyn? I'll give you a ride in my Cadillac." Jack gladly accepted the offer. But when Elliott reached the curb he discovered the automobile wasn't the Cadillac that Woody had promised. It was Totsy, Woody's brand-new, modestly priced, 1950 Plymouth. Woody had purchased the car with the royalties from the Weavers's recent recording of "So Long, It's Been Good to Know You." Jack reasoned it was far too late and out of the way to go home to his parent's house, so he gratefully accepted Woody's offer of the couch of his home in Coney Island.[31]

Late that next morning, something strange happened. Woody and Jack continued where they had left off the night before, playing their guitars and informally swapping songs. It wasn't long until Jack took to boarding with the Guthrie family, "another in a series of wayward kids who established residence with the Guthries over the years," according to Guthrie biographer Joe Klein. Elliott would later tell the BBC, "I spent twenty-four hours a day with [Woody] for a whole year. . . . I couldn't get enough of it. I was very happy to be in his company." It wasn't only Guthrie's music that intrigued the youngster. He studied Guthrie's mannerisms from every angle, watching as Woody dramatically lifted his cigarette to his lips in a swooping "S curve," noting that he would always dress in the same uniform of khaki work pants and moccasins. Elliott proved to be the most faithful of Guthrie's apprentices, but he soon learned that life with the balladeer was not entirely pleasant. "He was a very moody, cranky person," Jack recalled, and often "you had to kind of tiptoe around him."[32]

Jack's daily schedule soon fell into familiar patterns, often dictated by Woody's mood or consumption of alcohol, or his still undiagnosed illness. They would rise at five in the morning as Guthrie's three children would not allow them to sleep off the excesses of the night before. Jack recalled that four-year-old Arlo would begin each morning "by throwing things at me: toys and stuffed dolls. If that didn't work, he'd throw fire trucks and things [made] out of iron. That usually did the trick."[33]

With Marjorie out early to teach dance class, Woody and Jack would start each morning with a couple of mugs of Postum, a powdered coffee substitute, and prepare breakfast for the children. Once the household was settled, Woody and Jack would break out the whiskey and soda and the two would sip their drinks and play guitars for hours on end. Jack was not much of a drinker, so he tended to pull slowly, and as intermittently as possible, at his glass. Woody, on the other hand, was already "a heavy alcoholic," in Jack's estimation, and his return trips to the well were far more regular.[34]

One inevitable result of the morning's whiskey and soda sessions was that Woody would get drowsy around noon and retire to the bedroom for an afternoon siesta of some two or three hours. Upon awakening, Woody would collect the children and load them, with Jack riding shotgun, into Totsy for an afternoon ride out on the Belt Parkway. Elliott recalled there was little variation to the daily ritual. Woody would follow the same route every day, and they would visit nearby parks or grassy areas or wherever they could find "country-like areas . . . around the edge of Brooklyn." Occasionally, the two would go off together sans children. Jack remembered Woody as an erratic motorist, speeding and weaving on Manhattan's East Driver Drive, a bottle of wine tucked between his legs.[35]

Elliott admitted that he would have preferred to be out of New York entirely. He refused to warm to New York City and tired easily of the bustle and the crowds, the traffic, and the noise. But the opportunity to apprentice with Woody Guthrie was one too great to dismiss. He enjoyed the morning guitar sessions and savored the long car rides no matter how white knuckled. He would listen as Guthrie reminisced at length about his World War II adventures in the Merchant Marine and shared bawdy stories regarding Lead Belly.[36]

One day Woody, Jack, and the children piled into Totsy to visit Eric Von Schmidt, currently sharing a Westport studio with an artist friend. Woody was a primitive artist, self-trained, and something of a graffitist. He sketched and doodled incessantly, sometimes illustrating, occasionally defacing, his notebooks and writings with caricatures and comments. Jack, too, dabbled in the fine arts. He was a talented pencil-and-pen artist, with detailed sketches of tall ships and maritime scenes a specialty. Woody brought out the artist in Elliott. Elliott left behind a series of original sketches in Guthrie's care, most dating from 1951 through March 1952, with Woody providing occasional annotations in the margins. Among Elliott's drawings were a series of profiles of Woody, as well as titled portraits of Nora ("Puffy"), of modern dancers ("Buck Elliott's Acrojets"), of Guthrie jumping free off the torpedo-rocked S.S. *William B. Floyd* ("Woody's Mandolin Jump"), of Nora hiding beneath an oversized woman's chapeau ("Under Puffy's Hat"), and an untitled but particularly tender portrait of Woody playing guitar for his children. One sketch, "All Around My World," featured Elliott's depiction of his favorite things: a young man listening to records, bull riding scenes, and ships with tall masts. Ships and seascapes were, in fact, so familiar that Woody wrote in the margin of one moody sketch: "For Jack Elliott so loved the sea and the oceans and the waters that he gave them his only begotten life."[37]

Von Schmidt received his guests warmly, but a conversation on art technique was abandoned the moment Eric borrowed Jack's guitar and began to sing a series of duets with Woody. Not everyone was pleased. Before long there came a furious rapping of clenched fists at the studio door and an irate legal secretary from a downstairs office rushed in. "We're trying to run a law office down here and you're making a lot of noise!" "I came up here to get out of the way of lawyers!" Woody huffily sniffed. "I'm a lawyer myself!" Eric and Woody agreed to tone it down, but played on regardless of the protest. In the end, the music finally got the better of everyone and Eric's small studio was soon filled with personnel from the law office below. Woody had a gift of using his music to bring people of disparate backgrounds together and, as Elliott remembered, it wasn't long until the folksingers and the lawyers "were all tapping their feet and smiling."[38]

One afternoon Woody and Jack were in Totsy, cruising along the Belt Parkway. Woody was in the midst of another retelling of his service in the Merchant Marine. As Woody's story continued to spool, Elliott glanced distractedly out of the car's window and spied a ketch with familiar masts and rigging. The sails were not in terribly good condition; it appeared as if they had been patched, stitched together from burlap sacks. Elliott watched as the vessel made its way toward Sheepshead Bay and out to sea. Jack politely interrupted Guthrie's merchant marine saga, "Woody, there goes my army blanket and a good crew of young men on the good ship *Argosy*." Guthrie and Elliott watched in silence as the ragtag ketch sailed slowly by on its way to the Caribbean. For one moment, and just one moment, Elliott genuinely wished he had been able to afford the two-thousand-dollar fee to crew on the boat. But he reckoned at this moment of his life "I was in a better place, riding in Woody Guthrie's car."[39]

Guthrie was intrigued and perhaps a bit nonplussed by his eager protégé, but he recognized Jack's talents and his unorthodox musical tutelage continued. Though mostly celebrated as a guitar player and harmonica blower, Woody was also a rough-edged fiddler. He taught Jack how to back up what he called his "panther squall" fiddling with an appropriate rhythmic guitar accompaniment. In subsequent years, Jack recalled Woody's effect on the mechanics of his own guitar style proved invaluable, that playing a facile accompaniment behind "a real country fiddle" remained his "favorite way of playing guitar."[40]

Despite the fact that Woody was more than twice Jack's age, 39 years to Jack's 19, Guthrie thought enough of his friend to invite him to join a folk group he was forming. The quartet Woody had in mind would act as a rough-hewn alternative to the slick Weavers who were, improbably, riding high on the popular music charts. Woody's group was to feature Cisco Houston, Jack, Marianne "Jolly" Robinson, and himself. Though the outfit never got off the ground, Jack, to his delight, got to meet Cisco Houston, Guthrie's acknowledged best buddy, singing partner, and fellow Merchant Marine seaman.[41]

Nora Guthrie, Woody's daughter and the youngest of the three children in the Guthrie household, would recall that the years Elliott spent in her father's company were important to her father's own legacy. "It was a strange moment in time when my Dad was *losing* it," Nora told Elliott's daughter, Aiyana, during the filming of *The Ballad of Ramblin' Jack*. "I think, in some way, he knew it. He was losing his life. I think he was very grateful to have a protégé right there. There was some kind of very wonderful thing that happened in that moment when he was losing his life and here was this young guy saying 'How do you do this? How do you do that? What are you doing?' And I think in some way my Dad was so happy to hand over everything he knew and everything about himself that he *could* pass on. Because he knew that he didn't have time."[42]

Elliott proved to be an excellent student. He perfected most of Guthrie's mannerisms, musical and otherwise, becoming something of a doppelganger. He could perfectly mimic the drowsy cadences of Guthrie's speech and the rough eccentricities of Woody's guitar playing. Woody was not consciously grooming a protégé; Elliott remembered his tutelage as coolly informal. Woody was, in Elliott's estimate, "offended by the concept of teaching." "It would have been a lot easier if he could have showed me what I was trying to learn," Elliott admitted. But Woody was neither interested nor, perhaps, capable of extending any formal mentorship to his young friend. Elliott assimilated the nuances of Woody's guitar and vocal styles by watching him "play from every angle."[43]

Before long, Elliott had Guthrie's style down so perfectly that Woody's friends and admirers were offended by the eerie appropriation. Jack had, in effect, become Woody's ghost. He had made himself, in his own words, into an almost "perfect mimic" of Guthrie. He had Woody Guthrie down "to the very last movement and gesture and facial expression." "Some people said I thought I *was* Woody Guthrie," Jack recalled, but "Woody didn't seem to mind." Perhaps Woody didn't, but many of Guthrie's old friends were acutely aware that Jack was appropriating the mannerisms of an ailing man. Elliott recalled that many of Woody's friends "would be visibly shaken or make rude remarks" to his face. They challenged Jack to try to find out who he really was, to develop his own distinct musical persona. He understood that their arguments, though at times personal and hurtful, were well meaning. They wanted Elliott to find his own voice. But Elliott was satisfied in his role as Guthrie's finest and most worshipful apprentice. It probably would not be too far from the truth to say that the Jack Elliott of 1951–1952 *revered* Woody Guthrie. In that light, one can understand why Jack would later refer to Woody as "a cross between Jesus and Will Rogers and Mother Maybelle Carter."[44]

There was at least one serious price to pay for living and working alongside Woody Guthrie, who had written thousands of songs and several thousands of words of prose in a creative span cruelly cut short by illness.

If Jack harbored any notion of becoming a songwriter, he found the standard set by Guthrie was too daunting. Woody would spend hours at his typewriter, tapping away effortlessly on the keys. He sometimes fashioned a new song from something that happened that day or from a news clipping that caught his fancy. But Elliott also recalled the Woody of the early 1950s "spent a lot of time rewriting his old songs." As Guthrie captured in words nearly everything that went on around him, it was not long before Elliott, too, became the subject of one of Woody's songs: "All the Buck Elliott's around, eatin' sody crackers, rollin' on the ground." It has been said that the instrument that Guthrie played best was the typewriter, and it's true that the file cabinets of the Woody Guthrie archives brim with unrecorded songs and reams of unpublished text. Elliott told the *Worcester Phoenix*, "I used to look over [Woody's] shoulder as he'd sit there at the typewriter and knock off these songs just as quick as you could blink. And each time they'd be perfect and needed no correcting. So after watching that I realized there was no way I was gonna top *that*." Elliott made the decision right then and there that "it would be better if I just did what I did best: find the songs and interpret them the way they suited me." Though Elliott would exert little effort crafting his own songs, he understood the components of great songwriting and was profoundly moved by Guthrie's gift of telling a "terrible damn story" in song. In the songs of Woody Guthrie, Elliott found a "sort of an operatic sadness." It was a mix of journalism and poetry akin to "newspaper reportage, reciting the facts unemotionally, leaving it up to the listener to feel the emotions." For Jack Elliott, Guthrie's influence was "very profound."[45]

One facet of Woody's persona that Elliott did not necessarily embrace was an enthusiasm for socialism and the politics of the Left. "I was . . . much more interested in the cowboy thing than the politics of Woody Guthrie," he admitted. He was sympathetic to many of the causes Woody championed, but he was, both musically and spiritually, a free, apolitical spirit. Regardless, he admired the fearlessness that Guthrie brought to his art, lifestyle, and politics. "Woody was too honest, too real, for people to tolerate," Elliott reminisced. "They wanted things sugared up. Woody wouldn't do that." Neither, in his own way, would Jack Elliott.[46]

One benefit of his friendship with Guthrie was that Jack enjoyed access to many of the musicians, writers, and folklorists who, in a few years' time, would become the progenitors of America's nascent folk music revival. One night, Woody and Jack were sitting in *Mother Hubbards*, a small Greenwich Village eatery. The Weavers had an engagement at the Village Vanguard nightclub only a few doors down. During a stage break,

Pete Seeger strolled into the restaurant and Woody introduced Pete to his 19-year-old protégé. "Woody was one of the best liars that I had ever met," Elliott recalled, and it was with that caveat he recalled Guthrie giving him a pretty big buildup. Woody said, "Pete, say 'Hello' to Jack Elliott . . . The world's best guitar picker!" Though Woody's declaration appeared genuine, Elliott admitted, "I wasn't ready for it."[47]

By the spring of 1952, Guthrie's life seriously began to unravel. He and his wife, Marjorie, had separated in late autumn 1951. She had wearied of Woody's apparent alcoholism, of his philandering, and of his occasional, but very disturbing and frightening, outbursts. There was obviously something wrong, but no one knew what was fueling Woody's downward spiral. In the spring and summer of 1952, following an uncharacteristic physical attack on his estranged wife, Guthrie sought treatment for his alcoholism on three separate occasions at King's County, Bellevue, and Brooklyn State hospitals. It was at Brooklyn State Hospital that Woody learned that alcohol was only part of the problem. He was diagnosed as suffering from Huntington's chorea, the incurable disease that had left his mother to waste away in the insane asylum in Norman, Oklahoma. Upon his release from Brooklyn State Hospital in September 1952, Guthrie, frightened of his future prospects and distraught over the disintegration of his marriage, traveled to Topanga Canyon, outside of Los Angeles, to visit his friends Will and Herta Geer. It was there that Woody met Anneke Van Kirk Marshall, a free spirit who had moved to Topanga from New York City at the bequest of her actor-husband. Though Anneke was a newly-wed, she and Guthrie entered into a spontaneous affair, one that scandalized even the bohemian, open-minded cabal that populated Topanga. In January 1953 Woody and Anneke, unwelcome at Topanga, decided to return to New York City.[48]

In March 1953 Woody sought out Elliott, who had recently taken ownership of a rusting Model A Ford. He had purchased the car from a farmer for fifteen dollars and remembered "the engine was totally plugged up—it took me about ten days to get the thing running." Ignoring the car's shortcomings, Woody asked Jack if he would consider driving Anneke and himself in the Model A to Florida. Guthrie wanted to visit his friend, the writer and activist Stetson Kennedy, who had, until recently, been living in an abandoned bus on the edge of the Beluthahatchee Swamp. Beluthahatchee, a steamy, mosquito-infested wetland, was situated only a few miles outside of Jacksonville. Elliott agreed and the trio set off in the Model A, suffering frequent breakdowns and costly repairs. Regardless, Anneke remained particularly excited about the trip, bringing along a camera to record their adventure. She later collected her photographs in an oversized ledger book that documented their many visits to repair garages along the way: "Now this is another one of our many costly thrilling little break-downs. We certainly hated to see the hills roll by after each repair job," she wrote beneath one photograph in her elegant handwriting. Four days after leaving New York they arrived in Beluthahatchee, only to find that Kennedy had since moved on. But the derelict bus that served as his home, recently ransacked by the Ku Klux Klan, remained. The threesome moved in and set up house, but Elliott did not stay long, sensing immediately that he was the odd man out. Before he left, Elliott surrendered the title of the Model A to Guthrie, feeling it was the right thing to do; Woody had paid more in repairs than Jack originally had paid to purchase the vehicle. Shortly after Elliott left Beluthahatchee, Anneke and Woody's odd but peaceful repose was shattered when Guthrie absentmindedly poured gaso-line on a still smoldering campfire. The flames lit up his right arm, leaving him with painful, severe burns and lasting tendon damage. Woody would never again play his guitar with any facility. Six months later, Woody's arm was still crooked, bent in such a manner that he could no longer strum the guitar between the bridge and sound hole, forcing him to strum the instrument farther up the neck. Upon his return to New York, Woody partly compensated for the loss by composing *Skybally*. It was a grim play partly inspired by the UFO mania gripping the country, but the scenario also recounted the fateful campfire dousing. Although Elliott had departed Beluthahatchee prior to the accident, Woody chose to include Jack as a character in his dense and eccentric 48-page scenario, a phantom witness to the end of Guthrie's career as a musician.[49]

In the summer of 1953, a young Los Angeles–based folksinger by the name of Frank Hamilton arrived in New York City. Hamilton had fallen under sway of the 1950s folk song revival, his interest in the music nur-tured by the West Coast arm of People's Songs. Pete Seeger, the Weavers, Josh White, Woody Guthrie, and Lead Belly were all heroes to Hamilton, and he was held in regard as a tradition-steeped guitarist and banjo player. Hamilton had made arrangements to travel through the southeastern United States with Guy Carawan, a folksinging friend from Los Angeles. Carawan, too, was a member of People's Songs, a student of American folk music who played expertly on a variety of traditional instruments. Before setting off for the South, the two friends were in New York City to visit friends and to see the blues singer and guitarists Brownie McGhee perform at Feltons, a tavern in Harlem. It was at that Harlem saloon that Hamilton and Carawan would meet another fan of Brownie's, Jack Elliott.[50]

Elliott had befriended Brownie through Woody. McGhee was intrigued by Woody's young friend. Impressed by Jack's talent, Brownie nonetheless offered some sage advice that would take some years to absorb. "Jack and I would play the blues together and from that Jack picked up as much as he could—from me and others he met in New York and Brooklyn," Brownie told writer Bill Yaryan. "My advice to Jack was to play the blues you must come through yourself. You'll never be able and never will be a Woody or a Rev. Gary Davis or a Big Bill Broonzy. But you can be Jack when you apply what you learn from anyone."[51]

In the interval between McGhee's set, Hamilton and Carawan chatted with Elliott and mentioned their pending southern sojourn. Elliott was enthused by their plan, so much so that he asked if it was possible that he might come along. Carawan was reluctant to bring Jack on as they had only just met and he simply didn't know him that well. But Elliott tagged along with Frank and Guy for the duration of their stay in New York, and, after spending a week in his company, Carawan found himself genuinely impressed by Elliott's ability to "busk," to raise cash by singing on the street. Carawan was new at the game and had doubts that street singing would afford them petrol and the occasional meal, so he thought Elliott would prove to be an asset. Through Woody's mentoring Elliott was already an old pro at busking. Carawan noticed that Jack was completely at ease breaking out his guitar and singing for his supper at the top of his lungs, oblivious to the bemused stares and occasional ridicule of those who passed by. It was an early example of the "ineradicable quality" that folklorist John Greenway would assess as one of Elliott's (and Woody's) strongest traits, the "utter lack of self consciousness that one usually finds only in blind singers."[52]

So Jack was officially brought on and he climbed into Carawan's Plymouth without a change of clothes or an instrument case to house his Gretsch. The trio motored south through New Jersey, Delaware, and Maryland, stopping off in Washington, D.C., for a brief visit with Mike Seeger, the son of ethnomusicologist Charles and Ruth Crawford Seeger. They pushed on, Carawan and Elliott sharing the steering wheel as Hamilton had not yet tested for a license. Hamilton spent most of the trip in the backseat, practicing the banjo and singing through a deep catalog of folk songs he had committed to memory.[53]

One of those songs Hamilton sang was the haunting ballad "South Coast." The words had been written by Lillian Bos Ross, who had earlier composed an evocative poem, "The Monterey Coast," from which she sourced her ballad. Lillian Bos Ross was a pseudonym for Shanagolden

Ross. Ross had settled in the desolate area of California's Big Sur region where she lived among a small, fiercely private literary and artistic community that included author Henry Miller. Elliott was completely taken by the mysterious and haunting song and was determined to add it to his repertoire. The problem was Hamilton would only perform the atmospheric ballad when it rained; it was that kind of song. Elliott bided his time and prayed for bad weather.[54]

After visiting with Carawan's uncle in Mesic, North Carolina, and suffering a terrible sunburn from a long afternoon on a shrimp boat, the three pushed on to Asheville and Bascom Lamar Lunsford's Mountain Dance and Folk Festival. Lunsford was regarded, not inappropriately, as the "Minstrel of the Appalachians." He had been born in 1882 and was, at various stages in his long and productive life, a fruit tree salesman, a beekeeper, a lawyer, and a politician. Lunsford was a repository of several hundred authentic mountain ballads and folk songs that he performed on five-string banjo and fiddle and sang in a clinch-throated manner that belied his rather stiff, formal appearance. Politically, Lunsford was a reactionary, a dogged anti-Semite wary of the interest in American folk music by those on the Left. Carawan, Elliott, and Hamilton knew nothing of Lunsford's politics. They were only familiar with his Folkways recording *Smokey Mountain Ballads*, which they held in high regard. They introduced themselves as a trio of "folk-singers just come down from New York City," and that admission was enough to set off alarm bells. "You boys Communists?" Lunsford asked with suspicion. Hamilton and Elliott could barely contain their amusement, but Carawan, the most politically conscious member of the three, was troubled by the old man's antagonism.[55]

The trio continued their trek deep into the Smokey Mountains. They happened upon a fiddle and banjo contest where they met a colorful character by the name of Ted Sutton, a banjo player known among the locals as Maggie's Old Man. Sutton lived in nearby Maggie Valley, North Carolina, and hosted a weekly series of mountain music gatherings at Ted Sutton's Hillbilly Campground. It was late into a whiskey- and music-filled night when the three friends gladly accepted Sutton's offer of a night's lodging at his rustic home. Ted was greeted at the door by his simmering wife, and the Suttons, in Elliott's recollection, staged "a family feud in our honor." The next morning, the three traveled to Nashville where they attended the Saturday night Grand Ole Opry broadcast from the Ryman Auditorium. There they listened to the music of Roy Acuff, Grandpa Jones, and Hank Snow, laughed at the comic antics of Dave "Stringbean" Akeman, and marveled at the five-string banjo pyrotechnics of Earl Scruggs.[56]

Following Nashville, Elliott suggested they set off to New Orleans, where a friend from New York, Billy Faier, had recently taken up residence. Faier was a supremely talented five-string banjo player, but there was one problem. Elliott did not have Billy's new address or telephone number. So their first stop in New Orleans was to visit the Tulane University library in search of a telephone directory. Though they could not find a listing for a William Faier, they searched out a copy of *Mister Jellyroll*, Alan Lomax's biography of the great jazzman Jelly Roll Morton, and studied the map found inside. They finally chanced upon Billy at the famed Café du Monde on Decatur Street, just off the Mississippi River, not far from the Jax Brewery. Billy was sitting in a mysterious mist of white confectionary sugar used to powder the beignets, a local fried doughnut. Though Billy was surprised to find Elliott and his two folk-singing friends in New Orleans, he graciously invited everyone to his apartment off an alley on 912 Toulouse Street for an impromptu party. The music-making session lasted until sunrise.[57]

It was from this memorable sojourn that Elliott would craft his finest song, "912 Greens" (the title an "obtuse" reference to Jelly Roll Morton's "219 Blues"). "912 Greens" is, essentially, Ramblin' Jack's musical take on Jack Kerouac's *On the Road*. If Kerouac's novel was populated with troubled figures from America's psychic fringe, the cast of "912 Greens" featured only warm, homespun characters, friendly country folk who would graciously share their meals, their homes, their corn whiskey, their music, and their folkways. The worse bit of malfeasance in "912 Greens" is the tossed crockery of the "family feud" at the cabin home of Maggie's Old Man. "912 Greens" perfectly captures the wistfulness of that brief interlude when you are young and free and restless and healthy and filled with wanderlust. The song is also Elliott's one masterwork as a songwriter, marrying his gift for storytelling with a simple, but hauntingly evocative, guitar figure.[58]

If "912 Greens" owes more than a little something to Kerouac, it is not all that surprising. Woody was not the only literary and cultural icon whom Jack would befriend in the early 1950s. After returning to New York City from New Orleans, Elliott began a romantic liaison with an alluring, curly haired strawberry blonde by the name of Helen Parker. Parker, whose taste for alcohol was rarely sated, lived in a small apartment overlooking Bleecker Street at a time when Greenwich Village was still populated by authentic bohemians. Elliott remembered Parker as something of a "literary groupie." She had many relationships with men of a literary bent, and was once remembered by the otherwise proudly homosexual Allen

Ginsberg as the only girl he ever loved. She also boasted of relationships with Ernest Hemingway, *Mister Roberts* playwright Joshua Logan, and the novelist John Dos Passos.[59]

One afternoon in 1953, while at Helen Parker's apartment, Elliott was introduced to a young, struggling writer by the name of Jack Kerouac. Kerouac was immediately intrigued by Helen's cowboy boyfriend; Kerouac's antenna for offbeat, interesting people was acute. After listening to the Stetson-topped Elliott drawl through a few meandering yarns that seemed to go everywhere and nowhere at the same time, Kerouac told him, by way of a compliment, "I like the language of bums." That was all that Elliott had to hear before reaching for his guitar and performing a cycle of Guthrie songs. Though Elliott was not aware of it when they first met, he learned Kerouac was already "a big fan of Woody's." "That was one of the reasons he could relate to me," Elliott explained. "I was singing Woody Guthrie songs." Elliott would later describe Kerouac as "the literary offspring of Woody Guthrie."[60]

Long before it was published, Elliott and Parker listened, reportedly for three days and nights, to Kerouac as he sat on the floor of Helen's apartment and read passionately through the continuous roll of teletype paper on which he composed his novel *On the Road*. Elliott recalled he took a turn reading through the manuscript when Kerouac's voice gave out. Elliott loved *On the Road*, as "I'd already been hitchhiking and traveling all over, so I was the perfect audience."[61]

In the autumn of 1953, the actor-musicians Tom and Pat Clancy rented out the Cherry Lane Theater at 38 Commerce Street in Greenwich Village. The Clancys were producing and acting in such plays as Paul Vincent Carroll's *The Wise Have Not Spoken* and Sean O'Casey's *The Plow and the Stars*. Unfortunately, the productions, regardless of merit, were not bringing in audiences of considerable size, and they found themselves unable to meet the terms of the theater's rent. In December, the Clancys met and befriended Lou Gordon, a union official of left-wing pedigree. The Clancys asked Gordon if he would consider helping stage a series of folk music concerts at the Cherry Lane Theater. Proceeds from the concerts, which would start at midnight after the play had let out, would help defray rent costs. The concerts, advertised as "Swapping Song Fair," would feature a mix of established and new folk music talent.[62]

Jack Elliott's first professional concert was performed on the stage of the Cherry Lane Theater in the early winter of 1954. Hired on as support for Tom and Liam Clancy, Jack was paid the princely sum of $100, and he was in dire need of the money. He was barely supporting himself with odd jobs, such as a tree surgeon, he had, begrudgingly, taken on when his fortunes ebbed. To his dismay, Elliott's professional folk-singing debut was shortened to less than 30 minutes when Oscar Brand, an established "star" in New York City folk circles, arrived early and managed to negotiate some stage time of his own. It was a disappointment, but Jack was pleased to find both Helen Parker and Jack Kerouac had managed to make it to the theater for his professional debut. He recalled, "It was good to see [Kerouac] out there in the audience with a big smile." Kerouac had good reason to smile, sitting in the darkened audience and gently caressing the hand of Helen Parker.[63]

Though his name is often associated with Beat culture, Elliott candidly admitted he was not aware that a new literary movement was in the ascendant. Helen Parker hosted a series of parties at her apartment, and Elliott often found himself in the company of such erudite friends and future luminaries as Kerouac, Allen Ginsberg, Gregory Corso, William S. Burroughs, Alan Ansen, and David Amram. Though he was on a first-name basis with many of the scene's major players and enjoyed their company, he was not a writer and he stood apart from them, an outsider among outsiders. Near Christmas 1953, and at Neal Cassady's behest, Elliott and Kerouac had been planning to hitchhike to California, but the plan was scrapped when Kerouac "slumped into a paralytic depression."[64]

It was just as well, since a little bit of folk music history would have been lost. Elliott had wanted to get into the recording studio for some time. He learned that Woody was going to the Union Square office of Stinson Records where he planned on watching a session that was to feature Jack's friends Roger Sprung, Bob Carey, and Erik Darling. Elliott told Woody, "I would love to sing [...] on that." Bob Harris, the president of Stinson, was preparing the *American Folksay* album and would have likely welcomed Elliott, as he was not unwilling to bring in fresh talent. But Guthrie told Jack flatly that he was not yet ready. Though he would not get to record for Stinson, on January 18, 1954, Woody had a change of heart and brought Sonny Terry and Elliott to Moses Asch's Folkways Records office for an impromptu session. The surviving recordings, which are believed to be Guthrie's last, have, to date, not been commercially issued, save for a single, heavily edited performance of "Railroad Bill."[65]

Though the Asch recordings find an ailing Guthrie performing well below standard, the surviving reels importantly capture the only collaboration of Woody and his most celebrated disciple. Guthrie sings most of the lead vocals, accompanying himself on guitar, harmonica, mandolin, and fiddle. Elliott plays guitar throughout most, but not all, of the session, singing harmony and adding background vocals on a few songs. The first reel begins with a tuning-up session, followed by a microphone test of "New Morning Train" and an untitled guitar and harmonica instrumental. There are also attempts at such country music standards as "Rubber Dolly," "More Pretty Girls Than One," "This Train Is Bound for Glory," "Wabash Cannonball," "Old Time Religion," and "Roll on Buddy (Nine Pound Hammer)," before the reel spools out midway through a take of "Ezekiel Saw the Wheel." The second reel begins with a second attempt at "Ezekiel," followed by Woody and Sonny's twin blues harp performance of "Freight Train Blues." Elliott rejoins the session for trio performances of "Railroad Bill," "How Long Blues," "Bed on the Floor." There is also a third reel, undated, that is believed to be from the same session. This reel opens with a trio performance of "Put on My Traveling Shoes." Woody follows with a "Sukey Jump Tune" on solo fiddle before performing a series of guitar duets with Jack on "Rubber Dolly," "Ryestraw," "How Long Blues," and "Alabama Bound." There are also two additional songs with Sonny Terry sitting in ("Take This Hammer" and "Railroad Bill") before the reel ends with an ensemble performance of "Worried Man Blues." These sessions for Asch are the last studio recordings of Woody Guthrie.[66]

In May 1954 Jack Kerouac sat down at the typewriter at his mother's apartment in Richmond Hill, New York, and composed a long, rambling letter to Allen Ginsberg, filled with meditations on Buddhist practices and stories detailing the doings of mutual friends. Midway through, Kerouac mentioned that Helen Parker "Finally got rid of Jack Elliott the singing cowboy who apparently was costing her a lot of money." Kerouac wrote, ruefully, "poor Jack, he can't work, he's like the robin, he sings." Kerouac also related the story of an eventful stroll through Greenwich Village with Elliott. Jack was busking with Billy Faier when Bill Fox of Esoteric Records pulled up in his car to listen for a spell. Kerouac enthused that Elliott's audience quickly swelled to "a hundred and two children" from a nearby school and "an old Frisco wino with his bottle and broken pulpy nose." The ecstatic wino was so moved by Elliott's music that he reached into his shirt and pulled out a sandwich, offering it to Jack as a token of appreciation. Caught in the moment, Kerouac called over to Bill Fox, imploring his friend to "give these boys an audition for Esoteric."[67]

It would not have been a good fit. Esoteric Records was a small New York City–based jazz label, with little interest in folksingers. But Elliott's music had already come to the attention of Jac Holzman. Holzman, an electronics enthusiast and folk music fan, formed the Elektra Records label in 1950 while still a college student, issuing a series of ten-inch discs from

Jean Ritchie, Frank Warner, Cynthia Gooding, Hally Wood, Tom Paley, and Sonny Terry. Holzman had secured the services of Ed McCurdy and Oscar Brand for an album he was preparing titled *Bad Men and Heroes*. He brought Elliott onto the project as well, Jack contributing three "Bad Men" songs, solo guitar and harmonica versions of "Pretty Boy Floyd," "Jesse James," and "Charles Guiteau." The songs were recorded under the most informal of circumstances in the kitchen of Holzman's Greenwich Village apartment on West 10th Street. In lieu of royalties, Elliott was paid the modest sum of $10 per song and given his first professional recording credit. He would later enthuse "that was a fair deal compared to a lot of other deals I've made."[68]

One afternoon in the spring of 1954, Guthrie and Elliott turned up at the Sunday session at Washington Square Park. Woody was all but unrecognizable. He had grown a thick, dark beard, flecked with gray, and his hair was an unruly, unkempt mess. Elliott recalled Guthrie was, at that time, "not real flush, or in the best of health," but everybody at the Park knew who he was and crowded around, deferring to his celebrity. They played a few songs together on their guitars and collected donations in an empty beer cup they had found on the ground. Once the cup was filled, they brought the contents to the San Remo Bar on the corner of Bleecker and MacDougal Streets. They poured the coins onto the counter and found they had raised exactly $11.60. They each bought a beer to celebrate the windfall and converted the rest into paper money.[69]

Billy Faier was also visiting the park that afternoon. Faier had been asked to drive a friend's new Buick to California, a terrific opportunity, since he had a girlfriend he wished to visit in San Diego. Billy, hoping not to go it alone, was combing the Park for potential riders. The tenor saxophonist Brew Moore was sitting peacefully on a park bench when Billy drove through "shouting 'Anyone for the coast?'" "[T]here wasn't shit shaking in New York," Moore remembered, "so I said '[H]ell, yes.'" Moore was not a folkie, but a well-respected disciple of the bebop tenor saxophonist Lester Young. Though a native of Mississippi, Moore had moved to Manhattan, establishing himself as a fixture in the cabarets of Greenwich Village; such greats as Charlie Parker would have Brew "sit in" with their combos whenever they came to town. But with nightclub audiences thinning and interest in bebop on the wane, Moore accepted the offer of a free ride to the West Coast. That afternoon, Guthrie and Elliott also got wind of Billy's plans and they too decided to sign on. Woody figured they would set off for Topanga, promising to show Jack the parcel of land he was purchasing from his friend Bob DeWitt.[70]

The four musicians made for a lively traveling party. There was no shortage of open containers in the car, and alcohol loosened tongues and tempers. Jack thought that Billy was an awful driver and resented his "hogging" the wheel, but that was the least of the conflicts. It soon was apparent that Moore and Guthrie held strong opinions, often at odds. Guthrie had been going on for a stretch regarding one of his favorite topics, the struggle to get all of America under the umbrella of one big union. Moore listened patiently as Guthrie sang the praises of the union movement, but could finally hold his tongue no longer. "Woody, I know what you think about unions," Moore interrupted, "and how you're so in favor of them, but I've been in the New Orleans musicians' union . . . and all they do is mess me around." Woody munched on Moore's protest before answering stoically, "Well, Brew, nothing is sacred to me, not even unions. If that one needs fixing, you ought to help fix it. But nothing is sacred to me." By the time the Buick rolled into Texas, everyone was in need of a desperate break from one another. They stopped at a roadside restaurant, stretching their legs and dining on hamburgers. But before returning to the car, Billy, Jack, and Woody pulled out their instruments for an impromptu jam session. Faier asked Moore to bring out his tenor sax and join in, but Brew refused, explaining politely, "I don't play in your style, it wouldn't mix." Billy suddenly remembered Moore did not care much for country and western music, so he coaxed him into the session by suggesting they play some blues. Moore relented, pulled out his saxophone, and began to blow. But Guthrie was so mortified by Moore's bebop free-style improvisation that he surprised everyone with the announcement that he would have nothing else to do with Brew Moore. For the remainder of the trip, Woody would only speak to Brew through an intermediary. Moore recollected that Guthrie and he "were the only juice heads in the car so Woody would say to Jack or Billy, 'Would you ask Brew if he'd like to split a bottle of port with me,' and I'd say 'You tell Woody that's cool with me.'"[71]

Topanga Canyon, a stretch of land some twelve miles up the coast from Los Angeles, was more than a home to its residents. During the McCarthy era, the community served as a refugee camp for left-tilting cultural and political artists. A score of blacklisted writers, artists, and actors carved out a creative hamlet there, one of the few places they could ply their trade before an appreciative audience. Woody, a longtime friend of Topanga settlers Will Geer and his wife, Herta, was an unlikely property owner in Topanga. On an earlier visit, he had negotiated a down payment on a desolate eight-acre plot he dubbed "Pretty Polly Canyon," the name derived from the victim of the murderous folk ballad. Folksingers, settled and transient, were particular cultural heroes among the residents of Topanga, and such friends and fellow travelers as Pete Seeger and Cisco Houston would visit whenever they came to town.[72]

One occasional visitor to Topanga was Derroll Adams, a five-string banjo player and artist. Adams had been born in Portland, Oregon, in November 1925, but his earliest memories were of displacement. Derroll's family was nomadic, often forced to relocate at a moment's notice. This was, in part, a result of the dictates of Derroll's father's dual career as a suitcase salesman and engineer for Washington State's Bonneville Power Administration. As a result of the constant shuffling between towns and school systems, Adams formed few friendships in his young years, and his manner seemed as melancholic as the old country songs sung to him by his mother and grandmother. At sixteen, Adams ran away from home and signed up for a stint in the U.S. Army, but would serve only three and a half months before his parents discovered his whereabouts and had him "taken out." He returned to school, but upon reaching legal age Derroll enlisted for stints in the coast guard and the navy. But it was clear that Derroll was not military material. Suffering anxiety disorders, Adams received a "psycho-neurosis" discharge from the service and returned to the West Coast.[73]

His time in the military was not a complete waste. As a child, he had fooled around a little with a harmonica, but while in the service he made friends with some "boys from the southern states" who introduced him to the rippling sounds of the five-string banjo. Derroll took on assorted odd jobs, first as a logger, or more accurately as a "windfall bucker," and later as an apprentice to a broom maker who played banjo. Fortuitously, that broom maker happened to be Jim Garland, the former Kentucky coal miner and union agitator, who taught a young Pete Seeger and the Almanac Singers such agit-prop labor struggle songs as "I Don't Want Your Millions, Mister" and "The Murder of Harry Simms." Derroll found himself enchanted by the needle sharp notes of the five-string banjo, finding many similarities between the aural textures of the African American instrument and the traditional Japanese music that he loved. Soon he found a niche, if not an income, as an itinerant artist, which is about the time that he started hanging around Topanga Canyon. Adams was reportedly making his home in a nearby cave, where he passed the time painting, sketching, and practicing the banjo. He would occasionally descend from the mountain for the opportunity to attend one of Will Geer's legendary "hootenanny" parties, where enthusiasts of folk songs enjoyed all night sings.[74]

At first, Derroll preferred to simply soak in the atmosphere, but as his banjo skills blossomed, so did his confidence. Before long he began to jam with the Topanga musicians, once performing an evening of old-time banjo and guitar duets with Woody. Though Adams admired Woody's music he did not particularly admire the man. Adams was affable and friendly to a fault; Guthrie was something of a curmudgeon. Elliott recalled, "Derroll didn't get along with Woody. He didn't even *like* Woody. Derroll met Woody toward the end of Woody's career when Woody himself was not always in the best of health anymore and he wasn't in good spirits like when I first met him." Though Derroll was remembered as amiable, he was by nature a melancholic loner.[75]

The Buick finally arrived in San Diego. Billy went to find his girlfriend, Moore traveled to San Francisco, and Woody and Jack set off for Topanga. Woody brightened whenever he spoke of the eight-acre tract he had purchased, and when the two friends finally neared the Canyon, Woody gestured to Jack and said, "Theah's th' approaches to 'm'laand." Elliott had expected to see a gate or a winding road or something, but instead found himself craning his neck skyward at a "forty foot sheer cliff with hand and toe holds." "Ah got eight acres, theah,' says Woody. "Five vertical, 2 horizontal an' one Ah jist ain't found yet." Woody and Jack scaled the cliff. Woody explained that he had left behind a folded tent on his last visit, so they would be able to set up camp atop Pretty Polly Canyon. But Woody, who had been drinking Olympia Pale Ale most of the day, chose to wrap himself in the tent and fall fast asleep. With Guthrie out of sorts and with little to do, Jack decided he would let Woody sleep and go off on his own. He carefully scaled back down the cliff and set off for Topanga so he could look up Frank Hamilton. Hamilton had taken up residence in the makeshift town that was built around the Theatricum Botanicum, Geer's outdoor theater. He found Hamilton easily enough, but the visit lasted well into the night and Jack decided it would be impossible to find his way back to Woody. It was pitch-black outside and the cliff face of Pretty Polly Canyon was a treacherous piece of ground to circumnavigate even in the best of conditions. He decided to spend the night at Geer's theater and reunite with Guthrie early the next morning.[76]

The next morning, Elliott discovered Woody had gone off. He was not at Pretty Polly Canyon and no one had seen him. It was only then that Elliott learned from the locals that Woody was not welcome in Topanga, that his running off with Anneke Marshall in 1953 was not remembered fondly. That scandal had set off an unfortunate chain of personal and romantic misfortunes among the residents of Topanga, and Woody was now persona non grata. Though it would be nearly a year until Elliott would see Guthrie again, he did receive a long, typed letter from him. Woody informed him that he had taken off for Olympia, Washington, and that he had recently spent a night in a Montana jail. He also told Elliott that he was of the opinion that Los Angeles–area folksingers were "sissified."[77]

With Woody suddenly gone, and with no alternate plan, Elliott chose to remain at Topanga. He stayed through the summer of 1954 and sang cowboy ballads and Woody Guthrie songs between performances at the Theatricum Botanicum. Guthrie, the man, may have been unwelcome, but his songs were still beloved. It was near the end of the summer when some of Derroll Adams's friends, excited by Jack's music, urged his return to the scene. But Derroll was not interested. He was quite content on his own, painting and practicing the banjo. But his friends were very insistent, wanting, almost desperately, for Derroll to meet Jack. Adams admitted, "I didn't want anything to do with it, but somehow the guys found me." He agreed to the meeting and when he finally made it to Topanga, Derroll found Jack on the Theatricum Botanicum stage, performing an improvisational comedy sketch with Will Geer. Afterward, Derroll's friends brought him over for the introduction.[78]

Since arriving at Topanga, Elliott had been hearing stories about the mysterious Derroll Adams. Though he had never laid eyes on him, Elliott claims to have recognized him right away. Before the two men could trade more than a few shy words of greeting, everybody gathered was already pushing them toward the stage, wanting to hear them sing together. But Derroll was not, as Elliott had been warned, the chattiest guy around.

"You're Derroll Adams?" Jack asked.

"Yup."

"Do you have your banjo with you?"

"Nope."

"Yeah, well . . . Uh, Bess Hawes has a banjo. Maybe we could borrow it. Would you play on Bess' banjo?"

"Yeah, I suppose."

Someone ran off to fetch Bess's five-string banjo. As they waited for the instrument to arrive, Elliott queried Derroll on what songs he knew, rattling off a list of titles to no good effect. Finally he asked, "Do you know the 'Muleskinner Blues'?"

"Yup."

Derroll recalled that he and Jack "ended up on the stage doing "Muleskinner Blues . . . the only song we could think of that we knew together." To no one's surprise, except their own, the spirited guitar and banjo duet of "Muleskinner Blues" "went over like a ball." "Everybody was cheering and yelling," Derroll remembered. At that very moment, with the music ringing and the crowd cheering them on, Jack Elliott and Derroll Adams became fast friends.[79]

Elliott thought of Derroll as "the first guy I felt comfortable [playing music] with since Woody." They were not inseparable by any means; Adams remembered, at first, they were only "running around together loosely." They had their own lives and affairs to tend to, and both needed to earn, at the very least, a meager income. Elliott earned a few dollars as a resident cowboy singer at Knotts Berry Farm, a western-themed tourist attraction near Buena Park. Less reputable employment included a brief stint as a "faith-cured cripple" at a revival church outside of Los Angeles. "It was a little church run by this woman," Elliott explained to the *Chicago Sun-Times*, "and I had to pretend I was healed by her. I was supposed to have paralyzed legs, and I did such a good job of it that the next person in line actually got healed. The whole point of it was the power of suggestion." On one occasion, Derroll and Jack headed to San Francisco where they planned to busk on the streets. The street singing led to an impromptu date at the University of California in Berkeley where, as Jack remembered, they "played all night, 'til the cops threw us out." They were paid all of twenty-five cents, but they didn't seem to mind. Elliott recalled the Berkeley gig as "a lot of fun" and, in the summer of 1954, that seemed to be enough. Though the two friends were not bringing in much beyond subsistence earnings, Jack and Derroll began to play together constantly, honing their instrumental skills, working out functional, if hardly sweet sounding, harmony parts. They were diamonds in the rough, but they were original and soon established a funky repertoire of blues, ballads, and hillbilly songs.[80]

Around this time Elliott decided to hitchhike, sans Derroll, to San Francisco to catch a Pete Seeger performance at a local bookshop. Following Pete's program, the two friends chatted and Seeger informed him that the singer and guitarist K. C. Douglas was scheduled to perform on a blues bill across the Bay in Oakland. Seeger, aware of Elliott's interest in blues music, told him he thought K. C. was great and worth checking out. On Pete's recommendation, Elliott made his way to Oakland. He enjoyed the music of Douglas, but found himself completely enthralled by another musician on the bill, a virtual one-man band named Jesse Fuller. Fuller was not exactly a hard blues singer as much as a songster. He played, often simultaneously, the twelve-string guitar, harmonica, kazoo, washboard, and *fotdella*, a foot-operated bass of his own invention.[81]

Elliott was impressed by the music and spirit of Fuller. Though his admiration for Jesse's "San Francisco Bay Blues," composed in 1954, is well known, he also set himself down to learn several more of Fuller's songs, such as "High Sheriff from Baltimore" and "The Monkey and the Engineer." Initially, Jesse was not sure what to make of Elliott. Jesse told writer Michael Goodwin, "Jack came lookin' for me when he first came out to California. I was playin' in a little theater, and here comes Jack Elliott with his old easy walking shoes on, and wearin' some overalls that looked like somebody had poured Clorox down one side of 'em. So I didn't want to be bothered with him—I thought he was just tryin' to get all he could out of me and let me go. That's the way a lot of them are. Well, every which way I turned, Jack was right there. I couldn't get shut of that guy. But I come to find out that he was all right."[82]

Elliott was making new friends at every turn. One occasional visitor to the Theatricum Botanicum was the writer Rod Usher. Usher had befriended June Hammerstein, an aspiring actress and waitress from New York. Hammerstein was born in Long Island but was reared in Bay Ridge, Brooklyn. The daughter of a cinema projectionist, Hammerstein developed an early interest in film and theater. She studied drama in high school and, finding she had some talent, decided to make acting her vocation. She honed her skills with small parts in summer stock productions, eventually being offered the role of Luba in the theatrical production of *Darkness at Noon*. At the suggestion of actor Todd Andrews, who played a lead role in the play *Mr. Roberts*, Hammerstein relocated to Hollywood in 1954. She moved into a small apartment on a cul-de-sac named Woody Trail perched high in the Hollywood Hills and, within a few months, was contracted for a small role in the Hugo Haas film *Tender Hearts*. *Tender Hearts* was sold to Universal Pictures and garnered favorable reviews, but as she was still very much an unestablished actress with a thin résumé, Hammerstein modeled to make ends meet. Hammerstein accepted an assignment posing nude for Ruby Usher, a painter and art teacher. Usher had previously employed June on modeling assignments, and it was during one such sitting she met Ruby's son, Rod, as he peered admiringly at her from behind a slightly ajar door. Hammerstein remembered Rod as "a charming, brilliant, but ne'er do well writer, painter and bum, who absolutely fascinated me." Rod was also something of a folk-music fan and told June that he wanted her to accompany him to Topanga Canyon the following Sunday. As June recalled in her autobiography *Even When It Was Bad It Was Good*, the "person Rod wanted me to hear at Will Geer's Herb Farm and theatre was a folksinger named Jack Elliott."[83]

It was love at first sight, at least on Jack's part. He was so smitten with June he chose to abandon the rural charm of Topanga Canyon and move into her apartment on Woody Trail. One night while out on the town, June introduced Elliott to her friend the actor James Dean. Dean had been plying his trade onstage and on television but had only recently become a bankable film star due to the success of Elia Kazan's *East of Eden*. They met Dean in a parking lot outside of Googies, the famed Sunset Boulevard eatery frequented by cash-strapped Hollywood hopefuls. Dean pulled into the parking lot of Googies in style, gripping the wheel of his white Porsche Spyder, a cool platinum blonde in a white fur sitting beside him. June and Dean were sharing pleasantries when Dean took note of June's friend, a cowboy hat pulled down over his eyes and a guitar hanging off his shoulder. Turning his attention to Jack, Dean asked to hear a song. Elliott serenaded the actor for nearly an hour with a cycle of cowboy and Guthrie songs. Though he was not familiar with Dean's motion picture, June remembered Jack was totally charmed by his presence "and suddenly wanted to see Jimmy's films." Ramblin' Jack Elliott and James Dean would meet once more, under far more phantasmagorical circumstances.[84]

Much to June's surprise, Elliott began to talk of marriage. June enjoyed Elliott's rough-hewn music and was intrigued by his carefree, rambling lifestyle, but she was something of a free spirit and not anxious to marry. As Hammerstein (writing as June Shelley) offered in her autobiography, "I was enamored of Ramblin' Jack, but probably more in love with the music and the life . . . than with the man." As a student of the dramatic arts, June appreciated a good script. But everything that Jack Elliott did, onstage and in life, was entirely dependent on the moment and outrageously improvisational. It was especially maddening that Jack's casualness seemed to work for him. "As I got to know Jack better," June wrote, "I discovered he had no discipline at all, [that] his performance could as easily be 'off' as 'on.' But sometimes amazing things would happen when he got up in front of an audience, stopping songs in the middle to tell stories or jokes."[85]

After a maddeningly brief courtship, June accepted Jack's marriage proposal. In May 1955 the Elliotts were married at a civil ceremony in San Francisco, with Derroll Adams standing as Jack's best man. June found a vaguely dapper suit for Derroll in a local thrift shop for $3.10. But the suit hung awkwardly off his lanky frame and June was left "to pin it up for the wedding." Elliott also invited the Bay area boogie-woogie legend Burt Bales to the nuptials, but the pianist "didn't make it, somebody said he got drunk." Following the wedding, Jack and June hitchhiked slowly from California to New York City. The newlyweds spent one night as detainees in a New Mexico jailhouse, incarcerated as transients. Upon their arrival in New York, the couple made plans to meet with Jack's parents and old pal Woody Guthrie. Sadly, Woody was now a resident patient at Brooklyn State Hospital, his rambling days now behind him. The Elliotts told Woody they were planning to set off for Europe. Hammerstein acknowledged, "Europe . . . held no particular interest" to Jack, but she had consented to the marriage on the condition she could still embark on her long-planned trip. Dr. and Mrs. Adnopoz had given the newlyweds a generous cash wedding present, but June was determined not to use the gift except in case of an emergency. For their day-to-day expenses, June recalled that Jack had told her stories of how he and Woody "used to sing for their supper." "Well, if he could sing for his supper in America," June reasoned, "maybe he could sing for his supper in Europe too."[86]

Notes

1. Oscar Brand, *The Ballad Mongers: Rise of the Modern Folk Song* (New York: Funk & Wagnalls, 1962), 158–159; George Margolin, "Sidewalk Hootenanny," *People's Songs*, Vol. 2, No. 1–2, February/March 1947, 6; "Organization Page," *People's Songs*, Vol. 1, No. 1, February 1946, 3.

2. Kristen Baggelaar and Donald Milton, *Folk Music: More Than a Song* (New York: Thomas Y. Crowell Company, 1976), 274–275; Irwin Stambler and Grelun Landon, *The Encyclopedia of Folk, Country & Western Music* (New York: St. Martin's Press, 1984), 510; Mark Greenberg, "Ramblin' Jack: No Address, No Phone," *Frets*, Vol. 10, December 1988, 20–21; Roger Bull, "Ramblin' Jack Elliott Wandering This Way: Well Traveled, Well Versed Icon of the Folk Era Will Play Thursday at the Florida Theater," *Times-Union* (Jacksonville), 18 May 2004, Sec. Lifestyle, C-1.

3. Greenberg, "Ramblin' Jack: No Address, No Phone," 20–21.

4. Hank Reineke interview with Roger Sprung, Newton, CT, March 2002.

5. Jack Elliott, Noe Valley Ministry, San Francisco, 9 November 1999.

6. Hank Reineke interview with Roger Sprung.

7. Brand, *The Ballad Mongers*, 82–83.

8. Jack Elliott, Other End, New York City, 1 July 1975.

9. Randy Sue Coburn, "On the Trail of Ramblin' Jack," *Esquire*, April 1984, 82; Lee Winfrey, "In Woody's Image . . . and Beyond," *Miami Herald Sunday Magazine*, 18 April 1965, 8; Sheldon Harris, *Blues Who's Who* (New York: DaCapo Press, 1979), 173–174.

10. Steven Stolder, "Traveling Back with Ramblin' Jack Elliott," *NARAS Inforum*, www.grammy.com/features/jackelliot.html (accessed 22 May 1997); Woody Guthrie, *Struggle: Asch American Documentary #1* (Asch Records, No. 360), 1946; Woody Guthrie, *Ballads from the Dust Bowl* (Disc 610), circa 1947.

11. Stolder, "Traveling Back with Ramblin' Jack Elliott."

12. Edvins Beitiks, "Jack of Hearts," *San Francisco Examiner Sunday Magazine*, 4 August 1996, 10; Joe Klein, *Woody Guthrie: A Life* (New York: Alfred A. Knopf, 1980), 160.

13. Klein, *Woody Guthrie: A Life*, 78; Allan Taylor interview with Jack Elliott, *Shared Experience*, BBC Radio 2, broadcast 29 February 1996.

14. Stolder, "Traveling Back with Ramblin' Jack Elliott"; Beitiks, "Jack of Hearts," 10; Hank Reineke, "America's Love Affair with Fascism, and What It Did to Our Poets, Singers—from the 50's on," *Soho Arts Weekly*, Vol. 1, No. 2, 16 October 1985, 34-B.

15. Paolo Vites, "Ramblin' Jack Elliott," *On the Tracks*, No. 5, Spring 1995, 27.

16. Rob Patterson, "Guthrie Imitator Jack Elliott Has Grown into an American Original—and One of the . . . Monsters," *Austin American-Statesman*, 9 April 1998, XL Entertainment 10; Winfrey, "In Woody's Image . . . and Beyond," 8; John May interview with Jack Elliott, London, England, 12 February 2005. In an unpublished segment of his interview with Guthrie biographer Joe Klein, Elliott mentions he first saw Woody perform (with Betty Sanders and Pete Seeger) at a People's Songs hootenanny at 13 Astor Place in Manhattan in 1947.

17. Meg McConahey, "Travelin' Troubadour's Tales," *(Santa Rosa) Press Democrat*, 7 February 1999, Q15; Vites, "Ramblin' Jack Elliott," 27.

18. Vites, "Ramblin' Jack Elliott," 27; John May interview with Jack Elliott.

19. Vites, "Ramblin' Jack Elliott," 27; Winfrey, "In Woody's Image . . . and Beyond," 8.

20. Vites, "Ramblin' Jack Elliott," 27; Stolder, "Traveling Back with Ramblin' Jack Elliott."

21. Jack Elliott, *Woody Guthrie's Northwest: A Night of Music and Celebration*, Sky Church, Seattle, WA, 23 May 2001.

22. "Eric Von Schmidt, at 75; Musician, Artist—Eric Von Schmidt 75, Played Blues and Folk in Cambridge," *Boston Globe*, 5 February 2007, Obits 5E.

23. Dod Orsborne, "The Secret Adventures of Laundry Mark 45," *LIFE*, Vol. 25, No. 22, 29 November 1948, 104–120; Dod Orsborne, "The Phantom Islands," *LIFE*, Vol. 25, No. 23, 6 December 1948, 105–110; Jack Elliott, Bottom Line, New York City, 12 May 2000. The profile of Orsborne that sent Elliott to Connecticut to seek out Eric Von Schmidt was published in the February 1951 issue of *Argosy* magazine.

24. Joseph Sia, "Eric Von Schmidt—An Exclusive 'On the Tracks' Interview," *On the Tracks*, No. 4, Fall 1994, 22; Jack Elliott, Bottom Line, New York City, 12 May 2000.

25. Jack Elliott, Bottom Line, New York City, 12 May 2000.

26. Jack Elliott, *"Woody Guthrie's Northwest: A Night of Music and Celebration,"* Sky Church, Seattle, Washington, 23 May 2001; Jack Elliott, Unitarian Universal-

ist Church, Tucson, AZ, 10 April 1993, broadcast on station Community Radio KXCI, 91.3 FM, Tucson, AZ; Vites, "Ramblin' Jack Elliott," 27.

27. Vites, "Ramblin' Jack Elliott," 27; j. poet, "A Ramblin' Kinda Guy," *San Francisco Chronicle*, 1 October 2006, PK-46.

28. Jim Brown, Director, Harold Leventhal and Ginger Turek, Producers, *Woody Guthrie: Hard Travelin'* (video cassette).

29. Elliott, *Woody Guthrie's Northwest*.

30. Brown et al., *Woody Guthrie: Hard Travelin'*; Winfrey, "In Woody's Image . . . and Beyond," 8.

31. Brown et al., *Woody Guthrie: Hard Travelin'*.

32. Klein, *Woody Guthrie: A Life*, 364; Allan Taylor interview with Jack Elliott, "Shared Experience," BBC Radio 2, broadcast 29 February 1996.

33. Craig Harris, "A Mosaic of Stories," *Dirty Linen*, No. 63, April/May 1996, 17.

34. Harris, "A Mosaic of Stories," 17.

35. Harris, "A Mosaic of Stories," 17; "Joe Klein Interview Tapes—Ramblin' Jack Elliott—Topanga, Ca.," Woody Guthrie Foundation & Archives, 2000, 38.29.

36. Dave Hoekstra, "A Folkie's Land—Woody Guthrie Tribute Reveals Full Depth of Singer's Legacy," *Chicago Sun-Times*, 6 October 1996, Sec. Showcase, 21.

37. "Sketches," Woody Guthrie Archives—Artwork, Accessions 2004, 55.2, No. 1–9. "Sketches, Series #34, Drawings by Jack Elliott, Book #1."

38. Elliott, Unitarian Universalist Church, Tucson.

39. Jack Elliott, Bottom Line, New York City, 12 May 2000.

40. Karl Dallas, "Elliott Adnopoz—the Brooklyn Cowboy," *Melody Maker* 38, 28 September 1963, 10.

41. Joe Ross, "Ramblin' with Jack," *Folk Roots,* No. 115–116, January/February 1993, 40.

42. Nora Guthrie to Aiyana Elliott, *The Ballad of Ramblin' Jack* (Fox Lorber Centrestage/Winstar Video, WHE73134), 2001.

43. Jeff Stark, "Hard Travelin': Ramblin' Jack Has a Few More Stories to Tell," *Dallas Observer*, 9–15 April 1998, www.dallasobserve...ry=Ramblin' Jack Elliott (accessed 26 April 1998); John La Briola, "Ramblin' Man: Human Tumbleweed Ramblin' Jack Elliott Keeps on Rollin'," *Denver Westword*, 2 June 2005, www.westword.com/2005-06-02/music/ramblin-man/print (accessed 29 July 2007); Ross, "Ramblin' with Jack," 40.

44. Harris, "A Mosaic of Stories," 17; Stark, "Hard Travelin': Ramblin' Jack Elliott Has a Few More Stories to Tell"; La Briola, "Ramblin' Man: Human Tumbleweed Ramblin' Jack Elliott Keeps on Rollin'"; Buddy Blue, "Ramblin' Jack Elliott: The Rodeo Made Him Do It," *San Diego Union-Tribune*, 12 May 2005, Sec. Entertainment, 20.

45. Roger Catlin, "Ramblin' Jack Still a Cowboy at Heart: Ramblin' Jack Elliott at Home on the Road, the Motor Runnin'," *Hartford Courant*, 17 July 1992, E1; Beitiks, "Jack of Hearts," 10; Chris Flisher, "Living Legend: Ramblin' Jack Elliott Keeps Folk Standards High," *Worcester Phoenix*, 2–9 May 1997, www .worcesterphoe.../05/02/JACK_ELLIOTT.html (accessed 18 July 1997); Buddy Seigal, "Return Ticket: Folk Star Ramblin' Jack Elliott Has the Words and the Tunes," *San Diego Union-Tribune*, 13 April 2000, Sec. Night & Day, 31.

46. La Briola, "Ramblin' Man"; Rick Mitchell, "Ramblin' Jack Still Rustles Up Gems," *Houston Chronicle*, 8 April 1998, Sec. Houston, 1.

47. Jack Elliott, Tin Angel Café, Philadelphia, 17 May 1997.

48. Klein, *Woody Guthrie: A Life*, 387–389; Ed Cray, *Ramblin' Man: The Life and Times of Woody Guthrie* (New York: W. W. Norton, 2004), 359–362.

49. Bill Ellis, "Ramblin' Jack Elliott Earned His Nickname by His Mouth," *Memphis Commercial Appeal*, 31 March 2000, Sec. G, 2; Klein, *Woody Guthrie: A Life*, 389–391; Cray, *Ramblin' Man: The Life and Times of Woody Guthrie*, 363–364; Woody Guthrie, "*Skybally*" (1954), Woody Guthrie Foundation & Archives, Box 8, Folder 16.

50. Ronald D. Cohen, *Rainbow Quest: The Folk Music Revival & American Society, 1940–1970* (Amherst/Boston: University of Massachusetts Press, 2002), 3, 76.

51. Bill Yaryan, "Jack Elliott," *Folk Scene*, No. 10, August 1965, 4.

52. Cohen, *Rainbow Quest*, 3–4. John Greenway liner notes to *Ramblin' Jack Elliott* (Prestige-International Records, 13033), 1962.

53. Jack Elliott, "912 Greens," *Kerouac's Last Dream* (FolkFreak, FF 4005), 1981.

54. Lillian Bos Ross, *The Stranger: A Novel of the Big Sur* (New York: William Morrow, 1942); Katie Lee note to Chia Greer, Editor, "Sam Eskin Remembered—The Next Part . . .," www.passportjournal.org/Sam/part2.html (accessed 13 October 2007); Cohen, *Rainbow Quest*, 119–120.

55. Cohen, *Rainbow Quest*, 4–5; Kenneth S. Goldstein liner notes to *Minstrel of the Appalachians: Bascom Lamar Lunsford and His Banjo* (Riverside Folklore Series, RLP-12-645) (circa 1957).

56. Robert French, Michael Varhol, Richard Abramson, producers, *Banjoman* (Salad Production Company), 1975; Jack Elliott, "912 Greens," *Legends of Folk* (Red House Records, RHR CD 31), 1990.

57. Jack Elliott, Berkeley Blues Festival, University of California/Berkeley, 4 April 1970.

58. Bruce Sylvester, "Talk Talk: Ramblin' Jack Elliott," *Goldmine*, No. 442, 4 July 1997, 15.

59. Beitiks, "Jack of Hearts," 10.

60. Hoekstra, "A Folkie's Land"; Catlin, "Ramblin' Jack Still a Cowboy at Heart," E1; Gerald Nicosia, *Memory Babe: A Critical Biography of Jack Kerouac* (New York: Grove Press, 1983), 456.

61. Lew Herman, "Sounds: Ramblin' Man," *Creative Loafing (Charlotte)*, http://web.cln.com/archives/charlotte/newstand/c100999/sounds.htm (accessed 4 July 2001).

62. Sam Zolotow, "Charles Lederer to Guide Kismet," *New York Times*, 5 October 1953, 34; Israel G. Young, "Israel Young's Notebook," *Sing Out!* Vol. 18, No. 2–3, June/July 1968, 47; Cohen, *Rainbow Quest*, 105.

63. Catlin, "Ramblin' Jack Still a Cowboy at Heart," E1; John May interview with Jack Elliott.

64. Tom Clark, *Jack Kerouac* (San Diego: Harcourt Brace Jovanovich, 1984), 128.

65. Woody Guthrie, Jack Elliott, and Sonny Terry, "Railroad Bill," *The Ballad of Ramblin' Jack* (Vanguard Records, 79575-2), 2000; "Joe Klein Interview Tapes—Ramblin' Jack Elliott—Topanga, Ca.," 2000, 38.29; Smithsonian/Folkways Reference Recordings, CD 197: "Guthrie Dubs," CDR 198: "Guthrie Transfers," CD 205: "Guthrie Transfers."

66. Jeff Place, "Woody Guthrie's Recorded Legacy," in *Hard Travelin': The Life and Legacy of Woody Guthrie*," ed. Robert Santelli and Emily Davidson (Hanover, NH: Wesleyan University Press, 1999), 67; Klein, *Woody Guthrie: A Life*, 401; Guy Logsdon liner notes to *Woody Guthrie: Long Ways to Travel 1944–1949 The Unreleased Masters* (Smithsonian/Folkways Recordings, SF 40046), 1994, 10.

67. Jack Kerouac, *Selected Letters, 1940–1956*, ed. Ann B. Charters (New York: Viking Press, 1995), 412.

68. Chris Jorgensen, "An Interview with Ramblin' Jack Elliott," *DISCoveries*, Vol. 3, No. 10, October 1990, 99; Stolder, "Traveling Back with Ramblin' Jack Elliott."

69. poet, "A Ramblin' Kinda Guy," PK-46.

70. Mark Gardner liner notes to *Brothers and Other Mothers with Stan Getz, Al Cohn, Serge Chaloff, Brew Moore, Allen Eager: The Savoy Sessions* (Savoy SJL 2210), 1976.

71. Michael Pellecchia, "Paris on the Trinity," *Fort Worth Weekly*, 12 May 2004, www.fwweekly.com/content.asp?article=1151 (accessed 16 October 2007); Gardner liner notes to *Brothers and Other Mothers*.

72. Bess Lomax Hawes, *Sing It Pretty: A Memoir* (Urbana and Chicago: University of Illinois Press, 2008), 62–64; Klein, *Woody Guthrie: A Life*, 384–385; Cray, *Ramblin' Man: The Life and Times of Woody Guthrie*, 354–355.

73. Bill Yaryan, "Derroll Adams: Banjo Pickin' Expatriate," *Sing Out!* 17 December/January 1967–1968, 29–33; Dave Peabody, "The Banjo Man," *Folk Roots*, December 1990, 16–21.

74. Yaryan, "Derroll Adams: Banjo Pickin' Expatriate," 29–33; Peabody, "The Banjo Man," 16–21.

75. Jack Elliott, Bitter End, New York City, 26 October 2000.

76. Stan Darlington, "Jack Elliott and Derrol Adams," *Jazz Music*, Vol. 8, No. 5, September/October 1957, 8–9; Klein, *Woody Guthrie: A Life*, 402–403; Cray, *Ramblin' Man: The Life and Times of Woody Guthrie*, 368–369.

77. "Joe Klein Interview Tapes—Ramblin' Jack Elliott—Topanga, Ca."

78. Peabody, "The Banjo Man," 19.

79. Jack Elliott, Johnny D's, Somerville, MA, 13 May 1999.

80. Darlington, "Jack Elliott and Derrol Adams," 8; Hoekstra, "Jack Elliott Rambles into Town," *Chicago Sun-Times*, 8 June 1985, 21; Bill Yaryan, "Ramblin' Jack Elliott," *Sing Out!* Vol. 15, No. 5, November 1965, 27.

81. Barbara Dane, "Lone Cat Jesse Fuller," *Sing Out!* Vol. 16, No. 1, February/March 1966, 5–11; Irwin Stambler and Grelun Landon, *The Encyclopedia of Folk, Country & Western Music* (New York: St. Martin's Press, 1984), 252–254; Michael Goodwin liner notes to *Brother Lowdown* (Fantasy Records 24707), 1972.

82. Goodwin, *Brother Lowdown*.

83. June Shelley, *Even When It Was Bad . . . It Was Good* (Xlibris Corporation), 2000.

84. Shelley, *Even When It Was Bad . . . It Was Good*, 46.

85. Shelley, *Even When It Was Bad . . . It Was Good*, 44, 57.

86. Calvin Ahlgren, "'60's Folk Singer Ramblin' Jack Elliott Still Round and About," *San Francisco Chronicle*, 7 May 1989; June Shelley to Aiyana Elliott, *The Ballad of Ramblin' Jack*.

Rake and Rambling Boy   3

IN SEPTEMBER 1955, Jack and June boarded the French liner *Liberte* for LeHavre, France. The *Liberte* had once been the S.S. *Europa*, one of Germany's grandest ocean liners, but the Lloyd flagship had been surrendered to the French in 1946 as reparation following World War II. The *Liberte* now regularly ferried travelers between New York City and LeHavre. Upon their arrival in France, the Elliotts would need to transfer to the boat train for a short excursion across the English Channel to Southampton before traveling on to London.[1]

Once aboard the *Liberte*, Jack and June met Peggy Seeger, the daughter of musicologist Charles Seeger and composer Ruth Crawford Seeger. Peggy was blessed with a folksinging musical heritage, the sister of Mike and half-sister of Pete Seeger. The Elliotts learned that Peggy, a gifted five-string banjoist with a penchant for old-time music, was continuing on to Holland for a reunion with Mike. She promised them she would look them up when she returned to London.[2]

When the *Liberte* arrived at LeHavre, the Elliotts enjoyed their first glimpse of France before boarding the boat train to Southampton. They arrived in London in the early evening, booking a night's lodging in a nondescript bed-and-breakfast near Victoria Station. Though it was late by the time they settled their affairs, Jack and June decided to ride the underground to Piccadilly Circus and have their first look around. They arrived at Piccadilly near ten o'clock that evening.[3]

Though Elliott brought his guitar along, he had not planned on doing any busking that first night. There were relatively few people milling about, but it wasn't long before someone took notice of his cowboy hat and guitar case, a rare sight in central London. Suddenly, a voice boomed "Play the *Rock Island Line!*" Only hours after arriving in London, Elliott found himself fielding a request for an old Lead Belly song. "Where did you ever hear *that?*" Jack inquired. "Oh, it was a big hit!" Jack was nonplussed. He had imagined he had brought to England "a secret bag of songs that nobody had ever heard before." But he learned that night that Lead Belly's "Rock Island Line" had been a huge hit in Britain for the singer and guitarist Lonnie Donegan.[4]

Donegan was a star in England, the self-crowned "King of Skiffle." The skiffle phenomenon was to Great Britain what, in simplest terms, the folk music revival would become in America. It was a homegrown music movement that put instruments into the hands of nonprofessionals, mostly earnest and impressionable youngsters. The skiffle musician John Hasted contributed an explanative essay to *Sing Out!* reasoning that in the United States there was a tradition for songs from roots sources to "crossover" onto the popular music charts of the day. Circumstances in England were different. There was no populist interest in folk music; the study of folk song was mostly a formal, scholarly pursuit, an academic exercise. To Hasted's disappointment, England did not share an American-style populist tradition of "home grown guitar music, blues, [and] country and western singing." Instead, Britons had been served a menu of professionally performed music hall, pops, and classical music offerings. It was all very passive; you enjoyed your favorite songs in the comfort of your local theater or at home on the family radio, but you were rarely moved to make your own music. That all changed in the 1940s when jazz and blues music came to England's shore courtesy of American soldiers. Hasted noted the vibrant sounds "swept into the hearts of the young people," but these youthful adherents wanted to do more than listen. The American music had an innate do-it-yourself ethos, and the kids wanted to approximate the sounds and styles of the old blues record they were enjoying. But the skifflers, as they were soon called, did not sound much like the musicians and singers they admired; as late starters, they were not yet the most proficient of instrumentalists. But they were earnest and suffered no shortage of enthusiasm. Amateur skiffle bands, consisting of guitars, washboards, tenor banjoes, and all types of supplemental instruments, mushroomed. Skiffle's biggest star was Lonnie Donegan, a toothy, grinning Glaswegian who, by most accounts, held himself in high regard. Unlike most skifflers, Donegan was not some starry-eyed amateur. He had been a member of Chris Barber and Ken Colyer's jazz bands but brashly struck out on his own when he sensed the timing was right. Donegan soon recorded a number of hit singles, his biggest sellers often fashioned from American folk songs. In 1955, Donegan charted with fractured, hyperventilated versions of "John Henry" and Lead Belly's "Rock Island Line." He also helped popularize such American folk blues songs as "Jack O' Diamonds," "Lonesome Traveler," and "The Midnight Special." Donegan was also somewhat of a Woody Guthrie fan, at a time when there were not all that many in England, and in 1958 scored an unlikely hit single with Guthrie's "Grand Coulee Dam."[5]

England's obsession with skiffle caught them off guard, but the Elliotts had not arrived totally unprepared. Prior to leaving the United States, Pete Seeger had provided Elliott with a list of contacts: mostly Leftist musicians and scholars aligned with the more traditional, noncommercial, arm of the British folk scene. Among the names high listed were the ballad collector A. L. "Bert" Lloyd, the folksinger and song collector Ewan MacColl, and, most importantly, the American folklorist Alan Lomax, an old friend of Guthrie's who left the United States in 1950 to wait out the McCarthy-era blacklist.

Albert Lancaster "Bert" Lloyd was born on September 29, 1908, in London. An esteemed folksinger and ballad collector, Lloyd was one of the principal engines in the folk-music revival of the British Isles. Lloyd was a classic, self-made man, staunchly political, who embraced the concept that art must be used as a weapon in the class struggle. It was in this spirit that he helped found the Workers Music Association (WMA) in 1939, later to morph into the Topic Record Company of London. The first 78-rpm single issued by the WMA featured, not surprisingly, "The Internationale," the anthem of the Communist movement (more surprising was that the second and third disc of the WMA *also* featured the song). The gifted English folksinger and songwriter Ewan MacColl would press his first disc for Topic in 1950. MacColl was a perfect artist for the WMA; he was not only a gifted poet, actor, and musician, but also a committed champion of world socialism as well. The Topic Record Company would, in time, become less doctrinaire, documenting the traditional ballads and songs of the British Isles. But it would be some time before Topic lost its reputation as "that little red label." In June 1958, Topic signed a deal to handle the U.K. distribution of albums produced by Moses Asch and Folkways Records, including those of Pete Seeger, Paul Robeson, and Woody Guthrie. This arrangement helped introduce the work of many of America's finest folksingers to British audiences.[6]

Jack Elliott had barely touched down in England when the WMA approached him and asked him to record an album of Guthrie songs. The offer was extended at the behest of Alan Lomax. Bill Leader, an early recording engineer for Topic, recalled the details of Elliott's first session on a BBC radio program: "There was this fellow hit town, this cowboy, and his name was Rambling Jack Elliott. He agreed to make a record of Woody Guthrie songs for Topic. It was going to be, I think, pretty well amongst [Topic's] first 'long-playing' records to be released. The problem was we didn't have a tape recorder to record it on at that time. We hadn't managed to afford to buy a tape recorder. There weren't that many out to be bought! We couldn't afford the big, big stuff that EMI and Decca used, mainly designed and built by themselves anyway. It wasn't an 'off the shelf' culture in those days, you [couldn't] walk in and buy a tape machine as easy as that. But Ewan MacColl offered to do the recording for us. He got a high quality, portable tape recorder that was actually one . . . of thirteen made . . . to record the coronation for the BBC. . . . It worked very well."[7]

Elliott's first proper album, *Woody Guthrie's Blues*, was recorded in October 1955. Elliott's memories of his sessions for the WMA are, unfortunately, not always remembered as nostalgically. He has long maintained that he was never properly paid for his Topic recordings, noting, with delicious irony, that it was a company that represented itself as a "Workers Music Association" that cheated him of his due. In 1995, four decades after his first session for the label, Elliott was still bitter, noting sourly that Topic "sold thousands of copies of my record and never paid me any royalties for twenty years."[8]

In any event, *Woody Guthrie's Blues* (or *Woodie Guthrie's Blues* as per the LP's spine) remains one of the finest and most authentically interpreted series of Guthrie's songs by Jack Elliott or anyone else. He would recollect *Woody Guthrie's Blues* as "a little orange colored record, an 8" LP," bragging it was "the only 8" LP *ever* made." Though there is no such credit on the album, Elliott claims that it was Alan Lomax, not Bill Leader, who actually engineered *Woody Guthrie's Blues*, and that the album was recorded under the most informal of circumstances in the "living room [of] Ewan MacColl's mother's house" in West Prawle.[9]

The album leads with a Leftist chin. From the liner notes of *Woody Guthrie's Blues*: "Here we have 30 years of American history, as chronicled by Woody Guthrie—the 1913–14 strike of the Colorado mine workers; the Dust Bowl period; the New Deal days, and the wartime Atlantic convoys. Woody's ballads tell not only of the events, but of the people involved. The ones who get kicked around, and the ones who hit back. They are sung by Jack Elliott, who for four years or so was around and about with Woody, with guitar on his shoulder and harmonica round his neck."[10]

Woody Guthrie's Blues is comprised of six Guthrie originals ("Talking Columbia Blues," "Hard Travelin'," "1913 Massacre," "Ludlow Massacre," "Talking Dust Bowl Blues," and "Talking Sailor"), which Elliott performs on guitar and harmonica with all the dusty, authentic grit of the author himself. Elliott's versions are, for the most part, lifted directly from Guthrie's originals, sharing many characteristics of the 78s recorded for both RCA/Victor and Disc Records between 1944 and 1947.[11]

Thanks to the efforts of Guthrie discographers Guy Logsdon, Jim Kweskin, and Jeff Place, we know many of the original recording dates and year of release of Woody's sessions. In contrast, there is great confusion among discographers regarding the dating of many of Elliott's earliest recordings. Such confusion is due, in part, to the fact that Topic did not maintain formal records. Further obfuscation is the result of the original Topic/WMA recordings having been issued and reissued over the years, in multiple formats: 78 rpm, 8" LP, 10" LP, and 12" LP. The misinformation that has resulted is not entirely Topic's fault, as Elliott's own statements have often confused the matter. In 1996, Elliott hazily told *Dirty Linen* he believed *Woody Guthrie's Blues* was recorded "in the early part of 1956," but in a February 6, 1958, letter sent from the Elliotts to the labor music scholar Archie Green, June offered more exacting details. Green had obtained a copy of Elliott's Topic 78 rpm single "Talking Miner Blues"/"Pretty Boy Floyd" (two outtakes from the *Woody Guthrie's Blues* sessions, *released* in 1956), and was excited by the record. Green, a collector of "hillbilly" records with an interest in the songs and lore of the labor movement, was impressed by Elliott's deft handling of Guthrie's material. He wrote to Elliott in England to inquire where Jack had picked up such a rare gem as Guthrie's "Talking Miner Blues" as, prior to the pressing of the Elliott 78 rpm, there had been no extant recording of the song made by Woody or anyone else. June replied to Green's letter on Jack's behalf, apologizing for the tardiness of the reply ("Jack's a hell of a good guitar player but an awfully bad letter writer"). She continued: "Jack learned 'Talking Miner' off a pamphlet & 'Ludlow Massacre' off a record of Woodie's [sic] just a few months before he met Woody. . . . He lived with Woody, probably got to hear them sung during that time. Jack recorded those 2, along with 7 other Guthrie songs, Oct. 55. . . . Jack says Woody read a newspaper article that inspired the Ludlow song."[12]

June's response seems on the mark as "Talking Miner Blues" was, indeed, one of three songs written and recorded by Woody after he learned of a series of explosions on March 25, 1947, that tragically took the lives of 111 (of 118 miners) in the coal country of Centralia, Illinois. *People's*

Songs hurriedly published Guthrie's trio of grim ballads, all reportedly written the same day of his hearing the news, in a folio titled *Three Songs for
Centralia*, the referenced "pamphlet." Though Guthrie did record all three
of his Centralia ballads for Moses Asch in the days following the tragedy,
they would not be issued until 1994 when Smithsonian/Folkways released
the CD *Woody Guthrie: Long Ways to Travel 1944–1949*. Green also queried Elliott in his letter on the provenance of Guthrie's "talking blues"
method. "Never heard Woody say when & how he picked up on talking
songs," June wrote, answering for Jack. "They originated from East Texas,
& Woody spent some of his early life there."[13]

Elliott was proud of the *Woody Guthrie's Blues* album, as he later wrote
in a short note from Paris to San Francisco where his friend Norman Pierce
managed Jack's Record Cellar. The Record Cellar was a favorite haunt
of rare disc collectors, including Archie Green, and Jack gushed to Pierce
about his session for Topic and the first recording of "Talking Miner."
Elliott bragged he recorded "some other 78s" for the label and "have also
made a L.P. (8" diameter) called *Woody Guthrie's Blues*." The latter record,
Elliott noted with excitement, was comprised of "6 Songs—6!"[14]

In London, Elliott made plans to attend a program at Festival Hall
sponsored by the National Jazz Federation (NJF). Journalist Brian Nicholls was on hand to file a report for *Jazz Journal* magazine. Though Chris
Barber and Lonnie Donegan were the headlining acts, Nicholls was more
impressed by Elliott's unscheduled performance: "We met a most intrigu-
ing character at the beginning of the month—a real character, not one of
the pseudo-bohemians one meets around town nowadays. He was called
Jack Elliott and we came across him quite by chance in the Festival Hall's
Recital Room, singing folk blues and hillbillies. The occasion was one
of the NJF's 'New Orleans Encore' series and Jack Elliott was a surprise
guest artist. He certainly had the authentic touch, both in the material he
was singing and in his appearance—a sort of non dude cowboy outfit.
The audience loved it and he certainly brought a fresh touch to the recital
room." Nicholls was so impressed with Jack's performance that he practically "dived backstage" after Jack finished his set "to find out where he
had picked up this calibre of blues singing." Jack told Nicholls of his travels
across the United States, of his apprenticeship with Woody Guthrie, and of
time spent in "the Deep South" picking up "guitar playing and blues inflections as he went." Only a month into his first visit to England, Jack was
already being lauded as an informal ambassador of homegrown American
roots music. Nicholls also reported that Elliott, who cited the Reverend
Gary Davis for special mention, had "a lot to say about the enormous

number of great blues shouters who are virtually unknown outside their own small territory." "Jack had picked up everything by ear," Nicholls continued. "He can't read music, and the authentic blues sound he has acquired bears witness to his rough and ready tuition."[15]

Alan Lomax shared Nicholls's assessment. In the summer of 1955, Lomax had been field recording on Britain's outer islands, collecting material for Camedon's landmark series of long-playing discs *Folksongs of Great Britain*. His return to London that autumn had neatly coincided with Elliott's arrival. Acutely aware that his old friend Woody Guthrie was slowly disintegrating, Lomax seemed determined to keep his flame alive through the promotion of his protégé. Lomax had scripted a theatrical production based on *The Big Rock Candy Mountain*, the old hobo song popularized by Harry "Haywire Mac" McClintock, and convinced Joan Littlewood of the Theatre Royal to produce the play in time for the Christmas Pantomime. The Christmas Pantomime was an institution that was peculiarly British, though its origins dated to the ancient Greeks. Plays of the Christmas Pantomime were primarily based on myths, fairy tales, or folk songs and offered as family entertainment for audiences enjoying the vacation afforded by the holiday season. One night, while sharing a meal with the Elliotts, Lomax told Jack he would suggest to Littlewood, a former wife of Ewan MacColl's, that she cast him in the role of "The Cowboy." Lomax explained that "The Cowboy" role was the absolute plum role of the production; he could narrate the tale, sing, and play the guitar. Littlewood, already something of a legend for her uncompromising, agit-prop theatrical productions, found the idea of Jack joining the cast splendid, although she doubted Elliott was as authentic as he portrayed himself. Littlewood would later write, "We were putting on *The Big Rock Candy Mountain*, by Alan Lomax, for Christmas and he came along to join in on the fun . . . with a sackful of catchy tunes and Rambling Jack Elliott, the singing cowboy in tow. Mind you, Rambling Jack had never seen a cow in his life, being born and bred in New York. All the same, his cowboy hat and boots caused a sensation in Angel Lane, and brought the kids in. In fact, they followed him wherever he went."[16]

Littlewood and Lomax faced one problem casting Elliott in *The Big Rock Candy Mountain*. He was in England on a three-month tourist visa; without the appropriate government-issued work permit, he could not accept the offer. He had thus far been playing the skiffle cellars and ale houses in and around London for the promise of a small fee or a meal or a night's lodging, well below the radar of Britain's Home Office. But appearing on the London stage was an entirely different matter. Littlewood made arrangements for Jack to file the necessary application papers, arguing forcefully on his behalf that no British actor could convincingly play the part of an American cowboy singer in her production. "To our surprise," June mused, "the Home Office agreed."[17]

At the first rehearsal Littlewood gathered her regular troupe of players for casting and role assignments. She took immediate notice of June and, after learning of her theatrical background, offered her the role of "Jack." In the scenario, Jack is a young boy traveling with a hobo friend who meets and marries the daughter of a king. It is a happy turn of events that pleases everyone except the weary hobo who must push on, alone, "towards the mountain-country that may or may not exist." Not wanting to deal a second time with the Home Office, June adopted the pseudonym Terra Cotta ("Terry Cotta" in the program notes), homage to her red hair.[18]

The program described the stage setting as "a box of toy bricks that represent at various times the foothills of the Big Rock Candy Mountain: a hilly desert, a farm, Outer space and Beyond Bagdad [sic]." Aside from a brief biography of playwright Alan Lomax, Jack was the only other member of the cast or crew whose story would appear, puffed up, in the program: "Jack Elliott was a cowboy from California. He left the ranch to work in Rodeos—riding unbroken horses being his speciality [sic]—before his talents as a folksinger took him to Hollywood. He and his wife, June, are singing their way round the world and they have broken their journey in England to let Jack play in *THE BIG ROCK CANDY MOUNTAIN*. As soon as the run of the play is over they will be on their way again."[19]

The first public performance was set for December 26, 1955, at the Theatre Royal, in London's East End. *The Big Rock Candy Mountain* would total 21 performances during its two-week run. Due to its relatively short run, the show's schedule was somewhat exhausting, with no fewer than two performances a day from December 26 through New Year's Eve, along with additional matinee performances on January 1 and 3 and a special, one-off "late night" showing on January 6 before the final curtain on January 7, 1956. The *Times of London* wrote favorably of the production, finding it to be a thinly disguised adaptation of Samuel Beckett's *Waiting for Godot:* "In *The Big Rock Candy Mountain*, so an American folk-song tells us, there's a land that's fair and bright, where doughnuts grow on bushes, and you sleep out every night. Singing about it is, in other words, not unlike waiting for Godot; and there are points in which this 'folk-musical' of Theatre Workshop's, with a guitar playing cowboy (Mr. Jack Elliott) for chorus and a hobo and a young boy (Mr. Howard Goorney and Miss Terry Coster [sic], for heroes, recalls the legend of the two tramps in Mr.

Samuel Beckett's play." Jack's Stetson-topped, guitar-playing character was seated on the side of the stage through the entire performance, carrying the story and production forward with narration and singing of folk songs.[20]

Following one performance, Jack was introduced to Mai Zetterling, the Swedish actress known for her performances in the British films *Portraits from Life*, *The Lost People*, and *Quartet*. Zetterling was living in London when the BBC offered her the opportunity to host a television series on the arts. The first program of *Mai Zetterling Presents* would feature artists from opposite ends of the musical spectrum. Zetterling offset the rough and tumble guitar playing of her first guest, Jack Elliott, with the dignified classical piano music of Leonard Cassini. Elliott had only been in England for little more than three months but had already waxed a solo record, performed at Festival Hall, on the London stage, and BBC television. It was all very remarkable. Elliott later reflected, "I became a star in England after being just a bum in the States."[21]

The contacts that Pete Seeger had provided Elliott proved invaluable. Through MacColl and Lomax and their associates at the Workers Music Association, Elliott befriended many talented members of the British folk music scene. While in London the Elliotts were introduced to Seamus Ennis, the Irish folk song collector, recording artist, and master of the Uilleann Pipes. Ennis invited the Elliotts to visit Dublin, where he promised he would arrange an appearance on *Radio Erin*. They agreed, but after arriving in Dublin, they learned, with disappointment, that Jack would not receive a fee for the radio performance. But the staff supplied the Americans with something of equal value—a bellyful of Guinness Stout and two railroad coupons that would take them anywhere they wished to travel throughout Ireland.[22]

In Ireland, Elliott met the singer Margaret Barrie, who Lomax had "discovered" in 1951 when he chanced upon her busking on a street in Cork. Barrie played the five-string banjo and sang harshly, but movingly, through a catalog of traditional songs she had learned as a child. Elliott was particularly fond of her warbling of "The Wild Colonial Boy," which she sang out of the side of her mouth, since she was missing most of her teeth. He added the song to his rapidly expanding repertoire.[23]

Upon issue in the spring of 1956, *Woody Guthrie's Blues* was instantly heralded as a classic, cherished by a generation of British folk and blues guitarists. Elliott's best audiences were those who had been primed for American folk music through the affectations of skiffle but were now searching for the "real thing." Jack Elliott, cowboy hat pushed down over his eyes, drawling Woody Guthrie songs, and demonstrating remarkable instrumental skill on his Gretsch, seemed authentic beyond reproach. British finger-style guitarist John Renbourn recalled Elliott as one of two American folksingers influential in Britain's nascent folk music revival. Renbourn wrote: "Two musicians who played regularly in the London clubs, and who probably influenced would-be players in England as much as any, were Peggy Seeger and Jack Elliott. . . . His versions of Jesse Fuller's 'San Francisco Bay Blues' and Gary Davis' 'Cocaine Blues' were imitated widely by British pickers, but his influence extended even further. After he returned home he left behind quite a number of British Rambling Jack imitators fully equipped with ten gallon hats and mid-Atlantic drawls."[24]

It is true that it wasn't Elliott's music alone that commanded attention. Renbourn's mention of Jack's "ten-gallon hat" is revealing. British audiences in the 1950s were not unfamiliar with the sight of American cowboy singers parading around their stages and cinemas. But these cowboys were strictly of the Hollywood variety, smartly adorned with rhinestones, chaps, and silver spurs. Western film stars such as Gene Autry and Roy Rogers were not only icons in America, they were also celebrities of international renown. Their music and outfitting, however, was often a comical pastiche of the real thing. Jack's standard outfit of blue denim dungarees, plain stitched shirts, and neck bandanas was that of the unadorned, unaffected *working* cowboy, and his sartorial style would be faithfully assimilated by many of his folksinging peers in England and on the Continent. British music writer Ron Gould took note of Jack's casual "non-dude" outfit: "Jack was a young man, of course, but I remember a lined and weathered cowboy face straight out of a western movie. He looked to be completely covered in denim—you have to realize that in those days jeans were virtually unknown in [England]. . . . Jack was wearing the first pair of Levi's I'd ever laid eyes on. He had a big hat and cowboy boots [and] the nicest guitar I'd ever seen."[25]

Jack's Gretsch *Rancher* was a pretty nice guitar, but it is what Jack *did* with it that caused the most excitement among London clubgoers. Few people in London had ever heard anyone play in the Carter Family style, the basic component of Woody Guthrie and Jack Elliott's guitar methodology. On the surface, Mother Maybelle's technique was not the most complex of styles. But to get it sounding just right, akin to that stripped, bare bones, and authentically dusty sound that Guthrie and Elliott produced on the instrument, well, that was going to take a lot of wood shedding. The most intelligent, and poetic description, of Guthrie's guitar work was supplied by old friend Alan Lomax. On the occasion of a 1988 BBC film on Guthrie's life, Lomax explained that Woody's guitar "buzzes and

rumbles and bounces and jitters and skitters and sings all at the same time."
"It's a unique sound," Lomax continued. "It's like being in a big truck
and hearing the songs at the same time. 'Cause Woody was riding those
trucks and riding the trains and you hear the pulse of the drive wheel and
the whistle of the locomotive and all the racket of the wheels . . . It's all
going on with that guitar style of Woody's." As his earliest recordings for
Topic Records attest, in 1955 and 1956 it was also "going on" in the guitar
playing of Jack Elliott.[26]

    Woody was, sadly, out of commission, this time for good. In the spring
of 1955, the editors of *Sing Out!* solemnly noted that "Woody Guthrie,
the famed dust bowl balladeer, has been bed ridden in Brooklyn State
Hospital for the past few months. It looks like Woody will probably have
to be under hospital care for quite some time to come. Old friends and
acquaintances are urged to drop a note [to] Woody who sure needs some
good cheer these days." With Woody institutionalized, the import of
Elliott's carrying on the musical affects of Guthrie's legacy had increased.
But Elliott wasn't Woody Guthrie and he wasn't standing still; his musical education was continuing and broadening. As he rambled around the
British Isles and then Western Europe, Elliott would learn songs outside
of the Guthrie tradition. He began to incorporate all the little musical
nuances and filigrees that personalized his own guitar playing. He moved
away from a strict impersonation of Guthrie and smoothed his guitar style,
incorporating various little licks and tricks and bass runs. Later, when Elliott turned away from a repertoire that consisted mostly of Guthrie songs,
the lonesome sound of razor wire and railroad steel, the calling card of
Woody's sound, was discarded. The changes were incremental and probably not even conscious, but Elliott's new guitar and singing style was
more musical than Woody's, more accessible and pleasing to the ear.[27]

    Woody Guthrie's Blues was being deconstructed and studied by nearly
every serious student of traditional folk guitar in England. Copies were
finding their way to the turntables of serious jazz and blues music scribes
as well. Blues scholar Paul H. Oliver was impressed with Jack's "excellent imitation" of Woody, but suspicious of the record's political content:
"This disc has been issued by the Workers Music Association and one can-
not help but feel that there has been a somewhat deliberate use of this feature of Woody's work and Jack's admiration for the man, in the selection
that has been made." C. P. Stanton of Glasgow sent a transatlantic report
to the New York City–based folk-music magazine *Caravan*. Describing Elliott as a "citizen of the world . . . claimed by both America and Britain,"
Stanton lauded *Woody Guthrie's Blues* as "very down to earth working man

stuff," impressed that "Rambling Jack Elliott . . . sings, plays harmonica and strums, two at a time!"[28]

Jazz Journal offered *Woody Guthrie's Blues* as "the first of a series of small LPs inaugurated with [the] object of making known the many excellent blues-ballads of Woody Guthrie as performed by Jack Elliott. Elliott, a roving singer who caused quite a sensation amongst folk song lovers when he recently sang in London, spent some time wandering around the States with Guthrie and took the opportunity of learning many of his excellent songs. He sings these songs with delicacy, nice timing and a pretty sense of humour and accompanies himself expertly on guitar and mouthharp." *Jazz Music* commented: "Slightly larger than a normal 45 EP [*Woody Guthrie's Blues*] contains three tracks per side. The recording quality is amazing—exceptional balance. 'Talking Columbia Blues' is a very close follower to Guthrie's own version issued here several years ago. I like the rest of this wonderful little LP."[29]

With one "Massacre" per side, it was apparent *Woody Guthrie's Blues* would be held in high esteem by those on the Communist left. The authentic grit and radicalism and caliber of Elliott's performances were heralded by the serious students of folk song, those who held the cheerful robust skifflers in low regard. Ewan MacColl, who in a few years would infamously describe Jack's own protégé Bob Dylan as "a youth of mediocre talent," admitted that as a ballad singer Elliott was "one of the few to bring tears to my eyes." MacColl meant it as a compliment.[30]

Though there was no attempt to market *Woody Guthrie's Blues* in the United States, the album was available through international mail order. As such, only the most dedicated Guthrie fans in the States were aware of the record's existence; there really weren't any Jack Elliott fans yet in America. Two such Guthrie fans were Jon Pankake and Paul Nelson. It is a misuse of the term to describe Pankake and Nelson as "fans" of folk music, "fanatics" would be a more suitable term. In 1960, Pankake and Nelson were undergraduates at the University of Minnesota, among the most dedicated collectors of folk-music recordings in the Midwest. If these two friends shared strong enthusiasm on the subject of recorded folk music, they also shared strong opinions. They self-published many of their opinions in a mimeographed, small format digest called *The Little Sandy Review*. Initially, *The Little Sandy Review* carried no feature articles, only a series of entertainingly written, and more than occasionally poisonous, record reviews. Pankake and Nelson were young and brash; they were antiestablishment but only vaguely political and not at all beholden to the coterie of folk-music establishment types on either coast. As a result they did not fill the pages of their magazine with empty platitudes or professional niceties. They prided themselves on their ability to filter through the commercial dross that had sprouted in the post–Kingston Trio era. "We ridicule only the ridiculous," they told Irwin Silber of *Sing Out!* and their reviews were entertaining and, on occasion, unmerciful. Pankake and Nelson reserved much of their vitriol for such folk-pop performers as Harry Belafonte and Leon Bibb, and rarely had kind words for the well-scrubbed and buttoned down, collegiate type folk song groups. Though Pete Seeger was a hero of both men, even Pete's old group, the Weavers, were not spared what Silber described as the "sharp, unmitigated tone of their criticism." Pankake and Nelson's heroes were of the old school: Seeger, the solo artist, Woody Guthrie, Moses Asch, Lead Belly, the New Lost City Ramblers, but mostly hillbilly and delta blues performers. Though the amateur magazine's circulation was no more than 300 copies (200 to subscribers, 100 to bookstores), its influence was disproportionate to its small print run.[31]

Elliott's *Woody Guthrie's Blues* was reviewed, somewhat belatedly, in the second issue (April 1960) of *The Little Sandy Review*. The recording was feted as "a good tribute . . . by a man who knew him well." But American readers did not really yet know who this mysterious Jack Elliott was. Pankake and Nelson, in a sense, introduced Jack to U.S. folk-music fans, describing him as an "American folksinger and rambling man . . . who slams, slaps, and drawls out Woody Guthrie songs in a Texas-Oklahoma style." Though the review disputed Topic's contention that Elliott's "versions of these songs can be compared with Woody's when Woody was at his best," Nelson and Pankake begrudgingly acknowledged the songs "are well-done and sufficiently interesting," citing the grim and rarely recorded "1913 Massacre" and "Ludlow Massacre" as the disc's two finest performances, unknowingly echoing the sentiments of Ewan MacColl.[32]

The same time that critics and fans in England were being introduced to the music of Jack Elliott through *Woody Guthrie's Blues*, the man himself was busking in the streets and singing for his supper. Though the Elliotts used London as a home base, they regularly traveled to Paris and mainland Europe for sightseeing and fresh audiences. In London, the Elliotts ran into Earl Hugens, an American businessman. June had earlier met Hugens, whom she described as "a very rich real estate developer," while living in California. While in London on business, he invited the Elliotts to the River Humble in the South of England to visit a derelict boat he had purchased. The tide was out when the trio arrived and June found the boat "a very sad sight . . . on the mudflats, held upright by two wooden poles." Jack, on the other hand, could hardly contain his excitement. He immediately identified the craft as a neat copy of a Bristol Channel Pilot Cutter. *The Magnet*, as she would soon be rechristened, was built in 1890 and rerigged into a schooner. *The Magnet* ran 52 feet along her waterline and boasted a 12-foot bow spread, a deep keel, galvanized hardware, a low gaffe rig schooner with red sails, and "dead-eye" rigging. Elliott described the boat's cabin as "plainly appointed," which allowed for "a slight echo of the sound bouncing off the wood" so one could hear the "mooring lines creaking." Because Hugens had to return to the States, he asked the Elliotts if they would care to live aboard *The Magnet* and look after the craft in his absence. They agreed, and shortly after settling in, Dick Swettenham and Bill Leader of Topic arrived from London with a battery of recording equipment. Leader told the BBC that he and Elliott shared a number of sessions over the years "including one monumental one . . . on a yacht off Cowes on the Isle of Wight." Leader reminisced that since Elliott was not in possession of the proper work permit, "we decided we'd put ourselves in a situation where we'd claim we could've recorded it outside of [Britain's] territorial waters, which, in those days, was a modest three miles. Actually we weren't that far out . . . we were tied up to the quay! We dangled the ribbon down through the hatch and he sang for, I think it was, a couple of days, more or less. We did get a bit of sleep in between and he just recorded and recorded and recorded and . . . some wonderful material [came] out of that."[33]

Hugens had arranged the hire of Captain Henry Rooke of Yorkshire to sail *The Magnet* to the port city of Cowes on the Isle of Wight where she was to be refitted. Rooke was a no-nonsense sort, a descendant of the revered British admiral Sir George Rooke. Plans were made that, once refitted, Henry, Jack, and June would sail *The Magnet* to the Mediterranean and its final port-of-call, Gibraltar. In Gibraltar, Hugens would take possession of the craft. Rooke soon hired an assistant named Richard, a knowledgeable sailor and former British Olympian, to serve as first mate. June remembered when Henry and Richard met the Stetson-topped Ramblin' Jack they were a bit taken back, "astonished to find an American cowboy in such a situation." Any misgivings they might have had were quickly dispelled once Jack demonstrated his command of sailing practices. Elliott impressed everyone with his sail-rigging and knot-tying skills, and they found him a very capable helmsman as well.[34]

The Magnet was scheduled to sail to Spain, with port calls in Lisbon, Portugal, Tangiers, and Gibraltar. The first leg would take *The Magnet* across the Bay of Biscay to Lisbon. Jack was excited at the prospective adventure, this being his "first really long trip in a sailboat." The trip across the Bay of Biscay would take approximately seven days. Henry, Richard, and Jack would share sailing duties; June was assigned, much to her displeasure, to the galley as chief cook and bottle washer. The weather was rough during that first crossing, the waves turbulent, and June found the sailor's life an "unpleasant experience." She suffered from terrible bouts of seasickness and had shattered glass and "stranded sea-life" rain down upon her during one particularly violent stretch. Jack's account of that first trip was more stiff-lipped. Although *The Magnet* once tossed him overboard during a battering storm, he believed the craft "rode very comfortably."[35]

They winds were not the only factor to create waves. June quickly tired of the humorless Rooke, finding him an arrogant, difficult taskmaster. For starters, Rooke was displeased with June's talents as cook. He was particularly unhappy with the way June prepared such peculiarly British fare as Cornish pasties, which, to her lamentation, he "seemed to expect." Captain Rooke also derided the Elliotts at length for America's invention of the tea bag. He found the tea bag an abomination and demanded that the Americans learn how to brew and steep a proper pot of English tea. Unfortunately, the two Yanks could never get it quite right and, by Jack's estimate, Rooke had them toss some "fifty-six gallons" of otherwise perfectly potable water over the ship's side.[36]

Things took a darker turn when *The Magnet* sailed from Lisbon to Tangiers. Just as they set off, June recalled, a "monstrous ocean liner appeared at the entrance, being towed into port by a bevy of tugboats." A chorus of whistles and horns filled the air as the liner continued to sail into the harbor, *The Magnet* caught in her path. June wrote, "the color drained from Henry's face" as the great ship steamed closer toward an inevitable collision. Suddenly, one of the tugboats grabbed hold of *The Magnet* and successfully pulled her to safety, although the craft was tossed roughly against the dockside pilings. Richard and June managed to jump to safety, but Jack and Henry were caught on board. Both sailors were badly shaken by the incident but found themselves, miraculously, uninjured.[37]

With characteristic understatement, Jack would later recall *The Magnet* had suffered, but survived, "a little bumping with another boat." Earl Hugens was telephoned at once and arrived in Lisbon to inspect the damage. He decided to put *The Magnet* into dry dock for repair and to have the boat's faulty generator looked at. June chose the moment to pull Hugens aside and tell him in no uncertain terms that she wanted out. She had enough of Henry Rooke's arrogance, of her constant seasickness, and of cooking for the ungrateful captain. Hugens begged her to stay, but was enjoying little success until good-natured Richard interceded. He agreed to share the cooking and tea-brewing chores if June would remain. She reluctantly agreed.[38]

Jack and June were determined to make the best of the situation. Putting the craft in dry dock extended their stay in Lisbon by at least a week, affording the crew the opportunity to explore the beautiful region. Jack and June took in a bullfight and strolled through the city's many open-air markets. But not everyone was happy. For Captain Rooke, the sailing of *The Magnet* to Gibraltar was a straight delivery job and nothing more. By Jack's account, Rooke was not "interested in stopping and looking at the scenery," he only wanted to "get the boat to Gibraltar and fly home to his family."[39]

Next the crew set sail for Gibraltar. Although the boat had been repaired, the mechanics had not been able to fix the ship's generator, which still operated, but only barely. The Magnet made the two-hour sail to Gibraltar in excellent time, but they made the mistake of arriving at the island fortress in the middle of night. As a result of their generator troubles, The Magnet had no lights to signal their approach. Jack was well aware that without proper signaling, the British soldiers could very well "blow us right out of the water." So the crew decided to sail for Tangiers and attempt a return to the island during daylight. When they finally made it to Gibraltar, the British military personnel were clearly impressed when the captain read his celebrated surname off the tender list of *The Magnet*. Elliott was startled to learn that, centuries later, the mere mention of the revered Rooke name caused British sailors to snap to attention and salute.[40]

With the delivery of *The Magnet*, Henry Rooke signed off, returning to the Isle of Wight and his less troublesome position as yacht agent. "I think we were all glad to see Henry leave the boat," Jack admitted. "He was a stern captain." As had been planned, Hugens and his daughter met the crew at Gibraltar and joined them on the last leg of the sail to Valencia, Spain. Richard assumed the role of ship's captain, with Jack easily filling in for Richard as first mate.[41]

Richard had kept true to his promise to June. He even tried to make a sailor of her, teaching her to hold the helm and how to navigate by the stars. Late one night, June was alone on deck, manning the helm. Jack was in the chart house below, trying to sleep. But he was unusually restless and finally decided to join June. The eerie silence of the night was broken when Jack suddenly said "*What? Jimmy, is that you . . . ?*" James Dean had died in a tragic automobile accident on September 30, 1955, shortly after the Elliotts arrived in England. The news hit them hard. They were certain that Dean, their young, doomed Hollywood friend, had come on the wind to bid his last good-bye. June wrote in her memoir, "we both felt a presence, as if someone were on deck with us," recollecting the ghostly visit as "a peaceful moment." As *The Magnet* cut through the waves, June recalled, Jack grabbed his "guitar from the charthouse and played a quiet, sad song" for the ghost of James Dean.[42]

The Elliotts signed off once *The Magnet* made port in Valencia. They were due back in London as Elliott had earlier agreed to accompany the City Ramblers Skiffle Group on a late summer tour of Germany and Scandinavia. Hylda Sims, Russell Quaye, Tony Buquet, and John Pilgrim founded the City Ramblers in 1955, the ragtag ensemble often busking near Charing Cross Station on the streets of London. Pilgrim, whose stock in trade was a washboard and a pet monkey named Saki, would not last long. He had too many rows with Quaye, a man of similar high self-regard and crusty temperament. The City Ramblers, in some respects, were unique among the more "professional" London-based skiffle bands. Unlike such luminaries as Chris Barber or Lonnie Donegan, the City Ramblers did not come to skiffle after enjoying success as jazz musicians. The City Ramblers were barely musicians at all; they were a mix of disgruntled painters, self-proclaimed poets, and neo-beatniks. Hylda Sims's parents were Communists who had settled in London to enroll their daughter in a progressive school, where she learned to plunk out a few chords on the guitar. Quaye was several years her senior, a charismatic, edgy bohemian, a self-proclaimed anarchist with an intemperate reputation. Sims and Quaye had married and managed a series of art studios and skiffle clubs, central meeting places of London's subculture. Though Hylda and Russell were covocalists, the outfit was often billed as "Russell Quaye's City Ramblers," due to Russell's dogmatic, if impolitic, chauvinism.[43]

A German jazz promoter approached the City Ramblers and offered them the opportunity to tour Germany and Scandinavia in the summer of 1956. Though something of a gamble, the group was intrigued by the idea, purchasing a secondhand Chevrolet ambulance to serve as their makeshift tour bus. It was Quaye who invited his friends Jack and June to accompany them. Having the celebrated American cowboy singer Jack Elliott on the program would give the tour something of an international flavor.[44]

The tour was a disaster. There were personality conflicts, an endless series of disruptive automotive breakdowns, and it soon came to the band's attention that the German promoter was something of a violent "drunken lunatic." Elliott, too, shouldered some of the blame. As author Dave Arthur recalled vividly in *English Dance & Song* magazine: "Jack Elliott, who was still very full of his trans-American jaunts with Woody Guthrie in an old Model T Ford, insisted on demonstrating the technique that he and Woody had developed for slipping the gear without using the clutch. All you had to do was to listen to the engine and catch it at just the right speed. Unfortunately Jack never managed to catch it at just the right speed and, in consequence, subjected everybody to hundreds of miles of gear-crashing and body-numbing judders."[45]

Ramblin' Jack has, famously, never been charitable to skiffle music. He preferred the moody earthiness of genuine American folk song to skiffle's cloying and cheery pastiches. Regardless, he retained a lifelong fondness for his friends in the City Ramblers. He recalled Chris Bates, as a Louis Armstrong imitator who blew through a cornet mouthpiece with an attached metal funnel at the end. Russell Quaye, was a "very funny looking guy" who played the kazoo and a four-string guitar. Though Hylda Sims was probably the heart of the City Ramblers, Jack maintained she was not the most important member of the band. That designation was awarded to the amiable Tony Buquet, the band's wash tub bassist. "Tony was . . . a retired marine engineer who could fix cars," Jack recalled. "The Chevrolet ambulance broke down every night at midnight, wherever we were traveling. And Tony would have to wake up and get out and get it running again."[46]

There is not a lot of information regarding the City Rambler's tour. A broadside exists that advertises an August 20–21, 1956, engagement of the City Ramblers ("London's No: 1 Skiffle Group") featuring "Jack Elliott (USA): Gittar & Vocal") at the Bohéme Köln in Cologne, Germany. But the tour was neither the financial nor artistic success the band had hoped for. On September 12, 1956, they were in a Copenhagen, Denmark, recording studio, waxing a short program of fractured American folk songs, "When the Saints Go Marching In," "900 Miles," "(We) Shall Not Be Moved," and "Mama Don't Allow" among them. Jack sat in for only one song, contributing guitar and vocals to a spirited take of Lead Belly's "Midnight Special." The song was subsequently released on the EP *City Ramblers Skiffle Group*. Though the City Ramblers returned to Germany following the Copenhagen session, they finally decided to cut their losses and return to London. Jack and June chose to remain behind.[47]

Though strangers in a strange land, the Elliotts were confident they could successfully sing for their supper in Germany. In the years following World War II, Western Europe suffered no shortage of American military bases, and these enclaves were occasionally tapped as a source of income. Many of the bases were situated too far from a central city to make a special trip feasible. But on the occasions they did visit, the Elliotts found there was always someone who would assist in the staging of an impromptu gig. Payment for services rendered varied. It might be settled in the form of U.S. dollars or with local currency or with a bottle of whiskey or a hearty meal.[48]

The Elliotts had been in Europe for just over a year. They had chosen to stay in Frankfurt to test their fortunes at busking, but things had not gone as planned. Of all the countries they would visit, the Elliotts found Germany the least hospitable. June rued that singing on the streets there "was almost impossible." The Germans were not particularly fond of buskers, or transients of any sort, and any monies made from singing on the street were modest. Most pedestrians would go out of their way to avoid them. Occasionally, Elliott would benefit from the peculiar strength-in-numbers mind-set when a small, courageous few would pool and listen for a moment. But, invariably, the foot-tapping would cease when a dour businessman would confront them, sternly inquiring if their street performance was "sanctioned." In these instances, the Elliotts sorely missed Hylda Sims; she could speak fluent German and was able to deflect hostile inquires. With an autumnal cool creeping in, they lived briefly, and illegally, in a pitched tent on the outskirts of Frankfurt's old city. As an American Jew, albeit a nonpracticing one, Jack felt uneasy singing on the cold German streets. Some 45 years following Elliott's first visit to Germany, Jack embarrassingly recalled his unsuccessful attempts at busking on the streets of Frankfurt "to a lot of ex-Nazis and practicing Nazis five [sic] years after World War II."[49]

Occasionally, Jack and June would set off for a nearby American military base to visit the PX and enjoy delicacies from back home: hamburgers and malteds. It was while sipping at his malted in one PX that Jack heard the voice of an unfamiliar singer booming from the jukebox. The artist was Elvis Presley, from Tupelo, Mississippi, and Memphis, Tennessee, and the song was a ramped up take on the old "Big Mama" Thornton blues "Hound Dog." As the Elliotts had left the United States in September 1955, neither of them had any notion of the teen rock 'n' roll revolution back home.[50]

With the winter coming on the Elliotts decided to say *auf Wiedersehen* to Frankfurt. Knowing "friends of friends" in Switzerland, they were able to raise just enough cash for train tickets to Geneva. From Geneva, they could return to Paris. Paris was a city the Elliotts loved dearly and where they could eke out a living by playing on the streets and in the cafés. To Jack's delight, the "Muleskinner Blues," with its driving guitar rhythm and elongated yodel, would always draw an enthusiastic, and a relatively profitable, reception from the Parisians.[51]

But they did not stay in Paris for long. In late 1956, with winter coming on and their coffers adequately replenished, the Elliotts sought out the warmer climes of Spain. They made their way south, passing through Granada and Cordoba, and spent nearly a month in the Costa del Sol town of Torremolinos on the Mediterranean. Though he continued to sing for his supper, Elliott found the street audiences of Spain to be tough sells. The Spaniards would take one look at his wide brimmed cowboy hat and mistake him, with some derision, for a Mexican national. "They'd laugh and cover their mouths to be polite," Jack remembered. Lodging continued to be a challenge, but Jack found that a modest *pension* could be leased for as little as 30 *pesetas* a night (approximately one dollar). Elliott tried his best to continue with his street singing as it remained their only source of income, but even the most robust performance of the "Muleskinner Blues" would not open Spaniard pocketbooks in sufficient numbers. "I think I would have taken Spain by storm if I only could have translated [the lyrics] into Spanish," Elliott mulled. "I tried in the beginning." In some desperation, he modified the opening lyric of the "Muleskinner Blues" to the more region friendly *"Buenos Días, Capitan,"* but the results were hardly encouraging. In Barcelona, the Elliotts marveled at the sight of the actor Errol Flynn's yacht and savored the pleasures of a rare good meal. Jack believed Barcelona to be "the edge of good cooking" in Spain. "Below that," he added ominously, "you're on your own." After Spain, the Elliotts traveled to Tangiers and visited a string of Moroccan desert towns before returning, once again, to Paris.[52]

In Paris Jack told June he was no longer interested in making music as a solo artist. He wanted to wire his old friend Derroll Adams and see if he would want to join them in Europe. Reluctantly, June consented to Jack's wish. Their gypsy honeymoon through the capitals of the old world had not been without its trials, both personal and financial. Trying to make a go of it with Derroll tagging along would be difficult, but June finally acquiesced to the idea when she reasoned, optimistically, "day to day life with Jack might be easier on me if Derroll was around."[53]

Derroll was working with a logging outfit near Blue River, Oregon, when he received the letter. Though music was not Derroll's vocation, he would occasionally supplement his timber-man wages by singing late into the night at a nearby rowdy saloon called the Stage Coach. It was all good, unwholesome fun, but the offer to sail to England and reteam with

Jack Elliott sounded fun, too. June forwarded the fare that she and Jack had scraped together to pay for the transatlantic trip.[54]

On February 15, 1957, the Elliotts met Derroll as he stepped off the boat train at Victoria Station. True to form, Derroll had arrived bleary eyed, worn down, and painfully thin. He was still wearing his light California clothing, oblivious to the fact it was wintertime in England. June had the foresight to bring along a navy parka for Derroll to bundle himself into. But neither she nor Jack had counted on Derroll arriving sans banjo. The Elliotts arranged for a loan of a replacement banjo, and their first gig took place at Alexis Korner's Roundhouse in London the night of Derroll's arrival.[55]

Through Tony Buquet, Jack, June, and Derroll had found temporary lodging at a Waterloo communal house near the Old Vic Theatre, Lambeth. Dubbed "The Yellow Door" due to the garish coat of bright yellow paint splashed on the portal, June described their temporary home, charitably, as "near derelict." Its occupants tended to be cash-strapped artists, musicians, street people, and anarchists. One of their fellow tenants whom they befriended was a struggling songwriter named Lionel Bart, still a few years away from striking gold for his musical stage adaptation of Dickens's *Oliver Twist*.[56]

It seemed no one in England had ever heard anything as wild and wooly as the music of Jack Elliott and Derroll Adams. Though Adams had some notion that Elliott "already had the ball rolling" in England, enjoying some stature as an American folksinger abroad, he was surprised to learn the extent of Jack's celebrity. The two friends soon found themselves in great demand on the pub and skiffle club circuit, performing nightly to crowded, almost worshipful, audiences. They sang on the streets during the day and at night at such venues as The Skiffle Cellar, the Nucleus Coffeehouse, Les Cousins, and the Roundhouse. They had been playing around London for little more than a month when Jack and Derroll, against all logic, were contracted in March 1957 as entertainers at the Blue Angel in Berkeley Square. The Blue Angel was a high-society nightclub that attracted an upscale clientele of debutantes and royals. Jack and Derroll had been working the skiffle clubs, illegally, on tourist visas. But the opportunity to perform at such a posh club as the Blue Angel required them to obtain proper work permits from the Home Office, forcing Jack and Derroll to reenter the country from Paris to obtain them. The Blue Angel gig also compelled them to acquiesce to the professional nicety of finding a proper name for their unassuming guitar and banjo act. Such names as the

Topanga Canyon Boys and the Cowboys were considered and summarily rejected. They finally decided on the Rambling Boys. The name was a tip of the hat to the Carter Family classic "Rake and Rambling Boy."[57]

The Rambling Boys' engagement at the Blue Angel was an improbable triumph. "It was like a party in that place," Derroll recalled, noting that their residency had been "a big success . . . it was amazing." The posh engagement at the Blue Angel led to an equally unlikely performance before Princess Margaret. One night following a show at the Blue Angel, Jack and Derroll were introduced to Rory McEwan. McEwan was a gifted watercolor artist and an occasional folksinger. McEwan's father was Sir John McEwan, a conservative Scots politician who had been elected to the House of Commons in 1931. Through a combination of his own talent and his father's connections, Rory was made a member of the Queen's Cameron Highlanders. McEwan was a friendly, colorful fellow, in good standing with members of the Royal Family. When McEwan asked Jack and Derroll if they might have an interest in performing for a party at a friend's house, they had little reason to suspect that friend was Princess Margaret. Jack remembered Margaret, the 26-year-old sister of Queen Elizabeth, as "very hip," which was fortunate, as they chose to serenade the royal with "a slightly off-colour ditty." Because they were entertainers, Jack and Derrroll could appear at the function wearing their Stetsons and looking like cowboys. But June was expected to surrender to the niceties of the occasion. She borrowed a fancy gown for the event and was taught to curtsy.[58]

In early April 1957, *Melody Maker* reported the "Rambling Boys" were "now in their fourth week of cabaret at the *Blue Angel* in Mayfair." The Rambling Boys were a bit bewildered by all the goodwill. Enjoying the scene and the acclaim and the regular pay, they began to introduce a comedic element to their stage show. June noticed immediately that the more "down home" and folksy Jack and Derroll geared their performances, the more it amused and delighted the audience of sophisticates. They had become an act.[59]

The notoriety garnered by their engagement at the Blue Angel had surprised, and disappointed, many of Jack's fans on the English Left. Surely, this was not the same Jack Elliott who recorded the agit-prop masterpiece *Woody Guthrie's Blues*, who sang anguished accounts of the trials and tragedies of the copper miners of Calumet and Ludlow. At the Blue Angel, Jack and Derroll were not tapping the pocketbooks of moneyed progressives in service of the revolution. They were selling themselves as cabaret performers, mere entertainers, and many of Jack's political fans did not care for the change at all.

Though the company had been forged by socialist utopians, Topic Records knew commercial potential when they heard it and were anxious to record the Rambling Boys. In May 1957, Bill Leader, the recording engineer who had been involved in the production of *Woody Guthrie's Blues* and Elliott's sessions at Cowes on the Isle of Wight, recorded the Rambling Boys at Topic's London office. Though he had graduated from recording in a parlor or the hold of a schooner, Elliott still rued that his sessions for Topic were not too far removed from field recordings. "The first recording studio I ever got into at all was still very primitive," he recollected. "They had egg crates nailed on the wall as soundproofing!"[60]

Some of the material recorded was issued on the album *The Rambling Boys*. It was a very freewheeling album, one combining Jack's and Derroll's edgy, sardonic singing with some rough and tumble guitar and banjo playing. *The Rambling Boys* was wickedly entertaining, more accessible to folk-music fans more concerned with plectrums than politics. *Woody Guthrie's Blues* was comprised of mournful, occasionally brutal, songs. But many of the performances on *The Rambling Boys* were so eccentric that one couldn't help but smile. *The Rambling Boys* featured nine songs total, five of which included Jack and Derroll in tandem: "Rake and Rambling Boy," "Mother's Not Dead," "East Virginia Blues," "Danville Girl," and "Roll on Buddy." One of the oddest songs is Elliott's faithful re-creation of the spoken word monologue "State of Arkansas," borrowed from the Almanac Singers' *Sod Buster Ballads* 1941 album.[61]

The Rambling Boys also features the first of Elliott's performances of "Buffalo Skinners." Though often credited as the author of "Buffalo Skinners," Woody Guthrie did not write the song. The ballad first appeared as "Boggy Creek" in the John A. and Alan Lomax collection *Cowboy Songs and Frontier Ballads*, from whose pages Guthrie presumably gleaned it. Woody, as was his style, did rewrite many of the ballad's original verses, and it was the Guthrie version that caught Elliott's ear. Woody retitled his version "Buffalo Skinners," and it is under this name that it appears in the John and Alan Lomax collection *American Ballads and Folk Song*. Guthrie recorded the song for Moses Asch on March 24, 1945, and it appeared on *Struggle: Asch American Documentary No. 1*. Guthrie's performance of "Buffalo Skinners" is unusual as he performs the entire song on a single major guitar chord, while singing the melody in a minor key. It was an interesting, and oddly successful, experiment, one that Elliott hoped to duplicate when living with Guthrie in 1951. But when Elliott asked Woody to teach him the personalized guitar arrangement as featured on *Struggle*, Guthrie crankily refused. "It's on the record, Jack," he answered flatly, directing Elliott to a pile of 78-rpm records that sat on the floor near the parlor's upright piano. By Elliott's estimate, he listened to Woody's recording of "Buffalo Skinners" nearly "a hundred times . . . and all I could come up with was kind of my own misconstrued version of it." It is true that Jack's oft-imitated version of "Buffalo Skinners" musically shares little in common with Guthrie's version. Elliott built an exciting new arrangement around a minor key that effectively captured the drama of this ominous tale of betrayal and murder out on "the trail of the buffalo." But not everyone was taken by Jack Elliott's original and highly stylized arrangement. "Too Hollywood," Alan Lomax sniffed.[62]

Melody Maker deemed *The Rambling Boys* a success: "Many of their friends will be glad to have this memento of the Rambling Boys' Round House sessions. And they get full value for their money. That Guthrie-type guitar and Adam's [sic] incredible banjo must have been the most exciting things to hit British folk music in recent years." *The Spring 1958 LP Supplement* described the album as a "light-hearted selection of the Rambling Boys' most popular numbers. Little that's significant but lots of fun and with some instructive guitar and banjo." *Sing* offered, "As a pair of rambling boys it would be hard to find so plausible a pair of rogues as Elliott and Adams. Derroll is a perfect mate with a deep voice and a competent instrumental technique which, like Jack's, is very relaxed." Though it would be years before *The Rambling Boys* was available in the United States. *Sing Out!* would deem the album "one of the great records of American city singing. . . . Jack Elliott is at one of his peaks, Derroll Adams has a lot of humor in his voice, and together they blend with the familiarity of old friends in country harmony."[63]

The Rambling Boys was issued concurrently with Elliott's second solo album for Topic, *Jack Takes the Floor*. *Jack Takes the Floor*, a skeletal guitar and harmonica recording, documents Jack's early repertoire of traditional American folk songs and blues. Many of the album's eleven songs ("San Francisco Bay Blues," "Bed Bug Blues," and "Muleskinner Blues") would remain staples of Jack's live performances throughout his career. Simply, but tastefully, packaged, the front sleeve of the 10" album featured a black-and-white photograph of Jack in striped shirt and dungarees, his ever present cowboy hat propped back on his head and trademark Gretsch in hand. In Minneapolis in 1960, Bob Dylan, an earnest young Guthrie acolyte, would carefully study the iconic photograph on *Jack Takes the Floor*, recalling Elliott as "a character with certain careless ease, rakish looking, a handsome saddle tramp."[64]

The rear sleeve of *Jack Takes the Floor* features four paragraphs of liner notes, sadly uncredited, as they include this early, and beautifully descriptive, account of Jack's talents as a performing artist circa 1957:

> Jack Elliott takes the floor with the sort of programme that made him so popular with London skiffle club audiences when he was across here recently. Jack can hold the floor for hours, just standing with his guitar, talking, playing and singing. He chooses his repertoire from all parts of the States and from all the singers he has met or heard—songs learned from Gary Davis, Leadbelly [sic], Jimmie Rodgers, Woody Guthrie or songs he has picked up himself in his trips across the country. He starts a song with a beat that allows him to pick out strong rhythms and counter melodies with a plectrum on his battered old guitar. He might take a break in this number on his harmonica, which he has strapped around his neck, alternating between voice and harmonica so rapidly that, on disc, it sounds as if a second musician was sitting in on the session. His second song is quieter. A prison song or a blues perhaps. The plectrum is replaced by a wonderfully fluid finger style, as in "Cocaine." Jack's wry, dry humour always seeps through, and before long he tells some tall story or executes one of his startling impersonations. It might be Elvis Presley or Richard Dyer-Bennett or, as in "New York Town," a man he admires greatly: Woody Guthrie.[65]

Actually, with the exception of "New York Town," there is very little Guthrie (or Guthrie associated) material on the album. *Jack Takes the Floor* is a showcase of Elliott's talent as an innovative and earthy folk-blues guitarist and singer; a musician in the Guthrie tradition, perhaps, but now an amalgam of many idiosyncratic influences. It is one of Elliott's finest recordings, an extraordinary tapestry of traditional American folk song forms from bluegrass to blues, from southern field hollers to the displaced urban "folk songs" of Guthrie and Lead Belly.

As was so often the case, Elliott gleaned most of the material featured on *Jack Takes the Floor* from old records. In January 1942, Lead Belly recorded "Ol' Riley" for Moses Asch and the song was issued on the albums *Work Songs of the U.S.A. Sung by Leadbelly* and *Work and Play Party Songs Sung by Leadbelly*. "The Boll Weevil" was first recorded by Lead Belly as early as autumn 1934, but he would revisit the song at more than a half dozen recording sessions. "Grey Goose" (alternately titled "Gray Goose") was first recorded by Lead Belly in March 1935; that same session produced such other Jack Elliott–associated titles as "Alabama Bound," "Old

Rattler," and "Here, Rattler, Here." Another of Elliott's heroes, Ernest Tubb, recorded the "Mean Old Bed Bug Blues" as a single for Bluebird on October 27, 1936, in San Antonio, Texas.[66]

One of the gems of *Jack Takes the Floor* was Elliott's version of Guthrie's "New York Town," recorded by Woody on April 19, 1944 (under the title "My Town"), and released on the Asch folio *Woody Guthrie*. Elliott's fine version is famously, some might suggest *infamously*, prefaced by a spot on, if slightly schizophrenic, spoken-word "dialogue" between Jack and, well, Jack as Woody: "Well, I got a guest in the studio tonight," Jack drawls as the track opens. "It's my old partner and road buddy Woody Guthrie. Hey, Woody, how you been? I haven't seen you in . . . (Elliott briefly pauses). Seems like a year and a half now." In May 1957, when this song was recorded, it *had* been exactly a year and a half since the Elliotts last visited with Guthrie. When "Woody" responds to Jack's question, Elliott's dry-throated mimic of Guthrie's vocal timbre and inflection is masterful: "Well, Jack, about the same to *you*. Seems like about eighteen *years* to me. Let's get on with something good, what do you say? Some old time number like we used to sing together. Something like 'New York Town.' That's a good 'un." Jack and "Woody" trade verses throughout the song, Elliott seamlessly switching between the two distinct vocals.[67]

Jack Takes the Floor also features a fine version of Jimmie Rodgers's "Muleskinner Blues" (or "Blue Yodel #8"). "Muleskinner Blues" had been recorded by Woody Guthrie, Pete Seeger, and Cisco Houston for Asch on April 19, 1944, issued on *Folksay: American Ballads and Dances, Vol. 1*. But the song had already been a big regional hit down South for Bill Monroe and his Blue Grass Boys, and Elliott's version tends more toward Monroe's version, recorded October 7, 1940, at the Kimball Hotel in Atlanta, Georgia. Monroe was a member of the Grand Ole Opry by this time and it was the rare Saturday night at the Opry that Monroe did not perform "Muleskinner Blues."[68]

Elliott introduces "Cocaine Blues" with the preface, "I heard this from Reverend Gary Davis. Blind street singer. Preaches on the street corner about 135th street in Harlem." Davis was one of Elliott's guitar heroes, though he did not have the technique to perform in Davis's idiosyncratic style. Davis made his first commercial recordings for the American Recording Company (ARC) label of New York City in July 1935. Though he had one 78 rpm solo title to his credit, Davis served mostly as a guitar accompanist to such blues artists as Blind Boy Fuller and Bull City Red. Davis stayed on in New York City where he continued to perform, often on the streets, in his syncopated and highly sophisticated guitar style. Following his ordination as a Baptist minister in May 1937, Davis generally, but not without exception, turned away from the blues, but "Cocaine Blues" remained a favorite of the blues revivalists. No commercial recording of Davis performing "Cocaine Blues" was issued prior to 1957, so Jack's introduction to the song was, as he described on *Jack Takes the Floor*, learned firsthand from the reverend himself. "Dink's Song," another highlight, was most likely gleaned from the songbook *American Ballads and Folk Songs*; Elliott references the Brazos River in East Texas in his spoken word introduction, tellingly mimicking Alan Lomax's prefatory notes from that tome.[69]

Through recordings and live performances, Elliott's reputation amongst British folk-music enthusiasts continued to spread. Concurrently, a small backlash had developed among some in the old guard. The following review in *Jazz Journal* of *Jack Takes the Floor* made passing mention of the whispered brickbats: "Criticism has been leveled at Jack Elliott for what has been termed the 'lack of authenticity' in his singing—a criticism I find increasingly difficult to understand. I'll be frank and admit that my knowledge of folk songs and singers is limited to an interest which has developed only over the past eighteen months, but to me he is one of the finest of the contemporary singers. His voice and relaxed delivery have humility, and his wry sense of humour adds immeasurably to his performance. As far as guitar playing is concerned, it is always competent and tasteful and often rises to points of brilliance." For the most part, *Jack Takes the Floor* was welcomed as warmly as *Woody Guthrie's Blues*. The more perceptive critics noted that it was Elliott's own voice, and not that of Woody Guthrie's, that was in the ascendant. An article in *Sing* states: "Jack will take the floor again at the Hootenanny before you read this review. It will be nice to hear him again in the flesh; there is something about him that needs to be seen . . . to be believed. Topic's record is the next best thing—Jack being Woody, Jack being Leadbelly [sic], but best of all, Jack being Jack with his own refreshing voice."[70]

In the United States, *The Little Sandy Review* belatedly hailed *Jack Takes the Floor* as "the best of Elliott's English records" and Jack "as winning and as good a folksinger as I've heard in a long time." The album was praised for the manner in which it was assembled, not as a collection of studio tracks but as "a concert recording, complete with spoken introductions, chatter, imitations, and much fine singing." The review cited "Muleskinner Blues," "New York Town," "Cocaine," and "Dink's Song" as the album's highlights. The only missteps, according to Pankake and Nelson, were Jack's versions of Lead Belly's "Ol' Riley" and "Grey Goose," which were performed in too "daringly ethnic a manner." *Melody Maker* offered the album the spotlight treatment, headlining their review "Jack Elliott at His Best." Though the album contained "nothing particularly exciting," the album succeeded due to Elliott's "splendid" guitar work, his spoken word prefaces, and by the fact the performances are "as relaxed as any artist can get." "Personally, I was astonished to see yet another Jack Elliott LP—especially when it contained numbers already recorded," the review continued. "Once more, however, I've succumbed to the Elliott magic—in fact, I think it's his best to date."[71]

As suggested in the *Melody Maker* review, some of the songs on *Jack Takes the Floor* had only recently been issued. Topic was no longer the only British record company with Jack Elliott albums in the catalog. He had been approached by Doug Dobell, the proprietor of Dobell's Jazz Record Shop, 77 Charing Cross Road, in London, and asked to record a limited edition album for his "77" label. Not under exclusive contract to Topic, Jack agreed to sign on. The recordings were engineered under the direction of John R. T. Davies, a well-respected name in recording circles, often cited for his work with British jazz artists. In an article that appeared in *VJM's Jazz & Blues Mart* magazine, Davies recalled that Dobell "marketed these records from his shop, under the "77" label. . . . They didn't appear for sale anywhere else. We were faced with a big problem because of purchase tax, which stipulated that you could produce a hundred copies and not pay purchase tax but if you produced a hundred and one you'd have to pay tax on the lot. So many of those records only ran to a hundred copies, but this was usually enough to satisfy the immediate demand. If the demand was higher than 100, we could get around the purchase tax by making a separate issue of the same record."[72]

The resulting album, *Jack Elliot Sings*, has the dubious distinction of being the first to incorrectly spell Elliott's surname on an album sleeve. The notes on the rear sleeve credit Bill Colyer and Brian Harvey with the actual production of the record, with Davies listed as the engineer. *Jack Elliot Sings* was, as Davies suggested, originally released as a 10" LP, but as demand surpassed that first pressing of 100 copies, the eight songs that made up the original LP were halved and reissued as a twin set of EPs, unimaginatively titled *Jack Elliot Sings, Vol. 1* and *Jack Elliot Sings, Vol. 2*. It is difficult to determine exactly when the original pressing of *Jack Elliot Sings* was issued. In the April 6, 1957, issue of *Melody Maker* there is a mention that *Jack Elliot Sings* was complete and slated for release in the late spring. This, technically, made the Dobell record the true follow-up to Topic's *Woody Guthrie's Blues*.[73]

As suggested by *Melody Maker*, there was material overlap between Dobell's *Jack Elliot Sings* and Topic's *Jack Takes the Floor*. Taking a page from the old blues singers, Elliott demonstrated little allegiance to any particular record company and was not the least bit troubled by recording many of the same songs for a number of different labels. It is a credit to Jack's gift of improvisation that his many reinterpretations were rarely copies of earlier versions. Often his guitar work, his vocals, and, occasionally, even the lyrics changed subtlety with each new recording. The Dobell and Topic albums shared such titles as "San Francisco Bay Blues," "Muleskinner Blues," and "East Texas Talking Blues" ("Talking Blues," as per Dobell). But the Dobell album also featured unique material that showcased his talents as a blues interpreter. Lead Belly's "Alabama Bound" started off the album brilliantly, with Elliott easily handling the song's rollicking bass line. "Good Morning Blues," a traditional blues made popular, in part, through the recordings of Lead Belly and Brownie McGhee with Sonny Terry, was on display, as was "The Death of John Henry," which features a rare demonstration of Elliott's rough hewn slide guitar technique. Rounding out the album were "Fifteen Cents" and "Rocky Mountain Belle," two comedic songs, long favorites of the skiffle club audiences who continued to crowd his performances. Alexis Korner, who wrote the notes to the album, suggested that the inclusion of these comedy numbers was important, "a refreshing change from the many folk artists who believe that only mournful 'death and destruction' songs are truly good folk music."[74]

Elliott's amiableness was a welcome contrast to the high-mindedness and solemnity of such contemporary standard bearers as Ewan MacColl. Music writer and BBC radio personality Colin Irwin would write, "While the MacColl's were digging deep and doing it their way in dark corners of pubs, Rambling Jack happily wandered round Europe Woody-style doing it his way." Not everyone thought Elliott's approach was best, however. In his review of *Jack Elliot Sings*, critic Graham Boatfield thought it best that Jack not stray too far from the Guthrie template, in particular questioning his authenticity as a blues artist: "It does seem a pity to belabour the point, but this record would seem to reinforce the argument—white men are best employed singing white songs. Sorry for the racialism, but experience tends to bear it out. Jack Elliott doing Woody Guthrie songs is fine, so long as we are denied the original." Critic and blues scholar Paul Oliver found the record a mixed blessing: "If *Woody Guthrie's Blues* leans somewhat heavily on the social protest prop, *Jack Elliot Sings* is possibly aimed too much at popular appeal with humorous content."[75]

In the late spring of 1957, the Rambling Boys and June journeyed to Scotland for sightseeing and a visit with Rory McEwan's brother Jamie. Afterward, they set off for Paris so they could busk on the streets and replenish their coffers. They separated for a stretch, Derroll heading to Pamplona, Spain, where he planned to visit friends, take in a bullfight, and perhaps run with the bulls, the Elliotts setting off for Marseilles and St. Tropez. Derroll and Jack reunited, briefly, in St. Tropez, in early summer, but it wasn't long after that they separated again, the Elliotts drafted by a music-loving American businessman to assist in the sail of his yacht to the port cities of Cannes, Nice, and Portofino. In Portofino, Elliott found some welcome nightclub work at a small café, La Potiniere. Elliott's sets were so well received that the owner of the café asked him if he would be interested in staying for an extended run lasting straight through the end of summer. Elliott signed on, but only on the provision that Derroll would be hired as well. The manager agreed and Jack and June set forth on a mad scramble through St. Tropez and Juan-Les-Pins in search of Derroll. He was finally found in Nice, on the French Riviera.[76]

One night, after the Rambling Boys had finished their set at La Potiniere, June was introduced to "some people from the record industry [who] came down from Milano and said they wanted to record the guys." They had been approached by Walter Guertler, a Swiss-born record company executive who had spent most of his professional life in Milan. Guertler founded the Celson, Jolly, and Joker labels, though he had later combined Jolly and Joker under the acronym of SAAR (the Society of Reproduced Acoustic Articles). Guertler's offer of cash upfront was a welcome one, and Jack recalled that he and Derroll would record two albums' worth of material for Mercury Records "in about two days." June's memory of the session differed slightly, writing to friends that the "wonderful recording session in Milano for Mercury Records" took place over three days, not two. The facts and recording dates of the Milan sessions have always been a bit sketchy, due to the fact that for more than 50 years the recordings have been pirated, repackaged, released, and re-released in various configurations worldwide.[77]

To further confuse matters, in a 1990 interview, Derroll recalled that he and Jack "did about four records in Milan, Italy," but offered no titles or additional information to buttress his account. A four-song EP culled from the sessions did belatedly surface on the rare *Jack Elliot* [sic] *and Derrol* [sic] *Adams Sing the Western*, pressed March 10, 1959, and issued on the Italian *Hi-Fi Records* label. It was not until 1966 that a full 28 tracks surfaced on *Folkland Songs* and *Riding in Folkland*, two long playing albums released on

Guertler's Joker label. The music was more widely disseminated when, on January 17, 1967, Bounty Records, a British company (and subsidiary of Elektra Records) released a single, fourteen-track, version on the LP *Roll on Buddy—The Jack Elliott and Derroll Adams Story: Vol. 1*. The Bounty album was not distributed outside the United Kingdom, but it was a worthwhile collection, boasting a trio of unusual photographs and a set of thoughtful notes penned by the London-based American record producer Joe Boyd. A second volume on Bounty was promised, but a subsequent version was never released, though it was assigned a catalog number (Bounty BY 6046). In April 1967, Everest Records issued *Jack Elliot* [sic] in the United States, part of that label's "Archive of Folk Music Series." The Everest release is notorious for misspelling Jack's surname on the cover and for suggesting that Jack was dead in the liner notes. In 1973, the *Folkland Songs* LP was pirated by Spain's Gramusic label as *Canciones Folkloricas de USA*.[78]

In August 1957, Walter Guertler could be forgiven for not anticipating the number of gray market releases and outright bootlegs that would result. But he sensed he had captured something special on tape and promised to aggressively market the albums. In October 1957, June wrote to a friend in the States, "We've been in Italy for the last few months, and it certainly has been a lucky country for us: TV, club jobs and finally a wonderful recording session in Milano for Mercury Records." She explained that Mercury was planning to release "[One] 12" and 3 EPs (excellent records we hope) to be released in three months all over Europe—and maybe—the U.S.A."[79]

The material recorded by Guertler was far more demonstrative of the working repertoire of the Rambling Boys than the album recorded earlier for Topic (which would not be issued until 1958). Though Topic's *The Rambling Boys* featured nine songs, only four ("Buffalo Skinners," "I Wish I Was a Rock," "State of Arkansas," and "Mother's Not Dead") do not appear on the Milan session tapes. Of the 28 complete tracks that have surfaced, 20 feature tandem performances, five solo numbers by Derroll, and three guitar and vocal performances by Jack. (Elliott's version of "Hard Travelin'" is augmented by some occasional, but tasty, Sonny Terry–style blues harp.) Though four tandem songs ("Rake and Rambling Boy," "East Virginia Blues," "Roll On Buddy," and "Danville Girl") had been previously recorded for Topic, the new performances were sufficiently different to merit interest. June thought the Milan sessions "went well . . . in spite of the fact Derroll was drinking all day long." Though there is no evidence to suggest that Derroll's frequent pulls on the bottle had an adverse effect on the music, it is true the tape captured enough fumbled chord changes, mumbled lyrics, and unsynchronized starts and stops to suggest the atmosphere was entirely casual.[80]

Following the session, and much to the surprise of Jack and Derroll, June announced she had grown increasingly weary of acting as "nursemaid" to the Rambling Boys. She was tired of orchestrating the tangled affairs, both personal and professional, of both men. Derroll's eccentric behavior was exacerbated by his fondness for the bottled spirits that were continually proffered by well-meaning friends and fans. Derroll could be very amiable when drunk, and his banjo playing, which seemed almost an extension of him, was rarely affected. But his drinking caused Jack, on occasion, and June, more often, a fair share of grief. Derroll's indulgences coupled with Jack's own eccentricities had exhausted June's goodwill. Though Jack argued on Derroll's behalf, June stood firm in her decision and paid Derroll his half of the fee from the Milan sessions. She advised him to return to Paris, where she knew "he had made a lot of friends . . . and would be all right." Derroll chose to disregard June's stoic but well-meaning advice, choosing to ramble alone through Italy. "I stayed on in Milan and I bought a Lambretta with the money that I'd made from the records," Adams recalled. "I took off touring Italy, the banjo and me." Jack and June bought a Vespa motor scooter in Genoa and they set off for Rome, where Jack soon found employment singing, as a solo artist once again, at such nightclubs as the Brick Top and Via Veneto.[81]

Derroll found busking alone a difficult task. He told writer Bill Yaryan his bad luck coalesced in Pompeii, where he ended "up on [my] knees in a Catholic Church . . . my banjo broke, sick and hungry." With the assistance of some sympathetic prostitutes, Derroll was fed and cared for and, before long, he managed passage to Paris where, as June had originally suggested, he had friends to look after him. In Paris, he fell in love with Isabella, a talented artist and designer and the daughter of a local baron and village mayor. They were soon married, but Isabella's aristocratic family was unhappy with her choice of a husband. This unfortunate situation forced the newlyweds out of France, and they made Brussels, Belgium, their new home. With Derroll's assistance, Isabella went into the business of decorating display windows of "high couturier fashion shops." Things were going so well that Derroll no longer needed to play banjo to earn his keep. He told the BBC in 1960 that he enjoyed the creative outlet and steady income that the decoration job provided. As for his banjo picking, Derroll offered, contentedly, I "turned into what I like best, a *back porch* player. I play at home in the evening mostly . . . and for friends when they drop over."[82]

In October 1957, June wrote to a friend that she and Jack "were thinking about going to Greece next week for a month, sunshine, rocky islands, lots of boats." Traveling on the Vespa through Bari, Cofu, and Athens, they made it to the island of Hydra, where they befriended the Australian novelists George Henry Johnston and his wife, Charmian Clift. The Johnstons had relocated to Hydra in 1955, ostensibly to write undisturbed, but the couple garnered a reputation for spending a great deal of their time in the erudite, sometimes boozy, company of expatriates. The Elliotts were among their guests, staying in Hydra through Christmas 1957.[83]

They returned to Italy at the start of 1958, before choosing to set off on their Vespa to visit France, Switzerland, and Scandinavia. Their decision to travel north in winter on a motor scooter was unusual, the opposite of the wisdom found in the traditional lyric, "I'm going where the climate suits my clothes." Traveling through the snow capped Italian Alps on a motor scooter was a challenge, with Jack admitting he nearly "froze off my face" during the crossing. On one brutal stretch, Jack and June spied a little roadside café where they hoped to find a hot bowl of soup. A newspaper was lying on one of the tables, and though Jack could not read Italian, he immediately recognized the face of the gentleman in the black-and-white news photo: Jack Kerouac. "I *know* that guy!" Jack yelled, "That's my friend Jack Kerouac!" The patrons of the café looked up and stared blankly at the frost-bitten cowboy. Kerouac's *On the Road* had finally been published, nearly four years since he had first read the manuscript to Elliott on the floor of Helen Parker's apartment. Elliott realized the novel must have hit "big if he was on the front page" in Italy. He could not wait to get to the American bookstore in Paris so he could get a copy of *On the Road*.[84]

In Paris, the Elliotts headed for the famed Mistral bookshop on the Rue de la Bucherie. Jack was surprised to find old friends Allen Ginsberg and Gregory Corso there, preparing for a reading. Ginsberg was delighted to see Jack and took the opportunity to ask him to assist in the reading of excerpts from *On the Road* and to sing a few of Woody Guthrie's road songs.[85]

They next set off for Scandinavia. In Oslo, the Elliotts made the acquaintance of Eric Bye, an American expatriate who had managed to become one of Norway's most respected radio broadcasters. Bye, originally from Brooklyn, was a larger-than-life character; he was, at various times, a tugboat sailor, television host, author, and folksinger. Bye was also a

Guthrie fan who had translated Woody's lyrics into Norwegian slang, successfully capturing the nuances and spirit of the songs. Bye was profoundly
moved by Jack's handling of Guthrie's music and arranged for Elliott to appear as a guest on his radio show. He also convinced a friend in Norway's
fledgling television industry to include Jack on an early test broadcast.[86]

Warned that the weather was rough north of Oslo, Elliott wisely chose
to leave his guitar behind with a friend for safekeeping. The Elliotts continued motor biking northward, battling the elements: hailstorms, freezing
temperatures, and unpaved, gravel roads. One night, with the weather
worsening, they decided to take refuge at a hostel they had spied from
the road. They had been there just long enough to towel off and warm
themselves when Jack heard the strain of guitar music wafting down the
hallway. The guitar playing was unlike anything he had ever heard. The
guitarist was Arthur Tracey, the son of the South African musicologist
Hugh Tracey. He told Elliott that the exotic, infectious song he had been
playing was "Guabi, Guabi," a courting song learned from the playing of a
Bulawayo guitarist by the name of George Sibanda. Jack was charmed and
asked for an on-the-spot guitar lesson. Tracey obliged, but as the guitar
playing was unorthodox and complex, the African guitar style unfamiliar
to him, Jack was not able to get the song's tricky rhythm down. He asked
Tracey if the song had ever been recorded and was told it had appeared on
a difficult-to-find 10" disc titled *African Guitar*. Produced by Hugh Tracey,
African Guitar originally appeared on South Africa's Gallostone label but
was, at present, being distributed in Europe by London Records. Upon
his return to Paris, Jack managed to find the album in a specialty record
shop and set down with his guitar to woodshed. He was pretty successful
at replicating the song's intricate guitar setting, but the Swahili lyric proved
more troublesome, and he had to settle for singing the lines out phoneti-
cally. He was never quite sure what he was singing about.[87]

The Elliotts were due to return to Milan in the spring. Jack had been
contracted to tour Italy in May 1958 as part of a rock 'n' roll package
show starring the Platters. Between 1955 and 1958, the Platters, a Los
Angeles–based rhythm and blues group, scored a number of hit singles for
Mercury Records with such gems as "Only You," "The Great Pretender,"
"My Prayer," and "Twilight Time." Elliott would be a bit out of his element on the tour, serving as the bridging performer between the British
rock 'n' roll combo Colin Hicks and his Cabin Boys and the Platters. In
Milan, the Elliotts were introduced to the Platters at a cocktail reception,
but things did not get off to a great start. The Platters had arrived in Italy
from Switzerland, not in the best of moods as their luggage had been lost

in transit. The members of the tour were to travel by train, with a series of concerts planned for northern Italy, with visits to Rome, Florence, and Venice. Brian Gregg, the bassist for the Cabin Boys, recalled Elliott's solo spot was received with middling enthusiasm. The Italians had no notion of Woody Guthrie or authentic cowboy ballads; they were only interested in getting an earful of the Platters and American-style rock 'n' roll. Elliott was, once again, the odd man out.[88]

June wrote to a friend from Rome, suggesting they were contemplating a return to the United States in the autumn, following a sketchy plan to sing at the World's Fair in Brussels, which, they learned, was to include "The American Wild West Show and Rodeo." That summer the Elliotts traveled to Brussels to visit with Derroll and Isabella. Derroll, an amiable, spiritual man, harbored no hard feelings over the abrupt dissolution of the Rambling Boys. This was fortuitous as Jack had hoped to persuade Derroll into a reunion. He told Derroll about the "Wild West Show," how he was certain they could manage a gig singing cowboy songs at the exhibition. It was a crazy plan, but after meeting with the U.S. delegation, the Rambling Boys were contracted to sing to an international audience of tourists at the entrance to the American pavilion.[89]

"The American Wild West Show and Rodeo" attraction was not the only cowboy-themed entertainment in town. After arriving in Brussels, Elliott learned a second American rodeo company had recently set up business across town. This rodeo had not been sanctioned by the World's Fair committee; the strategy of the promoters was to siphon off some of the tourist money pouring into Brussels. Elliott thought it was well worth a visit, that perhaps the Rambling Boys could arrange a gig there as well. The rodeo was being staged on the outside of town, down in a valley near a derelict railroad bridge. But they could find no singing work there. They learned the shiftless promoters had already "absconded back to New York with about two million dollars," stranding a payroll of some 50 cowboys and 60 Sioux. The beleaguered team of cowboys, which included such legendary rodeo figures as Casey Tibbs, Bill Linderman, and Eddie Faulkner, were, against the odds, trying desperately to make a go of it. The cowboys had few other options; there simply was not enough cash to get everyone back home. But their plans were doomed from the beginning. The "Big Top" that had been erected for the rodeo was not held aloft by traditional tent poles, but by wind pressure generated from blowing ground fans. It worked, briefly, until the fabric tore, collapsing the "Big Top" to the ground. Since the cowboys did not have the tools, money, or materials to repair the tent, they hastened a decision to stage their rodeo in the open air. But the box office gate was negligible. It rained for several days, forcing the cowboys to ride their bucking horses in the mud. It was a dismal time and not long after the rodeo went bust, the cowboys were forced to sell their hats and boots to the locals in order to earn money for food. After listening to the cowboys tell their sad tale, Jack and Derroll set up behind the chutes and began to play a benefit for their forlorn, stranded countrymen. The homesick cowboys were grateful to hear the old songs. Elliott recalled there was not a dry eye to be found even though "We weren't singing sad songs, just the same old American stuff we'd been singing in England."[90]

The songs helped lift the morale of the cowboys and a party convened at a small tavern across the road. Bill Linderman removed his ten-gallon hat, proffering it as a makeshift collection plate, hitting up customers for donations. It wasn't long before the cowboys had collected nearly the equivalent of $50 in Belgian francs, buying wine, cheese, and bread with their windfall. Once the tavern closed, the party shifted to a nearby apartment where the cowboys asked Elliott to sing "Tom Joad." They enjoyed the song not for its great social commentary, but for the fact there was a character named "Preacher Casey" and Casey Tibbs's friends got a kick out of hearing his name. Afterward, the bronc rider George Williams pulled Elliott aside and, according to legend, taught him "Diamond Joe," the bitter and metaphoric saga of an unscrupulous drover who cheated the cowboys under his employ. Cisco Houston had already recorded "Diamond Joe" on the Folkways album *Cowboy Songs* (1952), and it is difficult to imagine that Elliott was not already conversant with the song through that recording. Regardless, the somber ballad of "Diamond Joe" became a favorite of Elliott's, and he promised the cowboys to record the song on his next LP.[91]

That opportunity would come soon. Elliott returned to London in the autumn of 1958 and met with Denis Preston, a bespectacled, goateed record producer of some notoriety. Preston's company, Record Supervision, Ltd., was interested in having Elliott record an album of western songs. Preston was one of Britain's few *truly* independent record producers, celebrated by the *Sunday Times* for combining "considerable technical expertise with business flair and a flamboyant personality." Preston would arrange the contracts of the artists he wished to record, oversee the sessions in his own studio, and then license the subsequent recordings to interested parties. In 1955, Pye Records became the first major label to license Preston's recordings and, with the capital resulting from that partnership, Preston built Lansdowne Studios in West London in 1956. In 1959, he entered into a similar partnership with EMI's Columbia Records label. It was shortly before striking the deal with Columbia that Jack Elliott turned up at Lansdowne, his trusty Gretsch slung across his shoulder.[92]

The sessions for *Ramblin' Jack Elliott in London* were held on November 5 and 7 of 1958. Jack Elliott, or rather *Ramblin'* Jack Elliott, as he was now more commonly known among friends and fans, would record, for the first time, the bitter saga of "Diamond Joe." The notes of Jack's first true 12" long-playing album offered: "Of all cowboy singers to be recorded in England (and, possibly, outside it as well) none is so impressive nor sounds so authentic as Jack Elliott. . . . Like all Westerners, Jack Elliott occasionally develops an attack of the wanderlust. It was during one of these bouts, when he was saddle-bumming his way around Europe, troubadour fashion, that he wandered into Denis Preston's office and arranged to cut the songs on this disc. Here is a man who obviously has a great repertoire, not only of western and country songs, but also of the original British ballads and folk tunes from which most Western songs sprung."[93]

Regardless of the album's glossy sheen, color cover photograph, and excellent production, *Ramblin' Jack Elliott in London* was the sort of record that Jack's fans, particularly the serious folk song types, had difficulty warming to. Preston had abandoned Topic's artistically successful, but commercially limiting, model. Gone were the great Woody Guthrie songs. Gone too was the razor wire guitar playing and railroad wail of Jack's harmonica. Preston had contracted the services of a serviceable but unremarkable country and western ensemble to accompany Elliott on the session. The long-playing album was structured around a program of old cowboy songs and ballads found in the public domain, the sort of material that Woody and Cisco had dusted off with far more success for Moses Asch in April 1944. Cisco's shadow looms large across *Ramblin' Jack Elliott in London*; nearly half of the LP's 12 tracks had been recorded by Cisco, including "Night Herding Song," "Chisholm Trail," "Rusty Jiggs and Sandy Sam," "Diamond Joe," and "I Ride an Old Paint."

It wasn't too bad of an album, but *Melody Maker* confirmed that Elliott's new offering seemed hardly the work of the same artist who had waxed *Woody Guthrie's Blues*. *Ramblin' Jack Elliott in London* featured a more "varied" program, with Elliott putting the songs "across with spirit and humour and a nicely authentic touch." But in the United States, *The Little Sandy Review* flatly called *Ramblin' Jack Elliott in London* "an out-and-out bad record," an outright "commercial" venture with little merit. "On almost every number," they wrote, "Jack takes off into the wild blue yonder of over-singing and makes Ed McCurdy at his broadest seem shy and subtle."[94]

It wasn't *that* bad, but it was, perhaps, time to take a break. After three years of "hard traveling," Jack and June made good on their promise to return home. *Melody Maker* broke the news in its November 15, 1958, issue: "Leaving London this week after a brief month's stay is American folksinger Jack Elliott. It is his fourth visit, coming at the end of a tour of seventeen countries."[95]

Just before he was to leave London for his return to California, *Melody Maker* loaned Elliott a long-playing copy of a new Guthrie LP, *Bound for Glory*. Folkways had released this "new" documentary-style album of mostly unissued Guthrie material in 1956. But it had only recently been licensed by Topic for distribution in England, appearing in record shops in the later half of 1958. *Melody Maker* arranged to tape-record Jack's first impressions of the Guthrie album, with the transcription published under the somewhat melodramatic title "This Record Made Me Cry, Says Jack Elliott."

Jack's tears were not the result of his hearing the voice of his ailing pal Woody Guthrie. Recitations of Guthrie's prose bridged the album's eleven musical tracks, and Elliott was profoundly moved by the peppery narration provided by Will Geer. "Will sounds just like what he is," Jack noted. "He's a friend of Woody's and understands what Woody has to say." Not a traditional record review, Elliott's article is nonetheless fascinating. Of all the songs collected on *Bound for Glory*, Elliott cited "Talking Fish Blues" as "by far the best one on there," with Guthrie's vocal "in about the best condition and shape I ever heard him." Elliott also offered that on "Talking Fish Blues," Woody's guitar "rolls right along . . . not dragging. It's got all sorts of tricky little things going on that sort of buoy the words up and rides them along." Of "The Sinking of the Reuben James," Elliott remembered that Guthrie composed the song (with contributions from the Almanac Singers) in response to the news that a German submarine had torpedoed a U.S. destroyer on October 31, 1941, ending the lives of 115 American seamen. Jack proudly noted, "Woody was on to Hitler long before a lot of people . . . and because of that some knucklehead like McCarthy branded him 'premature anti-fascist' after the war." Elliott estimated that Guthrie's success as a writer of children's songs was due to the fact that Woody was pretty much a grown-up kid himself: "He's got a sort of natural, uninhibited personality—more than any other white man I ever heard—and when he sings into the microphone something of Woody himself gets right on to that tape." Jack recalled "This Land Is Your Land" as "one we used to sing together" and opined the song "ought to be the U.S. national anthem." The only song to receive any criticism was "There's A-Better World A-

Comin,'" which "seems to stretch on about three times too long." "You might say it's monotonous," Elliott sheepishly allowed. "I might even say it myself. I doubt if you could stand anybody else in the world singing that song that length without going out of your mind."[96]

Not everyone was enjoying the new Guthrie album as much as Jack. The folklorist John Greenway, an appreciator of Guthrie's work, expressed mixed feelings. In a review published in *Western Folklore*, Greenway described the album, rather forthrightly, as "a brilliant conception . . . badly executed." In fact, Greenway was so disappointed he felt compelled to write Asch and ask "Why [was] Will Geer, who is here so obtrusively the actor . . . used for the narration instead of Jack Elliott?" Asch's blunt response was that "Jack Elliott was in England and Millard Lampbell who did the production wanted Will Geer. . . . I do not sway an editor in his conception." To be fair, Greenway did go on to commend Lampbell for his "kindness to Geer," acknowledging Geer's career had been sidetracked due to McCarthy-era "political stultification." But Greenway maintained Lampbell's "first duty was to Guthrie and Guthrie's material," and that Jack Elliott was, clearly, the only man for the job.[97]

The Elliotts returned to the United States in late 1958 and settled at June's apartment on Woody Trail in the Hollywood Hills. Jack found some work at a Costa Mesa boatyard, June supplementing their income with the occasional modeling assignment. Jack had not, of course, abandoned his career as a folksinger. *Caravan* reported that club owner Ed Pearl had reopened his Ash Grove nightclub on March 26, 1959, and that Jack Elliott had recently entertained there. Later that spring, Elliott had engagements at the Troubadour in West Hollywood and at the Club Renaissance in Los Angeles. In June 1959, Elliott dropped by for an unscheduled, but welcome, performance at the University of California at Berkeley Folk Festival.[98]

But Elliott's return did not last long. Pete Seeger recently had his passport returned following his battle with the House Un-American Activities Committee, and Pete was anxious to go abroad. He asked Jack to accompany him on a tour of England set for mid-September 1959. Jack signed on and, along with June, set off for New York, stopping off in Chicago en route. There they met Albert Grossman, a businessman and co-owner of Chicago's folk music club the Gate of Horn. Grossman's reputation was that of a shrewd businessman. Though somewhat leery, Jack accepted the impresario's invitation to a night on the town. Grossman brought the Elliotts to his nightclub, telling Jack there was money to be made in the folk song business, but an artist who did not have a national reputation would need good management. Grossman told Jack to write as soon as he returned from England, as he was interested in arranging a showcase for him at the Gate and would consider shopping his records around.[99]

On the eve of the Seeger tour, Elliott appeared at a matinee performance at Royal Festival Hall in London on September 19, 1959. The *Hootenanny* program featured a stellar lineup of folk talent from America, including the Weavers and the much-beloved blues duo Brownie McGhee and Sonny Terry. The souvenir program described Jack's appearance at the Royal Festival Hall, incorrectly, as "his debut as a concert entertainer." If there was any question that British folk-music fans were totally convinced that Elliott was a bona fide cowboy from the American Southwest, the following sentence from the program should put all doubt to rest: "But although singing in the lushness of the Festival Hall, Jack will remember the dry dustbowls of his native Oklahoma." Seeger's whistle-stop tour was set to commence immediately afterward and would include seven concerts throughout the United Kingdom, including visits to Liverpool, Birmingham, Edinburgh, Glasgow, and London. Pete and Jack would share co-billing, trading off the headlining and support slots. Following their solo sets, Seeger and Elliott would combine for the encores. Seeger was impressed with Jack's easygoing rapport with England's folk-music fans. Elliott was no longer dismissed by peers as little more than Woody's worshipful protégé. Four years of hard traveling throughout England and Western Europe had made Elliott nearly as famous as Pete Seeger among British audiences. One night in Scotland, Seeger learned, *literally*, what it was like to stand in Jack Elliott's shoes. Prior to their gig at the University of Glasgow, Seeger was combing through a nearby park on the river Kelvin, searching for an old log he could use in an axe-chopping work song demonstration. Seeger found a suitable log sitting atop a pile of autumn leaves, but when he went to retrieve it, he found himself chest deep in the river. With the concert less than an hour away, Seeger was spirited away to the hall by a sympathetic cabbie but forced to perform that night in Jack's dry, but awfully tight-fitting, shoes.[100]

Seeger's brief tour of the United Kingdom was an event with political undertones, so traditional news outlets as well as the folk-magazine press covered the concerts. One "first night" review noted the Seeger concert had been something of a challenge for him; not only did Pete face the "difficulty of standing up to his reputation, he had the task (unenviable at any time) of following Jack Elliott." *Sing!* featured a *Daily Herald* photograph of Pete, Jack, and June on the front cover of its December 1959 issue, describing this first-time pairing of Guthrie's two most important musical ambassadors as "the event of the year for folk song fans." The tour had some lasting effects. To pass the time between concerts, Elliott introduced Seeger to *We Didn't Mean to Go to Sea*, a storybook by the famed British author Arthur Ransome. The seventh in a series of Ransome's classic children's books, *We Didn't Mean to Go to Sea* recounts the adventures of the Swallows family children who accidentally drift off to sea in a small boat. Intrigued, Seeger read the book on Elliott's recommendation and after returning from England to his home in Beacon, New York, he bought a small, secondhand boat and began to sail on the polluted Hudson River.[101]

Following the tour with Pete, Elliott stayed in England. Promoters Roy Guest and Malcolm Nixon asked Elliott to appear as a special guest on two of the Roybert agency's "Folk Song—Blues—Country-Western and Music" package shows. The tour was to visit eight cities: Edinburgh, Glasgow, Sheffield, Liverpool, Birmingham, London, Manchester, and Leeds. Britain's homegrown hillbilly music ensemble Johnny Duncan and his Bluegrass Boys had been slated to play six of the eight dates, but scheduling conflicts necessitated that Elliott perform as Duncan's replacement at the Birmingham and London shows. [102]

The first week of October, Elliott appeared alongside Ewan MacColl and Peggy Seeger at a hootenanny at Saint Pancras Town Hall. Roy Guest would credit Britain's surging interest in *genuine* folk music to the efforts of Ewan MacColl and Malcolm Nixon and their "Ballad and Blues Organization." The club would regularly organize hootenannies as London, Glasgow, and Edinburgh, where fans were not only treated to stirring performances by such homegrown talent as A. L. Lloyd, Ewan MacColl, Seamus Ennis, and Dominic Behan, but also from "the best American folksingers around—people like Peggy Seeger and Jack Elliott."[103]

On November 14, Jack returned to Lansdowne to wax a second LP for Denis Preston. Once again, Preston was not at all interested in producing an Elliott album that featured the unadorned sound of his guitar and harmonica. Preston was a savvy producer who heard the blues motifs in Jack's music and wished to bring those elements to the forefront. The new album would offer a combination of songs by two of Jack's earliest musical heroes, Woody Guthrie, of course, but also Jimmie Rodgers, the "Singing Brakeman" from Meridian, Mississippi. Both Guthrie and Rodgers had been influenced as songwriters by African American musical forms, but Rodgers's songs were particularly affected by the blues artists he had come into contact with in Mississippi. Since Mississippi was a long way from London, Preston had to make do, bringing in two legends of the local jazz scene to accompany Elliott, the clarinetist Sandy Brown and trumpeter Al Fairweather.

The resulting album was titled *Rambling Jack Elliott Sings Songs by Woody Guthrie and Jimmie Rodgers*. A cursory scan of the Guthrie titles reveals an obvious attempt to feature only Guthrie songs not yet released on Topic. This was not accidental. Elliott had earlier signed an agreement with Topic, promising not to record any of the Guthrie material for another UK label for a period of seven years. The half-dozen songs that comprised the Guthrie side were new to fans collecting Elliott's British releases (Jack's Topic version of "So Long It's Been Good to Know You," recorded in 1956, would not see issue until 1963). Most of the versions were, as usual, cribbed from Woody's own recordings, and feature Jack's first commercial recordings of "Do-Re-Mi," "Dead or Alive," "Grand Coulee Dam," "I Ain't Got No Home in This World Anymore," and "Dust Storm Disaster." The Rodgers's side, on the other hand, was programmed with that artist's best-known material.

Although the songs for *Sings Woody Guthrie and Jimmie Rodgers* were recorded in November 1959, the tapes were shelved and not issued on LP until the early winter of 1961. The album, unjustifiably, received so little attention in the press that fans could have easily missed the record in their local music shop. In the past, *Melody Maker* would wax prosaic over a freshly minted Elliott recording, but this time the pop music weekly devoted no more than 36 words in its review. That brief citation was, at the very least, favorable: *Sings Woody Guthrie and Jimmie Rodgers* was selected as "an excellent choice for any folk fan," noting that Jack Elliott "on top of his form."[104]

Not everyone thought Elliott was "on top of his form." In a wonderful example of *The Little Sandy Review*'s trenchant sarcasm, Pankake and Nelson described the experience of listening to *Jack Elliott Sings the Songs of Woody Guthrie and Jimmie Rodgers* as akin to "the well known definition of 'mixed emotions': you feel like your mother-in-law just drove over a cliff with your new Ferrari." *The Little Sandy Review* held firm to its position that Elliott's music was not well served by Denis Preston, but the new album was not totally written off. Though Pankake and Nelson were genuine Guthrie fans, the side featuring the bluesy Rodgers's songs was billed as the better of the two, with Elliott capably tackling the material in a "nifty, freewheeling fashion." Oddly, no mention is made of Elliott's excellent solo guitar and vocal performance of "Dust Storm Disaster," which sounded as good and as genuine as any of the more stripped down Guthrie songs recorded for Topic.[105]

Regardless of the critical drubbing, Jack continued to enjoy a certain cache among the editors of *The Little Sandy Review*. The editors routinely forgave Elliott his musical trespasses, taking pains to note "no matter how far Jack goes astray, he is still the best purveyor of Woody Guthrie's songs that we have. He goes to the heart of the matter, and when he's in top form one gets the feeling that he and Woody sing from exactly the same place."[106]

On November 14, the same evening that work was completed on *Sings Woody Guthrie and Jimmie Rodgers*, Jack appeared on the BBC radio program *Saturday Club*. He refrained from singing any fresh material, choosing instead to perform the old standbys: "San Francisco Bay Blues," "Talking Blues," "Rusty Jiggs & Sandy Sam," "Rocky Mountain Belle," and "Muleskinner Blues." Ten days later, Elliott returned to Lansdowne to record a cycle of children's songs. The proposed album had been in the planning stage since his return, June excitedly writing to Woody on September 15 that "Columbia wants Jack to do an album of your kid's songs!!" The resulting EP *Kid Stuff—Rambling Jack Elliott Sings Children's Songs by Woody Guthrie*, was the first of Elliott's recordings to feature material solely designed for children. Interestingly, the EP is comprised of songs all entirely new: "Howdido," "My Daddy Flies a Ship in the Sky," "Why Oh Why," "The Fox and the Grey Goose," "Riding in the Car," and "Old Rattler." The record's subtitle is misleading since two of the songs were not from the pen of Woody Guthrie, but gleaned from Lead Belly and Pete Seeger. As with all of Elliott's recordings for English Columbia, *Kid Stuff* was handsomely packaged, the slipcase featuring a black-and-white photograph of Jack serenading a group of children on the street. The notes for *Kid Stuff* were composed by Elliott fan Alexis Korner. Korner, the blues singer-guitarist and an early disciple of Jack's music, had earlier penned the notes to *Jack Elliot Sings* for 77 Records. Korner, an unabashed folk music purist, had generated a small controversy when *Melody Maker* published his essay lambasting the practitioners of skiffle as amateurs whose music "rarely exceeds the mediocre." For the effort, Korner received a sack of angry letters from outraged skifflers, many asking him to defend his own musical credentials. To counter the accusation he was little more than a skiffler himself, Korner defended his pedigree, offering his "two or three sessions with Jack Elliott and Darrell [sic] Adams" as proof of his authentic brand. Korner likely lost more friends when he frostily rebutted that, "the main point in my article was not that all skifflers were 'prostituting the art.' It was that they were too inept, musically, to do so." Though Korner would make no secret of his low regard for the skifflers, he positively worshipped the music of Guthrie and Elliott. In his notes to *Kid Stuff*, Korner offered Guthrie as a "genius," anointing Jack as the "most worshipful admirer" of that genius.[107]

Following the session at Lansdowne, the Elliotts left for Paris, planning to push on to Israel after an interval. Jack and June's marriage was slowly disintegrating; she was certain the signs that the "marriage was in pieces" had been obvious to Pete Seeger on their recent tour. Though Jack was unaware of her intent, June's interest in Israel had little to do with sightseeing. She was quietly planning to settle for a term in Israel and engineer the end of their marriage. In Paris, Jack found work at the Café Contrescarpe, a derelict nightclub catering to an artsy crowd of bohemians and expatriates. There they were reunited with old friend and former Yellow Door roommate Alex Campbell, a Scottish folksinger who fancied himself a cowboy and had been hugely influenced by the music of the Rambling Boys. Campbell remembered the Contrescarpe as a "cabaret just behind the Pantheon on the Left Bank." Though Campbell would cite Derroll Adams as his greatest influence, he recalled that it was Elliott "who gave [us] the thrill of hearing for the first time many of Woody's songs and ballads, such as 'Ludlow,' '1913 Massacre,' and 'Pretty Boy Floyd.'" As a struggling musician, Campbell was impressed by Jack's talents as an entertainer; his music and personage seemed to cut through all social and class barriers. Elliott had an effective, if unusual, stage presence. As Bob Dylan would later write, "Most folk musicians waited for you to come to them. Jack went out and grabbed you." Long before Dylan, Campbell stood witness to Elliott's talent as a performing artist. Campbell had once worked a gypsy bar in Paris, playing guitar fills behind a vocalist friend. Elliott, too, was also in town, engaged at a slightly more upscale cabaret on the St. Germain des Pres. Most nights Elliott would finish up earlier than his friend and "would often pop around to sing us a few songs." Campbell recalled that "The yodel part on 'Muleskinner Blues' was always worth at least six glasses of wine from the customers and, of course, the gypsy singers loved him as well."[108]

Following his engagement at the Contrescarpe, the Elliotts boarded a train for Marseille. Their ship, of Turkish registry, sailed on December 18 and they arrived in Haifa, Israel, on Christmas Day. Upon arriving Jack dashed off a greeting to Woody via a photo postcard of "Tel Aviv seen from ancient Jaffa": "Merry X-Mas, Woody—Nothing special happening here today. Not a Christmas tree in sight." On January 28, 1960, the Elliotts sent Woody a much longer letter, June breathlessly recounting their adventures in Israel—"an exciting young country with miracles happening in front of your eyes." Since arriving, Jack had pulled out his guitar on a number of occasions to test the fortunes of busking on the street. The Israelis were very friendly, June reporting that most of the cities they visited had nightclubs that featured live music, and management "happy to hire an itinerant singer." Some club owners graciously offered the Elliotts accommodation in the storage rooms of their clubs, which helped stretch their meager funds. Following his return, Jack would tell the BBC that he went to Israel "without any previous arrangements or anything . . . walked into a place and said 'Here I am. Played a song and did all right. Sang and made a lot of friends."[109]

He would soon need those friends. Elliott was due back in London for a March 12 concert that would feature Jesse Fuller and the Rambling Boys, with support from Robin Hall, Jimmie MacGregor, and Leon Rosselson, but June told him she would not be accompanying him, that their marriage was over. She was planning to stay in Israel, where she hoped to find work and settle on a kibbutz. She suggested that he return to Paris, which, with great reluctance, he did, before returning to London. The dissolution of his marriage did not help his mood or music. Elliott admitted to becoming "totally disenchanted" with his music after that first visit to Israel. But he attributed this loss of enthusiasm less to the end of his marriage than to the fact the locals wanted him to perform Israeli songs. "I'm an American cowboy singer," Elliott recollected years later, "one of the best there is. I don't know how to sing Israeli songs worth a shit, but if you want to hear a good cowboy song, I'm the guy to ask."[110]

On March 10, two days before the concert at Islington Town Hall, Jack reunited with Derroll, and the Rambling Boys recorded a series of radio shows for the BBC radio program *Thursday Roundabout*. Ken Sykora, the host of *Thursday Roundabout*, assured listeners, "You'd recognize Jack Elliott in any British crowd by his bright checked shirt and his broad brimmed cowboy hat which, of course, he dons for certain, particular songs. His partner, Derroll Adams, is tall with a distinguished looking, Elizabethan looking beard, a single small gold earring and a well worn pair of working jeans." The two friends talked briefly of their meeting at Will Geer's, of Derroll's exposure to southern folk music during his stint in the armed services, of Todd Fletcher, the bull rider who inspired Jack to learn the guitar, and of Elliott's recent adventures in Israel. But mostly the program was built around the music of the Rambling Boys, Elliott and Adams playing both solo and in tandem. On March 24, the night that the third, and last, of the *Thursday Roundabout* radio programs was to be broadcast, Elliott took the floor at Portsmouth's Summa Cum Laude club. Afterward the Ballads & Blues Organisation arranged for Elliott to perform as the support act for the visiting American blues-folksinger Josh White at Islington Town Hall on April 9 and at the Midland Institute in Birmingham on April 11. [111]

Jack's old friend Jesse Fuller had arrived in England for a series of concerts that would introduce the songster to a new, worshipful audience. For someone who had never stepped foot on foreign soil, Fuller touched down in London as something of a conquering hero. This was, in no small measure, due to the efforts of Jack Elliott who, for the past four years, had primed British audiences with songs and tales of his friend "The Lone Cat." Jesse was amazed that everyone he met in England already seemed to know the "San Francisco Bay Blues." "Jack Elliott did that," Fuller would acknowledge. "He went to Europe and just rode that thing crazy there." Elliott also might have saved Fuller's life while in England. Jack and Jesse, the latter of whom was carrying his big twelve-string guitar and case on his shoulder, were walking through the busy London streets when Fuller absentmindedly stepped off the curb and into the path of automobile traffic. Jesse had been caught off guard as the cars in England traveled in the opposite direction than those in the States. Jack recalled Jesse "didn't see the car heading for him and I just grabbed him by the shoulder and put one hand on the guitar case and shoved him . . . back from the street. I said 'Jesse, you almost got hit by a car!'" Fuller replied coolly, "Aw, that's all right. I got *insurance!*"[112]

While in England, Jack met the writer Herb Greer, a young American novelist and playwright who had made London and Paris his home. Greer, only two years older than Jack, had already settled in London by 1952, where he continued his postgraduate studies at University College, followed by a two-year term at the Old Vic Theatre School in Bristol. Jack recalled him as tall and broad shouldered, totally bald with only one eye and a "serious looking goatee." He was also, in Jack's estimate, "an excellent guitar player." Interested in the art of underwater photography, Greer had recently earned a scuba diving certificate. He told Jack that he and a friend from France were planning a road trip to the village of Bodrum, on the banks of the Aegean Sea in southwestern Turkey. Two years earlier, local sponge divers of Bodrum had brought to the surface what appeared to be an ancient bronze statue and a clay urn. This surprising find brought a team of archaeologists to the area, spearheaded by the famed underwater treasure hunter and writer Peter Throckmorton. After nearly two years of intense exploration slowed only by the hassle of expedition underwriting and discouraging near misses, Throckmorton's team finally discovered the remains of the world's oldest undersea shipwreck. This Bronze Age ship, thought to date from 1400 B.C., was found just off Cape Gelidonya, near the coastal village of Finike. It was an exciting time and *National Geographic* offered a breathlessly adventurous, fully illustrated 21-page feature on the expedition authored by Throckmorton himself. Herb Greer was planning on visiting the site so he could test his newly acquired underwater photography skills, and he asked Jack if he would be interested in coming along.[113]

Greer's French friend backed out at the last minute so, equipped with guitars, photo equipment, and little else, Elliott and Greer doubled up on Jack's Lambretta and set off for the coast of southwestern Turkey. Elliott admitted that they had no "big musical mission" in mind when they packed their "two guitars on the back of that scooter." On May 11, Jack wrote to Woody from Brussels, telling him that they had left London in such a hurry that they had not brought along sleeping bags or a tent. Elliott planned to pick up these essentials while in Belgium. He hoped he might arrange a night's lodging with Derroll and Isabelle, but after arriving in Brussels on May 7 he learned the pair were on the Cote d' Azur. Luckily, Elliott found a group of Derroll's friends at the Café Welkom happy to help the travelers out in Derroll's absence. Elliott busked a bit that Saturday on the streets of Brussels and was invited to perform at a jazz club on Sunday, May 8. On Tuesday, he earned 110 francs ($2.20) at a rough and tumble tavern called Le Jambe de Bois ("The Wooden Leg"). From Brussels, the two planned stops in Munich and Vienna before heading to Yugoslavia and Bulgaria, and then Finike. It was a memorable trip for both men, though one fraught with difficulties. Jack wrote to Woody that they had suffered a series of flat tires traveling through Yugoslavia and the weather was uncooperative, having rained "all the way from Germany to Greece." It was a memorable time and Greer would adapt many of their encounters for his second novel *The Trip*.[114]

First published in 1963, Greer introduced *The Trip* as a *recit*, a seldom-used French term that Greer defined as a blend of fact and fiction. Both men were given pseudonyms: Greer is Eddy and Jack is Jerry, Eddy's guitar-playing American friend. *The Trip* was marketed as "the startling account of two scooter-riding, singing American cowboys who 'hit' Europe. What they discover about themselves and the Europeans they meet makes absorbing and amusing reading." Mimicking real life, *The Trip* had Eddy and Jerry singing on the street for their suppers, passing the hat and trading such songs as "Muleskinner Blues," "Hard Travelin'," "Gospel Plow," "The Wild Colonial Boy," and "Acres of Clams" as barter for coffee, food, and gasoline.[115]

On the road to Turkey, Jack had been periodically writing to June, hoping for reconciliation. On Friday, June 13, June wrote to Woody, telling him that Jack would soon be returning to Israel. Though she had no intention of getting back together with him, in early July the Elliotts settled for a time at a kibbutz not far from the Lebanon/Syria border. Elliott took a job in a car repair garage, with June writing to friends that Jack "comes home every night covered in grease. But he seems to enjoy it." He had not abandoned his music. On July 23, Elliott performed an hour-long concert for his Israeli neighbors, his rambling commentaries translated into Hebrew by an interpreter.[116]

The reconciliation that Jack had hoped for was not forthcoming. June had already made the decision to say farewell to Israel and travel, alone, to the Far East. She wrote to friends that Jack would likely be returning to the United States, confiding that they had written to Pete Seeger "to see if Jack can't get in on that annual concert [at] Carnegie Hall. . . . It would be nice if he had something to come home to."[117]

On October 6, 1960, Jack and Derroll were again in London, guests of *Thursday Roundabout*. Then, on October 26, Jack appeared on the *Easy Beat* radio program, performing "San Francisco Bay Blues" and a raucous "How Long Blues" before a worshipful audience of teenage music fans. British audiences clearly adored him. At the still tender age of 29, Ramblin' Jack Elliott was already a celebrated, legendary figure of England's insular folk-music world. But despite the acclaim and notoriety he enjoyed in the United Kingdom, Elliott admitted "the thrill of it all was beginning to wear thin." It was time to move on.[118]

In November 1960, Jack decided it was time to return home. "I came back to put a period to the end of the sentence," Elliott would tell *Newsweek* magazine. "I want to do something to make all the time I've spent seeing and hearing America worthwhile. Once I wished I had lived through the Depression and the dust bowl the way Woody had but now I don't want to live anyone's life but my own." Though Elliott left the United States in 1955 as little more than a busker and restless itinerant, he would finally return home an established recording artist and fledgling folk hero.[119]

Notes

1. June Shelley, *Even When It Was Bad . . . It Was Good* (Xlibris Corporation), 2000, 50. In the book *Guitar: An American Life*, Elliott told author Tim Brookes that he arrived in "England on September 8, 1955." In 1995 Elliott told Steve

Stolder (Steven Stolder, "Traveling Back with Ramblin' Jack Elliott") of the *NARAS Inforum* that he had "been in London about three weeks" when James Dean passed away on September 30, 1955.

2. Shelley, *Even When It Was Bad . . . It Was Good*, 50.

3. Shelley, *Even When It Was Bad . . . It Was Good*, 50; Jack Elliott, Bottom Line, New York City, 12 May 2000.

4. Jack Elliott, Bottom Line, New York City, 12 May 2000.

5. John Hasted, "Don't Scoff at Skiffle," *Sing Out!* Vol. 7, No. 1, April 1957, 28–30; Interesting studies on the skiffle music phenomenon include Chas McDevitt, *Skiffle: The Definitive Inside Story* (London: Robson Books, 1997), Michael Dewe, *The Skiffle Craze* (Aberystwyth, Wales: Planet, 1988), and Brian Bird, *Skiffle: The Story of Folk-Song with a Jazz Beat* (London: Robert Hale, 1958).

6. Mike Brocken, Alistair Bannfield, and Rod Stradling, "The Complete Topic Records Discography," www.mustrad.org.uk/discos/discog.htm (accessed 1 June 2008); "Topic Records' History," www.topicrecords.co.uk/Index_Link _Files/topic_records_history.html (accessed 1 June 2008); C. P. Stanton, "British Record Scene, No. 1 The Topic Label," *Caravan*, October/November 1958, 11; "U.S. Folkways Label for Britain," *Melody Maker*, 14 June 1958, 4.

7. "*Leader's Tapes*," BBC Radio 2, broadcast 27 March 1996; Ian Woodward, "The Robert Shelton Minnesota Transcripts: Part 6—Commentary and Interlude," *ISIS*, No. 93, October/November 2000, 23–24.

8. Stolder, "Traveling Back with Ramblin' Jack Elliott."

9. Craig Harris, "A Mosaic of Stories," *Dirty Linen*, No. 63, April/May 1996, 16; Stolder, "Traveling Back with Ramblin' Jack Elliott."

10. Liner notes to *Woody Guthrie's Blues* (Topic Records, T5), 1956.

11. Guy Logsdon, *Woody Guthrie: A Biblio-Discography* (Self-published, Revised 6 December 1999).

12. Harris, "A Mosaic of Stories," 16; June Elliott letter to Archie and Louanne Green, 6 February 1958, Archie Green Collection, Southern Folklife Collection, University of North Carolina at Chapel Hill.

13. June Elliott letter to Archie and Louanne Green, 6 February 1958, Archie Green Collection, Southern Folklife Collection, University of North Carolina at Chapel Hill; Guthrie's original version of "Talkin' Miner" (titled "Talkin' Centralia") can be found on *Woody Guthrie: Long Ways to Travel* (Smithsonian Folkways SF-CD 40046), 1994.

14. Jack Elliott letter to Norman Pierce, 24 June 1957, Archie Green Collection, Southern Folklife Collection, University of North Carolina at Chapel Hill.

15. Brian Nicholls, "A Jazzman's Diary: A Breath of the Real Thing," *Jazz Journal*, 8 November 1955, 25.

16. Joan Littlewood, *Joan's Book: Joan Littlewood's Peculiar History as She Tells It* (London: Methuen, 1994), 466–467; Shelley, *Even When It Was Bad . . . It Was Good*, 55–56.

17. Shelley, *Even When It Was Bad . . . It Was Good*, 55–56.

18. "Theatre Royal Stratford: The Big Rock Candy Mountain," *Times of London*, 28 December 1955, 5; Shelley, *Even When It Was Bad . . . It Was Good*, 55–56.

19. Program brochure for *The Big Rock Candy Mountain*, Theatre Royal, Angel Lane, Stratford, 16 December 1955.

20. J. P. Wearing, *The London Stage, 1950–1959, a Calendar of Plays and Players, Vol. 1, 1950–1957* (Metuchen/London: Scarecrow Press, 1993), 696; "Theatre Royal Stratford," 5.

21. Calvin Ahlgren, "'60's Folk Singer Ramblin' Jack Still Round and About, Elliott Logs Miles, Spins Yarns," *San Francisco Chronicle*, 7 May 1989, Sunday Datebook, 44; Shelley, *Even When It Was Bad . . . It Was Good*, 56–57.

22. John May interview with Jack Elliott, London, England, 12 February 2005.

23. John May interview with Jack Elliott.

24. John Renbourn, "Fingerstyle Guitar: Born of Skiffle and Blues," *Frets*, Vol. 10, No. 6, June 1988, 50.

25. Ron Gould, "The Legend of Ramblin' Jack," *Acoustic Music*, No. 29, September 1980, 14.

26. Alan Lomax comments from *Arena: Woody Guthrie*, British Broadcasting Company, Paul Lee, Director, Anthony Wall and Nigel Finch, Executive Producers, 1988.

27. "Woody Guthrie," *Sing Out!* Vol. 5, No. 2, Spring 1955, 36.

28. Paul H. Oliver, "Hard Travelling—Continuing the Story of Jack Elliott and Derroll Adams," *Music Mirror*, Vol. 4, No. 6, 16–17; Stanton, "British Record Scene, No. 1 The Topic Label," 14.

29. "S.T.," *Jazz Journal*, December 1956, 26; Frank Hurlock, *Jazz Music*, Vol. 8, No. 5, September/October 1957, 33.

30. Ewan MacColl, "Symposium: Topical Songs and Folksinging, 1965," *Sing Out!* Vol. 15, No. 4, September 1965, 12–13; Bill Yaryan, "Ramblin' Jack Elliott," *Sing Out!* Vol. 15, No. 5, November 1965, 27.

31. Irwin Silber, "They're All Talking about the Little Sandy Review," *Sing Out!* 10 (October/November 1960), 26–27; "Jon Pankake," in *Wasn't That a Time!: Firsthand Accounts of the Folk Music Revival*, ed. Ronald D. Cohen (Metuchen, NJ: Scarecrow Press, 1995), 105–114.

32. Jon Pankake and Paul Nelson, *The Little Sandy Review*, No. 2 (April 1960), 12, 15.

33. Shelley, *Even When It Was Bad . . . It Was Good*, 34, 58; Jim Gilchrist, "Woody, Bob and Me," *The Scotsman*, 12 February 2005, 22; Jack Elliott, Ceol Castle, Birmingham, England, 15 February 2005; The notes to *The Lost Topic Tapes: Cowes Harbour 1957* and *The Lost Topic Tapes: Isle of Wight 1957* (both issued in 2004) identified the tapes as having been recorded on May 14, 1957. But there are plenty of reasons to suspect this dating. In terms of simple chronology, June Elliott recalled that the recording session at Cowes preceded the spring 1956

sail of the *Magnet* to Valencia. Second, engineer Bill Leader is on record as having said that Elliott's sessions at Cowes took place over " a couple of days [with] a bit of sleep in between," not on a single date. Lastly, some of the material recorded at Cowes was offered for sale on 78 rpm discs issued on the Worker's Music Association label. These discs were already being reviewed in the music press as early as January 1957, five months prior to the May 14, 1957, date assigned in the notes of *The Lost Topic Tapes*.

34. Shelley, *Even When It Was Bad . . . It Was Good*, 58; Elliott, Ceol Castle.

35. Shelley, *Even When It Was Bad . . . It Was Good*, 58; Elliott, Ceol Castle.

36. Shelley, *Even When It Was Bad . . . It Was Good*, 58; Elliott, Ceol Castle.

37. Shelley, *Even When It Was Bad . . . It Was Good*, 61–62.

38. Shelley, *Even When It Was Bad . . . It Was Good*, 62; Elliott, Ceol Castle.

39. Elliott, Ceol Castle.

40. Elliott, Ceol Castle.

41. Shelley, *Even When It Was Bad . . . It Was Good*, 63; Elliott, Ceol Castle.

42. Shelley, *Even When It Was Bad . . . It Was Good*, 63; Colin Irwin, "Folk: Living Legend," *Melody Maker*, Vol. 59, 16 August 1980, 39.

43. Donny Lonnigan, "Hylda Sims and the City Ramblers," *Skiffle Party*, No. 3, 9–13; Dave Arthur, "Soho—Needless to Say: A Life of Russell Quaye, *English Dance & Song*, Vol. 46, No. 3 Autumn/Winter 1984, 2–5.

44. Arthur, "Soho—Needless to Say," 3.

45. Arthur, "Soho—Needless to Say," 3–4.

46. Jack Elliott on *Coffee Break Concert Series*, WMMS, Cleveland, Ohio, 17 August 1978.

47. Dewe, *The Skiffle Craze*, 112–113, 242–243; Promotional handbill reproduced in *Skiffle Party*, No. 3, 16.

48. Elliott on *Coffee Break Concert Series*; Shelley, *Even When It Was Bad . . . It Was Good*, 65.

49. Elliott on *Coffee Break Concert Series*; Shelley, *Even When It Was Bad . . . It Was Good*, 65; Arne Johnson, "Interview with Rambling Jack Elliott," *Wander*, 2000, www.ventnatormag.com/oct/ramblinjack.html (accessed 23 February 2002).

50. Elliott on *Coffee Break Concert Series*.

51. Shelley, *Even When It Was Bad . . . It Was Good*, 65; Jack Elliott, prefatory comments to "Muleskinner Blues," *Jack Elliott: Live at the Second Fret* (Prestige-International 13065), 1963.

52. Jack Elliott on *Across The Great Divide*, KPFA-FM Radio, 10 June 2001; Jack Elliott, McCabe's, Santa Monica, CA, 24 February 1996; Shelley, *Even When It Was Bad . . . It Was Good*, 67.

53. Shelley, *Even When It Was Bad . . . It Was Good*, 69.

54. Stan Darlington, "Jack Elliott and Derrol Adams," *Jazz Music*, Vol. 8, No. 5, September/October 1957, 9.

55. Darlington, "Jack Elliott and Derrol Adams," 9; Shelley, *Even When It Was Bad . . . It Was Good*, 70; Dave Peabody, "The Banjo Man," *Folk Roots*, December 1990, 19.

56. Shelley, *Even When It Was Bad . . . It Was Good*, 70; Bill Yaryan liner notes to *Derroll Adams Portland Town* (Ace of Clubs, SCL 1227), 1967.

57. Shelley, *Even When It Was Bad . . . It Was Good*, 70–71; Peabody, "The Banjo Man," 19.

58. Peabody, "The Banjo Man," 19; Shelley, *Even When It Was Bad . . . It Was Good*, 71; Robert Shelton, "Wandering Minstrel Is in Town," *New York Times*, 25 July 1961, 19; Jim Gilchrist, "Woody, Bob and Me," *The Scotsman*, 12 February 2005, 22.

59. Max Jones and Sinclair Traill, eds., "Rosy View of Skiffle," *Melody Maker*, 6 April 1957, 5; Shelley, *Even When It Was Bad . . . It Was Good*, 71.

60. Stolder, "Traveling Back with Ramblin' Jack Elliott."

61. Logsdon, *Woody Guthrie: A Biblio-Discography*.

62. John A. Lomax and Alan Lomax, eds., *Cowboy Songs and Other Frontier Ballads* (New York: Macmillan, 1938); John A. Lomax and Alan Lomax, eds., *American Ballads and Folk Songs* (New York: Macmillan, 1934); Jack Elliott, Johnny D's, Somerville, MA, 13 May 1999; Jack Elliott, Noe Valley Ministry, 9 January 1999.

63. "Capsule Reviews," *Melody Maker*, 5 March 1958, 15; "Gospel and Folk," *Melody Maker: Spring 1958 LP Supplement*, 5 April 1958, ii; "Titles from Topic," *Sing*, October 1958, 73; Josh Dunson, "A Far Country Come Nearer," *Sing Out!* Vol. 19, No. 1, April/May 1969, 33.

64. Bob Dylan, *Chronicles: Volume One* (New York: Simon and Schuster, 2004), 251.

65. Liner notes to *Woody Guthrie's Blues* (Topic Records, T5), 1956.

66. "Huddie Ledbetter Discography 1933–1949," in Charles Wolfe and Kip Lornell, *The Life & Legend of Leadbelly* (New York: HarperCollins, 1992).

67. Jack Elliott preface to "New York Town" from *Jack Takes the Floor* (Topic Records, 10T15), 1957.

68. Neil V. Rosenberg, *Bill Monroe and His Bluegrass Boys: An Illustrated Discography* (Nashville: Country Music Foundation Press, 1974); Logsdon, *Woody Guthrie: A Biblio-Discography*.

69. Jack Elliott preface to "Cocaine Blues" from *Jack Takes the Floor* (Topic Records, 10T15), 1957; Robert Tilling, *Oh, What a Beautiful City: A Tribute to Rev. Gary Davis 1896–1972* (Jersey Islands, UK: Paul Mill Press, 1992); John A. Lomax and Alan Lomax, eds., *American Ballads and Folk Songs* (New York: Macmillan, 1934).

70. Keith Goodwin, "Jack Elliott," *Jazz Journal*, June 1958, 16–17; "Titles from Topic," 73.

71. Pankake and Nelson, *The Little Sandy Review*, No. 2 (April 1960), 12–13, 15; "Jack Elliott at His Best," *Melody Maker*, 10 May 1958, 15.

72. Nick Dellow, "John R.T. Davies: The Ultimate Preservationist," *VJM's Jazz and Blues Mart*, www.vjm.biz/articles9.htm (accessed 10 April 2008).

73. Max Jones and Sinclair Traill, eds., "Rosy View of Skiffle," *Melody Maker*, 6 April 1957, 5.

74. Alexis Korner notes to *Jack Elliot* [sic] *Sings* (77 Records, 77 LP/1), 1957.

75. Irwin, "Folk: Living Legend," 39; Graham Boatfield, "Jack Elliott: Vol. 2," *Jazz Journal*, June 1958, 16–17; Paul H. Oliver, "Hard Travelling—Continuing the Story of Jack Elliott and Derroll Adams," *Music Mirror*, Vol. 4, No. 6, 17.

76. Shelley, *Even When It Was Bad . . . It Was Good*, 71–72; Peabody, "The Banjo Man," 19.

77. Shelley, *Even When It Was Bad . . . It Was Good*, 71–72; Peabody, "The Banjo Man," 19; Jack and June Elliott letter to Norman Pierce, 12 October 12 1957, Archie Green Collection, Southern Folklife Collection, University of North Carolina at Chapel Hill; Jack Elliott, Bitter End, New York City, 26 October 2000; "Walter Guertler, Biografia," http://it.wikipedia.org/wiki/Walter _Guertler (accessed 7 March 2009). Though the Milano sessions were, ostensibly, for Mercury Records, no material seems to have been issued on that label.

78. Peabody, "The Banjo Man," 19; Lee Palmer liner notes to *Jack Elliot* (Everest/ Archive of Folk Music, FS-210), 1967; Joe Boyd liner notes to *Roll on Buddy—The Jack Elliott and Derroll Adams Story: Volume 1* (Bounty BY 6036), 1967.

79. Jack and June Elliott letter to Norman Pierce, 12 October 1957.

80. Shelley, *Even When It Was Bad . . . It Was Good*, 74.

81. Shelley, *Even When It Was Bad . . . It Was Good*, 74; Peabody, "The Banjo Man," 19.

82. Bill Yaryan, "Derroll Adams: Banjo Pickin' Expatriate," *Sing Out!* December/January 1967, 32–33; Jack Elliott and Derroll Adams interview, *Thursday Roundabout*, BBC radio broadcast, taped 10 March 1960.

83. Jack and June Elliott letter to Norman Pierce, 12 October 1957.

84. Lew Herman, "Sounds: Ramblin' Man," *Creative Loafing* (Charlotte, NC), 9 October 1999, http://web.cln.com/archives/charlotte/newsstand/c100999/ sounds.htm (accessed 4 July 2001); Jack Elliott, Freight & Salvage, San Francisco, 29 October 1999.

85. Herman, "Sounds: Ramblin' Man."

86. Jonathan Tisdall, "Erik Bye, 1926-2004," *Aftenposten*, www.aftenposten.no/ english/local/article890961.ece (accessed 1 March 2009); Shelley, *Even When It Was Bad . . . It Was Good*, 79–80.

87. Jack Elliott interview with Robbie Osman, "*Across the Great Divide*," KPFA radio broadcast, 10 June 2001.

88. Jack Elliott, Ocean County Public Library, Toms River, NJ, 12 May 2002; Chas McDevitt, *Skiffle: The Definitive Inside Story*, 201.

89. June Elliott letter to Archie and Louanne Green, 6 February 1958, Archie Green Collection, Southern Folklife Collection, University of North Carolina at Chapel Hill.

90. *Jerry Jeff Walker's 48rd Birthday Concert*, Tried & True Music, Austin CableVision, Susan Walker and George Warmingham, Executive Producers, Norman Wright, Producer/Director, 1990; Jack Elliott, Bottom Line, New York City, 10 August 2000.

91. Jack Elliott, Bottom Line, New York City, 10 August 2000.

92. Paul Adams, "Denis Preston and the Record Supervision Story," *Singsong Entertainment Publicity*, December 2003, www.singsongpr.biz/news/lake3.htm (accessed 26 September 2007).

93. Charles Chilton liner notes to *Ramblin' Jack in London* (Columbia 33SX 1166), 1959.

94. "Blues and Folksong," *Melody Maker*, 29 August 1959, Supplement III; Jon Pankake and Paul Nelson, "Record Reviews," *The Little Sandy Review*, No. 4, Not known. 7–8.

95. Untitled, *Melody Maker*, 15 November 1958, 11.

96. Jack Elliott, "This Record Made Me Cry, Says Jack Elliott," *Melody Maker*, 13 December 1958, 15.

97. John Greenway, "Folk Song Discography," *Western Folklore*, Vol. 20, No. 2, April 1961, 150–151.

98. Shelley, *Even When It Was Bad . . . It Was Good*, 81; Stolder, "Traveling Back with Ramblin' Jack Elliott"; Zonweise Hubbard and Page Stegner, "Message from the West," *Caravan*, June/July 1959, 18; Sheldon Harris, *Blues Who's Who* (New York: DaCapo Press, 1979), 173–174; Eric Von Schmidt and Jim Rooney, *Baby, Let Me Follow You Down: The Illustrated Story of the Cambridge Folk Years*, 2nd ed. (Amherst: University of Massachusetts Press, 1995).

99. Shelley, *Even When It Was Bad . . . It Was Good*, 82; Joe Ross, "Ramblin' with Jack," *Folk Roots*, January/February 1993, 41.

100. Program brochure for *"Folk Song—Blues—Country-Western"* concert (Roybert [London] Limited and Malcolm Nixon, September 1959); Shelley, *Even When It Was Bad . . . It Was Good*, 82–83; Pete Seeger, "Johnny Appleseed, Jr.," *Sing Out!* Vol. 9, No. 3, Winter 1959/1960, 48.

101. Israel G. Young, "Frets and Frails," *Sing Out!* Vol. 9, No. 3, Winter 1959/1960, 34; "Pete Seeger with Jack and June Elliott . . . ," *Sing*, Vol. 5, No. 2, December 1959, Front Cover; David King Dunaway, *How Can I Keep From Singing: Pete Seeger* (New York: McGraw-Hill Book Company, 1981), 250.

102. "What's On and Who's Singing," *Sing*, Vol. 5, No. 1, September 1959, 7.

103. "What's On and Who's Singing," 7; Roy Guest, "British Isles Folk Scene," *Caravan*, August/September 1959, 45.

104. "Folk and Blues," *Melody Maker*, 4 February 1961, 14.

105. Jon Pankake and Paul Nelson, "Record Reviews," *The Little Sandy Review*," No. 13, 37–39.

106. Pankake and Nelson, "Record Reviews," *The Little Sandy Review*," No. 13, 37–39.

107. Jack and June Elliott postcard to Woody Guthrie, 15 September 1959, Woody Guthrie Foundation & Archives, Correspondence 2, Box 1, Folder 26; Alexis Korner, "Skiffle or Piffle," *Melody Maker*, 28 July 1956, 5; Alexis Korner liner notes to *Kid Stuff: Ramblin' Jack Elliott Sings Children's Songs by Woody Guthrie* (Columbia Records/Segment 8046), 1960.

108. Shelley, *Even When It Was Bad . . . It Was Good*, 83; Alex Campbell, *Frae Glesga Toon* (Woodham Walter, Essex, England: Folk Scene Publications, 1964), 36; Fair View, "Ramblin' Reminiscences of Ramblin' Jack Elliott," in *Praxis: One: Existence, Men and Realities*, ed. Stephen Pickering (Berkeley: No Limit Publication, 1972), 60.

109. Jack and June Elliott postcard to Woody Guthrie and the Gleasons, 25 December 1959, Woody Guthrie Foundation & Archives, Correspondence 2, Box 1, Folder 26; Jack and June Elliott letter to the Gleasons and Woody Guthrie, 28 January 1960, Woody Guthrie Foundation & Archives, Correspondence 2, Box 1, Folder 26; Shelley, *Even When It Was Bad . . . It Was Good*, 83–84; Jack Elliott and Derroll Adams interview, *Thursday Roundabout*, BBC radio broadcast, taped 10 March 1960.

110. Shelley, *Even When It Was Bad . . . It Was Good*, 83–84; Randy Sue Coburn, "On the Trail of Ramblin' Jack," *Esquire*, April 1984, 85.

111. Jack Elliott and Derroll Adams interview, *Thursday Roundabout*, BBC radio broadcast, taped March 10, 1960; *Melody Maker*, 15 March 1960; Monica Thapur (BBC) correspondence with Hank Reineke, 11 April 2007.

112. Michael Goodwin, *Brother Lowdown* (Fantasy Records 24707), 1972; Jack Elliott, Towne Crier Cafe, Pawling, NY, 12 July 1992.

113. Peter Throckmorton, "Thirty-Three Centuries Under the Sea," *National Geographic*, Vol. 117, No. 5, May 1960, 682–703; Jack Elliott, Tin Angel, Philadelphia, PA, 15 June 1996.

114. Herb Greer, *The Trip* (London: Hutchinson, 1963); Colin Irwin, "Folk: Living Legend," 42; Jack Elliott letter to the Gleasons and Woody Guthrie, 14 May 1960, Woody Guthrie Foundation & Archives, Correspondence 2, Box 1, Folder 26.

115. Greer, *The Trip*.

116. June Elliott letter to "Sid, Bob, Terri (Gleason) & Woody," 13 June 1960, Woody Guthrie Foundation & Archives, Correspondence 2, Box 1, Folder 26; June Elliott letter to the Gleasons and Woody Guthrie, 6 July 1960, Woody Guthrie Foundation & Archives, Correspondence 2, Box 1, Folder 26; June Elliott letter to the Gleasons, 24 July 1960, Woody Guthrie Foundation & Archives, Correspondence 2, Box 1, Folder 26.

117. June Elliott letter to the Gleasons, 24 July 1960, Woody Guthrie Foundation & Archives, Correspondence 2, Box 1, Folder 26.

118. Roger Catlin, "Ramblin' Jack Elliott Still a Cowboy at Heart," *Hartford Courant*, 17 July 1992, E1.

119. Robert Shelton, "Real Hung Up," *Newsweek*, 14 August 1961, 47.

Bleecker Street Blues   4

FROM AUTUMN 1955 THROUGH NOVEMBER 1960, Ramblin' Jack Elliott helped spread the songs and gospel of Woody Guthrie and
American folk music throughout Western Europe. Everywhere he
traveled, he introduced Guthrie's peerless catalog of ballads to audiences
who had little or no notion of either man. Elliott performed Woody's
songs, without apology, in the sometimes harsh and dissonant manner of
his mentor. The rough edges of Woody's songs were not smoothed, the
lyrics not diluted or expurgated for easier consumption. Elliott preserved
the simple, utilitarian sound of Guthrie's music, the rusty, lonesome guitar
married to the wail of a racked harmonica, and the effect was stunning.
There was something terribly forthright about Elliott's brand of American
folk music, and he engaged audiences with his deceptively easygoing, unhurried performing style. Elliott's no-frills approach touched a generation
of fledgling folk-music performers in England, particularly those put off by
the robust cheeriness of the skiffle crowd. Interestingly, Jack's antipathy
for Lonnie Donegan and his many adherents put him at odds with such
friends as Alan Lomax, and even with Woody himself. Lomax championed
the enthusiasm young Britons had demonstrated for skiffle and American
folk song, confident that skiffle was the portal through which youngsters
would be introduced to the rich wellspring of authentic folk song. But
Elliott was not on board with such long-range estimates. When the folk
boom hit America and England, Elliott groused, "Today's singers are kids
who grab guitars and jump aboard for a free ride." But Woody himself
admitted listening to the first records of such well-scrubbed folk groups as
the Kingston Trio and the Tarriers. He did not begrudge their commercial

success and even defended them against the purists. In Woody's mind, he was content in the knowledge that people were listening to "folk music and the folks like it."[1]

Elliott's decidedly American influence on a generation of fledgling singer-guitarists in the British Isles is incalculable; English guitarist John Renbourn recalled that Elliott "left behind a number of British Rambling Jack imitators." Among the more notable U.K.-based folksingers and roots-orientated guitarists that have, at one time or another, acknowledged their debt to Elliott are Ralph McTell, Bert Jansch, Alexis Korner, Wizz Jones, Long John Baldry, Alex Campbell, John Renbourn, and Davy Graham. Even Ewan MacColl, firmly of the old guard, had been impressed with Jack's talent, helping to arrange his first recordings for Topic and booking Woody's most worshipful protégé for his *Ballads and Blues* radio programs. But MacColl found himself increasingly frustrated by what he saw as the suffocating influence of American folk style on the British scene. He complained about established performers and "young kids from the streets of London trying to sound like Lead Belly or Woody Guthrie." MacColl found his countrymen's tendency to copy American folk song style to be particularly disturbing, especially "when our own tradition is so rich and untapped." Peggy Seeger, who married MacColl in 1958, agreed with her husband's assessment. In 1962, Seeger reflected, "Up until three or four years ago . . . . the American influence in England pre-dominated. Imitators of Big Bill Broonzy, Jean Ritchie, Jack Elliott, Lead Belly and others were the most popular performers around." In America, Jon Pankake and Paul Nelson of *The Little Sandy Review* also made some mention of this worrying trend in their review of *The Rambling Boys*. "Perhaps the American folk boom in England is overshadowing England's own fine folk tradition," they wrote in 1960, warning the Brits not to neglect their own hallowed roots.[2]

Andy Irvine was one of Jack's more notable disciples. Irvine, later the guitarist and singer of such seminal roots music groups as Patrick Street and Planxty, had been introduced to the music of Woody Guthrie through skiffle, and he befriended Elliott sometime around 1958. Elliott was a decade older that Irvine but had taken an immediate liking to the enthusiastic kid who once discreetly followed him home through the streets of London just so he could learn his address. Elliott demonstrated some of the nuances of Guthrie's guitar methods to Irvine and even gave him the prized gift of an old shirt that had once belonged to Woody. Irvine admitted he wore that old shirt "until it fell off my back."[3]

Irvine was already a Guthrie fan, so that first meeting with Elliott was fortuitous. Irvine had been corresponding with Woody through posts sent between himself and Bob and Sidsel Gleason, folk-music fans who admired Guthrie's music. With the blessing of hospital officials, the Gleason's arranged to transport Woody nearly every Sunday from Greystone Memorial Hospital in Morris Plains, New Jersey, to their home in nearby East Orange. There they would allow him the pleasures of a cigarette while soaking in a warm bath, and fed him the rare, and greatly appreciated, splendor of a hot home-cooked meal. The Gleasons had encouraged Woody's fans to write him in care of their home address and that call went, apparently, worldwide. England's *Melody Maker* sent a writer to the Gleasons who reported, "Letters arrive from all over America and Canada, and particularly from England, where Guthrie has always been held in high esteem." Following his return from England in November 1960, Elliott would dutifully visit the Gleasons' walk-up apartment most Sundays, usually finding Woody in the family parlor sitting amid a crowd of friends and admirers. Sidsel was, invariably, tucked away in the kitchen preparing dinner, and Jack recalled they would "be enjoying the aromas of her cooking and anticipating eating her great food." Everyone brought their guitars, of course, and there was a lot of singing and trading of songs—mostly Woody's songs, as that was his preference. Bob Gleason was something of a home audio hobbyist and he recorded the Sunday afternoon sessions in the family parlor. The friends who traveled out to East Orange each Sunday would change from week to week, but the crowd of regular well-wishers included Elliott, Alan Lomax, Pete Seeger, Dave Van Ronk, Peter LaFarge, Oscar Brand, John Cohen, Ralph Rinzler, Ed Badeaux, and Lionel Kilberg.[4]

In 1960 Jon Pankake and Paul Nelson had reverently mailed out the first three issues of *The Little Sandy Review* to Woody via the Gleasons. They were no doubt surprised when they received a letter back. As Guthrie was not in any physical condition to respond, he asked the Gleasons to send regards on his behalf. They praised the magazine, adding, "Woody asked me to thank you for the wonderful review on Jack Elliott. He said it's about time America realized that Jack is one of the greatest of the young folksingers. And if it weren't for Jack Elliott, I'm sure that Woody's music wouldn't be loved all over England. Jack has carried the gospel of Woody far and wide through the British Isles, Europe and Isreal [sic]. In Isreal [sic], even though the people couldn't understand a word of what he sang, they sat entranced as he sang Woody's songs."[5]

Elliott's status as the preeminent Guthrie interpreter was confirmed when Moses Asch approached him and asked if he would be interested in recording an album of Woody's children's songs for Folkways. It is not clear why Asch decided to have Elliott re-record the cycle of songs that comprised Woody's *Songs to Grow On* albums, which were still available. In fact, *every* recording in the Folkways catalog was available; Asch refused to let any title fall out of print regardless of how little an album sold. Interestingly, Elliott confided in a BBC-Radio 2 interview that the collection of Guthrie's children's songs on the album he recorded for Asch were "learned directly off [Woody's] own album" rather than firsthand from the author himself.[6]

It is possible that Asch was interested in collecting as many of Guthrie's children's songs as would fit on the now standard 12" long-playing record. With the exception of Woody's "How Di Do" (labeled "How Dja Do" on Folkways FC 7501), the 15 remaining titles that comprise Elliott's version of the *Songs to Grow On* album could only be found scattered across three 78-rpm folio sets issued by Folkways and Disc between 1946 and 1951. By the 1950s Asch reissued many of the songs on two separate 10" albums, *Songs to Grow On, Vol. 1, Nursery Days* (FC 7005) and *Songs to Grow On for Mother and Child* (Folkways 7015, 1950/1953). Most of the songs recorded by Elliott for his *Songs to Grow On* were subsequently issued, though Asch chose to edit out two performances from the final LP, "Bling Blang" and "Hobo's Lullaby." The plaintive "Hobo's Lullaby," written by the caustic Wobbly songwriter Goebbel Reeves, might have stretched the definition of "children's song" too far anyway, but it was probably left off of the album because it had not been written by Guthrie.[7]

Elliott's *Songs to Grow On by Woody Guthrie* masquerades as a bona fide Woody Guthrie album in almost every sense. Asch is credited for the album's sleeve design, which is, at best, workmanlike in its presentation, rescued only by a trio of "Original Drawings by Woody Guthrie" featured on the front and back covers. The included eight-page booklet contains a full page and a half of Guthrie's prose, the lyrics to all 18 featured Guthrie songs, 20 additional line drawings by Woody, and a full-page black-and-white photograph of Woody on the last page. The recording is respectfully dedicated to the memory of Cathy Ann "Stackabones" Guthrie, the eldest child of Woody and Marjorie, who had perished in a house fire in February 1947. Though the second page of the booklet features a small black-and-white photograph of Elliott, no biographical information is included.[8]

Songs to Grow On by Woody Guthrie is one of the forgotten treasures of Elliott's early discography. Elliott loved Guthrie's children's songs, and this affection is reflected in the performances. Elliott told the BBC that Guthrie's talent as a writer of children's songs was primarily because "Woody kept his childishness" through adulthood. But Guthrie also retained the "cantankerousness" of a child, and Elliott agreed that interaction with Woody was, at times, "difficult." He told the *Chicago Sun Times*, "Woody was a cantankerous sort of guy. I got along with him, but many people did not. They did not like his oddness. Woody was a hobo from Oklahoma, and he carried that with him forever." On another occasion, Elliott reminisced that Woody's second wife, Marjorie Mazia Guthrie, once sadly confided to him, "Sometimes I don't think it's possible to be a great artist and also be a great human being in the same body."[9]

The *New York Times* briefly described *Songs to Grow On* as a record that best served "as [an] introduction to sounds and simple rhythms and simple tunes," offering no commentary on the merit of the songs or of Elliott's contribution. In her "Survey of Children's Records" published in *Sing Out!* Henrietta Yurchenco compared and contrasted Elliott's Folkways recording to Woody's own *Songs to Grow On* and *Songs to Grow On for Mother and Child*. "Although Woody and Elliott (who imitates him to a tee) do some of the same songs," Yurchenco wrote, "the two records are sufficiently different to warrant buying them both." *The Little Sandy Review* was one of the few journals to recognize Elliott's *Songs to Grow On* as an important contribution to the Guthrie canon, as crucial, in its own way, as Woody's *Dust Bowl Ballads*. The magazine devoted four full paragraphs to the album, analyzing Guthrie's skill as a writer of songs "crammed full of activity and motion, pictorially vivid, filled with fascinating phrases, noises and things for kids to do." Elliott is offered as "an early disciple of Guthrie," one of the few musicians to "master . . . all the stylistic nuances and profundities required to bring [the songs] to life." In England, Ken Phine of *Sing* agreed that Woody's children's songs were an integral, if mostly overlooked, facet of his legacy: "Jack Elliott makes his Folkways debut with Woody's *Songs to Grow On*. Guthrie's original recordings are still in the Folkways catalogue, missed by many because they are buried in the kiddie's section."[10]

Ewan MacColl and Peggy Seeger performed a series of concerts in the United States, commencing October 1960 and finishing at Carnegie Hall on December 3. A crowded postconcert party was held at Albert Grossman's suite on Central Park West, and in attendance were Oscar Brand, Tom, Liam, and Pat Clancy, Cisco Houston, Tom Paley, Pete and Toshi Seeger, and Robert Shelton. Izzy Young, the veritable New York City folk scene gadfly, missed the Carnegie concert but managed to find his way to Grossman's apartment later that evening. He was still there when Elliott arrived near four in the morning, having completed his late-night set at Gerdes where he had been engaged for a week's residency. Young had caught several of Jack's performances that week, impressed by his skills as a raconteur and uncanny ability to channel Woody Guthrie. That week, Izzy would note in his journal, "Jack is a legend to the younger kids and they are flocking to hear him everywhere he sings in NYC."[11]

The winter of 1960–1961 brought with it a brutal cold, and early on December 3, as Elliott readied himself for his Saturday-night engagement at Gerdes, the temperature on the street was well below freezing. On stage, Elliott had made light of the bitter cold that greeted his return to the United States. "I was afraid that I was gonna freeze to death when I got to New York after being in balmy England," Jack acknowledged, but "the cold suits me fine." Elliott did confess he was having a problem getting acclimated to the steam-heated apartments of the city. There was little of that in England.[12]

Jack's first residency at Gerdes Folk City, which began on November 29, was something of a homecoming. Brother John Sellers was the emcee and Jack had earlier met Brother John while in London. Sellers had accompanied Big Bill Broonzy on the blues singer's 1957 tour, and Jack told the crowd at Gerdes that British audiences "sure went mad for them." Jack met Brother John a second time on the Boulevard St. Germain des Pres in Paris. On that occasion, Sellers was working with Sidney Bechet, the New Orleans–born clarinetist. Bechet had performed with Jack's early hero Bunk Johnson as early as 1908, and Elliott hoped to see Bechet while in Paris. But Bechet and Sellers were performing at a posh and pricey Paris nightclub. "I never did get over to see him," Jack drawled with a hint of disappointment. "Never could work up the price. It was a pretty high class joint. I used to bump into him on the street all the time." It was no wonder. While Brother John collected a nice fee for entertaining a nightclub filled with Parisian sophisticates, Elliott was on the street outside singing for spare change.[13]

That night at Gerdes, Jack opened with "Howdido," one of Guthrie children's songs recently waxed for Asch. He then moved easily into Fuller's "San Francisco Bay Blues," an unusual guitar scratch version of "Gambler's Blues," and Ray Charles's "I Got a Woman." They were followed by a suitably solemn "Diamond Joe" and a jaunty take on Woody's "Car Song (Riding in My Car)." He prefaced his gentle reading of Elizabeth Cotten's "Freight Train" with the news that Libba herself would soon be in New York for a concert date. The haunting "South Coast" closed the set, Jack talking at some length about the desolate Big Sur country.

On Tuesday, December 7, the Weavers replaced Jack on the bill at Folk City. But Elliott was immediately booked for a three-night stay

(December 15–17) at One Sheridan Square, "in the heart of Greenwich Village." Referencing the arctic cold holding the city in its icy grip, the newspaper advertisement screamed: "Throw Away Your Snow Shovels and *Dig* Ramblin' Jack Elliott & Guests!" Elliott had been home for little more than a month and was already working steadily.[14]

It was around this time that Jack would meet the person who would change his life as profoundly as Woody Guthrie. Elliott has long maintained that the first new face he encountered following his return to the States was that of a 19-year-old folksinger from Hibbing, Minnesota, by the name of Bob Dylan. According to an oft-recollected tale, Elliott returned to New York City from London, staying that first night at a hotel room on West 57th Street. The following morning he reportedly boarded a bus for the 30-mile ride to Greystone Hospital and a reunion with his ailing mentor. It was at Greystone, the morning of his return, that Elliott, reportedly, would meet Dylan for the first time at Guthrie's bedside. The tale has long been part of the mythology surrounding Dylan, Ramblin' Jack, and Woody Guthrie, but the facts belie this romantic scenario. By most accounts, Dylan was still en route to New York City from Chicago when Elliott landed in November 1960.[15]

In September 1960, Dylan was, technically, studying at the University of Minnesota. But his interest was not on his studies but on the folk-music scene that had coalesced around "Dinkytown," an area adjacent to the Minneapolis campus, a rough equivalent of New York's Greenwich Village. Dave Whitaker, a legend among the local bohemians, was an artist, poet, and bibliophile who suggested that Dylan read Woody Guthrie's occasionally fanciful autobiography *Bound for Glory*, first published by E. P. Dutton in 1943. Dylan was entranced by *Bound for Glory* and its romantic depictions of hoboes and rattling boxcars and set out to learn all he could about Guthrie. Dylan was introduced to Guthrie's recordings at the house of his friend Ellen Baker, whose father had a decent collection of *Peoples Songs* bulletins and Woody's old 78s. His passion for the music of Woody Guthrie would soon manifest itself on the stages of such Minneapolis coffeehouses as the Ten O'Clock Scholar and the Purple Onion. Dylan admitted to becoming something akin to a "Woody Guthrie jukebox." His interest in Guthrie was not entirely musical; there was a spiritual element to it as well. In a 1987 BBC radio program, Dylan remembered "I was completely taken over by [Guthrie]. By his spirit, or whatever. You could listen to his songs and actually learn how to live, or how to feel. He was like a guide."[16]

Jon Pankake, for one, wasn't terribly impressed by Dylan's talent as a Woody Guthrie interpreter. He flatly told Dylan he was wasting his time in the effort, that Woody already had a protégé, and a great one at that. It was Pankake who introduced Dylan to the music of Jack Elliott, playing him his cherished copy of Topic's *Jack Takes the Floor*. Dylan recalled that the moment Jack's voice "blasted into the room," he realized he had been bested; Jack had already mastered Woody's songs and style. Though the Jack Elliott on *Jack Takes the Floor* was not singing the same material that Dylan had been performing in Minneapolis, Dylan was impressed by the roguish singer who "sounds just like Woody Guthrie, only a leaner, meaner one." Pankake allowed Dylan to listen to his collection of Elliott records. Dylan would later tell Robert Hilburn of the *Los Angeles Times*, "It's like being a doctor who has spent all these years discovering penicillin and suddenly [finding out] someone else has already done it." In Dylan's own estimate, "Elliott had indeed already gone beyond Guthrie, and I was still getting there." The only consolation, Dylan figured, was that Jack was reportedly in "a self-imposed exile" in Europe. Dylan hoped he would stay there.[17]

If Elliott did, in fact, meet Bob Dylan at Guthrie's hospital bedside it is likely that meeting occurred in late January or early February 1961. Time and again, Elliott recounted arriving at Greystone only to find Dylan already there. Jack described Dylan as "strange but interesting," a young kid with "full, round cheeks and big soulful eyes, sporting a peach-fuzz beard and wearing a funny hat." Dylan told Jack he was nineteen years old, the same age he had been when he first met Woody.[18]

The pilgrimage to Guthrie's bedside is one of the most sacred and enduring tales of Dylan's legend. But the Guthrie that Dylan met at Greystone was a mere shadow of the man who had written *Bound for Glory* and recorded all those wonderful sides for Moses Asch. Pete Seeger recalled, "The last few years [Woody] really couldn't speak at all. Just a blur came out of his mouth. Bob Dylan visited him but I doubt they had much of a conversation. He was just one more young fellow with a guitar." By Elliott's account the Guthrie he met at Greystone in 1960 "was really beginning to show the effects of his disease, to the point where he could barely play the guitar any more. He could still walk and talk, but his speech was very garbled." Though Jack was certain Woody "knew who was with him in the room . . . he really couldn't communicate." In 1986, Bob Dylan was asked by a caller to Bob Fass's WBAI radio program if he would share his reminiscences about his first meeting with Woody Guthrie. Dylan was, uncharacteristically, forthright with his answer: "I never knew Woody

Guthrie when he was traveling around," Dylan replied. "[The caller will] probably have to ask Jack Elliott about that. I knew Woody in his last days . . . his situation pretty much deteriorated from when he was out *Ramblin' Round*. It was a thrill. I remember it was a thrill. I made a pilgrimage and a journey and I accomplished what I'd set out to do."[19]

Regardless of when they first met, Elliott recalled his visit with Woody and Bob at Greystone lasted only an hour or so. Jack was charmed by Dylan and appreciated that the kid was not only "profoundly awed with respect and admiration for Woody," but demonstrated "a lot of good feeling towards me too." Dylan told Elliott he had carefully studied his Topic records, particularly admiring his "singing of Woody Guthrie songs." "He told me that he had six of 'em back in Minnesota," Jack remembered, "all those Topic records recorded by Derroll Adams and myself. It finally dawned on me that he was a big, big fan of mine. Later I read in some book that he didn't even buy [them], he stole them from his friends!"[20]

In his memoir *Chronicles, Volume One*, Dylan does not recount his bedside visit with Guthrie and Elliott. But, shortly following his arrival in New York City, Dylan did send a postcard to friends in Minneapolis, excitedly telling them he had met not only Woody but Elliott as well. To further confuse matters, Elliott remembers he and Dylan left Greystone together, sharing a bus ride back to Manhattan. Elliott maintains that it was Dylan who told him that Cisco Houston would be performing soon at Gerdes and that the Gleasons were hosting informal Sunday afternoon visits with Woody at their East Orange apartment.[21]

Though long part of Dylan mythology, it is doubtful the story could have played out as remembered here. Houston had performed at Gerdes from the third week of November 1960 through November 27, followed by Elliott's own residency. But Dylan's arrival in New York City wasn't until late January (reportedly January 24) 1961. Though there is no reason to doubt Elliott first met Dylan at Guthrie's bedside, it is unlikely he met him, as the legend goes, "the very next day after my return." It is more likely that Elliott first made Dylan's acquaintance some two to three months following his return to the States. In such a scenario, Dylan telling Elliott that Cisco was to soon perform at Gerdes would make more sense as Cisco was scheduled to return to Gerdes the third week of February 1961.[22]

Elliott also maintained that it was Dylan who *personally* introduced him to the Gleasons (Jack and June had, of course, been corresponding with Woody through the Gleasons as early as 1958) but, again, the facts prove otherwise. John Cohen, the musician and cofounder of the New Lost

City Ramblers, was a regular visitor of Woody's at Greystone and had photographed Elliott sitting with Woody at his hospital bedside shortly following his return to America. One of these photographs was featured, all too briefly, in the Guthrie documentary *Arena: Woody Guthrie*. On New Year's Day 1961, Cohen shot a series of moving black-and-white portraits of Woody and Jack sitting in the Gleasons' parlor: Woody, sitting on the sofa, guitar in hand, with Elliott, sprawled out on the floor, looking over his left shoulder at his old friend with unreserved admiration. There are no photographs of Dylan and Woody sharing a similar moment of repose at Greystone or the Gleasons'. In April 1961, Woody was transferred to Creedmoor State Hospital in Queens, New York, effectively ending the Sunday afternoon gatherings at the Gleasons' apartment.[23]

Regardless of the circumstances, Dylan and Jack became fast friends. They hung out and played guitars together, shared bottles of wine, and attended the noisy open-mike nights at Gerdes and the Gaslight. Elliott was not all that fond of playing the taverns of Greenwich Village. The audiences who frequented England's folk clubs were *listeners*, polite and respectful. In contrast, Elliott found patrons of Greenwich Village night-clubs to be "rude, noisy and inattentive." Elliott was impressed by Dylan who could cut through the din with his guitar playing. It was rough and raw, much like his vocals, but Jack offered, "I could tell by his angle of attack, his attitude and the way he sang that he was going to be great." Suze Rotolo, Dylan's girlfriend at the time, remembered Elliott would call Bob to the stage during his performances, but little music was made. The two friends performed "together more as a comedy duo than serious folksingers." It wasn't all fun and games. The two traded songs and it was likely through Elliott that Dylan learned a series of songs that Guthrie had written in 1949 for a government health services radio program. Woody had been commissioned to write a song cycle on the decidedly unmusical subject of venereal disease, machine gunning out at least nine such songs. Elliott remembered a handful of them, which he taught to Dylan. After returning to a friend's apartment in Minneapolis near the end of 1961, Dylan played four of Woody's "VD Songs" for Tony Glover's reel-to-reel recording deck, unwittingly rescuing at least a few of them from near obscurity.[24]

If Jack's apprenticeship with Guthrie had earlier made him the magnet of complaints by Woody's friends, now Elliott's friends were warning him that Dylan was trying to steal the wind from his sails. June Elliott had returned to the United States in 1961 following her adventures in the Far East, setting off for Greenwich Village and a meeting with Jack. June was not interested in reconciliation; she wanted to be granted a proper divorce. Elliott told her to meet him at the Bitter End, promising to introduce her to his own protégé. Elliott proudly introduced Dylan as his "son," but June did not care much for his "offspring." She thought Dylan needed a haircut and was put off by his outright imitation of Elliott's cultivated musical persona. It was difficult to figure out exactly of whom Dylan was a doppelganger. Was he pretending to be Woody Guthrie or Jack Elliott? "I kind of thought he was imitating Woody," Jack would later tell Max Jones of *Melody Maker*, "but he said he wasn't, that he learned those songs from various hobos he met on the road. I didn't argue about it. I dug him, and I guess he reminded me of myself a little when I was younger. In those days he had a repertoire of wonderful hobo songs, some of which I'd never heard before. He was singing worse than I was at the age of 20 or so, but although he hurt my musical ear at times, I was the loudest clapper in the audience. I wanted to applaud that man for stepping into the Guthrie-Cisco Houston tradition."[25]

Dylan hurt the "musical ear" of others as well. In May 1961, only a few months into his apprenticeship with Jack, Dylan returned to Minneapolis as Woody Guthrie reincarnate. Jon Pankake told Robert Shelton that suddenly Dylan had found a "new voice . . . talking in the Okie accent. He had the costume and the hat and everything. . . . His guitar was shockingly out of tune. . . . He was shrieking-ly off key and said that 'if Woody's guitar didn't go out of tune, he would *tune* it out of tune. I thought he was terrible," Pankake mused, "but I was fascinated by him."[26]

Back in Greenwich Village, Izzy Young, proprietor of the Folklore Center, found himself fascinated by Ramblin' Jack Elliott. Izzy agreed to produce Jack's first bona fide concert in New York City at Carnegie Chapter Hall. The concert was scheduled for Saturday night, February 16, 1961. The event was announced, with Izzy's usual flair, in the Folklore Center's newsletter: "Jack Elliott in his first concert in America after five years in England, France, Japan [sic], Greece, Yugoslavia and many other places. We hope Jack will stay here for a while this time." Izzy could not recall if he saw Elliott perform prior to his return to the States in November 1960. "I may have seen him at a hootenanny," Izzy mused, "but I didn't really know him." Izzy certainly knew *of* Jack, but only through the Topic imports he sold through his store and from stories culled from the pages of Eric Winter's British folk-music digest *Sing*. In Izzy's estimation, Elliott's return to the United States was "the best thing that ever happened." There were already whispers that he was not exactly the cowboy he claimed to be, but Izzy did not care about the rumors. "I never asked anybody for their 'purity' credentials," Izzy reminisced. "I didn't give a shit if he was a genuine cowboy or not a genuine cowboy, if he really knew how to ride a horse or not ride a horse, or if he knew how to work a thirty-two gear truck. I didn't care about that. I liked what he was doing on stage. I didn't worry about whether or not he was authentic. I never thought about that for a second. I liked what he did. . . . People talk about authenticity. I'm not interested if somebody is pure black or pure Jewish. I'm just interested if they're singing well. And he did it better than anybody else."[27]

The Elliott concert at Carnegie Chapter Hall on 57th Street and Seventh Avenue (an intimate venue that Elliott described as "Upstairs, in the attic, 'bout a hundred seats") was a true homecoming affair. It was attended by an assortment of Jack's friends, old and new. Alan Lomax, who had recently returned from England, was there as was "Cap'n" Hinkley, Jack's harbor pilot neighbor from Brooklyn. Woody's former wife, Marjorie, and her 13-year-old son Arlo were also in attendance, as was Dylan. Dylan sat up front with Eve McKenzie, whose husband, Mac, was a founding member of Woody and Cisco's beloved National Maritime Union. In an interview with the *Telegraph*, McKenzie told writer Mitchell Blank that in 1961, Jack "was one of those very few people who could stand toe-to-toe with Bobby on the stage and not be one-upped or blown away. He was an absolutely incredible performer."[28]

The concert was a huge artistic success. Young was rarely moved to write reviews of the performances he attended, noting "I go to concerts to enjoy myself. I don't usually write about them." But the Elliott concert profoundly moved him. Many of the principal players of folk music's old Left had gathered at Carnegie Chapter Hall, and suddenly all the old ideals of solidarity and progressive politics did not seem part of some distant past. "The reason I wrote about that particular concert was it was almost like going back to the 1940s," Izzy reminisced 46 years later. "I said 'Hey, the 1940s are still going on in '61! All those people are still around." Following the concert, Izzy wrote in *Sing Out!* "Jack Elliott came into his own as a folksinger and natural showman at his last concert in NYC. Alan Lomax made the last statement official with an off the cuff speech introducing the second half—explaining how Jack had once been known as a shadow of Woody Guthrie, and later of Blind Lemon Jefferson and how he had learned and imitated their styles and techniques. And now he had broken the 'sound barrier' with a presentation of Jack Elliott himself. He gave freshness to the songs which are considered 'standard' material and demonstrated tremendous versatility by doing blues and music hall songs, too. His set of Woody Guthrie songs was so moving and authentic that

Marge Guthrie was seen crying and she wasn't the only one. People say I never applaud at folk concerts. They're wrong. I became part of a wall of applause that just wouldn't let him go."[29]

Indeed, the "wall of applause" was so fervent and long-lasting that Elliott only "convinced everyone to leave by inviting the people to come down to Gerdes to hear Cisco Houston." Cisco was, in fact, holding the stage, for the last time, at Folk City, with support from the Grandison Singers and the guitarist Bruce Langhorne. Many friends and fans followed Jack from Carnegie to Gerdes, the party continuing late into the night. Few realized that Cisco's weeklong engagement at Gerdes would be his last. He had been diagnosed with an inoperable form of cancer and told his days weren't long. Weakened by the disease, Cisco brought to the stage a succession of friends who helped carry him through the engagement, among them a young Arlo Guthrie. Arlo would write eloquently of the night in February 1961 when, to his surprise, Cisco called on him to sing a song. Arlo acutely recalled every circumstance, from his terrible, almost incapacitating, stage fright to the sympathetic applause from those in the audience. But he mostly remembered the moment as bittersweet. Arlo's "painful agony of birth" as an artist would always coincide with Cisco's farewell. Cisco passed away at his sister's home in San Bernardino, California, on April 29, 1961.[30]

Elliott's Carnegie Chapter Hall concert was unusual since proper concert engagements were still rare. Most of his gigs were before crowded and boisterous coffeehouse and tavern audiences. But Jack's success even brought his parents into Manhattan. Dave Van Ronk remembered being at Gerdes for a Jack Elliott gig: "I was sitting at the table with the artist Harry Jackson, Bobby Dylan and Dr. and Mrs. Adnopoz," Van Ronk told Robbie Woliver, a future owner of Folk City. "[Jack's parents] were very prominent people in Brooklyn. His father was chief of surgeons in a hospital, and the family had been in medicine for several generations—and that Jack had turned into such a bum and furthermore, changed his name, was a great source of grief. . . . Jack was on stage having some trouble tuning his guitar and the audience was hushed, a very rare occurrence in that room. Mrs. Adnopoz, sitting about two chairs from me, was just staring at him, raptly, and she lets out a stage whisper, 'Look at those fingers—such a surgeon he could have been!'"[31]

Alan Lomax had returned to the United States in 1958, finding a home among the throng of folksingers, artists, and bohemians of Greenwich Village. Alan befriended George Pickow, the husband of ballad singer Jean Ritchie, a talented shutterbug who had photographed a well-scrubbed Jack

Elliott playing guitar in Washington Square Park for a 1955 *Cosmopolitan* magazine photo feature. Lomax enlisted Pickow as a cinematographer on *Blues, Ballads & Bluegrass*, a fascinating portrait of the Greenwich Village folk-music scene circa 1961. The low-budget film captured images of many seminal figures of the nascent folk-music revival: the New Lost City Ramblers, Roscoe Holcomb, Ernie Marrs, Doc Watson, Clarence Ashley, Willie Dixon, Memphis Slim, Jean Ritchie, Peter LaFarge, and Jack Elliott. After performing Gary Davis's "Candyman," Elliott offers, "That's my favorite song . . . *right now*. That song got me all over Europe everywhere I went." He also performs an eerie, note perfect reading of Guthrie's "Talking Sailor (Talking Merchant Marine)." "What I like to sing, mostly, is some of Woody Guthrie's songs," Elliott admits in a cool, drawled preface. "Woody is about the best singer, guitar picker, composer, song-writer I've ever heard or seen or come up against or heard about." Jack also sings Guthrie's World War II talking blues in the author's own voice and the effect is stunning.[32]

Lomax thought highly of Elliott, continuing to work on his behalf. Lomax would tell *Newsweek* magazine in 1961, "Jack has a weird, wild, wonderful Will Rogers quality. He's coming into his own now—a kid who can astonish and delight the multitude doing whatever he wants to do. I'd rather listen to Jack than any of the other young people." It was through the efforts of Lomax that Elliott would make his first records for Prestige-International. Prestige-International, a small record company headquartered in the Manhattan suburb of Bergenfield, New Jersey, was already well respected as one of America's finest jazz and blues labels. In the late 1950s, the label began to record and market long-playing albums by some of the finest artists of the contemporary folk-music scene, including Bonnie Dobson, Ed McCurdy, Ewan MacColl, Peggy Seeger, Frank Warner, Jean Ritchie, and Cynthia Gooding, usually under the supervision of Kenneth Goldstein.[33]

Elliott's signing with Prestige-International was an important milestone. In England, Elliott was a bona fide legend, but in the United States he was hardly known outside of Greenwich Village and Topanga. The recordings he had made for Topic, 77 Records, and English Columbia were not easily available in the States. Elliott's contemporary, Dave Van Ronk, reasoned that in 1960 or 1961 a budding folk or blues singer was not going to get anywhere professionally without an album to his credit. Izzy Young agreed that albums were important, though he was less certain that having a long-playing record on your résumé was a guarantee of employment. "Everybody wanted to have a record," Izzy recalled. "But the concept of making money out of recordings to get 'well known' to do concerts and bigger clubs. . . . It wasn't that clear." Izzy wasn't underestimating the importance of the LP. "You needed a record to get started in the growing *radio* industry," Izzy explained. "The music industry was growing too. So everybody wanted to be part of that." But Izzy knew even the best folk-singers struggled to secure nightclub jobs of financial merit. The relative few enjoying success were more than recording artists; they were stage performers who radiated charisma. Charisma, fortunately, was a trait that Jack Elliott had in abundance. In Dylan's estimate, Jack Elliott was "a brilliant entertainer, something that most folk musicians didn't bother with."[34]

In July 1961, Prestige-International released *Jack Elliott Sings the Songs of Woody Guthrie*. The album has long been heralded as one of Elliott's essential recordings, subsequently reissued on a variety of labels in the United States, Great Britain, and Japan. Following the two augmented studio albums for Denis Preston, Elliott's LP for Prestige-International was a refreshing return to the stripped-down acoustic guitar and harmonica sound of his early Topic recordings. Channeling 14 of Guthrie's greatest songs, *Jack Elliott Sings the Songs of Woody Guthrie* stands as a testament to his interpretive genius.

Folklorist John Greenway, an unabashed Elliott fan, was tapped by Goldstein to contribute the liner notes. Though the album was comprised entirely of songs composed by Guthrie, Greenway heard Elliott's maturation as an artist in his own right. "Elliot [sic] is not a mere imitator of Woody Guthrie," Greenway wrote. "Guthrie evolved a unique guitar style, but he was never more than an indifferent performer of that style; Elliot has perfected it. Guthrie's singing too, was imperfect; Elliot has refined that singing. . . . This, in short, is what Jack Elliott has accomplished in his years in England, away from Woody: a refinement of Guthrie's singing and playing style, an amalgamation of Woody's genius and his own genuine talents into a compound better than either alone."[35]

On *Jack Elliott Sings the Songs of Woody Guthrie*, Jack finally came out of Guthrie's shadow as a guitarist. He streamlined Guthrie's style by smoothing out the "buzzes and skitters" of Woody's guitar methodology. Throughout the album, particularly on such songs as "Tom Joad" and "Dust Storm Disaster," Jack's knowledge of the Guthrie songbook is nothing short of masterful. Jack's guitar playing is near perfect, showcasing a seamless union of Guthrie's dusty, rough and tumble style with his own smooth, less angular style of country music flat-picking.

The release of Elliott's new collection of Guthrie songs was important for various reasons. Many of Woody's original and most famed recordings were not easily accessible. Moses Asch could hardly be blamed. He continued to issue many of Guthrie's recordings on his Folkways label, but they were most readily available in libraries and schools, though select titles were distributed through such national chains as the Sam Goody record stores. In a sense, it was through Elliott's first album for Prestige-International, and Cisco Houston's album of Guthrie songs for Vanguard, that a new generation of folk-music fans would be introduced to his music. Of the thousands of ballads that Guthrie composed and the hundreds he recorded, the songs he is best remembered for are the two dozen that Ramblin' Jack, Cisco, and Pete Seeger sang tirelessly. Beginning in the early 1960s, many aspiring Guthrie-style folk guitarists studied Jack's Prestige-International record as reverently as the finger style players worshipped the recordings of Mississippi John Hurt and the Reverend Gary Davis. For youngsters introduced to Woody's music during the "folk boom," Jack Elliott was acknowledged as the real deal, a singer as authentic as Woody Guthrie himself.[36]

The reviews of *Jack Elliott Sings the Songs of Woody Guthrie* were uniformly positive, with many bordering on the ecstatic. *Sing Out!* combined their review of the album with Vanguard's similarly titled *Cisco Houston Sings the Songs of Woody Guthrie*. Cisco's effort was described as one of his "finest, most impassioned recordings." This was true despite the fact that Cisco, as was his style, smoothed out almost all of Guthrie's rough edges. But *Sing Out!* admitted to being "put in a tough spot to have to report that a second disc, covering approximately the same ground as Cisco's, is an even more impressive offering." Elliott's interpretations of Guthrie's songs are described as "far closer in spirit" to Woody's originals, the guitar work a "strong, polished extension of Woody's own distinctive style."[37]

The *Journal of American Folklore* also chose to compare and contrast the two albums. Acknowledging Elliott as the one true "perfected performer of Guthrie's songs," the review nonetheless gives the edge to the Vanguard offering as it features "some of the best Houston we have." "Houston was not Guthrie, as Elliott is trying to be," the review huffily continues, "yet some of his renditions are closer to Guthrie's than Elliott's." This is arguable, but the review concedes that Jack's guitar work is artful and "uses a beautifully developed form of Guthrie's guitar style."[38]

Greenway's review of the album for *Western Folklore* was suspect as he had contributed the sleeve notes. Undeterred, Greenway described Elliott as one "who has made his life work in folk song the memorialization [sic] of Woody Guthrie." This was, perhaps, a poor choice of words on Greenway's part, as Woody was very much alive. Greenway heralded

Elliott's Prestige-International debut as a "magnificent record" and "an essential purchase for all Guthrie admirers." He also noted that Elliott's performance is not merely a "mechanical imitation, but a refinement of the elements that made Guthrie the unique performer that he was in the 1940s." Robert Shelton agreed. Writing for the *New York Times*, he called the album "a little classic," while celebrating Elliott as "the most faithful interpreter of the Guthrie songbook and the Guthrie manner."[39]

The good notices continued to pour in. Josh Dunson in *Mainstream* found *Jack Elliott Sings the Songs of Woody Guthrie* to be his "best." Dunson, a writer for *Broadside* and the author of the small, but important, study, *Freedom in the Air: Song Movements of the '60s*, felt that Jack's recordings for English Columbia were marred by "an immature effort to imitate Woody's accent." Taking a page from *The Little Sandy Review*, Dunson disparaged the Preston albums as a contrived "play for the English audience's country and western taste." On Elliott's new recording, Dunson found that Jack had abandoned such affectations. Dunson continued: "This record, I think, is Jack's best, because on it, he gets his guitar and his voice complimenting each other. He brings Woody's songs of past years up to date in a meaningful way. 'Tom Joad,' Guthrie's condensation of Steinbeck's *Grapes of Wrath*, moves people who never lived in the years of the dust bowl and migration westward, for Woody's poetry is made vivid by Jack's artful handling. 'Dust Storm Disaster' and '1913 Massacre' have a guitar behind them whose sharp, distinct notes, placed just right, bring a lonesome music to the poetry of people's troubles." Although Dunson's *Freedom in the Air* was principally a study of the songs and songwriters of the burgeoning topical song movement of the early 1960s, of which Jack Elliott was not a part, Dunson does note in his "Suggested Reading and Listening List" that "The best interpreter of Guthrie is his young friend Jack Elliott, and *Jack Elliott Sings the Songs of Woody Guthrie* shifted the attention of thousands from Odetta and Bikel to Guthrie."[40]

The Little Sandy Review had the most enthusiastic review. "Gone is all the rigidity and stiffness of some of his Topic recordings," Pankake and Nelson enthused in the five-page review: "He now plays and sings as if he owned the whole world." They described the album as "the greatest batch of Guthrie songs, bar none, since Woody himself was forced to hang up his guitar," and they continued: "Best of all is the SPIRIT in which Jack sings these songs—it is the same spirit in which they were originally written and sung. It is an incarnation of the Guthrie vision of America . . . merging with a daring, understanding, tremendously mature new talent. Jack seems to have the gift of greatness."[41]

Shortly following the album's release, Elliott and the Stevens Gospel Singers were booked for a two-week residency at Folk City beginning July 20. On July 25, the *New York Times* published Shelton's "Wandering Minstrel Is in Town," a glowing review of Jack's residency. Often reprinted in Ramblin' Jack's press kit, it was the first important feature on Elliott to be published in the mainstream press since his return to the States. Shelton wrote: "With a gift of mimicry and a remarkable ear for the cadences of the speech and song of the American plains, Mr. Elliott hails from everywhere. He has so thoroughly mastered the idiom of genuine American folk song that he not only mirrors a tradition, but also in many respects has refined and improved upon it. . . . Mr. Elliott drones and ambles, phrases with the tobacco-chewing casualness of a plainsman serenading his horse or girl. His singing is low-pressured, unhurried and done with a sort of interior concentration that can elude many in the audience with its subtlety. Yet, with all the laconic passion of the true folksinger, Mr. Elliott artfully compresses the cry and assertion of a century of rural experience."[42]

On July 29, WRVR, New York City's newest FM station, broadcast a twelve-hour program of live folk music from the Riverside Church near Harlem. Izzy Young and Bob Yellin, the five-string banjo picker of The Greenbriar Boys, had hastily assembled the program from a pool of nearly 50 volunteer performers, including the Reverend Gary Davis, Dave Van Ronk, John Herald, Tom Paxton, Victoria Spivey, Bob Dylan, John Cohen, and Jack Elliott. Pete Karman of the tabloid *New York Mirror* singled out Elliott and Dylan for special mention: "Just returned from five years in Europe where he was called the 'most American' of U.S. folksingers, Rambling Jack Elliot [sic] . . . offered cowboy and outdoor tunes. Bob Dylan, of Gallup, New Mexico, played the guitar and harmonica, simultaneously, and with rural gusto." The *New York Times* sent Robert Shelton to cover the anarchic event, who famously referenced that evening's "antics of Rambling Jack Elliott."[43]

The "antics" that Shelton referred to took place during "Acne," Dylan and Elliott's off-the-cuff lampoon of "Doo-Wop" music. As Dylan chords along in an appropriate musical setting, he freestyles teen angst verses such as "I'll get me a shotgun/.22 Rifle/I got for my birthday/I'll kill my parents/'Cause they don't understand/They don't dig a teenager at all." Elliott, for his part, coos, wails, and cries "Doo-Wop" in the background in such an unself-conscious manner that even Dylan breaks out into a laugh midsong. Though "Acne" was a complete throwaway, more telling is the brief comment Jack made following the song. Elliott had performed his own set at Riverside earlier that afternoon as he had business to attend to that evening. "I'm supposed to be at Gerdes Folk City now singing for some other people," Elliott explained during the late hours of the broadcast, "but I just couldn't tear myself away from here." Prophetic words from a man who in a few years would be considered an "unreliable" booking by a score of managers, concert promoters, and club owners.[44]

Less than a month after the release of *Jack Elliott Sings the Songs of Woody Guthrie* and Shelton's glowing review of Jack's Gerdes residency, the nationally circulated magazine *Newsweek* dedicated a page to Elliott. Shelton wrote the *Newsweek* feature, though his profile was published without credit. Titled "Real Hung Up," the essay recounted the standard Elliott biography for a national audience of nonfans. Though the article would bring an unprecedented windfall of publicity, such national recognition would come at some cost. Perhaps as a preemptive measure, Jack decided to "come clean" regarding his Brooklyn origin. "I was born on a 45,000-acre ranch in the middle of Flatbush," Jack told Shelton. "I've been lying for years. . . . My real name is Elliot Charles Adnopoz and that name really bugs me." He continued, "When I was 9, I was hung up on cowboys and Buck Elliott sounded like a cowboy's name. Later I changed it to Jack. I was real hung up on Gene Autry for a year. But then I met a real cowboy and found out he didn't look like Gene Autry at all. I've hated Autry ever since and campaigned against him for years."[45]

It is not clear why Elliott chose this moment and *Newsweek* magazine to reveal the facts of his middle-class upbringing, to publicly admit he was not a genuine cowboy from out West. It is likely he accepted that Greenwich Village was only a few subway stops from Brooklyn and the truth was bound to come out. His parents, after all, had already been to Gerdes to watch him perform, and his background was no longer a secret to many in the community. As a visitor to England and the continent, distance allowed the former Elliot Adnopoz to convincingly pass himself off as a drawling and dusty, Oklahoma-born cowboy singer. The admission was likely a preemptive strike, but he discovered, to his surprise, that few really seemed to care. Just as Izzy Young did not care about anyone's "purity credentials," most reasonable people on the folk scene felt the same way. Dave Van Ronk laughed because in the early 1960s, every city-billy singer was fudging the details of his or her middle-class background. Van Ronk reminisced that his friend Barry Kornfeld once wrote a song titled "What Was Your Name in the Bronx?" which lampooned the score of city-born kids who reimagined themselves as proletarian singers, the earnest musical sons and daughters of farmers and laborers.[46]

Dylan was the exception. He reportedly fell to the floor of the Café Figaro, laughing hysterically, when he learned Elliott was not the genuine cowboy he believed him to be. Of course, Dylan (the former Robert Allen Zimmerman) had reason to overreact; he was a shadow figure himself with his own secret. But through Elliott's revelation, Dylan was witness to the awkward consequences of telling the truth, for Jack would now suffer the unfortunate sobriquet "Last of the Brooklyn Cowboys." Jack hated the term, offering forthrightly that the nickname "really offends me." Elliott was quick to point out that historians believed the outlaw William H. Bonney, better known as Billy the Kid (one of the most celebrated icons of the old West), was likely born in New York City circa 1859. In truth, the Brooklyn Cowboy tag was rarely invoked as a term of derision. For many fans, the nickname was endearing. But it is true the appellation was often employed by shallow critics wishing to brand Elliott's music as less than authentic. Arlo Guthrie later attempted to appropriate the name, titling one of his best-selling Warner Bros. albums *The Last of the Brooklyn Cowboys*. But the nickname did not stick with Woody's physical son. It stayed resolutely with Woody's spiritual son, Ramblin' Jack.[47]

Robert Shelton found nothing inauthentic about Elliott's music. Shelton was an influential tastemaker of the Greenwich Village folk scene, and his anointment of Elliott as the "folksinger's folksinger" no doubt helped boost Jack's career. Having already offered effusive praise of Elliott's roguish charisma in the sacrosanct pages of the *New York Times* and *Newsweek*, Shelton's unflagging support was further evident following *Sing Out!* magazine's "Hootenanny at Carnegie Hall" on September 16, 1961. The program featured Pete Seeger, Alan Mills and Jean Carignan, the Country Gentlemen, Hedy West, Bessie Jones, and Jack Elliott. The following Monday, the *New York Times* carried Shelton's review: "Rambling Jack Elliott dipped into the Woody Guthrie songbook with more than customary aplomb, earnestness and humor. Judging from the heated reception he got, Mr. Elliott is on the road to popularity." There is little doubt that Jack was enjoying his brief reign as *the* man of the Village folk scene. He was a hero at home, but such acclaim would be short lived. On September 29, 1961, the *New York Times* ran "Bob Dylan: A Distinctive Folk Song Stylist," Shelton's ultraenthusiastic review of Dylan's residency at Gerdes. By September 30, Bob Dylan's and Jack Elliott's lives and careers would, irrevocably, be changed. In his journal entry of October 13, less than a month following Shelton's review of Dylan at Gerdes, Izzy Young solemnly opined "After listening to Jack Elliott for two nights last week I now think he will not 'make' it."[48]

Elliott could have been forgiven if he had thought he had already "made it." That autumn, he had been invited to perform at the Ash Grove in Los Angeles. He would share the bill with the Texas blues singer and guitarist Lightnin' Hopkins. The residency would last nearly three weeks, running from October 20 through November 12.

A writer from the showbiz bible *Variety* covered the program: "Lightnin' Sam Hopkins makes his L.A. debut in a rare excursion from the Negro district of Houston, where the master of the blues has grown into legend. Coupled with Ramblin' Jack Elliott's natural folk-ballads, show offers two distinct musical mediums in a serious reflection of deep-seated American culture. . . . Balladeer Elliott looks and sounds like a typical cowboy, yodels with the best and has tone control that is amazingly displayed in sustained areas that are smooth and clear. Most of his material is pure folklore. Interest is limited to buffs of this kind of Americana, though a fine version of Bessie Smith's 'Nobody Knows You When You're Down and Out' has universal appeal. He specializes in Woody Guthrie songs, scoring handsomely with 'Tom Joad,' suggested by the 'Grapes of Wrath,' and a delightful comedy treatment of 'Shade of the Old Apple Tree.' Attempt is not for pretty sounds or stylized arrangements, but on telling a story as naturally as possible."[49]

While Jack was out West, Dylan was performing in New York to mixed reviews. Art D'Lugoff, the owner of the Village Gate nightclub, recalled the young Bob Dylan, desperate for a gig, would often "audition for me right on the street." Lugoff remembered, "I liked him, but he sounded just like Woody Guthrie. And since I knew Woody Guthrie, why would I want a second-rate version? I'd rather have Ramblin' Jack Elliott." Many of Elliott's friends in the Village felt the same. They considered Dylan little more than a young upstart who brashly assumed the role of Guthrie's heir apparent without actually having done any real hard traveling. This was glaringly apparent during Gerdes's hoot nights. As Jack recalled in an interview with *Melody Maker*, "The first time Bob got up on the stage and sang it was such a direct and obvious imitation of my whole style that the people sitting next to me were astounded—and offended *for* me. They said 'Look at him. He's stealing the wind from your sails!' I felt like I had to defend him . . . because everybody else was so angry about it. But I couldn't feel that upset—though it was very, very obvious what he was doing." On some level, Dylan seems to have accepted the fact he would not unseat Elliott as Woody's most worshipful protégé and began to distance himself from the comparisons. "I knew that I wasn't really the best at doing Woody Guthrie imitations," Dylan later told the BBC, "I never *really* was about doing a Woody Guthrie imitation. Jack Elliott was the expert at that." Regardless, it probably did not help Elliott's career that Albert Grossman, Dylan's new manager, was whispering in important ears that Dylan was the next big thing and that Jack's star was in decline.[50]

As a stage and recording artist, Elliott chose to perform, almost exclusively, songs from a bygone era. In and of itself this should not have been a problem. After all, the "folk boom" was in full bloom and one could establish a pedigree with a deep song bag of Guthrie ballads, sentimental hillbilly songs, and cowboy laments. Jack's repertoire was vast, but it offered little in the way of variety. Perhaps more fatefully, Jack simply did not possess Dylan's fire. Passing from favor was Jack's rather laconic manner, the very cool and unhurried style that had brought him so much attention and acclaim in England. John Rockwell, writing in the *New York Times*, offered that Jack's performances do not "really offer anything new, but one doesn't go to an Elliott concert for novelties. One goes for the seemingly endless repository of songs, the occasional flashes of energetic vocalism, the wandering anecdotes and, above all, for the simple, sleepy charm of the man." Rockwell's words painted a perfect portrait of Ramblin' Jack's performance style, but they also underscored the marked contrast between Elliott's "sleepy charm" and Dylan's fire. In an article in the April 26, 1962, issue of the *Village Voice*, J. R. Goddard references the excitement that the early Bob Dylan performances conjured, describing Dylan as a "real enfant terrible" who can "muster a growling, grumbling force backed up by flailing guitar which can drive you wild."[51]

By the autumn of 1961 Harold Leventhal, Woody's manager, had successfully negotiated the rights to adapt his "autobiography" *Bound for Glory* for the stage. Leventhal was very enthused about securing the rights, telling friends he hoped he could have the production ready for Broadway's season of 1962–1963. He had not yet shared his thoughts as to whom he would cast as Woody. It was a part that many thought Jack Elliott was destined, and desperate, to play. Jack told Robert Shelton, "I've got to play that part. No one else can really do it. I know—I've been playing it for ten years now." Izzy Young agreed that Elliott should be offered the lead role, not simply because he was a gifted mimic who "slavishly followed" Guthrie, but "because he's a natural genius as an entertainer and belongs on TV, movies and the stage." But the 1962–1963 Broadway season passed without the appearance of, or any further rumor about, a Guthrie stage program. Leventhal quietly set the *Bound for Glory* project on the back burner.[52]

It hardly mattered. Less than five months after *Jack Elliott Sings the Songs of Woody Guthrie* hit the racks, Prestige-International's Kenneth Goldstein was readying a second LP of freshly minted Elliott material. The new album, simply titled, *Ramblin' Jack Elliott*, featured twelve new performances that displayed Jack's talents as an interpreter of songs *not* from the pen of Woody Guthrie. As they had for Elliott's first collection for Prestige, Goldstein handled production duties, with Rudy Van Gelder engineering. Goldstein brought to the project guitarist John Herald and mandolin player Ralph Rinzler, both members of the bluegrass outfit the Greenbriar Boys. Herald and Rinzler perfectly augmented Elliott's guitar playing on four of the more hillbilly-orientated tracks. *Ramblin' Jack Elliott* was released in December 1961 and immediately hailed as one of his finest recordings. The album capably demonstrated that Jack Elliott was more than "Boswell to Guthrie's Samuel Johnson," as Greenway had charged. Elliott's talents as an earthy folk guitarist, nuanced singer, and unabashed entertainer were apparent on the new album.[53]

"Jack's feel for many different kinds of emotion and people and songs comes over in *Ramblin' Jack Elliott*," wrote Josh Dunson in *Mainstream*. *Western Folklore* was effusive, describing *Ramblin' Jack Elliott* as "the outstanding record of a professional folksinger made during the last year." *The Little Sandy Review* hailed the album as "Jack's finest American recording. A little bit of everything for everybody." In a subsequent issue, Pankake and Nelson revisited the album, awarding the disc four out of four stars. Their enthusiasm had not waned with time: "Jack's performances sparkle with originality and wit, and his showmanship still maintains the needed respect necessary for his folk material."[54]

There was a little something for everyone on *Ramblin' Jack Elliott*. The album featured an eclectic mix of ragtime blues ("San Francisco Bay Blues"), traditional songs ("The Cuckoo"), hillbilly standards ("The Last Letter," "Sadie Brown," "Roll in My Sweet Baby's Arms," "Tramp On the Street"), music hall songs ("I Belong to Glasgow"), and, for the first time, a nod to the rhythm and blues style of Ray Charles ("I Love Her So/I Got a Woman"). In spite of Herald's and Rinzler's fine contributions, the songs for which Elliott would be best remembered ("San Francisco Bay Blues" and "South Coast") featured his lone guitar as accompaniment.

Another acclaimed solo performance from *Ramblin' Jack Elliott* was "Railroad Bill," a finger-picking classic soon to become a staple of every folksinger's song bag. Elliott had recorded the song as early as 1954 (with Woody Guthrie and Sonny Terry) for Moses Asch, and again for Topic and John R. T. Davies. The latter two performances remain unreleased; the Asch recording was issued 46 years later on *The Ballad of Ramblin' Jack* soundtrack. In his notes to *Ramblin' Jack Elliott*, John Greenway charged, "The almost chaotic amalgamation of maverick stanzas in this piece makes it impossible for Elliott to assign credits," but Jack had, in fact, learned "Railroad Bill" from Hobart Smith. Years later, Jack sheepishly allowed, "I think I played it better than the guy I learned it from." Hobart Smith, a legendary old-time five-string banjoist was, in Elliott's estimation, "one hell of a picker," but musically crippled to some extent by his obsession with the instrument: "[Smith] played the guitar and made it sound like a 5-string banjo," Elliott told one nightclub audience. "He played the piano and *it* sounded like a 5-string banjo."[55]

In December 1961, Manny Greenhill arranged a northern city tour for Lester Flatt, Earl Scruggs, and the Foggy Mountain Boys. Northern "citybillies" would soon be swooning over the high, lonesome singing and dazzling instrumental prowess of such bluegrass musicians as Bill Monroe, Don Reno and Red Smiley, and the Stanley Brothers. The records of the Foggy Mountain Boys were particularly revered; their Mercury recordings featured Earl's revolutionary and exciting three-finger roll style of banjo playing. Greenhill's master stroke was to bring on Jack Elliott as support. The tour commenced on Friday evening, December 1, with a performance at Boston's Jordan Hall. On Saturday night, the Flatt and Scruggs/ Jack Elliott bill performed at the Ethical Culture Society Auditorium in Queens, the second of two folk festival performances staged that day. Jack watched from the curtains as Scruggs, one of his boyhood heroes, went through the paces with the Foggy Mountain Boys. Though "hillbilly" music was rarely successfully staged in New York City, Robert Shelton wrote in the *New York Times* that by night's end "the emotional range of bluegrass was deepened in a way that even sophisticated city listeners could not resist." As for Jack's set, Shelton thought, "Mr. Elliott was at his best in an unaccompanied night herding cowboy song and in Woody Guthrie material. But too often he traded eccentric antics for the moving singing of which he is capable." During the evening's final set, Jack joined Flatt and Scruggs for an impromptu version of the Carter Family's "Worried Man Blues." It was Shelton's belief that the encore signaled the "closing of the gap between city and country [and] was a stirring symbol of where the folk-music revival is going."[56]

In the late 1940s, a young Jack Elliott had listened to Flatt and Scruggs on the Opry broadcasts and learned a thing or two from their old 78s. But by 1961 Elliott seemed to be having some converse effect on his boyhood heroes. He was partly responsible for the band's experimentations with "modern" folk songs. On March 18, 1962, only a few months following their tour with Jack, Flatt and Scrugg's recorded *Folk Songs of Our Land*, which included, for the first time, such Guthrie classics as "Philadelphia Lawyer (Reno Blues)" and "This Land Is Your Land." That same year the bluegrass legends issued *Hard Travelin'* on Columbia, which, again, revisited the Guthrie songbook. Along with the title track, Lester and Earl recorded the haunting "Pastures of Plenty" (and Woody's "New York Town" as well, though the latter song did not make the final cut). Bluegrass fans were not particularly happy with their heroes change in repertoire, blaming Columbia Records and the city folksingers for the shift from tradition-based tunes of the southern mountains to a song cycle more familiar to college students weaned on folk music.[57]

As interest in folk music extended beyond the usual coterie of academics, political Lefties, and those musically simpatico, money started changing hands. Crass "entertainment industry" writers, most of whom had little or no knowledge of the historical and political aspects of the art of folk song, were dispatched to review traditional musicians as if they were cabaret acts. Elliott would fall victim to one such scribe in January 1962. He had accepted an offer to perform at Le Hibou in Ottawa, Canada, one of only a few nightclubs there to spotlight folk-music artists. *Daily Variety*, Hollywood's entertainment industry bible, chose to send their man in Canada to catch one of Elliott's sets, resulting in a garish account published in the trade paper's "New Acts" column. Sadly, the dispatch was exactly what one might have expected from an entertainment industry stringer: "Jack Elliott, chanter with guitar, has been around the circuits for some ten years but seven of them were spent in Europe. Abroad, Elliott got big mileage out of the Europeans liking of the American cowboy idea. Probably the closest he comes to a saddle is the bridge on his guitar. Despite this, he handles his items solidly and with an aura of authenticity. He warbles and plunks pleasantly, gabs with sharp wit, and varies his offerings. Stanza caught was too long, but he can slice it if needed. Elliott already has a number of disks on both sides of the Atlantic. With good handling, he would work nicely in niteries and on tv or radio."[58]

Jack returned to New York City in late January and was immediately drafted by Pete Seeger to assist in the recording of some "old west" ballads for Columbia Records. On January 21, Elliott recorded a fine solo of "Buffalo Skinners," and on the January 23 he shared an afternoon session with Seeger, Harry Jackson, and Sandy Bull. That same night, Jack returned to the Gerdes stage. Ed McCurdy was acting as emcee that evening and

Cynthia Gooding was on hand to record Elliott's set for her radio program on WBAI, New York's Pacifica station. McCurdy explained that additional microphones were there to "put on tape a couple of things which will be tightened into a couple of hour presentations to be submitted . . . to prospective buyers for a syndicated radio show across the country." Elliott's set that night included Will Fyffe's "I Belong to Glasgow" and "South Coast," both recently issued on *Ramblin' Jack Elliott*, as well as Woody's "Talking Sailor (Talking Merchant Marine)" and "The Story of the Goo-Goo," a monologue cribbed, with permission, from humorist Orson Bean.[59]

The second annual University of Chicago folk festival was held in early February 1962. The program was organized by the students and featured an eclectic mixture of mostly traditional and some city performers. This year the lineup of talent included the New Lost City Ramblers, Big Joe Williams, Jean and Edna Ritchie, the Bluegrass Gentleman, the Reverend Gary Davis, Clarence Ashley, the Staples Singers, Doc Watson, and Jack Elliott. Shel Kagan, a writer and record producer (he would later minister albums for artists as varied as Jack Elliott, the Velvet Underground, and Pink Floyd's David Gilmour), was in Chicago, and remembered Elliott as an affable, populist entertainer. Kagan was impressed when Elliott turned around midway through his set to sing exclusively "to those unfortunates who had been seated on stage behind the performers."[60]

The year 1962 turned out to be a busy, and important, one for Elliott and every other professional singer of folk songs. Within two years the so-called folk boom would peak, remembered by many as one more passing pop music fad. Hardly a careerist, Elliott reminisced to a Memphis newspaper, "I guess there was a whole folk boom happening. I wasn't aware of it, I was just singing and picking like always. But it seemed like we were pretty busy." On February 23, the City College of Manhattan hosted an evening of folk music for the benefit of the Student Non-Violent Coordinating Committee (SNCC). Jack shared the bill with John Cohen, Bob Dylan, John Herald, Ralph Rinzler, Jerry Silverman, Dave Van Ronk, the Tarriers, and the New World Singers. In late March, he returned to Gerdes for a week-long residency with the Grandison Singers. The pairing proved so popular that both acts were "Held over by Popular Demand" for a second week. Elliott was still the toast of Greenwich Village, and as Izzy Young had earlier reported in *Sing Out!* fans truly were "flocking to hear him everywhere he sings in NYC." The newspaper ads placed by Folk City in the *Village Voice* described Jack as a "Rambler of 45 States and most of Europe," which wasn't entirely accurate but close enough.[61]

The same week Elliott had taken the floor at Gerdes, another signifi-
cant cultural milestone had taken place. On March 19, Columbia Records
released *Bob Dylan*, the singer's first long-playing recording. The album
featured versions of songs by Jesse Fuller ("You're No Good"), Blind
Lemon Jefferson ("See That My Grave Is Kept Clean"), and Roy Acuff
("Freight Train Blues"), as well as two Dylan originals, "Talkin' New
York" and "Song to Woody." Dylan had recorded two takes of Guthrie's
"(As I Go) Ramblin' Round" at the session, but both were left in the can.
The song had recently appeared on the Guthrie tribute LPs recorded by
Elliott and Cisco and, after all, who needed the comparisons? Interestingly,
Dylan had recorded songs by many of the same artists whose work figured
prominently on Elliott's own recordings, though he wisely chose not to
record the *same* songs closely associated with his friend. The influence of
Elliott on the young Dylan is clearly evident on the Columbia album, with
nods to Elliott's growling blues inflections and his playful yodels. Elliott
was suitably impressed and recalled Bob's "first record sounds like me. I'm
kind of proud of that."[62]

Though Dylan's record did not sell terribly well, news of its release
caused a mild buzz in the folk music circles of Greenwich Village and Minneapolis. Paul Nelson told Robert Shelton, "I remember seeing Bob and
Jack Elliott on stage at Folk City one Monday night, shortly after [Dylan's]
first record came out." Nelson and Jon Pankake were "curious" to gauge
Dylan's popularity among the coffeehouse audiences of New York City.
"We didn't know [Dylan] was the 'new hope' or anything like that," Nelson remembered. "That night [at Gerdes], he played piano a lot. At that
time, he and Jack were indistinguishable from each other—almost—but
not much of that got on record."[63]

On April 12 Jack recorded his third long-playing record for Prestige-
International, *Country Style*, which featured a sampling of the finest "hillbilly" songs he had learned when cutting his musical teeth back in the
1940s. John Greenway was tapped a third time to contribute the notes.
He boldly proclaimed, "Elliott is clearly the greatest of the professional
folksingers working today, a young man of uniquely variable voice accompanied by his uniquely variable guitar (augmented on this record
by his chest harmonica). . . . On this record Jack goes *Country Style* . . .
plaints and complaints to women, chronicles of locomotives, old dead dogs
and moribund soldiers, green-eyed horses and brown eyed-ladies, aching
joints, and roads closed up for repairs—in short, the stuff of rural life in
the middle of the 20th century." Many of the songs were new to folkies
but standards among country music fans and regular listeners of the Grand

Ole Opry. Many of Elliott's versions were plainly derived from the commercial recordings of two of his biggest musical heroes, Ernest Tubb and Roy Acuff. Tubb had recorded "Mean Mama Blues," "Low and Lonely," "The Soldier's Last Letter," and "Take Me Back and Try Me One More Time" between 1941 and 1945. Two famous railroad songs, the "Wreck of the Old 97" and "The Wabash Cannonball," can be traced back to the origin of recorded country music, but the songs were widely disseminated through the early recordings of Roy Acuff and the Smokey Mountain Boys. Though *Country Style* did not feature any performances of songs by Guthrie, Elliott did choose to record "Those Brown Eyes," recorded by Woody and Cisco for Moses Asch on April 19, 1944, and issued as the B-side of a 78 rpm single.[64]

One of the songs best remembered from *Country Style* was Elliott's interpretation of Jimmie Driftwood's "Tennessee Stud." The song, which first appeared on Driftwood's 1958 album for RCA *The Wilderness Road*, told an episodic tale of a cowboy's tangles with Indians, gamblers, and a recalcitrant future father and brother-in-law, to win the hand of his sweetheart "with the golden hair." In 1959 the best-selling country music singer Eddy Arnold charted Driftwood's song, bringing it to number five on the country music chart and sneaking it onto the pop music Top 50 hit singles as well. Elliott's sparkling guitar arrangement brought a more folksy edge to the song; *Sing Out!* declared, rightfully, that Driftwood's song only "became a standard in citybilly repertoire after Jack sang it around."[65]

One of the less celebrated, but more interesting songs, on *Country Style* was "The Arthritis Blues," composed by Baldwin "Butch" Hawes, the husband of fellow Almanac Singer Bess Lomax Hawes (the sister of Alan Lomax). Hawes suffered from arthritis of the spine, and "The Arthritis Blues" was his darkly humorous attempt to document his struggle with the disease. Hawes had recorded the song for Moses Asch, with the assistance of Tom Glazer, Pete Seeger, and Bess, in the mid-1940s, and a collection of songs from that session was finally issued in 1951 as the 10" Folkways album *Lonesome Valley*. Though it is likely that Elliott learned "The Arthritis Blues" from that album, it is not impossible he learned the song directly from Hawes. Butch and Bess had settled in Topanga Canyon and were residing there when Jack and Woody rolled through in the summer of 1954.[66]

The Little Sandy Review considered Jack's decision to record an album of country and western standards a "daring step." They noted, "folkniks have never displayed much more than contempt for this type of music. . . . [But] much of the music that Jack sings here is certainly more valid than the folkum dribblings of all those 'trios.'" Josh Dunson, writing in *Mainstream*, also noted, "there are many folk-singers who look down on country music as being too sentimental, and maybe sometimes it is, but when Jack starts singing some of the songs that come from Ernest Tubb, Red Foley and Jimmie Rodgers . . . you fully know that he is taking seriously the songs' message about old parents, lost loves and arthritis. There is no cynical overstatement." *Sing Out!* was so impressed with *Country Style* that they reviewed the album twice. The first review offered that most "composed" country music suffered from "sentimentality [that] can spill over into bathos," but *Country Style* proved "style can overcome subject matter . . . and Elliott has style to spare." The second *Sing Out!* review was equally enthusiastic.[67]

In May, a little more than a month after recording *Country Style*, Elliott returned to Philadelphia for a residency at the Second Fret. He was a favorite performer there, having earlier graciously filled in as an unpaid replacement for the ailing Cisco Houston. On Friday evening, May 18, a team of recording engineers from Prestige-International was sent to Philadelphia to document Elliott's performance. The Prestige team was hoping to cobble together a usable album from the idiosyncratic stage show.[68]

In July, Jack traveled to Hyannis, Massachusetts, a resort village on Cape Cod, where he was to share a weekend engagement with Prestige-International label mate Bonnie Dobson at the Ballad and Banjo Room. Elliott left New York for Hyannis in his Bell Telephone repair truck, a forlorn utility vehicle he had bought secondhand in the early winter of 1962 to help him get to some of his more distant, and, occasionally more lucrative, bookings. Some were the result of Jack's signing with Folklore Productions, Manny Greenhill's Boston-based booking agency. By 1962, Folklore Production's talent roster included Joan Baez, the Reverend Gary Davis, Bonnie Dobson, Jack Elliott, Lester Flatt and Earl Scruggs, the New Lost City Ramblers, the Greenbriar Boys, Tony Saletan, and Jackie Washington.[69]

In August, Monitor Records was readying the first American release of the two albums Elliott had recorded for English Columbia in the late 1950s. Michael Stillman and Rose Rubin founded Monitor in December 1956 in New York City. They were principally interested in making available collections of folk and classical music from the Soviet Union and other nations of the Eastern Bloc, but soon expanded to offer music from the nonsocialist world as well. Through Denis Preston, Monitor licensed *Ramblin' Jack Elliott in London* (retitled *Ramblin' Cowboy*) and *Ramblin' Jack Elliott Sings Woody Guthrie and JimmieRodgers*. With three albums on

Prestige-International, two on Monitor, and one on Folkways (his Topic recordings had not yet been issued on a 12" format in the United States), there seemed to be no shortage of Elliott albums to be found in the better record shops.[70]

On September 8 and 9, the Philadelphia Folksong Society staged the first Philadelphia Folk Festival on a small farm outside of Paoli, Pennsylvania. Gene Shay, a local folk music radio broadcaster who helped organize the event, recalled the Society had lofty ambitions, hoping to put on a first-rate festival with only $150 in the treasury. With the assistance of the Martin Guitar Company of Nazareth, Pennsylvania, they slowly built a roster of first-rate performers: Jack Elliott, Reverend Gary Davis, Bonnie Dobson, Professor Clarence Johnson and Mabel Washington, Mike Seeger, the five-string banjo wizard Bobby Thompson, and Pete Seeger. Prestige-International taped the entire two-day program. From the resulting tapes, the label issued *Philadelphia Folk Festival, Vol. 1*, which included fine versions of Elliott performing "Night Herding Song," "Talking Fishing Blues," and a rousing, yodeling version of the "Muleskinner Blues."[71]

That autumn Elliott traveled to the University of Illinois for a campus Folksong Club concert on November 20. One young fan in attendance that evening was Roger Ebert, then a student reporter for the campus news-sheet the *Daily Illini*, who later became a nationally syndicated film critic and television personality. Ebert was the sort of fan who enjoyed a well-staged concert; he did not quite know what to make of Ramblin' Jack. He acknowledged Elliott's "songs and . . . singing were very good" and his "guitar work . . . excellent. His voice was flexible and his stage manner was humorous and entertaining," but Ebert suggested the concert contained too much "folklore" and too little folk music. He lamented that "some of the anecdotes seem rather far-fetched, and certainly one can be interested in folk lore without possessing an undying passion for stories of Mike Seeger's maid, the train station in Venice or the historical accuracy of the Kingston Trio's folksong research." Though Ebert shared his generation's interest in folk music, it was clear that he had little understanding that Elliott's annotations were part of what made him unique.[72]

One of Manny Greenhill's early publicity leaflets rightfully heralded Elliott's talents as a musician, but made note of his skills as a "Raconteur" and "Comedian" as well. On occasion, Jack would go off on extended stream-of-consciousness monologues, forgetting (or choosing not) to play guitar or sing a full song for an entire set or two. More often than not, his legendary, if occasionally meandering, tales were endlessly fascinating.

As Arlo Guthrie noted, Elliott "knows more about sailing and trucking and horses and cowboys (and girls) and this whole country than the combined cabinets of the United States, and can tell you about anything and everywhere in the shortest or longest space of time, depending on how he feels and who he's with." Ebert was not alone in not understanding this component of Elliott's art; concerts were often cat-called with impatient demands to "shut up and sing." Nearly 38 years later, in his review of the documentary film *The Ballad of Ramblin' Jack*, Ebert harkened back to his memories of the Elliott concert (and a subsequent performance at Chicago's Old Town School of Folk Music). "He was more a personality than a great singer," Ebert opined. "It wasn't so much what he did as what he stood for." Few Chicago-area Elliott fans shared Ebert's assessment, however, and in February 1963 he returned as a main stage artist at the University of Chicago's third folk festival.[73]

By the spring of 1963, folk music's popularity had increased exponentially, but mainstream interest would come at artistic and authentic cost. On Saturday night, April 6, ABC-TV broadcast *Hootenanny*, the debut airing of the network's half-hour weekly folk music show. As Pete Seeger was the acknowledged dean of America's folksingers, everyone assumed he would be among the program's first guests. But ABC-TV was interested in selling soap, not providing a platform to a suspected Communist sympathizer. Journalist Nat Hentoff broke the story of Seeger's blacklisting in his *Village Voice* column of March 14, 1963, challenging musicians, many of whom owed their careers to Pete, to boycott the program. Elliott declined the offer to appear, but his decision was less political than personal. He told a reporter from *Variety*, that *Hootenanny* "is not a hootenanny, and if I did the program, I couldn't stand up and sing again, or sit down to dinner again, with Pete Seeger." He described his friend as "the greatest folksinger of them all and the originator of the whole idea of hootenanny."[74]

The most talented of the new folksingers did not need *Hootenanny*, however, as an increasing number of colleges, including Swarthmore, Yale, and Cornell, decided to try their hand at festival production. Queens College in Flushing, New York, with the support of the Cultural Affairs Committee of the College's Student Association, planned their own festival in April. Early rumors held that the festival would feature Seeger, Sleepy John Estes, Sonny Terry, the Freedom Singers, Jack Elliott, and the New Lost City Ramblers. Seeger and the Freedom Singers were unable to make the date, however, leaving the bill top heavy with "citybilly" performers: Bonnie Dobson, Jack Elliott, Dave Van Ronk, Jim Kweskin, and Harry and Jeannie West. The *New York Times* was enthusiastic, noting "Jack Elliott's tangy western yodeling and Dave Van Ronk's moving, visceral blues growling have been heard here before, but all wear well."[75]

Shortly after the Queens festival, Elliott traveled to Boston. Jack had signed on for ten days in mid-April at the Unicorn in Cambridge. Coincidentally, Bob Dylan was due to perform in Boston at the Café Yanna. Following their respective Saturday-night bookings on April 20, Dylan and Elliott met up with Joan Baez, also in town for a solo recital. The following afternoon, the trio convened at Club 47 on Palmer Street in Cambridge. Club 47 hosted an open-mike program every Sunday, and those gathered on April 21 were to witness something special. Before the hoot concluded, they had been treated to performances by Dylan, Elliott, Baez, Eric Von Schmidt, Geoff Muldaur, the newly formed Jim Kweskin Jug Band, Jim Rooney, the Charles River Valley Boys, Bob Neuwirth, and Carolyn Hester. In was a true "Hootenanny." Every performer was limited to three songs; in Jack's case, two songs and a retelling of his notorious, and impolitic, "Provincetown faggot joke." Afterward, Dylan, Jack, and Von Schmidt climbed onstage for an impromptu performance of a Woody Guthrie song. Following the hoot, many of the participants and a few hangers-on made their way to Geoff and Maria Muldaur's apartment. It was a crowded, smoky affair, with more than 30 people squeezed into a few small rooms. The music making continued into the night. Elliott recalled one magical moment when Dylan stood in the center of the room and began to sing a new song he had recently written, "Who Killed Davey Moore?" It was impressive. Dylan had Woody's gift of fashioning stinging songs from somber newspaper stories.[76]

That May, Elliott had a weeklong residency at the Gaslight Café, an engagement that proved so popular that manager Sam Hood held him over an additional two weeks. The first week Jack had shared the bill with fellow Prestige-International and Folkways label mate Pat Webb, a talented blues guitarist who, with his wife, Charlotte Daniels, had recently recorded an album of mostly bluesy songs for Prestige. The second week Webb and Daniels had moved on and Elliott's supporting acts were folksinger Bob Carey, moonlighting from his usual gig with the Tarriers, and the up and coming comedian Bill Cosby.[77]

George Wein and the Newport Folk Foundation announced in the spring of 1963 that the event would return, after a two-year hiatus, as a three-day affair in late July. The talent roster would include more than 70 high-profile artists for five major concerts and some 20 workshops. Every performer, regardless of drawing power, would work for scale. Though

Elliott was scheduled to perform on the main stage on Sunday July 28, the final night, he also appeared at Saturday afternoon's "Blues Session" workshop with Brownie McGhee and Sonny Terry, Mississippi John Hurt, Dave Van Ronk, John Hammond, Jr., and John Lee Hooker. Hardly a dedicated blues singer and guitarist, Elliott was a bit out of his depth among this lineup of blues artists, but as he was one of the last performers on the bill, his folksy take made for a seamless segue into Saturday evening's program. Elliott sang only two songs at the workshop, a talking blues and Jimmie Rodgers's "Waiting for a Train," before ceding the stage to Erik Darling and Brownie and Sonny who finished things off with a blistering "Walk on Blues."[78]

On Sunday afternoon Elliott performed on Newport's Porch 2 at a guitar and banjo workshop that featured Sam Hinton, Mother Maybelle Carter, Doc Watson, Mississippi John Hurt, and Dorsey Dixon. Here Jack was a bit more in his element, playing Guthrie's "Pretty Boy Floyd" and the Reverend Gary Davis's "Candy Man." On Sunday evening Pete Seeger brought out Elliott, who tore immediately into a program of crowd-friendly material, the rhythmic thumping of "San Francisco Bay Blues," "Muleskinner Blues," and Blind Lemon Jefferson's "Black Snake Moan," closing with a playful finger pick through "Guabi, Guabi" and a riveting performance of "Diamond Joe." Vanguard Records selected the latter for their "best of" souvenir LP recording of the event.[79]

In the early summer of 1963, Shel Silverstein, a writer and illustrator whom Elliott had met in Rome in 1958, stood as best man at a perfunctory civil service ceremony at City Hall for Elliott's brief marriage to his girlfriend Patty. It was also in the summer of 1963 that Kenneth Goldstein issued Jack's fourth, and final, album for Prestige-International, *Jack Elliott at the Second Fret*. Recorded May 18, 1962, it would represent the first commercial release of an Elliott club engagement. *Jack Elliott at the Second Fret* is an interesting album since not a single song had appeared on Elliott's earlier recordings for Prestige-International. The album's producers, Shel Kagan and Esmond Edwards, seemed to have ignored the usual record company practice of building an artist's "live-in-concert" recording around his "best of" or "greatest hits" material. Regardless, American fans were treated to a live album that was not only representative of Elliott's club engagements, but was comprised of fresh material as well. It is true that half of the ten songs had already seen issue in England: "Muleskinner Blues," "Salty Dog," and "The Boll Weevil" had been included on *Jack Takes the Floor*; "Talking Sailor" appeared on *Woody Guthrie's Blues*; and "Talkin' Miner" had been issued as a 78 rpm record for the WMA.

But the LP featured recorded debuts of "Cool Water," a western classic made popular through the recordings of the Sons of the Pioneers; "How Long Blues," which Jack learned off a record by Jimmy Yancey; Goebel Reeves's "Hobo's Lullaby" (reportedly Guthrie's favorite song); and a faithfully raucous reading of Lead Belly's "Rock Island Line."[80]

Goldstein saw fit to give Greenway a respite from contributing notes to Jack's latest release. Producer Shel Kagan filled in, writing perceptively: "This recording is, in a sense, the 'essential' Jack Elliott. Previous studio recordings, made under technically perfect conditions, have revealed him to be an artist of stunning capabilities. Here, relaxed and working before a group of responsively warm people (the applause is *not* canned), Jack has ample room to reveal himself as a human being. . . . Many of the reasons for his popularity stand out on this recording. His ability to talk about the things he's done and the people he has known in a wry, peppery, kidding-himself style provides endlessly fascinating material for spell-binding audiences. He is a no fooling around professional artist who just loves to fool around. There are few songs or picking techniques which he has not mastered. But he is liable, on stage, to do at any time that which occurs him to do."[81]

Since Jack's reputation as a performer was built in large part on his outrageously improvisational and eccentric live performances, it is surprising that *Jack Elliott at the Second Fret* was the only solo recording issued through 1976 that attempted to capture his stagecraft. Not that everyone was satisfied with the final result. Jon Pankake and Paul Nelson continued to maintain a peculiar love/hate relationship with Elliott, scratching out the following with their poisoned pens: "Never a performer noted for his artistic consistency (like some Shakespearean actors, he is brilliant only in flashes), Elliott sounds tired, uninterested, and affected on his in-person album, *Jack Elliott at the Second Fret*. His mannerisms seem forced and often show signs of freezing into mere grotesque vocal tricks (as in 'How Long Blues' and 'Rock Island Line,' two rather pathetic burlesques), and his long introductions wander pointlessly in bewildered circles. The element of self-parody is strongly present. It is unfortunate that Prestige recorded him in such a mood; the results are a rather tawdry and overdone album." Ed Kahn in *Western Folklore* thought otherwise. He described *Jack Elliott at the Second Fret* as "another record of quality to which we have been accustomed. His respect for tradition and his personal honesty have permitted him to present a wide variety of songs which interest him for one reason or another, regardless of their origin."[82]

In 1963, Elliott found himself on Columbia Records, Dylan's label. Columbia's president, Goddard Lieberson, had inaugurated "The Columbia Legacy Series," a collection of recordings that would attempt "to make explicit, vivid and meaningful various historic, artistic and cultural events and periods in our common heritage through the combination of the written word, the picture, the spoken word and, in some cases, sound itself." One of the ideas for the series was a documentary study of the American "Old West." Lieberson brought together such luminaries as the folklorist B. A. Botkin, Pete Seeger, Elliott, the western artist and singer Harry Jackson, Ed McCurdy, Carolyn Hester, and Sandy Bull to assist on the scholarly, erudite project. The resulting album, *The Badmen*, was released in September 1963.[83]

Elliott brought to *The Badmen* a riveting, solo performance of "Buffalo Skinners," his first studio recording of the song for an American label. He also joined Seeger and McCurdy in a spirited reading of the outlaw ballad "Jesse James," from which Guthrie had cribbed the melody for his own song "Jesus Christ." Elliott and Seeger also performed in tandem on the outlaw ballads "Billy the Kid" and "Belle Starr." Though there was no extant recording of Guthrie performing "Belle Starr," *Sing Out!* reported, "Pete Seeger and Jack Elliott set Woody Guthrie's 'Belle Starr' poem to a tune that both felt would be 'how Woody would have done it.'" Seeger and Elliott's musical contribution to "Belle Starr" was, ultimately, disregarded, as Ludlow Music's 1963 copyright of the song credits both "Words & Music" only to Guthrie himself.[84]

The Badmen, offered as a deluxe boxed set of two long-playing albums and a nearly 70- page accompanying book of historical text and photographs, was perhaps *too* attractive a package. Robert Shelton's short-lived magazine *Hootenanny* opined that folk music fans might opt not to remove the discs from their sleeves "for fear of soiling one of the finest jobs of packaging and annotating the record industry has yet produced." *Hootenanny* did manage to unseal their copy, with Joe Boyd instantly anointing *The Badmen* as one of the "150 Best Recordings of American Folk Music." *Western Folklore* was not unimpressed, but more restrained in its praise. Describing *The Badmen* as "perhaps the most elaborate recorded production ever seen in the field," the album was nonetheless dismissed as "strangely lacking in musical content." The blame was laid squarely on the producer's choice of recording artists. *Western Folklore* argued, not unconvincingly, for all its sheen the album featured "not one traditional singer," which, in a sense, was true. The *New York Time*'s Robert Shelton defended the musicians; he argued they were "skillfully chosen" and "tradition-steeped," who approached the songs without resort to "the current rage for exaggeration and slickness." Shelton summarily dubbed *The Badmen*: "a splendid fusion of folk art, graphics, social history and the recording craft."[85]

Kenneth Goldstein left Prestige-International near the end of 1962, and by 1963 the label had morphed into a company called Prestige/Folklore. Jack's back catalog had been reissued with new catalog numbers and, in the case of *Jack Elliott Sings the Songs of Woody Guthrie*, with new cover art as well. Perhaps spurred by Goldstein's departure or simply hoping to find a better deal, Elliott was casting about for a new record label.[86]

Elliott's first choice was Columbia. Bob Dylan was on Columbia and it was apparent that John Hammond had managed to do some good things for both him and Pete Seeger. Interestingly, Dylan did play a role in arranging a new recording contract for Jack, though not with Columbia. Jack asked Dylan for a letter of introduction to John Hammond and Dylan obliged. It was not a very formal note. It was little more than "a funny letter," an in-joke of sorts, with Dylan describing Elliott as "my long lost buddy who abandoned me at the age of twelve." Jack recalled Hammond as a "very cordial and charming man" who received Dylan's note in the manner it was intended. "I'll tell you what," Hammond told Elliott. "We've just invested a heck of a lot of money in Bob, and your style being so similar to Bob's, we could never afford to sign you now. But I recommend Vanguard. You go over there and say hello to my friend. Tell him I sent you."[87]

Hammond's friend at Vanguard was Maynard Solomon, who had founded the Vanguard Recording Society in 1950 with his brother Seymour. In 1963, they added Jack Elliott to their roster of folksinging talent, which included Joan Baez, Ian and Sylvia, Doc Watson, John Hammond, Jr., Buffy Sainte-Marie, Eric Andersen, the Rooftop Singers, and the Greenbriar Boys. Unfortunately, Jack's stay at Vanguard wasn't long. Jack and Manny Solomon's relationship soured following creative differences and a silly, bitter row over a set of wickedly funny and unpretentious liner notes submitted by Elliott's friend Shel Silverstein. Of Manny Solomon, Jack would admit, "I ended up hating that guy. He was just so square."[88]

Elliott's first album for Vanguard was *Jack Elliott*, recorded in the summer of 1963. It had an old-timey feel and featured a wide variety of songs and styles, close in spirit to *Ramblin' Jack Elliott*, his second album for Prestige-International. Aside from a stirring "1913 Massacre," no other Guthrie song was featured. Instead, there were recording debuts of such disparate material as "Guabi, Guabi," "Sowing on the Mountain," "Roving

Gambler," "House of the Rising Sun," "Shade of the Old Apple Tree," Blind Lemon Jefferson's "Black Snake Moan," and Derroll Adams's "Portland Town." Six of the songs were recorded solo with guitar, two songs with Jack's guitar and Bill Lee's bass as the only accompaniment, and one song as a guitar and five-string banjo duet with Erik Darling. The remaining three songs were recorded with various combinations of guitarists, including John Herald, Ian Tyson (of Ian and Sylvia fame), and Monte Dunn.[89]

There were other special contributors to the LP. A few months following the release of his second album *The Freewheelin' Bob Dylan*, Dylan joined Elliott, Darling, and Lee on a raucous version of the A. P. Carter standard "Will the Circle Be Unbroken." Dylan's spirited harmonica contribution was credited to "Tedham Porterhouse," an alias necessitated by Dylan's contractual obligation to Columbia. Blues singer and fellow Vanguard artist John Hammond, Jr., was also brought in to contribute some mouth harp on Jack's revisit of "Roll on Buddy." The Vanguard album would not see release for nearly a year.[90]

Rory McEwen had written Elliott from England that summer, asking if he would be interested in returning for a short concert and club tour. Elliott signed on, as did Carolyn Hester, and their first concert was scheduled for September 12 in Edinburgh. Though Jack's return to England was received warmly, he was hardly embraced as the conquering hero. Following a concert at Royal Festival Hall, Elliott agreed to share a few words with *Melody Maker*, but the resulting profile only limply warmed up the now two-year-old revelation that Jack was, once, Elliot Charles Adnopoz. On September 18, Elliott and Hester performed at the Kingston & Surbiton Folk Club for the club's "Folksong Jamboree," and the tour ended three nights later with a "folk song and country and western concert" at London's Royal Albert Hall. Nearly 5,000 fans caught performances by Elliott, Steve Benbow, the Ian Campbell Folk Group, Cyril Davies and his All-Stars, Jacqueline McDonald, and the Spinners. *Melody Maker* noted that Jack retained "a special place in the fans affection." Before returning to the United States, Elliott agreed to an appearance on the BBC 1 television program *TONIGHT*.[91]

In October 1963, Eric Winter, editor of *Sing*, was advanced a set of thoughtful notes, composed by Paul Nelson and Jon Pankake, to be featured on the rear sleeve of Topic's *Talking Woody Guthrie*, the company's first 12" collection of Elliott material. Only Jack's "So Long, It's Been Good to Know You" would be new to fans. Otherwise, *Talking Woody Guthrie* was programmed with six songs culled from *Woody Guthrie's Blues* and three performances issued in 1956 on 78 rpm discs. The notes printed in *Sing* (which differ slightly from the notes eventually published on the LP) were almost entirely complimentary. But Pankake and Nelson also charged that Elliott's transition from the "serious Guthrie mode of expression" to "the good-timeyness of Oakland's Jesse Fuller and into the country-western music of Jimmie Rodgers, Hank Williams and Rose Maddox," damaged his reputation as the finest contemporary Guthrie interpreter. They felt that his recent performances of such grim ballads as "1913 Massacre" and "Ludlow Massacre" "no longer rang as true as they once did." In his own review of *Talking Woody Guthrie*, Winter seemed to agree. He argued that the Jack Elliott of *Woody Guthrie's Blues* was "a hip-swinging, fast-singing boy who hits the Guthrie note just right. . . . Jack has since become, judging by recent performances, Jack Elliott singing Jack Elliott." Such criticism, of course, was ironic. Elliott was now being faulted for being his own man, for *not* presenting himself as the ghost of Woody Guthrie. In early 1964, Topic would reissue augmented 12" long-playing versions of *The Rambling Boys* and *Jack Takes the Floor* as *Roll on Buddy* and *Muleskinner*, respectively.[92]

Though Bob Dylan initially wanted to be regarded as Guthrie's peerless protégé, his dream was dashed when he was introduced to the music of Woody's authentic protégé. It was a bitter pill, but Dylan acknowledged that, as an interpreter of Guthrie, "Elliott was far beyond me." But Dylan had an ace up his sleeve, telling the *Los Angeles Times*, "I knew I had something Jack didn't have." Dylan had Woody's gift of crafting songs about the things that were happening all around him.[93]

Sadly, it was not a gift bestowed on Jack Elliott. But if Jack wasn't destined to be the world shaker that Dylan would quickly become, he remained an artist revered by nearly every old-school folkie. On January 25, 1964, Elliott appeared at Philadelphia's Town Hall, the top bill of a program that featured the Greenbriar Boys and Judy Roderick. *Tune Up* described Jack as "the best example of an urban folksinger who has come forth with a style and manner of his own. He is an excellent performer who stands head and shoulders above his contemporaries." The concert was an outstanding success, with *Hootenanny* magazine reporting that fans hailed the evening as "the best event of the season."[94]

Vanguard finally released *Jack Elliott* in the early summer of 1964. But nearly a year had passed since the album was recorded and the music scene had shifted dramatically in the interim. Seventy million Americans tuned into the *Ed Sullivan Show* on February 9, 1964, to watch the Beatles perform. The so-called British Invasion had arrived and suddenly the folk songs everyone had been singing seemed quaint and old hat. No one was immune. Photographer Douglas Gilbert had been following Dylan around the Village for a time, and his camera captured Bob and Jack contemplating the album jacket of the first Rolling Stones LP. Elliott's Vanguard recording was possibly his best-produced album to date, but in terms of sound and repertoire, the disc was anachronistic and largely ignored by the mainstream press. *Sing Out!* one of the few magazines to offer a review, stated that "Jack Elliott is one of a handful of performers who work within the confines of folk-style, but still function as individual creative artists." But the magazine also made clear that there was nothing terribly new on the album. The best *Sing Out!* could offer was that "Woody Guthrie's '1913 Massacre' and 'Diamond Joe' lose nothing for having been on earlier Elliott recordings." "As a re-creator of American folk music," the review concluded, "Jack Elliott is a major talent." But the inference was that a "re-creator" could only take the music so far.[95]

On June 9 Bob Dylan, who could no longer be mistaken as a "re-creator," set off for Columbia's studios in Manhattan to record his fourth album, *Another Side of Bob Dylan*. Elliott's long-rumored participation in that legendary session was entirely by accident. He had been walking down the street when he happened upon Dylan and his friend Victor Maimudes as they climbed out of a taxi. Elliott almost missed him. Dylan no longer resembled Woody Guthrie; gone were the denim work shirts and laced work boots of *The Times They Are A-Changin'* era. This proletariat uniform had been replaced with stylish clothing and gleaming boots of Spanish leather. Dylan sported a new haircut as well, the tangled curls of Woody Guthrie replaced by something more stylish. Dylan told Elliott that he was on his way to a recording session and asked Jack if he would care to come along.[96]

The Dylan cognoscenti long traded the story of an early demo of "Mr. Tambourine Man" cut as a duet with Elliott. The genesis of the rumor could be traced to John Cohen's interview with Roger McGuinn in the December 1968/January 1969 issue of *Sing Out!* McGuinn explained that the Byrds first learned "Mr. Tambourine Man" off a dub from the record producer Jim Dickson. Dickson was a friend of Dylan's, and McGuinn recalled, "Dylan laid this dub on him with Dylan and Jack Elliott singing. It hadn't been released on the previous album because of a contract release problem with Jack. [The demo] was sloppy, the words weren't clear. It was groovy though [and] had its charms." Fellow Byrd David Crosby's recollection of the dub was less charitable. He recalled the Dylan/Elliott demo as "truly awful—two guys that were not too sharp on staying in tune." The worthiness of the outtake was somewhere in between those two estimates.

The existence of the demo was confirmed with the release of a fragment on the *Highway 61 Interactive* CD-ROM in 1995.[97]

Following the release of *Highway 61 Interactive*, Elliott was as surprised as anyone that the outtake had surfaced. He had long assumed the original version of "Mr. Tambourine Man" would not be included on *Another Side of Bob Dylan* as it "was a very poor recording . . . roughly done." But it wasn't so much "roughly done" as underrehearsed. Elliott did not know all the words. "Mr. Tambourine Man" was an almost totally new song to him, having heard Dylan sing it only once before at his home in Woodstock. Dylan surprised everyone, including producer Tom Wilson, when he asked Elliott, who had been watching the session from an adjacent room, to accompany him in the studio. "Jack, sing on this." There was a single false start as Jack was standing too far from Dylan's vocal microphone. Wilson punched in, telling Dylan, "If he's gonna sing that much, you got to get him closer. Sing over his shoulder there, Jack. Get behind him. . . . That's right." Elliott sang some tentative harmony on the famous chorus but the long-fabled performance was cut from the final album. Dylan himself had not yet committed all the lyrics to memory, and the occasional mumbles captured on tape were not Jack's alone. For reasons unknown, both the false start and complete takes were, apparently, assigned the same Columbia reference number (CO 82221). The complete duet was released officially in 2005 on *Bob Dylan: No Direction Home: The Bootleg Series Vol. 7*.[98]

In 1963 Dylan and Jack both performed on Newport's main stage. Riding the winds of change, Dylan sang duets with Joan Baez ("With God on Our Side") and Pete Seeger ("Playboys and Playgirls") and closed with a stirring, ensemble treatment of "Blowin' in the Wind." Jack, on the other hand, sang songs by Blind Lemon Jefferson and "Diamond Joe" and "Muleskinner Blues." The times they were a changin' but, clearly, Ramblin' Jack was not. He was not scheduled to perform at Newport 64, but went anyway with friends to enjoy the weekend. On the last day of the festival, July 28, Dylan and Elliott were sitting in the front seat of Bob's blue Ford station wagon saying their good-byes. The car's radio was playing softly in the background when suddenly Eric Burdon and the Animals' electrified version of "The House of the Rising Sun" came on. The song had been recorded by both Dylan and Elliott, but neither had yet heard this seminal "folk-rock" reworking. Simultaneously, Elliott and Dylan pointed their fingers at the car's dashboard radio and called out "That's *my* version!"[99]

On November 1, 1964, the Village Gate hosted the first *Broadside* magazine "Topical Song Workshop." *Broadside* founders Gordon Freisen,

Agnes "Sis" Cunningham, and Pete Seeger had inaugurated the series as a "singing newspaper," an "in-performance" companion to disseminate the topical songs they were publishing in their monthly bulletin. The Village Gate was completely sold out for the afternoon gathering. The *New York Times* noted, "The 500 teenagers and young adults there were charging the atmosphere to get this first-Sunday-of-each-month enterprise off to a flying start." Seeger acted as emcee for the afternoon's program, introducing the crème de la crème of Greenwich Village's topical songwriters and performers: Barbara Dane, Eric Andersen, Phil Ochs, Tom Paxton, Bernice Johnson-Reagon, Len Chandler, Buffy Sainte-Marie, Patrick Sky, and Julius Lester. Seeger sternly reminded those assembled not to attend future *Broadside* hoots "if you expect to hear your favorite star sing his latest hit song." These were the best of the new topical songs for America's new tough times, and the theme of civil rights was foremost on the agenda. Near the end of the nearly three-hour program, Phil Ochs announced, jokingly, "We have the traditional surprise guest with us to sing a *topical song from another day,* Ramblin' Jack Elliott." Ochs thought highly of Elliott, writing that he was not only Guthrie's finest disciple but "one of the finest folk musicians in the country. He has developed a stage personality that can move from light hilarity to tragic depth with surprising ease. He presents himself almost as a reincarnation of Guthrie, complete with cowboy hat, drawling tones, and western mannerisms. His growing stage maturity and his sense of theater has made him less of an imitator and more of an interpreter." Though Elliott was not destined to be a world shaker, few would deny his credentials were impeccable and his musical integrity unassailable. Through presence alone, Elliott reminded every songwriter in the room they were all Woody's children. That afternoon Elliott offered a suitably taut reading of Guthrie's "1913 Massacre." He was followed by Patrick Sky who performed "Mahogany Row," Ernie Marr's melancholy song of Harlem brothel life, its melody freely borrowed from "1913 Massacre." The two songs formed a perfect bridge, demonstrating how the old and new could inform each other. Though Elliott did not compose "topical" songs, he carried the old ones into the present, showing a new generation of rebels how it had been done in the past.[100]

Notes

1. Alan Lomax, "Skiffle: Why Is It So Popular?" *Melody Maker*, 31 August 1957, 3; Alan Lomax, "Skiffle: Where Is It Going?" *Melody Maker*, 7 September 1957, 5; Ronald D. Cohen, ed., *Alan Lomax: Selected Writings 1934–1997* (New

York: Routledge, 2003), 135–138; Robert Shelton, "Real Hung Up," *Newsweek*, 14 August 1961, 47; Robert C. Smith, "Woody Guthrie Today (Part Two)," *Melody Maker*, 18 June 1960, 4.

2. John Renbourn, "Fingerstyle Guitar: Born of Skiffle and Blues," *Frets*, Vol. 10, No. 6, June 1988, 50; Irwin Silber, "Ewan MacColl: Folksinger of the Industrial Age," *Sing Out!* Vol. 9, No. 3, Winter 1959/1960, 7–9; "Peggy Seeger: The Voice of America in Folksong," *Sing Out!* Vol. 12, No. 3, Summer 1962, 4–8; Jon Pankake and Paul Nelson, *The Little Sandy Review*, No. 2, April 1960, 16.

3. Andy Irvine notes to "Seaman Three" on *Folk Friends 2* (FolkFreak FF 3003/4), 1981; Andy Irvine: Bio, www.andyirvine.com/bio/bio-2.html (accessed 4 December 2008).

4. Guy Sterling, "How Friends and Music Eased a Folk Legend's Pain," *Sunday Star-Ledger*, 24 July 2005, Sec. 4, 1, 8; Robert C. Smith, "Woody Guthrie Today" (Part One), *Melody Maker*, 11 June 1960, 5; Joe Klein, *Woody Guthrie: A Life* (New York: Alfred A. Knopf, 1980), 425–428.

5. Bob and Sidsel Gleason, "Letters to the Editors," *The Little Sandy Review*, No. 5, July 1960, 37–38.

6. Allan Taylor interview with Jack Elliott, *Shared Experience*, BBC Radio 2, broadcast 29 February 1996.

7. Guy Logsdon, *Woody Guthrie: A Biblio-Discography* (Self-published, Revised 6 December 1999), 51–52, 71; Jeff Place correspondence with Hank Reineke, 10 October 2007.

8. Notes to *Songs to Grow on by Woody Guthrie, Sung by Jack Elliott* (Folkways Records, FC 7501), 1961.

9. Allan Taylor interview with Jack Elliott; Mary Houlihan, "A Side She Never Saw," *Chicago Sun-Times*, 6 September 2000, Sec. 2, 44.

10. Herbert Mitgang, "Some with Music," *New York Times*, 28 January 1962, 97; Henrietta Yurchenco, "Survey of Children's Records," *Sing Out!* Vol. 13, Summer 1963, 55; Jon Pankake and Paul Nelson, "Record Reviews," *The Little Sandy Review*, No. 18, 8–9; Eric Winter, "DISCussion," *Sing*, Vol. 6, No. 4, December 1961, 39; Ken Phine, "For the Record," *Sing*, Vol. 6, No. 2, October 1961, 16.

11. Robert Shelton, "Ewan MacColl, in Debut Here, Offers Concert of Folk Music," *New York Times*, 5 December 1960, 44; Israel G. Young, "Frets and Frails," *Sing Out!* Vol. 11, February/March 1961, 84; Israel G. Young, "Israel Young's Notebook," *Sing Out!* Vol. 18, No. 3, August/September 1968, 12.

12. Jack Elliott, Gerdes Folk City, 3 December 1960.

13. Jack Elliott, Gerdes Folk City, 3 December 1960.

14. "One Sheridan Square: Ramblin' Jack Elliott & Guests" (advertisement), *Village Voice*, 15 December 1960, 12.

15. Paul Jarvey, "Ramblin' Jack Elliott Wanted to Be a Cowboy," *Worcester Telegram & Gazette*, 10 October 1993, Sec. Datebook, 9.

16. Anthony Scaduto, *Bob Dylan: An Intimate Biography* (New York: Grossett & Dunlap, 1971), 43–44; Mitchell Blank, "I Read a Book Today, Oh Boy

. . .," *The Telegraph*, No. 45, Spring 1993, 77–81; Bob Dylan to Elliott Mintz, "Statements on Woody Guthrie," *California*, April/May 1987. Partly broadcast as "*Woody Guthrie: Hard Travelin'*," BBC-2, October 1987; Bob Dylan liner notes to *Folkways: A Vision Shared—A Tribute to Woody Guthrie and Lead Belly* (Columbia Records OC 44034), 1988.

17. Bob Dylan, *Chronicles: Volume One* (New York: Simon and Schuster, 2004), 252; Robert Hilburn, "How to Write Songs and Influence People," *Guitar World Acoustic*, February 2006, 30.

18. Craig Harris, "A Mosaic of Stories," *Dirty Linen*, No. 63, April/May 1996, 17; John May, "Woody, Bob and Me," *The Telegraph*, 19 February 2005, Sec. Arts, 7. To further complicate matters, Jack's friend Wavy Gravy—the former Hugh Romney—told Robbie Osman of KPFA radio that it was he who first introduced Jack Elliott to Bob Dylan at Gerdes Folk City. Ordinarily, Gravy's story could be dismissed as apocryphal, a twist of cultural history revisionism. But in the autumn of 1967 Elliott told Reprise Records publicist Andy Wickham a somewhat similar yarn. "I remember the first time I saw Bobby Dylan," Jack told Wickham. "He was singin' and pickin' at some little concert and after the show I went over and introduced myself."

19. Pete Seeger comments from *Arena: Woody Guthrie*, British Broadcasting Company, Paul Lee, Director, Anthony Wall and Nigel Finch, Executive Producers, 1988; May, "Woody, Bob and Me," 7; Lew Herman, "Sounds: Ramblin' Man," *Creative Loafing (Charlotte)*, http://web.cln.com/archives/charlotte/new stand/c100999/sounds.htm (accessed 4 July 2001); Bob Dylan to Bob Fass, *Radio Unnameable*, WBAI-FM radio program, 21 May 1986.

20. John Wesley Harding, "The Wanted Man Interview: Ramblin' Jack Elliott," *The Telegraph*, No. 50, Winter 1994, 14; Steven Stolder, "Traveling Back with Ramblin' Jack Elliott," *NARAS Inforum*, www.grammy.com/features/jack elliot2.html (accessed 22 May 1997).

21. Robert Shelton, *No Direction Home: The Life and Music of Bob Dylan* (New York: Beech Tree Books/William Morrow, 1986), 92.

22. Harding, "The Wanted Man Interview," 13; "Rambling Jack Elliott—1st American Concert in 5 Years, Carnegie Chapter Hall" (advertisement), *Village Voice*, 16 February 1961, 5; "Cisco Houston, Singer, Dies; Toured India for U.S. in 1959," *New York Times*, 30 April 1961, 86.

23. Two of John Cohen's photographs of Woody Guthrie and Jack Elliott together at the Gleasons can be found in *On the Tracks*, #7. Vol. 4, No. 1, 15 June 1996, 40–41. Cohen's photograph of Elliott visiting Woody Guthrie at Greystone Memorial Hospital can be seen briefly in the documentary film *Arena: Woody Guthrie*.

24. May, "Woody, Bob and Me," 7; Suze Rotolo, *A Freewheelin' Time: A Memoir of Greenwich Village in the Sixties* (New York: Broadway, 2008), 126–127.

25. Max Jones, "Dylan, Me and the Legend of Woody Guthrie," *Melody Maker*, 29 May 1965, 6; Rob Patterson, "Guthrie Imitator Jack Elliott Has Grown into an

American Original—and One of the . . . Monsters," *Austin American-Statesman*, 9 April 1998, XL Entertainment, 10.

26. Robert Shelton (ed. Ian Woodward), "The Robert Shelton Minnesota Transcripts: Jon Pankake," *ISIS*, No. 88, December 1999/January 2000, 22.

27. Hank Reineke interview with Izzy Young, New York City, 20 September 2007; Folklore Center Concert Schedule Newsletter, February/March 1961.

28. Bob Atkinson, "Ramblin' with Jack Elliott," *Sing Out!* Vol. 19, No. 5, March/April 1970, 3; Israel G. Young, "Frets and Frails," *Sing Out!* April/May 1961, 47; Blank, "I Read a Book Today, Oh Boy . . .," 80.

29. Reineke interview with Izzy Young; Young, "Frets and Frails," *Sing Out!* April/May 1961, 47.

30. Young, "Frets and Frails," *Sing Out!* April/May 1961, 47; Arlo Guthrie, "House of the Rising Son," *Esquire*, September 1984, 82.

31. Robbie Woliver, *Bringing It All Back Home: Twenty Five Years of American Music at Folk City*, New York: Pantheon Books, 1986, 51.

32. Noel Clad and George Pickour, "Greenwich Village—1955," *Cosmopolitan*, April 1955, 87; Alan Lomax, host, George Pickow, cinematographer, *Blues, Ballads and Bluegrass*. 1961.

33. Shelton, "All Hung Up," 47.

34. Reineke interview with Izzy Young; Dylan, *Chronicles: Volume One*, 251.

35. John Greenway liner notes to *Jack Elliott Sings the Songs of Woody Guthrie* (Prestige/International, 13016), 1961.

36. Israel Young (ed. Josh Dunson), "Moses Asch: Twentieth Century Man, Part II," *Sing Out!* Vol. 26, No. 2, 1977, 25–26; Jim Capaldi, "Conversation with Mr. Folkways: Moe Asch," *Folk Scene*, Vol. 6, No. 3, May 1978, 14–20 and Vol. 6, No. 4, June 1978, 2–4; Peter Goldsmith, *Making People's Music: Moses Asch and Folkways Records* (Washington, DC: Smithsonian Institution Press, 1998).

37. "Folk Music Round-Up," *Sing Out!* December 1961/January 1962, 55, 57.

38. D. K. Wilgus, "Record Reviews," *Journal of American Folklore*, April/June 1962, 181–182.

39. John Greenway, "Folk Song Discography," *Western Folklore*, Vol. 21, No. 2, April 1962, 150. Robert Shelton, "Americana for the Tyro." *New York Times*. 1 October 1961, X16.

40. Josh Dunson, "Off the Record: The Restless Art of Ramblin' Jack," *Mainstream*, Vol. 16, No. 2, February 1963, 62–63; Josh Dunson, *Freedom in the Air: Song Movements of the '60s* (New York: International Publishers, 1965), 119.

41. Jon Pankake and Paul Nelson, "Record Reviews," *The Little Sandy Review*, No. 16, 29–33.

42. "Gerdes Folk City: Stevens Gospel Singers, Jack Elliott" (advertisement), *Village Voice*, 20 July 1961, 8; Robert Shelton, "Wandering Minstrel Is in Town," *New York Times*, 25 July 1961, 19.

43. Pete Karman, "Riverside Radio Broadcasts All-Day Folk Music Program, *New York Mirror*, 6 August 1961 (as reproduced in Rotolo, *A Freewheelin' Time*, 93); Robert Shelton, "Folk Music Heard on 12-Hour Show," *New York Times*, 31 July 1961, 15.

44. Paul Cable, *Bob Dylan: His Unreleased Recordings* (New York: Schirmer Books, 1978), 14.

45. Shelton, "All Hung Up," 47.

46. Hank Reineke, "Dave Van Ronk: From the '50s and the Beats, to the '60s and Dylan and Ochs, Until Now," *Soho Arts Weekly*, No. 220, 28 November 1990, 38-A.

47. Chris Flisher, "Living Legend: Ramblin' Jack Elliott Keeps Folk Standards High," *Worcester Phoenix*, 2–9 May1997, www.worcesterphoe.../05/02/JACK _ELLIOTT.html (accessed 18 July 1997).

48. Robert Shelton, "Hootenanny Held at Carnegie Hall," *New York Times*, 18 September 1961, 35; Robert Shelton, "Bob Dylan: A Distinctive Folk Song Stylist," *New York Times*, 29 September 1961, 31; Israel G. Young, "The Izzy Young Notebooks," *The Telegraph*, No. 56, Winter 1997, 59.

49. Dale, "Ashgrove, L.A.," *Variety* 224, 1 November 1961, 76.

50. Colin Irwin, "Living Legend," *Melody Maker*, No. 55, 16 August 1980, 39; David Hinckley, "Art D' Lugoff," *On the Tracks*, No. 2, Fall/Winter 1993, 45; Ian Woodward, "The Wicked Messenger #3743," *ISIS*, No. 74, August 1997, 15.

51. Robert Palmer, "Ramblin' Jack to the Rescue," *New York Times*, 9 August 1977, 28; j. poet, "A Ramblin' Kinda Guy," *San Francisco Chronicle*, 1 October 2006, PK-46; J. R. Goddard, "Records: Bobby Dylan," *Village Voice*, 26 April 1962, 7.

52. Shelton, "All Hung Up," 47; Israel G. Young, "Frets and Frails," *Sing Out!* October/November 1961, 51.

53. Greenway liner notes to *Jack Elliott Sings the Songs of Woody Guthrie*.

54. Josh Dunson, "Off the Record: The Restless Art of Ramblin' Jack," *Mainstream*, Vol. 16, No. 8, August 1963, 62–63; Greenway, "Folk Song Discography," 150; Jon Pankake and Paul Nelson, *The Little Sandy Review*, No. 29, March/April 1964; Jon Pankake and Paul Nelson, *The Little Sandy Review*, No. 28, 26–27.

55. John Greenway liner notes to *Ramblin' Jack Elliott* (Prestige/International 13033), 1961; Jack Elliott, Second Fret, Philadelphia, PA, circa 1962.

56. Ronald D. Cohen, *Rainbow Quest: The Folk Music Revival & American Society, 1940–1970* (Amherst/Boston: University of Massachusetts Press, 2002), 172; Robert Shelton, "Bluegrass Music by Earl Scruggs," *New York Times*, 4 December 1961, 49.

57. Neil Rosenberg notes and discography to *Flatt & Scruggs 1959–1963* (Bear Family Records BCD-15559), 1992.

58. Gorm, "New Acts," *Variety*, No. 225, 31 January 1962, 60; Israel G. Young, "Frets and Frails," *Sing Out!* 12, February/March 1962, 51.

59. Jack Elliott, Gerdes Folk City, 23 January 1962; Notes to *Folk Classics—Roots of American Folk Music* (Columbia/Legacy 45026), 1989.

60. Shel Kagan liner notes to *Jack Elliott at the Second Fret—Recorded Live* (Prestige/International 13065), 1963; Cohen, *Rainbow Quest*, 171.

61. Israel G. Young, "Frets and Frails," *Sing Out!* April/May 1962, 47; "Gerdes Folk City: Grandison Singers/Jack Elliott" (advertisement), *Village Voice*, 22 March 1962, 13; Israel G. Young, "Frets and Frails," *Sing Out!* February/March 1961, 84; Bill Ellis, "Ramblin' Jack Elliott Earned His Nickname by His Mouth," *Commercial Appeal* (Memphis), 31 March 2000, G2.

62. Michael Krogsgaard, "Bob Dylan: The Recording Sessions (Part One)," *The Telegraph*, No. 52, Summer 1995, 76; Meg McConahey, "Travelin' Troubadour's Tales," *Santa Rosa Press-Democrat*, 7 February 1999, Q15.

63. Robert Shelton (ed. Ian Woodward), "The Robert Shelton Minnesota Transcripts: Paul Nelson," *ISIS*, No. 91, June/July 2000, 25.

64. John Greenway liner notes to *Jack Elliott: Country Style* (Prestige-International 13045), 1962.

65. Introduction to "Tennessee Stud," *Sing Out!* Vol. 19, No. 5, March/April 1970, 6.

66. Bess Lomax Hawes, "Butch Hawes 1919–1971," *Sing Out!* Vol. 21, No. 2, January/February 1972, 19–20; Bess Lomax Hawes, *Sing It Pretty: A Memoir* (Urbana and Chicago: University of Illinois Press, 2008).

67. Jon Pankake and Paul Nelson, "A Lot of Jack," *The Little Sandy Review*, No. 28, 27; Josh Dunson, "Off the Record: The Restless Art of Ramblin' Jack," 62–63; Jay Smith, "City Folk," *Sing Out!* Vol. 14 January 1964, 87; Jon Pankake, "Country Music," *Sing Out!* Vol. 15, No. 4, September 1965, 90.

68. Booklet notes to *Ramblin' Jack Elliott: Country Style/Live* (Fantasy FCD 24754-2), 1999.

69. Robert Shelton, "Hyannis Welcomes Folk Music," *New York Times*, 28 July 1962, 11; Israel G. Young, "Frets and Frails," *Sing Out!* Vol. 12, April/May 1962, 46.

70. Douglas Martin, "Michael Stillman, 87, Founder of Innovative Record Company," *New York Times*, 27 April 2003, N48; "Obituary 1: Rubin, Rose," *New York Times*, 12 September 1999, 48.

71. Daniel Shearer, "Weekend Jamboree," *Princeton Packet*, 16 August 2001 www.groovelily.com/2001/08/16/philadelphia-folk-festival-preview (accessed 12 February 2009).

72. Roger Ebert, "Elliott Concert," *Autoharp*, Vol. 3, No. 2, 30 November 1962; Roger Ebert, "Rambling Jack Rambles Here, Leaves Folk Songs, Anecdotes," *University of Illinois Daily Illini*, 21 November 1962.

73. Ebert, "Elliott Concert"; Ebert, "Rambling Jack Rambles Here"; Arlo Guthrie liner notes to *Ramblin' Jack Elliott: Bull Durham Sacks & Railroad Tracks* (Reprise 6387), 1970; Roger Ebert, "Ramblin' Man: Documentary Can't Pin Down Jack Elliott's Life," *Chicago Sun-Times*, 8 September 2000, Sec. Weekend

Plus, 32; John Cohen and Ralph Rinzler, "The University of Chicago Folk Festival," *Sing Out!* Vol. 11, April/May 1961, 8.

74. David King Dunaway, *How Can I Keep from Singing: Pete Seeger* (New York: McGraw-Hill, 1981), 217; "Jack Elliott Joins Ranks of 'Hoot' & Holler Boys in Ban on ABC-TV Show," *Variety*, April 24, 1963, 26. Israel G. Young, "Frets and Frails," *Sing Out!* Vol. 13, Summer 1963, 63.

75. Robert Shelton, "Queens College Folk Festival Begins on an Authentic Note," *New York Times*, 7 April 1963, 83; Israel G. Young, "Frets and Frails," *Sing Out!*, 13, February/March, 1963, 65; Ronald D. Cohen, *A History of Folk Music Festivals in the United States* (Lanham, MD: Scarecrow Press, 2008).

76. *Broadside* (Boston), Vol. 11, No. 4, 19 April 1963, 7; Eric Von Schmidt and Jim Rooney, *Baby, Let Me Follow You Down: The Illustrated Story of the Cambridge Folk Years*, 2nd ed. (Amherst: University of Massachusetts Press, 1995), 172–173; Bruce Sylvester, "Talk Talk: Ramblin' Jack Elliott," *Goldmine*, Vol. 23, No. 14, Issue 442, 4 July 1997, 15.

77. "Cabaret Tonight," *New York Times*, 4 June 1963, 34; "Cabaret Tonight," *New York Times*, 12 June 1963, 38.

78. Robert Shelton, "Newport Folk-Music Festival Opens 3-Day Run Before 13,000," *New York Times*, 27 July 1963, 9; "Newport Folk Festival" (advertisement), *New York Times*, 16 June 1963, 92; Newport Folk Festival, *Blues Session*, Porch One, 27 July 1963, Library of Congress Sound Recording, Control no. 00584933.

79. Newport Folk Festival, *Banjo and Guitar Workshop*, Porch Two, 28 July 1963, Library of Congress Sound Recording, Control no. 00584944; Newport Folk Festival, *Evening Concert*, 28 July 1963, Library of Congress Sound Recording, Control no. 2006657054; *Evening Concerts at Newport, Vol. 1* (Vanguard VRS 9148), 1964.

80. Israel G. Young, "Frets and Frails," *Sing Out!* Vol. 13, No. 4, October/November, 1963, 63; Shel Silverstein liner notes to *Jack Elliott* (Vanguard VRS-9151), 1964.

81. Shel Kagan liner notes to *Jack Elliott at the Second Fret—Recorded Live* (Prestige/International 13065), 1963.

82. Jon Pankake and Paul Nelson, "A Lot of Jack," *The Little Sandy Review*, No. 28, No year given. 27; Ed Kahn, "Folk Song Discography," *Western Folklore*, Vol. 22, No. 4, October 1963, 297.

83. Goddard Lieberson, Producer, *The Badmen: Stories & Pictures* (Columbia Records Legacy Collection L2S 1012), 1963, 69; "The Columbia Legacy Series" (advertisement), *New York Times*, 8 December 1963, 566.

84. Woody Guthrie, *American Folksong* (New York: Oak Publications, 1961), 28; Woody Guthrie, "Belle Starr," *Sing Out!* Vol. 15, No. 5, November 1965, 22–23.

85. Joe Boyd, "The 150 Best Recordings of American Folk Music," *Hootenanny*, May 1964, 62; Ed Kahn, "Folk Song Discography," *Western Folklore*, Vol.

23, No. 3, July 1964, 224; Robert Shelton, "Fused Folk Arts," *New York Times*, 27 October 1963, 130.

86. Israel G. Young, "Frets and Frails," *Sing Out!* Vol. 12, No. 4, October/November 1962, 51.

87. Stolder, "Traveling Back with Ramblin' Jack Elliott."

88. Stolder, "Traveling Back with Ramblin' Jack Elliott."

89. Silverstein notes to *Jack Elliott*.

90. The vaguely western sounding name "Tedham Porterhouse" was only one of Dylan's many early pseudonyms. He was, more famously, billed as "Blind Boy Grunt" on recordings made for *Broadside* magazine in 1962.

91. Eric Winter, "Focus on Folk," *Melody Maker*, 31 August 1963, 16; "Anglo-US Marathon of Jazz, Folk," *Melody Maker*, 21 September 1963, 4; Karl Dallas, "Elliott Adnopoz—the Brooklyn Cowboy," *Melody Maker* 38, 28 September 1963, 10; "Folk Success," *Melody Maker* 38, 28 September 1963, 10; Correspondence from Ian Woodward, 19 February 2007.

92. Paul Nelson and Jon Pankake, "What's Happened to Jack Elliott?" *Sing*, October 1963, 77; Eric Winter, "Behan—Way Back When: New Records Reviewed," *Sing*, November/December 1963, 93.

93. Dylan, *Chronicles: Volume One*, 251; Robert Hilburn, "Rock's Enigmatic Poet Opens a Long-Private Door," *Los Angeles Times*, 4 April 2004; Robert Hilburn, "How to Write Songs and Influence People," *Guitar World Acoustic*, February 2006, 30.

94. "Jack Elliott, The Greenbriar Boys, Judy Roderick—In Concert: Town Hall, January 25, 1964," *Tune Up*, Vol. 2, No. 2, December 1963; Len Packer, "Our Man in Philadelphia," *Hootenanny*, May 1964, 60.

95. Douglas R. Gilbert, *Forever Young: Photographs of Bob Dylan* (Cambridge, MA: DaCapo Press, 2005), 108–109; Jay Smith, "Records in Review," *Sing Out!* Vol. 15, No. 3, July 1965, 79, 81.

96. John May interview with Jack Elliott, London, England, 12 February 2005.

97. John Cohen, "Interview with Roger (Jim) McGuinn of the Byrds," *Sing Out!* Vol. 18, No. 5, December 1968/January 1969, 9; Steve Silberman, "An Egg Thief in Cyberspace: An Interview with David Crosby," *Goldmine*, Vol. 21, No. 14, 7 July 1995; *Bob Dylan: Highway 61 Interactive* (Columbia/Graphix Zone), 1995.

98. *Bob Dylan: No Direction Home—The Soundtrack* (Columbia/Legacy C2K 93937), 2005; Jack Elliott, Tin Angel, Philadelphia, PA, 18 May 1995; *Bob Dylan: Highway 61 Interactive*.

99. Jack Elliott, Bitter End, New York City, 26 October 2000.

100. Robert Shelton, "First Edition of 'Singing Paper' Is Issued Hot Off the Guitars," *New York Times*, 2 November 1964, 59; Broadside Hootenanny, 1 November 1964 (FT-9547 Dub), Southern Folklife Collection, University of North Carolina at Chapel Hill; Phil Ochs, "The Guthrie Legacy," *Mainstream*, Vol. 16, No. 8, August 1963, 36.

Do-Re-Mi

5

THOUGH VANGUARD HAD ISSUED HIS *Jack Elliott* album, Elliott continued to moonlight as a recording artist for Columbia's "Special Products" division. In 1950, Goddard Lieberson and musical director Lehman Engel chose *Pal Joey* as the first of Columbia's celebrated series of "recorded re-creations" of classic American musicals. The albums were not original cast recordings but, instead, polished, lovingly engineered studio re-recordings. In 1964, Lieberson managed to attract several of Broadway's most talented actor/singers to assist on a studio re-creation of *Oklahoma!* The cast for the retooling would include footlights legend John Raitt (the father of blues/rock singer Bonnie Raitt), singer/actress Florence Henderson, and 1962 Tony award–winner Phyllis Newman. Improbably rounding out the cast of Broadway's finest was Ramblin' Jack Elliott. He had been cast as Will Parker, the shy rodeo cowboy sweet on the flirtatious farm girl Ado Annie. In March 1964, Elliott was busy at work at Columbia's 30th Street studios, contributing the lead vocal to Rodgers and Hammerstein's "Kansas City" and singing a duet with Phyllis Newman on "All Er Nothing." Photographs from the *Oklahoma!* session show the Stetson-topped Elliott appearing somewhat out of character in thick-framed black eyeglasses, standing stiffly before a Columbia microphone as he sang alongside members of the men's chorus. Elliott did not need a guitar to provide the accompaniment on this assignment; he had the strength of Franz Aller's 37-piece orchestra for support.[1]

Lieberson also contracted Elliott to appear on *The Mormon Pioneers*, the seventh installment of the *Columbia Records Legacy Collection* historical series. Elliott seemed less comfortable with the material here than with the cowboy songs for *The Badmen*, but his performances of "Root Hog or Die," "The Mormon Battalion Song," and "Tittery-Irie-Aye" nonetheless rang true. It is possible Elliott was already familiar with a variant of "Root Hog or Die" through one of Woody Guthrie's Sacco & Vanzetti ballads. Released in the autumn of 1965, *The Mormon Pioneers* included folksingers Oscar Brand, Ed McCurdy, Clayton Krehbiel, and Elliott, though all of Jack's cuts were recorded solo with only an acoustic guitar for backing. The *Journal of American Folklore* was somewhat more impressed with *The Mormon Pioneers* than it had been with *The Badmen*: "Short as it falls of the ideal, this recording is a significant contribution to Americana." Similar to its review of *The Badmen*, the *Journal* again faulted Lieberson's employ of nonauthentic artists to sing the songs of Mormonism. "The choral heresy is not absent," the review goes on, "and the solos range from the overly dramatic performances of Ed McCurdy and Oscar Brand to the perhaps too Southern renditions of Jack Elliott. What was the status of guitar and banjo in the Mormon communities?" the *Journal* asked. Tellingly, neither Columbia album featured the credit that Elliott appeared "Courtesy of Vanguard Records." Such an omission suggests that Elliott was not under any formal contract with Vanguard and remained, as always, a free agent. Elliott proudly confirmed his career-long untethered status, telling one writer flatly, "I never was signed exclusively with anybody or record label." He chose this route as freedom from a contract allowed him to forgo the tensions of having to "go through the excruciating process of getting divorced from a record label. I . . . was free to move and nobody ever gave me any complaints when I signed to do an album with someone else."[2]

On February 27, 1965, the Folk Song Society of Minnesota presented "Jack Elliott—America's Finest Urban Folksinger in His First Minnesota Appearance." The concert was scheduled to take place at the Main Ballroom of the Coffman Memorial Union building at the University of Minnesota, Dylan's alma mater, had he graduated. The day before the concert, a complimentary profile of Elliott was published in the *Minnesota Daily*. The article studiously noted that though Elliott first made his mark as an interpreter of Woody Guthrie, his repertoire had since "grown to include hundreds of songs besides those Guthrie taught him, and even many of non-Southwestern origin. He is so absorbed in the Southwestern style, however, that songs, regardless of origin, take on the flavor of the old west."[3]

It was true. Through his own research and friendships with kindred spirits such as Peter LaFarge, Sam Hinton, and the western artist Harry Jackson, Elliott earned a reputation as one of the folk scene's preeminent singers of cowboy songs. Elliott's talent and gritty repertoire of cowboy ballads brought him to the attention of the country and western singer Johnny Cash, a best-selling artist for Columbia who, in 1965, was interested in recording concept albums documenting America's pioneering heritage. When researching song titles for inclusion on *Johnny Cash Sings Ballads of the True West*, he consulted the standard texts, such as the western song anthologies by John and Alan Lomax and Frank Dobie. Cash also combed through the repertoires of contemporary artists who performed authentic cowboy songs, such as Elliott, who taught Cash "The Death of Mister Garfield," the odd ballad recorded by the Rambling Boys in 1957 that eerily, and casually, details the assassination of President James A. Garfield by Charles Guiteau in 1881. Cash was intrigued by the song and wrote in the notes, "This song was brought to me by folksinger Jack Elliott. . . . It is eighty years old and to my knowledge has never been recorded." The song had been recorded by both Bascom Lamar Lunsford and Derroll Adams, but it was obvious that Cash learned the song firsthand from Elliott himself. Cash could not help but tool with the song's lyrics, and the version he eventually waxed for Columbia shared only occasional similarities with earlier versions. Oddly, Columbia wrongly assigned the writing credit of the "Mr. Garfield" ballad to Elliott.[4]

Jack had first met Johnny Cash in 1962 at the Gaslight Café on Mac-Dougal Street. He had long been a fan of Cash's music; the singer performed an eclectic mix of country and western songs, rockabilly numbers, ballads, and novelty tunes. Elliott was surprised when he strolled into the Gaslight only to find the legendary country singer onstage. He was not on the bill; Cash was in town on business and just checking out the Greenwich Village folk scene. The Gaslight Café was nearly a grotto, one of the smallest cabarets on the street. Cash was a large man whose presence could hardly be missed, and he was soon cajoled into performing. Jack recalled that Johnny "had to stand at an angle, because he was too tall for that stage." Cash was something of an anomaly; he was a hero to fans of country and western music, a man who's deeply held religious faith and old-fashioned patriotism were lauded by country music's traditionally conservative, right-of-center audience. But Cash was a deeply principled man who believed America's flag-waving liberties should extend to the new generation of American rebels. Cash's favorite songs were those that told a story, particularly ones with a moral, and in 1962, the best stories were being fashioned by the singer-songwriters of Greenwich Village. Cash was an early champion of Bob Dylan and soon befriended such Village luminaries as the songwriter-performer Peter LaFarge and the dusty-voiced, cowboy singer Ramblin' Jack Elliott.[5]

On March 12, 1965, Elliott and Cash shared a recording session at the Columbia Record Studios in Nashville. The only song issued from that session was Elliott's own "Cup of Coffee," a humorous, shaggy-dog spoken-word monologue, that is buoyed along by a bouncy, four-chord guitar progression and a catchy refrain. The refrain was so memorable that "Cup of Coffee" might have enjoyed potential as a hit single on the country music charts, if only it had been coupled to a more traditional set of rhyming verses. Elliott's "Cup of Coffee" spools out an engaging, humorous tale of an alcohol-fueled truck driver's visit with a friend. The Cash/Elliott version was released in May 1966 on the Cash album *Everybody Loves a Nut*. The album was programmed, in Elliott's own words, with mostly "silly songs." The casual session with Elliott was a side project to Cash's own solo enterprise, but their music making was remembered warmly by both men. Cash would later write to Elliott, telling him, "Nashville is still talking about you, asking about you. [Columbia] will never get over that session we did together. They still would like for me to try and get you to sign with them." It is impossible to determine if Cash's assertion that a deal with Columbia was truly considered or only wishful thinking, as it is difficult to imagine Elliott passing on an offer to record a solo album for the label. There are suggestions that the version of "Cup of Coffee" waxed for Columbia was as much Cash's song as Elliott's. Cash biographer Michael Streissguth relates that Elliott and Cash more or less worked out "Cup of Coffee" together as the two men and Cash's wife, June Carter, drove from Manhattan to visit Dylan at his retreat in the upstate town of Woodstock.[6]

In May 1967, a year following the release of Cash's *Everybody Loves a Nut*, Elliott was a guest of *Radio Unnamable*, Bob Fass's free-form late-night program. Elliott had trooped up to New York City's WBAI studios following his set at the Gaslight, playing a solo acoustic version of "Cup of Coffee" for the folks in radioland. As the song wound down, Fass commented politely, "When I went and I listened to the Johnny Cash version of the song, after I heard your version of the song, I think yours cuts his to ribbons." "Well, mine is based on his," Elliott conceded, confusingly adding, "But then his [version] is based on my original." Though it is doubtful Elliott made any real money from Cash's recording of "Cup of Coffee," he warmly recollected, "I still get little annual reports that [*Everybody Loves a Nut*] sold ten copies in Australia."[7]

On Saturday night, April 17, 1965, New York City's Town Hall and *Sing Out!* hosted "Hootenanny Town Hall: Tribute to Woody Guthrie, Songs of, by, for and to Woody Guthrie." Scheduled that evening were Pete Seeger, Jack Elliott, Logan English, Sonny Terry, Brownie McGhee, Patrick Sky, Marianne "Jolly" Robinson, and Woody's 18-year-old son Arlo. Though already suffering the effects of Huntington's disease, Woody had been well enough to attend the first tribute concert held in his honor on March 17, 1956, at Manhattan's Pythian Hall. But his physical condition had long since deteriorated to the point that he could no longer speak clearly or control his flailing limbs and Woody was now largely confined to his hospital bed. It was this knowledge that caused Robert Shelton to note that many of the artists who performed at Town Hall "had trouble keeping their comments about Mr. Guthrie in the present tense." The Town Hall concert wasn't the first, nor would it be the last, of the Guthrie tributes, but it was the template for those that followed. In Shelton's view, the concert was "an emotional tribute to a dying man who has yet to receive his full recognition as a writer who belongs with Robert Burns and Walt Whitman in the awesome fraternity of great national poets."[8]

Elliott next traveled to Dallas, Texas, but it might have been best if he had chosen to remain in New York. Elliott had an important and rare concert date of his own scheduled at Town Hall later that month, one that now seemed in jeopardy. Izzy Young broke the news in his *Sing Out!* column, reporting "Jack Elliott ripped his ankle and has it in a cast due to some fancy riding in the streets of Dallas on those new fangled roller skates that are the current rage." Izzy had the story partly right. In truth, Elliott had been tested, and bested, by a friend's skateboard. He had taken a bad tumble at the base of the hill and was taken directly to Dallas's Parkland Hospital, where the doctors confirmed that he had broken his leg.[9]

The Elliott concert at Town Hall, scheduled for Friday evening, April 30, 1965, was, in some ways, a litmus test. The popularity of rock 'n' roll had surged in 1965, and the relatively few "commercial" folk-music artists who enjoyed marquee status were beginning to feel the cooling effects at the box office. Not everything on the horizon seemed bleak. Oak Productions presented a concert of the New Lost City Ramblers and Elizabeth Cotten at Town Hall on January 30, 1965, and Izzy wrote, triumphantly, that the New Lost City Ramblers, against all odds, nearly filled the house. He enthusiastically wrote, "Concerts like this are happily proving that the market for city folk music isn't dead by any means. . . . I'd like to see Jack Elliott do as well in his Town Hall concert." Izzy's wish came true when an audience of nearly one thousand, just shy of a sellout, gathered to catch Elliott's solo recital at Town Hall. Vanguard Records planned to record the evening's performance for an "in concert" album.[10]

The concert, produced by Harold Leventhal, started off somewhat tentatively with Elliott hobbling out onstage in western attire, his foot in a cast where his cowboy boot should have been. Propped upright on a set of crutches, he smiled widely, shyly acknowledging the warm greeting of his fans. A friend carried his guitar out to center stage. Once settled, Elliott started the program with a robust take of Jesse Fuller's "San Francisco Bay Blues" and closed some two hours later with a plaintive rendering of Woody's "Ramblin' Round" ("As I Go Ramblin' Around"). Sandwiched in between were songs by Dylan ("Don't Think Twice, It's All Right"), Jimmie Driftwood ("Tennessee Stud"), Jimmie Rodgers ("Sadie Brown"), Lead Belly ("Blind Lemon Jefferson"), and Will Fyffe ("I Belong to Glasgow"). He also scored handsomely with "Lovesick Blues" (the Irving Mills and Cliff Friend yodel popularized by Hank Williams), Woody's "Talking Columbia," and also sang songs by artists as diverse as Ray Charles, Derroll Adams, and Reverend Gary Davis.[11]

The concert was an outstanding success. Robert Shelton was among those who routinely charged that Ramblin' Jack too often misused his talent. But at Town Hall Shelton triumphantly reported "Elliott . . . spread his own air of informality around the room. But it was not the undisciplined sort of performance that has marred some of his nightclub and festival appearances." In Shelton's view, Elliott had, at long last, become his own man. The Town Hall concert was proof that Jack was no longer merely "an alter ego of Woody Guthrie," but an artist who had, at long last, synthesized his many musical influences and turned the amalgam into something very much his own. "Mr. Elliott has gone to the very top of his art," Shelton conceded. "In his folk singing, his guitar playing and gently paced humor, what he did last night can justifiably be called art."[12]

The British promoter Roy Guest was preparing a series of concerts for early summer and he planned to feature a sampling of the best folk music artists America had to offer. Signing on were Elliott, Josh White, Jr., Reverend Gary Davis, Derroll Adams, Julie Felix, and, for her first appearance in England, Buffy Sainte-Marie. For Elliott it was an opportune time to travel overseas; his Vanguard album had been belatedly released in England on the Fontana label, and two of his early Prestige-International LPs had been issued on the British Stateside imprint. England, too, was weathering the current rock 'n' roll storm, and the younger, career-minded, folk song enthusiasts found they had two options. They could marry the old songs to the new sound, much like the Animals had done with "The House of the Rising Sun," or they could, to paraphrase Dylan, "Wrap themselves to

the tree with roots"; that is, give no quarter to the mods with their electric guitars and folk-rock sound. The entrenched folk song hardliners and
old-timers, the group most likely to buy the latest Ramblin' Jack Elliott
long-playing record, shared mixed feelings for Elliott's new album, with
many regarding the Vanguard/Fontana LP as a step backward.

Ewan MacColl remained the unrepentant Leftist and purist. He was
hardly impressed with Jack's new album, publicly declaring that Elliott
had gone soft. MacColl told Bill Yaryan of London's *TV World*, "Jack was
best as an interpreter of Guthrie material. As time went by, he became
instrumentally more accomplished. Later his guitar work got too 'souped
up' with beat-type arrangements and chords. His voice became soft and his
Guthrie songs too mannered. His cowboy hats won't go in England today.
Only the younger kids will listen to him." Rory McEwen was no dyed-
in-the-wool radical, but he, too, thought Elliott had changed and that the
change was not for the better. McEwen felt as early as 1959 that Jack had
become less and less the proletariat singer and "more of an entertainer."
As proof, he offered that Elliott was singing fewer Guthrie songs, instead
lacing his set with more "comedy stuff." Alex Campbell, the Scot cowboy
singer and an early disciple of Jack and Derroll, proved a more loyal friend.
He agreed that Elliott had changed but believed the transformation was
not necessarily for the worse. Campbell, too, dated the change to the time
when Jack first left England to play on the continent. That's when Elliott
"gradually dropped his Guthrie material," Campbell opined. "People there
wanted variety in a cabaret act. Jack couldn't be just Woody." Roy Guest
privately fretted that perhaps Elliott had gone "commercial" and was no
longer a suitable performer for this 1965 concert tour sponsored by the
austere Cecil Sharp House. To Guest's credit, he decided to bring Jack
over regardless of the critics.[13]

The excitement of Jack's return to England for a full-fledged tour was
partially muted. Dylan had just finished a brief, but rapturously received
seven-date tour of British theaters. Ostensibly, Dylan was still considered
a folksinger in most circles; his concerts in England, for the very last time
anywhere, were performed with only an acoustic guitar and racked harmonica. But Dylan had long abandoned traditional music, and his concerts were now comprised entirely of self-penned material, mostly culled
from his *Freewheelin'*, *The Times They Are A-Changin'*, and *Another Side of
Bob Dylan* albums. British audiences were, indeed, seeing another side of
Dylan, as America's enfant terrible had been slotting a number of recently
written (and heretofore unissued) songs into his engagements, such as
"Mr. Tambourine Man" and "Gates of Eden." Fans and the British press

swooned, and Dylan was asked to return to London on the first of June to record a television program for the BBC program *Tonight*.[14]

Elliott was as surprised as anyone regarding Dylan's meteoric rise, but did not, publicly at least, begrudge his protégé's success. He was well aware Dylan had professional and artistic ambitions that bordered on the ruthless. In contrast, friends (and detractors) found Elliott to be *too* easygoing, *too* undisciplined, and not terribly career-minded. He continued to live, as he always had, in the moment, rarely concerning himself with long-range plans or career goals. He later rued that professional and financial success eluded him because he "didn't have the right kind of energy—you know, combative, competitive." Dylan, on the other hand, could be, and often was, merciless with those who challenged or compromised his artistic vision. Dylan could not understand Jack's rather cavalier attitude to his own music and career. He once complained that Elliott had "too many friends," which, on the surface, seemed the oddest of accusations. But Dylan was well aware that surrounding oneself with too many friends and scene makers and hanger-ons easily drained energy that might otherwise be channeled into more creative pursuits. Moreover, Dylan had the services of Albert Grossman. It had not escaped Jack's notice that while Dylan was pulling in $2,000 a night at theaters, he was still playing nightclubs, two sets an evening, for $200.[15]

That is not to say England's folkies had turned against Elliott, that all of the reaction to the Fontana issue of the *Jack Elliott* Vanguard album was unfavorable. *Melody Maker* assured, "Jack Elliott sings well in a friendly, unpretentious fashion and he is caught in pretty keen form." He still had plenty of admirers in England.[16]

The first show of the U.K. tour took place at Acton Town Hall on May 26, and the BBC was there to record a short interview with Jack for the *Midday Spin* radio program. Max Jones of *Melody Maker* also grabbed a brief interview that afternoon, but Jones was more interested in Jack's take on Dylan's recent doings than with Elliott's own. Jack did not seem to mind. He good-naturedly referenced Dylan's great propensity for artful songwriting, but admitted the lyrics of some of the bard's more recent efforts were "a little bit vague. . . . Woody wasn't vague and that's one way in which Dylan has departed from him." Elliott found himself genuinely touched by Dylan's new songs and defended his friend's right to explore the boundaries of his art. Elliott cited "A Hard Rain's A-Gonna Fall" as an example of Dylan's imaginative use of language. "A lot of people say his songs are full of images that don't mean anything," he told Jones. "But

I don't get tired of hearing those words—and I don't know what some of them depict."[17]

The tour included dates in Birmingham, Manchester, Liverpool, Romford, Bristol, London, Croydon, and Glasgow. The Elliott who visited England this time around was, at best, only a semiambulatory "Rambling Boy." The program distributed at the concerts dutifully reported, "It should be noted in this programme that Jack's limp is due to a recent skate-board accident and will not, we hope, be permanent." Not all of the concert engagements ran as smoothly as Guest might have hoped. There apparently was a bit of self-medication going on and Elliott was, reportedly, out of sorts in Glasgow. The *Sunday Times* reported when the plane that carried the lively entourage landed, most of the cast were already "well gone." At the concert, Elliott reportedly spent a good portion of his set, as one angry letter put it, "messing up Guthrie and Dylan songs." A disappointed fan at the Glasgow show wrote *Sing Out!* complaining that Elliott took the stage "somewhat inebriated," mumbled his way through a dire set, and lost his picks. Jack's biggest success that night was not a traditional folk song or Guthrie classic but the drunken reverie of the music hall song "I Belong to Glasgow." "This from the top-of-the-bill artiste at a concert of American folk music just doesn't wash," the letter writer sniffed.[18]

In part due to Dylan's meteoric rise, Guthrie's legend had continued to grow. In October 1965, the Macmillan Company issued *Born to Win*, a previously unpublished collection of Guthrie's writings and sketches. Among the book's treasures is a flattering pencil sketch of Guthrie by Jack Elliott. The portrait of Woody was so complimentary that it caused Guthrie to scribble beneath his Barrymore-like profile "Jack Elliott drew me thissa way and I sure do hope I look this good." *Sing Out!* asked Elliott to write a review of *Born to Win* and he obliged. Jack recalled feeling both "proud and embarrassed" that one of his sketches had been selected for inclusion. Elliott had been unaware that a new book from his old friend was forthcoming, having "stumbled" upon *Born to Win* entirely by accident, spying copies sitting atop a cashier's desk at a Greenwich Village bookseller. As for the merit of *Born to Win*, Elliott championed that, at long last, "a bit of the real Woody" was being issued. He preferred this publication of Guthrie's "rugged free style" writings to the recent spate of blatantly commercial and slick recordings of Guthrie songs that had been "bitched up" by "pop and fop" groups. Jack cited the "Bellyfonte [sic] Singers" recent performance of Guthrie's "Hard Travelin'" as antithetical to Woody's dusty art. In Jack's mind, the Belafonte Singers were emblematic of the

Tin Pan Alley dross that had infected recent folk song recording. In *Born to Win*, Guthrie's "laughs and grim jokes and some very sad parts" were presented in equal measure, and Jack welcomed the book's publication "so the world can learn a little more about this great man."[19]

Elliott composed his review of *Born to Win* on the afternoon he was scheduled to appear at the Village Gate to accept an award on Woody's behalf. The men's magazine *Cavalier*, with Robert Shelton as musical editor, had chosen to honor Woody and promote the new tome with their "Hooey" award, a well-meaning but empty platitude. Jack was not particularly sure it was the best time to be accepting awards on anyone's behalf, but he had already agreed. The problem wasn't the award itself; it was the timing of the trophy ceremony. He had since married a third time (his 1963 marriage to Patty was short lived) and Jack's third wife, Polly, was not only nearing the last stages of her pregnancy, but already two days overdue. Jack had already chosen a name should his first child be born a male: "Woody." He feared his "big little woman" might have the baby right there on the floor of the Village Gate, but luck prevailed and she did not. On October 17, 1965, Polly gave birth to a daughter, Maggie Guthrie Elliott.[20]

On Saturday night, November 13, Pete Seeger finally found a television audience long denied him. Seeger and producer Sholom Rubinstein had secured financing to inaugurate a modest series of programs on folk music. Ever since the *Hootenanny* debacle, Pete had designs of presenting a program of authentic folk music for television broadcast. The series was to be titled *Rainbow Quest*, a name Seeger had previously used earlier for his Folkways album of 1960. *Rainbow Quest* would be taped on the threadbare set of the WNJU television studios in Newark, New Jersey, and broadcast in the New York metropolitan area on Channel 47. The potential audience for the series would be limited. WNJU could only broadcast at ultrahigh frequency, and few television sets in the greater metropolitan area were equipped with the converters that allowed reception. But Seeger reasoned it was a start, and on the first program the 46-year-old musician opened with a few Woody Guthrie songs before bringing out the Clancy Brothers with Tommy Makem, and topical songwriter Tom Paxton. Though WNJU slotted *Rainbow Quest* between such disparate fare as teen pop music programs and gruesome bull fights from Mexico City, the *New York Times* conceded Seeger's program was, just as the veteran folksinger conceived, "free of the slightest trace of show business ostentation." The *Times* television reporter confidently predicted *Rainbow Quest* would garner Channel 47 its "first certain Emmy Award."[21]

Elliott missed the television premiere of *Rainbow Quest* as he was per-
forming that same night at the Gaslight Café on MacDougal Street. The
Gaslight was promoting Elliott in their newspaper advertisement as the
"Famous Folk Recording Artist," and in 1965 this was still the case. Chas.
O'Hegarty, the British Balladeer, was second-billed for the duration of
Elliott's residency, which was to last through Thanksgiving weekend. On
November 26, Jack performed at Carnegie Hall as part of *Folksong '65*, an
impressive folk and blues "package" show that combined Tom Paxton, John
Hammond, Jean Ritchie, and the New Lost City Ramblers with blues legends Son House, Big Joe Williams, Skip James, and Bukka White. In many
respects, Elliott shared more in common with the aging blues singers than
with the city folksingers. Though only 34, he had already been around the
world. He seemed less a contemporary artist than the youngest member of
the old guard. Because of his association with Woody Guthrie, Ramblin'
Jack was counted among that select group of folksingers whose histories
and careers were inseparably interconnected to the Woody Guthrie/
Cisco Houston/Lead Belly/Pete Seeger axis.[22]

It was in such company that Elliott agreed to appear on the CBS television program *Camera 3*. On Sunday morning, December 12, *Camera 3*
broadcast a half-hour program titled "Woody Guthrie's California to the
New York Island." Based on a script by Millard Lampell and featuring
the songs and prose of Woody, the program was a coproduction of CBS
television and the Guthrie Children's Trust Fund. The program, mixing
music with spoken word passages, featured Pete Seeger, Jack Elliott, Bernice Reagon, and Ed McCurdy.[23]

It had been well over a decade since Woody first introduced a shy Jack
Elliott to Pete Seeger. Pete witnessed Elliott's transformation from Woody
Guthrie protégé to an artist of international acclaim. Seeger had earlier
dedicated several paragraphs to Elliott in his *Sing Out!* column "Johnny
Appleseed, Jr.," offering Jack as a self-made man who weathered "years
of discouragement" only to come out the other side having "slowly made
himself into one of the finest pickers and singers and all-around entertainers I've ever seen on a stage." In many ways, Seeger and Elliott were
cut from the same cloth. Both men were dreamy romantics, and Seeger
probably glimpsed some of his younger self in Elliott. "When some people
find that Jack Elliott was born in Brooklyn, he with his cowboy hat and
boots, rough lingo and expert guitar playing—their first reaction is, 'Oh,
he's a fake.' They're dead wrong," Seeger wrote. "Jack reborned himself
in Oklahoma. He didn't just learn some new songs. He changed his whole
way of living."[24]

Following the *Camera 3* taping, Seeger asked Elliott to appear as a guest on *Rainbow Quest*. He agreed and at WNJU, Elliott met with Seeger, Rubinstein, and songwriter Malvina Reynolds. Though she resembled a demure, favorite grandmother, Malvina was a composer of barbed topical songs, a talent she honed in the late 1940s as a dues-paying member of People's Songs. Reynolds was passing through New York City when Pete, who charted Malvina's song "Little Boxes" in 1963, invited her to the taping. Reynolds was far from her home in Berkeley, California, and she learned from Elliott that he was planning to abandon New York for the "Garden of Eden" that was California following his *Rainbow Quest* appearance.[25]

After his return from England in November 1960, Elliott had been residing on a more or less permanent basis in and around New York City, primarily in his room at the Earle Hotel and later in the lush suburb of Short Hills, New Jersey. But he was not looking forward to another grim New York winter, so he planned to set off with his wife and new daughter for the West Coast. By the end of 1965, many of New York City's most dynamic record companies had pulled up stakes, relocating entirely or opening "more happening" sister offices in and around Los Angeles. Once the record companies abandoned Manhattan, it was only a matter of time until the artists followed. Seeger made note of Elliott's planned migration in his prefatory comments to Jack's *Rainbow Quest* appearance: "I've got a young fellow who's just about to leave for the West Coast. . . . He was born in the East but was re-born out West. He met Woody Guthrie and decided a life of rambling was for him. . . . Woody Guthrie not only got me started traveling around the country but this young fellow [too]. The young fellow's name is Jack Elliott. Jack's had a problem though. He could never make up in his mind whether he liked horses best or sailboats best. He loves 'em both. So . . . he's going to live right near the edge of the sea out there in California. He'll be able to ride a horse when he wants to and sail a boat when he wants to."[26]

That night on *Rainbow Quest* Elliott sang "Diamond Joe," "Portland Town," and "San Francisco Bay Blues." Prior to the taping, Elliott met the famed maritime artist John A. Nobel, who made his home on the banks of the Hudson River. Elliott was so impressed with Nobel's work he dedicated his *Rainbow Quest* performance of Woody's "Talking Sailor (Talking Merchant Marine)" to him. Jack and Pete followed with a tandem performance of the "Muleskinner Blues," Seeger contributing the very same up-the-neck banjo break he had worked out in 1944 when he recorded the song for Moses Asch with Woody and Cisco. The program closed with Seeger trading his banjo for a bowl mandolin and leading the tandem guitars of Elliott and Reynolds through "Woody's Rag." The sixth episode of *Rainbow Quest* featuring Ramblin' Jack was broadcast throughout the New York metropolitan area on December 18, 1965.[27]

Though Elliott had not released an album of fresh material since his Vanguard issue of 1964, LPs bearing his name continued to come to light. In January 1966, Joker Records of Italy took fresh interest in the mostly un-issued master tapes recorded by Elliott and Adams in Milan in 1957 for Mercury Records. In 1958, the brothers Walter and Ernesto Guertler formed the Joker and Jolly record labels. The Jolly imprint was to release contemporary recordings, while Joker was to offer budget-priced versions of previously issued material. The Joker albums would prove to be nothing short of a musical treasure chest for collectors of Jack Elliott's music.[28]

It is unfortunate that it took nearly a decade for fans to hear the material recorded in Milan. Walter Guertler had only managed to issue the EP *Jack Elliot and Derrol Adams Sing the Western*. In 1966, Guertler decided to make use of the 28 complete monophonic takes held in the vault, marketing the vintage recordings as two separate 12" inch albums in "Stereo Rama Sound," that is, electrically rechanneled for stereo. The first of these albums, *Jack Elliot & Derrol Adams—Folkland Songs*, was pressed on January 28, 1966. The companion album, *Jack Elliot & Derrol Adams—Riding in Folkland*, was produced three days later. Nearly everything about the packaging was stingy and anonymous, and Joker continued an unfortunate tradition by misspelling the name of both artists on the jackets. There were no photographs of Jack or Derroll, no recording information, no sleeve notes to explain the genesis of the songs to the record collector. The Joker albums were not to be sold outside of Italy, though it wasn't long before copies surfaced in adjourning countries. Fans lucky enough to chance upon the two quasi-bootlegs assumed the collections were comprised of outtake material from the Topic Record sessions. This was understandable, as very few fans were aware that the Rambling Boys' recording legacy extended beyond the United Kingdom. By the time that word circulated among enthusiasts that a fresh collection of previously unissued Rambling Boys material had been made available, the mysterious Joker albums had already disappeared. This was unfortunate, as the recordings that Jack and Derroll made in Italy were as fascinating and eclectic as anything they had waxed for Topic.[29]

Topic's own back catalog of Jack Elliott 78 rpm, 8", and 10" albums had finally been made available on 12" long-playing albums beginning in 1963, but for American fans the Topic LPs were to be found, if at all, as costly imports, stocked only by the most esoteric of record shops. This all changed in March 1966 when the Delmark Record Company of Chicago released the first Topic reissue LP *Talking Woody Guthrie* on its own label. Delmark was known among record collectors as a small, independent company whose hip catalog brimmed with recordings of vintage and contemporary Chicago blues and jazz. Delmark's entry into the business of marketing folk music was an uncharacteristic, and rather puzzling, move as it was so ill-timed. By 1966 rock 'n' roll and "folk-rock" were firmly in the ascendant, with interest in the "one man and his guitar" sound not only on the wane but mostly dead. Regardless, Delmark was planning to distribute a series of folk music albums of which *Talking Woody Guthrie* was to be the first ("Jack Elliott's best albums are known to be the one's he cut in England for Topic," the label boasted).[30]

Delmark placed a handful of advertisements in the press trumpeting the album: "Elliott's legendary Topic recordings made available in the U.S. for the first time," they bragged. The production of the "new" version of *Talking Woody Guthrie* was credited to Robert G. Koester, the founder of Delmark, but the album was a straight copy of the 1963 Topic LP of the same name. To his credit, Koester commissioned a new set of liner notes, which helped establish the historical context and significance of the original Elliott recordings. Blues scholar Paul Oliver was responsible for the erudite, although oddly not credited, essay that accompanied the release. Unfortunately, *Talking Woody Guthrie* did not garner much attention from either the mainstream or pop-music press. Sales of *Talking Woody Guthrie* were downright sluggish and proved to be the *only* album to see release in Delmark's proposed "Folk Music Series."[31]

If the "new" Elliott album escaped the notice of American record buyers, it had not passed unnoticed by those engaged in folklore studies. In an essay studying the recent spate of albums featuring the music of Guthrie, the *Journal of American Folklore* refused to "deny the importance" of Woody's effect on the American folk-music revival. But the journal concluded as a *genuine* folksinger he "interpreted the folk to the non-folk, but had little or no effect on the folk tradition." It was a harsh assessment and, to no one's surprise, the record by Woody's celebrated protégé fared even less well. "One wonders what Guthrie, who hated sham and pretense," the review mocked, "would really think of such productions as *Talking Woody Guthrie* by Jack Elliott (Delmark DL-801, from Topic masters of a decade ago)." Not everyone agreed with that assessment, with the folklorist and labor scholar Archie Green, an early Elliott admirer, offering a welcome contrarian view. Writing in *Western Folklore*, Green cited *Talking Woody*

Guthrie as one of only a handful of contemporary *commercial* recordings where union songs were "reduced to the democracy of the marketplace." Green was particularly impressed by Elliott's handling of "Talking Sailor," a song he described as a "faded war snapshot," not generally remembered even among enthusiasts of union songs. Green offered praise for *Talking Woody Guthrie* and for Elliott's guitar playing on "Talking Sailor," describing it as "evocative of the Liberty Ship's pounding motor and straining propeller as well as Woody's style."[32]

Ramblin' Jack still wasn't making much money from the sales of albums. His decision to record as a "free agent" afforded him freedom but little else. When asked by a journalist if he was "glad" he played his cards in such a manner, Elliott later admitted, "I'm not glad about anything because I haven't made any money in the record business." It was only through club and concert engagements that he managed to stay on the road and eke out a living. In early April 1966, Jack was booked for a two-week residency at the Ice House in Pasadena, California. Elliott was the nightclub's top bill, supported by the comedy trio "The Uncalled for Three" and a local folksinging duo Bob and Terry. *Variety* sent down a particularly uninformed writer to catch Jack's act and the review started unpromisingly with the faux pas that Jack was "fresh back on U.S. nitery scene after a six year stay in Europe." Though Elliott was described, in near Shakespearean terms, as a "slight, clown-like, tragic little man," the critic was totally charmed by Jack's act, noting his uncanny ability to establish "immediate rapport with his under-fed, poor boy look." Jack's set included the usual mix of Dylan ("Don't Think Twice, It's All Right") and Ray Charles ("Drown in My Own Tears"), but he also scored with retreads of "Nobody Knows You When You're Down and Out," "Candy Man," and "Cocaine Blues."[33]

One of Elliott's favorite new venues was the Jabberwock at 2901 Telegraph Avenue and Russell Street in Berkeley. The Jabberwock sat only a few blocks from the University of California campus and was a popular meeting place for both students and faculty. Elliott had agreed to perform at the club for two "off night" (Monday and Tuesday) performances that June. But the gigs were so satisfying and well received and the audiences so welcoming that Jack returned for no fewer than six additional midweek performances on July 5–7 and 12–14. The staff of the Jabberwock advertised their good fortune with a modest handbill that read, "Tues.–Thurs. Both Weeks. Ramblin' Jack Elliott who has played everywhere, will be here."[34]

Jack did seem, increasingly, to be here, there, and everywhere. He returned to Newport nearly a year to the day in 1965 when Dylan stole the show, and a good part of the audience, by going electric. Newport's "talent and folklore coordinator," Ralph Rinzler, promised the 1966 event would be less of a circus and would offer a return to the basics; it would even include craft demonstrations to reinforce "this is a folk festival, not just a folk music festival." Though he had not performed at Newport '65, Elliott seemed to be everywhere at the 1966 event. On Friday afternoon, July 22, he appeared at workshops for both guitar and balladry. On Saturday, July 23, he performed at the "Ballad Swapping" workshop as well as the "West of the Mississippi" program on the main stage. On Sunday, July 24, he returned to participate in the grand finale. Following Newport, Elliott rambled down to the Playhouse in Woodstock, New York, where he celebrated his 35th birthday with a Monday night concert on August 1.[35]

On January 17, 1967, nearly one year after *Folkland Songs* and *Riding in Folkland* had been issued in Italy, Elliott's fans in the United Kingdom were given the opportunity to hear a selection of the circulating material through a more official channel. Bounty Records, a subsidiary of the U.K. division of Elektra Records, collected the fourteen tracks found on the *Riding in Folkland* album, shuffled the album's A and B sides, and resequenced the tracks for *Roll on Buddy—The Jack Elliott and Derroll Adams Story: Volume 1.* Joe Boyd, an American record producer based in London and working for Elektra, was brought in to contribute a set of notes. Boyd finally helped to clear up *some* of the mystery surrounding the music's provenance, but his notes were frustratingly thin on detail. Boyd reported that Jack was "delighted" when he heard the news that Elektra was planning to release the collection properly. He reportedly told Boyd that he remembered being "well paid" for the sessions in Milan and "thought the tapes were quite good." In a bit of well-meaning hagiography, Boyd offered Jack and Derroll as the "only 'citybillies' who ever really made it into the ranks of the true originals; the only middle-class sons worthy of mention alongside Lead Belly, Woody, and Jimmie Rodgers. Boyd promised that a second collection, presumably lifted from *Folkland Songs*, would soon follow. Unfortunately, that second collection would not come to light. Unless they had friends on the continent who could ferret out the original Joker release of *Folkland Songs*, fans in the United Kingdom were left with only half of *The Jack Elliott and Derroll Adams Story.*[36]

In early February 1967 Elliott returned to New York City for a three-week residence at the Gaslight Café. Midway through the wintry engagement, Woody's nineteen-year-old son, Arlo, was brought in by club manager Sam Hood and added to the bill. The young Guthrie had been playing the New York City area, on a mostly semiprofessional basis, for nearly a year. In many regards, Arlo was not at all different from a score of other young, struggling folksingers hustling for gigs. Arlo haunted all the usual venues that hosted open-mike nights, occasionally earning a small fee for a coffeehouse performance. But he mostly worked the basket houses, playing for friends and bemused tourists. Arlo had not planned on a career as a professional musician; it was something that he sort of backed into.[37]

Elliott had known Arlo since the first-born son of Woody and Marjorie was still shy of four years old. Elliott was tickled to see Arlo hone his talent as a raconteur and folksinger and blossom as a performing artist. Andy Wickham of Reprise Records opined, "If Woody was Arlo's physical father, then Jack was his professional father." Arlo told *Guitar Player* magazine nearly the same, offering as a *performer* his greatest musical influence was neither his father nor Bob Dylan. It was "Ramblin' Jack Elliott probably more than everybody else." Arlo would cite Jack's idiosyncratic guitar technique and his singing style as the pillars of his own unhurried, chatty manner. But it was only when Arlo's fame expanded beyond the New York to Boston folk-music axis that he fully appreciated the full breadth of Elliott's influence. On his first trip to London as a "professional" singer in the autumn of 1966, Guthrie admitted, "I'd written enough songs for fifteen minutes in a set, and I did my Dad's songs for thirty. The rest were songs that Jack had recorded that had nothing to do with Dad. Everywhere I went people would say 'Oh, that's great—you know Jack Elliott songs.'"[38]

It was through the albums of his father, of Cisco Houston, and of Ramblin' Jack, that Arlo formed his earliest repertoire of time-worn classics. In the notes to his own collection of cowboy songs, *Son of the Wind*, Arlo wrote, "Ramblin' Jack taught me 'Ridin' Down the Canyon,' 'South Coast' and 'Old Paint.' But more than teaching me the words, Jack taught me how to make these songs come alive." Elliott may have been the template for Arlo's performing style, but he was also helpful to the young Guthrie in more economically meaningful ways. Once, when Arlo was still in the nascent days of his career and no one really knew who he was, he received a long-distance telephone call from Elliott. "Listen," Jack told him, "I'm supposed to go to Missouri. I can't make the date. They're gonna give me five hundred dollars to play the week. I told them 'My friend Arlo can come.'" "Arlo who?" "He's Woody's son," Jack would reply. That answer was, usually, enough for the doors to open magically.[39]

Arlo's emergence as a recording artist neatly, if sadly, overlapped with the last breath of his father. Woody Guthrie passed away at Creedmoor

State Hospital in Queens, New York, on October 3, 1967. Elliott was in Santa Fe, New Mexico, living temporarily in an abandoned railway carriage with friends Barry and Patti McGuire, when he got the news. Elliott had been hanging around Santa Fe's Seton Village, escaping the pain of a third failed marriage. He was in the process of buying a horse from rancher and saddle shop owner Slim Green. Elliott would credit the horse, a 12-year-old cow pony named Young Brigham, for carrying him "through the shock of Woody's passing" and his personal blues.[40]

On the bright side, Elliott had recently been signed to Reprise Records, a subsidiary label of the Warner Bros. Corporation, founded by the crooner Frank Sinatra in 1960. Reprise was belatedly trying to make inroads into the youth market, snagging artists as diverse as Arlo Guthrie and the Jimi Hendrix Experience. Shortly after the new record deal was announced, Elliott met his future wife, Martha, a young actress and fellow free spirit, in a Sausalito boatyard. In November, Elliott was in Los Angeles to record his first album for Reprise, with sessions scheduled at United Recorders on Sunset Boulevard and Gold Star Studios on Santa Monica Boulevard. The guitarist Bruce Langhorne, an old friend of Jack's from Greenwich Village, was brought on as producer, but it was an assignment he would soon regret. Though Langhorne was familiar with Elliott's undisciplined ways, he was nonetheless surprised that his painfully cavalier attitude extended to the studio. Langhorne had assembled a skilled group of musicians sympathetic to Elliott's muse. Mitch Greenhill (the son of Jack's former manager Manny Greenhill) and Mark Spoelstra were brought in to augment Elliott's own acoustic guitar. Richard Greene (of the Jim Kweskin Jug Band, fresh from a stint as fiddler for Bill Monroe) was on fiddle, Bill Lee on organ, Peter Childs on Dobro, and "Mad" Eric Hord offered support on guitar, electric auto-harp, and harmonica. Jack O'Hara and Peter Childs would handle the album's bass guitar arrangements. But Andy Wickham, a friend of Phil Ochs's and a Warner Bros. publicist, dropped in on one *Young Brigham* session, only to find Langhorne visibly rattled, frustrated at the chaos that ensued outside the control booth. Elliott was clearly enjoying himself. This was not necessarily bad, as some of that spirit and energy would be reflected on the LP. But Jack could not, or would not, focus, and the sessions bordered on the anarchic. Langhorne told Wickham flatly, "I do wish that this album was a little more important to Jack," which was hardly the testimonial the publicist had been seeking. Following the recording of *Young Brigham*, Elliott remained in Los Angeles where he was co-billed with Doc Watson, Brownie McGhee, and Sonny Terry for a 10-night residency at the Ash Grove. It was always good to be back onstage and also, for the first time since 1964, back in the record business.[41]

On January 20, 1968, Carnegie Hall played host to "A Musical Tribute to Woody Guthrie," a musical and spoken-word program saluting Woody's life and work. The event was to be part memorial, part benefit, and part celebration, modeled after the 1956 Guthrie tribute concert at Pythian Hall. Harold Leventhal, who had helped stage that earlier concert, was now producing the memorial program at Carnegie, which was to benefit the Guthrie Children's Trust Fund and the Committee to Combat Huntington's Disease. Millard Lampell, a colleague of Guthrie's from his days with the Almanac Singers, adapted and staged the Carnegie program. Lampbell's script read as a dramatic narrative, featuring the best elements of Woody's music and prose. There were two performances planned for that Saturday at Carnegie; a matinee at 2:30 in the afternoon, and a second performance to follow at 8:30.[42]

The first advertisement for the event appeared on January 5 in the *New York Times*. Billed to appear was a startling "all-star" lineup of contemporary folk-music talent: Judy Collins, Bob Dylan, Arlo Guthrie, Richie Havens, Brownie McGhee and Sonny Terry, Odetta, and Pete Seeger. The spoken-word excerpts from Woody's prose that bridged the musical performances were to be shared equally by Woody's folksy-voiced old pal Will Geer as well as by the more distinguished voice of Robert Ryan, the Chicago-born actor long associated with left/liberal causes.[43]

To the surprise of many, Jack Elliott was not asked to perform. It was an unfortunate omission, which caused some lingering hard feelings, but Harold Leventhal pointed out, some thought defensively, some thought honestly, that it was not all that easy to *find* Elliott at any given time. Izzy Young was angered by Elliott's omission. Some 40 years after the Carnegie program, Izzy sighed, "I can't understand to this day why the Woody Guthrie Foundation people and Harold Leventhal didn't want Jack Elliott." Outraged, Izzy telephoned Leventhal and Pete Seeger, frostily telling them, "If you don't put on Jack Elliott, I'm going to make a protest demonstration . . . by myself in front of the Hall." Izzy was further rankled when he attended a rehearsal and discovered Pete Seeger *teaching* some Woody Guthrie songs to several performers on the program. Elliott was angered at the slight but resigned to the fact that he would not be performing. "Look, Izzy. Don't complain. I'll just come to the concert," Young recalled Elliott telling him. "No, you've *got* to be on the concert," Izzy replied. "If anybody should be on a Woody Guthrie concert, it's *you*!"[44]

It was partly through Izzy's intervention that Jack Elliott made it onto the Carnegie stage that night. Elliott met with Leventhal, and to Harold's credit, was officially brought onto the program. But Elliott's hurt at being passed over would not be easily forgotten. Several months following the concert, *Rolling Stone* reported Jack was still "a bit angry" with Leventhal, which may have been something of an understatement.[45]

Regardless of the backstage drama, the concert was a worthy celebration of Woody's life and art. Dylan's emergence from long seclusion caught the attention of an international team of newspaper journalists, and Guthrie's reputation soared as a result of the coverage. The deification of Woody Guthrie had already begun, but Izzy Young believed few of the musicians had performed at their best that night. He thought Elliott was "distracted," that he hadn't "done as well as I expected him to do. I thought he was a little weak." In Izzy's opinion, Elliott "didn't feel at home" on the Carnegie stage, that the backstage wrangling had drained him of his spirit. Izzy was adamant "the only person who brought Woody Guthrie 'up' [that evening] was Bob Dylan and his friends from Woodstock." Although most performers chose not to stray far from Guthrie's more famed material, Dylan chose to perform an obscure song of Woody's, "Dear Mrs. Roosevelt," a heartfelt paean to the widow of President Franklin Delano Roosevelt. Izzy contended that Dylan's take on "Dear Mrs. Roosevelt" was the "best song on the program."[46]

"Dear Mrs. Roosevelt" was a highlight, but Dylan had not been the only artist to shine. Though Elliott playfully sang "Howdido," one of Guthrie's best-loved children's songs, it was his steely revisit of "1913 Massacre" that held the audience spellbound. The *New York Times* noted that Elliott "was his customarily splendid disciple of Woody, his old touring companion and mentor." In a dispatch sent off to the *Sydney Morning Herald*, journalist Lillian Roxon described Elliott "in cowboy hat, looking as he always has, a little like Guthrie." He sounded a lot like him too, with his vocal imitation on "Howdido" nothing short of eerie. Both Carnegie concerts were recorded, and Leventhal was planning to issue the musical highlights on a series of future LP releases.[47]

One month following the Carnegie memorial, *Young Brigham* was released. The newly founded underground newspaper *Rolling Stone* offered a genuinely enthusiastic review, as did the mainstream *New York Times*. Robert Shelton of the *Times* described the new disc as "one of [Jack's] best," giving the tip of the cap to Reprise for their rescuing of "second time around artists." In Shelton's view, Reprise had offered Elliott and other seasoned artists access to "excellent production values when other

[labels] felt they were no longer commercially viable." Shelton, a sometimes critical but longtime Elliott supporter, applauded producers Bruce
Langhorne and Andy Wickham (who had stepped in when Langhorne had
had enough), for their role in creating an album that "rings as much with
tradition as it does with modernity."[48]

Young Brigham starts off beautifully with Elliott's take on Tim Hardin's
"If I Were a Carpenter." "Carpenter" wasn't technically a new song,
though by Elliott's standards it was. On "Carpenter," Jack tuned the first
and sixth strings of his guitar to D, thereby allowing him to finger-pick
with the option of playing three open D notes. This created a genuinely
original scoring that sounded contemporary due to the "eastern" influence
of the arrangement. Robert Shelton would describe Elliott's performance
of "Carpenter" as "an experimental quasi-rag," though this may have been
a mistake of the *Times* typesetter; Shelton most likely had written "raga,"
which would make more sense. Guthrie's "Talkin' Fisherman" followed,
the guitar playing sparkling and perfect. Jack's version of "Tennessee Stud"
featured the fiddle talents of Richard Greene and proved to be popular
among fans. Following the release of *Young Brigham*, few shows would pass
when the song was not requested by some overexuberant or boozy fan in
the audience. Elliott eventually grew tired of performing the "Tennessee
Stud," refusing to play it no matter how desperate the request. "The horse
died," Jack would drawl acidly.[49]

"Night Herding Song," the old cowboy work song previously recorded by Elliott at his 1959 session for Denis Preston, is yet another gem.
Discussing Jack's version on *Young Brigham, Rolling Stone* astutely pointed
out that Jack's weary vocal positively dripped with authenticity. "Elliott
sounds so much like Almeida Riddle or Maybelle Carter," the review offers, "it's hard to believe that Jack Elliott was really born in Brooklyn."
Though well intentioned, the last sentence clearly demonstrates how even
the most sympathetic critic felt the need to get that *Brooklyn* qualifier into
the review. Lead Belly's "Rock Island Line" closes out side one. The
"Rock Island Line" of *Young Brigham* sounds an awful lot like the version on *Recorded Live at the Second Fret*, augmented this time around with
instrumental support.[50]

The beautiful, lonesome old railroad song "Danville Girl" opens the
album's side two, but the *Young Brigham* version is somewhat of a misfire.
"Danville Girl" (issued under the title of "Poor Boy") had been recorded
by Woody Guthrie and Cisco Houston on April 19, 1944. Unfortunately,
the elements that made the plaintive ballad as sung by Woody and Cisco
such an affecting piece of music are absent here. Elliott's version is an

anarchic misread, his vocals stretching and howling to comic effect. "912 Greens," Jack's famed travelogue song, made its first (and belated) appearance on vinyl but only in snapshot. This was a missed opportunity as "912 Greens" remained the one indisputable masterwork of Elliott's few attempts at songwriting. Andy Wickham hinted that Elliott's recording of the song was almost an afterthought. Wickham recalled that Elliott had been meandering "frivolously through a new Arlo Guthrie song," when Langhorne asked in exasperation "Don't you have any songs of your own?" Elliott responded with an impromptu performance of "912 Greens" that rang beautiful and eloquent. But the version was also abridged and, therefore, less than definitive.[51]

"912 Greens" is followed by a perfect solo acoustic rendition of "Don't Think Twice, It's All Right," the first Dylan song to appear on a Jack Elliott LP. Dylan's "Don't Think Twice, It's All Right" was first recorded by the "Minnesota Mover" circa November 1962 in Studio A at Columbia Recording Studios, New York City, subsequently appearing on Dylan's second album for Columbia (*The Freewheelin' Bob Dylan*, released May 27, 1963). For decades Elliott has shared a story that he taught himself "Don't Think Twice, It's All Right" from a friend's copy of *Freewheelin'*. Jack had recorded the Dylan classic once before, at the summer 1963 sessions that produced his eponymous debut album for Vanguard. Though that recording was left off the album at the time of its release, it was later issued on the collection *Ramblin' Jack Elliott—Best of the Vanguard Years*, released in October 2000. But it was Elliott's version of "Don't Think Twice, It's All Right" from *Young Brigham* that set an army of fledgling finger style guitarists to diligently work through the arrangement, much as they had for Mississippi John Hurt's "Spike Driver Blues" a few years earlier.[52]

The penultimate track of the album is a surprising one; a raucous cover of the out-and-out rock 'n' roll song "Connection." Penned by Rolling Stones bandmates Mick Jagger and Keith Richards, "Connection" first appeared on the Stones Decca album *Between the Buttons* (released in January 1967). It was very much a new song when Elliott recorded it later that November. *Rolling Stone* enthusiastically branded Elliott's "Connection" as "the most startling piece of country-rock ever laid down." It wasn't, but it was one of the album's more inspired performances and song choices. Elliott would retain his enthusiasm for the song. Some 20 years after *Young Brigham*, he would record a noticeably stripped-down version for producer Roy Rogers. That version appeared on *The Long Ride*, Jack's 1999 album for Hightone Records.[53]

Young Brigham closes with Woody Guthrie's "Goodnight, Little Arlo," the first commercial appearance of the song. Woody recorded a variant of "Goodnight, Little Arlo," a charming lullaby for his son, at the winter 1947 sessions for Moses Asch that produced, among others, such children's songs as "Grassy Grass Grass (Grow Grow Grow)," "Needle Sing," and "Bling Blang." Elliott apparently learned the song directly from Woody's singing around the Guthrie home circa 1951 for the young Arlo. The decision to have a rare Guthrie song to bring the curtain down on Reprise's *Young Brigham* was welcome, but not accidental. Its inclusion was likely the result of a deliberate and not-too-subtle cross-promotion effort of the Warner Bros. marketing department, hoping to further boost Arlo's rising star for the label. The track begins with Elliott asking, "Arlo? Can you hear me? I'm out in Californee. I'm sitting here in a recording studio with a lot of old buzzards—funny people. We're going to sing you a little song. I been hearing about you and I seen your picture on your latest album cover and I just want to say I think you've been burning the candle at both ends, kid. And it's time you got a little sleep. You're only nineteen and you're starting to look thirty-eight." At the time of the song's recording, Elliott was a world-weary 36 years old. That spring Jack toured in support of *Young Brigham*, starting with a week's residency at the Ash Grove in May 1968.[54]

The eighth annual Newport Folk Festival was scheduled for late July. Wednesday, July 24, was feted as "Children's Day," and Newport impresario George Wein had brought together a seasoned panel of performers to welcome the children, of all ages, who made the annual pilgrimage. Jim Kweskin acted as master of ceremonies, with the cast including Taj Mahal, Eric Von Schmidt, Pete Seeger, Bernice Reagon, Mississippi Fred McDowell, Reverend Fredrick Kirkpatrick, Sam Hinton, and Jack Elliott. Though the afternoon skies were unfriendly and gray, the performers brought their own sunshine, and fans enjoyed an eclectic mix of blues, freedom songs, and jug band music.[55]

Those fans attending Newport '68 could be forgiven if they did not recognize Elliott. He looked nothing like the artist they remembered. Gone was the western-attired, underfed, dusty clone of Woody Guthrie. The new Jack Elliott was a man of the times. He sported a full, dark beard, shaggy hair, a modern shirt with prints, a thin necklace and circular, horn-rimmed glasses à la Beatle John Lennon. Gone, too, were the traditional denim blue jeans Jack had always favored, now replaced by acid washed dungarees. It was all too sudden of a change for some. Jack's old friend Jesse Fuller made his disgust for Jack's new look entirely plain. Jesse was surprised at seeing Elliott "with the spots of bleach spilled all over his jeans." "I thought he was a cowboy!" Fuller said in disgust. Though Elliott's physical persona had undergone a substantial change since moving to California, he remained, musically, the completely unadorned cowboy singer. He proved that his talents as a singer of cowboy songs had not diminished with a well-received set of "Old West" ballads at a rain-soaked Newport workshop. Though only 36, Elliott was something of an elder statesman; a much beloved transitive figure who bridged mossy folkies to contemporary blues-rockers. Janis Joplin, the whiskey-voiced blues-rock vocalist from San Francisco, made her Newport debut in 1968, whiling away the downtime with Elliott and a bottle of Southern Comfort.[56]

Elliott was scheduled to perform on Saturday night's "Country Music for City Folks" program, but he was also scheduled to take part in the most anticipated event of Newport '68: the festival's memorial program for Woody Guthrie. Though illness had prevented Guthrie from participating in any of the Newport gatherings, the Oklahoman's presence had been felt from the very beginning. In 1959, road buddies Pete Seeger and Cisco Houston sang Woody's songs and told stories of their old friend, unwittingly planting the seeds for the "cult of personality" that was to develop around him. On Friday and Saturday afternoons of Newport '68, the promoters slated two separate "Songs of Woody Guthrie" workshops and on Sunday evening, George Wein presented a gala "Tribute to Woody Guthrie" on the main stage. Though not of the emotional caliber of the Carnegie Hall memorial held earlier that year, the event nonetheless drew one of the festival's biggest crowds. Wein promised a reunion of some of the original Almanac Singers, as well as performances by Pete Seeger, Jack Elliott, Arlo Guthrie, Millard Lampell, Lee Hays, Sam Hinton, Alan Lomax, Odetta, Reverend Fred Kirkpatrick, Oscar Brand, and others. Arlo and Jack, respectively the natural and spiritual sons of Woody Guthrie, sang a song together in tribute to the original rambling man.[57]

By 1968 entrepreneurial rock music promoters began staging outdoor multiact rock 'n' roll festivals on the order of the biggest and best of the folk-music festivals. One of the first was the Sky River Rock Festival held on a farm outside of Sultan, Washington, the last weekend of August 1968. It was the model and forebear of the more celebrated Woodstock Arts and Music Exposition Festival of August 1969. Prior to their more fabled appearances at the Woodstock festival, artists such as Carlos Santana and Country Joe and the Fish performed at the Sky River event, sharing the bill with Jack Elliott and a handful of other folksingers. But the folkies seemed increasingly out of their element, performing almost as fill in acts between stage and band changes.

There was no getting around the fact that *commercially*, folk music had been supplanted by rock. Elliott found himself playing mostly to audiences of hippies and flower children, which may have accounted, in part, for the dramatic makeover of his physical persona. It was that audience that Elliott played before when, at the end of September 1968, he shared a three-night engagement with Lester Flatt and Earl Scruggs and the Foggy Mountain Boys at Bill Graham's Avalon Ballroom in San Francisco.

Elliott returned to the Ash Grove in early March 1969, his residency spanning two weekends, March 7–9 and March 14–16. March 8 had been an extremely busy day for Elliott; he agreed to appear on two separate radio shows earlier that morning to promote the Ash Grove gigs, and later visited Topanga Canyon for an afternoon "folk session" with friends. Despite his popularity, a critic from the *Los Angeles Times* offered Elliott as a "minor folk legend . . . unpredictable and difficult to describe." But that same critic found himself charmed by Jack's informal stage manner. As was his custom, Elliott wandered, troubadour style, through the audience with his guitar, pulling people in close with the "gentle intensity" of his singing. "He seems so eccentric," the *Times* continued, "that no one could ever take him seriously as a singer. Yet, when he's singing he is so intense and effective that he seems incapable of small talk between songs."[58]

In the spring of 1969 Elliott became a father for the second time when Martha, his fourth wife, gave birth to their daughter Aiyana. Shortly afterward, Elliott was witness to another birth for which he shared parentage, the launching of the sloop *Clearwater* before a crowd of 2,000 well-wishers at the Gamage shipyard in South Bristol, Maine, on May 17. Pete Seeger's dream of building a replica of a 19th-century Hudson River sloop was transformed into an unlikely reality thanks to an enthusiastic coalition of sailors, historians, environmentalists, folksingers, and hippies. On June 27, Captain Allen Aunapu and the first all-volunteer crew of the *Clearwater*, which included such musical sailors and land lubbers as Ramblin' Jack Elliott, Don McLean, Reverend Fredrick Douglas Kirkpatrick, Louis Killen, Len Chandler, and Jimmy Collier, set sail down the Damariscotta River toward the Atlantic Ocean for the 40-mile cruise to Portland, Maine. Portland was to host the first of a series of 25 waterfront fund-raising concerts. Pete's son Daniel documented the maiden voyage of the *Clearwater* as she sailed from Maine to lower Manhattan. Dan Seeger's resulting 30-minute documentary film *Clearwater* features a few glimpses of Elliott helping to haul the bowline, as shanty master Louis Killen directed the effort with the rousing work song "South Australia."[59]

The *Clearwater* and Ramblin' Jack Elliott sailed to Rhode Island for a stopover at the Newport Folk Festival. Jack was scheduled to perform on Sunday, July 20, 1969, one of a cabal of Warner Bros. artists to be featured at the festival. Joe Smith, then a vice president of the Warner Bros. label, recalled Newport '69 as "a marvelous festival and a very important one for us," with the Everly Brothers, Arlo Guthrie, Jack Elliott, and Joni Mitchell scheduled to perform. Smith also had a particular interest in Sunday afternoon's "Young Performers" showcase, as the event was to feature the newly signed artist Van Morrison. Warner Bros., sparing no expense to promote and coddle their artists at the festival, hired out Newport's posh Viking Hotel for a company dinner to which all of the artists and their families were invited. Elliott shared Newport's Sunday program with Seeger and the "Hudson Sloop Group," Sonny Terry and Brownie McGhee, John Hartford, and the African finger-style guitarist Jean-Bosco Mwenda.[60]

The Newport '69 souvenir program made note that "Jack Elliott . . . has sung all over the world, and when he wasn't singing, he was talking—about his music, or someone else's, or more than likely, trucks or boats." The program also correctly pointed out that although he had recorded "innumerable records," Elliott was "best experienced in person—when you can catch up with him. His talented picking and rare insouciance are better experienced than described." That year at Newport, Elliott rambled at length about trucks and boats and, for the first time, spaceships. Jack was on the Newport stage when Apollo 11 astronaut Neil Armstrong made history as the first human to set foot on the surface of the moon. The Newport staff had a small television sitting off stage so they too could witness history in the making. It was Elliott's turn to perform and, watching the telecast, he counted off the rungs as Armstrong began his descent down the ladder and onto the moon's surface. "He's just stepping on the moon right about now," Jack informed the crowd, knowing full well that astronauts Neil Armstrong, Edwin "Buzz" Aldrin, and Michael Collins were, without doubt, the ultimate rambling boys.[61]

Jack's friend Johnny Cash had also performed at Newport '69, and, later that summer, Elliott visited Cash at the singer's lakefront home outside of Nashville. The two friends were on a boat with their fishing lines resting in the water when Cash asked, "Hey, Jack. Are you going to this Woodstock thing?" Strangely, Jack had not yet heard of the Aquarian Arts and Exhibition Festival that was to be held in August on Max Yasgur's farm in Bethel, New York. Cash told Elliott he did not know all that much about the proposed festival, only that Dylan had recently sent him a letter cautioning the singer to refuse an invitation to play. A resident of Woodstock, Dylan did not want all those hippies in his backyard. "Well, if you're not going," Elliott told Cash, "I ain't going either. That's settled." As the eyes of the nation focused on the estimated half-million music fans that chose to congregate at the Woodstock event for "Three Days of Peace and Music," Elliott was some 2,900 miles to the west, settling into an eight-night engagement at the Candy Company nightclub on El Cajon Boulevard in San Diego.[62]

Elliott had been in Nashville to wax his second album for Reprise. Prior to flying to the Music City, Elliott had been hanging around Hollywood with such friends as actors Sterling Hayden and Dan Blocker, the latter of whom was enjoying success as Eric "Hoss" Cartwright on the popular television western *Bonanza*. Though no tinsel-town gadfly, Elliott had been around long enough to meet and befriend many of Hollywood's most promising young actors, Robert and David Carradine, Dennis Hopper, and Kris Kristofferson among them. He was occasionally offered a small role in the films his friends were appearing in, but his cameos rarely escaped the editor's scissor. In his otherwise favorable review of Kris Kristofferson's film *Cisco Pike*, Ralph J. Gleason, one of the deans of rock music journalism, mentioned Ramblin' Jack was among the casualties of that film's "cut scenes and dropped bits." It was also rumored that Elliott had been offered a small part in the Universal film *The Last Movie* starring Dennis Hopper. This rumor was partly confirmed by Elliott at a concert at the University of California in Berkeley when he off-handedly mentioned Kris Kristofferson was "pinch hitting for me in my latest movie I didn't do down in Peru." Elliott also befriended the actor Dennis Olivieri, then enjoying a semblance of teen scene popularity as one of *The New People*, a short-lived Aaron Spelling television drama about a gaggle of college students marooned on an island in the South Pacific. Olivieri was also a musician and songwriter, parlaying his television fame into a record contract with VMC Records. He drafted Elliott as a guitarist for his notoriously weird and decidedly non–bubble gum LP *Come to the Party*, a cultish blend of acid/psychedelic/folk-rock. It is difficult to hear Elliott's contribution on the final LP; the music was so totally outside of Jack's realm and the album's final mix prominently featured only the piano, organ, harpsichord, and bass.[63]

To some Jack Elliott critics, Olivieri's *Come to the Party* was only slightly more avant garde and cultish than Elliott's newest album for

Reprise. *Bull Durham Sacks & Railroad Tracks* was reportedly recorded in two marathon sessions of 12 hours each, with Bob Johnston manning the control board. Johnston, who had worked with such Elliott compadres as Cash and Dylan, had, essentially, brought in the same outfit of musicians with whom Dylan had recently recorded his *Nashville Skyline* album in February 1969: Kenny Buttrey on drums, Charlie McCoy on bass, Pete Drake on the pedal steel, Norman Blake and Charlie Daniels on guitar, and Bob Wilson on piano. The album was recorded at Woodland Sound Studios and Columbia Recording Studios in Nashville, with Elliott sleeping over at Johnston's house on the night between the two sessions. Oddly, Johnston's name is missing from the album's credits. Producer credits were assigned solely to Charlie Daniels and recording engineer Neil Wilburn. It was rumored that Johnston shared many of the same problems that Bruce Langhorne had encountered when recording the notoriously studio-wary Elliott. Elliott admitted the album was recorded in haste and most of the songs were "done in two takes. I always work like that—if I don't do it in three takes I've lost it." Elliott left town almost immediately following the sessions, dumping the resulting reels on Johnston to sort out. Elliott remembered the album was entirely "put together by Bob Johnston. . . . I didn't help him. I wasn't even around. I don't know why he included all the noise and sound effects and funny things." In Jack's mind, he did nothing wrong in ceding control of the album to Johnston. But Elliott admitted the resulting LP was nothing if not "very weird." Johnston oddly chose to include some of Elliott's meandering, and often pointless, studio banter between musical tracks. The inclusion of such segments was not Elliott's idea. Jack remembered, "Bob Johnston is sort of a headstrong individual. He does things his own way. I didn't ask him about it [since he'd] been producing a lot of good Johnny Cash records and some Bob Dylan albums. And I thought 'He really knows his stuff. I can just leave him to it.'"[64]

The sound mosaic that was the *Bull Durham* album could have been even odder. At some interval during the session, engineer Neil Wilburn packed his recording gear and a set of directional microphones into a car and set off for the highways circling Nashville. Wilburn was hoping to capture the sounds of the big trucks on the road as they shifted gears. He planned to graft the gear-shifting sounds onto the *Bull Durham* soundtrack, but his plans went awry when an unsympathetic trucker menacingly threatened him with a tire iron.[65]

On Saturday night, September 20, Elliott enjoyed unprecedented exposure as a guest on the ABC Television program *The Johnny Cash Show.*

Taped at the Ryman Auditorium, *The Johnny Cash Show* was a surprise hit of the ABC Television network's fall schedule, showcasing a veritable who's who of country, rock, and folk music artists and bands. Elliott was on the 14th program of that first season, sharing the stage with "Mama" Cass Elliott, the Staple Singers, John's brother Tommy Cash, the Carter Family, and the Statler Brothers. The show opened with Cash singing "Goin' to Memphis." He then brought out Jack: "You know, I've done a lot of traveling in my time. Anyplace, I guess, that you could mention: from Maine to California to Alaska to Europe . . . Asia. Done a lot of traveling. But nobody I know—and I mean nobody—has covered more ground and made more friends and sung more songs than the fellow you're just about to meet right now. He's got a song and a friend for every mile behind him. Say 'Hello' to my good buddy Ramblin' Jack Elliott."[66]

Then, suddenly, he was on national television, Ramblin' Jack standing among a thistle of plastic foliage on the Ryman stage, surrounded by a bank of blinking television cameras. Dressed in a beige corduroy jacket, cowboy hat, checkered neckerchief, and round lens eyeglasses, Elliott launched into a smooth, nearly perfect rendering of Tim Hardin's "If I Were a Carpenter." Following the performance, Cash called Elliott over to join him on a center stage bench. As Elliott walked toward Cash, he smiled at the cameras, sending out mumbled greetings to both "Bob" and "Arlo," both of whom had already appeared on the Cash program earlier that season.

The two friends sat down across from each other, acoustic guitars cradled in their arms. Cash told Elliott, "I've got a singing welcome for you" and, indeed, Johnny had composed, or was, perhaps, provided with, an introductory, cornpone novelty song to commemorate Jack's appearance on the show. Cash strummed through a simple chord change and sang:

"Ramblin' Jack, Ramblin' Jack,
I sure am glad that you could ramble back."

Elliott was to take the next verse, but it was then that things began to go awry. Elliott had forgotten to retune his guitar for the duet; the instrument was left in the open-D tuning he used for "Carpenter." As the show was recorded "live" Cash could only look on and laugh as Elliott strummed discordantly across the strings. Fittingly, Jack's reply verse went:

"Well, my boots are dusty and my head's a mess,
I just flew in from the West."

Cash took the next verse:

"Well, I was talking 'bout you and someone said

I believe Ramblin' Jack's dead."

Elliott: "Well, that somebody must have been crazy as Hell, 'cause you'd be the first guy I'd tell."

Then Cash and Elliott launched into the pleasant but lightweight travelogue song "Take Me Home." The version from the broadcast would be featured more than three decades later on the soundtrack album of the film *The Ballad of Ramblin' Jack.* In the liner notes to the CD, Aiyana Elliott credited Cash as the composer of "Take Me Home," writing "Johnny Cash wrote 'Take Me Home' for Jack's appearance on his show," but this was not the case. "Take Me Home" was cowritten by J. H. Clement and A. L. Reynolds and the song had already appeared on the Johnny Cash LP *Everybody Loves a Nut,* the same album that featured Cash and Elliott's take on Jack's own "Cup of Coffee."[67]

Elliott returned to the road while Reprise readied *Bull Durham Sacks & Railroad Tracks.* On October 31 through November 2, he shared a co-bill at the Ash Grove with his old friend Jesse Fuller. Elliott then made his way east to New York City in early November for a two-week residency at the Gaslight Café. Both the *New York Times* and *Daily Variety* sent down reporters, as Jack's return to Manhattan was heralded as a cultural event of some magnitude. Elliott had not performed a solo concert in New York City for over three years. Sam Hood, the son of the Gaslight's original owner, had recently taken control of the cabaret's affairs. He arranged for Elliott's residency, a smart business tactic *Daily Variety* deemed "a decisive move in the café's favor." *Variety* offered Elliott as a charismatic "hardcore pro," noting that in contrast to the new breed of folksingers, Jack "spends the bulk of his time living what he sings about rather than singing about how he would like to live." The Gaslight residency showcased the usual mélange of songs from the pens of Guthrie and Dylan, with the Dylan material clearly in the ascendant. The *Times* noted Elliott performed no fewer than four Dylan compositions on one program alone, stitching together two of his old friend's Greenwich Village–era songs ("Don't Think Twice, It's All Right" and "With God on Our Side") with his more recent Nashville-era offerings ("Lay Lady Lay" and "I'll Be Your Baby Tonight)." On the occasions that Jack moved into the more contemporary material, his performances nearly begged for the bow of a fiddle or the wail of a pedal steel. But there would be none of that. "Too restless to be burdened by electric equipment," *Variety* explained, "Elliott has developed his style around a firmly strummed folk guitar and simple but vivid balladeering." Elliott's Gaslight residency brought all of his friends out of the woodwork, many climbing onstage to share in the music-making. Clearwater mate

Len Chandler was there, as was Rosalie Sorrels and the anthropologist Harry Smith. The always curmudgeonly Dave Van Ronk was there as well, shouting devilishly at Elliott from the back of the nightclub, "You're getting worse every time I see you."[68]

Notes

1. Richard Ridge notes to *Oklahoma!* (Sony/Columbia, SK 61876), 1964, 2002; Stanley Green, "The Original Cast Preserved," *New York Times*, 22 May 22 1960, X13.

2. Goddard Lieberson (producer), *The Mormon Pioneers* (Columbia/Legacy, LS 1024), 1965; *Ballads of Sacco & Vanzetti, Commissioned by Moses Asch—1945, Composed & Sung by Woody Guthrie—1946–47* (Folkways Records, FH 5485), 1960, 1961; D. K. Wilgus, "Records in Review," *Journal of American Folklore*, October/December 1966, 634; Chris Jorgensen, "An Interview with Ramblin' Jack Elliott," *DISCoveries*, October 1990, 99.

3. "Jack Elliott—America's Finest Urban Folksinger in His First Minnesota Appearance, February 27, 1965," concert poster; Maury Bernstein, "Folksinger Jack Elliott to Appear at Union Saturday," *Minnesota Daily*, 26 February 1965, 10–11.

4. Steve Turner, *The Man Called Cash—The Life, Love and Faith of an American Legend* (Nashville: W Publishing Group, 2004), 110; Johnny Cash, *Ballads of the True West* (Columbia C2L 38 M/C2s 838), September 1965.

5. Roger Bull, "Ramblin' Jack Elliott Wandering This Way: Well Traveled, Well Versed Icon of the Folk Era Will Play Thursday at the Florida Theater," *Times-Union* (Jacksonville), 18 May 2004, Sec. Lifestyle, C-1.

6. Hank Reineke, "An Interview with Ramblin' Jack Elliott: See How All Those Stories Get Twisted," *Aquarian Arts Weekly*, 17 April 1985, 10–11; Johnny Cash, *Everybody Loves a Nut* (Columbia CS 9292/CL 2492), 1966; Johnny Cash letter to Jack Elliott, 13 December 1967, *Young Brigham* (Reprise Records, 6284), 1968; Michael Streissguth, *Johnny Cash—The Biography* (Cambridge, MA: Da Capo Press, 2006), 121.

7. Reineke, "An Interview with Ramblin' Jack Elliott," 10–11; Jack Elliott to Bob Fass on *Radio Unnamable*, WBAI-FM, New York City, circa May 1967.

8. Robert Shelton, "Guthrie Honored by Folk Concert," *New York Times*, 19 April 1965, 38; *Hootenanny—Town Hall: Tribute to Woody Guthrie*, recorded 17 April 1965, New York City. Reference recording. Ralph Rinzler Folklife Archives and Collections, Smithsonian Institution, CDR-0549.

9. Izzy Young, "Frets and Frails," *Sing Out!* Vol. 15, No. 3, July 1965, 73–75; Steven Stolder, "Traveling Back with Ramblin' Jack," *NARAS Inforum*, www.grammy.com/features/jackelliott.html (accessed 22 May 1997).

10. "Oak Productions Presents the New Lost City Ramblers and Guest Artist Elizabeth Cotton" (advertisement), *New York Times*, 17 January 1965, X5; "Harold Leventhal Presents Jack Elliott" (advertisement), *New York Times*, 18 April

1965, X6; Izzy Young, "Frets and Frails," *Sing Out!* Vol. 15, No. 2, May 1965, 77.

11. Ramblin' Jack Elliott, *The Essential Ramblin' Jack Elliott* (Vanguard Records, VSD 89/90), 1976; Robert Shelton, "Folk Bill Given by Jack Elliott," *New York Times*, 1 May 1965, 18; Peter Brown, "Maybe Music: First of the Brooklyn Cowboys, Last of the Real Folksingers," *Welcomat* (Philadelphia), 6 October 1993, 42.

12. Shelton, "Folk Bill Given by Jack Elliott," 18.

13. Bill Yaryan, "Jack Elliott," *Folk Scene*, No. 10, August 1965, 3–4.

14. Michael Krogsgaard, *Positively Bob Dylan: A Thirty Year Discography, Concert & Recording Sessions Guide, 1960–1991* (Ann Arbor, MI: Popular Culture, 1991), 27.

15. J. H. Tompkins, "Dreaming Dreams, Talkin' Blues: Folk Legend Ramblin' Jack Elliott Has Some Stories to Tell," *San Francisco Bay Guardian*, 22 August 2001, 39; Chris Samson, "Ramblin' Along with a Little Help from His Friends: Folksinger Jack Elliott Visits Record Store to Promote His New CD of Duets with Old Friends," *Petaluma Argus-Courier*, 3 April 1998, http://home.comcast.net/~2samsons/Chris/Writing/Musicians/elliott.html (accessed 26 December 2005).

16. "Ramblin' Jack in Fine Form—and Dylan in Disguise," *Melody Maker*, 17 July 1965, 11.

17. Max Jones, "Max Jones Meets Ramblin' Jack Elliott: Dylan, Me, and the Legend of Woody Guthrie," *Melody Maker* 40, 29 May 1965, 6; Monica Thapur, BBC Archives, letter to Hank Reineke, 11 April 2007.

18. Mamie Lang, "A Bow to the West," *The Sunday Times* (London), 5 January 2003; Ken M' Kay, "International Letters: Lack of Responsibility . . .," *Sing Out!* Vol. 16, No. 4, September 1966, 76.

19. Woody Guthrie (Robert Shelton, ed.), *Born to Win* (New York: Macmillan, 1965), 152; Jack Elliott, "Book Review: Woody Guthrie Revisited," *Sing Out!* Vol. 15, No. 6, January 1966, 79, 81.

20. Jack Elliott, "Book Review: Woody Guthrie Revisited," 79, 81; Izzy Young, "Frets and Frails," *Sing Out!* Vol. 15, No. 6, January 1966, 89.

21. Jack Gould, "TV: Pete Seeger Makes Belated Debut," *New York Times*, 15 November 1965, 75.

22. "Ramblin' Jack Elliott/Chas. O'Hegarty, Gaslight Café" (advertisement), *New York Times*, 19 November 1965, 42; "Felix G. Gertsman presents 'Folk Song '65—Folk Show of the Year'" (advertisement), *New York Times*, 14 November 1965, X2.

23. "Camera 3 Presents . . . Woody Guthrie's 'California to the New York Island,'" (advertisement), *New York Times*, 11 December 1965, 67.

24. Pete Seeger, "Johnny Appleseed, Jr.," *Sing Out!* Vol. 14, No. 1, February/March 1964, 71.

25. Susan Wengraf, *Love It Like a Fool: A Film about Malvina Reynolds* (Berkeley, CA: Red Hen Films, 1977).

26. Sholom Rubinstein, Producer, *Pete Seeger: Rainbow Quest #6, Malvina Reynolds & Jack Elliott* (VHS) (New York: Norman Ross Publishing, undated.

27. Guy Logsdon, *Woody Guthrie: A Biblio-Discography* (Self-published, Revised 6 December 1999), 50.

28. "Biografia: Walter Guertler," http://it.wikipedia.org/wiki/Walter_Guertler (accessed 1 March 2009).

29. *Jack Elliot* [sic] *and Derrol* [sic] *Adams, Folkland Songs* (Joker SM 3023), 1966; Jack *Elliot* [sic] *and Derrol* [sic] *Adams, Riding in Folkland* (Joker SM 3024), 1966.

30. "Jazz Record Mart's Own Classified Ads: Announcements" (advertisement), *Sing Out!* Vol. 16, No. 2, April/May 1966, 61.

31. "Jazz Record Mart: Folk Music Series" (advertisement), *Sing Out!* Vol. 16, No. 4, September 1966, 55; Paul H. Oliver, "Rambling Blues: The Saga of Derroll Adams and Jack Elliott," *Music Mirror*, Vol. 4, No. 5, 1957, 20–21.

32. "Record Reviews: From the Record Review Editor—Woody Guthrie," *Journal of American Folklore*, April/June 1967, 204; Archie Green, "Folksong on Records," *Western Folklore*, Vol. 27, No. 1, January 1968, 74–75.

33. Jorgensen, "An Interview with Ramblin' Jack Elliott," 99; Joex, "Ice House, Pasadena, April 5," *Variety*, No. 242, 13 April 1966, 67.

34. "The Jabberwock," www.chickenonaunicycle.com/Jabberwock%20Shows.htm (accessed 1 March 2009).

35. Robert Shelton, "Newport Starts Its Folk Festival," *New York Times*, 22 July 1966, 20; "Who Makes Music and Where," *New York Times*, 31 July 1966, 86; Program for the 1966 Newport Folk Festival.

36. Joe Boyd notes to *Roll on Buddy—The Jack Elliott and Derroll Adams Story: Volume 1* (Bounty Records, BY 6036), 1967.

37. "Ramblin' Jack Elliot—Gaslight Café" (advertisement), *Village Voice*, 2 February 1967, 33; "Ramblin' Jack Elliot/Arlo Guthrie—Gaslight Café" (advertisement), *Village Voice*, 16 February 1967, 29; Susan Braudy, "As Arlo Guthrie Sees It . . . Kids Are Groovy. Adults Aren't," *New York Times Sunday Magazine*, 27 April 1969, 56.

38. Michael Brooks, "Woody & Arlo," *Guitar Player*, Vol. 5, No. 5, August 1971, 35; Randy Sue Coburn, "On the Trail of Ramblin' Jack Elliott," *Esquire*, April 1984, 84; Andy Wickham, "About Our Talky Cowboy Friend, Ramblin' Jack Elliott." Warner Bros./Reprise Records promotional flyer, 1968.

39. Arlo Guthrie notes to *Son of the Wind* (Rising Son Records, RSR 0003), 1991; Jeff Tamarkin, "Arlo Guthrie at 50: In the House of the Rising Son," *Goldmine*, No. 111, August 1997, 47.

40. "Producer's Note" on *Young Brigham* (Reprise Records, RS 6284), 1968; Jack Elliott, Towne Crier Café, Pawling, NY, 12 July 1992.

41. Wickham, "About Our Talky Cowboy Friend, Ramblin' Jack Elliott"; Richie Unterberger, *Turn! Turn! Turn! The '60s Folk-Rock Revolution* (San Francisco: Backbeat Books, 2002), 247.

42. Woody Guthrie, *A Tribute to Woody Guthrie* (New York: TRO Ludlow Music/Woody Guthrie Publications, 1972); "A Musical Tribute to Woody Guthrie" (advertisement), *New York Times*, 5 January 1968, 40.

43. "A Musical Tribute to Woody Guthrie," 40.

44. Hank Reineke interview with Izzy Young, New York City, 20 September 2007.

45. Barry Gifford, "A Friendly Tribute for Ramblin' Charles Adnopoz," *Rolling Stone*, Vol. 2, No. 3, 20 July 1968, 6, 22.

46. Reineke interview with Young.

47. Lillian Roxon, "The Guthrie Concert" for the *Sydney Morning Herald*, in *Bob Dylan: A Retrospective* (New York: William Morrow, 1972), 211; Robert Shelton, "Tribute to the Life and Legend of Woody Guthrie," *New York Times*, 22 January 1968, 31.

48. Barry Gifford, "Young Brigham, Jack Elliott," *Rolling Stone*, Vol. 1, No. 7, 9 March 1968, 20; Robert Shelton, "Separating Pop from Pap," *New York Times*, 26 May 1968, D36.

49. Shelton, "Separating Pop from Pap," D36.

50. Gifford, "Young Brigham, Jack Elliott," 20.

51. Logsdon, *Woody Guthrie: A Biblio-Discography*, 53; Wickham, "About Our Talky Cowboy Friend, Ramblin' Jack Elliott."

52. Krogsgaard, *Positively Bob Dylan*, 21; Jack Elliott, "Jack Introduces Don't Think Twice" from *Legends of Folk* (Red House Records RHR CD 31), 1990.

53. Gifford, "Young Brigham, Jack Elliott," 20.

54. Logsdon, *Woody Guthrie: A Biblio-Discography*, 39; Jack Elliott preface to "Goodnight, Little Arlo" on *Young Brigham* (Reprise RS 6284), 1968.

55. "Newport Folk Festival" (advertisement), *New York Times*, 30 June 1968, D4; Robert Shelton, "Eighth Folk Fete Opens in Newport," *New York Times*, 25 July 1968, 29.

56. Arlo Guthrie, *This Is the Arlo Guthrie Book* (New York: Amsco Music Publishing, 1969), 32–33; Barbara Dane, "Lone Cat Jesse Fuller," *Sing Out!* Vol. 16, No. 1, February/March 1966, 8; Edvins Beitiks, "Jack of Hearts," *San Francisco Examiner Magazine*, 4 August 1996, 10.

57. David Green, *Folk Artists '69* (Providence, RI: C. Nigro Publishing Company, 1969), 2–3.

58. Robert Hilburn, "Ramblin' Jack Elliott on Stage at Ash Grove," *Los Angeles Times*, 14 March 1969, H18.

59. Daniel Seeger, Producer, *Clearwater* (Poughkeepsie, NY: Hudson River Sloop Clearwater, 1976); *Newport Folk Festival—1969* (program book), Concert Hall Publications, 1969, ed. James K. Rooney; David King Dunaway, *How Can I Keep from Singing: Pete Seeger* (New York: McGraw-Hill, 1981), 288; Douglas Robinson, "Sloop Will Sail Up the Hudson in Campaign for Clean Water," *New York Times*, 2 August 1969, 53.

60. John S. Wilson, "Folk Fete Shines without Superstars," *New York Times*, 22 July 1969, 32; "Newport Folk Festival" (advertisement), *New York Times*, 22 June 1969, D8; Bob Sarlin, *Turn It Up! (I Can't Hear the Words; The Best of the New Singer-Songwriters* (New York: Simon & Schuster, 1973).

61. *Newport Folk Festival—1969* (program book); Beitiks, "Jack of Hearts," 10.

62. Brian Mansfield, *Ring of Fire: A Tribute to Johnny Cash* (Nashville: Rutledge Hill Press, 2003), 54.

63. Jack Elliott, Berkeley Blues Festival, University of California–Berkeley, 4 April 1970; Ralph J. Gleason, "Perspectives: Kristofferson's Fine Flick," *Rolling Stone*, 13 April 1972, 38.

64. Colin Irwin, "Folk: Living Legend," *Melody Maker*, No. 55, 16 August 1980, 39; Production notes to *Ramblin' Jack Elliott: Me & Bobby McGee* (Rounder CD 0368), 1995; Hank Reineke, "An Interview with Ramblin' Jack Elliott: See How All Those Stories Get Twisted," *Aquarian Arts Weekly*, 17 April 1985, 10–11; Jack Elliott, Turning Point Café, Piermont, NY, 17 May 1995.

65. Jack Elliott, Turning Point Café, Piermont, NY, 17 May 1995.

66. *The Johnny Cash Show*, Nashville, TN, broadcast on ABC Television, 20 September 1969, Bill Carruthers, Stan Jacobson, Producers.

67. *The Johnny Cash Show*; Aiyana Elliott and Dick Dahl notes to *The Ballad of Ramblin' Jack—Original Soundtrack from the Motion Picture* (Vanguard 79575-2), 2000.

68. "Coming Events," *Bluegrass Express*, Vol. 1, No. 4, November/December 1969, 17; Pine, "Village Gaslight," *Variety*, No. 256, 12 November 1969, 75; Mike Jahn, "Jack Elliott Sings Dylan and Guthrie in Return to City," *New York Times*, 15 November 1969, 44; Bob Atkinson, "Ramblin' with Jack Elliott," *Sing Out!* Vol. 19, No. 5, March/April 1970, 4.

Jack takes the floor. Photographer: Terry Cryer

Sleeve of Woody Guthrie's Blues *(Topic Records T-5, 1956).*
Author's Collection

Elliott and his trusty Gretsch jams with Rory McEwan as wife June Elliott looks on. Photographer: Terry Cryer

Sharing a few pints and songs with wife June and Rory McEwan. Photographer: Terry Cryer

Front cover sleeve of the rare EP Jack Elliott Sings Vol. 2 *(77 Records, 77 EP/2, 1958).*

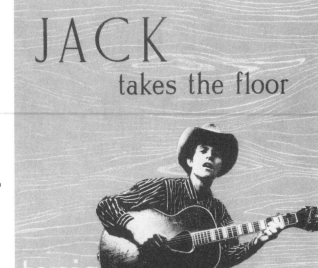

Sleeve of Jack Takes the Floor *(Topic Records 10-T-15, 1958).* Author's Collection

Sleeve of The Rambling Boys *(Topic 10-T-14, 1958).* Author's Collection

Elliott duets with the famed British blues guitarist Alexis Korner. Photographer: Terry Cryer

Elliott playing guitar with British blues harmonica pioneer Cyril Davies and Alexis Korner.
Photographer: Terry Cryer

Elliott meets Muddy Waters backstage at Conway Hall, London, October 1958. Photographer:
Terry Cryer

FOLK-SONG

BLUES COUNTRY-WESTERN

MUSIC CONCERT

Souvenir program from the Ballad and Blues Association's Folk-Song–Blues–Country-Western Music *concert of September 1959.* Courtesy of Ronald D. Cohen

Artist biography as it appeared in the brochure of the Ballad and Blues Association's Folk-Song–Blues–Country-Western Music *concert of September 1959.* Courtesy of Ronald D. Cohen

Jack Elliott

It is not accidental that Jack is called "Ramblin' Jack." Since he was a boy he has wandered all over the States and Europe singing folk songs and talkin' blues. Now, fame is catching up with him. This tour marks his debut as a concert entertainer. But although singing in the lushness of the Festival Hall, Jack will remember the dry dust-bowls of his native Oklahoma. We welcome this great young entertainer whom Roybert is launching, and we hope that he will stay to sing on a further tour in Britain.

Jack and June Elliott and Pete Seeger on the front cover of the December 1959 issue of Eric Winter's Sing *magazine.* Courtesy of Ian Woodward

Pete Seeger with Jack and June Elliott during Pete's recent British tour—the event of the year for folk song fans. TWO SEEGER SONGS—see pages 26 and 27

Photo: Daily Herald

Sleeve of Kid Stuff *(Columbia/Segment SEG 8046, 1960).* Author's Collection

Izzy Young's Folklore Center newsletter of February/March 1961 promotes Elliott's first New York City recital at Carnegie Chapter Hall, February 18, 1961.

AN EVENING OF FOLK

jack elliot

j
a
n
25

ᵀʰᵉ greenbriar boys

Handbill for Town Hall *concert, Philadelphia, Pennsylvania, January 25, 1964.* Courtesy of Ronald D. Cohen

judy roderick

AT

town hall

BROAD & RACE
PHILA., PA

Ticket Prices : $1.75 - 2.25 - 2.75 - 3.25 All seats are reserved. Due to the extreme length of the concert, show begins at 8.00 PM SHARP !

Tickets Available at ; The Gilded Cage, 261 So. 21 St. Lockers, 21 So. 18 St. Phila. Folk Workshop, 1344 Jerome St.(1 block south of Hunting Park) The Second Fret 1902 Sansom St.

Mail Order ; Box 5156 Phila. 41, Pa. Send check or money order and stamped, self addressed envelope to "AN EVENING OF FOLK ".

Record album advertisement for Vanguard's Jack Elliott (VRS—9151, 1964). Author's Collection

Woody Guthrie, Jack Elliott, and Bob Dylan share the cover of the Vol. 1, no. 4 issue of the Karl Dallas magazine Folk Music (London, 1964). Courtesy of Ian Woodward

"The Folksinger's Folksinger!"
---- NEW YORK TIMES

FOLK SONG SOCIETY OF MINNESOTA presents

JACK ELLIOTT
AMERICA'S FINEST URBAN FOLKSINGER
IN HIS
FIRST MINNESOTA APPEARANCE

"In the button-down world of commercialized folk singing,
one of the few authentic voices is the tenor of
Rambling Jack Elliott." -- NEWSWEEK

"Jack Elliott sounds more like me than I do." -- Woody Guthrie

"My favorite folksinger." -- Alan Lomax

Saturday, February 27, 1965 -- 8:30 P.M.

COFFMAN MEMORIAL UNION (MAIN BALLROOM)
UNIVERSITY OF MINNESOTA
Minneapolis, Minnesota

TICKETS $1.50
Available at the door,
and:
The Podium
The Scholar
CMU Ticket Booth
YDFL Office, 348 CMU

(Presented in cooperation with
University Young Democrats)

Poster for Jack Elliott *concert, Coffman Memorial Union (Main Ballroom), University of Minnesota. February 27, 1965.*

Record album advertisement for Bull Durham Sacks & Railroad Tracks *(Reprise 6387, 1970).*
Author's Collection

Brooklyn's Foremost Cowboy:
RAMBLIN' JACK ELLIOTT

"Jack stands alone because he's somewhere between being a little in
front and a little behind us all."
– Arlo Guthrie

"Mr. Elliott's main assets are his total recall of the down-to-earth type of
song Mr. Guthrie created and a relaxing informality. In his husky
phrasing and hip cowboy manner, he made the smoke in the small
basement club seem as if it was coming from a pile of freshly raked
autumn leaves."
– Mike Jahn, N.Y. Times

"He plays fine guitar, sure. He interprets good songs by good
songwriters in his personal, unique style, but it's those things joined
with a total lack of uptightness, gentle warmth, great sense of humor,
natural story-telling, and an ability to immediately connect with his
audience that ties all of Ramblin' Jack together."
– Changes Magazine, N.Y.

His Best Is His Latest-On Reprise
Bull Durham Sacks & Railroad Tracks

SING OUT!
THE FOLK SONG MAGAZINE
VOLUME 19/NUMBER 5   MARCH/APRIL/1970 $1.00

Ramblin' with Jack Elliott.

Elliott on the front cover of the March/April 1970 issue of Sing Out! *magazine.* Author's Collection

Hartford, Connecticut, August 21, 1988.
Author's Collection

Hartford, Connecticut, August 21, 1988.
Author's Collection

Outside the Half Moon, Putney, London, July 22, 1991. Photographer: Robert Wylie

Concert program book for Legends of Folk Music, *Westport, Connecticut, May 14, 1994.* Author's Collection

Advertisement for South Coast *CD.*

Pleasance Bar, Edinburgh, Scotland, February 17, 2005. Photographer: Gordon McKerracher

Backstage in the dressing room of the Arches, Glasgow, Scotland, May 17, 2006. Photographer: Gordon McKerracher

Walking beneath the famed glass-wall railroad bridge "The Heilanman's Umbrella," Glasgow, Scotland, May 17, 2006. Photographer: Gordon McKerracher

"Backstage at the Borderline, London, May 16, 2006. Photographer: Alain Fournier

Promotional photograph from the Red House Records Press Kit for South Coast *(1995, RHR CD 59).* Michael Crouser

Reason to Believe   6

IN THE MONTHS PRIOR TO THE RELEASE of *Bull Durham Sacks & Railroad Tracks*, Jack seemed uncharacteristically excited about the artistic and commercial prospects of the album. In November 1969, he was traveling by car, with *Sing Out!* writer Bob Atkinson, to Pete and Toshi Seeger's home on the Hudson River in Beacon, New York. Pete was in London, but Elliott found singer-songwriter and *Clearwater* mate Don McLean (of "American Pie" fame) visiting with Toshi. Elliott had been carrying around a test pressing of *Bull Durham* and played it for McLean and the others. Atkinson reported that everyone agreed the LP was "a fantastic example of what happens at a recording studio when things are left to just happen." Elliott was so enthused he offered, "It's the first time I'm really *there*; I've never been able to get *me* onto a record before." Elliott told *Sing Out!* that the *Bull Durham* album was "the only one out of twenty seven others that he likes and would recommend to anyone."[1]

Few would share that sentiment. Even when measured against Elliott's own back catalog of generally eccentric studio albums, *Bull Durham Sacks & Railroad Tracks* remains an anomaly. Though *Bull Durham* is, without question, the most unusual and controversial release of his career, it conversely remains Elliott's only truly *contemporary* album. Featuring songs from such friends as Johnny Cash, Bob Dylan, Tim Hardin, and Kris Kristofferson, *Bull Durham* seems a concerted effort to drag Elliott out of the dust bowl and into the present. Released in February 1970, *Bull Durham* reflected the country-rock of Dylan's *Nashville Skyline*, the Grateful Dead's *Workingman's Dead* and *American Beauty*, and Johnny Cash's best-selling concert albums from Folsom Prison and San Quentin. It would be a stretch to suggest *Bull Durham* anticipated the energy of country music's "outlaw" movement, but there were similarities. Such Austin-based "outlaws" as Willie Nelson and Waylon Jennings had slipped from Nashville's musical straitjacket. They were not stripping country music of its heart, only of its bloated and schmaltzy, Chet Atkin's country-pop orchestrations. By fusing the best elements of rock and country with blues and jazz, the Texans were giving country music a much-needed reinvigoration. The "outlaw" country movement also enjoyed a certain rebel chic among a cabal of more enlightened rock music fans and critics.[2]

Bull Durham kicked off promisingly with a galloping bass riff that slid easily into a jaunty take on Kris Kristofferson's "Me and Bobby McGee." On most of the album, Jack sings from the chest in a rich baritone, modulating throughout. A blues-drenched reinterpretation of Cash's "Folsom Prison Blues" is another highlight, the emphasis on the flattened, bluesy aspect of the song only hinted at in Cash's original version. Tim Hardin's small but celebrated catalog of original songs is once again revisited, Elliott offering a perfectly gentle, wistful version of "Reason to Believe," which sounds an awful lot like Rod Stewart's own version released a year later. "I'll Be Your Baby Tonight," recorded two years earlier by Dylan for his ruminative, meditative, and mystical *John Wesley Harding* album, gets the full Nashville treatment on *Bull Durham*, Elliott reimagining the simple and sparse love ballad as a bona fide honky-tonk outtake from *Nashville Skyline*. "Don't Let Your Deal Go Down" is little more than a toss away, as it appears only in fragmentary form, but fans are at least treated to a showcasing of Jack's bluegrass-style guitar skills. If side one had ended there, the first act of *Bull Durham* would have been considered a perfunctory success. Unfortunately, Bob Johnston bafflingly closed the side with the self-indulgent, quasi-psychedelic "spoken-word" (for lack of a better term) track "We Come Here Not Chicago Dutchland for the Alles Brink Hoof Geslaffen Mocker." The track begins with a brief segment of studio chatter captured on microphone, not too dissimilar to the album's earlier "Rapping and Rambling" intercessions. Arlo Guthrie had recently done the same thing, albeit more tastefully, prior to his performance of Mississippi John Hurt's "My Creole Belle" on his *Running Down the Road* album. As side one winds down, Elliott is heard giving a halting recitation of "One Too Many Mornings," a lonesome lament featured on Dylan's *The Times They Are A-Changin'* album of 1963. In February 1969, Dylan had recorded a far less ethereal, more countrified, version with Johnny Cash, and the song was clearly on Elliott's mind. But on *Bull Durham*, Jack's recitation is soon swallowed into a swampy pool of echo and reverb. It quickly descends into an offensive, anarchic cacophony of pidgin German and cries of "Seig, Heil!"[3]

Side two opens more promisingly, with Elliott "Rapping and Rambling" about the events that caused him to learn "Don't Think Twice, It's All Right" from a friend's copy of the *The Freewheelin' Bob Dylan*. But as Elliott had already waxed his definitive rendition of the song on *Young Brigham*, the belated introduction on *Bull Durham* was, at best, two years too late. The spoken word preface does, arguably, serve some thematic purpose, dovetailing neatly into the triad of Dylan songs that follow. "Lay Lady Lay" is near-perfectly realized, ringing with lush acoustic guitars and the tasteful accents of Pete Drake's electrified pedal steel. On "Girl from the North Country," Elliott mused that he rescored the song's guitar setting to C, as on *Freewheelin'* Dylan played "it in G on the record, but that's not the right key for my voice." There were other more practical, musically salient reasons that Elliott changed the song's original key. He notes that in C the second chord in the progression moves into "an E minor, which *I know how to play*. . . . They had a B minor chord in there and I've had a lot of trouble learning a B minor chord." Elliott's version is an interesting one as the song is performed almost as a dramatic recitation. Elliott's Beat-era style recitation effectively brings out the melancholic poetry of the original Dylan lyric. It remains among the most unusual, but perhaps best, of Elliott's many reinterpretations of Dylan's classic songs. "Tramp on the Street" follows, a song first recorded for Prestige-International on the album *Ramblin' Jack Elliott*. On *Bull Durham*, Elliott provides a satisfactory, but workman-like, performance of no great note. Jelly Roll Morton's "Michigan Water Blues"/"Don't You Leave Me Here" follows, Elliott seamlessly coupling the fragments for an interesting demonstration of flat-picked guitar blues. This sojourn is followed by yet another pointless "Rapping and Rambling" intercession, Jack attempting to learn the provenance of the song "Blue Mountain." The album closes with the ballad "With God on Our Side," another classic song from the pen of protest-era Dylan. Elliott's version, though suitably plaintive, is hardly representative of the song's merit; five of the nine verses have been pruned from Dylan's original version, with the song now losing its agit-prop potency due to the culling of the lyric.[4]

Reprise made an attempt to market Jack's album in a more aggressive fashion than it had for *Young Brigham*. The publicity department at Warner Bros. took out a full page ad in *Sing Out!* ("Brooklyn's Foremost Cowboy," the ad touted, with Jack's Stetson-topped head transposed on the shoulders of the Statue of Liberty). There was also a double-page spread in the trades featuring a worshipful letter from a fan. A four-page profile on Elliott ran in the less than cerebral, but widely distributed, tabloid magazine *Country-Western Stars*, alongside such lightweight features as "The Truth about Bobbie Gentry's Marriage" and "June and Johnny Cash: How Their Baby Is Changing Their Lives." On the eve of *Bull Durham*'s release, Reprise issued a 60-second radio spot to those radio stations featuring a sympathetic format. The promotional disc featured Elliott deftly finger-picking his way through Dylan's "Don't Think Twice, It's All Right," offering Jack's wistfully remembered spoken-word preface from *Bull Durham* as narration. John Hartford, the derby-topped songwriter and banjo player, was brought in to contribute his own folksy touch to the commercial. This was helpful as Hartford was currently enjoying a high media profile due to the success of "Gentle on My Mind" and for his frequent guest appearances on the popular television variety program *The Glen Campbell Show*. The *Bull Durham* radio commercial was followed by a second promotional item, a white label radio-only 45-rpm disc featuring "Me and Bobby McGee" as the A side and "Girl of the North Country" as the B side. A commercial stock copy of the same 45-rpm single was issued soon after to little public notice or commercial effect.[5]

Reprise label mate Arlo Guthrie was drafted to write the liner notes for *Bull Durham*. It is unclear what he *really* thought of the new album. Arlo had only recently released his third album for the label, *Running Down the Road*, which featured Woody's "Oklahoma Hills" and his own Woodstock anthem "Coming into Los Angeles." Like his old friend Jack Elliott, Arlo was mixing and blending disparate musical styles, juxtaposing delicate readings of such material as Mississippi John Hurt's "My Creole Belle" and Pete Seeger's "Living in the Country" with the grungy psychedelic electric guitar feedback cacophony of the title track. It is likely that Arlo's notes for *Bull Durham* were as thoughtfully crafted as his album. Although he did not offer any direct criticism of Jack's latest LP, the younger Guthrie did not particularly wax prosaic about it either. Arlo began his notes: "This obviously is the back of Ramblin' Jack's Album, but Ramblin' Jack has never been captured by an album before and most likely he never will be." As an opening salvo, Arlo's assessment was probably not the sort of blessing the publicity staff at Reprise had imagined.[6]

The reviews of *Bull Durham* were, to say the least, mixed. *Sing Out!* offered an almost apologist take on the album: "Jack by his very nature could never make a 'perfect' record in the usual sense. The looseness, the recklessness, the imperfections are what make Jack Elliott and this record such joys." But *Rolling Stone* found absolutely nothing joyful about Elliott's latest and launched the following missile: "Somebody has convinced Ramblin' Jack Elliott, who is surely one of America's greatest living folksingers, to get very, very drunk and record an album with some people who sound like the dregs of Nashville's studio musicians. The whole package is an affront to one sensibilities [sic] . . . and one gets the distinct impression that Ramblin' Jack is being cruelly mocked. A very ugly record." The album wasn't *that* bad, but *Rolling Stone* had been doling out a lot of rough press to albums produced by Bob Johnston. Dylan's new double album effort on Columbia, *Self-Portrait* (released June 8, 1970), mostly recorded in Nashville under the aegis of Johnston, had been famously raked over the coals by critic Greil Marcus, who opened his review with the question "What is this shit?"[7]

To help promote *Bull Durham*, Ed Pearl booked Elliott for a weeklong residency at the Ash Grove, stretching from February 24 through March 1. On the very night U.S. newspapers reported that the Chicago 7 were free on bail and the war in Vietnam was continuing to rage, Jack wistfully prefaced Woody's "Talking Sailor" as "a song from the late, great World War II," remembering, "We were knights in shining armor then." The *Los Angeles Times* noted Elliott was, at heart, a "fundamentally undisciplined" musician, but marveled at his "unique ability to take the songs of Woody Guthrie . . . and transform what might otherwise be sheer nostalgia into contemporary relevance."[8]

"A lot of people wonder what Jack Elliott's doing at a Blues festival," offered one emcee, on Saturday, April 4, the third and final day of the 1970 Berkeley Blues Festival. "It's very simple," he continued. "Happened to see him a couple of months ago and decided we just had to bring him to Berkeley." Jack was the odd man out at this blues-drenched, once-in-a-lifetime event, which included Big Mama Thornton, Sonny Terry and Brownie McGhee, Bukka White, Jesse Fuller, Robert Pete Williams, Furry Lewis, T-Bone Walker, Reverend Robert Wilkins, Reverend Gary Davis, the Georgia Sea Isle Singers, K. C. Douglas, and Luther Allison. The souvenir program justified Elliott's presence by offering that as "friends with many older bluesmen, Jack Elliott has popularized many of their songs." Elliott ambled onstage to near rapturous applause; *Rolling Stone* would note, with some sarcasm, the "white kids who'd come out to hear the blues in Berkeley loved Jack Elliott the best, and that, perhaps, was inevitable, having something to do with 'roots.'" He fittingly launched into the well-worn blues couplet "Michigan Water Blues"/"Don't You Leave Me Here."[9]

Ramblin' Jack was scheduled to perform on Saturday night's closing bill, sandwiched between Oakland's own L. C. "Good Rockin'" Robinson and the Georgia Sea Isle Singers. *Rolling Stone* reported, with cynicism, that although the nation's best and most authentic blues artists had been showcased that weekend, the mostly white audience reserved "the best reception . . . for Jack Elliott." *Rolling Stone* described Elliott as "a method folksinger," "a pretty good guitar player," and an "authentically lousy singer." The response from the *New York Times* was muted; they described Elliott's set as "fine" but, ultimately, "anticlimactic."[10]

If the news accounts were grudging in their praise, Reprise Records was, undoubtedly, happy with the set that Jack delivered that afternoon. Two-thirds of the songs performed had been lifted from his two most recent albums for the label. But Elliott's brewing schism with Warner Bros. was coming to the fore. In his prefatory comments to "Me and Bobby McGee," Elliott allowed for a moment of cynicism when he offered, "Somebody told me that I wasn't going to be here tonight. . . . They heard it on the radio. Well, you can't believe everything you hear on the radio." Then, after a long, reflective pause, Elliott coolly noted, "I may get here yet." The audience laughed, but Elliott continued on, taking an unsubtle shot at Warner's distribution system. "Here's a little thing I recorded. Should be out shortly in the stores. . . . May even already be out. . . . It was released about two months ago."[11]

Following the blues festival, Elliott climbed into his Volkswagen bus and made his way to Chicago's Quiet Knight, where he had been booked for a lengthy residency beginning April 8 and concluding 11 days later. It was a long haul from California and his fatigue was apparent during his opening-night performance. The *Chicago Tribune* reported that Elliott arrived in the Windy City "less than beady eyed and bushy tailed" but soon found himself "revivified" after a tumbler of tequila found its way to him onstage. The *Tribune* also admitted that watching Elliott onstage in 1970 was nothing if not a "weird, anachronistic delight." Jack eventually settled down and, on the last night of his residency, a writer from *Billboard* stopped by to report that Elliott "won the crowd over with his easy manner and fine singing." Obviously not an informed critic, the *Billboard* scribe went on to describe Elliott's guitar work, somewhat dubiously, as "not up to the caliber of Guthrie."[12]

Jack continued to tour in support of *Bull Durham*, traveling to New York City for a series of shows at the Village Gaslight. Kris Kristofferson, a friend whose career as a recording artist and film actor was blossoming, met Elliott in Manhattan and invited him down to the A & R Recording Studio to listen to the final mixes of *Ned Kelly*, the soundtrack album of his latest film. Elliott and Kristofferson spent a good deal of the week together, visiting with the author and songwriter Shel Silverstein and attending a number of Kris's scheduled photo shoots. Kristofferson was being profiled by a *New York Times* freelancer, and one night, after Elliott excused himself to head off to his gig at the Gaslight, Kris watched as he disappeared from sight. He told the writer in no uncertain terms that Ramblin' Jack was "one of the greats."[13]

Following the Guthrie memorial concerts at Carnegie Hall in January 1968, Woody's fans on the West Coast were feeling slighted. Harold Leventhal agreed that a second Guthrie celebration should be arranged, and on September 12, 1970, the Hollywood Bowl hosted a West Coast version of "A Musical Tribute to Woody Guthrie." Though Dylan, to the disappointment of many, chose to pass on this second tribute, the program suffered no shortage of folk and folk-rock stars. Joan Baez, Jack Elliott, Arlo Guthrie, Richie Havens, Country Joe McDonald, Odetta, Earl Robinson, and Pete Seeger had all agreed to perform, with the proceeds, again, to benefit the Committee to Combat Huntington's Disease. Will Geer returned to bridge the musical performances with recitations of Guthrie's prose. Peter Fonda, the actor, fresh from his *Easy Rider* success, assisted Geer with the spoken-word segments.

The Hollywood Bowl concert would signal the final, official send-off for Guthrie. For Jack Elliott, Woody was, increasingly, a figure in the rearview mirror. This is not to say that Elliott had abandoned his songs or forgotten his inspiration. He told *Guitar Player* magazine, "I have always created my own sources, but I still sing Woody's songs. . . . People don't think I'm imitating Woody, I still feel like I am in a way . . . like he's looking over my shoulder." Elliott's musical refocus, a shift from the old-school songs of Guthrie and Cisco and Jimmie Rodgers to the songs of contemporary songwriters, was not something new. He had recorded Dylan's "Don't Think Twice, It's All Right" in Vanguard's studios not long after the song was written. Though Vanguard chose not to release Elliott's version, the fact that the song was recorded at all was a clear indication that Elliott was already beginning to explore the work of his friends, the new "city" songwriters. Not everyone agreed that Elliott's experiments with contemporary songs made the best use of his gifts. Izzy Young believed that once Elliott made the decision to become an *interpreter* of contemporary singer-songwriters, the quality of his music and performances suffered. Izzy sighed, it was only after Elliott "started singing Bob Dylan songs" that he "gave up" on his old friend.[14]

Though some old-timers were not happy that Elliott's music had changed, Jack had been cultivating a new generation of admirers, musicians who respected him as an artist in his own right. In England, many young practitioners of skiffle passed through folk music and folk-blues to establish international reputations as rock 'n' roll performers. Rod Stewart, whose smoke-tinged vocals more than hinted at Jack's influence, was a big fan as a young man. Stewart told *Rolling Stone* he would not be nervous about meeting Dylan, but would be absolutely "awestruck in front of Jack Elliott." Elliott recalled a time when Stewart, already an established and wildly successful rock 'n' roll singer, cornered him under a folding umbrella at a beach party, serenading him with "ten or fifteen old Jack Elliott tunes" that he had learned off his old Topic records. Elliott was honored since Stewart "knew them perfectly and . . . did them exactly the way I used to do them back then." But he also found the episode to be embarrassing, as the rock legend "sang them like I used to sing them and I think I'm a little better singer now." Mick Jagger of the Rolling Stones described Jack as "one of my earliest inspirations." In a Toronto hotel room, Jagger told Elliott he first heard Jack's music as a child. Jagger and his schoolmates had listened wide-eyed as Stetson-topped Jack Elliott busked for change on a busy railroad platform near Jagger's hometown. Jagger's band mate Keith Richards was in his second year of art school when he walked into the school's water closet to find "three guys sitting around playing a guitar, doing Woody Guthrie and Ramblin' Jack Elliott stuff." It was through Jack and Woody and the disciples left in their wake that Richards would develop his passion for American blues artists, such as Jesse Fuller and Big Bill Broonzy. In January 1991, Beatle Paul McCartney appeared on the popular MTV music series *Unplugged* before a television audience of millions. McCartney prefaced his take of "San Francisco Bay Blues" with the somewhat cheeky comment he had learned the song off "a record that I had by Ramblin' Jack Elliott, son of T. S." Donovan Leitch, better known simply as "Donovan," was yet another great fan of Jack Elliott and Derroll Adams. As a young man, Donovan had been taken by the records he had heard of Woody Guthrie. When the word had spread throughout London music circles about Ramblin' Jack's engagement at the Peacock folk club, Donovan sought out Woody's finest protégé, sitting, worshipfully, "at Jack's feet, with a pint, and try to figure out how it was done."[15]

He was revered by American musicians as well. The folkies held him in high esteem, of course, but he also befriended members of the Grateful Dead, forming long-lasting friendships with Bob Weir and Jerry Garcia. Garcia shared the same August 1 birthday as Elliott, and respected Jack's music and the cultural history that surrounded him. Elliott's mentorship with Guthrie gave him a certain cache that very few singers could boast of and undeniably boosted his own legend. But to the free-spirited Aquarian generation, Elliott's nomadic and seemingly untethered lifestyle was equally celebrated. Elliott was, at this time in his career, regarded more as a West Coast artist than a Greenwich Village folkie. He had lost touch with what was happening in New York folk circles and, with the notable exception of an entertaining profile published in the March/April 1970 issue of *Sing Out!* he had pretty much disappeared from the pages of the magazine for the duration of the 1970s. As a resident of California, Elliott played as many local gigs as his schedule allowed and audience demand would permit, performing at the Berkeley Folk Festival in October 1970 and at the Matrix on November 20 and 21. That is not to say Elliott ignored New York City. Two days following that last Matrix show, Elliott was onstage at the Anderson Theater on Manhattan's Lower East Side, sitting in with the Grateful Dead and playing mouth harp. It seemed as if Ramblin' Jack was floating between disparate musical worlds.[16]

This was never more apparent than in January 1971, when he returned to Nashville's Ryman Auditorium to tape his second guest spot on Johnny Cash's ABC television show. He was among a handful of musical artists who could hang comfortably among both the long-haired disciples of the Grateful Dead and the unnaturally coiffed and chiffon-gowned Carter Family Singers. Cash, too, was an independent spirit, always pushing the envelope and trying to book nonmainstream musical guests on his hit television show. June Carter offered at the beginning of the January 6 program, "We really have a nice show tonight. I'm excited about it because it kind of reflects the whole music scene today." Cash agreed, adding, "There's somebody for everybody tonight. Some really great artists that you don't get to see on television all that often." This was not conflated opinion: featured on Cash's program were Greenwich Village songwriter Eric Andersen, the cornpone music and comedy team of Homer and Jethro, country music chanteuse Connie Smith, Ramblin' Jack Elliott, and two guitar-slinging outfits of the highest order, the Tennessee Three with Carl Perkins, and Derek and the Dominos featuring Eric Clapton. If Elliott's first appearance on the show in 1969 was only half-transcendent, his second turn would more than make up for it. Cash introduced Jack as "a young fellow that's rambled here, he's rambled there, he's rambled everywhere. We're glad he rambled back to be with us." Following that introduction, the cameras swung to an adjoining stage where, dressed in jeans, tie-dyed pullover, cowboy hat, and racked blues harp, a bespectacled Elliott launched confidently into "Muleskinner Blues." Elliott was accompanied by a trio of Nashville's finest session players, including guitarist

Norman Blake and five-string banjo picker Randy Scruggs (the son of Earl Scruggs). Jack held the final yodel of the song for nearly 38 seconds, moving the country music traditionalists at the Ryman to rapturous applause. He returned to the West Coast and on February 18 and 19, performed for an audience of flower children at San Francisco's Matrix.[17]

Ed Pearl of the Ash Grove had a long interest in folk music and politics, but feared the audiences who visited his nightclub thought the music was little more than cabaret fare. In April 1971, Pearl organized an ambitious month-long series titled "Miners, Mines and Music." The idea was to offer a multimedia presentation that would bring together films, taped speeches, vintage and contemporary photographs, music performances, and discussion groups to examine the history and continuing struggles of the mining community. Pearl launched the series on April 20 with Ramblin' Jack (whom the *Los Angeles Times* was fast to point out was an apprentice to "Woody Guthrie, whose music was heavily tied to social comment") and the Morris Brothers, deemed the "official balladeers" of Joseph Yablonski's campaign to take control of the United Mine Worker's Union. The program was such a success that Pearl arranged a second miner's program featuring Mike Seeger and Sara Ogan Gunning, half-sister of Aunt Molly Jackson, who had taught Pete Seeger and others such songs as "Girl of Constant Sorrow" and "I Hate the Capitalist System."[18]

In the summer of 1971, the Los Angeles PBS affiliate KCET made plans to produce a series of nine 30-minute television programs documenting an assortment of "in studio" performances by local musicians. The series was to be called *Boboquivari*, reportedly a term used by the Papago tribe of Arizona to describe the narrow canyon that formed where a grouping of large mountains joined together. Freddie King, the Texas blues guitarist, and his band were the first performers on the program, succeeded in the following weeks by Tim Buckley, the Sir Douglas Quintet, Roberta Flack, Lightnin' Hopkins, the Roger Kellaway Cello Quartet, Kris Kristofferson, Odetta, and Ramblin' Jack. Elliott was chosen to perform on the final program since it was the producer's opinion that he represented a dying tradition. "Most of the songs that Elliott sings have been handed down orally from garage mechanics, hobos, cowboys, workers and other singers—people he met during his travels," the PBS press release informed prospective affiliates. The release also warned station general managers that Ramblin' Jack's program would differ from the first eight, and more conventional, installments of *Boboquivari*: "Elliott . . . is as unpredictable in his delivery as an 'authentic folksinger' should be. His *Boboquivari* performance, during which he starts singing one song, changes his mind and starts another, then abandons the microphone to wander into the audience and tell some of his rambling tales, is no different."[19]

Though television was no longer an anathema to Elliott, it was surprising to see his performance on *Boboquivari* turn out as well as it did. He opened with a spirited romp through Kristofferson's "Me and Bobbie McGee," responding to the strong, enthusiastic applause with the caution "Careful about that clapping. . . . Ain't too good for your hands. Especially if you been out there picking cotton or . . . driving a truck or something like that." His second song was Molly O'Day's "Tramp on the Street," the old chestnut he had waxed for both Prestige-International and Warner Bros. Elliott next smiled warmly and looked shyly at the studio audience sitting cross-legged on the floor before him. "I'm glad you could come," he drawled. "I didn't have a chance to hardly call up a lot of friends of mine. I just got into town this afternoon. . . . Seems most of them are here anyway." Though in control, Elliott appeared a little uncomfortable under the bright television lights, the center of a tangle of cables and cameras and microphones. Elliott noted some of his discomfort during the performance: "I live up in the country and we don't have cameras and machinery and stuff like that. . . . Every time I get near telephone wires, highways now . . . I feel the weirdness of the machinery and them cats that operate the machinery." During the taping an audience member took note of Jack's oversized belt buckle that featured a Diesel Semi. "I didn't get that buckle for show business reasons," Elliott assured the fan. "I got that buckle because I'm crazy about trucks." Guthrie's "Talking Dust Bowl," Hardin's "If I Were a Carpenter," and Elliott's own "912 Greens" rounded out the set, and the taping went pretty well, all things considered.[20]

Though *Bull Durham Sacks & Railroad Tracks* would be the last freshly minted Ramblin' Jack album for some time, that did not mean that "new" albums bearing his name were not being stocked in record shops. In 1971, the U.K.-based Marble Arch Records licensed the rights to distribute a copy of the 1959 release *Ramblin' Jack Elliott in London*. As that earlier LP had long since fallen out of print, the Marble Arch edition, titled, simply, *Ramblin' Jack Elliott*, was a thinly disguised sham, repackaged to resemble a new release with no revised notes to establish that it consisted entirely of previously issued material. To further enhance the deception, the reissue featured a cover design unique to the edition, an uncredited and contemporary psychedelic pastiche of the Henry Diltz photograph of Elliott featured on the rear sleeve of *Young Brigham*.

In late June 1971, he was in New York City to attend the Madison Square Garden Championship Rodeo. Afterward, Jack was to set off for the Mariposa Folk Festival in Toronto, Canada, the second weekend in July. Elliott had brought along an old friend, David Amram, the musicologist and colleague of the late Jack Kerouac. As the two friends chatted and watched the cowboys run through their bruising paces, Amram filled the empty intervals by sketching out lyrics to a new song, "Going North," on the back of the rodeo program book. The song was a celebration of Elliott's "Going North" to Mariposa, and Amram brought his folk-singing friend into the studio to record the song, later featured on the album *No More Walls*.[21]

On January 12, 1972, Columbia Records issued *A Tribute to Woody Guthrie, Part One*, a single LP of highlight performances culled from the January 1968 Carnegie Hall memorial concert. In April 1972, Warner issued *A Tribute to Woody Guthrie, Part Two*, a second LP documenting the Guthrie tribute at the Hollywood Bowl in September 1970. (It wasn't until 1976 that the two LPs were, sensibly, brought together as a set on the Warner Bros. label.) The early reviews of the album were generally favorable, with Nat Hentoff writing at some length about the disc in the *New York Times*. Though Elliott once fretted he "had a feeling that Nat Hentoff was not a friend of mine," the sometimes acerbic critic wrote that although "the results are not all incandescent," the outstanding performers were "Dylan, Seeger, Arlo Guthrie and Jack Elliott. The latter, who worked so long to be Woody's mirror image, has grown into himself, thereby making his tribute all the more affecting." Ira Meyer of *Sing Out!* thought the album was something less than the sum of its parts, that it would be best to hear the original Guthrie versions. Meyer's lukewarm appraisal wasn't critical enough to satisfy folksinger and *Sing Out!* editorial board advisor Michael Cooney. In his review, Cooney railed against Baez and Collins for singing too sweetly, at Odetta and Collins (again) for being overly emotive, and at Dylan and Arlo for "competing for 'Farthest-Out Screaming Rock Arrangement.'" Only Pete Seeger, Earl Robinson, and Elliott were spared Cooney's wrath, as, in his opinion, these three friends of Woody's intuitively knew "how to stay out of the way of a song."[22]

If Elliott knew how to stay out of the way of a song, he also had a talent for staying clear of strong record sales. He toured incessantly, playing taverns and festivals, coffeehouses and concerts, but in the 1970s there was rarely a new product to promote. It hardly mattered. Elliott seldom carried boxes of LPs to sell at concerts and almost never talked about records or recording sessions or did a hard sell from the stage. He continued to make a nominal living, traveling the backwaters and cities for a night or two before moving on, never staying long in one place. In 1972, Elliott embarked on a tour of Australia with singer-songwriter Cat Stevens, commencing at Brisbane's Festival Hall on August 24, and concluding on September 11 at the WACA in Perth, with visits to Sydney, Melbourne, and Adelaide in the interim. An Australian rock music news magazine reported that Elliott "was added to the *Zimmering* concerts because Stevens' [sic] wanted Jack to replace Alun Davies' [sic] spot of opening the show." Davies was Stevens's lead guitarist and "Cat Stevens is apparently a perfectionist so he thought Jack was more appropriate." Things went so well that, after a three-and-a-half-week break, Elliott was brought back for the tour's second leg through the United States and Canada, commencing at the Shrine Auditorium in Los Angeles on September 29 and concluding on November 12 at Toronto's Massey Hall, with visits to New York City, Miami Beach, Tampa, Chicago, Cleveland, and South Bend, Indiana.[23]

Though the tour with Stevens was relatively profitable for Jack, it was also a time when his musical ego was severely tested. Stevens's career was at its commercial peak and many of the concerts were large venue affairs, with audiences comprised mostly of rock 'n' roll fans who knew Cat from such AM hits as "Wild World," "Moonshadow," "Peace Train," and "Morning Has Broken." As his opening act, Jack appeared nightly onstage before rows of empty chairs or, perhaps worse, seats filled with indifferent, gossiping rock fans restless to see the main event. The *Los Angeles Times* made note that the audience at the Shrine "was so ready for Stevens that it seemed to totally ignore Ramblin' Jack Elliott's twenty minute opening set." Things apparently got a bit better the second night at the Shrine. Describing him as "a tiny, well-worn gnome of a man," *Billboard* reported that Elliott started off the evening "with a much appreciated mini-set" consisting of songs culled from the records of Dylan and Kristofferson "rather than the old trail songs that usually characterize his appearance." In the Windy City, the *Chicago Tribune* described the Stevens/Elliott pairing as "unfortunate." Though Jack did his best to connect to the crowd, the *Tribune* suggested that an arena "was neither the time nor place for him. It's amazing that he stuck it out as long as he did." When Jack announced to the crowd that he was signing off, the audience burst rudely into cheers. *Melody Maker* of England sent a correspondent to the show in Miami Beach to catch Cat's set. Reporting that "It was good to see Ramblin' Jack Elliott again," the correspondent noted he had not changed much over the years, continuing to draw from the songbooks of Woody Guthrie, Bob Dylan, and Kris Kristofferson. Elliott was not able to take the stage at New York's Philharmonic Hall as he had fallen ill, replaced at the last minute by an otherwise anonymous brother and sister singing duo.[24]

Jack returned to the welcoming bosom of the Ash Grove in January 1973. He performed best in a more relaxed and intimate setting, where hipper, more attentive audiences hung on his every word. But the advent of the New Year did not bring anything fresh to the set list. As always there was "San Francisco Bay Blues," "House of the Rising Sun," "Don't Think Twice, It's All Right," "I'll Be Your Baby Tonight," "Reason to Believe," and "If I Were a Carpenter." Though the program was nothing if not familiar, Jack remained one of Ash Grove's favorite performers, never more so than when he would casually stroll through the rows of small tables, carrying his guitar chest high, intimately serenading those in the audience. Jack often made this trademark stroll near the end of the program, occasionally walking straight outside and into his waiting mini-bus. One newspaper marveled at Elliott's ability to "stroll through the audience and sing right into the customer's eyes" as he did this night at the Ash Grove, concluding the program with "If I Were a Carpenter." The *Los Angeles Times* reported, quite accurately, that Elliott's performance of the song "generates a depth of feeling that Bobby Darin, and perhaps even [Tim] Hardin, never dreamed of." Referencing Jack's recent tour, critic Richard Cromelin wrote, "it's nice to imagine the day when Cat Stevens will be supporting Jack Elliott on a national tour, instead of vice versa."[25]

On January 23, Elliott was scheduled to appear at a high-profile multi-tiact concert event at the State University in Manhattan, Kansas. The concert was designed to celebrate the music and influence of bluegrass banjo legend Earl Scruggs and would feature the Earl Scruggs Revue, as well as many of Earl's youthful disciples and friends: Joan Baez, David Bromberg, the Byrds, Ramblin' Jack, Tracy Nelson and Mother Earth, Doc and Merle Watson, and the Nitty Gritty Dirt Band. Producers Robert French, Richard G. Abramson, and Michael C. Varhol were planning to document the concert on 16-mm film. Elliott flew into Kansas, but upon his arrival it was clear he was a little worse for wear. Though suffering laryngitis, Elliott told the filmmakers, "This is one time that I *had* to sing, I *wanted* to sing and there wasn't *no way* I wasn't going to sing." Backed by guitarist David Bromberg, Elliott bravely soldiered through a short set that included a hoarse but inspired "Me and Bobby McGee" and a gentle reading of "912 Greens." The resulting concert film, *Banjoman*, premiered at the John F. Kennedy Center for the Performing Arts in Washington, D.C., in 1975. Though the low-budget film spawned a pleasant soundtrack album, the documentary was never picked up for national release and soon disappeared.[26]

On March 17, Jack signed on to support the New Riders of the Purple Sage at the band's Saturday night concert at the University of New York, Stonybrook. The Long Island concert was merely a warmup for the big event the following night in New York City. On Sunday evening, Elliott and the New Riders were scheduled to join the Grateful Dead for their sold-out concert at Madison Square Garden's Felt Forum. The concert was to be broadcast live on WNEW-FM, New York City's premier rock 'n' roll radio station. As was the case with the Cat Stevens tour, Elliott was game for the challenge but, once again, clearly out of his element. He opened his set with "Salt Pork, West Virginia," possibly the most rock 'n' roll–sounding song of his repertoire, but was greeted with only lukewarm applause. After a totally unacknowledged run through of the old chestnut "Anytime," Elliott gazed around the Forum, a 3,500-seat theater in the basement of the Madison Square Garden complex. Referencing the rodeos he had attended at the Garden as a child, Elliott remarked, "You know, it's a real gas for me to be here in this particular building [though] it was the old Madison Square Garden that bent my head." It wasn't the same. He was caught awkwardly between two eras. He peered out from beneath the brim of his Stetson at an arena filled with long-haired hippies in tie-dyed shirts, rather than horses and cowboys. Perhaps unwisely, Elliott began to play through the elongated, spoken-word monologue that was "Cup of Coffee." But he sensed almost immediately that his choice was a complete miscalculation and wound the song down abruptly. He gamely attempted to get through to the young, rock 'n' roll audience with songs he thought might be familiar to them: Dylan's "Don't Think Twice, It's All Right" and "I'll Be Your Baby Tonight," and "House of the Rising Sun," a traditional song charted by Eric Burdon and the Animals. The problem was the capacity audience at the Felt Forum was looking forward to the Grateful Dead and the ensuing party, not a mossy old folksinger with an acoustic guitar and nostalgic memories of a 1940 rodeo. Indeed, the only song that Elliott connected with that evening was "Ain't Nobody's Business," and even then the distinguishable rise in the audience was the result of the blunt reference in the lyric to cocaine and champagne.[27]

It was a tough time. Elliott's marriage to Martha had ended and he left California for transient residencies in small towns in and around Colorado and Utah. Around this time, he was conscripted by music journalist and radio disc jockey Jay Meehan to visit the KMOR radio station in the canyon town of Murray, Utah, near Park City. Meehan was host of a program called *Mellow Country*, but the show was really built around the music that would later be described as "Americana," a roots-orientated mix of folk, delta blues, classic honky-tonk, bluegrass, singer-songwriter, and the music of the fermenting Austin scene. Meehan was part of a contingent of displaced Los Angeles young people who had relocated to Park City, hoping to build an artistic and musical community of fellow free spirits. Elliott was a frequent visitor to the cattle ranch of the family of Grateful Dead lyricist John Barlow near Cora, Wyoming. It was at the Barlow ranch that he met a young woman and local "Deadhead," affectionately known as Muffin, who brought the folksinger to meet the residents of Park City. Muffin introduced Elliott to Meehan, and Meehan introduced Elliott to the saloons of Park City where, he was promised, singing and tequila were plentiful. Elliott was no stranger to the residents. Meehan remembered, "During the 60s many of us had become huge Jack Elliott fans and had taken in his act at the Ash Grove, Golden Bear and various other L.A. folk and blues venues. When word spread that Jack was staying among the faithful . . . it was a pretty big deal for all of us."[28]

Meehan occasionally hosted "in studio" performances by local folk and country music artists, setting up chairs, microphones, and a beer-filled cooler for the visiting artists. Elliott agreed to visit KMOR, but Meehan found the legendary Ramblin' Jack to be "defensive and somewhat brooding. . . . He still had obvious issues over Dylan and not getting the credit he thought he deserved from the mentoring process." But once Elliott's voice went out over the airwaves, the small studio fast became crowded. Initially, Meehan remembered, a "half-dozen or so street aficionados," had come along and found "comfort zone niches along the walls," but once he began to perform, the true Ramblin' Jack fans, "off duty cab drivers, bar keeps and bikers . . . began filtering in." Among the visitors was Guthrie Thomas, a singer-songwriter and guitarist, recently signed to RCA on the recommendation of Hoyt Axton. Thomas would later finagle a stint as music coordinator for Hal Ashby's production of the Woody Guthrie bio-pic *Bound for Glory*, attempting, unsuccessfully, to teach David Carradine how to play and sing in the Guthrie style. Elliott was a friend of Thomas's, having penned the notes to his *Sitting Crooked* LP. Guthrie, who was a pretty good guitar player, had brought along his instrument, and he and Elliott traded songs throughout the broadcast. Muffin had the foresight to slip a reel-to-reel tape onto the machine to capture some of what went down that evening. Afterward, Thomas asked for a dub of the recording, of which a half album of material was excerpted, pressed onto vinyl, and sold, without Elliott's consent or authorization, at Thomas's gigs as *Dear Ginny*. Elliott was not pleased when he learned of the album's existence, though the pressing reportedly ran to only 500 copies.[29]

In the summer of 1973, Elliott embarked on a short tour with John Prine, the Chicago area songwriter and an early candidate as the "new Dylan." He wasn't, but Prine shared Dylan's gifts for the cutting turn of a phrase, his best songs beautifully crafted short-story vignettes. Though his earliest albums for Atlantic had only sold in modest numbers, Prine was something of a cult favorite and a darling of the critics. Prine recalled his pairing with Ramblin' Jack and hanger-ons as a modest "tour of nothing but Colorado ski-towns . . . playing mostly to locals in movie theaters." It was the antithesis of the early winter tour with the New Riders; everything was more relaxed and folksy and unpressured. Everyone traveled together in Elliott's Winnebago, eight eccentrics and Jack's fabled car-driving dog Caesar. Prine recalled the RV was peopled with characters that seemed to have fallen "off of Ken Kesey's bus." Among those traveling with the musicians was a friend of Jack's, the comedian Kelly Green, remembered by Prine as "tall, black, and gay." Green opened each concert with a verse or two of "I'm an old cowhand from the Rio Grande." Prine couldn't help but notice that the hard-drinking "cowboys out in the front row didn't know if they liked that or not." Elliott was not too concerned; he remembered Green simply as "a good comedian" who, importantly, "knew how to keep the danger at bay." The tour soon spilled beyond Colorado's borders, Prine and Elliott scheduled to play two shows at the Egyptian Theater in Park City, Utah. Prine, his longtime manager Al Bunetta, and Elliott had flown into Salt Lake City for the gig, where they were met at the airport by a member of the advance team and Jay Meehan. Meehan recalled everyone immediately set off for the airport lounge and a marathon elbow-bending session, and by the time they arrived at the Egyptian "the promoters were irate with all of us." Though two shows had been scheduled, a decision was hastened to stage only a single concert and honor all the tickets sold.[30]

Later that summer Elliott performed before an audience of 30,000 at the first Ozark Mountain Folk Fair in Eureka Springs, Arkansas. The Ozark festival blended an interesting mélange of artists that encompassed the blues (Johnny Shines, John Lee Hooker, Big Mama Thornton, Mance Lipscomb, James Cotton), bluegrass (the Earl Scruggs Revue, Lester Flatt and the Nashville Grass, John Hartford), country-rock (Nitty Gritty Dirt Band, Ozark Mountain Daredevils), along with those more difficult to categorize (experimental guitarist Leo Kottke, singer-songwriter Loudon Wainwright III, and Ramblin' Jack). That summer Elliott returned to Burbank,

California, to tape a segment of Burt Sugarman's late-night NBC-TV music program *The Midnight Special.* The show had made its debut earlier that year, featuring an eclectic lineup of performers from the worlds of rock, folk, and soul. Elliott's episode, broadcast August 3, 1973, was no different. Soul singer Al Green was the host that evening, introducing performances by the rock band Foghat, Bobby Womack, Livingston Taylor, the Stylistics, and Freeman and Murray. Elliott, no longer concerned with promoting his Reprise catalog, returned to old favorites, romping merrily through Jesse Fuller's "San Francisco Bay Blues."[31]

In September the Metro nightclub in Greenwich Village hosted Elliott for a three-night residency. The *New York Times* sent down a reviewer who described him as "the most faithful upholder of the Woody Guthrie spirit before the public today," reminding readers of Elliott's influence on a generation of singers and poets. That same weekend, Elliott was again featured on *The Midnight Special.* This time, Seals and Crofts played host to Paul Butterfield's Better Days, Arlo Guthrie, Leo Kottke, T. Rex, and Uriah Heep. After performing two songs from his most recent records for Reprise ("Gypsy Davy" and "Bling, Blang"), Arlo brought Elliott out: "Seals and Crofts have asked me to introduce to you a good friend of mine, Ramblin' Jack Elliott. Jack's gone though, Jack's *gone.* He's *long gone.* He's gone fishing!" Indeed, he had, Elliott plunking laconically through Woody's "Talkin' Fisherman."[32]

Jack traveled to Vancouver for a residency at the Egress in late October, before returning to California for a November 4 gig as part of the California State College at Sonoma's "Bluegrass on an Autumn Afternoon" program. Jack was on the bill that afternoon as the briding act between Clover, a Mill Valley roots-rock band, and "Old and in the Way," a bluegrass-oriented side project of Grateful Dead guitarist Jerry Garcia and "Dawg" music mandolin player David Grisman. Near the concert's end, Jack was invited to join Garcia and Grisman onstage, handling lead vocal duties on "Tramp on the Street" and Jimmie Rodgers's "All Around the Water Tank," the network of Grateful Dead tapers on hand to record the collaboration for posterity.

In December 1973, *Rolling Stone* reported that Elliott was one of a "series of surprise guests" at Mickey Newbury's "Country Party Benefit" for the Pacifica radio station KPFA-FM. His performance was erratic, *Rolling Stone* reporting that Elliott was "just in from Hawaii and mildly high on acid." Later Jack was joined onstage by the singer-songwriter Tom Jans.[33]

In late January 1974, Elliott set off for a ten-day tour of Japan, with concerts planned for Tokyo, Okayama, Fukuoka, Osaka, and Kyoto. He was supported on the tour by Masato Tomobe, whom Jack later described as "the Japanese Bob Dylan," a slight, earnest young man with acoustic guitar and racked harmonica. The tour followed a more or less circular route, beginning and finishing at Tokyo's Yomiuri Hall. Bellwood Records, a subsidiary of the King Record Co., Ltd., of Tokyo, recorded both Jack's opening 12-song set of January 25 and his final 19-song concert of February 2. The first Tokyo concert went well, but he admitted to feeling somewhat "shy" onstage, concerned the language barrier might be too high a hurdle to surmount. Though renowned for his skills as a raconteur and shaggy-dog yarn spinner, Elliott would need to connect with the Japanese on the strength of his music alone. He succeeded, as the resulting live album *Ramblin' Jack Elliott—Live in Japan* attests. Sadly, no rare songs or unusual one-offs from either Tokyo concert were featured on the Bellwood release. The album, offered exclusively to the Japanese market, consisted primarily of cool revisits of Jack's best-known songs from his Prestige, Vanguard, and Reprise catalogs. This was a missed opportunity, since the Tokyo concerts included recordings of such previously unissued gems as "Salt Pork, West Virginia," Lead Belly's "Grey Goose," and Eddy Arnold's "Anytime." Other rarely performed songs, such as Dylan's "With God on Our Side," Woody's "I Ain't Got No Home," and the playful guitar instrumental "Guabi, Guabi" (all performed on January 25), were, disappointingly, left on the cutting room floor of Bellwood.[34]

There wasn't enough time built into the frenetic tour to enjoy any real sightseeing. The winter skies were grim and dismal and many of the concert venues sterile, Elliott writing that the concert in Okayama commenced in a "concrete sports stadium and cold." Following a more pleasing evening in a "modern brand new hall" in Fukuoka, Elliott, Tomobe, and crew made their way to the gray, windy coast so Jack could have the opportunity to survey the fishing boats and small islands off in the mist. By nightfall the travelers were back in Fukuoka. After enjoying a sauna and sake, Elliott was brought to an American-style western-themed nightclub called the Chuck Wagon, which featured a house band performing electrified country and western music. Jack sat in for one song, a celebrated guest of honor.[35]

In April Elliott appeared at the Golden State Bluegrass Festival in San Rafael, California. The festival played host to an impressive field of roots music talent: Norman Blake, Vassar Clements, Doug Dillard, the Greenbriar

Boys with John Herald and Frank Wakefield, Richard Greene, Emmy Lou Harris, John Hartford, Maria Muldaur, Jim and Jesse McReynolds, Ralph Stanley, and Doc and Merle Watson. Dylan's friend Bob Neuwirth was among those in attendance and he sent a dispatch to *Rolling Stone*, describing the event as "the nicest one since the Newport Folk Festival in 1964 or the famed Monterey Pop Festival of 1967." Neuwirth noted, with some surprise, that Elliott "rambled in from Motown, whipped it on 'em, got five encores, more than anyone at the festival."[36]

It is true that when Jack was on his game, there were few singers who could so successfully engage an audience predisposed to his type of folk music. The problem was that he was appearing before fewer and fewer audiences steeped in the Woody Guthrie–Cisco Houston school of American folk music. The old-timers found Elliott's Lead Belly–inspired "high singing" style and brash and powerfully stroked guitar rhythms effective and inspiring. But those with little knowledge of Lead Belly found Elliott's authentic replications odd and eccentric. He was not interested in retooling the songs for contemporary audiences.

It was a somewhat discouraging time, but the problems he faced were not always the fault of indifferent audiences. Elliott was a moody performer and, rather than try to bring a recalcitrant audience around, he often chose the path of least resistance, playing a set "for the tourists" and attempt to get through the booking on reputation alone. In February 1975, he agreed to a residency at the Main Point in Bryn Mawr, Pennsylvania. Elliott had difficulty connecting until the final night of February 15 when, following a rapturously received reading of Woody's "Talking Sailor," he scolded, "I've been waiting for three nights for you folks to come alive. . . . Fell asleep on stage a couple of nights ago," insinuating that it was the fault of the audience that things had not clicked that week.[37]

There was still plenty of work to be found, though one had to rack up more mileage between the better paying and more prestigious bookings. In the early summer of 1975, Elliott returned to Japan for a second series of concerts and a few weeks of sightseeing. Afterward he made his way back to California following a stopover on the island of Guam. But Jack's return to the States was necessarily brief. In a few days, he was due in Toronto for a performance at the 11th annual Mariposa Folk Festival. Mariposa had replaced Newport as Elliott's favorite "grand scale" folk festival. He admitted that he found the backstage atmosphere to be less competitive than Newport and was soon extolling the virtue of Mariposa's "good vibes" to colleagues. After Mariposa, he returned to the United States, steering to Cambridge, Massachusetts, for a nightclub engagement. But after the fresh air, blue skies, and green scenery of Mariposa, Elliott found Boston's brick streets to be twisted and barely navigable. He sighed, with no small measure of exasperation, that the "streets are all built on a curve so you can't find your way around no how. You'll go around in circles if you don't look out. There's not a ninety degree corner in the whole city." He next boarded a train for New York City for a three-night booking at the Other End.[38]

In February 1974, Paul Colby had opened a second nightclub adjacent to his Bitter End, calling it "the Other End." He secured both a liquor license (the Bitter End sold only coffee and ice cream treats) and an impressive roster of recording and standup comedy talent to entice audiences to visit his new club. In July 1975, the Other End played host to Tracy Nelson and Mother Earth, Jim Dawson, the comedian Martin Mull, and Glenn Yarbrough and the Limeliters. It was a new nightclub, but one with an old vibe, and it was in this spirit that Colby booked his friend Ramblin' Jack.[39]

"It's been a long time since I've been in this city," Elliott noted shortly after taking the stage. "The jet lag probably hasn't caught up with me yet." He asked for the audience's forbearance should he appear to be "talking strangely or anything. I just came through several time zones all in one day." Those gathered that evening would not be disappointed, sensing that, in some ways, Elliott had always lived in a time warp. He opened with "San Francisco Bay Blues" before moving briskly through a set of Guthrie and Dylan songs, with a little bit of the Grateful Dead thrown in for good measure. Midway through the evening's set he surprised the crowd with an extremely rare revisit of "a sentimental old song that I used to sing when I was just starting to play the guitar." He tilted into a low-key, unhurried, and perfect reading of Ernest Tubb's "Filipino Baby," a post-War-era classic of the "Texas Troubadour." Elliott closed his first night's set with Tim Hardin's "Reason to Believe," and there was every reason to believe that the following two nights at Colby's nightclub would prove to be something special.[40]

News of Elliott's appearance had circulated among the cabal of Greenwich Village folkies, and on Thursday evening, the Other End was filled to capacity with fans and well-wishers. Rosalie Sorrells, Bobby Neuwirth, Logan English, and Phil Ochs were among those celebrating Jack's return to Manhattan. Just after the lights had gone down prior to Elliott's second set, the shadow of another old friend appeared in the nightclub's portal. With the audience's backs to him, Bob Dylan slipped quietly into the darkened cabaret and watched the remainder of Elliott's performance from a small, candlelit table in the back of the room. Dylan had only recently moved back to the Village, taking up semipermanent residence in a Houston Street loft, only a short stroll from the Other End. Though Dylan was, characteristically, maintaining a low profile, he was no longer a recluse. During the last week of June, Dylan had made a series of unannounced, low-key appearances both onstage and in the audience of a number of Greenwich Village nightclubs. Elliott mixed things up a little on Thursday, bringing "House of the Rising Sun," "Tom Joad," "912 Greens," and Dylan's own "I Threw It All Away" to the set, closing with "Cup of Coffee." Following the gig, Dylan and Elliott sat at a corner table and chatted quietly over a glass of white wine and a tumbler of tequila, surrounded by a small circle of friends and hangers-on.[41]

News of Dylan's visit to the Other End quickly circulated, and on Jack's final night, July 3, the club was filled to capacity. He opened, as was his custom, with "San Francisco Bay Blues." A writer from the *New Yorker*, who had attended Elliott's show the previous night, described Jack's final engagement as "magical," sensing that everyone gathered somehow "seemed to know it would be." At the conclusion of the first set, the usual racket filled the room: the settling of tabs, the cleaning of the tables, and the turnover of the audience. When the cabaret's sound engineer set up a second microphone stand and chair during intermission, the Other End was rife with rumors that Dylan would be "sitting in." Jack ambled onto the stage and sang a few songs before moving, hesitantly, into Dylan's "With God on Our Side." After singing a verse or two of that *The Times They Are A-Changin'* classic, Elliott peered off into the darkened back corner and asked, "Bob, you want to help me out on this?"[42]

Dylan climbed onto the stage to rapturous applause and, following an interval of microphone juggling, sat to Elliott's immediate right. The duo launched into a bouncy, if only occasionally transcendent, version of Woody Guthrie's "Pretty Boy Floyd." Elliott handled the lead vocal and rhythm guitar chores, Dylan contributing a high vocal harmony and ornamenting the melody with a simple guitar line. A perfunctory stab at a duet on Leroy Carr and Scrapper Blackwell's "How Long Blues" followed, to no great effect. "How Long Blues" did not finish as much as it sort of simply died away, causing Elliott to look sheepishly up from his cowboy hat and offer, "We really didn't have any time to rehearse anything, you dig? We haven't jammed in about seven years, I guess . . . so it takes a little tuning up." But instead of revisiting another old song, Dylan had something else in mind. Dissatisfied with the buzzing guitar on which he was playing, Dylan traded instruments with Elliott and began to finger an unusual chord progression. Jack attempted to follow along at first, but soon thought the better of it and slipped into the shadows, leaving Dylan alone in the spotlight. Dylan was performing a new song, not properly introduced this night, but referred to for years as "St. John, the Evangelist" among the Dylan tape-trading community. In less than a month, Dylan would record "Abandoned Love" (the song's true title) for Columbia, with full instrumental accompaniment and under the working title of "Love Copy." The song would not see official release until Columbia issued the Dylan box-set retrospective collection *Biograph* in October 1985. Regardless, Dylan fans fortunate enough to score a copy of the legendary "Other End" bootleg consider Dylan's solo acoustic version to be the preeminent performance of the song.[43]

Dylan signed off after "Abandoned Love" and Jack, wisely, invited Bobby Neuwirth to the stage. Dylan had proven, once again, that he was a tough act to follow. Elliott eventually returned for a few songs, the evening closing with Jack and Logan English's spirited duet of "This Land Is Your Land." The *New Yorker* reported that following the show, Elliott and Dylan retired to an adjourning room and, much as they had the night before, "drank until closing." Though no one could have predicted it at the time, music historians often date the genesis of Bob Dylan's famed "Rolling Thunder Revue" to Elliott's Other End residency. It was on that night that Dylan handed Elliott a glass of red wine and said, "Neuwirth and I were just talking about an idea, where we'd get a bus and travel around and sing and do little concerts in little halls." It would be an informal, pared-down affair, Dylan explained, consisting only of himself and Neuwirth, Joan Baez, and Ramblin' Jack. "You in?" Dylan asked. "Count me in," Jack replied enthusiastically.[44]

Elliott returned to New York in September 1975 for a full five nights at the Other End. He was suffering from an autumnal cold, with the *New York Times* reporting that due to his ailment Elliott's "singing style, always technically limited, sounded more diffident than ever." It hardly mattered, with the writer acknowledging that Elliott's stage shows were essentially critic proof, that his "easy phrasing, delicately agile guitar playing and warmly idiosyncratic personality" helped him win fans and fill nightclubs even without the benefit of record company promotion. Neuwirth was in the audience for at least one of Elliott's engagements that week, the two friends walking over to Neuwirth's nearby apartment after the club had closed. Neuwirth placed a long distance call to Dylan, who had left Manhattan for California. Neuwirth and Dylan chatted for nearly an hour before Neuwirth suddenly proffered the telephone handset to Elliott.

"Hey, Jack. Remember that thing we talked about?" Dylan asked. "Yeah."
"It's gonna happen," Dylan promised. "It's gonna happen in November."
"Well, I'll see ya," Jack replied, returning the receiver to Neuwirth. He
made the mental note that the exchange was among the shortest conver-
sations that he had ever had with Dylan, who was hardly a magpie by
anyone's standards.[45]

The "thing" Dylan and Elliott had "talked about" was the Rolling
Thunder Revue. The Revue was scheduled to visit 23 cities for a total of
31 performances, beginning on October 30, 1975, at the War Memorial
Auditorium in Plymouth, Massachusetts, and ending on December 8 at
Manhattan's Madison Square Garden. The New York City performance
was publicized as "The Night of the Hurricane." Dylan was planning to
use his high public profile to bring attention to the plight of Rubin "Hurricane" Carter, a former middleweight boxing champion imprisoned since
1965 for the murder and robbery of two men in a Paterson, New Jersey,
tavern. Though he had been rambling and playing gigs his entire adult life,
Elliott had never been on a rock 'n' roll tour of several months' duration.
He was concerned about how many sets of clean clothes he would need
to bring along. On the eve of the tour, he innocently asked Dylan, "Are
we going to have a chance to do laundry? How many pairs of jeans are
you taking along?" Dylan told Elliott he was bringing along "Just one pair
of Lees."[46]

Dylan was back in New York City by mid-October, moving himself
and other members of the Rolling Thunder Revue into the Gramercy Park
Hotel on Lexington Avenue. The first, tentative rehearsals were held, most
informally, on acoustic guitars in various rooms of the Gramercy. Later,
more formal, and electrified, sessions took place at Studio Instrument Rehearsals at both their mid-Manhattan and Chelsea locations. Elliott recalled
there were at least two weeks of rehearsals before the Revue left Manhattan for Cape Cod, Massachusetts. Once on the Cape, there was yet another
week of rehearsals at the Seacrest Motel in North Falmouth, Massachusetts.
On the day prior to the Revue's first official performance in Plymouth, a
dress rehearsal was staged in the Seacrest lounge. The audience for the first
performance of the Rolling Thunder Revue was a gaggle of unsuspecting
elderly women who had gathered at the Seacrest for a Mah-Jongg tourna-
ment. They watched with amusement, some confusion, and, occasional,
bewilderment as the poet Allen Ginsberg, also along for the ride, read
through "Kaddish," a long, turbulent prayer to his mother.[47]

Though the first concert at the small Memorial Auditorium in Plymouth
was a bit ragged, the atmosphere was electric. UPI sent a correspondent

who reported that, "The close physical proximity of the worshipped and the worshippers . . . lent an eerie overtone to the show." The *New York Times* noted that Elliott followed the singer Ronee Blakely in the program, and entertained the audience of college students with "a few typically relaxed and ingratiating tunes." Things got somewhat stranger when, during Elliott's solo spot, UPI reported that Dylan, face hidden behind a garish "Bob Dylan" Halloween mask, "drifted onstage for a duet with folk singer Ramblin' Jack Elliott." Later, backed by Roger McGuinn's five-string banjo, Elliott sang "Rake and Rambling Boy," introducing the Carter Family classic as the "song Derroll Adams sang at my first wedding ever."[48]

As the script for the musical program already ran nearly five hours (it would later be pruned to four and a half hours), there was little variation to Elliott's set. And as half of his four-song slot was supported by the Revue's touring band, informally dubbed "Guam" by its members, Elliott's gift for mixing improvisational theater with music was greatly hindered. Most Rolling Thunder Revue performances began with a nine-song prelude performed by Guam, with lead vocals shared somewhat equally between Neuwirth, T-Bone Burnett, Steven Soles, Mick Ronson, and Ronee Blakely. Elliott watched from the wings as Neuwirth closed Guam's portion of the evening with "Ramblin' Jack," an introductory song Neuwirth had composed for the occasion. Neuwirth's lyric made note of Elliott's unapologetic lifetime of rambling for which he "never gives a reason or a damn."

Elliott's segment began with a solo acoustic (on occasion Rob Stoner would accompany on bass guitar) two-song spot, followed by another two-song slot with Elliott accompanied by the full band. Getting into the spirit of things, Ramblin' Jack would even occasionally perform with an electric guitar strapped to him, perhaps for the only time in his career. Jack's acoustic spots would invariably consist of such fare as "Me and Bobby McGee," "South Coast," "Pretty Boy Floyd," and the "Muleskinner Blues." The amplified set consisted of a mix of such songs as "Salt Pork, West Virginia," "If I Were a Carpenter," and "Rake and Rambling Boy." Occasionally, Jack would get more adventurous and stretch out a bit as he did at the Boston Music Hall on November 21, adding Woody's "Grand Coulee Dam" and an extremely truncated version of his own "912 Greens," but such changes were the exception rather than the rule. Dylan, too, stayed close to the script, particularly for the electric performances, arriving onstage directly following Elliott's set, and usually launching into "When I Paint My Masterpiece." Dylan would then continue with a five-song electric set before bringing out Joan Baez for a series of acoustic duets.

After an intermission, Baez and Roger McGuinn contributed solo spots of their own, and Dylan would conclude the program with still another electric set, often bringing down the final curtain with a cast ensemble performance of "This Land Is Your Land" or Paul Clayton's "Gotta Travel On."

Prior to the tour, Dylan had arranged the hire of a film crew. The filmmakers were conscripted to not only document the Rolling Thunder concerts on celluloid, but to shoot informal cinema verite segments as well, with the musicians doubling as actors. Dylan had brought in an off-off Broadway playwright and occasional screenwriter named Sam Shepard to contribute on-the-scene dialogue for his proposed art-film.[49]

The film that would result from the hundreds of hours of footage shot was *Renaldo and Clara*, a title derived from the names of the two principal characters in the film. Though Elliott is featured in both the original four- and subsequent two-hour cut of *Renaldo and Clara*, many of his best scenes, filmed, scripted, or otherwise plotted, did not escape the editor's scissors. Some scenes that did include Elliott were incoherently edited or presented only in truncated flashes. A year after his experience with the Rolling Thunder Revue, Sam Shepard published his *Rolling Thunder Logbook*, a diary-styled companion to the tour that offered an interesting peek behind the curtain. Though they had not met prior to Rolling Thunder, Shepard was immediately intrigued by Elliott, famously describing him as a "wandering, mythical, true American minstrel." Shepard specifically wrote Elliott into several of his proposed scenarios, and his book offers fascinating glimpses of what Ramblin' Jack fans might have been treated to had the film been steered to reflect Shepard's, rather than Dylan's, vision.[50]

Elliott loved traveling with the Rolling Thunder Revue and admitted he found himself "lost" at the tour's conclusion. The musicians had become almost like family. This was demonstrated most clearly in December 1975 at the Forum de Montreal when Elliott received news that his mother had passed away. With Elliott feeling understandably blue, Dylan arranged for him to take part in a short scene he was filming with Joan Baez and the actor Harry Dean Stanton. The crew later arranged for Elliott to attend the funeral, hiring a limousine to bring him afterward to the Revue's penultimate show before the prison population of the Correctional Institution for Women in Clinton, New Jersey. Larry Sloman, a freelance writer documenting the tour for *Rolling Stone*, recalled his surprise that Elliott was so composed after arriving at Clinton following his long, sad day. Sloman was equally astonished to find Elliott's performance so well received: the audience of incarcerates was composed, primarily, of African American women. Many of the performers that afternoon, including Joni Mitchell and Dylan himself, were received with some derision. But Sloman noted, for whatever the reason the inmates related to Jack Elliott, "this bizarre-looking Brooklyn cowboy playing a funky '50s rock 'n roll song." There was something so sincere and genuine about his music it was hard not to like him. Then suddenly, following the media circus at Madison Square Garden that was "The Night of the Hurricane" (December 8), the tour was over. In the early morning hours of December 9, Elliott, Joni Mitchell, Roger McGuinn, and Bobby Neuwirth sat at the bar of the Other End, drinking until five in the morning. For Elliott, it was back to the grinding nightclub circuit, a single bar stool, and a lone acoustic guitar. He traveled to Colorado, where he had taken up residence, but soon returned to California, wondering what to do next.[51]

On January 25, 1976, Jack stopped off at the Grateful Dead's office in San Rafael, California, to sort through his mail. Jack's appearance at the office surprised one member of the Dead staff who asked Elliott why he wasn't in Houston for the "Night of the Hurricane 2," a regrouping of the Rolling Thunder Revue at the Astrodome. The staffer handed Elliott a copy of that week's edition of *Daily Variety*, where his name was prominently featured as one of the artists appearing at the event. Confused, Jack immediately found out where the cast and crew were staying, then called the hotel and asked for Bobby Neuwirth. The start of the concert was only a few hours away. Neuwirth grabbed the telephone and asked Elliott why he wasn't in Houston. A hotel room had already been booked for him and his name was on the marquee. But it was too late. There was simply not enough time to fly to Houston and still make the concert. How could this have happened?[52]

In the spring of 1976, Dylan was scheduled to return to the road with a second incarnation of the Rolling Thunder Revue. Most shows were scheduled to pass through cities of the Deep South, with excursions into Texas, Oklahoma, Colorado, and Utah. Most members of the first Rolling Thunder Revue had already signed on, but Jack, mysteriously, had not been formally brought aboard. He had been replaced by Kinky Friedman, the satiric Texan songwriter who famously outraged redneck country music fans with his provocative lyrics. Just prior to the second incarnation of Rolling Thunder, Elliott traveled to Dylan's home in Malibu. He asked Dylan directly whether or not he should expect an invitation, but Dylan mumbled and "hemmed and hawed" and refused to answer the question directly, telling Elliott he did not "have anything to do with the people that are choosing about who gets to go." Jack clearly did not believe that for a moment. On April 18, 1976, the Rolling Thunder Revue 2 tour, minus Ramblin' Jack, commenced at the Civic Center in Lakeland, Florida.[53]

It was a disappointment but it was a time for bad news. Little more than a week prior to the second Rolling Thunder tour, Elliott's friend Phil Ochs committed suicide at his sister's home in Far Rockaway, Queens, New York. The day following the death, his family announced plans for a memorial concert. Elliott was contacted and promised the Ochs family that he would be there to pay tribute. Dylan, to the disappointment of many, would not attend.[54]

On May 23, 1976, Elliott appeared onstage for the only time with the Rolling Thunder Revue 2. Dylan and the entourage were to perform at Colorado State University's Hughes Stadium in Fort Collins. The concert was the Revue's second to last performance and it was a cursed, dismal, rain-soaked affair captured on film for the appropriately titled NBC television special *Hard Rain*, broadcast September 14, 1976. Elliott was pulled onstage by Neuwirth as Dylan ran through a particularly guttural, full-band version of "A Hard Rains A-Gonna Fall." Elliott can be spied, briefly, on the NBC broadcast of the event, standing alongside his Rolling Thunder tour replacement, Kinky Friedman, singing along on the refrain of "Hard Rain."[55]

The "Concert Tribute to Phil Ochs by His Many Friends" was staged on May 28, at the Felt Forum in Manhattan. Tickets sold out almost immediately, despite the fact that no official roster had been advertised. The concert featured a combination of spoken-word and musical performances, the personal often mixing uneasily with the political. WHYY, the public television affiliate from the Philadelphia/Wilmington, Delaware, area, filmed the night's events, the program tilting, as ever, to the hard left. Ed Sanders of the Fugs and Allen Ginsberg read from their tracts, the radical lawyer William Kunstler spoke, as did Jerry Rubin and former U.S. Attorney General Ramsey Clark, an old friend of Phil's. Musically, the program offered performances by a veritable who's who of the Greenwich Village folk scene: Pete Seeger, Fred Hellerman, Ed McCurdy, Oscar Brand, Peter Yarrow, Dave Van Ronk, Eric Andersen, Tom Rush, Tim Hardin, Melanie, Patrick Sky, Bob Gibson, Len Chandler, David Blue, Odetta, David Amram, and Ramblin' Jack. Rather than perform "Joe Hill," the song he recorded with Phil in 1968 to the tune of Woody's "Tom Joad," Elliott chose to sing Woody's "Pretty Boy Floyd" and Phil's own Guthrie tribute "Bound for Glory." The critic Robert Palmer found the program well intentioned but old hat; "Ramblin' Jack Elliott, Len Chandler and

Peter Yarrow might as well have been performing for a 1960's audience," Palmer sniffed.[56]

It wasn't a great time to be earning a living as a folksinger. By the mid-1970s, it was difficult to purchase a Ramblin' Jack album anywhere in the United States except at the best-stocked secondhand shops. Though he had been on a high-profile tour with Dylan only a year earlier, playing nightly to audiences of thousands, Elliott's early albums for Prestige-International, Prestige-Folklore, Monitor, and Vanguard had long since fallen out of print. His more "recent" solo efforts for Reprise/Warner Bros. were also difficult to manage, though you could still find a remainder of *Bull Durham Sacks & Railroad Tracks* on eight-track if you were lucky. This sorry situation was partly remedied in 1976 when Vanguard decided to celebrate America's Bicentennial, and move old product, by digging into their mostly moribund back catalog. Vanguard was in the process of issuing a series of retrospective LP sets called "Twofers," that is two records for the price of a single LP. Most were comprised of "Best of" or "Greatest Hits" material, but other former Vanguard artists had entire, unabridged albums paired and re-released as "*Essential*" collections. This was easy enough for the artists who had stayed long enough with the company to establish some sort of back catalog, but Elliott's proposed set proved more troublesome as there had not been a second disc to augment 1964's *Jack Elliott*. In the end, Jack's fans would benefit as Vanguard was forced to dig a little deeper into their archives and examine the unissued material they held. More than a decade after it had been recorded, an edited program of Elliott's April 30, 1965, concert at New York's Town Hall was mastered and released commercially as the second act of *The Essential Ramblin' Jack Elliott*. The following year, Fantasy Records of Berkeley, California, issued its own two-disc retrospective *Ramblin' Jack Elliott—Hard Travelin': Songs by Woody Guthrie and Others*. Prestige's back catalog had been sold to Fantasy in 1971; by the end of the decade, the label began to market two-album sets of previously issued but long out-of-print materials. In Elliott's case, Fantasy chose to reissue, complete and unabridged, Elliott's first, and best, two releases for Prestige-International, *Jack Elliott Sings the Songs of Woody Guthrie* and *Ramblin' Jack Elliott*.[57]

There was still interest in Ramblin' Jack Elliott, and it was not unusual to find him on the telephone, chatting with an endless parade of small-town journalists to promote an upcoming appearance at a local nightclub or tavern. But, tellingly, the questions asked of him rarely touched on his own musical legacy or current doings. More often than not, journalists were only interested in probing his friendships with Woody Guthrie and Bob Dylan. If and when the occasional, intelligent interview did appear, it was rarely published between the covers of a genuine music-orientated magazine. By the end of the 1970s, Elliott had all but disappeared from the pages of *Rolling Stone* and *Sing Out!*

There were exceptions, of course. *Billboard* sent a reporter to attend a February 11, 1977, Elliott gig at McCabes Guitar Shop in Santa Monica. It was a good notice, though Elliott was explained away to readers as a lone "troubadour carrying a tradition whose founders are now mostly dead or rock convertees." Jack's 40-minute set included the usual, well-worn chestnuts ("San Francisco Bay Blues," "House of the Rising Sun," "Pretty Boy Floyd," and "Don't Think Twice, It's All Right"). *Billboard* concluded, not unrespectfully, that Elliott's principal strength as a performing artist remained his uncanny ability "to share his devotion with those of like tastes and in this albeit modest undertaking succeeds." The *Los Angeles Times* was also at McCabes, describing Elliott "as a somewhat erratic performer. His whimsical, spaced-out manner is accepted as part and parcel of the Elliott persona." The *Times* rued that Elliott's set was mostly comprised of the same old songs that he had been performing for years on end. One exception this night was the Grateful Dead's "Friend of the Devil," which he nailed, leading the writer to comment that Elliott "could delve advantageously into more contemporary material." This may have been so, but for the most part he seemed to exist in a musical time warp, and somehow a more modern Ramblin' Jack would miss the point. As the *Times* noted: "Elliott's vocal-guitar style is as loose, rattletrap and picturesque as a Dust Bowl refugee's jalopy, and it works for him because he offers not just voice and words but a total personality. It's real, and you take your chances with it."[58]

Even if Elliott chose to imbue his set list with more contemporary songs, for whom would he record such material? Elliott had not waxed a solo album for any record company throughout the 1970s. Royalties, long past due, from the sales of old albums continued to anger him. Part of the problem was that he had recorded for so many different labels, and many of those were small independents that went bankrupt, were abandoned, or were bought up by a conglomerate. The original contracts, if there had been any at all, had hardly been formal and, in the best of cases, only hazily recalled. Regardless, Elliott defended his decision to remain a free agent and record for whomever he pleased. He had, by his own account, developed a "total mistrust" of record labels since "I'd been ripped off so many times by record companies that I never had any hope of ever getting a square deal." His status as a free agent always allowed him to record for any company that offered. "I never was signed exclusively," he recalled with some satisfaction. As long as he wasn't any label's exclusive property, he was free to jump from label to label "when I signed to do an album with someone else." This strategy, borrowed from the old bluesmen, most of whom died penniless, was not terribly successful. Though he was spared the "excruciating process of getting divorced in court from a record label," the fact remained that Elliott had not been able to make much money in the record business. He complained often and bitterly that he was the recipient of few royalty statements.[59]

He held special vitriol for Reprise Records, which, more than the other labels, to hear him tell it, repeatedly deflected his request to be paid his royalties. According to Elliott, Warner Bros. response was always the same, that he had not yet "sold enough [copies] to pay the recording costs. . . . I called them and they told me I owed *them* $43,000." It was at moments like this that Elliott wondered where all the money went for the thousands of copies of *Young Brigham* and *Bull Durham* he had signed for fans over the years. Once his relationship with Reprise/Warner Bros. soured, Elliott made the conscious, partly understandable, but totally unorthodox decision to abstain from future recording projects. If he wouldn't get paid for the records he was making, why bother to make them at all? Elliott would not record a new solo album until the spring of 1980. Though he had lost interest in recording his own albums, he would occasionally guest on the LPs of such friends as Earl Scruggs, John Prine, David Amram, Steven Fromholz, and Jamie Brockett.[60]

Elliott was well aware that his real meal ticket was the fee he collected for his nightclub and concert engagements. He certainly did not need a record company to find work at the folk clubs. He remained a popular performer on that circuit, but the number of clubs that specifically catered to folk-music audiences was in fast decline. By cutting himself off from the recording studio and the planning of new albums, Elliott also unburdened himself of the responsibility of freshening up his stage show with the occasional new song. Jack's repertoire was expansive, but not bottomless, and by the mid-1970s, few new songs had been incorporated into his set list. Elliott's musical malaise did not go unnoticed by his most loyal fans or the most sympathetic of music journalists. He defensively told the *San Francisco Examiner*, "I've sung the same 25 songs forever. I'm too lazy to learn any new ones." In 1976, Kristin Baggelaar and Donald Milton authored *Folk Music: More Than a Song*, an encyclopedia of folk-music artists, instruments, and history. Elliott's entry is respectful and complimentary, but it is telling that at age 45 Jack was already referenced not as a contemporary artist but as a "nostalgic figure of the folk revival era."[61]

In August 1977, Jack returned for a three-night engagement at the Bottom Line in Manhattan. Elliott was reportedly out of sorts, and the *Times*'s music critic Robert Palmer complained that Jack's "sodden, lugubrious late show" was rescued only by a compelling version of "912 Greens." "This was prime Ramblin' Jack Elliott," Palmer opined. "The story completely overshadowed the singing and picking that preceded it, suggesting that the folkies gestalt, as created and lived by performers of Mr. Elliott's generation was not about making music as much as it was about celebrating America, the America Jack Kerouac was celebrating in *On the Road*."[62]

That October, Elliott appeared at the University of California's Greek Theater in Berkeley to help out Mimi Fariña and her "Bread and Roses" organization. Elliott ambled onstage, seemingly unprepared, as usual, and apparently in no hurry to get things started. After a lengthy stab at tuning his guitar, he looked out over the blessedly patient crowd and offered dryly and with a little frustration, "I tuned this guitar in Corpus Christi." It all added to the legend.[63]

The year 1978 was an out-of-tune time, a year of near misses and out-and-out disasters. To start off, Elliott nearly became history himself when he flipped over his beloved Land Rover on Sunset Boulevard after a night's drinking with Jerry Jeff Walker. Then Dylan's Rolling Thunder Revue film *Renaldo and Clara* finally opened in New York and Los Angeles on January 25, 1978, to a firestorm of criticism. Elliott found the film fascinating; "a strange, mysterious movie" is how he described it, though he had to admit he did not really understand it at all. *Renaldo and Clara* offered only the vaguest of storylines, no continuity, scenes assembled into a baffling, cryptic mosaic. Elliott was able to fit the pieces together to some extent, but only for the reason that he had been part of the opus. But he admitted he "couldn't imagine anyone who wasn't in [the film] getting much enjoyment out of it." He confessed he had sat through *Renaldo and Clara* a total of five times. "I don't think I could stand to watch it again," he admitted. "I was impressed that I had the endurance to watch it that many times." Indeed, Dylan's film crew had reportedly shot nearly 200 hours of footage. Editing the footage down into a film that was somewhat cohesive was such a challenge that, Elliott noted, Howard Alk, the film's editor, "died during the effort."[64]

Interestingly, *Renaldo and Clara* was not the only film to feature, and misuse, the talents of Ramblin' Jack in 1978. That summer, *Rolling Stone* announced that Elliott was to star in *Honky Tonk Nights*, "a film shot in

California about an aging ex-stripper who wants to be another Dolly Parton." Songwriter Rick Nowels, who would later go on to better things as a Grammy-winning songwriter and producer, told *Rolling Stone* that the film would feature the music of the California-based Hot Licks (minus frontman Dan Hicks) and Jack Elliott. "It's the first time Jack's been backed by a pop setting and not just acoustic guitar," said Nowels, with little regard for reality. *Rolling Stone* promised that both the film and accompanying soundtrack album were "due this summer," though this deadline passed with no sighting of either project. It is not entirely clear why Jack agreed to lend his talents to this production. *Honky Tonk Nights* was directed by Charles Webb, a pseudonym for Charles De Santos, whose resumé boasted a score of X-rated adult films. In fact, most of the *Honky Tonk Nights* cast were aging starlets recruited from the ranks of the adult-film industry. Adult-film actresses Georgina Spelvin (*The Devil in Miss Jones*) and the single-named (never a good sign unless you are Odetta) Serena also signed onto the project. Though Elliott's screen time amounted to little more than a few minutes here and there, he was second-billed in the film and marketing only to Carol Doda, the infamous San Francisco stripper who plied her trade at North Beach's Condor Club. Doda's notoriety was due to the fact she was among the first strippers to undergo silicone breast enhancements. *Honky Tonk Nights* was plagued by many of the same no-budget elements of your usual run-of-the-mill adult film: poor lighting, zero production values, wooden acting, and cringe-worthy dialogue. Perhaps referencing this film, Elliott candidly told a Minnesota newspaperman, "My motion picture career has subsided to a new low." Hiding behind a droopy mustache, Elliott assumed the role of Bill Garvey in *Honky Tonk Nights*, a Stetson-topped country music legend, who agrees to mentor Dolly Pop, a moody, frustrated, and occasionally violent, saloon singer.[65]

In the early winter of 1978 Elliott trooped out to Chicago to lend his distinctive vocal to the "Hobo Chorus" of John Prine's "The Hobo Song," the closing number of Prine's critically acclaimed album *Bruised Orange*. On May 11, he appeared at the Great American Music Hall in San Francisco and on July 14, he was in Berkeley for a Woody Guthrie Birthday celebration, sharing the stage with a host of other performers including Woody's son, Joady Ben Guthrie. Joady, a fine guitarist, doubled Elliott's own guitar on such songs as "I Ain't Got No Home," "Riding in My Car," and "Buffalo Skinners." Prior to performing "I Ain't Got No Home," Elliott recalled, "This is the first song I sang in public," as he and Joady tried to settle on the proper guitar key. After some fumbling, Joady made the suggestion "Let's do it Woody's way." Elliott cautioned "Oh,

OK. I hope I can remember that." In August, Elliott was in Cleveland to perform at a new club called Bobbie McGee's, visiting station WMMS early that morning to sing and chat and promote the show. That autumn, he was back in California for a series of concerts including a November 1 engagement at the Boarding House in San Francisco. He was teamed with songwriter Tim Hardin for a two-night, four-set Friday and Saturday night engagement at McCabe's in Santa Monica on November 10 and 11, 1978. Tim told Elliott he was related to the fabled western outlaw John Wesley Hardin, and Jack had no reason not to take him at his word.[66]

In early 1979, Elliott returned to the Other End in Greenwich Village for a co-bill with Mimi Fariña. The *New York Post* sent down a music writer who described Ramblin' Jack as "a bit of the hobo . . . a bit of the hustler." Though his set remained more or less static, Elliott's music was beginning to transform itself into something different. The *Post*'s critic was one of the first to notice the subtle change in the performance style, Jack trading his usual rough 'n' tumble singing and guitar playing for something more gentle, though no less intense: "The vibrato in his voice last night hinted at the yodel he sometimes offers and his guitar playing had it's usual unassuming confidence."[67]

In 1979, Elliott met Barbara Dodge, a self-styled poet and artist. Starting that summer she became a small part of his show, climbing onstage and reciting intense poems during the interlude, Jack lightly strumming his guitar, Beat style, in the background. Described as "tall, bold and absolutely stunning," one newspaperman recounted Dodge as "coiffeured [sic] in that just-come-through-the-hedge-backwards look." Dodge was blessed with a husky voice that lent a gravitas to her poetry, which was stylistically free form and often difficult to follow. Journalist Larry Scanlan reported that she explained to an audience of bemused Texans that poetry "is by its nature incomprehensible." "By that yardstick," Scanlan wrote, "hers was a dizzying success." Elliott was clearly taken by Dodge, telling friends, "She leadeth me through the darkened tunnels where cowboys fear to tread."[68]

The entry of Dodge into Elliott's life may have been fortuitous, her arrival coincident with a time that he was in need of a true friend. In a preconcert profile published in the days prior to his July 1979 concert at the Great American Music Hall, the wear and tear of traveling America's back roads for too long were made plain: "In recent years, Ramblin' Jack Elliott's life hasn't been successful. In some ways, the myths he invented for himself turned out to be too much to live up to. Acting out, on a 24 hour-a-day basis, the role of the American cowboy isn't easy: all that two-fisted drinking and the endless days on the road and the nights sleeping in the back of pick-up trucks or on borrowed floors."[69]

Things were not only getting increasingly tougher for folksinging cowboys, they were getting tougher for the folk community as a whole. In 1979, producer Frank J. Russo tried to resurrect the Newport Folk Festival after an absence of nine years. Russo had arranged to host a three-day event over Labor Day weekend at Newport's Fort Adams State Park and managed to book an impressive slate of performers: Taj Mahal, David Bromberg, Ramblin' Jack, Leon Redbone, Bob Gibson, Tom Rush, Buffy Sainte-Marie, Muddy Waters, Don McLean, Mary Travers and Peter Yarrow, John Hammond, Elizabeth Cotten, Sweet Honey in the Rock, and Roosevelt Sykes. It was a dream bill, circa 1968, but some argued it was fatally topped with a slate of old-timers, not the Village singer-songwriters of *Fast Folk* who were creating new songs for new days. Ticket sales were so sluggish that Russo was forced to cancel the festival or else face almost certain financial calamity. It seemed to be one more nail in the folk coffin.[70]

Though Newport was off, Elliott headed east anyway that September as he had been paired with Bob Gibson at the Cellar Door in Washington, D.C. It had been about two years since he had played the nation's capital, reportedly, falling asleep onstage in the middle of his set. This evening, Elliott sat off at the bar and listened with nostalgia as Gibson was joined by his old singing buddy Hamilton Camp. When it was time for Jack to take the stage, he pulled his Stetson down over his eyes and went to work, performing a couple of Woody's talking blues and "I Belong to Glasgow." The *Washington Post* grumpily noted Elliott's "songs were seldom as long as his introductions and never quite as colorful," but admitted that the "long and amusing anecdotes . . . is what Ramblin' Jack Elliott has always done best." A reviewer from the *Washington Star* echoed this sentiment, reporting that Elliott "tells wonderful stories in that marvelously off-centered way." The critic was also of the opinion that Ramblin' Jack "still picks the guitar as well as he, and Woody Guthrie ever did." He also managed to stay awake throughout the gig, which was always a plus.[71]

There were some gigs we might have preferred sleeping through. On November 12, Elliott traveled to the Keystone Club in Palo Alto, California, for a noisy fund-raising concert to benefit local radio station KFAT. His performance was a bit ragged, his voice mostly shot, and the audience mostly indifferent. Prior to singing "Buffalo Skinners," Jack explained away his wobbly vocals by telling the crowd he had "just recently returned from Texas where I picked up this hoarse/horse . . . in my throat." He moved into Guthrie's "Talking Fishing Blues" (Woody's son Joady was in attendance to lend support), but the noise in the club steadily increased, causing Jack to remark, "Now I know why Willie [Nelson] has a band." Elliott scolded the crowd, asking them to "think about all those good people out there in radio land," but this only caused the crowd to shout and talk all that much louder. "I was playing down in Texas last week and I thought it was kind of rowdy down there—but actually it was very quiet compared to here," Elliott sniffed. When someone in the crowd suggested that he tell everyone to simply "shut up," Elliott responded, "I never tell people to 'Shut up.' I try to leave that up to their own intelligence." Midway through his fourth song, a mostly ignored rendition of "Old Shep," he lost his cool and told the rude crowd to "Shut up." Things came to an even more unpleasant head during "Arthritis Blues" when Elliott finally blew up. He told the audience "You folks are really rude. You know that? I don't give a shit. . . . I don't have to live here. I live on the road. I live in the Holiday Inn. One night here ain't gonna kill me. I'll be back in Texas pretty soon."[72]

Following a couple of better-received gigs in Santa Cruz and Emoryville, California, Elliott, as promised, returned to Texas, where he was booked for a December 21, 1979, performance at San Antonio's Jam Factory. He was in fine form, among friends again, and the crowd hung on his every word. A local music scribe perceptively noted that at 49, Elliott "can no longer brandish power and volume, hit all the high notes or slap his cowboy hat against his thigh to adrenalize [sic] an audience. What Elliott now offers instead are subtler, more mature renditions of three decades of folk music. The musical seduction is all the more satisfying for its slow unfolding." Indeed, Elliott's music had changed. There were fewer "over-the-top" performances, less high-end singing and yodeling. Through years of honing his time-tested repertoire, Elliott had smoothed out all the angles and rough edges, turning such old ballads as "Buffalo Skinners" and "Pretty Boy Floyd" into subdued, intimate set pieces that pulled audiences in with their subtleties. Part of this change could be credited to Barbara Dodge; she constantly championed him as a great artist in his own right, reminding everyone of Elliott's contribution to the art of folk song. It did sometimes seem that Jack's very real accomplishments were, at best, dimly remembered, at worse, nearly forgotten, by a new generation of folk-music enthusiasts. Dodge told *Melody Maker* that the Elliott she knew was "an enigma. . . . He's a real Walter Mitty, he's in his own world. He's stunned the entire world." That assessment might have been overreaching, but Dodge seemed to be attempting to rebuild Jack's self-esteem as his musical ego had taken a fair battering over the past few years. A newspaper noted that Dodge was clearly not using Elliott's fame to advance her own career, that during her poetry interlude "she read neither too much nor too little, made no attempt to upstage a man she clearly cares for and refused his invitation to share the stage with him at the end." In four months, with Barbara Dodge at his side, Jack would finally end his decade-long estrangement from the recording studio and tape one of his finest albums.[73]

Notes

1. Bob Atkinson, "Ramblin' with Jack Elliott," *Sing Out!* Vol. 19, No. 5, March/April 1970, 9.

2. One of the most entertaining accounts of the Texas "outlaw" music scene is Jan Reid's *The Improbable Rise of Redneck Rock* (New York: DaCapo Press, 1977). Reid reports Jack Elliott was well known in the late 1960s' Texas music circles due to his appearances at the Chequered Flag, an Austin coffeehouse and early proving ground for such singer-songwriters as Townes Van Zandt and Jerry Jeff Walker.

3. Michael Krogsgaard, "Bob Dylan: The Recording Sessions—Part Two," *The Telegraph*, No. 53, Winter 1995, 71.

4. Ramblin' Jack Elliott, *Bull Durham Sacks & Railroad Tracks* (Reprise RS 6387), 1970.

5. "Brooklyn's Foremost Cowboy: Ramblin' Jack Elliott" (advertisement), *Sing Out!* Vol. 19, No. 5, March/April 1970, 44; "Rambling Jack Elliott: The Man Who Ran from the City," *Country-Western Stars*, Vol. 1, No. 4, July 1970, 46–49.

6. Arlo Guthrie notes to *Bull Durham Sacks & Railroad Tracks*.

7. Hoyle Osborne, "Record Reviews," *Sing Out!* Vol. 19, No. 6, June/July 1970, 35–36; "Record Review: Bull Durham Sacks & Railroad Tracks, Jack Elliott," *Rolling Stone*, No. 60, 11 June 1970, 50; Greil Marcus, "Self Portrait No. 25," *Rolling Stone*, No. 63, 23 July 1970, 16–19.

8. Michael Sherman, "Ramblin' Jack Elliott on Ash Grove Stage," *Los Angeles Times*, 26 February 1970, C20.

9. Program brochure for the Berkeley Blues Festival, 2–4 April 1970; John Lombardi, "The Truth Will Never Die," *Rolling Stone*, No. 57, 30 April 1970, 10.

10. Lombardi, "The Truth Will Never Die," 10; Michael Lydon, "Sing Your Own Blues," *New York Times*, 19 April 1970, 101.

11. Jack Elliott, Berkeley Blues Festival, University of California–Berkeley, 4 April 1970.

12. Lynn Van Matre, "Music: Legendary Rambler," *Chicago Tribune*, 10 April 1970, C16; George Knemeyer, "Ramblin' Jack Elliott, Quiet Knight, Chicago," *Billboard* 82, 2 May 1970, 28.

13. Craig McGregor, "Pop: I'm Nobody's Best Friend," *New York Times*, 26 July 1970, 68; Jack Elliott, Turning Point Café, Piermont, NY, 17 May 1995.

14. "Pro's Reply," *Guitar Player*, Vol. 8, No. 10, October 1974, 6; Hank Reineke interview with Izzy Young, New York City, 20 September 2007.

15. Chris Jorgensen, "An Interview with Ramblin' Jack Elliott," *DISCoveries*, Vol. 3, No. 10, October 1990, 99; Stanley Booth, "The Playboy Interview: Keith Richards," *Playboy*, Vol. 36, No. 10, October 1989, 59–68, 114–115, 143; Paul McCartney, *MTV Unplugged*, rec. 25 January 1991, Limehouse Studios, London; Donovan Leitch, *The Autobiography of Donovan: The Hurdy Gurdy Man* (New York: St. Martin's Press, 2005), 60; Jack Elliott promotional handbill (author's collection), circa 1983.

16. Atkinson, "Ramblin' with Jack Elliott," 2–10.

17. Bill Carruthers, Stan Jacobson, producers, *The Johnny Cash Show*, Nashville, TN, broadcast on ABC Television, 6 January 1971.

18. Robert Hilburn, "Folk Music Mixes Social, Political," *Los Angeles Times*, 20 April 1970, F9.

19. "Jack Elliott Rambles onto PBS Pop-Rock Series," PBS Press Release, "Boboquivari #9, Ramblin' Jack Elliott," undated; "Program Information," PBS Press Release, "Boboquivari #9, "Ramblin' Jack Elliott," KCET Los Angeles, undated; Hollie I. West, "Preview: Boboquivari," *Washington Post*, Times Herald, 4 August 1971, B6.

20. Ramblin' Jack Elliott, "Boboquivari, #9," broadcast 29 September 1971, KCET, Los Angeles.

21. David Amram notes to *No More Walls* (Flying Fish Records 752), 1979.

22. "A Tribute to Woody Guthrie Part 1 and Part 2" (advertisement), reproduced in Michael Krogsgaard, *Positively Bob Dylan: A Thirty Year Discography, Concert & Recording Sessions Guide, 1960–1991* (Ann Arbor, MI: Popular Culture, 1991), 77; Nat Hentoff, "Woody Guthrie Still Prowls Our Memories," *New York Times*, 16 April 1972, D28; Michael Cooney, "Record Reviews—The Woody Guthrie Tribute: Another View," *Sing Out!* Vol. 22, No. 2, March/April, 1973, 43; Ira Meyer, "Record Reviews: A Tribute to Woody Guthrie," *Sing Out!* Vol. 21, No. 4, May/June 1972, 41.

23. "Random Notes," *Rolling Stone*, No. 121, 9 November 1972, 6.

24. Robert Hilburn, "Cat Stevens Celebration at the Shrine," *Los Angeles Times*, 3 October 1972, D8; Shelly Heber, "Talent in Action: Cat Stevens/Ramblin' Jack Elliott," *Billboard* 84, 4 November 1972, 40; Lynn Van Matre, "A Joyous Celebration," *Chicago Tribune*, 16 October 1972, B18; Mike Kerrigan, "Caught in the Act: Cat Stevens," *Melody Maker*, 11 November 1972, 53.

25. Richard Cromelin, "Jack Elliott Rambles Back," *Los Angeles Times*, 1 February 1973, H15.

26. Jack Elliott and Earl Scruggs comments sourced from the film *Banjoman* (Robert French, Richard G. Abramson, and Michael C. Varhol, Producers), 1976.

27. Jack Elliott, Felt Forum, New York City, WNEW 102.7 FM radio broadcast, 18 March 1973.

28. Jay Meehan letter to Hank Reineke, 24 March 2007.

29. Ed Robbin, *Woody Guthrie and Me* (Berkeley, CA: Lancaster-Miller Publishers, 1979), 83; Jay Meehan letter to Hank Reineke, 24 March 2007.

30. G. Brown, "Asked and Answered: John Prine," *Denver Music Examiner*, www.examiner.com/x-363-Denver-Music-Examiner~y2008m6d5-Asked-and-answered-John-Prine (accessed 10 June 2008); Jay Meehan letter to Hank Reineke, 24 March 2007; *Bobby Bare and Friends* (Bare Works, 1985), Steven J. Greil, Executive Producer/Producer; Jim Yockey, Director; Pam Zimmerman, Writer/Associate Producer.

31. "Random Notes," *Rolling Stone*, No. 138, 5 July 1973, 5; "Television," *New York Times*, 3 August 1973, 61.

32. John Rockwell, "Jack Elliott Dips Anew into Woody Guthrie Era," *New York Times*, 1 October 1973, 45.

33. "Random Notes," *Rolling Stone*, No. 132, 12 April 1973, 5.

34. Jack Elliott notes to *Ramblin' Jack Elliott—Live in Japan* (King Bellwood Records, OFM 1002), 1977.

35. Elliott notes to *Ramblin' Jack Elliott*.

36. "Random Notes," *Rolling Stone*, No. 162, 6 June 1974, 28.

37. Jack Elliott, Main Point, Bryn Mawr, PA, 15 February 1975.

38. Jack Elliott, Other End, New York City, 1 July 1975.

39. "Paul Colby's the Other End in the Village" (advertisement), *Village Voice*, 30 June 1975, 93.

40. Jack Elliott, Other End, New York City, 1 July 1975.

41. "Nights at the End," *New Yorker* 51, 28 July 1975, 19–20.

42. Joe Kivak, "Abandoned Love," in *Encounters with Bob Dylan: If You See Him, Say Hello*, ed. Tracey Johnson (San Francisco: Humble Press, 2000), 90–91; "Nights at the End," *New Yorker*, No. 51, 28 July 1975, 19–20.

43. Jack Elliott, Other End, New York City, 3 July 1975; Paul Cable, *Bob Dylan: His Unreleased Recordings* (New York: Schirmer Books, 1978), 111.

44. "Nights at the End," 19–20; Jack Elliott, Bitter End, New York City, 9 May 2001.

45. John Rockwell, "Jack Elliott Sings Winningly at Club," *New York Times*, 26 September 1975, 23; Jack Elliott, Bitter End, New York City, 9 May 2001.

46. Krogsgaard, *Positively Bob Dylan*, 109; Nick Cristiano, "Ramblin' Jack and the Monsters of Folk Tour," *Philadelphia Inquirer*, 17 April 1998, www.phillynews.co...h_and_science/BLUE20.htm (accessed 26 April 1998).

47. Sam Shepard, *Rolling Thunder Logbook* (New York: Penguin Books, 1978); Larry Sloman, *On the Road with Bob Dylan: Rolling with the Thunder* (New York: Bantam Books, 1978).

48. "Dylan, Baez Open Tour," *Dallas Morning News* from UPI feed, 4 November 1975, 10; John Rockwell, "Bob Dylan Tour Lands on Plymouth Rock,"

New York Times, 1 November 1975, 60; Jack Elliott, War Memorial Auditorium, Plymouth, MA, 30 October 1975.

49. Shepard, *Rolling Thunder Logbook*, 13.

50. Shepard, *Rolling Thunder Logbook*, 14.

51. Fish Griwkowsky, "Ramblin' Jack, Well Rambles: Storytelling Legend Shares His Thoughts," *Edmonton Sun*, 12 March 2004, www.canoe.ca/News Stand/EdmontonSun/Entertainment/2004/03/12/pf-379355.html (accessed 29 January 2005); Sloman, *On the Road with Bob Dylan*, 355–356; John Wesley Harding, "The Wanted Man Interview: Ramblin' Jack Elliott," *The Telegraph*, No. 50, Winter 1994, 28; Jack Elliott, Speakeasy, New York City, broadcast by Bob Fass on *Radio Unnamable*, WBAI-FM, New York City, 2000; John Rockwell, "Folk-Rock Stars Give a Concert at Jersey Prison," *New York Times*, 8 December 1975, 35; Frank Rose, "Back Pages: New York—Dylan: Knocking on Hurricane's Cell, *Circus*, No. 128, 2 March 1976, 52.

52. John Wesley Harding, "No Exit: Talkin' Bob Dylan Blues with Ramblin' Jack Elliott, *Bam (Bay Are Music) Magazine*, 2 June 1995, 41; John May interview with Jack Elliott, 12 February 2005.

53. Harding, "The Wanted Man Interview," 28–29.

54. Marc Eliot, *Death of a Rebel: Starring Phil Ochs and a Small Circle of Friends* (Garden City, NY: Anchor Books/Doubleday, 1979); Michael Schumacher, *There but for Fortune: The Life of Phil Ochs* (Boston: Hyperion Books, 1996); Robert E. Tomasson, "Phil Ochs a Suicide at 35; Singer of Peace Movement," *New York Times*, 10 April 1976, 26.

55. *Hard Rain*, NBC Television, Top Value Television, Broadcast 14 September 1976.

56. Robert Palmer, "The Pop Life: Friends of Phil Ochs Sing a Tribute to Him Tonight at the Felt Forum," *New York Times*, 28 May 1976, 59; John J. O'Connor, "TV Weekend," *New York Times*, 8 July 1977, 61; Robert Palmer, "Friends Perform in Ochs Concert," *New York Times*, 30 May 1976, 41; "Phil Ochs Memorial Celebration," WHYY-TV/Philadelphia-Wilmington, broadcast on PBS 9 July 1977.

57. *Harrison Tape Guide* (New York: Weiss Publishing, 1975), 18.

58. Richard Cromelin, "At McCabes: Gamblin' Gambol with Ramblin' Jack," *Los Angeles Times*, 14 February 1977, D12; Susan Peterson, "Talent in Action: Ramblin' Jack Elliott/Kajsa Ohman," *Billboard*, Vol. 89, 26 February 1977, 39–44.

59. Chris Jorgensen, "An Interview with Ramblin' Jack Elliott," *DISCoveries*, October 1990, 99; Jeff Stark, "Hard Travelin': Ramblin' Jack Elliott Has a Few More Stories to Tell," *Dallas Morning Observer*, 9–15 April 1998, www.dallas observe...ry=Ramblin'Jack Elliott (accessed 26 April 1998).

60. Jorgensen, "An Interview with Ramblin' Jack Elliott," 99.

61. Michael Goldberg, "Ramblin' Jack Elliott Sings the Same Old 25 Songs," *San Francisco Examiner*, 15 July 1979; Kristen Baggelaar and Donald Milton, *Folk Music: More Than a Song* (New York: Thomas Y. Crowell, 1976), 120.

REASON TO BELIEVE 243

62. Artie Traum, "When Legends Meet: Rambling Jack and the Master of Meditation," *Oak Report: A Quarterly Journal on Music & Musicians*, Vol. 2, No. 1, 1981, 1; Robert Palmer, "Ramblin' Jack to the Rescue," *New York Times*, 9 August 1977, 28.

63. Jack Elliott on *Bread & Roses: Festival of Acoustic Music—Greek Theater, U.C. Berkeley* (Fantasy Records F-79009), 1979.

64. Boris Weintraub, "Jack Elliot, for 25 Years A-Ramblin'," *Washington (D.C.) Star*, 17 September 1979; Craig Harris, "A Mosaic of Stories," *Dirty Linen*, No. 63, April/May 1996, 17; Tom Surowicz, "Hard Travelin'," *Twin Cities Reader*, April 26 through May 2, 1989.

65. "Random Notes," *Rolling Stone*, No. 267, 15 June 1978, 61–62; Arthur Chang and Charles Webb, Producers, *Honky Tonk Nights* (Tapeworm Productions, 1988).

66. Jack Elliott and Joady Guthrie, "Woody Guthrie Birthday Celebration," Berkeley, CA, 14 July 1978; Jack Elliott on *Coffee Break Concert Series*, 17 August 1978; "Tim Hardin Due at McCabes," *Los Angeles Times*, 10 November 1978, H27.

67. Ira Mayer, "Jack Elliott's Still Ramblin' On," *New York Post*, 17 May 1979, 34.

68. Larry Scanlan, "Ramblin' Jack—the Performer Peaks," unknown publication, author's collection, 24 December 1979.

69. Goldberg, "Ramblin' Jack Elliott Sings the Same Old 25 Songs."

70. "Newport Folk Festival—A Revival of a Great Tradition" (advertisement), *New York Times*, 10 August 1979, C2.

71. Mike Joyce, "Gibson and Elliott," *Washington Post*, September 17, 1979; Weintraub, "Jack Elliot, for 25 Years A-Ramblin'."

72. Jack Elliott, Keystone Club, Palo Alto, CA, 12 November 1979, KFAT radio broadcast.

73. Scanlan, "Ramblin' Jack—the Performer Peaks"; Colin Irwin, "Living Legend," *Melody Maker*, 16 August 1980, 39.

Detour 7

O N APRIL 20, 1980, Jack Elliott and Barbara Dodge traveled to Germany for an appearance at the Cologne Folk Festival. His set that afternoon was nothing short of brilliant. Folk music fans watched, worshipfully, as Elliott played and sang "San Francisco Bay Blues," "Buffalo Skinners," "Diamond Joe," "Muleskinner Blues," "Pretty Boy Floyd," "South Coast," "Talkin' Fishing Blues," "Freight Train Blues," and "Don't Think Twice, It's All Right." The songs had been rearranged to suit Elliott's new style, his singing understated and cool, a facile guitar perfectly underpinning the lyrics. But Elliott's masterful turn at Cologne was merely the prelude to a more significant event. Carsten Linde, the roots-music festival promoter and author-editor of *Folksongs aus Amerika*, had convinced Jack to end his decade-long boycott of the recording studio.[1]

The resulting effort, *Kerouac's Last Dream*, remains one of Elliott's finest recordings. Though billed as a coproduction of Elliott, Barbara Dodge, and Carsten Linde, the album's real production hero was recording engineer Günter Pauler, who expertly captured the most intimate and austere nuances of Jack's voice and guitar. On no preceding recording had Elliott's vocals been more wistful and weary, his guitar playing as gentle and confident. It's true that, on the surface, *Kerouac's Last Dream* seemed to offer little that was new. Of the ten songs comprising the final cut, only two had not appeared on an earlier solo album. The first of these, "Blue Eyes Crying in the Rain," had enjoyed recent popularity due to Willie Nelson's fine version that appeared on his *Red Headed Stranger* album. The second song to make a *solo* debut was "Cup of Coffee." Technically, "Cup of

Coffee" had already appeared on Johnny Cash's *Everybody Loves a Nut* album for Columbia, but Cash handled the main vocal on that recording, leaving Elliott little to do but contribute the occasional yodel. Otherwise, *Kerouac's Last Dream* was programmed with material long familiar to his fans. But the songs never sounded better, Elliott smoothing all the rough corners, making each his very own. Perhaps anticipating criticism of his decision to re-record so many familiar songs, Elliott contributed a note of explanation in the album's booklet: "Somebody is singin an old song cause the new ones don't have any spirit of life. But if life shall go on and if we are to live we must have certain things, air, water, wood. Here is a man who is building a better canoe. . . . I have been asked, sometimes, why I don't learn new songs. These are old ones and I have sung them for a long time. They are good and I think they shall always be good."[2]

Kerouac's Last Dream was recorded on April 24 and 25, 1980, at Tonstudio St. Blasien, Northeim, West Germany. Tonstudio, according to Linde, was "a small studio built into the wine cellar of a former medieval abbey" and "Elliott was fascinated by doing a new recording after a long break which had already lasted far too many years. There he was: cowboy hat, red bandana his beautiful guitar in hand and an equally cute woman by his side . . . enjoying what he was doing in a relaxed mood."[3]

"Relaxed" is probably the operative word here as Elliott handled the well-worn material with the brilliant, understated confidence of his finest "live" performances. Put at ease by the tranquil wine-cellar setting, the songs passed easily through him. Listening to the playback a few days following the sessions, Linde recalled no one involved in the production "was amazed by how intense and great [the performances] sounded through the recording machine because we knew that these were Ramblin' Jack's best recordings so far." Elliott provisionally agreed, careful to note that "there can never be a best record, only better ones."[4]

Elliott recorded more material at Tonstudio than could fit on a standard album. Left off the original version of *Kerouac's Last Dream* were fine, if less than perfect, versions of "Detour," "Don't Think Twice, It's All Right," "The Soldier's Last Letter," "Night Herding Song," and "Mean Mama Blues." More interestingly, Elliott also taped such previously unrecorded songs as Roy Acuff's "Freight Train Blues," Dylan's "I Threw It All Away," and Gene Autry's "Riding Down the Canyon." There was nearly enough material recorded for a follow-up album, but the outtakes would not see issue for another seventeen years.

Shortly after the *Kerouac's Last Dream* sessions, Elliott and Champion Jack Dupree, the New Orleans–born, expatriate blues pianist, appeared on the popular German television pop music program *Rockpalast.* Dupree was a fairly well-known figure throughout Europe. He had left the United States in 1958, eventually settling in a number of Western European countries, influencing a generation of fledgling blues piano players. Elliott made his way to WDR television's Studio B soundstage and found that *Rockpalast* was taped live before a young audience sitting sprawled out, uncomfortably, on the studio floor. The studio lights were hot and the room temperature was made worse by Elliott's decision to wear a green long sleeve pullover and western neckerchief, causing sweat to bead beneath the brim of his cowboy hat. He opened his half of the program with a workmanlike, nonchatty, 10-song set before joining Champion Jack on guitar and vocal for an impromptu, rollicking version of "MacNeil (Salt Pork, West Virginia)." The program was broadcast on July 28, though Jack's original 10-song set was pruned to a mere four songs for the telecast.[5]

The summer of 1980 brought Elliott home to North America, briefly, for the folk festival season. On the first of July, he was in Boston for a multiact "folk revival" show at the Paradise Rock Club, featuring Mimi Fariña, Tom Paxton, and Josh White, Jr. Later that month, Elliott traveled to Jericho Beach Park, British Columbia, for the third Vancouver Folk Festival. It was his first appearance at the event, the festival program describing him as "a walking Library of Congress of folk music," the artist who bridged "the gap between the last of the hobos, cowboys and other repositories of American folk songs who were dying out in the forties and the new revival generation of the sixties."[6]

Following the Vancouver event, Elliott and Dodge crossed the Atlantic again for an appearance at the 16th annual Cambridge Folk Festival, scheduled for the first weekend of August. At a Holiday Inn outside of Cambridge, Elliott granted a nearly four-hour audience to writer Colin Irwin, a musician and BBC personality who served as one of the festival's master of ceremonies. Irwin asked Elliott why it took him nearly 17 years to find his way back to England, with Jack replying, "That's a good question and I don't know how to answer it." His life in the States, Jack explained, kept him plenty busy, "traveling back and forth from coast to coast like a shuttle-cock. It's almost as if I forgot there was anything outside of America." He revisited some old tales as well, the conversation peopled with such familiar names as Kerouac, Guthrie, and Dylan. He admitted he had gotten "a bit careless" over the past decade with his career, particularly as a recording artist. He off-handedly mentioned that a new album had recently been recorded in Germany, but provided few details. As always, the specter of Bob Dylan loomed large in Irwin's excellent profile, published in *Melody Maker* a week following the Cambridge event. Elliott remained steadfastly loyal to his old friend, even when Irwin and Dodge tried to get him to admit to some lingering bitterness at Dylan's success and appropriation of his style. But Jack would have none of it. "Bob had the good sense to take the good things of Woody Guthrie and absorb them without copying Woody's faults and weak spots," Jack straight forwardly answered.[7]

The Cambridge Folk Festival had been recorded by the BBC. A 50-minute television documentary was broadcast that October on BBC-2, featuring performances by Lonnie Donegan, Silly Wizard, Don McLean, Richard and Linda Thompson, Leo Kottke, Claudia Schmidt, and Jack. The BBC film captures Elliott performing a playful version of "Don't Think Twice, It's All Right" as well as a wistful "If I Were a Carpenter." Jack's musical segment was prefaced in the film by yet *another* interview with Colin Irwin, who gamely tried to get a reluctant Elliott to share his memories of his first meeting with Dylan. Jack obliged, but was clearly bored with the subject. When asked to explain, yet again, why he chose to stay away from England for so many years, Jack curtly replied, "Well, I was on vacation" and left it at that. The BBC Transcription Service offered a professionally engineered, six-song excerpt of Elliott's commanding performance at the Cambridge Folk Festival to interested radio affiliates.[8]

Following the Cambridge event, Elliott and Dodge were due to perform at a far more intimate gig at the Amberley Folk Club in Sussex. The August 4 performance was booked by Stan Wigg, an old friend who knew Elliott from the 1950s. That night, Jack dedicated "South Coast" to Wigg, who was probably unaware, until Elliott casually mentioned it while onstage, that he had nearly missed the date. It seems that after removing his Stetson at a leisurely breakfast at their hotel that morning, Jack had absentmindedly left the hat on the floor beneath the dining table. He was hours out from London when he realized he had left his beloved hat behind, necessitating a lengthy and untimely U-turn back to the hotel. At the Amberley, the reception was nothing short of rapturous, the crowd keyed in on all the history that surrounded Ramblin' Jack. He responded by performing at his best, even agreeing to a request by an excited guitar enthusiast for a rare, bright flat-picking demonstration of the Carter Family's "Wildwood Flower." Near the end of the concert, Elliott was riffing between verses of his own "Cup of Coffee" when he told the rapt audience something he had not been able to say in years: "Oh, I got a new album coming out. I didn't think I'd ever do that, it's been ten years now since I did an album. It's coming out soon on the Folk Freak label. It's called *Kerouac's Last Dream*, which is based on some dream that Jack Kerouac had written down . . . that I had some million selling hit. But I never had no hit record—you know *that*. But this is gonna be one, I think."[9]

In October 1980, Carsten Linde brought together an assortment of traditional singers from Western Europe, the British Isles, and the United States, calling them his Folk Friends. This was the first time since 1978 that Linde had arranged a gathering of his Folk Friends, the first meeting having produced a fine LP collection by the same name. For 12 days, Linde recorded the musical goings-on at the the the Fortuna Windmill in Struckum, a small village in the north of Germany, as well as at his own cellar studio in St. Blasien, Northeim. The musicians whom Linde assembled for the second incarnation of his Folk Friends included many of Western Europe's finest artists: Davey Arthur, Alex Campbell, Finbar Furey, Dick Gaughan, Andy Irvine, Wizz Jones, Dolores Keane, Werner Lammerhirt, and Danny Thompson. There was also a sprinkling of American talent, including Derroll Adams, Guy and Candie Carawan, and Ramblin' Jack, who contributed a song or two. Photographs from the gathering show Elliott appearing pensive and unsmiling, seemingly less at ease than his bright-eyed musical colleagues. Regardless, Elliott recorded essential versions of "Don't Think Twice, It's All Right," and "Me and Bobby McGee" (the latter with Werner Lammerhirt on second guitar), with both performances included on the 1981 gatefold double album *Folk Friends 2*.[10]

The early 1980s found Jack often splitting his time between North America and Western Europe, his touring bringing him to the outermost fringes of both continents. In 1981, Elliott was in Anchorage, Alaska, for two concerts at the Warehouse, on January 16 and 17. Summer found him performing on Britain's Channel Islands, halfway between southern England and northern France. At the Benjamin Meaker Theatre on the isle of Jersey, Elliott was in fine form, performing the rare one-offs "Kentucky Waltz" and Hoagy Carmichael's "Hong Kong Blues." One newspaperman wrote, "the happy faces and loud applause were proof that we were glad that this man is living in our lifetime." Following a gritty, heartfelt performance of "House of the Rising Sun," the same critic offered that if singer Eric Burdon of the Animals had first heard Elliott's version "he wouldn't have bothered booking studio time."[11]

In 1982, Elliott was performing at a Houston cabaret called Rockefellers when he was approached backstage by Dee Brown and Bruce Bryant, two fans and talented filmmakers who thought he would make an interesting subject for a documentary film. Brown had been in California when he first saw Elliott perform on a 1959 twin bill with the Chambers Brothers at Rolf Cahn's Berkeley nightspot the Blind Lemon. Though Brown had been introduced to Elliott's music through "lefty friends," it was actually Jack's handling of such traditional material as "The Cuckoo" that blew him away. Bryant had been introduced to Elliott's music through Brown, though he had to wait some time before getting to see Jack perform. "We went to see him for the first time at a big show in Texas, but he didn't show for some reason," Bryant remembered, laughing off this less-celebrated aspect of Jack Elliott fandom. In the early 1970s, Bryant, Brown, and their friend Charlie Hargrave opened a little club with the big name of the Sweetheart of Texas Concert Hall and Saloon in their hometown of Houston. One of their first missions was to book Elliott, but Bryant made the mistake of taking Elliott out for an adventure in a hot air balloon on the afternoon of that first concert. The trip started out innocently enough, but the balloon ride was interrupted when Jack insisted on bringing the basket down in a cow pasture so he could, as Bryant recalled, tape-record "audio of the cattle 'talking to us' when we landed in the middle of the herd." This unplanned adventure made Elliott late for the gig, but the Houstonians at the Sweetheart forgave his tardiness when he treated them to a masterpiece of spontaneous musical theater. Onstage that night, Jack cued up the tape he had made of ambient cattle sounds and sang the traditional cowboy lullaby "Night Herding Song" over the recording. It was this sort of eccentric magic that Brown and Bryant hoped they might capture on film.[12]

Elliott was intrigued by the film proposal but he wasn't in Houston on a musical mission. He had been spending a lot of time in nearby Galveston, having signed on as an enthusiastic member of an all-volunteer crew helping to rehabilitate the *Elissa*. The *Elissa* was a three-mast, iron-hulled sailing ship built in 1877 at an Aberdeen, Scotland, shipyard and brought to Galveston in July 1979. In October 1980, a volunteer program was commissioned to assist on the rehab of the *Elissa*, the decision attracting a coalition of enthusiastic locals, sailors, history buffs, and Ramblin' Jack. Bryant and Brown shot some footage of Elliott at work on the *Elissa*, but the heart of the documentary was to be built around a musical performance at Houston's Anderson Fair nightclub. The filmmakers brought in a remote truck from Austin for the shoot, but Bryant remembered the fader was inoperable and "we could only do cuts. That may have been a blessing in disguise as it forced us to keep it simple." That night at Anderson Fair, Elliott performed "Muleskinner Blues," "Night Herding Song," "Cup of Coffee," "Don't Think Twice, It's All Right," "912 Greens," and "Diamond Joe." Elliott, as usual, provided the requisite tension, catching the filmmakers off guard when he wandered away from the microphone mid-set to say hello to an old guitar-playing friend who happened to be performing with violinist Stephen Grappelli at a nightclub across the street.[13]

Aside from the performance footage, the resulting film, *Ramblin' Jack in Texas*, featured testimonials from Arlo Guthrie, Barbara Dodge, and Austin-based singer Jerry Jeff Walker; the latter opined that Jack was the first folksinger he had met who was not overbearingly grim, that had fun with the music. The filmmakers shot segments of Jack talking at length about Woody and Dylan and others, and also caught him running through the paces atop a frisky, cutting horse. One of Brown's favorite memories was of cameraman Bob Brandon bravely climbing alongside his subject so he could capture Elliott singing a sea chantey high in the rigging of the *Elissa*. The original intent was for *Ramblin' Jack in Texas* to be sold to PBS, but to Brown's diappointment the network "showed little interest and we had little knowledge about how to go about doing anything else with it." It probably did not help that Elliott seemed ambivalent with the final result. This was a shame as the documentary captures, in Bryant's estimation, Jack Elliott "at the top of his game." The problem wasn't *Ramblin' Jack in Texas*, the problem was Ramblin' Jack himself. He was notoriously camera shy for a public figure, admitting to "psychotic fits" as a result of flash photography. He told singer John Wesley Harding, bluntly, "I never like the way I look in pictures," and he tried his best to stay far away from cameras, which is tough when you're in show business. For someone with a healthy ego who spent the better part of his life onstage, Elliott did not particularly enjoy being the center of attention. Robert Shelton noted early on, "Jack was always a little unsure of himself, easily hurt behind his Stetson-topped, Marlboro-country cool." Elliott screened the footage of *Ramblin' Jack in Texas* and Bryant recalled, "I don't think Jack liked the way he looked [in the film], but later he felt good about it." Brown concurs, remembering, "I always felt he didn't like it. However, he recently said he *did* like it. Things change." Bryant remains hopeful that *Ramblin' Jack in Texas*, perhaps re-edited, might yet be made available for the home video market.[14]

If working on the rehabilitation of the *Elissa* brought Elliott great satisfaction, it had not brought in any income. He needed to go back to work, but things were getting increasingly tough on the road. The commercial popularity of folk music continued its decline, with many clubs shuttering their doors. One casualty was Boston's renowned folk-music club the Idler, which would close in the autumn of 1982. Idler manager Len Rothenberg still hoped to make a go of it and temporarily shifted the club's operation to the Ryles Club in Inman Square. He dubbed his temporary nightspot "Not at the Idler," showcasing Ramblin' Jack on October 12 and a twin bill of Jesse Winchester and Shawn Colvin on October 13 and 14. But it was simply not like the old days, the crowds just weren't coming.[15]

There was still a hootenanny spirit in the air, but musical gatherings to benefit political causes were no longer solely the provenance of the folk music community. In December 1982, Elliott had been invited to participate in the "Freedom Jam" at Uncle Charlie's in Corte Madera, California. He had been brought on as a special guest by his friend Bob Weir of the Grateful Dead and the "Jam" included performances by Bill Kreutzmann, John Cipollina of Quicksilver Messenger Service, Barry Melton of Country Joe and the Fish, Peter Walsh, and Norton Buffalo. After performing a set of his own, Weir introduced Elliott who ambled onstage and joined the Dead guitarist for duets of "San Francisco Bay Blues" and "Muleskinner Blues." A band member's request to Jack to perform "Tennessee Stud" was quickly deflected, as always, but Elliott acquiesced to what he would describe as a "diminished, downtown version" of "Don't Think Twice, It's All Right," a Grateful Dead–style accompanying fluid guitar line dancing around his own finger-picked guitar and lyrical free improvisation.[16]

Playing with rock stars was fun, but Elliott was a folksinger to the core and the early 1980s brought tough times. There were the stirrings of a new, smaller-scale, singer-songwriter movement. Elliott was not unaware of it, but watched from the sidelines. In early winter of 1983, his father took ill and Jack, for the first time since the mid-1950s, stepped off the road and settled in for a six-month vigil on Long Island. One of the few projects he allowed himself during this somber period was an appearance in Jim Brown's documentary film on the life of Woody Guthrie, *Hard Travelin'*. His contribution was a slow stroll with Arlo through Washington Square Park. Elliott reminisced about first meeting Woody at the party at 120 University Place, and the afternoon rides on the Belt Parkway in Totsy with Woody at the wheel, and Arlo, Joady, and "Puffy" (Nora) giggling in the backseat. Brown also filmed a fascinating musical segment featuring Elliott, Guthrie, and Sonny Terry performing such classics as "New York Town" and "Hard Travelin'." He also performed a solo note-perfect reading of Guthrie's "Talking Sailor (Talking Merchant Marine)." Though the old talking blues did not make the film's final cut, it was included on the film's accompanying soundtrack album. *Hard Travelin'* was produced for the U.S. television market and first broadcast on the New York City PBS affiliate WNET-TV on March 7, 1984.[17]

Elliott was not able to watch the local PBS television screening of *Hard Travelin'* with his father. Dr. Abraham Adnopoz passed away in August 1983, leaving Jack to settle the details of his father's estate. The months

preceding and following his father's death had been a reflective, meditative time. He had been away from the nightclubs, away from the smoky
bars, away from the endless procession of one-night stands, away from the
bottles and shot glasses being proffered by friends and fans. He stayed with
friends in and around Westport, Connecticut, and contemplated his next
move.

That October, Elliott was hanging around the seaport town of Mystic
when he was approached by Randy Sue Coburn, a freelance writer on
assignment from the decidedly unfolksy men's magazine *Esquire*. Coburn
had been commissioned to profile the wandering folk-music legend for an
upcoming issue, but her first order of business was simply trying to locate
the peripatetic troubadour. It took Coburn two months to *find* Elliott who,
she reported, was temporarily living outside of Mystic in a small motor
home mounted atop a 1977 Dodge pickup. Coburn's resulting profile,
"On the Trail of Ramblin' Jack Elliott," was one of the finest essays on the
folksinger, reintroducing America to one of its forgotten musical heroes.
Initially, Elliott was not in much of a mood to chat. He and Coburn needed
to go "on the road" so he could clear his head. This tactic was apparently
successful, as once he got to talking, the interview lasted nearly three days:
"We drove all around Connecticut with a rent-a-car in the rain," Elliott
recalled. "I had to keep moving in order not to feel bored, 'cause I was
telling her the same damn stories that I had told millions of times before.
I was tired of talking about myself. But I wanted to do it with freshness
and vigor. . . . And to be able to tell it right, I had to get into a sort of
mood where it's enjoyable. You can't force things like that. But by driving around in the rain, and getting lost in Connecticut and Rhode Island,
looking at deserted beaches and stuff. . . . That kind of scenery and that
kind of movement got us in a good mood." Coburn not only recounted
Elliott's standard biography, she touched on the many career and personal
frustrations suffered in recent years, the personal and professional costs of
a lifetime of rambling. Coburn noted the recent death of his father and
Jack's troubles with pharmaceuticals and alcohol, which, surprisingly, led
to a brief dalliance with Christianity, shortly following Dylan's conversion
in 1979. "It isn't always easy being known as an inspiration to the rich and
famous when you're neither yourself," Coburn wrote, perfectly capturing
Elliott's battered spiritual state. The welcome publicity came out of the
blue and Elliott was mostly pleased with the resulting *Esquire* profile. He
did dismiss Coburn's assertion that a "prestigious independent label is now
interested in recording him. All he needs are new songs, some of which
he hopes he can write if he can just find a new house to settle into." "Oh,

I don't know if that's true," Elliott told the *Aquarian Arts Weekly* the following spring. "Well, it was at that time that I was maybe thinking about talking to one of those small folk labels like 'Mountain Railroad.'" As for Elliott's promise of writing "new songs," "No, I was gonna, but I didn't do it," he answered unapologetically. "The inspiration passed like a fart in the wind."[18]

In August 1984, Elliott settled in the town of Newcastle, a quaint New England village nestled between the Sheepscot and Damariscotta rivers in southeastern Maine. Newcastle was the home of Peter Throckmorton, the underwater archaeologist who had supervised the exhumation of the shipwreck in the Mediterranean Sea that Elliott had visited with Herb Greer in 1960. Elliott had settled into a temporary residency in a small dory shack that sat adjacent to the Throckmorton home. The shack was so contained that Elliott bragged he needed to feed less than three cords of wood into two iron pot-bellied stoves to warm him through the winter. Throckmorton was a genial host who would invite Jack into the kitchen of his own home, where the two men shared stories over glasses of Jim Beam. His tongue loosened by the whiskey, Throckmorton would spool through his salty repertoire of entertaining, profanity-laced stories. Elliott listened with fascination, sometimes writing down the best of Peter's stories in his notebook. He was of the notion he might be able to turn some of those tales into songs, but, as was too often the case, Elliott never did get around to writing those songs. The old songs, as always, would have to do.[19]

On occasion, the old songs were still in demand. On Friday evening, February 24, 1984, Elliott was due in Cambridge, Massachusetts, for a concert at Harvard University's Paine Hall. Here, he would not have to shoulder the burden of carrying his rusting show on his own. Concord Productions, the company responsible for the booking, saw to it that Elliott would share the bill with two old, bluesy, and equally road-tested friends, Dave Van Ronk and guitarist/songster Spider John Koerner. Days prior to the gig, the *Boston Globe* identified Elliott, Van Ronk, and Koerner as a "triple threat trio . . . three key factors to the '60s folk revival." Which was a nice way of saying it was to be a nostalgia show.[20]

Prior to the concert at Paine Hall, Jack consented to a brutally honest telephone interview with the *Providence Journal-Bulletin*. He told the *Bulletin*'s Tony Lioce that he was "numb, pretty burned out, just licking the wounds of the last thirty years." It was a grim assessment of a stalled career, hardly the standard promotional fare an artist might engage in to help fill the seats at an upcoming concert date. Jack admitted that playing music was no longer fun for him, that he played now only for necessity, as a means of making money: "I haven't enjoyed myself in a long, long time." Elliott admitted he was happiest when touring England in the 1950s, as the audiences back then were so much more "appreciative."[21]

Elliott admitted that some of his problems were self-inflicted, the result of his drinking, now somewhat under control. Jack told much the same to a writer from *Fast Folk* magazine, who found Jack nursing a glass of tonic water at the bar, explaining how old friend and Rolling Thunder colleague Bob Neuwirth "had been central in helping him to overcome his battle with alcohol." Elliott admitted to Lioce that while touring with the Rolling Thunder Revue, he was "drunk the entire time. I didn't even realize I was on that tour until afterwards when they charged me two thousand dollars for my liquor bills."[22]

There were other sources of frustration. His friends agreed that *Kerouac's Last Dream* was one of his finest recordings, but Jack's "new" album was now nearly four years old. It was 1984 and no American label seemed interested in picking it up. Elliott had ignored the U.S. recording industry for more than a decade, and he found the record business had become more fickle in his absence. *Kerouac's Last Dream* had turned into something of a nightmare. "I haven't been able to sell it to any of the American companies," Jack told Lioce. "Everybody agrees it sounds really good, but nobody'll release it. I could release it myself—if I could come up with the cash to buy it back from the Germans. Imagine that? I've got to buy my own record back from somebody else."[23]

On Friday afternoon, February 24, Jack left Maine for the drive south to Cambridge, a cold New England rain falling as he neared Boston. Jack made his way to Paine Hall, a small auditorium of 435 seats, but found the crew had not yet set up for the sound check. So he set off on foot to find a place to eat, settling on the Acropolis, a popular local restaurant. Afterward, Jack jogged back to Paine Hall where he found Van Ronk, only recently arrived, waiting for him backstage and warming his hands. Jack admitted, "It was nice to be back in old Cambridge again. There's a certain kind of magic that seems to still be there." He surveyed the audience and came to the conclusion that many in the crowd were, for better or worse, "still living in the sixties." To underscore his observation, Elliott casually dropped the name of the old Club 47 into one of his spoken-word interludes during the show. Elliott sarcastically remarked the mere *mention* of the fabled club brought forth "a lot of sighs out in the audience and two or three people fainted." In truth, Jack did not really do all that much talking that night. He had not been onstage for some time and, in his own words, was "feeling shy." But sharing the bill with such old friends as Van Ronk and Spider John took a lot of the pressure off his shoulders.[24]

Following the Harvard gig, Elliott left Boston and headed south for New York, the rain following him clear to Greenwich Village. Jack had a February 25 show at Folk City on West 3rd, with two shows scheduled for eight and eleven that evening. Like the many legendary musicians who still played there, Folk City too was struggling to meet the rent. The nightclub now offered as much comedy and improvisational theater as it did folk music, but it was operating against the odds and its time wasn't long.

"New York seems more exciting than usual," a smiling Elliott told the crowd after climbing onstage, "more exciting than ever." There was still a trace of rust in Elliott's performance. He opened the first set with the "Salty Dog Blues," but started into mumbling and improvising verses when his memory faltered. "Buffalo Skinners" started promisingly, but he soon lost the thread of the song, explaining that the ballad now seemed somehow "unreal to him." He reasoned that living in wintry, wet New England for the past year had left him unable to sing "Buffalo Skinners," a "wild, old, dusty song," with any grit or conviction. He later blew the dust off Gene Autry's "Riding Down the Canyon," the Hollywood-western classic, but fumbled through the chord changes and only half recollected the words. Musically, the first set was less than hoped for, but Elliott's storytelling abilities remained intact, and he easily charmed the friendly Village audience. Jack had been away from the stages of New York City for far too long, and his fans were grateful to have him back.[25]

If the early set was distracted and halting, the late-night set was a modest return to form. Elliott wisely chose to open with the always-dependable "San Francisco Bay Blues." "Riding Down the Canyon" was revisited as well, still not perfect, perhaps, but a wonderfully engaging performance all the same. At one point, Elliott started to flat-pick the chord progression of the "Salty Dog Blues," which had given him so much trouble during the first set, but he soon abandoned the song with the explanation, "I can't take too much salt." Following a particularly well-tendered and poignant reading of the Bahamian lullaby "All My Trials" that quieted the room, Elliott leaned forward on his bar stool and whispered softly into the microphone "This is nice. . . . If show business could always be like this, I'd be working all the time." An audience member's request for the old cowboy song "I Ride an Old Paint" was fulfilled with Elliott, perhaps tellingly, choosing to sing the song's melancholy, desperate final verse twice. He closed the evening with a suitably dusty reading of Woody's "So Long, It's Been Good to Know You." With a nod of acknowledgment and a tip of the Stetson, Elliott stepped off the Folk City stage and out of the spotlight. He still had it.[26]

Jack left for Texas shortly following the Folk City shows, but soon returned to New England. He also accepted a late summer invitation to perform at the 23 annual Philadelphia Folk Festival. Arlo Guthrie had also been booked to play the festival, so it was arranged that Jack would meet him at his home near Washington, Massachusetts. Together they would set off with Arlo's band Shenandoah for Schwenksville, where both were to perform on Sunday, August 26. "We've never been booked alone together before," Arlo confusedly told a Philadelphia-based newspaperman during a prefestival telephone interview from his home. Guthrie hedged a bit when questioned if he and Jack would perform in tandem. Guthrie admitted that he really wasn't certain if there would be any type of collaboration. Jack "must know thousands and thousands of songs," Guthrie continued, noting that neither he nor Jack "ever rehearse." That night, Ramblin' Jack and Arlo performed together onstage, as everyone knew they would.[27]

Jack returned to Greenwich Village for two shows at Folk City on September 22, 1984. These were performances by the Ramblin' Jack of old. He masterfully balanced his storytelling sojourns with a set laced with seldom performed folk and country music chestnuts. Earlier that afternoon, Elliott had been interviewed by Robbie Woliver, one of the nightclub's co-owners, for a book he was writing on the history of the famed club. The trip down memory lane left Jack feeling a little old and nostalgic. Afterward, he stared at the walls of the club with its display of hundreds of aged, yellowing eight-by-ten photographs of past performers. The faces staring back at him were friends and colleagues, many long gone. Two days before the Folk City gig, Elliott had unfolded the morning newspaper and learned that Steve Goodman, the singer-songwriter, had died at the age of 36. Jack admitted to rarely buying newspapers; he was content to thumb through an issue once or twice a week. The reading of newspapers had become a "strange, frightening thing." It seemed that every time he opened one, he would read a "mention some friend of mine has died." On September 6, Ernest Tubb, the "Texas Troubadour" and one of Jack's earliest musical heroes, had succumbed to emphysema. Earlier in the year Tom Jans, the singer-songwriter, had been found dead in his California home. Elliott dedicated part of his Folk City set to the memory of Tubb, performing the singer's biggest hit "Walking the Floor Over You." "Not one of my favorite songs in the world," Elliott admitted, "but it's very typical of some of the first things I ever heard by Ernest Tubb." He also sang the singer's World War II–era classic "Seaman's Blues." Noting he had recorded the song with Arlo Guthrie and Sonny Terry on this very stage, Elliott began to sing a rousing version of Woody's "New York Town." But the song was aborted when he lost interest midway through and stopped completely. "That song used to be a lot more meaningful to me when I was closer to [Woody] at that time period," he offered as limp explanation for the abrupt curtailment.[28]

In the autumn of 1984 Elliott had been temporarily nesting out on the Point of Newport, Rhode Island. He had not been performing regularly as autumn passed into winter, but he would still arrange an occasional gig in the New England area to freshen his wallet. On Saturday evening, November 17, Elliott appeared alongside U. Utah Phillips and Rosalie Sorrels at Arlington Town Hall. On Sunday, December 9, he performed at Newport's Blue Pelican Jazz Club. On a frigid night when "the wind was howling" off the coast, a writer from a local Newport paper stopped by the Blue Pelican. He described Elliott as "a master who's been just about everywhere, played with just about everyone, gathered hundreds, maybe thousands of songs in that bag of his, and now delivers it all with subtle, inner strength and wisdom."[29]

Elliott was playing a gig in Toronto on New Year's Eve when a frigid 1984 gave way to an equally cold 1985. He had recently purchased a new truck to carry him from show to show, but the vehicle's heating system was not working properly so he, naturally, chose to drive to Florida where the climate would better suit his clothes. But Elliott's time in the sun was cut short. He was due back in New York City for a February 15 engagement at Folk City. He left the area surrounding Okefonokee around seven that morning for the long drive to Greenwich Village. Parking the vehicle in a New Jersey suburb, Elliott set off for the nightclub by taxi. After telling the cabbie he had just arrived from the Sunshine State so he could play this single date at Folk City, the bored driver glanced at Elliott's cowboy hat and guitar case and asked, "Oh, what is it, amateur night?"[30]

Following the two sets at Folk City, Elliott headed for Nashville. He had accepted an offer from country singer Bobby Bare to appear on his TNN television program *Bobby Bare and Friends*. It was a relaxed taping, Elliott and singer-songwriter John Prine filling the hourlong program with a handful of songs and amusing reminiscences of old tours and friends. Jack sat in with Bare's house band "Pulleybone" for an electrified version of "Muleskinner Blues," while Prine performed a group of songs from his latest LP, *Aimless Love*.[31]

On June 18, promoter George Wein announced the Newport Folk Festival would return to Fort Adams State Park on the weekend of August 3 and 4 for the first time in 16 years. Wein promised "this year we will go back to the time before Dylan went electric." Though Wein admitted, "I don't think we can recapture the old days," it wasn't from lack of trying. When the roster of performers was announced, the majority of artists were from the era of the last gathering in 1969: Joan Baez, Arlo Guthrie, Ramblin' Jack, Bonnie Raitt, Tom Paxton, Doc Watson, Taj Mahal, and Dave Van Ronk. Elliott was uncharacteristically pleased and excited to return to Newport. He told a newspaper reporter, "I drove five days and five nights to get here, with no sleep, from Oregon—just to come to one gig—and I wasn't doing it for the money. I'm going on the energy of an image that I remember from the past." Elliott delivered a nostalgic, well-received 30-minute set before a crowd of 6,500. Elliott's segment set the tone for the weekend. He reached back and sang a couple of Woody's old talking blues and "Tom Joad." There was little balance between the old and the new, however, and nearly lost among the old guard were such fresh faces as Bill Morrissey, Greg Brown, and Buskin and Batteau. The *Boston Globe* were among the newspapers that noted the dearth of fresh talent at Newport '85, but reported the younger performers had the last laugh since "the relative newcomers to the scene received several of the loudest and longest ovations from the crowd."[32]

Wavy Gravy asked Elliott to lend his services to the "Cowboys for Indians" benefit concert that he was organizing at the Berkeley Community Theater for October 14, 1985. Wavy promised a stellar lineup of talent that would include Kinky Friedman, Dave Nelson of the New Riders of the Purple Sage, Bob Weir, Peter Rowan, Jerry Jeff Walker, Kate Wolf, and Floyd Westerman. Wavy had chosen this particular Monday as it was Columbus Day, "the day the Indians found Columbus wandering aimlessly on the beach." Friedman canceled at the last minute but his absence hardly registered when fellow Texan Stevie Ray Vaughan, the talented blues guitarist, filled in as his replacement. Elliott performed three solo songs at the benefit, "Buffalo Skinners," "San Francisco Bay Blues," and "Old Shep," before Weir came out to join Jack on second guitar for "Whinin' Boy Blues."[33]

Elliott enjoyed these multiartist bills, as he enjoyed sharing the stage with old friends. One of his favorite events was Jerry Jeff Walker's annual Birthday Bash. On March 15, 1987, Walker, the country singer-songwriter ("Mr. Bojangles" and "Up Against the Wall, You Redneck Mother"), hosted the first of his birthday celebrations at Austin's Paramount Theater. The inaugural got under way with excellent sets by David Bromberg and Paul Siebel. As the lights dimmed following the interval, Jerry Jeff brought out another old friend: "Starting off the second half is going to be my good friend and mentor, a man I look up to [as he started] my interest in performing and playing songs: a wild man, the man that can't be tamed or tied down, Ramblin' Jack Elliott." Walker was a true fan, recounting in his autobiography that Elliott had been the template for many aspiring singers as himself.[34]

That spring Elliott was in Charleston, West Virginia, for the first of many visits to the *Mountain Stage* radio show. *Mountain Stage* host Larry Groce was, by his own admission, a big fan who had been trying to get Elliott to perform in Charleston since the program's inception. Elliott played five songs that evening and the audience hung on his every word. After his opening song, "Diamond Joe," was so enthusiastically received, Elliott relaxed and said, "This makes that long drive through Ohio worthwhile." The pendulum was swinging back.[35]

On August 28, 1987, Elliott made his way to the Long Island town of Westbury, where Arlo Guthrie and Shenandoah were performing at the Westbury Music Fair, an intimate theater-in-the-round. Arlo had run into Jack a few weeks earlier and had invited him to Westbury to sit in. July 14 would have been Woody's 75th birthday and Arlo had planned something special to celebrate the occasion. Three songs into his regular program, Arlo performed several of Woody's classic songs and talked a little about his famous father. He recalled there was always an endless stream of "strange people" making their way in and out of their household in Howard Beach, including "one guy who was a friend of my Dad's. They used to travel around a lot together and every once in a while he'd stop by the house. As a matter of fact," Arlo continued, "when I was a little kid he'd come to visit us one night and stayed for four years!" With that Arlo brought out Ramblin' Jack to great applause. Oddly, their first collaboration was not one of Woody's songs at all. It was "Anytime," the Herbert "Happy" Lawson/Eddy Arnold classic that Arlo had recorded in 1972 for his *Hobo's Lullaby* album. Arlo had likely gleaned the song from Jack, as it was one of Elliott's concert perennials. They soon moved into a rollicking take of Woody's "Do-Re-Mi," the two old friends trading verses before closing out with the Jimmie Rodgers's blue yodel "Waiting for a Train." Following the performance, Elliott walked off stage with a wave and a smile, and Arlo surveyed the crowd from his seat behind an electric piano. He shook his head. "I could spend a lot of time telling you some weird stories about

Jack," Arlo mused, thinking out loud. This comment caused one member of the audience to shout, "We've got the time, Arlo!" Arlo looked up and laughed. "You *don't*, believe me!"[36]

On January 20, 1988, three of Elliott's heroes were to be inducted into the Rock and Roll Hall of Fame. It was only the second year of the newly founded awards ceremony, which was to take place at the posh Waldorf Astoria Hotel in Manhattan. Dylan was to be feted as was, more improbably, Woody Guthrie and Lead Belly. The family of Woody Guthrie was pleased but did not quite know what to make of the honor. Woody's daughter Nora, who attended the banquet along with her brother Arlo, candidly expressed her confusion: "I didn't see my father's influence on rock and roll. We're here to see other people's perspective on it."[37]

Plans were made for singer-songwriter and Guthrie fan Neil Young to present the award to Arlo and Ramblin' Jack Elliott, the two principal torch-bearers of Woody's art. But there was a problem. Though the award ceremony was only several hours away, no one had been able to locate Elliott. The committee had been told that he was on the road, out west, where even his agent could not find him. Elliott's daughter finally reached him by telephone in Texas. "Call your agent right away!" she excitedly told him. His curiosity piqued, Elliott called his agent who promptly told him to drop whatever he was doing, go straight to the airport, and "Get on a plane and go to New York." Elliott's first reaction was "You get on a plane and go to Hell, buddy. I don't like New York." But once Elliott was filled in on the details, he had an immediate change of heart. Not only were Woody and Lead Belly to be feted, Elliott would find himself in the company of such old friends as Dylan, Arlo, and Pete Seeger. He would also rub elbows with the royalty of rock 'n' roll: George Harrison and Ringo Starr, Mick Jagger, the Beach Boys, Bruce Springsteen, Elton John, Billy Joel, and John Fogerty. This was the place to be and, for once, someone was hip and thoughtful enough to invite him.[38]

But it wasn't to be. The message had been received too late. The plane was delayed and by the time Jack arrived at the Waldorf Astoria he had missed the opportunity to coaccept the honor on Woody's behalf. Arlo was already onstage, receiving the award. "You could figure a lot of things in this world, but this isn't one of them," Arlo conceded in his acceptance speech. "I'm fairly positive that if my Dad was alive today, this is one place he *wouldn't* be . . . or he would've showed up drunk." There was a smattering of faux rebel applause from those who could afford the thousand-dollar plate dinner, but mostly there was a ripple of nervous laughter in the room. Nearly everyone was dressed to the nines, but Elliott rolled into the

Waldorf wearing "a red plaid lumberjack shirt and my dirty old cowboy hat," the same clothes he had on in Texas when he first got the news. The awards ceremony concluded with the obligatory all-star jam. By this time Elliott had made his way to the stage where he stood, sans guitar, between Arlo and Neil Young. Suddenly, Bob Dylan, wearing facial makeup and sporting a cape, glanced over at the cowboy in the dirty Stetson. Dylan smiled as he passed on his way to the center microphone stand. "Whady-yaknow? It's Jack. Hi, Jack." Dylan turned as he and George Harrison launched into "All Along the Watchtower."[39]

It was nice to stand alongside music legends, but among many folk-music enthusiasts there was no bigger living legend than Ramblin' Jack. On April 28, 1989, Elliott was scheduled to perform at the World The-ater in St. Paul, Minnesota. Elliott was the top-bill of three "Legends of Folk" brought to St. Paul by Bob Feldman of Minneapolis's Red House Records. Red House was a small, independent label with a good reputa-tion. Feldman had signed and recorded a number of performers based around the Minneapolis–St. Paul area, and most were impressed by his sense of fair play and the guaranteed quality of his label's CD releases. The concept of getting Ramblin' Jack Elliott, one of his earliest heroes, to record for Red House was a case of Feldman "bringing it all back home." Part of the difficulty of snagging Elliott was that through most of the 1980s no one was ever sure where Elliott was at any given time. For most of the decade Jack was on the road, staying with friends or living out of his mo-tor home, out of contact with nearly everyone, including his agent. Bob Feldman really wanted Elliott to record for Red House and his persistence would finally pay off. *Folk Roots* magazine bragged, "The fact that Red House was able to find Elliott and bring him to town surprised more than a few concert promoters who had tried and failed in the past." The "Leg-ends of Folk" deal was finally consummated when Feldman signed Elliott, Spider John Koerner, and Bruce "U. Utah" Phillips for a concert and the recording of a possible live album.[40]

Feldman arranged to have the witty and loquacious Phillips welcome the concertgoers and handle the Master of Ceremonies duties. Originally, Feldman wanted the three to close the show together, but Elliott report-edly balked at the suggestion. Much like his mentor Woody, Elliott pre-ferred to play solo and sidestep the whole feel-good grand finale ritual. He had always been an idiosyncratic singer and guitarist, not resistant to adding or subtracting measures of a song, throwing off the timing of musicians around him. "I'm not in the habit of getting together with the other acts on the bill, no matter how much I may love and adore them," he offered, a bit grumpily. Elliott's solo set at the World Theater was nothing short of riveting. In a review that appeared in the U.K.-based magazine *Folk Roots*, one critic commended Red House for their efforts. "Not only did they get the first U.S. recording of Elliott in over 30 years," the reviewer opined, "they may have taped one of his finest performances."[41]

Though *Folk Roots* misidentified the date of Elliott's last U.S. recording, they were correct in their praise of his performance. Elliott's set was so commanding, his vocal and guitar playing so perfect and his phrasing effortless, there was at least some initial scuttlebutt that Feldman was considering putting aside his original concept of a *Legends of Folk* ensemble album. It was reported that Red House was thinking of issuing a solo album, tentatively titled *The Legendary Jack Elliott*, culled from his 40-minute set.[42]

Red House was not the only company interested in seeing Ramblin' Jack return to the record business. In 1986, Arlo Guthrie, no longer an artist for Warner Bros., formed his own independent label, Rising Son Records. Arlo wanted his start up company to issue the music of other artists as well and, in the spring of 1989, the *Minneapolis Star-Tribune* reported that Guthrie had already "made arrangements to produce some sessions with Ramblin' Jack and release them on his own label." The sessions for Guthrie's Jack Elliott project were partly recorded in the North Carolina studio of Lamon Records. Lamon had been in the business since 1962, maintaining offices in Nashville and Monroe, North Carolina. Guthrie's wife, the former Jackie Hyde, was producing the Elliott project. Elliott recorded for some two weeks at the Moody's studio in North Carolina, but it was by no means an intense two weeks. They recorded a few solo tracks of Jack performing Woody songs, a fourteen-minute rendering of "912 Greens," as well as a few songs with instrumental backing. In October 1990, Elliott sighed that the Lamon project was "still very much in the planning stages. It's been dragging on for a year now." Back at the Guthrie farm in Massachusetts, Jackie had shared the early playbacks with Arlo, who found the results less than satisfying. He thought that Elliott was singing off-key on a number of the songs and that Jack's handling of such material as his father's "Oklahoma Hills" left a lot to be desired. Jack had not yet heard the tapes; he wasn't certain if Arlo's criticisms were valid. But as Elliott regarded Arlo as one of the premier interpreters of Woody's songs, he acquiesced to his opinion and the recordings were shelved.[43]

There was one "new" Elliott album issued as the 1980s neared a close. In the summer of 1989, Big Beat Records released *Talking Dust Bowl—The Best of Ramblin' Jack Elliott*. Big Beat had licensed the tracks from Fantasy

Records, which retained the rights to Elliott's earliest albums for Prestige-International. *Talking Dust Bowl* featured sixteen songs from *Jack Elliott Sings the Songs of Woody Guthrie* and *Ramblin' Jack Elliott*. In his review of the new compilation, Jack's old friend Wizz Jones wrote that he was pleased to see these tracks made available in England again. An early disciple of Jack Elliott's, Jones remembered, "Skiffle was in at the time and strangulated versions of Woody Guthrie songs appeared in the charts while in the back rooms of smoky pubs Jack Elliott showed us how they should be sung. You can hear how he sounded then, on this record which has several definitive performances of Woody's songs and talking blues."[44]

This was all true, but Jack's most steadfast fans had those early albums burned into their collective psyche. They remembered how Ramblin' Jack "sounded then." They wanted to hear how he sounded *now*. They would soon find out.

Notes

1. Carsten Linde, *Folksongs Aus Amerika* (Frankfurt am Main: Fischer-Taschenbuch-Verlag, 1982); Jack Elliott, Cologne Folk Festival, Cologne, Germany, 20 April 1980.

2. Jack Elliott liner notes to *Kerouac's Last Dream* (FolkFreak FF 4005), 1981.

3. Carsten Linde liner notes to *Kerouac's Last Dream* (Appleseed Recordings 1021), 1997.

4. Linde liner notes to *Kerouac's Last Dream*; Elliott liner notes to *Kerouac's Last Dream*.

5. Setlist for *Rambling Jack Elliott*. WDR Studio-B, Köln, 28 July 1980. Rockpalast. www.rockpalastarchiv.de/setlist/set1980.html#jack/ (accessed 19 August 2009).

6. Program brochure for *Vancouver Folk Festival*, Jericho Beach Park, 18–20 July 1980.

7. Colin Irwin, "Folk: Living Legend," *Melody Maker 55*, 16 August 1980, 39.

8. *The 16th Annual Cambridge Folk Festival* (television broadcast), BBC Company, Channel BBC-2, transmission date 25 October 1980, Don Sayer, Producer.

9. Jack Elliott, Amberley Folk Club, Black Horse, Amberley, Sussex, 4 August 1980.

10. Carsten Linde liner notes to *Folk Friends 2* (FolkFreak 3003/4), 1981.

11. "Ramblin' Jack Elliott," *Daily Times*, Anchorage, AK, 11 January 1981; Alan Sheridan, "Ramblin' Jack Has His Audience in Raptures," *Jersey Evening Post*, 14 August 1981, 13.

12. Hank Reineke interview with Dee Brown and Bruce Bryant, 4 September 2008.

13. "History of Elissa," www.galvestonhistory.org/elissa-history.asp (accessed 25 February 2009); Reineke interview with Dee Brown and Bruce Bryant.

14. Reineke interview with Dee Brown and Bruce Bryant; John Wesley Harding, "The Wanted Man Interview: Ramblin' Jack Elliott," *The Telegraph*, No. 50, Winter 1994, 23; Robert Shelton, *No Direction Home: The Life of Bob Dylan* (New York: Beech Tree Books/William Morrow), 1986, 102.

15. Jeff McLaughlin, "Gracenotes: The End of an Era at the Idler in Cambridge," *Boston Globe*, 27 September 1982, Sec. Arts/Film.

16. Jack Elliott, Uncle Charlies, Corte Madera, CA, 21 December 1982.

17. Jim Brown and Harold Leventhal, Producers, *Woody Guthrie: Hard Travelin'*, a Ginger Group/Harold Leventhal Management film, Jim Brown, Director, 1984; Soundtrack from the film *Woody Guthrie: Hard Travelin'* (Arloco Records, ARL-284), 1984; Jon Pareles, "TV Reviews, Woody Guthrie: Hard Travelin'," *New York Times*, 7 March 1984, C22.

18. Randy Sue Coburn, "On the Trail of Ramblin' Jack," *Esquire*, April 1984, 80; Hank Reineke, "An Interview with Ramblin' Jack Elliott: See How All Those Stories Get Twisted," *Aquarian Arts Weekly*, 17 April 1985, 10–11.

19. Jack Elliott, Bitter End, New York City, 26 October 2000.

20. Ernie Santosuosso, "Weekend: City Eyes Two Sites for Summer Concerts," *Boston Globe*, 17 February 1984, Sec. Arts/Films.

21. Tony Lioce, "Jack's Had It: Ramblin' Jack Is 'Burned Out' from 30 Years of Folksinging," *Providence Journal-Bulletin*, 24 February 1984, Sec. Weekend, 1.

22. Lioce, "Jack's Had It"; Richard Chanel, "Ram-Ram-Ramblin' Jack," *COOP/Fast Folk*, September 1982, 25.

23. Lioce, "Jack's Had It."

24. Jack Elliott, Folk City, New York, 25 February 1984.

25. Jack Elliott, Folk City, New York, 25 February 1984.

26. Jack Elliott, Folk City, New York, 25 February 1984.

27. David Lee Preston, "Echoes of Past Will Fill the Air at Folk Festival," *Philadelphia Inquirer*, 24 August 1984, F-18.

28. Jack Elliott, Folk City, New York, 22 September 1984.

29. R. E. Reimer, "Ramblin' Jack Empties Weathered Bag of Classics," *Newport (R.I.) Daily News*, 10 December 1984, 6.

30. Jack Elliott, Folk City, New York, 15 February 1985.

31. *Bobby Bare and Friends*. Bare Works, 1985; Steven J. Greil, Executive Producer/Producer; Jim Yockey, Director; Pam Zimmerman, Writer/Associate Producer.

32. Ernie Santosuosso, "Newport Folk and Jazz Lineups Announced," *Boston Globe*, 19 June 1985, Sec. Arts and Film, 65; "Newport Folk Festival Returns after 16-Year Absence," *Atlanta Journal-Constitution*, 4 August 1985, A23; Jeff

McLaughlin, "After 16 Years, Folk Festivals and Crowds Return to Newport," *Boston Globe*, 4 August 1985, Metro, 67.

33. "Benefit Concert to Aid Indians," *San Francisco Chronicle*, 5 October, 1985, 36; Seva Foundation handbill, circa 1987 (author's collection).

34. "Jerry Jeff Walker's Birthday Bash," Paramount Theater, Austin, TX, 15 March 1987; Jerry Jeff Walker, *Gypsy Songman* (Emeryville, CA: Woodford Press, 1999).

35. Jack Elliott, Mountain Stage, Charleston, WV, 12 April 1987.

36. Arlo Guthrie and Shenandoah, Westbury Music Fair, Roslyn, NY, 28 August 1987.

37. Jon Bream, "Rock Hall of Fame Induction, Program Provided Contrast in Good, Bad Vibes," *Star Tribune* (Twin Cities), 21 January 1988, Sec. Variety, 16E; "Rock Hall of Fame Ceremonies Fail to Unite Beatles," *Star Tribune* (Twin Cities), 21 January 1988, Sec. News, 07A.

38. Chris Jorgensen, "An Interview with Ramblin' Jack Elliott," *DISCoveries*, Vol. 3, No. 10, October 1990, 99; "Rock and Roll Hall of Fame," *Rolling Stone*, No. 521, 10 March 1988, 8–17, 97.

39. Gary Graff, "Great Music, Strange Words at Rock Induction," *Detroit Free-Press*, 22 January 1988, Sec. FTR, 5C; Harding, "The Wanted Man Interview," 29.

40. T. D. Mischke, "U. Utah Phillips, Spider John Koerner, Ramblin' Jack Elliott: World Theatre, St. Paul, MA [sic], USA," *Folk Roots*, No. 74, August 1989, 57–60.

41. Jon Bream, "Legends about Ramblin' Jack Amaze Him as Much as Public," *Star-Tribune* (Minneapolis), 23 April 1989, Sec. Ent, 01F; Ian Anderson, "Ramblin' Jack Elliott, Spider John Koerner, U. Utah Phillips: Legends of Folk, Red House RHR CD31," *Folk Roots*, No. 85, July 1990, 43.

42. Jorgensen, "An Interview with Ramblin' Jack Elliott," 98.

43. Bream, "Legends about Ramblin' Jack," 01F; Jorgensen, "An Interview with Ramblin' Jack Elliott," 98.

44. Wizz Jones, "Ramblin' Jack Elliott: The Best of Ramblin' Jack Elliott—Talking Dust Bowl," *Folk Roots*, No. 74, August 1989, 42–43.

Sowing on the Mountain   8

O N SATURDAY NIGHT, March 17, 1990, the fourth annual Jerry
  Jeff Walker Birthday Bash was held at the Paramount Theater
  in Austin. Through the swapping of old songs and telling of tall
tales, the Bash was to celebrate "the cowboy way of life." To that end,
Walker brought along such friends as Jack Elliott, rodeo legend Larry
Mahan, Guy Clark, Patsy Montana, Chris Wall, U. Utah Phillips, and
a very young Nanci Griffith (as a last-minute replacement for an under-
the-weather Ian Tyson). It was a Stetson-topped, magical concert, one
that featured a series of relaxed, low-key musical performances bridged by
Phillips's masterful storytelling. Elliott sang the ballad of "Diamond Joe,"
but really brought the house down with a shambling, chaotic take on
"Strawberry Roan." Though the concert was being taped for television
broadcast by a local cable station, a writer from the *Austin-American Statesman* noted, "Elliott . . . demonstrated that the show wasn't terribly well
rehearsed when his crib-sheets for the lyrics of 'Strawberry Roan' became
mixed up. He amiably ad-libbed through the songs to howls from the full
house at the Paramount."[1]

The moment caught Elliott at his most endearing; rescuing a performance from the brink of disaster by refusing to acknowledge that things
had gone awry. No matter how tangled or off center a performance might
turn, Elliott would plow on, seemingly oblivious to the onstage chaos.
His longtime fans realized the half-drawled loopy sidebars and lengthy
discourses were as much part of the performance as the songs themselves,
but the experience rattled the uninitiated and added to his legend. Though
he was no slouch in the self-mythologizing department, Elliott was well

aware that many of the shaggy-haired stories told about him had been ex-
aggerated beyond belief. He would complain that people had a tendency
to recall those isolated occasions when "I did something unusual or bad
and recount it forever." "Those people don't ever go out on the road,"
Jack said in his defense. "They don't know what it's like." Of course, Elliott also bristled when people said *good* things about him. He was often
described as a "living legend" or a "folk hero" by well-meaning fans, fellow musicians, and members of the press. But he grumbled, "I've heard
it millions of times and for the past 25 years. . . . It's a good feeling but it
doesn't put potatoes on the table, gas in the tank, or pay the bills. . . . But
at least people treat me nice."[2]

Elliott's banjo-playing pal Derroll Adams was to turn 65 on November 27, 1990, and his friends thought a celebration of his life and music
was in order. They managed to book a small town hall on the evening of
October 5 in Kortrijk, Belgium, not far from Derroll's home in Antwerp.
Happy Traum, the guitarist and former editor of *Sing Out!* was asked to
perform; he was also assigned the difficult task of locating Ramblin' Jack,
the "human tumble-weed." Derroll wrote that it was through Traum's efforts that they were finally able to track down Elliott who, as always, "was
off somewhere in America singing and playing, living in a camper." The
night at "De Stadsschouwburg" was a celebration of Derroll's life, music,
and influence on banjo players and guitarists across Western Europe. The
evening's last sets were reserved for the Americans, the program having
gone on for nearly four hours before Ramblin' Jack was brought out. The
Rambling Boys were, once again, reunited. They sang the tragic ballad of
"Willie Moore," and though they had trouble remembering all the words,
nobody really cared. The evening closed with the entire cast performing
Derroll's antiwar ballad "Portland Town," a song popularized by Joan
Baez nearly three decades earlier. The tribute concert had been recorded,
with highlights issued on CD the following year as *Derroll Adams—65th
Birthday Concert.*[3]

Elliott returned to the continent in the summer of 1991 for a series of
appearances encompassing both thousands-strong folk festivals and more
intimate pub engagements. Though the festival appearances were the more
financially amendable gigs, Elliott preferred performing in small, closeted
spaces. He visited England as well, but hardly anyone was aware of it until after he had gone. Ian Anderson, the editor of *Folk Roots*, rued in the
pages of the magazine that it was "extraordinary" that someone of Elliott's
stature should be bypassed by those who booked Britain's summer traditional music festivals. Here was Jack Elliott, relegated to performing at the

Half Moon Pub in Putney and in a similarly small folk club in Penzance. "What were all the major festival organizers thinking of?" asked Anderson, rhetorically. But if British festival organizers chose to pass on Elliott, those on the continent did not. He appeared with Derroll Adams at Rudolstadt's "Tanz und Folkfest" that July and in August at both the "Festival Intercelt-ique" in Lorient, France, and Denmark's famed Tonder Festival.[4]

On May 7 and 8, 1992, Elliott attended a pair of Dylan concerts at the Community Theater in Berkeley and the Warfield Theater in San Fran-cisco. Dylan's new passion seemed to be the deconstruction of his classic song catalog, and his so-called "Never Ending Tour," often left critics and fans baffled by its intent. Elliott remained steadfastly loyal; he refused to trash Dylan or the sometimes chaotic music he chose to play onstage, although he once remarked that he thought his old friend seemed bored and unhappy. He admitted to the *Telegraph* he preferred Dylan's "early and middle work to anything he's done lately," though, to offset the negative vibe, he quickly added, "he's still capable of moments of brilliance." Some of the energy Dylan displayed at the Warfield might have rubbed off on Elliott. One week following Dylan's shows in the Bay area, Jack traveled to Charleston, West Virginia, to perform on *Mountain Stage*. His program featured the usual mélange of familiar songs, but he seemed more attuned with his muse, scoring with a rousing take on Roy Acuff's "Freight Train Blues" and perhaps his finest recorded version of Woody's "Ludlow Mas-sacre." When host Larry Groce offered that Elliott hopped freight trains with Woody Guthrie, Jack corrected that oft-cited, but totally false, at-tribution: "Woody told me stories about riding freight trains. I've only been on one. I didn't care for it too much. I forgot to bring along my easy chair."[5]

There was no escaping the ghost of Woody Guthrie. To celebrate the occasion of Woody's 80th birthday, a concert was scheduled for July 12, 1992, part of New York City's Central Park Summer Stage free music series. Pete Seeger, Arlo Guthrie, Suzanne Vega, Nanci Griffith, Billy Bragg, and the Disposable Heroes of Hiphoprisy were on hand to pay tribute to Woody, mixing Guthrie's own songs and folk-style ballads with current rap and topical songs. By any measure of justice, Ramblin' Jack Elliott should have been there too, especially as he was already in the area. Though he wasn't scheduled to play Manhattan, Elliott was due to perform July 12 on a small stage at the Towne Crier Café, a Mexican restaurant nestled in the hamlet of Pawling, New York, some 75 miles northeast of the city. That night at the Café, Elliott made note of his omission during his preface to "Pretty Boy Floyd": "I understand they're having a big . . .

celebration in honor of Woody. This would have been his 80th birthday today. Not actually *today*. July 14th is his birthday. Theoretically, I should be there, I suppose. But I didn't know about it. They probably didn't know how to get a hold of me. It's alright."[6]

But it wasn't allright. In an interview published less than a week following the Guthrie tribute, Elliott was still "feeling a bit stung" by his exclusion, repeating what he told the small crowd at the Towne Crier Café. He *should* have been there.[7]

Elliott's exclusion would not be the only perceived slight of 1992. He was also, far more famously, not asked to perform at Columbia Record's high-profile "30th Anniversary Concert Celebration" for Bob Dylan. He admitted to being downright "insulted" by the omission, especially as the official roster included a number of artists whose only connection to Dylan was that they were label mates on Sony/Columbia. He did not blame Dylan for the slight. "I figure Bob didn't have much to do with putting it together," Elliott sighed. He blamed the businessmen of Columbia, the corporate bean counters "who probably never heard of me."[8]

Interestingly, it was the occasion of another, less formal, splashy celebration that would signal the first step in Elliott's rehabilitation as a recording artist. In July 1994, he traveled to Minneapolis to perform at a Guthrie birthday event organized by Red House Records. Following the gig, Bob Feldman, still enamored of Elliott's performance at the 1989 "Legends of Folk" concert, approached him, asking if he would be willing to go into the studio and record a solo album. Feldman, well aware that Jack had not recorded a full album of songs for an American label for nearly a quarter of a century, wanted desperately to rectify that sorry situation. "Jack, when's the last time you did a studio album, you know, as opposed to a live album?" "Gee, Bob, it was about twenty-eight years ago." "Jack, you might die before you do another studio album!" "Yeah, that's right," Jack replied flatly, unmoved. "So what?"[9]

Elliott did not really want to return to the studio, and was, in fact, a little wary of Feldman's enthusiasm. "He kind of talked me into it," Elliott told *Country Spotlight*. "Waved a bunch of money in my face and bribed me." He was not entirely sure why Feldman thought the time was right: "We'd already done a live album together and I don't think it sold very well. I was amazed he wanted to make another one." Elliott finally relented when he decided he needed gas money to get out of Minneapolis.[10]

Feldman arranged the hire of Pachyderm Studios of Cannon Falls, Minnesota, 35 miles south of Minneapolis, nestled deep in a 50-acre forest. Elliott would describe Pachyderm as "a fancy hotel in the woods" that boasted an indoor swimming pool and sauna, and was but a short stroll from a nearby trout-filled stream. Feldman arranged for Jack to record over three consecutive nights, each session lasting four hours. There was little preplanning, Feldman wisely choosing to roll the tape and see what came of it. Elliott confessed he chose the easiest route, performing "all my favorites because I can do them easily and quickly. . . . It was like spinning through the pages of a comic book." He recorded somewhere in the neighborhood of 25 songs. Occasionally, Feldman would ask for a second attempt at a song and Jack would comply with the request. There would be no third takes. If any song necessitated a third take, it was time to move on. It was all very informal and once the sessions ended, Jack had recorded his first studio album since *Kerouac's Last Dream* in 1980 and his first solo American studio album since *Bull Durham Sacks & Railroad Tracks* in 1970.[11]

Following the session Jack was riding in Bob Feldman's BMW on the highway heading toward Minneapolis. Feldman was playing back some of the material that had been recorded that evening, and Elliott found himself, unusually, pleased with the results. In a classic demonstration of how not to do business, it was only *after* the album had been recorded that Jack and Feldman discussed terms. There was no written contract, only a verbal agreement hashed out over a beer or two. It was an uncharacteristic display of trust from a man who held a long, public feud with the recording industry, but Elliott deemed Feldman an upright, friendly guy and admitted being, at this late stage of his career, "tired of being paranoid about record companies."[12]

Of the 12 songs chosen for *South Coast*, only Woody's "Pastures of Plenty" and Ian Tyson's "Will James" were "new" to fans. It was also easy to tell that these two songs had not been overplayed. Jack sang the verses of "Pastures of Plenty" out of order and absentmindedly left out the second verse to "Will James." Regardless, the well-worn songs he chose to program on the new CD all benefited from his weathered vocals and dusty guitar playing.

Red House released the *South Coast* CD on May 23, 1995, and the notices were uniformly positive. *Folk Roots* acknowledged though there was very little "new" material on the CD, that Elliott's "fettle is . . . in remarkably fine order," Jack successfully negotiating "the misty pitfalls of his own reputation." *Stereo Review* noted "no serious folk collection should be without" *South Coast* as Elliott's "plain spoken vocals" and guitar work were "seminal . . . commanding and moving." *Living Blues* described *South Coast* as "essential," offering Elliott as "one of those vocalists who can't sing at all by any conventional standard, but who can put across a song with tremendous emotional force."[13]

Later that autumn, Elliott's fans found a second "new" CD in the bins of their local record shop. In October 1995, Rounder Records of Cambridge, Massachusetts, issued *Me & Bobby McGee*, a collection of previously released material that Jack had recorded for Warner Bros. in 1967 and 1969. Rounder wisely chose to excise all of the "Rapping and Rambling" segments from *Bull Durham*, which, arguably, ruined the commercial prospect of that original LP. Elliott was not happy when he learned of the Rounder CD. He complained, "Those two LPs have been re-released on a single CD . . . without my permission. When you're as big and crooked as Warner Bros., you don't have to get permission from anybody."[14]

On January 4, 1996, the National Academy of Recording Arts and Sciences (NARAS) released the final nominations for the forthcoming Grammy Awards presentation. *South Coast* was one of the five albums nominated in "Best Traditional Folk Album" category, competing against Norman and Nancy Blake's *While Passing Along This Way*, Ali Akbar Khan's *Then and Now*, and Laurie Lewis and Tom Rozum's *The Oak and the Laurel*. Rounding out the nominations was Dave Van Ronk's *Another Time and Place*. Elliott told a local newspaper that he and Van Ronk had made a friendly wager beforehand that "whoever won would get a Cuban cigar from the other one." The presentation for "Best Traditional Folk Recording" was scheduled for the afternoon of February 28, 1996, several hours prior to the worldwide television broadcast. Elliott arrived in high style, ambling into the Shrine in downtown Los Angeles wearing a tuxedo made of denim. It was a copy of the famous tuxedo custom-made for crooner Bing Crosby by Levi Strauss & Co. in 1951. Producer Bob Feldman was also on hand. It was as big a deal for Red House as it was for Elliott. The small, independent label had never received a Grammy nomination, and Feldman told the *Minneapolis Star-Tribune* that Red House staffers were waiting nervously at the telephones for the winner to be announced. Late that afternoon, Feldman called and shared the joyous news: Ramblin' Jack Elliott had won.[15]

Backstage Elliott told reporters "It's my first Grammy," almost not believing his good fortune. He also admitted that this was the first time he had actually *seen* the Grammy program as "I don't have television where I live." Elliott's acceptance speech was short but heartfelt. He acknowledged the memory of his parents and that of Woody Guthrie, who convinced "me to play a guitar and not drive a truck." Though Elliott was extremely gratified to win the Grammy, he graciously acknowledged the moment as bittersweet. His old pal Van Ronk would be going home empty-handed, which didn't seem fair. But Van Ronk would have his revenge. The crusty old blues singer made good on his wager and delivered a fine Cuban cigar to Elliott; Jack recalled he "took one puff of that cigar and it nearly tore my throat out."[16]

The success of *South Coast* did more than just motivate the staff at Red House. Elliott told *Dirty Linen* that "I'm getting a whole new attitude about my possibilities as a recording artist. I'm more interested in the idea of doing more records." Playing through a set of old songs, no matter how tried and true, simply would not be an option. He would need fresh material or, at the very least, a new angle on the old material.[17]

The news of Jack's Grammy win was, perhaps, less surprising than the scuttlebutt that he had *already* returned to the recording studio to tape material for his *next* album. The genesis of Elliott's *Friends of Mine* album dated to 1995, when he and blues guitarist Roy Rogers were cast as guitar-playing hoboes in the doomed independent film *The Barrow Gang*. As with any extras employed in film work, Elliott and Rogers found they had plenty of free time between takes, the two new friends sitting on a railroad platform playing their guitars. Rogers, who had not really known Jack prior to the film's production, found he was enchanted by Elliott's music. There was something endearing about Jack's deceptively simple guitar method and the long, loopy stories and fragmented discourses that poured so easily from him. In 1989, Rogers had produced the Grammy-winning CD *The Healer* for John Lee Hooker, the legendary Detroit blues singer and guitarist. In Elliott, Rogers found another roots-music hero and standard-bearer whose musical reputation was in need of rehabilitation.[18]

Rogers had a good ear and intuitively knew what worked and what did not. After listening to Jack sing and play for a while, he realized that Elliott was so much more than a run-of-the-mill folksinger. The songs he chose throughout his career cut across a wide swath of American music: blues, country and western, dust bowl balladry, with a dash of rock 'n' roll and popular song. It was in this light that Rogers steered the *Friends of Mine* project, the album to reflect the musical essence of Jack Elliott. Rogers noted the songs chosen for the project covered "a lot of different territory in American music . . . but we didn't set out to make a nostalgic record. He's not a historical guy, he's right here now."[19]

On February 2, 1996, slightly less than a month *prior* to the Grammy award presentation, Arlo Guthrie was in San Francisco for a performance at the Fillmore Auditorium. That afternoon, Guthrie met Elliott and Rogers at Prairie Sun Recording Studios in nearby Cotati to record the old Gene

Autry/Smiley Burnette classic "Ridin' Down the Canyon." It had been previously recorded by both artists, Elliott recording a solo version at the *Kerouac's Last Dream* sessions in 1980, Arlo including the song on *Son of the Wind* in 1991. The version they would record in Cotati would ultimately find itself as the lead track of a forthcoming album of folksy duets that Rogers was planning. The project was off to a great start, magic created that afternoon by two acoustic guitars, bass, snare drum, and violin. Even the cranky, hipper-than-thou, post-modern music writers at the *Village Voice* were not immune to its charm, describing Jack and Arlo's version as "swinging . . . perfect, slow rolling. But it also has great taste and, beyond that, great dignity."[20]

Less than a week following his Grammy triumph, Elliott and Rogers were joined by Bob Weir for a session at San Francisco's Russian Hill Recording Studios. Nearly 25 years earlier, Weir had handed Elliott a copy of the Grateful Dead's *American Beauty* LP and underlined "Friend of the Devil" on the album's jacket. "Learn this song, Jack," Weir told him, and Elliott obliged. "Friend of the Devil" had been long a concert staple of Elliott's, but he had yet to record the song. The version recorded with Weir was less folksy than Jack's stage version or the Dead's original, more wistful and gentle, befitting a man of some years.[21]

Friends of Mine was recorded in bits and pieces as old friends passed through town. This unhurried schedule was fine with Jack, who was enjoying a rare and late turn in the limelight following his Grammy win. The honors, in fact, were beginning to multiply. On March 9, 1996, he accepted the Bill Graham Lifetime Achievement Award at the Bay Area Music Festival and was conscripted to take part in the all-star musical tribute to Graham at San Francisco's Warfield Theater.[22]

On May 28, 1996, Tom Waits and Elliott met at Prairie Sun for one of the album's more anticipated duets. Waits, the gravel-voiced, cult-hero, singer-songwriter first heard Elliott's music while working as a doorman at a San Diego coffeehouse where *Young Brigham* was played continually over the house system. Through the years, Waits remained a fan, impressed by the cultural history surrounding Elliott. He told the *San Francisco Examiner* that Jack's "story is also the story of the country." In Waits's estimation, the yarns that tumbled out of Elliott should be recorded for posterity and archived at the Library of Congress. For *Friends of Mine*, Waits contributed an unrecorded original song, "Louise," written by his wife, Kathleen Brennan, and himself. Elliott was enamored of the tune and gave it his highest praise: "If you didn't know it, you might think it's an old song."[23]

Friends of Mine was recorded over 21 months, beginning with the February 2, 1996, session with Guthrie and concluding on October 14, 1997, with a solo recording of a rare Elliott original. That song, "Bleecker Street Blues," was a heartfelt, spoken-word get-well card to old friend Bob Dylan. Elliott composed the meditative song on May 29, 1997, directly upon learning that Dylan had been hospitalized with a serious heart infection. Dylan recovered, and Elliott admitted to nearly regretting having written the song, feeling "a little silly having even bothered to go out of my way . . . because he didn't even seem to care."[24]

Much as he had for his John Lee Hooker project, Rogers brought together an impressive roster of talent to duet with Elliott: Guthrie and Weir and Waits, of course, but also Peter Rowan, Rosalie Sorrels, Emmylou Harris, Nancy Griffith, John Prine, Jerry Jeff Walker, and Guy Clark. Rogers was pleased with the album's progress and was cheered to find Jack's friends all "delighted" to be in the studio with him. "You have to understand," Rogers worshipfully told one California newspaper, "Jack's position in this musical realm is exalted."[25]

During the time that the songs comprising *Friends of Mine* was being recorded, Elliott, somewhat reluctantly, got himself involved in another long-term project. Jack's daughter with Martha, Aiyana, was now a talented student in the film studies program at New York University. One of her first assignments was to create a video profile of someone she found interesting. As her estranged father happened to be performing in New York that week, Aiyana and a friend, Tyler Brodie, went to see Jack's show, where she chatted with her father and videotaped the evening's performance. After Aiyana screened the footage for her teacher and classmates, the consensus among them was that she should consider developing the short video into a full-length feature. Elliott agreed to help his daughter with her film project, not fully realizing what he was getting himself into. Elliott later mused, "My daughter . . . asked me if it would be OK if she took my picture. . . . . I said 'Sure, fire away!' So she poked this movie camera in my face and left it on for three years."[26]

On June 14, Elliott returned to New York City for a rare concert appearance at the Westbeth Theater in Manhattan. A few days prior to the engagement he granted the *New York Daily News* an interview, which heralded the aging folksinger's appearance as his "first New York show in a decade." This was not entirely accurate, but it was true that Elliott had not performed a genuine solo *concert* in the Big Apple since 1965. The event had been partly orchestrated by Aiyana, so a camera crew could capture one of her father's concerts in its entirety. The house was near capacity when Elliott ambled onto the stage, but Jack, unfortunately, was not able to rise to the occasion; the concert was mostly a flat, uninspired affair. The show opened, promisingly, with a fine version of Woody's "New York Town," and some minor excitement was generated when Elliott invited old friend and displaced Texan Kinky Friedman onstage for an impromptu duet of the tragic dog ballad "Old Shep." But it was far from his greatest concert. He forgot words to songs he had sung a million times before, watching warily as the cameras panned around him, distracting him and destroying his natural rhythm.[27]

That September, the Rock and Roll Hall of Fame and Museum in Cleveland sponsored a conference celebrating and studying the impact of Woody Guthrie on American popular music. The weeklong celebration of all things Guthrie culminated with a concert at Severance Hall on September 29. The concert featured several respected and enduring holders of the Guthrie flame (Ramblin' Jack, Fred Hellerman, and Arlo Guthrie), one moonlighting rock music icon (Bruce Springsteen), and a score of young, contemporary performers (Ani DiFranco, the Indigo Girls, and Billy Bragg). All of the musicians were artists who, in their own personal style, had helped to carry on the tradition of Woody Guthrie. Backstage, nearly all the performers made it a point to pay their respects to Ramblin' Jack, Woody's old road buddy. Journalist Dave Hoekstra, reporting on the event for the *Chicago Sun-Times*, noted that even among the stars, "The old cowboy stood out. Each time a guest artist spotted the ramblin' man, they stopped to pay homage. You don't cross a restless heart." Though most of Cleveland's rock 'n' roll fans had gathered that night to catch a glimpse of Springsteen, the musicians themselves crowded in the wings to watch Elliott sing a primal, suitably tortured "1913 Massacre." Elliott's wrenching performance reminded everyone gathered that it was Woody Guthrie, not Bruce Springsteen, who was the uncontested star of this show.[28]

The *Friends of Mine* recording project continued at its leisurely pace, but the completed album would soon be in the can. On January 14, 1997, Elliott traveled to Nashville to record with old friends John Prine, Emmylou Harris, and Nanci Griffith. Prine and Elliott recorded a twin guitar, suitably gruff, and solemn version of Dylan's "Walls of Red Wing," a dimly remembered Guthrie-style ballad trimmed from *The Times They Are A-Changin'* album of 1963. In contrast, Elliott's rough vocal on Townes Van Zandt's "Rex's Blues" was beautifully counterbalanced by the sweet, angelic voices of Harris and Griffith. Jack had wanted to include a song by Van Zandt, the famed singer-songwriter from Fort Worth, Texas, who passed on at age 52 and was a treasured, if troubled, friend. Elliott would dedicate his *Friends of Mine* CD to his memory.[29]

Friends of Mine was scheduled for release on March 17, 1998, with a party planned at Nashville's Café Milano. Elliott was joined at the reception by such friends and recording mates as Harris, Griffith, Guy Clark, and Roy Rogers. A photographer from *Country Music* caught Elliott with a wide smile, arms draped around Griffith and Harris, enjoying the attention and company of good friends. Following the album's release, Elliott was invited by the owners of a Petaluma, California, record store for a meet-and-greet with fans to sign copies of the new CD. That afternoon, Elliott was asked by a journalist why he had recorded so little from 1970 through 1995. Elliott answered that the "long drought" was due to the fact that making records was "hard work," and because he rarely cashed royalty checks from record sales, why bother with the process?[30]

Though he had become increasingly more comfortable with the process, Elliott remained estranged from the recording business. The recent awards and accolades from critics and fellow musicians did not translate into financial success. The triumph of *South Coast* at the 1996 Grammy Awards was certainly heartening, and in the week following the television broadcast, sales of the CD soared 145.9 percent. But that still only meant an additional 200 copies sold. Through mid-March 1996 sales of *South Coast* continued to sell above their pre-Grammy rate, but as the month closed sales leveled off to where they had started. Jack was clearly disappointed, acknowledging the album "hasn't sold very well." But even if it wasn't moving out of stores in appreciable units, the time in the spotlight Elliott enjoyed following his Grammy win had paid dividends of a different sort. For starters, the Grammy reminded everyone that Ramblin' Jack was still out there, playing his guitar, singing all the old songs as they were meant to be sung, and still doing his thing. Suddenly, Ramblin' Jack found himself very much in demand. "I used to do only sixty concerts a year," he told a writer from the *Honolulu Star-Bulletin*, but "that may double 'cause of that damn Grammy."[31]

Elliott's media profile had never been higher and he was suddenly the recipient of a lot of good press following the release of *Friends of Mine*. On the eve of a tour to promote the album, Elliott's thumbnail photograph and words reached an audience of millions when he appeared, most unexpectedly, in the pages of the glossy "A List" celebrity magazine *People Weekly*. Such exposure would surely have been a boon for a younger, and perhaps hungrier, musician. But Elliott was 67 years old and slowing down. He had crisscrossed America for so long and so often that his love of traveling was slowly dying away. He told a New Jersey–based newspaper that, for all his newfound fame, he genuinely missed the simpler times, the good old days. The hard traveling with Woody Guthrie in the 1950s was more exciting than the current touring routine of "twelve concerts in a row with a day off for laundry." He acknowledged that although professional folksinging inhabited a "less intense" corner of the showbiz world, it remained show business all the same. "In my heart," Elliott continued, "I feel more of a kinship with cowboys than with folksingers."[32]

Elliott's weariness began to creep into many of the interviews he granted, and he was clearly nonplussed by his late career notoriety. He complained to the Santa Rosa *Press-Democrat*, "I'm competing with ten million other famous people in show biz. . . . You can be on the cover of *LIFE* magazine and three weeks later no one knows who you are." Part of his curmudgeonly demeanor was the result of his age and attendant creakiness; all this attention had come too late in the game. He could no longer shake off the little aches and pains; they had to be endured. He began to suffer from a persistent, dry cough that made nightclub engagements difficult to get through. His legendary rambles had long since disintegrated into an endless string of one-night stands, and Elliott somberly noted cities he once thrilled to were "not quite as nice the second time around." He told one Austin newspaperman, "You know how everyone thinks I love traveling? Well, I did want to see the world, and I'm glad I saw it when I did—before they went out and ruined it completely."[33]

But the road was where he made his living, and there would be no changing that. In the spring of 1998, Hightone Records announced that Elliott would be teaming with label mates Dave Alvin, Chris Smither, and Tom Russell as one-fourth of the "Monsters of Folk." The nationwide tour was scheduled to kick off at Seattle's Tractor Tavern on April 7 and conclude on April 22 at Boston's Sculler's Jazz Club. They would visit 12 cities, two shows often scheduled for each night. In Alexandria, Virginia, and Philadelphia, Pennsylvania, extra shows were added due to the high demand. It was a tight schedule, and though Elliott was excited about touring with the "Monsters," he clearly was no longer comfortable performing so many dates in such short proximity. Though far older than his fellow "Monsters," he had been chosen to handle the vocals for a lion's share of the collaborative material, and many of his performances were nearly ruined by his dry cough. The shows were constructed in a democratic, round-robin fashion, every performance bookended by the foursome opening and closing with Guthrie's "Hard Travelin'" and "Do-Re-Mi." The encore each evening usually featured a medley of train songs

("Wabash Cannonball," "The Wreck of the Old '97," and the "Rock Island Line"). Occasionally, the "Monsters" would coax Elliott into a free-wheeling take on the old Carter Family song "Dixie Darlin'," and Tom Russell often had Jack colorfully play-act the vocal of "Deacon Black" in his horse thief saga "The Sky Above and the Mud Below."

The concerts were enthusiastically received. The *Philadelphia Inquirer* noted that Elliott's presence "dominated" the concert at the city's Tin Angel nightclub and "provided the only stress in an otherwise loose and laid-back evening." A writer from the *Village Voice*, in attendance at the "Monsters" show at Manhattan's Bottom Line, accurately described the songs as "the music of grizzled, self-sufficient roamers who keep body and soul together where musicians always have—on the road." The *Boston Globe* noted there was no one greater than Jack Elliott "at making time-worn folk classics shine like new."[34]

The old America Jack remembered and treasured may have passed into history, but the country still had a long memory and would, to its credit, recognize its folksinging heroes. On October 28, 1998, the White House announced the winners of the prestigious National Medal of Arts award, established by a decree of Congress in 1984. Among the twelve honorees for 1998 were the actor Gregory Peck, rock 'n' roll piano legend Antoine "Fats" Domino, the opera soprano Roberta Peters, the novelist Philip Roth, architect Frank Geary, and Ramblin' Jack Elliott. The ceremony took place shortly after 11:15 a.m. on the South Lawn of the White House. Elliott was the second artist to be presented with the medal by President William Jefferson Clinton. In his introduction, Clinton noted, "it was hearing his first Woody Guthrie record that transformed him into the man Sam Shepard called a 'wandering, true American minstrel.' In giving new life to our most valuable musical traditions, Ramblin' Jack has, himself, become an American treasure." Following the presentation, Elliott recalled on a radio program that he was the only honoree that day, maybe ever, to wear a cowboy hat. The medal ceremony was a "rather formal" event ("I had to wear a tie," Jack remembered), and after Clinton draped the nearly four-pound medal around his neck, Jack joked that he "couldn't walk for a week after." He was terribly nervous about being in such posh company. As he stepped up to meet the president, Jack shyly said, "It's wonderful to meet you, Bill. Is it all right to call you 'Bill'?" Clinton smiled warmly and replied "Of course, Jack." Then the First Lady, Hillary Rodham Clinton, stepped toward him. Jack recalled he thought it might be best if he introduced himself to Mrs. Clinton. "I'm Ramblin' Jack Elliott," he told her. The First Lady broke into a big grin, "I know *you*, Ramblin' Jack!" Mrs.

Clinton had addressed him in a twangy southern accent and Elliott recalled the exchange as wonderfully informal, as if the two of them were meeting casually out on "the back porch in Arkansas."[35]

The honors continued to pour in. In December 1998, NARAS announced the slate of nominees for February's Grammy award for the "Best Traditional Folk Album." Jack's *Friends of Mine* was nominated and would compete against Norman Blake's *Chattanooga Sugar Babe*, *Slant 6 Mind* by former Red House–label mate Greg Brown, *Long Journey Home* by the Chieftains, and *Southern Banjo Sounds* by Mike Seeger. It was time to retrieve his denim tuxedo from storage.

On February 21, 1999, the morning of the Grammy telecast, the CBS news and arts program *Sunday Morning* broadcast a nine-minute segment on Elliott. Though partly a career retrospective, with the usual Guthrie and Dylan references, narrator Charles Osgood steered the segment toward the present. A CBS camera crew had filmed Elliott's performance at various locations, and viewers were treated to fragments of "Buffalo Skinners," "Don't Think Twice, It's Alright," "South Coast," and "Rex's Blues" (the latter with guest Emmylou Harris). There was also footage of Elliott and future wife, Jan Currie, wandering through a Sausalito Bay boatyard, rehearsing "He Was a Friend of Mine" with Nanci Griffith, an enthusiastic testimonial from producer Roy Rogers, and a fascinating glimpse of his receiving the National Arts medal. The segment closed at Sweetwater, the cozy music room in Mill Valley, California, long a favorite watering hole of Jack's. The segment closed with Elliott performing Jelly Roll Morton's "Whinin' Boy Blues" to a hushed, reverent audience.[36]

Later that afternoon, Elliott would appear on television for a second time. Bay area television journalist Kate Kelly, of the CBS affiliate KPIX *5 Reports*, informed viewers, "there's something for just about everyone in this year's crop of Bay-area Grammy nominees." She then presented a series of short video vignettes of Bay-area musicians who had been nominated for a Grammy: rock guitarist Joe Satriani, gospel artist Walter Hawkins, the new-age string instrumentalist Alex DiGrassi, and the chamber music ensemble Kronos Quartet. Leading off the segment was Ramblin' Jack, who sat on a darkened nightclub stage, cowboy hat pushed down over his eyes, flat-picking out the rhythm to his own "Cup of Coffee." Kelly recounted an occasionally fanciful account of Jack's life, reporting "Ramblin' Jack Elliott used to buck broncos before he picked up a guitar and sang about American life. He's crossed paths with Woody Guthrie, Jack Kerouac, and James Dean. Now Ramblin' hangs his hat near Tomales Bay." The segment concluded with Elliott standing comfortably at the bar of the Old Western Saloon in Point Reyes Station, demystifying his art: "If you can tap your foot slowly, strum the guitar a couple of whacks, give it a sense of time passing slowly—that's what music is for me." After the news crew packed their equipment, Elliott shuffled out onto the street and found, to his surprise, he was now a genuine celebrity. Someone approached him and asked excitedly, "By any chance, are you Ramblin' Jack Elliott?" "Used to be," Elliott answered.[37]

Elliott did not win a second Grammy for *Friends of Mine*, but it hardly mattered. In late March 1999, he had already reteamed with Roy Rogers for a follow-up CD. It would feature duets with his two recent "Monsters of Folk" comrades Dave Alvin ("East Virginia Blues") and Tom Russell ("Cup of Coffee" and "The Sky Above and the Mud Below"), as well as an eerie reading of the classic "St. James Infirmary" recorded with Van Ronk. Elliott also chose to resurrect another old song. In 1968, the Macmillan Company had asked Elliott to choose a song for the forthcoming collection *Something to Sing About: The Personal Choices of America's Folk Singers*. He had selected the old ballad "A Picture from Life's Other Side," a gloomy old country song that was a favorite of Woody Guthrie's. Elliott had never recorded the song and Rogers brought in Maria Muldaur to share the vocals. Elliott also took solo turns on Woody's "Ranger's Command," "Diamond Joe," and Dylan's "With God on Our Side" to great effect. Tom Waits and his wife, Kathleen Brennan, offered another new gem of a song, "Pony," to the Elliott and Rogers project. "Pony" allowed Jack to assume the role of the slightly drunk rogue in the style employed for "I Belong to Glasgow." Rogers and Elliott also composed two new songs, "Now He's Just Dust in the Wind" and "True Blue Jeans," the latter of which sounds like less of a song than a demo for a television commercial. Rounding off the disc were classic, and previously recorded, songs by Ernest Tubb ("Take Me Back and Try Me One More Time") and Mick Jagger and Keith Richards ("Connection"). Rogers completed postproduction work by mid-summer and *The Long Ride* was scheduled for release on September 14, 1999. The Hightone Records press release trumpeted *The Long Ride* as Elliott's "most ambitious recording ever." It wasn't, but that was hardly the point. Roy Rogers had actually coaxed and ministered the release of not one but two very fine studio albums from him in a couple of years.[38]

Perhaps due to the absence of such "big name" guest vocalists as Tom Waits and Bob Weir, *The Long Ride* received less attention in the media than its predecessor. *The Long Ride* seemed as if it were *Friends of Mine 2*, minus the rock stars. Regardless, the *San Francisco Chronicle* found *The Long*

Ride to be "superior" to Jack's last effort: "Elliott's the source; he's a link to our collective past that most of us will only ever know about from books. That still doesn't explain exactly what he does," the review added, "but he's getting much closer to capturing it on disc." In what was becoming a welcome tradition, Elliott learned in January 2000 that *The Long Ride* had, once again, been Grammy nominated as Best Traditional Folk Recording. On February 23, the Grammy Awards presentation was held at the Staples Center in Los Angeles but, for a second time, Elliott left the ceremony empty-handed.[39]

On January 21, 2000, Aiyana Elliott's *The Ballad of Ramblin' Jack* was screened at the prestigious Sundance Film Festival. Prior to the screening at Sundance, held each year in the trendy hamlet of Park City, Utah, Jack had yet to view any of the footage that Aiyana had shot over the previous three years. He was not sure what to expect. Sundance planned to show the film on five separate occasions throughout the week, with Elliott reportedly attending at least three of those screenings. In a March 26 mailer, Aiyana recalled the greatest reward of making the film was finally "getting to watch the film sitting next to Jack." She recalled her father being "deeply moved," admitting he was "somewhat confused by some of the personal aspects of the film." Indeed, Jack was caught off guard by the honest, occasionally *brutally* honest, portrayal. To many of Elliott's colleagues, Aiyana's cinema portrait unfairly painted him as an eccentric, absentee father, remote and self-absorbed. For his part, Elliott admitted to watching the film and wishing, in his own words, "to disappear through the floor" during some of the film's more wrenching moments. He had not expected it. The film had been originally conceived as more or less a standard rock 'n' roll documentary. But once the film's editor, David Baum, spooled through the footage of Aiyana's mother, Martha, candidly discussing Aiyana's childhood and Elliott's shortfalls as a parent, he had little doubt the estranged relationship between daughter and father was the emotional heart of the film. Elliott's marriage to Martha was not long lasting, so Aiyana did not have the opportunity to spend any truly meaningful time with her legendary itinerant father. This would change. The production of the film took a full three years to complete, and this was followed by a lengthy promotional press campaign. By the time the cycle of the film had run its course, Aiyana and her father would get to know each other as well as they could manage.[40]

Those who led more traditional lives could relate sympathetically to Aiyana's plight, but it's interesting that the musicians she interviewed for the film all understood that Jack had no choice but to follow his muse.

One of the most revealing moments occurred when Arlo Guthrie, who certainly knew better than anyone the personal toll exacted on a child of a famous parent, stared uncompromisingly into Aiyana's camera lens and suggested she might never find the source of her father's wanderlust. "Maybe there's parts of him that you're never going to know," Arlo opined. In a more grandfatherly manner, Dave Van Ronk shared his belief that Jack might have led a happier life if he had settled down in the traditional manner. But that would have come at a cost. "The world would have gotten one more, good family man," Van Ronk reasoned, "and in exchange we would have lost Jack Elliott. From my detached point of view . . . we got the better of the deal."[41]

On February 6, 2000, Elliott learned that Derroll Adams had passed away. Derroll's health had been in decline for some time and for the last few years he had been mostly confined to a wheelchair. In 1998, Hans Theessink, the Dutch blues singer and guitarist, had contacted Derroll and his wife, Danny Adams, and told them of his plans to gather Derroll's friends and colleagues for a tribute album celebrating his life and music. Theessink signed on a stellar cast of singers and musicians: Arlo Guthrie, Donovan, Allan Taylor, Dolly Parton, Ralph McTell, Wizz Jones, Happy Traum, and Youra Marcus. Of course, no tribute would be complete without a song or two from Ramblin' Jack. Elliott's contribution was taped at the Peter Miller studio in San Francisco, where he recorded two solo songs ("The Cuckoo" and "Wish I Was a Rock") and one duet with Arlo ("Muleskinner Blues"). Theessink had hoped that Derroll might live to hear the completed tribute CD, but that wish ended with his passing. The completed album, *Banjoman—A Tribute to Derroll Adams*, was launched officially at Denmark's Tonder Folk Festival at a noontime press reception on Friday, August 23, 2002. On the festival's final day, August 25, Elliott, Arlo, Donovan, Allan Taylor, and Youra Marcus performed many of the featured songs at a concert that was, fittingly, more celebration than memorial.[42]

On March 6, 2000, *Variety* reported that Jeff Lipsky's company, Lot 47 films, had acquired the North American rights to distribute *The Ballad of Ramblin' Jack*. Lipsky, a former director of marketing and distribution at Samuel Goldwyn Films, called Aiyana's film "a great American story . . . the funny and tempestuous tale of a father and his daughter." Later that same month, Aiyana and coproducer and writer Dick Dahl traveled to Austin for the South by Southwest Film Festival, where they picked up a prize for *Ballad* from controversial filmmaker Michael Moore in the "Best Documentary" category.[43]

In April 2000, Elliott recorded two of Woody's children's song, "Curley Headed Baby" and "I'll Write and I'll Draw," for the Rounder Records release *Daddy-O Daddy! Rare Family Songs of Woody Guthrie.* The multiartist recording featured performances by Joe Ely, Jimmie Dale Gilmore, Taj Mahal, Cissy Houston, Billy Bragg and the Blokes, and Woody himself. Woody's recording of "Howdy Little Newlycome" was sourced from near 50 hours of informal tape recordings of his songs that Guthrie had made at his home for music publisher Howie Richmond. The songs for *Daddy-O Daddy* were recorded at House of Blues Studios-West in Encino, California. Elliott's vocals and acoustic guitar were augmented by a country-accented rhythm section. Producer Frankie Fuchs, a lifelong friend of the Guthrie family's, recalled Elliott's reaction when she played back one of the original Richmond cassette demos of Woody. Jack had not heard any of Guthrie's homemade Richmond recordings and was taken back when Guthrie's bone-dry vocals cut through the transom of the magnetic tape. "Sound just like he did the day I met him," Elliott told Fuchs. It should have. The Guthrie recording dated from 1951, the same year that Elliott first met Woody. One month following the session, Elliott was asked if he was preparing to perform either of the two "new" Guthrie songs at his upcoming gig in Providence, Rhode Island. Jack candidly admitted that he had sung the lyrics off a sheet "in the studio, so I haven't learned them yet. It takes me an awful long time to learn a song so I'm reluctant to put a new batch of songs together with any frequency. My learning speed is slow."[44]

The official world premiere of *The Ballad of Ramblin' Jack* was held on August 9, 2000, at Manhattan's Loews AMC Theater near Times Square. Though the premiere was an invitation-only event, there were more friends and fans gathered than seats available. The screening was delayed until the aisles were cleared. Following the screening, Lot 47 hosted a party on the rooftop of the theater. A microphone stand had been set up on the rooftop so Elliott and such well-wishers as Van Ronk, Odetta, and Eric Andersen could sing a few songs. Elliott performed a rough but spirited duet with Van Ronk on Woody's "Riding in My Car," but the press quickly pulled him away for photo shoots and interviews. The publicity campaign by Lot 47 Films had officially started, keeping Elliott plenty busy for months.

The *Ballad of Ramblin' Jack* opened for business on August 16 at the Film Forum in Greenwich Village, New York City's premiere independent film house. The film's west coast premiere followed on August 25 at the Nuart cinema in Los Angeles. The *New York Times* called the documentary a "touching and acutely perceptive" portrait of Elliott, "a poignant case study of a peculiarly American obsession: the mania for self-invention." The *Boston Globe* described the film as "extraordinary" and suggested it perfectly revealed "the murky place between past and present, between history and reality, where most legends really dwell." In the *Chicago Sun-Times*, critic Roger Ebert noted, deliciously, that the documentary seemed to "hover intriguingly between homage and revenge." Though the film fared less well in the tabloids, it suffered no critical drubbings. The *New York Post* awarded the film two and a half stars and described it as "bittersweet . . . often funny but overlong." The *New York Daily News* was a bit more enthusiastic, awarding the film three of four stars. "America loves a legend," the review began, "and the more outsized the better. But what happens when you try to pin down the person behind the myth?"[45]

The media splash surrounding the release of *The Ballad of Ramblin' Jack* brought other surprises. On August 15, 2000, Jack found himself back on the Vanguard label, which had been sold by the Solomon Brothers to the Welk Music Group conglomerate in 1985. Aiyana and Dick Dahl had prepared a thoughtfully compiled soundtrack album to accompany the theatrical release of their film. Initially, Elliott was not particularly enthused at the prospect of Aiyana producing the album. Though Jack could not control his image on the motion picture screen, he was not about to cede control of his music to his daughter. Aiyana recalled her father's "mistrust of people in the record business is so great that when Dick and I were producing the record, it extended to us." Nonetheless, the soundtrack was released and the resulting CD was a fascinating document that stood easily independent of the film it had been designed to support.[46]

Only three of the album's 20 tracks ("Pastures of Plenty," "Rake and Rambling Boy," and "The Cuckoo [Reprise]") had been collected from earlier albums. The most notable of the "historic" recordings was the Moses Asch recording of January 1954 (mistakenly dated "1953" in the notes) of Woody Guthrie, Ramblin' Jack, and Sonny Terry performing "Railroad Bill." Bob Dylan and Ramblin' Jack's spirited take on "Acne," Eric Von Schmidt's lampoon of teenage angst songs, was first broadcast on a New York City radio program in the summer of 1961. "Acne" had long been in the tape libraries of Dylan fans, but it was now offered here for everyone's amusement. Interestingly, Elliott was not too happy to see "Acne" released. "It embarrasses me to listen to it. . . . Of all the stuff to put out," he rued afterward. "Muleskinner Blues" and "Take Me Home" were sourced, respectively, from the 1971 and 1969 broadcast tapes of *The Johnny Cash Show*. "Candy Man" and "Talking Sailor" were culled from the rare 1961 film *Ballads, Blues and Bluegrass.* "San Francisco Bay Blues" was culled from the 1965 *Rainbow Quest* television appearance with Pete Seeger. An alternate version of "The Cuckoo" as well as "If I Were a Carpenter" and "The Car Song" were taken from performances recorded at the 14th annual Cowboy Poetry Gathering in January 1998. "Don't Think Twice, It's All Right" and "1913 Massacre" were recorded on April 21, 1998, at the "Monsters of Folk" gig at the Bottom Line cabaret in Greenwich Village. A great "Hard Travelin'" was excerpted from Elliott's guest spot on a CBS radio program in 1998. Jack's shaggy-dog trucking song "Cup of Coffee" was taken from the soundtrack of *Ramblin' Jack in Texas.*[47]

The film soundtrack was not the only "new" Elliott CD to be released on Vanguard/Welk in 2000. The company was celebrating its 50th anniversary, and part of that celebration involved looking back at the company's glorious history as one of the premier classical and folk music labels. On October 31, 2000, Vanguard issued *Ramblin' Jack Elliott—Best of the Vanguard Years.* Though Elliott had only recorded a single studio LP consisting of a dozen songs for the label in the summer of 1963, the resulting *Best of* album forced the company to dig deeper into their tape library. Though no true Ramblin' Jack fan would dismiss his original Vanguard LP as lightweight, the label's Halloween 2000 release of 13 outtakes from the archives made it clear that Vanguard had a second, equally worthy, studio album in the can.

In May 2001, Happy Traum, the guitarist, folksinger, and owner of the music instruction company Homespun Tapes, brought Elliott and Arlo Guthrie together at his studio in Woodstock to record the tutorial *The Songs and Guitar of Ramblin' Jack Elliott.* Traum caught Elliott playing from multiple angles with split screens, Jack's weathered and creased hands casually running through a demonstration of some of the guitar techniques he had picked up over the past 50 years. Though something less than a formal music lesson, the Homespun recording was a valued artifact, with Elliott and Arlo trading Woody stories. Jack also demonstrated the idiosyncratic finger-style guitar pattern Woody used for all his famed talking blues songs, a technique that Elliott admitted to never getting to sound just right.[48]

In August 2001, Elliott celebrated his 70th birthday with friends at the home of Roy and Gaynell Rogers. One gift arrived in the form of a telegram sent by an estranged old friend: "Happy Birthday, Jack. This Land Is Your Land. Bob." Jack told writer John May of the *Telegraph* that Dylan's welcome greeting was "plagiarism—but who cares?" The fact that Dylan had bothered to send him the note was one of the best gifts he received that year.[49]

It was important to Jack that Dylan remembered him. On New Year's Day 2004, Dylan's long-anticipated memoir *Chronicles, Vol. 1* was published. If Elliott had been concerned that Dylan had forgotten him, that the rock legend no longer recognized his contributions to his own musical and philosophical development, all of Jack's fears were now dispelled. In the final chapter of his book, "River of Ice," Dylan recounts his introduction to Elliott's music through "an imported record, a very obscure one" that held pride of place in Jon Pankake's collection in Minneapolis. In his book, Dylan described Elliott as "the King of the folksingers" and a "master of musical tricks." Jack read *Chronicles* while on an airplane flying east for a series of concerts, pleased and humbled by Dylan's kind words, the official acknowledgment he had long waited for and thought he would never get. Jack told the *San Diego Union-Tribune* that after reading the memoir he sent Dylan "a thank-you note. I'm feeling better about him. I thought it was a wonderful book."[50]

Dylan's memoir was not the only blast from the past that Elliott experienced in 2004. On October 26, Hightone Records issued a pair of budget-priced CDs of unreleased material that he had recorded for the Topic label. The collections were titled *The Lost Topic Tapes: Cowes Harbour 1957* and *The Lost Topic Tapes: Isle of Wight 1957*. The album titles were something of a misnomer; these recordings had not been lost or misplaced. The recordings had been, for the most part, abandoned by the label. In 1995, Topic had issued *Ramblin' Jack—The Legendary Topic Masters*, but that collection consisted entirely of previously released material. It was as if no one at Topic was aware of the trove of unreleased Jack Elliott material that was available to them. Topic had transferred most of the material they had recorded from the 1940s through the 1950s to the National Sound Archive, under the auspices of the British Library. There the material rested undisturbed and only barely cataloged. That changed in 1998 when the Scotsman Robert Wylie, a lifelong fan of Elliott's music, contacted the National Sound Archives and began making inquires. The Archives told him the tapes, in their present condition, were not available for playback as 40 years of age and neglect had exacted a toll. It took nearly a year of restoration work to enable a successful transfer of the original tapes to CD safety copies but, once completed, Elliott's issued material on Topic would be doubled.[51]

Surprisingly, Topic was not all that interested in releasing the *Lost Topic Tapes*. The company feared that a collection of Elliott recordings, no matter how historic, simply would not sell in Britain; Jack's visits to the United Kingdom had become rare events. As Elliott continued to perform regularly in the United States, Topic suggested it might be best if the material was released on an American label. Eventually a deal was struck with Hightone Records, the company issuing the CDs as budget-priced loss leaders. But with little promotion, the set was met with middling sales.

One satisfying result of the *Lost Topic Tapes* was that Ramblin' Jack's name was again being bandied about in England and, on February 14, 2005, Elliott was in London to accept a Lifetime Achievement honor from the BBC at their annual Folk Awards program. Elliott was introduced by radio broadcaster Bob Harris, who respectfully, if inaccurately, described him as one of the "all time great narrative songwriters." Elliott thanked the usual suspects for the honor as well as the "the schoolteacher and whiskey salesman who put me and Pete Seeger up that night in Glasgow who told me always mix half and half . . . water with my scotch. Thank *you*. Saved my life." Elliott then set off on a short tour of the United Kingdom that included visits to Birmingham, Leeds, Newcastle, Dublin, and London.[52]

In March 2006, Elliott traveled to the South by Southwest Festival in Austin, Texas. He performed a solo show at the Tambaleo nightclub on Friday, March 17, and was the top-billed performer the following evening at a midnight hootenanny sponsored by ANTI Records at Austin's Central Presbyterian Church. The hootenanny, which the *Tucson Weekly* called the "hottest ticket" of the week, featured Billy Bragg, Jolie Holland, Tim Fite, Joe Henry, and the Los Angeles hip-hop artist Busdriver. Elliott closed the hoot with the Carter Family's mournful "Engine 143," with friend and Nashville string-wizard Marty Stuart accompanying on mandolin. The entire cast joined Jack for the obligatory Guthrie finale that included "Pretty Boy Floyd" and "Plane Wreck at Los Gatos (Deportee)." The folks at ANTI were clearly taken by Elliott, this "organic anarchist" troubadour revered by a new generation for whom street credentials meant everything.[53]

ANTI Records was a subsidiary of the Epitaph label, known among those in the industry as an uncompromising punk/alternative rock specialty imprint. ANTI had been broadening their catalog of late, while careful to maintain the label's outlaw image. In 2006, Elliott signed on, telling fans in Boston one night, "I don't know what they're anti, but I'm all for it." Aiyana Elliott wanted her father to title his new album " Not for the Tourists," as the CD would mostly feature fragments of dimly recollected, seldom performed material from the deepest recesses of Jack's repertoire. The working title was something of a family joke. One night Aiyana and Dick Dahl were sitting around listening to Jack as he informally played through a series of fragmented folk songs and blues he almost never performed onstage. Dahl asked Elliott why he chose not to perform these off-beat songs at his concerts and Jack answered curtly, "They're not for the tourists." It was Aiyana who really pushed her father to return to the recording studio. After all, it was 2006 and Elliott's last studio effort, *The Long Ride*, had been released in 1999.[54]

I Stand Alone was produced by Ian Brennan. Brennan had worked with Elliott before, having produced "Power to the People," a free concert held on August 26, 2001, that featured everyone from "Punk-Laureate" Jello Biafra to the Gospel legends the Holmes Brothers to Ramblin' Jack at San Francisco's Crissy Field, right off the Bay. Brennan agreed to distribute Elliott's new album on the ANTI label, which had already issued albums by singer-songwriters Tom Waits, Nick Cave, and Billy Bragg, and country music legends Merle Haggard and Porter Wagoner. Of his new record label, Elliott admitted to the *San Francisco Bay Guardian*, "I've never been with a hip company before."[55]

The new album, *I Stand Alone*, was marketed, somewhat deceptively, as a *Friends of Mine*–style collection of duets. Though Elliott had recorded the album as a solo, Brennan chose to burnish the spare recording, bringing an assortment of musical friends onto the project after the fact. Elliott was not entirely pleased with this decision, made without his consent. He sarcastically described ANTI as the "Best record company I ever had. They put people on the record and didn't ask me."[56]

Though far from his best album, the CD was an interesting one. Three songs featured on *I Stand Alone* can be traced to Harry Smith's seminal *Anthology of American Folk Music*, released by Folkways in 1952, which remains one of the finest, most influential collection of rural folk music assembled. The Carter Family's mournful "Engine 143," an occasional inclusion in Elliott's live performance, is found on the set as is "Willie Moore," as recorded by Burnett and Rutherford. "Old Blue," which Elliott had recorded 50 years earlier for Topic, appears on the Smith collection as "Old Dog Blue" by Jim Jackson (though Elliott's version also shares much in common with Cisco Houston's, waxed for Vanguard in 1959). The track listed as "Call Me a Dog" was most likely based on the Brunswick 78 by Dick Justice titled "Old Black Dog Blues." Elliott borrowed "Mr. Garfield" from the repertoire of Derroll Adams, who gleaned it from Bascom Lamar Lunsford. There is also a short snippet of Lead Belly's tribute to the silver screen's first "Blond Bombshell," actress Jean Harlow. Elliott also allowed for a tip of the Stetson to honky-tonk hero Ernest Tubb with faithful versions of "Driving Nails in My Coffin" and "Careless Darling." "Remember Me" was the classic hillbilly lament penned by Scotty Wiseman and recorded by T. Texas Tyler. Hoagy Carmichael's quirky, saloon and opium-laced tale "Hong Kong Blues" is the album's only concession to "popular music." The album also features Elliott's third (and, arguably, least successful) revisit of the Carter Family's "Rake and Rambling Boy." The album concludes with the spoken-word track "Woody's Last Ride," which clocks in, disappointingly, at a mere 1 minute, 38 seconds. "Woody's Last Ride" was recorded mostly due to the prodding of Aiyana, credited as the album's associate producer. Aiyana had long been intrigued by her father's story recounting the last cross-country ride he made in 1954 with Woody, Billy Faier, and Brew Moore in tow, and hoped he might wed those memories to a wistful guitar accompaniment à la "912 Greens." It was a great idea but, sadly, one not brought to fruition on *I Stand Alone*.

A few weeks before the album's release, Elliott made his way to Salt Lake City to perform on the *Prairie Home Companion* radio show on June 24. Jack opened his segment with the recently recorded "Call Me a Dog" and "Engine 143," though, typically, he made absolutely no mention of his forthcoming album to host Garrison Keillor, wasting a wonderful promotional opportunity.[57]

ANTI Records released *I Stand Alone* on July 11, 2006. Though the album was not nearly his best, it had its moments and the reviews were uniformly positive. The *Los Angeles Times* was happy to see Jack return to a gritty, stripped-down format where most of "the cuts are just voice and guitar, marked by Elliott's idiosyncratic time measurements and creaking, croaking voice." *Vanity Fair* was enthused by the retro feel of the album: "There's no doubt Ramblin' Jack Elliott represents a different time in America, a bygone era of campfire hootenannies, boxcar trains and true outlaws. The moment he lets out that gravelly, whiskey-soaked bawl, you're transported." The *Boston Globe* wrote, "*I Stand Alone* distills Elliott's artistry to its very core (and it's very best)." On December 8, 2006, NARAS announced that *I Stand Alone* had been chosen as a Grammy nominee in the "Best Traditional Folk Album" category. It was Elliott's fourth consecutive studio album to be chosen, but he lost out to Bruce Springsteen's *We Shall Overcome: The Seeger Sessions*.[58]

Many thought *I Stand Alone* would be the last studio recording they would hear from him, but in August 2008 ANTI Records announced that Elliott had returned to the studio for a new recording project under the aegis of producer/musician Joe Henry. Henry was ideally suited to the task, having previously ministered albums by Mavis Staples, Ani DiFranco, Mary Gauthier, Bettye LaVette, Solomon Burke, Billy Preston, and Allen Toussaint. It was particularly helpful that Henry, himself a roots rocker of some pedigree, was already a fan of Elliott's music, conversant with the tradition of which he was part. Henry, who had accompanied Elliott on a tour of Italy in November 1993, had recently produced Elliott's idiosyncratic take on the *Highway 61 Revisited* classic "Just Like Tom Thumb's Blues" for the soundtrack album of Todd Hayne's *I'm Not There: Suppositions on a Film Concerning Dylan*. A half century of singing had honed Elliott's weathered croak into an instrument of its own, and Henry, intrigued by the world-weary sophistication of his singing, was interested in crafting Elliott's first, true blues album, selecting songs from a catalog of titles dating from the Depression era. The new album, *A Stranger Here*, was recorded at the Garfield House in South Pasadena, California, on July 21–24 and 27–29, 2008, and released in the United States on April 7, 2009. Elliott, on vocals and acoustic guitar, was provided evocative, textural support from such musicians as keyboardist/arranger Van Dyke Parks (piano and vibraphone), David Piltch (upright bass), Greg Leisz (guitar, mandolin, mandola, and Dobro), Jay Bellerose (drums and percussion), David Hidalgo (acoustic guitar and accordion), and Keefus Ciancia (piano and keyboards). In November 2008, a half year prior to the album's scheduled arrival, ANTI issued a CD sampler of songs from new and forthcoming label releases. The sampler's closing track was Elliott's ethereal take on Blind Willie Johnson's gospel blues "Soul of a Man," with early evidence suggesting that Henry's moody production was masterful and that *A Stranger Here* would be counted among the artist's best work. The CD featured Elliott's wrecked vocal interpreting songs by such blues singers as Blind Lemon Jefferson, Reverend Gary Davis, Furry Lewis, Son House, Mississippi John Hurt, Lonnie Johnson, Walter Davis, Brownie McGhee, and Leroy Carr. With the exception of "How Long Blues" and "New Stranger Blues," most of the songs on the album were new to his repertoire, Elliott readily admitting that he needed to sing and recite the mostly unfamiliar lyrics from studio cheat sheets. On the eve of the album's release, Elliott told the Santa Rosa *Press-Democrat* that recording *A Stranger Here* was a challenge as he consciously tried "to sing like a 90-year-old blues singer." It was a difficult transition, Elliott admitted, as "I've been singing like a 60-year-old folksinger all my life."[59]

Though it is likely his role in the promotion and preservation of Woody Guthrie's musical legacy will be what he is best remembered for, Ramblin' Jack Elliott's influence on 20th-century music is incalculable. Though he has left behind hundreds of musical disciples the world over, Elliott, oddly, has left no true protégé. There was, he explained, a reason for that.

"Music is a part of life experience," he told journalist Meg McConahey.
"The kids today are not experiencing what I experienced. That America
is not here—it's a figment of our past." Elliott often sighed that the
Depression-era music of Woody Guthrie is so now far removed from
contemporary American youth consciousness that he never thought of
grooming a protégé; he simply did not "have that burning need to pass my
mantle or the flame." It has been charged that Jack Elliott's music is anachronistic, that he is as much historian as entertainer, a caretaker of a dying
art. There is some truth to that, with Elliott lamenting that the America he
remembered and cherished has long been in the rearview mirror. "I used
to be in love with the good ol' USA," he told the *Ithaca Journal*, but "it's
kind of like being a history teacher . . . I don't get romantic about it." That
is arguable, as it is the heartbeat of the old America that pulses through all
of Elliott's music. He once claimed, unapologetically, "That modern day
people don't really have the pioneer blood. I keep the old songs around in
their original state, although a lot of people don't know what I'm talking
about."[60]

For those who do, Ramblin' Jack Elliott's music has kept the memories, the struggles, and promise of the old America very much alive into
the 21st century.

Notes

1. *Jerry Jeff Walker 48th Birthday Concert*, Paramount Theater, Austin, TX, 17
March 1990, produced by Austin Cablevision and Tried & True Music, Su-
san Walker and George Warmingham, Executive Producers, Norman Wright,
Producer and Director; Pete Szilagyi, "Candles to Cheer a Cowboy—Jerry Jeff
Walker Blows Them Out at Rambling Concert," *Austin American-Statesman*, 18
March 1990, Sec. City/State, B2.

2. Jim Farber, "The Ballad of a Runaway Ramblin' Man: Even Folk Legend
Jack Elliott's Daughter Can't Pin Him Down," *New York Daily News*, 30 July
2000, Sec. Showtime, 14–15; Joe Ross, "Ramblin' with Jack: Joe Ross Talks to
an American Legend," *Folk Roots*, January/February 1993, 43.

3. Derroll Adams liner notes to *Derroll Adams—65th Birthday Concert* (Waste
Productions, WP 9101), 1991; Greg Swain, "Derroll Adams 65th Birthday Concert, Kotrijk, Belgium," *Folk Roots*, No. 90, December 1990, 47–48.

4. Ian Anderson, "Rambling Jack Elliott: Half Moon, Putney, London," *Folk
Roots*, No. 99, September 1991, 51.

5. John Wesley Harding, "The Wanted Man Interview: Ramblin' Jack Elliott," *The Telegraph*, No. 50, Winter 1994, 30; *Mountain Stage* radio program,
Capitol Theater, Charleston, WV, 10 May 1992.

6. *New York Times* New Service, "Musicians to Remember Woody Guthrie," *Tulsa World*, 9 July 1992, Sec. Today, 5C; Jack Elliott, Towne Crier Café, Pawling, NY, 12 July 1992.

7. Roger Catlin, "Ramblin' Jack Elliott Still a Cowboy at Heart," *Hartford Courant*, 17 July 1992, Sec. CT Living, E1.

8. Harding, "The Wanted Man Interview," 29; David Hinckley, "Rambling Jack Is Back: Pedigreed Folkie Giving First New York Show in a Decade," *New York Daily News*, 12 June 1996, Sec. Now, 40.

9. Marianne Horner, "Ramblin' Jack Elliott: The Road Less Traveled," *Country Song Roundup*, Vol. 50, No. 445, 1998, 64; Monica Collins, "Ramblin' Man: Emmy-Winning [sic] Cowboy Folk Singer Regales with Tales of Travels," *Boston Herald*, 14 July 1998, Sec. Arts, 33.

10. Horner, "Ramblin' Jack Elliott," 64.

11. Craig Harris, "A Mosaic of Stories," *Dirty Linen*, No. 63, April/May 1996, 16; Sylvia Rubin, "Rising Stars: Six Lesser-Known Bay Area Artists in the Spotlight with Grammy Nominations," *San Francisco Chronicle*, 25 February 1996, Sec. Sunday Datebook, 28; Sylvia Rubin, "Reluctant Ramblin' Jack Went Back into the Studio: Best Traditional Folk Album 'South Coast,'" *San Francisco Chronicle*, 25 February, 1996, Sec. Sunday Datebook, 28.

12. Horner, "Ramblin' Jack Elliott," 64.

13. Colin Irwin, "Ramblin' Jack Elliott: South Coast (Red House Records RHR CD59)," *Folk Roots*, No. 146–147, August/September 1995, 73; Alanna Nash, "Ramblin' Jack Elliott, South Coast," *Stereo Review*, September 1995, 93; JDK, "Short Takes: Ramblin' Jack Elliott, South Coast," *Living Blues*, No. 123, Vol. 26, No. 5, September/October 1995, 103.

14. Bruce Sylvester, "Talk Talk: Ramblin' Jack Elliott," *Goldmine*, Vol. 23, No. 14, Issue No. 442, 4 July 1997, 14–15.

15. David Rolland, "Ramblin' Jack Elliott of Marshall Wins Grammy," *Point Reyes Light*, 7 March 1996; Jon Bream, "Red House Records Grabs a Grammy," *Star-Tribune* (Minneapolis), 29 February 1996, 04B.

16. Rolland, "Ramblin' Jack Elliott of Marshall Wins Grammy."

17. Harris, "A Mosaic of Stories," 119.

18. Rick Mitchell, "Ramblin' Jack Still Rustles Up Gems," *Houston Chronicle*, http://cgi.chron.com/con...s/cover/0409elliott.html (accessed 25 October 1998).

19. Mike Perry, "On the Road: Ramblin' Jack Elliott Lives Up to His Nickname—Except When the Conversation Turns to Music," *No Depression*, No. 14, March/April 1998, 58–63.

20. Patrick Carr, "Creaky Beauty," *Village Voice*, 7 April 1998, 81, 85.

21. Robert Makin, "Gotham Nights: Good Times with Ramblin' Jack Elliott," *Courier-News*, 16 April 1998, E9.

22. "Isaak Steals the Show at Bammies: He Wins Five Awards, including Top Musician," *San Jose Mercury News*, 10 March 1996, 11.

23. Edvins Beitiks, "On the Road," *San Francisco Examiner*, 4 August 1996, Mag, 24; Jeff Stark, "Hard Travelin': Ramblin' Jack Elliott Has a Few More Stories to Tell," *Dallas Observer*, 9–15 April 1998.

24. Buddy Seigal, "Return Ticket: Folk Star Ramblin' Jack Elliott Has the Words and the Tunes," *San Diego Union-Tribune*, 13 April 2000, Sec. "Night and Day," 31.

25. Meg McConahey, "Travelin' Troubadour's Tales," *Santa Rosa Press-Democrat*, 7 February 1999, Q15.

26. Mike McGonigal, "Film: Aiyana Elliott," *New York Press*, Vol. 13, No. 33, 16–22 August 2000, 36, 38; Jack Elliott, Bitter End, New York City, 26 October 2000.

27. David Hinckley, "Rambling Jack Is Back: Pedigreed Folkie Giving First New York Show in a Decade," *New York Daily News*, 12 June 1996, Sec. Now, 40.

28. Dave Hoekstra, "A Folkie's Land—Woody Guthrie Tribute Reveals Depth of Singer's Legacy," *Chicago Sun-Times*, 6 October 1996, Sec. Showcase, 21.

29. Jack Elliott dedication note to Townes Van Zandt on *Friends of Mine*.

30. Hazel Smith, "People: Jack's Friends," *Country Music*, July/August 1998, 7; Chris Samson, "Ramblin' Along with a Little Help from His Friends: Folksinger Jack Elliott Visits Record Store to Promote His New CD of Duets with Old Friends," *Petaluma Argus-Courier*, 3 April 1988, http://home.comcast.net/~2samsons/Chris/Writing/Musicians/elliott.html (accessed 26 December 2005).

31. Kris Goodfellow, "What Is a Grammy Worth?" *New York Times*, 24 February 1997, D9; Rick Mitchell, "Ramblin' Jack Still Rustles Up Gems," *Houston Chronicle*, 8 April 1998, Sec. Houston, 1; Tim Ryan, "Ramblin' Through Town: Folk Legend Jack Elliott Has a Knack for Takin' a Good Story and Makin' It His Own," *Honolulu Star-Bulletin*, 7 June 1996, http://starbulletin.com/ . . . /06/features/story1.html (accessed 2 March 1997).

32. "Picks and Pans: Talking with . . . Ramblin' Jack Elliott—Just the Two of Us," *People Weekly*, Vol. 49, No. 12:28(1), 30 March 1998; Makin, "Gotham Nights," E9.

33. McConahey, "Travelin' Troubadour's Tales," Q15; Rob Patterson, "Guthrie Imitator Jack Elliott Has Grown into an American Original—and One of the . . . Monsters," *Austin American-Statesman*, 9 April 1998, XL Entertainment, 10.

34. Fred Beckley, "An Evening of Just Plain Folk," *Philadelphia Inquirer*, www.phillynews.co...h_and_science/BLUE20.htm (accessed 26 April 1998); Robert Christgau, "The Sound of the City: Men without Women," *Village Voice*, Vol. 43, 5 May 1998, 72; Scott Alarik, "Folk Foursome Throws Scullers Pickin' Party," *Boston Globe*, 24 April 1998, D8.

35. *West Coast Live—Radio Show to the World* with Sedge Thompson, 21 January 1999 (radio broadcast).

36. "Ramblin' Jack Elliott" segment on *CBS Sunday Morning with Charles Osgood*, broadcast 21 February 1999.

37. "5 Reports" on Bay-area artist Grammy nominees with Kate Kelly, KPIX-TV, broadcast 21 February 1999; McConahey, "Travelin' Troubadour's Tales," Q15.

38. Milton Okun, ed., *Something to Sing About! The Personal Choices of America's Folk Singers* (New York: Macmillan, 1968), 83–87; Hightone Records Press Release: "Ramblin' Jack Elliott—The Long Ride—Release Date: September 15, 1999."

39. Denise Sullivan, "Review: Ramblin' Jack Elliott—The Long Ride (High Tone)," *San Francisco Chronicle*, 15 September 1999, www.sfweekly.com/issues/1999-09-15/record2html (accessed 4 July 2001).

40. Aiyana Elliott and Dick Dahl, "Ramblin' Films" mailing, 26 March 2000; Jim Catalano, "Elliott Brings 50 Years on the Road to Ithaca," *Ithaca Journal*, 11 September 2003, www.theithacajournal.com/entertainment/stories/20030911/culturalevents/232881.html (accessed 29 January 2005).

41. Arlo Guthrie and Dave Van Ronk to Aiyana Elliott, *The Ballad of Ramblin' Jack* (Fox Lorber Centrestage/Winstar Video, WHE73134), 2001.

42. Hans Theessink, "The Making of the CD," liner notes to *Banjoman: A Tribute to Derroll Adams* (Rising Son Records RSR–2102-2), 2002; Eugene Graham, "Tonder 2002: Old and New Celtic and Danish Music," *Folk World*, www.folkworld.de/23/e/tonder.htm (accessed 1 March 2009).

43. Dana Harris, "Lot 47 Buys 'Jack' Rights: Docu Chronicles Life of Folk Music Icon Elliott," *Variety*, 6 March 2000.

44. Frankie Fuchs liner notes to *Daddy-O Daddy: Rare Family Songs of Woody Guthrie* (Rounder Records 11661-8087-2), 2001; Bob Gulla, "Ramblin' Man: Jack Elliott Rides into Providence," *Providence Phoenix*, 11–18 May 2000, www.providencephoenix.com/archive/music/00/05/11/LOCAL.html (accessed 29 January 2005).

45. Stephen Holden, "Film Review: A Down-Home Ramblin' Persona from Brooklyn," *New York Times*, 16 August 2000, E5; Loren King, "Candid View of a Folk Legend, Flaws and All," *Boston Globe*, 25 August 2000, Sec. Living, C5; Roger Ebert, "Ramblin' Man—Documentary Can't Pin Down Jack Elliott's Life," *Chicago Sun-Times*, 8 September 2000, Sec. Weekend Plus, 32; Hannah Brown, "Movies: Ramblin' on Jack," *New York Post*, 16 August 2000, 64; Elizabeth Weitzman, "Trying to Catch Dad's Drift—'Ballad' Director Hit the Road to Get to Know Her Folkie Father," *New York Daily News*, 16 August 2000, 44.

46. Mike McGonigal, "Film: Aiyana Elliott," *New York Press*, Vol. 13, No. 33, 16–22 August 2000, 36, 38.

47. Tristam Lozaw, "Ramblin' Man: Woody Guthrie Lives On," from Guitar.com (20 September 2001), http://www.ramblinjack.com/rjsrc/sk_092001.html (accessed 15 May 2008).

48. Happy Traum, producer, *The Songs and Guitar of Ramblin' Jack Elliott* (Woodstock, NY: Homespun Video, VD-RJE-GT01), 2001.

49. John May, "Woody, Bob and Me—Who Taught Bob Dylan to Sing Like Woody Guthrie? Rambling Jack Elliott. John May Met Him," *Telegraph*, 19 February 2005, Sec. Arts, 7.

50. Bob Dylan, *Chronicles: Volume One* (New York: Simon and Schuster, 2004), 250; Buddy Blue, "Ramblin' Jack Elliott: The Rodeo Made Him Do It," *San Diego Union-Tribune*, 12 May 2005.

51. Stuart Ross, "Recordings Go a Ramblin'," *The Living Tradition*, No. 61, March/April 2005, 24–26; Michael John Simmons, "Ramblin' Jack Elliott: American Folk Troubadour's Early Recordings Unearthed Across the Pond," *Acoustic Guitar*, Vol. 15, May 2005, 18.

52. "BBC Radio 2 Folk Awards," Brewery Arts Centre, London, 14 February 2005.

53. Upstarter/Linda Ray, "Behind the Music: Pop Finally Starts Paying Attention," *Tucson Weekly*, 30 March 2006, www.tucsonweekly.com/gbase/Music/Content?oid=80400 (accessed 31 December 2008).

54. James Reed, "Elliott Isn't Done with His Ramblin'," *Boston Globe*, 11 May 2006, Sec. Arts, E8; Kimberly Chun, "Ramblin' Man," *San Francisco Bay Guardian*, http://cgi.sfbg.com/printable_entry.php?entry_id=1209 (accessed 23 November 2007).

55. Chun, "Ramblin' Man," *San Francisco Bay Guardian*; "Mudnow: The Community Coalition for Lower Utility Bills—Ian Brennan Presents" (advertisement), *San Francisco Bay Guardian*, 15 August 2001, 10.

56. Chris Jay, "Jack of All Trades—Folk Legend Jack Elliott Still Rambles On," *Ventura County Reporter*, 3 May 2007, www.vcreporter.com/article.php?id=4609&IssueNum=122 (accessed 13 June 2007); j. poet, "A Ramblin' Kinda Guy," *San Francisco Chronicle*, 1 October 2006, PK-46.

57. *A Prairie Home Companion with Garrison Keillor*, Abravanel Hall, Salt Lake City, UT, broadcast on National Public Radio 24 June 2006.

58. Richard Cromelin, "Regular Folk, Yet Not," *Los Angeles Times*, 7 July 2006, E-39; James Reed, "Ramblin' Jack Elliott, Aged to Perfection: 'I Stand Alone' Stands with Folk Legend's Best," *Boston Globe*, 9 July 2006, Sec. Arts/Entertainment, N-5.

59. Gina, "Ramblin' Jack in Studio with Joe Henry," ANTI Records Press Release, 15 August 2008, www.antilabelblog.com/?p=674 (accessed 1 March 2009); John Beck, "Legendary Musician Has Seen and Done It All and Still Has a Twinkle in His Eye," *Santa Rosa Press Democrat*, 5 April 2008.

60. McConahey, "Travelin' Troubadour's Tales," Q15; Jim Catalano, "Elliott Brings 50 Years on the Road to Ithaca," *Ithaca Journal*, 11 September 2003; Ross, "Ramblin' with Jack," 41.

Discography 1
Ramblin' Jack Elliott—Basic Official Discography: Extended Play/Long Playing Records/Compact Discs

THE FOLLOWING LIST INCLUDES THE RECORDINGS issued on EP, LP, and compact disc (CD) that feature Ramblin' Jack Elliott as a solo artist, as one-half of the Rambling Boys or, as in the case of *Badmen and Heroes* or *Legends of Folk*, as a principal performer. Variants, reissues, and foreign pressings of Elliott's solo albums have been documented and cross-indexed. Recordings are listed chronologically by date of release.

Badmen and Heroes. Elektra EKL-16 (10" LP), 1955, Ed McCurdy, Jack Elliott, and Oscar Brand; notes by Kenneth S. Goldstein. Jack Elliott: vocal, guitar, and harmonica.
Side 1
    Band 2. "Charles Guiteau"
Side 2
    Band 2. "Pretty Boy Floyd"
    Band 4. "Jesse James"

Woody Guthrie's Blues. Topic Records T-5 (8" LP), 1956, notes, anon. Jack Elliott: vocal, guitar, and harmonica.
Side 1
    Band 1. "Talking Columbia Blues"
    Band 2. "1913 Massacre"
    Band 3. "Hard Traveling"
Side 2
    Band 1. "Talking Dust Bowl Blues"
    Band 2. "The Ludlow Massacre"
    Band 3. "Talking Sailor Blues"

Badmen Heroes and Pirate Songs and Ballads. Elektra Records 129 (12" LP), 1957. Long playing reissue album combining *Badmen and Heroes* (Elektra EKL-16) with Dick Wilder's *Pirate Songs* (Elektra EKL-18).
Side 1
Band 2. "Pretty Boy Floyd"
Band 4. "Jesse James"
Band 6. "Charles Guiteau"

Jack Elliot Sings. 77 Records 77 LP/1 (10" LP), 1957, notes by Alexis Korner. Jack Elliott: vocal, guitar, and harmonica.
Side 1
Band 1. "Alabama Bound"
Band 2. "Good Morning Blues"
Band 3. "Talking Blues"
Band 4. "Rocky Mountain Belle"
Side 2
Band 1. "Jesse Fuller's San Francisco Blues"
Band 2. "Fifteen Cents"
Band 3. "Muleskinners"
Band 4. "John Henry"

Jack Elliott Sings, Vol. 1. 77 Records 77 EP/1, 1958 (7" EP), notes by Alexis Korner. Jack Elliott: vocal, guitar, and harmonica.
Side 1
Band 1. "Muleskinners"
Band 2. "Rocky Mountain Belle"
Side 2
Band 1. "Fifteen Cents"
Band 2. "Good Morning Blues"

Jack Elliott Sings, Vol. 2. 77 Records 77 EP/2, 1958 (7" EP), notes by Alexis Korner. Jack Elliott: vocal, guitar, and harmonica.
Side 1
Band 1. "John Henry"
Band 2. "Talking Blues"
Side 2
Band 1. "San Francisco Blues"
Band 2. "Alabama Bound"

The Rambling Boys. Topic Records 10-T-14 (10" LP), 1958; Jack Elliott and Derroll Adams; notes by John Hasted. Jack Elliott: vocal, guitar, and harmonica; Derroll Adams: vocal and five-string banjo.

Side 1

Band 1. "Rich and Rambling Boy" (with Derroll Adams, vocal and five-string banjo)

Band 2. "Buffalo Skinners"

Band 3. "Wish I Was a Rock" (Derroll Adams, vocal and five-string banjo)

Band 4. "State of Arkansas"

Band 5. "Mother's Not Dead" (with Derroll Adams, vocal and five-string banjo)

Side 2

Band 1. "East Virginia Blues" (with Derroll Adams, vocal and five-string banjo)

Band 2. "The Old Bachelor" (Derroll Adams, vocal and five-string banjo)

Band 3. "Danville Girl" (with Derroll Adams, vocal and five-string banjo)

Band 4. "Roll on Buddy" (with Derroll Adams, vocal and five-string banjo)

Jack Takes the Floor. Topic Records 10-T-15 (10" LP), 1958, notes, anon. Jack Elliott: vocal, guitar, and harmonica.

Side 1

Band 1. "San Francisco Bay Blues"

Band 2. "Ol' Riley"

Band 3. "Boll Weevil"

Band 4. "Bed Bug Blues"

Band 5. "New York Town"

Band 6. "Grey Goose"

Side 2

Band 1. "Muleskinner's Blues"

Band 2. "Cocaine"

Band 3. "Dink's Song"

Band 4. "Black Baby"

Band 5. "Salty Dog"

Jack Elliot and Derrol Adams Sing the Western. Hi-Fi Records EPM 10147, 1959. Jack Elliott: vocal and guitar; Derroll Adams: vocal, five-string banjo, and harmonica.

Side 1

Band 1. "Roll in My Sweet Baby's Arms"

Band 2. "San Francisco Blues"

Side 2
  Band 1. "Ain't It a Shame"
  Band 2. "Salty Dog"

Ramblin' Jack Elliott in London. Columbia Records 33 SX 1166 (12" LP), 1959, notes by Charles Chilton. Jack Elliott: vocal and guitar with instrumental accompaniment. Recorded in London, England, November 14, 1959.
Side 1
  Band 1. "Rusty Jiggs and Sandy Sam"
  Band 2. "Git Along Little Dogies"
  Band 3. "Sadie Brown"
  Band 4. "Night Herding Song"
  Band 5. "Chisholm Trail"
  Band 6. "Fifteen Cents and a Dollar"
Side 2
  Band 1. "Rocky Mountain Belle"
  Band 2. "Talking Blues"
  Band 3. "Diamond Joe"
  Band 4. "In the Willow Garden"
  Band 5. "I Ride an Old Paint"
  Band 6. "Jack O' Diamonds"

Kid Stuff—Rambling Jack Elliott Sings Children's Songs by Woody Guthrie. Columbia Records/Segment 8046 (7" EP), 1960, notes by Alexis Korner. Jack Elliott: vocal and guitar; Alexis Korner: mandolin; Jack Fallon: string bass. Recorded in London, England, November 24, 1959.
Side 1
  Band 1. "Howdido"
  Band 2. "My Daddy"
  Band 3. "Why, Oh, Why?"
Side 2
  Band 1. "The Fox"
  Band 2. "Riding in My Car"
  Band 3. "Hey, Rattler!"

Jack Elliott. Collector Records JEA 5 (7" EP), 1960, notes by Alexis Korner. Jack Elliott: vocal, guitar, and harmonica. Reissue of four songs from *Jack Elliot Sings* (77 Records 77 LP/1).
Side 1
  Band 1. "Muleskinners"
  Band 2. "San Francisco Bay Blues"

Side 2
   Band 1. "Alabama Bound"
   Band 2. "Talking Blues"

Rambling Jack Elliott—Blues 'n' Country. Collector Records, American Folk
Series, JEA6 (7" EP), 1961, notes by Elizabeth-Ann Colville. Jack El-
liott: vocal, guitar, and harmonica. Reissue of four songs from *Jack Elliot
Sings* (77 Records 77 LP/1).
Side 1
   Band 1. "Fifteen Cents"
   Band 2. "Good Morning Blues"
Side 2
   Band 1. "Rocky Mountain Belle"
   Band 2. "John Henry"

Rambling Jack Elliott Sings Songs by Woody Guthrie and Jimmie Rodgers. Co-
lumbia Records 33 SX 1291 (12" LP), 1961, notes by Alexis Korner.
Jack Elliott: vocal and guitar; Sandy Brown: clarinet; Al Fairweather:
trumpet; Alexis Korner: mandolin; Jack Fallon: string bass; Danny Le-
van: violin. Recorded in London, England, November 5 and 7, 1958.
Side 1
   Band 1. "Do-Re-Mi"
   Band 2. "Dead or Alive"
   Band 3. "Grand Coulee Dam"
   Band 4. "Dust Storm Disaster"
   Band 5. "It Ain't Got No Home"
   Band 6. "So Long, It's Been Good to Know You"
Side 2
   Band 1. "T for Texas"
   Band 2. "Waitin' for a Train"
   Band 3. "Jimmy the Kid"
   Band 4. "Mother, the Queen of My Heart"
   Band 5. "In the Jailhouse Now"
   Band 6. "Whippin' the Old T.B."

Woody Guthrie's Songs to Grow on Sung by Jack Elliott. Folkways Records
FC 7501 (12" LP), 1961, notes by Woody Guthrie. Jack Elliott: vocal,
guitar, and harmonica.
Side 1
   Band 1. "Jig Along Home"
   Band 2. "Car Song"
   Band 3. "Swim Swim"

Band 4. "Don't You Push Me Down"
Band 5. "Why Oh Why"
Band 6. "Put Your Finger in the Air"
Band 7. "Wake Up"
Side 2
Band 1. "Pretty and Shiny-O"
Band 2. "Clean-O"
Band 3. "Pick It Up"
Band 4. "Dance Around"
Band 5. "How Dja Do"
Band 6. "My Little Seed"
Band 7. "Build a House"
Band 8. "Needle Song"
Band 9. "We All Work Together"

Jack Elliott Sings the Songs of Woody Guthrie. Prestige-International INT
13016 (12" LP), 1961, notes by John Greenway. Jack Elliott: vocal,
guitar, and harmonica.
Side 1
Band 1. "Hard Traveling"
Band 2. "Grand Coulee Dam"
Band 3. "New York Town"
Band 4. "Tom Joad"
Band 5. "Howdido"
Band 6. "Talking Dust Bowl"
Band 7. "This Land Is Your Land"
Side 2
Band 1. "Pretty Boy Floyd"
Band 2. "Philadelphia Lawyer"
Band 3. "Talking Columbia"
Band 4. "Dust Storm Disaster"
Band 5. "Riding in My Car"
Band 6. "1913 Massacre"
Band 7. "So Long"

Ramblin' Jack Elliott. Prestige-International INT 13033 (12" LP), 1961,
notes by John Greenway. Jack Elliott: vocal and guitar; Ralph Rinzler:
mandolin; John Herald: guitar.
Side 1
Band 1. "Sadie Brown"
Band 2. "East Virginia Blues" (with Ralph Rinzler, mandolin and John
Herald, second guitar)

Band 3. "I Belong to Glasgow"
Band 4. "The Cuckoo"
Band 5. "Roll in My Sweet Baby's Arms" (with Ralph Rinzler, mandolin and John Herald, second guitar)
Band 6. "South Coast"
Side 2
Band 1. "San Francisco Bay Blues"
Band 2. "The Last Letter" (with Ralph Rinzler, mandolin and John Herald, second guitar)
Band 3. "I Love Her So/I Got a Woman"
Band 4. "Candyman"
Band 5. "Tramp on the Street" (with Ralph Rinzler, mandolin and John Herald, second guitar)
Band 6. "Railroad Bill"

Monitor Presents Jack Elliott: Ramblin' Cowboy. Monitor Records MF 379, 1962, notes, anon. Jack Elliott: vocals, guitar with instrumental accompaniment. American reissue of *Ramblin' Jack Elliott in London* (Columbia Records 33 SX 1166).

Ramblin' Jack Elliott Sings Woody Guthrie and Jimmie Rodgers. Monitor Records MF 380/MFS 380, 1962, notes, Robert Shelton, excerpts from "A Man to Remember: Woody Guthrie." U.S. issue of *Rambling Jack Elliott Sings Songs by Woody Guthrie and Jimmie Rodgers* (Columbia 33 SX 1291). Program identical.

Country Style. Prestige-International INT 13045 (12" LP), 1962, notes by John Greenway. Jack Elliott: vocals, guitar, and harmonica. Recorded April 12, 1962.
Side 1
Band 1. "Mean Mama Blues"
Band 2. "Low and Lonely"
Band 3. "The Wreck of the Old 97"
Band 4. "Old Shep"
Band 5. "Wabash Cannonball"
Band 6. "Brown Eyes"
Band 7. "Love Sick Blues"
Side 2
Band 1. "Arthritis Blues"
Band 2. "Take Me Back and Love Me One More Time"
Band 3. "The Tennessee Stud"
Band 4. "Those Brown Eyes"

Band 5. "Detour"
Band 6. "The Soldier's Last Letter"

Jack Elliott at the Second Fret—Recorded Live. Prestige-International 13065 (12" LP), 1963, notes by Shel Kagan. Jack Elliott: vocal and guitar. Recorded at the Second Fret, Philadelphia, PA, May 18, 1962.
Side 1
Band 1. "Muleskinner Blues"
Band 2. "Cool Water"
Band 3. "Talking Miner"
Band 4. "Boll Weevil"
Band 5. "How Long Blues"
Side 2
Band 1. "Salty Dog"
Band 2. "Tyin' Knots in the Devil's Tail"
Band 3. "Hobo's Lullaby"
Band 4. "Talking Sailor"
Band 5. "Rock Island Line"

Talking Woody Guthrie. Topic Records 12 T 93 (12" LP), 1963, notes by Paul Nelson and Jon Pankake. Jack Elliott: vocal, guitar, and harmonica. Reissue of *Woody Guthrie's Blues,* augmented with one previously unreleased song and three songs from earlier Topic 78 rpm recordings.
Side 1
Band 1. "Talking Columbia Blues"
Band 2. "Pretty Boy Floyd" (from Topic T.R.C. 98/2)
Band 3. "Ludlow Massacre"
Band 4. "Talking Miner Blues" (from Topic T.R.C. 98/1)
Band 5. "Hard Traveling"
Side 2
Band 1. "So Long, It's Been Good to Know You" (Previously unreleased)
Band 2. "Talking Dustbowl Blues"
Band 3. "1913 Massacre"
Band 4. "Rambling Blues" (from Topic T.R.C. 103/B)
Band 5. "Talking Sailor Blues"

Roll on Buddy. Topic Records 12 T 105 (12" LP), 1964, notes by Alexis Korner. Jack Elliott: vocal, guitar, and harmonica; Derroll Adams: vocal and five-string banjo. Reissue of *The Rambling Boys* (Topic 10-T-14) augmented with previously unreleased material.

Side 1
  Band 1. "Rich and Rambling Boys"
  Band 2. "Buffalo Skinners"
  Band 3. "I Wish I Was a Rock" (Derroll)
  Band 4. "It's Hard Ain't It Hard" (Previously unreleased)
  Band 5. "All Around the Water Tank" (Previously unreleased)
  Band 6. "Mother's Not Dead"
Side 2
  Band 1. "East Virginia Blues"
  Band 2. "The Old Bachelor" (Derroll)
  Band 3. "Danville Girl"
  Band 4. "The State of Arkansas"
  Band 5. "The Death of Mr. Garfield" (Derroll)
  Band 6. "Roll on Buddy"

Muleskinner. Topic Records 12 T 106 (12" LP), 1964, notes, anon. Jack Elliott: vocal, guitar, and harmonica. Reissue of *Jack Takes the Floor*, augmented with one previously unreleased recording and one earlier Topic 78 rpm recording.

Side 1
  Band 1. "San Francisco Bay Blues"
  Band 2. "Ol' Riley"
  Band 3. "The Boll Weevil"
  Band 4. "Bed Bug Blues"
  Band 5. "New York Town"
  Band 6. "Old Blue" (from Topic T.R.C. 103/A)
  Band 7. "Grey Goose"
Side 2
  Band 1. "Muleskinner Blues"
  Band 2. "East Texas Talking Blues" (Previously unreleased)
  Band 3. "Cocaine"
  Band 4. "Dink's Song"
  Band 5. "Black Baby"
  Band 6. "Salty Dog"

Jack Elliott Sings the Songs of Woody Guthrie. Prestige-Folklore 14011 (12" LP), 1964. Reissue of *Jack Elliott Sings the Songs of Woody Guthrie* (Prestige-International INT 13016).

Ramblin' Jack Elliott. Prestige-Folklore 14014 (12" LP), 1964. Reissue of *Ramblin' Jack Elliott* (Prestige-International INT 13033).

Hootenanny with Jack Elliott. Prestige-Folklore 14019 (12" LP), 1964. Reissue of *Jack Elliott at the Second Fret—Recorded Live* (Prestige-International 13065).

Country Style. Prestige-Folklore 14029 (12" LP), 1964. Reissue of *Country Style* (Prestige-International INT 13045).

Jack Elliott. Vanguard Records VRS-9151 and VSD-79151 (12" LP), 1964, notes by Shel Silverstein. Jack Elliott: vocal, guitar, and harmonica; Erik Darling: five-string banjo; Monte Dunn: guitar; Sylvia Fricke: beads; Bill Lee: bass; John Herald: guitar; John Hammond: mouth harp; Tedham Porterhouse (Bob Dylan): mouth harp; Ian Tyson: guitar; Eric Weissberg: bass.
Side 1
    Band 1. "Roving Gambler"
    Band 2. "Will the Circle Be Unbroken?"
    Band 3. "Diamond Joe"
    Band 4. "Guabi Guabi"
    Band 5. "Sowing on the Mountain"
    Band 6. "Roll on Buddy"
Side 2
    Band 1. "1913 Massacre"
    Band 2. "House of the Rising Sun"
    Band 3. "Shade of the Old Apple Tree"
    Band 4. "Black Snake Moan"
    Band 5. "Portland Town"
    Band 6. "More Pretty Girls"

Jack Elliott. Fontana TFL 6044 (12" LP), 1965. British issue of *Jack Elliott* (Vanguard VRS-9151/VSD-79151). Program identical.

Country Style. Stateside Records SL 10143 (12" LP), 1965. British issue of *Country Style* (Prestige-International INT 13045).

Jack Elliott Sings the Songs of Woody Guthrie. Stateside Records SL 10167 (12" LP), 1965. British issue of *Jack Elliott Sings the Songs of Woody Guthrie* (Prestige-International INT 13016).

Encore! Ramblin' Jack Elliott in London. Encore 194/E.M.I. Records (12" LP), 1965. Reissue of *Ramblin' Jack Elliott in London* (Columbia 33 SX 1166).

Ramblin' Jack Elliott. Victor Record Company/Prestige SJET-7838 (12" LP), 1966. Japanese issue of *Ramblin' Jack Elliott* (Prestige-International INT 13033).

Folkland Songs. Joker Records SM 3023 (12" LP), 1966. Jack Elliott: vocal, guitar, and harmonica; Derroll Adams: vocal, five-string banjo, and harmonica.
Side 1
Band 1. "Muleskinner's Blues"
Band 2. "How Long Blues"
Band 3. "Precious Jewel"
Band 4. "Death of John Henry"
Band 5. "Ain't It a Shame" (from Hi-Fi Records EPM 10147)
Band 6. "East Virginia Blues"
Band 7. "Stern Old Bachelor"
Side 2
Band 1. "Cigarettes and Whiskey"
Band 2. "The Cuckoo"
Band 3. "Salty Dog Blues" (from Hi-Fi Records EPM 10147)
Band 4. "I'm Going Down the Road"
Band 5. "Rich and Rambling Boy"
Band 6. "Death of Mr. Garfield"
Band 7. "I'm Gonna Walk the Street in Glory"

Riding in Folkland. Joker Records SM 3024 (12" LP), 1966. Jack Elliott: vocal, guitar, and harmonica; Derroll Adams: vocal, five-string banjo, and harmonica.
Side 1
Band 1. "Wreck on the Highway"
Band 2. "Portland Town"
Band 3. "Danville Girl"
Band 4. "The Tramp on the Street"
Band 5. "Worried Man Blues"
Band 6. "San Francisco Bay Blues" (from Hi-Fi Records EPM 10147)
Band 7. "900 Miles"
Side 2
Band 1. "Hard Traveling"
Band 2. "More Pretty Girls Than One"
Band 3. "Freight Train"

Band 4. "Talking Blues"
Band 5. "I'm Sad and I'm Lonely"
Band 6. "Roll on Buddy"
Band 7. "Roll in My Sweet Baby's Arms" (from Hi-Fi Records EPM 10147)

Talking Woody Guthrie. Delmark Records DL 801 (12" LP), 1966, notes, anon. American reissue of *Talking Woody Guthrie* (Topic 12 T 93). Program identical.

Roll on Buddy—The Jack Elliott and Derroll Adams Story: Volume 1. Bounty Records BY 6036 (12" LP), 1967, notes by Joe Boyd. Reprogrammed British reissue of *Riding in Folkland* (Joker Records SM 3024).
Side 1
Band 1. "Roll on Buddy"
Band 2. "More Pretty Girls"
Band 3. "Freight Train"
Band 4. "Talking New York"
Band 5. "Hard Travelin'"
Band 6. "Sad and Lonely"
Band 7. "Roll in My Sweet Baby's Arms"
Side 2
Band 1. "Crash on the Highway"
Band 2. "Portland Town"
Band 3. "Danville Girl"
Band 4. "Tramp on the Street"
Band 5. "Worried Man Blues"
Band 6. "San Francisco Bay Blues"
Band 7. "Nine Hundred Miles"

Jack Elliott Sings the Songs of Woody Guthrie. Transatlantic Records, XTRA 5043 (12" LP), Great Britain, 1967. Reissue of *Jack Elliott Sings the Songs of Woody Guthrie* (Prestige-Folklore 14011).

Jack Elliot. Archive of Folk Music/Everest Records FS 210 (12" LP), 1967, notes by Lee Palmer. Jack Elliott: vocal, guitar, and harmonica; Derroll Adams: vocal, five-string banjo, and harmonica (uncredited).
Side 1
Band 1. "More Pretty Girls Than One"
Band 2. "Roll on Buddy"
Band 3. "Death of John Henry"
Band 4. "Salty Dog Blues"

Band 5. "Talking Blues"
Band 6. "I'm Gonna Walk the Street in Glory"
Side 2
Band 1. "Cigarettes and Whiskey"
Band 2. "Danville Girl"
Band 3. "Worried Man Blues"
Band 4. "San Francisco Bay Blues"
Band 5. "Roll in My Sweet Baby's Arms"
Band 6. "I'm Going Down the Road"

Young Brigham. Warner/Reprise 6284 (12" LP), 1968, notes by Johnny Cash. Jack Elliott: vocal, guitar, and harmonica; Peter Childs: Dobro, bass; Richard Greene: fiddle; Mitch Greenhill: guitar; Eric Hord: guitar, harmonica, electric autoharp; Bruce Langhorne: tabla; Bill Lee: organ; Jack O'Hara: bass; Mark Spoelstra: guitar. *Young Brigham* was simultaneously released in Great Britain as *Young Brigham* (Reprise RSLP-6284) and in Japan as *Young Brigham* (Victor Record Company SJET-8051/ SREP 7230).
Side 1
Band 1. "If I Were a Carpenter"
Band 2. "Talking Fisherman"
Band 3. "Tennessee Stud"
Band 4. "Night Herding Song"
Band 5. "Rock Island Line"
Side 2
Band 1. "Danville Girl"
Band 2. "912 Greens"
Band 3. "Don't Think Twice, It's All Right"
Band 4. "Connection"
Band 5. "Goodnight Little Arlo"

Jack Elliott Sings the Songs of Woody Guthrie. Prestige 7453 (12" LP), 1968. Reissue of *Jack Elliott Sings the Songs of Woody Guthrie* (Prestige-Folklore 14011).

Bull Durham Sacks & Railroad Tracks. Warner/Reprise Records 6387 (US) (12" LP), 1970, notes by Arlo Guthrie. Jack Elliott: vocal and guitar; Norman Blake: guitar; Kenny Buttrey: drums; Charlie Daniels: guitar; Pete Drake: steel guitar; Charlie McCoy: bass; Bob Wilson: piano. Issued in the United States on cassette (Reprise CRX 6387), and eight-track tape as (Reprise M86387).

Side 1
  Band 1. "Rapping and Rambling"
  Band 2. "Me and Bobby McGee"
  Band 3. "Rapping and Rambling"
  Band 4. "Folsom Prison Blues"
  Band 5. "Rapping and Rambling"
  Band 6. "Find a Reason to Believe"
  Band 7. "I'll Be Your Baby Tonight"
  Band 8. "Don't Let Your Deal Go Down"
  Band 9. "Rapping and Rambling"
  Band 10. "We Come Here Not Chicago Dutchland for the Alles Brink
    Hoop Geslaffen Mocker"
Side 2
  Band 1. "Rapping and Rambling About"
  Band 2. "Don't Think Twice, It's All Right"
  Band 3. "Lay, Lady, Lay"
  Band 4. "Rapping and Rambling"
  Band 5. "Girl from the North Country"
  Band 6. "Rapping and Rambling"
  Band 7. "The Tramp on the Street"
  Band 8. "Rapping and Rambling"
  Band 9. "Michigan Water Blues"
  Band 10. "Don't You Leave Me Here"
  Band 11. "Rapping and Rambling"
  Band 12. "Blue Mountain"
  Band 13. "With God on Our Side"

Ramblin' Jack Elliott. Marble Arch MALS 1385 (Great Britain) (12" LP),
  1971, notes by Charles Chilton. British reissue of *Ramblin' Jack Elliott in
  London* (Columbia Records 33 SX 1166). Program identical.

Ramblin' Jack Elliott. Prestige 7721 (12" LP), 1971. Reissue of *Ramblin' Jack
  Elliott* (Prestige-Folklore 14014).

Country Style. Prestige 7804 (12" LP), 1972. Reissue of *Country Style*
  (Prestige-Folklore 14029).

Jack Elliott. King Records/Vanguard SR-843 (Japan) (12" LP), 1974. Japanese issue of *Jack Elliott* (Vanguard VRS-9151/VSD-79151). Program
  identical.

Canciones Folkloricas De USA. Gramusic GM 289 (12" LP), 1974. Spanish issue of *Folkland Songs* (Joker Records SM 3023). Program identical, with Sides 1 and 2 reversed.

Ramblin' Jack Elliott/Guthrie Thomas—Dear Ginny. Rarer Records, no catalog number (12" LP), 1975, notes by Ramblin' Jack Elliott and Guthrie Thomas. Side 1 features a program of Guthrie Thomas studio recordings. Side 2 features an unauthorized "bootleg" recording of Elliott's appearance on Jay Meehan's *Mellow Country* program broadcast on KMOR radio, Murray, Utah. Pressing reportedly ran to only five hundred copies.
Side 2
    Band 1. "San Francisco Bay Blues"
    Band 2. "Instrumental"
    Band 3. "Cup of Coffee"
    Band 4. "Danville Girl"
    Band 5. "Don't Think Twice, It's All Right"
    Band 6. "912 Greens"

America. Joker Records SM 3767-2 (2 × 12" LP), 1975. Re-issue collection pairing *Folkland Songs* (Joker Records SM 3023) with *Riding in Folkland* (Joker Records SM 3024).

The Essential Ramblin' Jack Elliott. Vanguard Records VSD-89/90 (2 × 12" LP), 1976. VSD-89 is a reissue of *Jack Elliott* (Vanguard Records VRS-9151/VSD-79151). VSD-90, previously unreleased, was recorded at Town Hall concert, New York City, April 30, 1965.
VSD-89
Side 1
    Band 1. "Roving Gambler"
    Band 2. "Will the Circle Be Unbroken?"
    Band 3. "Diamond Joe"
    Band 4. "Guabi Guabi"
    Band 5. "Sowing on the Mountain"
    Band 6. "Roll on Buddy"
Side 2
    Band 1. "1913 Massacre"
    Band 2. "House of the Rising Sun"
    Band 3. "Shade of the Old Apple Tree"

Band 4. "Black Snake Moan"
Band 5. "Portland Town"
Band 6. "More Pretty Girls"
VSD-90
Side 1
Band 1. "San Francisco Bay Blues"
Band 2. "Buffalo Skinners"
Band 3. "Sadie Brown"
Band 4. "Don't Think Twice, It's All Right"
Band 5. "Blind Lemon Jefferson"
Band 6. "Ramblin' Round Your City"
Side 2
Band 1. "Talkin' Columbia"
Band 2. "Tennessee Stud"
Band 3. "Night Herding Song"
Band 4. "Love Sick Blues"
Band 5. "I Belong to Glasgow"

Ramblin' Jack Elliott—Live In Japan. King Bellwood Records OFM 1002 (12" LP), 1977, notes by Jack Elliott. Jack Elliott: vocal and guitar. Recorded on January 25 and February 2, 1974, at Yomiuri Hall, Tokyo, Japan.
Side 1
Band 1. "San Francisco Bay Blues"
Band 2. "Me and Bobby McGee"
Band 3. "House of the Rising Sun"
Band 4. "Don't Think Twice, It's All Right"
Band 5. "Night Herding Song"
Band 6. "Old Shep"
Side 2
Band 1. "Reason to Believe"
Band 2. "Roll in My Sweet Baby's Arms"
Band 3. "Rock Island Line"
Band 4. "Diamond Joe"
Band 5. "Black Snake Moan"
Band 6. "Car Car Song"
Band 7. "Pretty Boy Floyd"

Ramblin' Jack Elliott—Hard Travelin': Songs by Woody Guthrie and Others. Fantasy Records F-24720 (2 × 12" LP), 1977, notes by David Bromberg and John Greenway. Gatefold 2 LP reissue of *Jack Elliott Sings the Songs*

of Woody Guthrie (Prestige-International INT 13016) and *Ramblin' Jack Elliott* (Prestige-International INT 13033).
Side 1
  Band 1. "Hard Traveling"
  Band 2. "Grand Coulee Dam"
  Band 3. "New York Town"
  Band 4. "Tom Joad"
  Band 5. "Howdido"
  Band 6. "Talking Dust Bowl"
  Band 7. "This Land Is Your Land"
Side 2
  Band 1. "Pretty Boy Floyd"
  Band 2. "Philadelphia Lawyer"
  Band 3. "Talking Columbia"
  Band 4. "Dust Storm Disaster"
  Band 5. "Riding in My Car"
  Band 6. "1913 Massacre"
  Band 7. "So Long"
Side 3
  Band 1. "Sadie Brown"
  Band 2. "East Virginia Blues"
  Band 3. "I Belong to Glasgow"
  Band 4. "The Cuckoo"
  Band 5. "Roll in My Sweet Baby's Arms"
  Band 6. "South Coast"
Side 4
  Band 1. "San Francisco Bay Blues"
  Band 2. "The Last Letter"
  Band 3. "I Love Her So/I Got a Woman"
  Band 4. "Candyman"
  Band 5. "Tramp on the Street"
  Band 6. "Railroad Bill"

Kerouac's Last Dream. FolkFreak Records FF 4005 (12" LP), 1981, notes by Jack Elliott and Barbara Dodge. Recorded on April 24 and 25, 1980, at Tonstudio St. Blasien, Northeim, West Germany.
Side 1
  Band 1. "Buffalo Skinners"
  Band 2. "Pretty Boy Floyd"
  Band 3. "Cup of Coffee"

Band 4. "Roving Gambler"
Band 5. "Blue Eyes Cryin' in the Rain"
Band 6. "The Cuckoo"
Side 2
Band 1. "Talkin' Fishin'"
Band 2. "1913 Massacre"
Band 3. "Carpenter"
Band 4. "912 Greens"

Talking Dust Bowl—The Best of Ramblin' Jack Elliott. Big Beat Records WIK 86 (12" LP), 1989, notes by Brian Hogg. British compilation of sixteen songs sourced from *Jack Elliott Sings the Songs of Woody Guthrie* (Prestige-International INT 13016) and *Ramblin' Jack Elliott* (Prestige-International INT 13033).
Side 1
Band 1. "Pretty Boy Floyd"
Band 2. "The Cuckoo"
Band 3. "Roll in My Sweet Baby's Arms"
Band 4. "Talking Dust Bowl Blues"
Band 5. "Tom Joad"
Band 6. "New York Town"
Band 7. "Riding in My Car"
Band 8. "So Long (It's Been Good to Know You)"
Side 2
Band 1. "Grand Coulee Dam"
Band 2. "Railroad Bill"
Band 3. "East Virginia Blues"
Band 4. "Talking Columbia Blues"
Band 5. "South Coast"
Band 6. "The Last Letter"
Band 7. "Tramp on the Street"
Band 8. "This Land Is Your Land"

Ramblin' Jack Elliott—Hard Travelin': Songs by Woody Guthrie and Others. Fantasy Records FCD 24720-2, 1989, notes by David Bromberg and John Greenway. CD issue of the LP *Ramblin' Jack Elliott—Hard Travelin': Songs by Woody Guthrie and Others* (Fantasy Records F-24720). "I Love Her So/I Got a Woman" omitted from program as "CD could not accommodate the entire length of the original double-album." Released in Great Britain as *Ramblin' Jack Elliott—Hard Travelin': Songs by Woody Guthrie and Others* (CDWIK 952).

Track 1. "Hard Traveling"
Track 2. "Grand Coulee Dam"
Track 3. "New York Town"
Track 4. "Tom Joad"
Track 5. "Howdido"
Track 6. "Talking Dust Bowl"
Track 7. "This Land Is Your Land"
Track 8. "Pretty Boy Floyd"
Track 9. "Philadelphia Lawyer"
Track 10. "Talking Columbia"
Track 11. "Dust Storm Disaster"
Track 12. "Riding in My Car"
Track 13. "1913 Massacre"
Track 14. "So Long"
Track 15. "Sadie Brown"
Track 16. "East Virginia Blues"
Track 17. "I Belong to Glasgow"
Track 18. "The Cuckoo"
Track 19. "Roll in My Sweet Baby's Arms"
Track 20. "South Coast"
Track 21. "San Francisco Bay Blues"
Track 22. "The Last Letter"
Track 23. "Candyman"
Track 24. "Tramp on the Street"
Track 25. "Railroad Bill"

Legends of Folk. Red House Records RHR CD 31, 1990. Ramblin' Jack Elliott, Spider John Koerner, and U. Utah Phillips recorded at the Old World Theater, April 28, 1989.
Track 8. "Talkin' Fishin'"
Track 9. "Jack introduces *Don't Think Twice*"
Track 10. "Don't Think Twice, It's All Right"
Track 11. "Quoting Thoreau"
Track 12. "On the Range of the Buffalo"
Track 17. "Old Shep"
Track 21. "912 Greens"

Jack Elliott Plus Live/Jack Elliott. Vanguard/King Records KICP 2027, 1990. Japan only CD reissue of the LP *Jack Elliott* (Vanguard Records VRS-9151 and VSD-79151) *The Essential Ramblin' Jack Elliott* (Vanguard Records VSD-89/90) minus "I Belong to Glasgow." Part of the label's "Vanguard Folk Revival 20" series.

Track 1. "Roving Gambler"
Track 2. "Will the Circle Be Unbroken?"
Track 3. "Diamond Joe"
Track 4. "Guabi Guabi"
Track 5. "Sowing on the Mountain"
Track 6. "Roll on Buddy"
Track 7. "1913 Massacre"
Track 8. "House of the Rising Sun"
Track 9. "Shade of the Old Apple Tree"
Track 10. "Black Snake Moan"
Track 11. "Portland Town"
Track 12. "More Pretty Girls"
Track 13. "San Francisco Bay Blues"
Track 14. "Buffalo Skinners"
Track 15. "Sadie Brown"
Track 16. "Don't Think Twice, It's All Right"
Track 17. "Blind Lemon Jefferson"
Track 18. "Ramblin' Round Your City"
Track 19. "Talking Columbia"
Track 20. "Tennessee Stud"
Track 21. "Night Herding Song"
Track 22. "Lovesick Blues"

Ramblin' Jack Elliott—Kerouac's Last Dream. Wundertute Musik TUT CD 72.163, 1993, notes by Ramblin' Jack Elliott and Barbara Dodge. German CD reissue of the LP *Kerouac's Last Dream* (FolkFreak Records FF 4005).
Track 1. "Buffalo Skinners"
Track 2. "Pretty Boy Floyd"
Track 3. "Cup of Coffee"
Track 4. "Roving Gambler"
Track 5. "Blue Eyes Cryin' in the Rain"
Track 6. "The Cuckoo"
Track 7. "Talkin' Fishin'"
Track 8. "1913 Massacre"
Track 9. "Carpenter"
Track 10. "912 Greens"

Ramblin' Jack Elliott Sings Woody Guthrie and Jimmie Rodgers and Cowboy Songs. Monitor Records MCD 71380, 1994. CD reissue of *Ramblin' Jack Elliott Sings Woody Guthrie and Jimmie Rodgers* (Monitor Records

MF 380) and *Monitor Presents Jack Elliott: Ramblin' Cowboy* (Monitor Records MF 379).
Track 1. "Do-Re-Mi"
Track 2. "Dead or Alive"
Track 3. "Grand Coulee Dam"
Track 4. "Dust Storm Disaster"
Track 5. "I Ain't Got No Home"
Track 6. "So Long, It's Been Good to Know You"
Track 7. "T for Texas"
Track 8. "Waitin' for a Train"
Track 9. "Jimmie the Kid"
Track 10. "Mother, the Queen of My Heart"
Track 11. "In the Jailhouse Now"
Track 12. "Whippin' That Old T.B."
Track 13. "Rusty Jiggs and Sandy Sam"
Track 14. "Git Along Little Dogies"
Track 15. "Sadie Brown"
Track 16. "Night Herding Song"
Track 17. "Chisholm Trail"
Track 18. "Fifteen Cents and a Dollar"
Track 19. "Rocky Mountain Belle"
Track 20. "Talking Blues"
Track 21. "Diamond Joe"
Track 22. "In the Willow Garden"
Track 23. "I Ride an Old Paint"
Track 24. "Jack O'Diamonds"

Jack Elliott Plus Live/Jack Elliott. Vanguard/King Records KICP 2523, 1994. Japan only CD reissue of *Jack Elliott Plus Live/Jack Elliott* (Vanguard/King Records KICP 2027). Part of the label's "Vintage Folk Series 2300." Program identical.

South Coast. Red House Records RHR CD 59, 1995, notes by Guy Clark, Joan Baez, Jackson Browne, Ian Tyson, Greg Brown, Jerry Jeff Walker, John Wesley Harding, Doc Watson, Bob Weir, Artie Traum, Peter Rowan, Chance Browne, Zachary Richard, Floyd Red Crow Westerman, Stefan Grossman, Tim Grimm, Bruce Pratt, Rory Block, Buck Ramsey, Tom Russell, and Jeremy Slate.
Track 1. "Pastures of Plenty"
Track 2. "If I Were a Carpenter"
Track 3. "Cocaine Blues"

Track 4. "I Ain't Got No Home"
Track 5. "Will James"
Track 6. "The Buffalo Skinners"
Track 7. "Rake and Rambling Boys"
Track 8. "South Coast"
Track 9. "Talkin' Dust Bowl"
Track 10. "Mean Old Bedbug Blues"
Track 11. "Ludlow Massacre"
Track 12. "San Francisco Bay Blues"

Ramblin' Jack Elliott—Me & Bobby McGee. Rounder Records 0368, 1995, notes by Arlo Guthrie, Johnny Cash, and Scott Alarik. CD reissue of the LP *Young Brigham* (Reprise 6284) and *Bull Durham Sacks & Railroad Tracks* (Reprise Records 6387) minus the "Rapping and Rambling" segments and "Danville Girl," "Connection," "Goodnight Little Arlo," "Girl from the North Country," and "Michigan Water Blues/Don't You Leave Me Here."
Track 1. "Me & Bobby McGee"
Track 2. "Folsom Prison Blues"
Track 3. "Reason to Believe"
Track 4. "I'll Be Your Baby Tonight"
Track 5. "Don't Let Your Deal Go Down"
Track 6. "912 Greens"
Track 7. "If I Were a Carpenter"
Track 8. "Talking Fisherman Blues"
Track 9. "Tennessee Stud"
Track 10. "Night Herding Song"
Track 11. "Rock Island Line"
Track 12. "Don't Think Twice, It's All Right"
Track 13. "Lay Lady Lay"
Track 14. "Tramp on the Street"
Track 15. "With God on Our Side"

Ramblin' Jack—The Legendary Topic Masters. Topic Records TSCD477, 1995, notes by Wizz Jones. British CD reissue of *Talking Woody Guthrie* (Topic Records 12 T 93), *Muleskinner* (Topic Records 12 T 106, minus "Bed Bug Blues," "Old Blue," "Grey Goose," "Cocaine," "Black Baby," and "Salty Dog Blues") and *Roll on Buddy* (Topic Records 12 T 105), minus Derroll Adams's solo performances, "Rich and Rambling Boys," "Buffalo Skinners," and "State of Arkansas."
Track 1. "Talking Columbia Blues"

Track 2. "Pretty Boy Floyd"
Track 3. "Ludlow Massacre"
Track 4. "Talking Miner Blues"
Track 5. "Hard Traveling"
Track 6. "So Long It's Been Good to Know You"
Track 7. "Talking Dustbowl Blues"
Track 8. "1913 Massacre"
Track 9. "Rambling Blues"
Track 10. "Talking Sailor"
Track 11. "San Francisco Bay Blues"
Track 12. "Ol' Riley"
Track 13. "The Boll Weevil"
Track 14. "New York Town"
Track 15. "Muleskinner's Blues"
Track 16. "East Texas Talking Blues"
Track 17. "Dink's Song"
Track 18. "It's Hard Ain't It Hard"
Track 19. "All Around the Water Tank"
Track 20. "Mother's Not Dead"
Track 21. "East Virginia Blues"
Track 22. "Danville Girl"
Track 23. "Rich and Rambling Boys"
Track 24. "Roll on Buddy"

Jack Elliott & Derrol Adams—Selection of America. Gold Sound/Promo Sound
  AG DCD-768, 1996. Czech 2 CD reissue of *America* (Joker Records
  SM 3767-2). Program of disc 1 is identical to *Folkland Songs* (SM 3023).
  Program of disc 2 is identical to *Riding in Folkland* (SM 3024).
CD 1
Track 1. "Muleskinner's Blues"
Track 2. "How Long Blues"
Track 3. "Precious Jewel"
Track 4. "Death of John Henry"
Track 5. "Ain't It a Shame" (from Hi-Fi Records EPM 10147)
Track 6. "East Virginia Blues"
Track 7. "Stern Old Bachelor"
Track 8. "Cigarettes and Whiskey"
Track 9. "The Cuckoo"
Track 10. "Salty Dog Blues" (from Hi-Fi Records EPM 10147)
Track 11. "I'm Going Down the Road"

Track 12. "Rich and Rambling Boy"
Track 13. "Death of Mr. Garfield"
Track 14. "I'm Gonna Walk the Street in Glory"
CD 2
Track 1. "Wreck on the Highway"
Track 2. "Portland Town"
Track 3. "Danville Girl"
Track 4. "The Tramp on the Street"
Track 5. "Worried Man Blues"
Track 6. "San Francisco Bay Blues" (from Hi-Fi Records EPM 10147)
Track 7. "900 Miles"
Track 8. "Hard Traveling"
Track 9. "More Pretty Girls Than One"
Track 10. "Freight Train"
Track 11. "Talking Blues"
Track 12. "I'm Sad and I'm Lonely"
Track 13. "Roll on Buddy"
Track 14. "Roll in My Sweet Baby's Arms" (from Hi-Fi Records EPM 10147)

Jack Elliot & Derrol Adams—Cowboy Songs. Cameo/Promo Sound AG/Cedar CD 3589, 1996. Selection of songs compiled from *America* (Joker Records SM 3767-2).
Track 1. "Death of Mr. Garfield"
Track 2. "Hard Traveling"
Track 3. "Wreck on the Highway"
Track 4. "Muleskinner's Blues"
Track 5. "Death of John Henry"
Track 6. "Portland Town"
Track 7. "How Long Blues"
Track 8. "Precious Jewel"
Track 9. "900 Miles"
Track 10. "Salty Dog Blues"
Track 11. "I'm Gonna Walk the Street in Glory"
Track 12. "Freight Train"
Track 13. "I'm Sad and I'm Lonely"
Track 14. "Ain't It a Shame"
Track 15. "The Cuckoo"
Track 16. "Stern Old Bachelor"

Jack Elliott Sings the Songs of Woody Guthrie. P-Vine Records/Blues Inter-
actions PCD 5140, 1997. Japan only CD reissue of the LP *Jack Elliott
Sings the Songs of Woody Guthrie* (Prestige-International 13016). Part of
the label's *Coffee House Folkie Sounds* series.
Track 1. "Hard Traveling"
Track 2. "Grand Coulee Dam"
Track 3. "New York Town"
Track 4. "Tom Joad"
Track 5. "Howdido"
Track 6. "Talking Dust Bowl"
Track 7. "This Land Is Your Land"
Track 8. "Pretty Boy Floyd"
Track 9. "Philadelphia Lawyer"
Track 10. "Talking Columbia"
Track 11. "Dust Storm Disaster"
Track 12. "Riding in My Car"
Track 13. "1913 Massacre"
Track 14. "So Long"

Ramblin' Jack Elliott. P-Vine Records/Blues Interactions PCD 5219, 1997.
Japan only reissue of the LP *Ramblin' Jack Elliott* (Prestige-International
13033). Part of the label's *Coffee House Folkies Sounds* series.
Track 1. "Sadie Brown"
Track 2. "East Virginia Blues"
Track 3. "I Belong to Glasgow"
Track 4. "The Cuckoo"
Track 5. "Roll in My Sweet Baby's Arms"
Track 6. "South Coast"
Track 7. "San Francisco Bay Blues"
Track 8. "The Last Letter"
Track 9. "I Love Her So/I Got a Woman"
Track 10. "Candyman"
Track 11. "Tramp on the Street"
Track 12. "Railroad Bill"

Kerouac's Last Dream. Appleseed Recordings 1021, 1997, notes by Carsten
Linde (uncredited), Ramblin' Jack Elliott, and Jim Musselman. CD
reissue of the LP *Kerouac's Last Dream* (FolkFreak Records FF 4005),
augmented with previously unreleased material.

Track 1. "Pretty Boy Floyd"
Track 2. "Blues Eyes Crying in the Rain"
Track 3. "Freight Train Blues" (Previously unreleased)
Track 4. "Talkin' Fishin'"
Track 5. "Roving Gambler"
Track 6. "Cuckoo"
Track 7. "Don't Think Twice, It's All Right" (Previously unreleased)
Track 8. "Soldier's Last Letter" (Previously unreleased)
Track 9. "1913 Massacre"
Track 10. "Buffalo Skinners"
Track 11. "Night Herding Song" (Previously unreleased)
Track 12. "Mean Mama Blues" (Previously unreleased)
Track 13. "I Threw It All Away" (Previously unreleased)
Track 14. "Detour" (Previously unreleased)
Track 15. "Riding Down the Canyon" (Previously unreleased)
Track 16. "Cup of Coffee"
Track 17. "912 Greens"

America—Jack Elliot & Derrol Adams. Cedar/Music of the World/Promo Sound AG CD 12543, 1997. Selection of songs compiled from *America* (Joker Records SM 3767-2).
Track 1. "The Tramp on the Street"
Track 2. "Muleskinner's Blues"
Track 3. "Precious Jewel"
Track 4. "Ain't It a Shame"
Track 5. "East Virginia Blues"
Track 6. "Cigarettes and Whiskey"
Track 7. "I'm Going Down the Road"
Track 8. "Rich and Rambling Boys"
Track 9. "I'm Gonna Walk the Streets in Glory"
Track 10. "Worried Man Blues"
Track 11. "Wreck on the Highway"
Track 12. "Danville Girl"
Track 13. "More Pretty Girls Than One"
Track 14. "900 Miles"
Track 15. "Talking Blues"
Track 16. "Roll on Buddy"
Track 17. "Roll in My Sweet Baby's Arms"
Track 18. "San Francisco Bay Blues"

Ramblin' Jack Elliott—Live in Japan. Vivid/Bellwood Records VSCD 706, 1997. Japan only CD reissue of the LP *Ramblin' Jack Elliott—Live in Japan* (King Bellwood Records OFM 1002).
Track 1. "San Francisco Bay Blues"
Track 2. "Me & Bobby McGee"
Track 3. "House of the Rising Sun"
Track 4. "Don't Think Twice, It's All Right"
Track 5. "Night Herding Song"
Track 6. "Old Shep"
Track 7. "Reason to Believe"
Track 8. "Roll in My Sweet Baby's Arms"
Track 9. "Rock Island Line"
Track 10. "Diamond Joe"
Track 11. "Black Snake Moan"
Track 12. "Car Car Song"
Track 13. "Pretty Boy Floyd"

Hootenanny at a Second Fret/Hootenanny with Jack Elliott. P-Vine Records/ Blues Interactions PCD 5308, 1997. Japan only CD reissue of the LP *Jack Elliott at the Second Fret—Recorded Live* (Prestige-International 13065)/*Hootenanny with Jack Elliott* (Prestige Folklore FL 14019). Part of the label's "Coffee House Folkies Series."
Track 1. "Muleskinner Blues"
Track 2. "Cool Water"
Track 3. "Talking Miner"
Track 4. "Boll Weevil"
Track 5. "How Long Blues"
Track 6. "Salty Dog"
Track 7. "Tyin' Knots in the Devil's Tail"
Track 8. "Hobo's Lullaby"
Track 9. "Talking Sailor"
Track 10. "Rock Island Line"

Friends of Mine. Hightone Records HCD 8089, 1998, notes by Susanna Clark, released March 17, 1998. Jack Elliott: guitar, 12-string guitar, vocals; Arlo Guthrie: guitar and vocal; Ruth Davies: bass; Tom Rigney: violin; Jimmy Sanchez: drums, snare drum; Peter Rowan: guitar, vocal, and mandolin; Norton Buffalo: harmonica; Rosalie Sorrels: vocal; Tom Waits: guitar and vocal; Billy Wilson: accordion; Roy Rogers: slide guitar; Emmylou Harris: vocal; Nanci Griffith: vocal; John Prine: guitar

and vocal; Jerry Jeff Walker: guitar, vocal, and harmonica; Guy Clark: guitar and vocal; Bob Weir: guitar and vocal.
Track 1. "Riding Down the Canyon" (with Arlo Guthrie)
Track 2. "Me and Billy the Kid" (with Peter Rowan)
Track 3. "Last Letter" (with Rosalie Sorrels)
Track 4. "Louise" (with Tom Waits)
Track 5. "Rex's Blues" (with Emmylou Harris and Nanci Griffith)
Track 6. "Walls of Red Wing" (with John Prine)
Track 7. "Hard Travelin'" (with Jerry Jeff Walker)
Track 8. "He Was a Friend of Mine" (with Jerry Jeff Walker)
Track 9. "Dark as a Dungeon" (with Guy Clark)
Track 10. "Friend of the Devil" (with Bob Weir)
Track 11. "Reason to Believe"
Track 12. "Bleecker Street Blues"

Jack Elliott. Vanguard Records/King Records KICP 3006, 1998. Japan only CD reissue of LP *Jack Elliott* (Vanguard Records VRS-9151 and VSD-79151). Part of the label's *Vanguard Folkie Sound Collection.*
Track 1. "Roving Gambler"
Track 2. "Will the Circle Be Unbroken?"
Track 3. "Diamond Joe"
Track 4. "Guabi Guabi"
Track 5. "Sowing on the Mountain"
Track 6. "Roll on Buddy"
Track 7. "1913 Massacre"
Track 8. "House of the Rising Sun"
Track 9. "Shade of the Old Apple Tree"
Track 10. "Black Snake Moan"
Track 11. "Portland Town"
Track 12. "More Pretty Girls"

Early Sessions—Ramblin' Jack Elliott with Derroll Adams. Tradition Records/ Rykodisc TCD 1083, 1999, released April 6, 1999. Selection of songs compiled from *America* (Joker Records SM 3767-2).
Track 1. "More Pretty Girls Than One"
Track 2. "Roll on Buddy"
Track 3. "Death of John Henry"
Track 4. "Salty Dog Blues"
Track 5. "Talking Blues"
Track 6. "I'm Gonna Walk the Street in Glory"
Track 7. "Cigarettes and Whiskey"

Track 8. "Danville Girl"
Track 9. "Worried Man Blues"
Track 10. "San Francisco Bay Blues"
Track 11. "Roll in My Sweet Baby's Arms"
Track 12. "I'm Going Down the Road"

Country Style/Live. Fantasy FCD-24754-2, 1999, notes by John Greenway and Shel Kagan, 1999. CD reissue of the LPs *Country Style* (Prestige-International 13045) and *Jack Elliott at the Second Fret—Recorded Live* (Prestige-International 13065).
Track 1. "Mean Mama Blues"
Track 2. "Low and Lonely"
Track 3. "The Wreck of the Old 97"
Track 4. "Old Shep"
Track 5. "Wabash Cannonball"
Track 6. "Brown Eyes"
Track 7. "Love Sick Blues"
Track 8. "Arthritis Blues"
Track 9. "Take Me Back and Love Me One More Time"
Track 10. "The Tennessee Stud"
Track 11. "Those Brown Eyes"
Track 12. "Detour"
Track 13. "The Soldier's Last Letter"
Track 14. "Muleskinner Blues"
Track 15. "Cool Water"
Track 16. "Talking Intro"
Track 17. "Talking Miner"
Track 18. "Boll Weevil"
Track 19. "How Long Blues"
Track 20. "Salty Dog"
Track 21. "Tyin' Knots in the Devil's Tail"
Track 22. "Hobo's Lullaby"
Track 23. "Talking Intro"
Track 24. "Talking Sailor"
Track 25. "Rock Island Line"

The Long Ride. Hightone Records HCD 8107, released September 14, 1999, notes by Tom Russell. Jack Elliott: vocals and guitar; Joe Craven: mandolin, fiddle, banjo; Derek Jones: bass; Roy Rogers: electric guitar, slide guitar, stumpfiddle; Jim Sanchez: drums; Bruce Gordon: accordion; Dave Van Ronk: vocals, guitar; Maria Muldaur: vocals; Dave

Alvin: vocals, guitar; Norton Buffalo: harmonica; Tom Russell: vocals, guitar; Andrew Hardin: guitar.
Track 1. "Connection"
Track 2. "Cup of Coffee" (with Tom Russell)
Track 3. "Ranger's Command"
Track 4. "Pony"
Track 5. "St. James Infirmary" (with Dave Van Ronk)
Track 6. "Picture from Life's Other Side" (with Maria Muldaur)
Track 7. "East Virginia Blues" (with Dave Alvin)
Track 8. "The Sky Above and the Mud Below" (with Tom Russell)
Track 9. "Take Me Back and Try Me One More Time"
Track 10. "Now He's Just Dust in the Wind"
Track 11. "True Blue Jeans"
Track 12. "Diamond Joe"
Track 13. "With God on Our Side"

The Long Ride. P-Vine Records/Blues Interactions, Inc. PCD 5556, 1999. Japan CD issue of *The Long Ride* (Hightone Records HCD 8107). Program identical.

Young Brigham. Reprise Records/WEA International WPCR-10718, 2000. Japan CD issue of the LP *Young Brigham* (Reprise 6284). Program identical.

The Ballad of Ramblin' Jack—Original Soundtrack from the Motion Picture. Vanguard Records 79575-2, 2000, notes by Aiyana Elliott and Dick Dahl.
Track 1. "Introduction by Johnny Cash" (*The Johnny Cash Show*, September 1969, previously unreleased)
Track 2. "Muleskinner Blues" (*The Johnny Cash Show*, September 1964, previously unreleased)
Track 3. "Cuckoo" (Cowboy Poetry Gathering, Elko, NV, 1998, previously unreleased)
Track 4. "Hard Travelin'" (*Gill Gross Show*, WCBS Radio, 1998, previously unreleased)
Track 5. "Railroad Bill" (with Woody Guthrie and Sonny Terry, New York City, January 1954, previously unreleased)
Track 6. "Buskin'"
Track 7. "Pastures of Plenty" (from *South Coast*, Red House Records RHR CD 59)

Track 8. "Rake and Ramblin' Boy" (from *The Rambling Boys*, Topic Records 10-T-14)

Track 9. "San Francisco Bay Blues" (from Pete Seeger's *Rainbow Quest*, 1965)

Track 10. "Candy Man/Talkin' Sailor Blues" (from the film *Ballads, Blues and Bluegrass*)

Track 11. "Acne" (with Bob Dylan, Riverside Church, New York City, July 29, 1961, previously unreleased)

Track 12. "Don't Think Twice, It's All Right" (Bottom Line, New York City, 1998, previously unreleased)

Track 13. "Take Me Home" (with Johnny Cash, *The Johnny Cash Show*, 1969, previously unreleased)

Track 14. "If I Were a Carpenter" (Cowboy Poetry Gathering, Elko, NV, 1998, previously unreleased)

Track 15. "Car Song" (Cowboy Poetry Gathering, Elko, NV, 1998, previously unreleased)

Track 16. "900 Miles" (Odetta, D.A Pennebaker recording, New York City, previously unreleased)

Track 17. "Cup of Coffee" (Anderson Fair, Houston, TX, from the film *Ramblin' Jack in Texas*)

Track 18. "Introduction by President Clinton"

Track 19. "1913 Massacre" (Bottom Line, New York City, 1998, previously unreleased)

Track 20. "Cuckoo (Reprise)" (from *Kerouac's Last Dream*, FolkFreak Records FF 4005)

Ramblin' Jack Elliott—The Best of the Vanguard Years. Vanguard 79573-2, 2000, notes by Randy Poe. CD reissue of LP *Jack Elliott* (Vanguard Records VRS-9151 and VSD-79151) augmented with previously unreleased material. Part of the *Vanguard Sessions* series.

Track 1. "Roving Gambler"

Track 2. "Will the Circle Be Unbroken?"

Track 3. "Diamond Joe"

Track 4. "Guabi Guabi"

Track 5. "Sowing on the Mountain"

Track 6. "Roll on Buddy"

Track 7. "1913 Massacre"

Track 8. "House of the Rising Sun"

Track 9. "Shade of the Old Apple Tree"

Track 10. "Black Snake Moan"
Track 11. "Portland Town"
Track 12. "More Pretty Girls"
Track 13. "Danville Girl" (Previously unreleased)
Track 14. "John Hardy" (Previously unreleased)
Track 15. "Dark as a Dungeon" (Previously unreleased)
Track 16. "Hard Ain't It Hard" (Previously unreleased)
Track 17. "Don't Think Twice, It's All Right" (Previously unreleased)
Track 18. "I Got a Woman" (Previously unreleased)
Track 19. "Railroad Bill" (Previously unreleased)
Track 20. "I Never Will Marry" (Previously unreleased)
Track 21. "At My Window" (Previously unreleased)
Track 22. "Blue Eyed Elaine" (Previously unreleased)
Track 23. "Wildwood Flower" (Previously unreleased)
Track 24. "Ranger's Command" (Previously unreleased)
Track 25. "Willie Moore" (Previously unreleased)

Young Brigham. Collector's Choice Music CCM-198-2, 2001, notes by Johnny Cash. CD reissue of the LP *Young Brigham* (Reprise 6284). Program identical.

Bull Durham Sacks & Railroad Tracks. Collector's Choice Music CCM-199-2, 2001, notes by Arlo Guthrie and Richie Unterberger. CD reissue of LP *Bull Durham Sacks & Railroad Tracks* (Reprise Records 6387). Program identical.

The Rambling Boys. Vivid Sound Corporation VSCD 261, 2002. Japan CD reissue of the LP *Roll on Buddy* (Topic Records 12 T 105).
Track 1. "Rich and Rambling Boys"
Track 2. "Buffalo Skinners"
Track 3. "I Wish I Was a Rock"
Track 4. "It's Hard Ain't It Hard"
Track 5. "All Around the Water Tank"
Track 6. "Mother's Not Dead"
Track 7. "East Virginia Blues"
Track 8. "The Old Bachelor"
Track 9. "Danville Girl"
Track 10. "The State of Arkansas"
Track 11. "The Death of Mr. Garfield"
Track 12. "Roll on Buddy"

Woody Guthrie's Blues. Vivid Sound Corporation VSCD 266, 2002. Japan only CD reissue of the LP *Talking Woody Guthrie* (Topic Records 12 T 93).
Track 1. "Talking Columbia Blues"
Track 2. "Pretty Boy Floyd"
Track 3. "Ludlow Massacre"
Track 4. "Talking Miner Blues"
Track 5. "Hard Traveling"
Track 6. "So Long It's Been Good to Know You"
Track 7. "Talking Dustbowl Blues"
Track 8. "1913 Massacre"
Track 9. "Rambling Blues"
Track 10. "Talking Sailor"

Jack Takes the Floor. Vivid Sound Corporation VSCD 267, 2002. Japan only CD reissue of the LP *Muleskinner* (Topic Records 12 T 106), augmented with two tracks from *Songs Against the Bomb* (Topic Records 12001).
Track 1. "San Francisco Bay Blues"
Track 2. "Ol' Riley"
Track 3. "The Boll Weevil"
Track 4. "Bed Bug Blues"
Track 5. "New York Town"
Track 6. "Old Blue"
Track 7. "Grey Goose"
Track 8. "Muleskinner's Blues"
Track 9. "East Texas Talking Blues"
Track 10. "Cocaine"
Track 11. "Dink's Song"
Track 12. "Black Baby"
Track 13. "Salty Dog"
Track 14. "Brother, Won't You Roll Down the Line?"
Track 15. "There Are Better Things to Do"

Ramblin' Jack Elliott—The Lost Topic Tapes: Cowes Harbour 1957. Hightone Records HCD8175, 2004, notes by Robert Wylie and Jack Elliott.
Track 1. "Intro"
Track 2. "Hard Travelin'"
Track 3. "Big Rock Candy Mountain"
Track 4. "Old Rattler"

Track 5. "Talking Columbia Blues"
Track 6. "Streets of Laredo"
Track 7. "Jack O' Diamonds"
Track 8. "Rusty Jiggs & Sandy Sam"
Track 9. "Tom Joad"
Track 10. "Acres of Clams"
Track 11. "Freight Train"
Track 12. "Chisholm Trail"
Track 13. "Crawdad Song"
Track 14. "Black Girl"
Track 15. "Tom Dooley"
Track 16. "Rocky Mountain Belle"

Ramblin' Jack Elliott—The Lost Topic Tapes: Isle of Wight 1957. Hightone Records HCD8176, 2004, notes by Robert Wylie and Jack Elliott.
Track 1. "Intro"
Track 2. "T for Texas"
Track 3. "Howdido"
Track 4. "I Thought I Heard Buddy Bolden Say"
Track 5. "Crash on the Highway"
Track 6. "Candy Man"
Track 7. "Ballad of John Henry"
Track 8. "Car Song"
Track 9. "Roll in My Sweet Baby's Arms"
Track 10. "Old Blue"
Track 11. "Don't You Leave Me Here"
Track 12. "Why O Why"
Track 13. "In the Shade of the Old Apple Tree"
Track 14. "Oklahoma Hills"
Track 15. "Rock Island Line"
Track 16. "Closing/Railroad Bill"

Ramblin' Jack Elliott—Live at Tales from the Tavern—Volume One. Tales from the Tavern 023, 2005, notes by Ron and Carole Ann Colone. Recorded "in concert" on February 12, 2003, at Mattei's Tavern, Los Olivos, California.
Track 1. "Introduction of Ramblin' Jack"
Track 2. "It's Going to Be an Unusual Evening"
Track 3. "Take Me Back and Try Me One More Time"
Track 4. "Remarks about Jelly Roll Morton"
Track 5. "Whinin' Boy Blues"

Track 6. "Introduction to the 'Night Herding Song'"
Track 7. "The Night Herding Song"
Track 8. "Introduction to 'The South Coast' and Frank Hamilton"
Track 9. "The South Coast"
Track 10. "Introduction to 'Don't Think Twice'"
Track 11. "Don't Think Twice, It's All Right"
Track 12. "Introduction of Robert Carradine"
Track 13. "Tom Joad"
Track 14. "Introduction of 'Buffalo Skinners'"
Track 15. "Buffalo Skinners"
Track 16. "Introduction to '912 Greens'"
Track 17. "912 Greens"

I Stand Alone. ANTI Records 86814, 2006.
Track 1. "Engine 143"
Track 2. "Arthritis Blues"
Track 3. "Old Blue"
Track 4. "Driving Nails in My Coffin"
Track 5. "Rake and Rambling Boy"
Track 6. "Hong Kong Blues"
Track 7. "Jean Harlow"
Track 8. "Call Me a Dog"
Track 9. "Careless Darling"
Track 10. "Mr. Garfield"
Track 11. "My Old Dog and Me"
Track 12. "Leaving Cheyenne"
Track 13. "Remember Me"
Track 14. "Willy Moore"
Track 15. "Honey, Where You Been So Long?"
Track 16. "Woody's Last Ride"

Vanguard Visionaries: Ramblin' Jack Elliott. Vanguard 73153-2, 2007. CD compilation of *Jack Elliott* (Vanguard Records VRS-9151 and VSD-79151, minus "Sowing on the Mountain," "Roll on Buddy," "Shade of the Old Apple Tree," "Portland Town," and "More Pretty Girls Than One") and with the addition of "John Hardy," "Don't Think Twice, It's All Right," and "I Got a Woman" from *Ramblin' Jack Elliott—The Best of the Vanguard Years* (Vanguard 79573-2).
Track 1. "1913 Massacre"
Track 2. "Will the Circle Be Unbroken?"
Track 3. "Don't Think Twice, It's All Right"

Track 4. "John Hardy"
Track 5. "Guabi Guabi"
Track 6. "House of the Rising Sun"
Track 7. "Black Snake Moan"
Track 8. "Roving Gambler"
Track 9. "Diamond Joe"
Track 10. "I Got a Woman"

The Musical Grandfather & Father of Bob Dylan: Woody Guthrie & Jack Elliott.
Avid Entertainment AMSC 944, Great Britain, 2008, notes by Tony
Russell. CD compilation of previously issued material from *Woody
Guthrie's Blues* (Topic Records T-5), *Jack Elliot Sings* (77 Records 77
LP/1), *Badmen and Heroes* (Elektra EKL-16), and Topic T.R.C. 98, 103
and 104 78 rpm singles.
Disc 2
Track 1. "Pretty Boy Floyd"
Track 2. "Jesse James"
Track 3. "Charles Guiteau"
Track 4. "Alabama Bound"
Track 5. "Good Morning Blues"
Track 6. "Talking Blues"
Track 7. "Rocky Mountain Belle"
Track 8. "San Francisco Bay Blues"
Track 9. "15 Cents"
Track 10. "Muleskinner Blues"
Track 11. "John Henry"
Track 12. "Talking Miner Blues"
Track 13. "Pretty Boy Floyd"
Track 14. "Old Blue"
Track 15. "Rambling Blues"
Track 16. "Streets of Laredo"
Track 17. "Boll Weevil"
Track 18. "Talking Columbia Blues"
Track 19. "1913 Massacre"
Track 20. "Hard Traveling"
Track 21. "Talking Dust Bowl Blues"
Track 22. "Ludlow Massacre"
Track 23. "Talking Sailor Blues"

A Stranger Here. ANTI Records 87005, 2009, notes by Joe Henry. Jack
Elliott: vocals and acoustic guitar; Greg Leisz: acoustic guitar, mando-

lin, mandola, Dobro, and Weissenborn; David Piltch: upright bass; Jay
Bellerose: drums and percussion; Keefus Ciancia: piano and keyboards;
David Hidalgo: acoustic guitar and accordion; Van Dyke Parks: piano
and vibraphone.
Track 1. "Rising High Water Blues"
Track 2. "Death Don't Have No Mercy"
Track 3. "Rambler's Blues"
Track 4. "Soul of a Man"
Track 5. "Richland Women Blues"
Track 6. "Grinnin' in Your Face"
Track 7. "The New Stranger Blues"
Track 8. "Falling Down Blues"
Track 9. "How Long Blues"
Track 10. "Please Remember Me"

Discography of Singles on 78 RPM/45 RPM

(1956) Talking Miner Blues/Pretty Boy Floyd (Topic T.R.C. 98, Great
Britain)

(1956) Old Blue/Rambling Blues (Topic T.R.C 103, Great Britain)

(1956) The Streets of Laredo/Boll Weevil (Topic T.R.C. 104, Great
Britain)

(——). *Le Canzoni Del West—Montagne E Foreste Del Sud* ("Mountains and
Forests of the South") (Signal Records S 137, Italy): "Muleskinner's
Blues/How Long Blues"

(——) *Le Canzoni Del West—I Canti Della Frontera* ("Songs of the Frontier") (Signal Records S 142, Italy): "I'm Going Down the Road/Stern
Old Bachelor"

(——) *Le Canzoni Del West—I Pericoli Della Pista* ("Dangers of the Road-
way") (Signal Records S 144, Italy): "Wreck on the Highway/Danville
Girl"

(1965) More Pretty Girls/Roll on Buddy (Fontana TF 575, Great Britain)

(1965) Rocky Mountain Belle/Rusty Jiggs and Sandy Sam (Columbia DB
7593, Great Britain)

(1968) Connection/Foggy River (Previously unreleased) (Reprise 0828)
(White label promo)

(1970) Radio Spots For: *Bull Durham Sacks and Railroad Tracks* (Reprise
PRO 373) (White label promo)

(1970) Me and Bobby McGee/Girl of the North Country (Reprise 0900) (White label promo)

(1970) Me and Bobby McGee/Girl of the North Country (Reprise 0900) (Stock copy)

Discography 2
Albums and Samplers on
EP/LP/CD That Feature
Recordings by Ramblin' Jack Elliott

T HE FOLLOWING LIST IS A SELECTIVE, not complete, listing of recordings on EP, LP, and compact disc (CD) that feature Jack Elliott as a guitarist and/or vocalist. Only recordings that offer material unique to these albums are included. For example, Elliott's one song contribution to *Folk Songs for Children* (Prestige-International Records 13073, 1963) will not be found on this list as the song included on that LP ("Howdido") was previously issued on *Jack Elliott Sings the Songs of Woody Guthrie* (Prestige-International INT 13016, 1961). Recordings are listed chronologically by date of release.

City Ramblers Skiffle Group. Storyville Records SEP 345, 1957. Recorded on September 12, 1956, in Copenhagen, Denmark.
"Midnight Special" (with Jack Elliott, shared vocal and guitar)

Songs Against the Bomb. Topic Records 12001, Great Britain (12" LP), 1959. The two tracks said to include Elliott (on guitar) were reportedly recorded at a "Ballads and Blues" gathering circa 1958.
"Brother, Wont You Join in the Line?" (with Peggy Seeger and Ewan MacColl)
"There Are Better Things to Do" (with Peggy Seeger)

The Badmen. Columbia Legacy L2S 1012/LS 1012 (2 × 12" LP), 1963, notes by B. A. Botkin, Sylvester L. Vigilante, Harold Preece, James Horan, and Goddard Lieberson. "Songs, Stories and Pictures of the Western Outlaws from Backhills to Border 1865–1900." "Songs of

the Badmen" sung by Pete Seeger, Ed McCurdy, Jack Elliott, Harry Jackson, Carolyn Hester, and Jaques Menahem with "guitar interludes and accompaniments" by Charlie Byrd and Sandy Bull. The musical performances were released on LP in France as *Les Veritables Chansons Des Hors-La Loi Du Far West* (Serp Disques MC 7011).
Side 1
Band 3. "Billy the Kid" (with Pete Seeger)
Band 6. "The Buffalo Skinners"
Side 2
Band 4. "Jesse James" (with Pete Seeger and Ed McCurdy)
Band 8. "Belle Starr" (with Pete Seeger)

Come for to Sing: Folksongs Sung by Eric Von Schmidt, Carolyn Hester, Jackie Washington, Jack Elliott, Rolf Cahn. Pathways of Sound 1033 (12" LP), 1963. Jack Elliott: vocal, guitar, and harmonica on four songs.
Side 1
Band 2. "The Car Song"
Band 10. "Night Herding Song"
Side 2
Band 5. "Haul on the Bowline"
Band 9. "Candy Man"

Philadelphia Folk Festival, Vol. 1. Prestige-International 13071 (12" LP), 1963. Recorded September 8 and 9, 1962, at the Philadelphia Folk Festival, Wilson Estate, Swedesford Road, Paoli, PA. This compilation album features performances by Bonnie Dobson, Professor Clarence Johnson, Mabel Washington, Mike Seeger, Sonny Miller, and Jack Elliott. All three of Elliott's performances were issued on CD in the United States as *The Prestige/Folklore Years, Vol. 4: Singing Out Loud* (Prestige CD 9904, 1995). "Talking Fishing Blues" was issued on *Philadelphia Folk Festival—40th Anniversary* (Sliced Bread Records 74440, 2001).
Side 1
Band 4. "Night Herding Song"
Band 6. "Talking Fishing Blues"
Side 2
Band 1. "Muleskinner Blues"

The Folk Scene. Elektra Records SMP 6 (12" LP), 1963, notes by Jack Holzman (uncredited). Jack Elliott, vocal and guitar. Released in Great Britain as *The Folk Scene* (Golden Guinea GGL 0265).
Side 1
Band 5. "Talking Dust Bowl" (Previously unreleased)

Hootenanny. Prestige Folklore FL 14020 (12" LP), 1964, notes by H. G. MacGill. Though this LP features cover graphics unique to this edition, the program is identical to Prestige-International 13071.
Side 1
Band 4. "Night Herding Song"
Band 6. "Talking Fishing Blues"
Side 2
Band 1. "Muleskinner Blues"

Hootenanny. Aravel Records AB 1003 (12" LP), 1964. Festival recordings by Pete Seeger, Jack Elliott, the Country Gentleman, Oscar Brand, Jean Ritchie, and David Sear. Released in Great Britain as *Hootenanny* (Ember NR-5016).
Side 1
Band 3. "San Francisco Bay Blues"
Side 2
Band 4. "Railroad Bill"

Evening Concerts at Newport, Vol. 1. Vanguard Records VRS 9148/VSD 79148 (12" LP), 1964. Recorded live at the 1963 Newport Folk Festival. Released in Great Britain as *Evening Concerts at Newport, Vol. 1* (Fontana TFL 6041). Issued on CD in the United States as *The Newport Folk Festival 1963: The Evening Concerts, Vol. 1* (Vanguard 77002, 1991) and in Japan as *The Newport Folk Festival 1963: The Evening Concerts, Vol. 1* (King KICP-2039).
Side 1
Band 3. "Diamond Joe"

Oklahoma! Columbia Records OS 2610 (12" LP), 1964. Released on CD in the United States as *Oklahoma!* (Sony Classical/Columbia/Legacy SK61876, 2002).
"Kansas City" (with Men's Chorus)
"All Er Nothin'" (with Phyllis Newman)

The Mormon Pioneers. Columbia Legacy LS1024 (12" LP), 1965, notes by Carl Carmer, Leroy P. Hafen, Thomas E. Cheney, and Goddard Lieberson. Musical contributions by Jack Elliott, Ed McCurdy, Oscar Brand, Clayton Krehbiel, and the Mormon Tabernacle Choir.
Side 1
Band 2. "Tittery-Irie-Aye"
Band 5. "The Mormon Battalion Song"
Side 2
Band 5. "Root Hog or Die"

A Tribute to Woody Guthrie, Part Two. Warner Bros. Records BS 2586 (12"
LP), 1972, notes by Millard Lampbell. Released in Great Britain as *A
Tribute to Woody Guthrie, Part Two* (CBS 64861).
Side 2
Band 4. "Howdido"
Band 6. "1913 Massacre"

A Tribute to Woody Guthrie. Warner Bros. Records 2w 3007 (2 × 12" LP),
1972, notes by Millard Lampell. Released on LP in Great Britain as *A
Tribute to Woody Guthrie* (CBS 64861) and in Germany as *A Tribute
to Woody Guthrie* (Warner Bros. 66051). Issued on CD in the United
States as *A Tribute to Woody Guthrie* (Warner Bros. Records WB/WEA
26036-2, 1989).
Record 2, Side 2
Band 4. "Howdido" (from Warner Bros. Records BS 2586)
Band 6. "1913 Massacre" (from Warner Bros. Records BS 2586)

Woody Guthrie's "We Ain't Down Yet." Cream Records CR 1002 (12"
LP), 1976. "Poetry & Prose of the Prophet Singer Narrarated by Jess
Pearson, featuring musical performances by Arlo Guthrie, Ramblin' Jack
Elliott, Will Geer, Peter Yarrow, Hoyt Axton, John Hartford, the Dil-
lards, and Seals & Crofts." Released in Germany on 12" LP as *Woody
Guthrie's "We Ain't Down Yet"* (Cream INT 148-104). Issued on CD in
Great Britain as *Woody Guthrie's "We Ain't Down Yet"* (Diablo Records
812, Great Britain, 1994).
Side 1
Band 6. "The Great Historical Bum"
Side 2
Band 1. "The Grand Coulee Dam"

Banjoman—The Original Soundtrack. Sire Records SA 7527 (12" LP), 1977.
Concert highlights from the Manhattan, Kansas, Earl Scruggs Revue
program featuring Jack Elliott, the Nitty Gritty Dirt Band, Joan Baez,
Doc and Merle Watson, and the Byrds. Also released in Germany as
Banjoman—The Original Soundtrack (Sire 200 242-320) and in France
(Sire 2C 070 61930).
Side 2
Band 1. "Me and Bobby McGee" (Jack Elliott: vocal and guitar; David
   Bromberg: second guitar)
Band 8. "Billy Fehr" [sic] (aka "912 Greens," Jack Elliott: vocal and
   guitar)

Bread and Roses. Fantasy Records F-79009 (2 × 12" LP), 1979. This multiartist album was recorded live at the "Festival of Acoustic Music," Greek Theater, University of California, Berkeley, October 1977. It was issued on CD in the United States as *Bread & Roses: Festival of Acoustic Music, Vol. 1.* (Fantasy Records FCD-79009, 2004) and in Japan as *Bread & Roses: Festival of Acoustic Music, Vol. 1* (P-Vine PCD-3162). Disc 1, Side 1. "San Francisco Bay Blues"

Folk Friends 2. Folk Freak Records FF 3003/4 (2 × 12" LP), 1981, notes by Carsten Linde. Issued on CD in West Germany as *Folk Friends 2* (Wundertute CD Tut 72.150, West Germany, 1990).
Side 2
Band 5. "Don't Think Twice, It's All Right"
Side 4
Band 1. "Me and Bobby McGee"

Woody Guthrie: Hard Travelin'—Soundtrack from the Film. Arloco Records 284 (12" LP), 1984. Issued on CD in the United States as *Woody Guthrie: Hard Travelin'—Soundtrack from the Film* (Rising Son Records RSR0013, 2000).
Side 1
Band 3. "Hard Travelin'" (with Arlo Guthrie: guitar and vocal; Sonny Terry: harmonica)
Band 7. "New York Town" (with Arlo Guthrie: guitar and vocal; Sonny Terry: harmonica)
Side 2
Band 3. "Talking Sailor (Talking Merchant Marine)"

Derroll Adams—65th Birthday Concert. Waste Productions WP 9101, notes by Derroll Adams, Belgium, 1991. Recorded live at "De Stadsschouwburg," Kortrijk, Belgium, on October 5, 1990.
Track 18. "Willie Moore" (with Derroll Adams)
Track 19. "Don't Think Twice, It's All Right"
Track 20. "Portland Town" (with cast)

Tanz & Folkfest Rudolstadt '91. He-Deck (no catalog no. or date of issue).
Track 17. "Willie Moore" (with Derroll Adams)

Sing Out for Seva. Arista Records GDCD 4067, notes by Tamara Klamner "with help from Seva staff and friends," 1999. Recorded live at Berkeley Community Theater, May 15, 1998.
Track 1. "Don't Think Twice, It's All Right"

'Til We Outnumber Them. Righteous Babe Records, RBR019D, 2000. Recorded live on September 29, 1996, at Severance Hall, Cleveland, Ohio. Released in Japan as 'Til We Outnumber Them (P-Vine PCD-5600).
Track 1. "Hard Travelin' Hootenanny" (with cast)
Track 3. "1913 Massacre"
Track 18. "Talkin' Dust Bowl Blues"
Track 19. "This Land Is Your Land" (with cast)

Rockin' Patriots. Rhino/Wea Records R2-74268, 2001.
Track 1. "This Land Is Your Land" (with Joe Feliciano, Alvin Young-blood Hart, Bill Miller, and Dar Williams)

Daddy-O Daddy: Rare Family Songs of Woody Guthrie. Rounder 11661-8087-2, 2001, notes by Frankie Fuchs.
Track 9. "I'll Write and I'll Draw"
Track 13. "Curly Headed Baby"

Banjoman: A Tribute to Derroll Adams. Rising Son Records RSR-2102-2, 2002. Released in Western Europe as Banjoman: A Tribute to Derroll Adams (Blue Groove BG-1420, 2002). Released in Japan as Banjoman: A Tribute to Derroll Adams (Vivid NACD-3201).
Track 3. "The Cuckoo"
Track 10. "Muleskinner Blues" (with Arlo Guthrie)
Track 19. "The Rock"

The Gift—A Tribute to Ian Tyson. Stony Plain Records SPCD 1322, 2007.
Track 12: "Will James"
Track 16: "Bonus Track: An interview with Ramblin' Jack Elliott and Buddy Cage"

Ramblin' Jack Elliott Recordings Featured on Other Artists' Records
Recordings listed chronologically.

Tom Rush: Tom Rush. Elektra EKL 288/ EKS 7288 (12" LP), 1965. "Do-Re-Mi"

Johnny Cash: Everybody Loves a Nut. Columbia CS 9292/CL 2492 (12" LP), 1966, notes by Mort Goode. Reissued on CD on Johnny Cash—

The Man in Black: Vol. 3, 1963–1969 Bear Family Records BCD 15588 FI (1995/1996).
"A Cup of Coffee" (Jack Elliott, yodel)

Derroll Adams: *Portland Town.* Ace of Clubs Records/Decca SCL 1227 (12" LP), 1967, notes by Bill Yaryan.
"Portland Town" (Jack Elliott, guitar)

Phil Ochs: *Tape from California.* A&M Records SP 4148 (12" LP), 1968, notes by Phil Ochs. CD Reissue on Collector's Choice Music CCM-138, 2000.
"Joe Hill" (Jack Elliott, guitar)

Dennis Olivieri: *Come to the Party.* VMC Records VS 130 (12" LP), 1970. Elliott is credited as a guitarist on this album but his contribution is uncertain.

The Earl Scruggs Revue—Anniversary Special, Volume One. Columbia Records PC 33416 (12" LP), 1975, "Special Thanks" notes by Bob Johnston. Also released in Great Britain as *The Earl Scruggs Revue—Anniversary Special, Volume One* (CBS 808210) and the Netherlands as *The Earl Scruggs Revue—Anniversary Special, Volume One* (CBS S 80821). CD reissued as *The Earl Scruggs Revue—Anniversary Special: Vol. One and Two* (Gott CD-021).
"Song to Woody" (Elliott shares vocals with Johnny Cash, Earl Scruggs, and the New Riders of the Purple Sage)
"Passing Through" (Elliott shares vocals with Joan Baez, Leonard Cohen, Buffy Sainte-Marie, the Pointer Sisters)

Jamie Brockett: *North Mountain Velvet.* Adelphi Records AD 1028 (12" LP), 1977. CD reissued in Japan on Airmail Recordings 1013, 2002.
"South Coast" (Jack Elliott: vocal and guitar)
"Just Stopped by to Get a Cup of Coffee" (Jack Elliott: vocal/harmony vocal)

John Prine: *Bruised Orange.* Asylum Records 6E 139 (12" LP), 1978. Elliott contributes the most prominent vocal to the album's "Hobo Chorus." CD reissued on Oh Boy Records OBR 006, 1989.
"The Hobo Song"

David Amram: *No More Walls.* Flying Fish GRO 752 (12" LP), 1979. CD reissue on Flying Fish Records FF 752, 1997.
"Tompkins Square Park Consciousness Expander" (Jack Elliott: guitar)

David Amram: *Home Around the World*. Flying Fish Records 094 (12" LP), 1980. CD reissued as *David Amram & Friends—At Home/Around the World* (Rounder/Flying Fish LC 4588, 1996).
"Home on the Range" (with Odetta)
Frummox II (Steven Fromholz and Dan McCrimmon). Felicity Records FR003 (12" LP), 1982.
"The Angel" (Jack Elliott: backup vocal)

Rod McKuen: *Early Harvest*. Delta/Laser Light 12445, 1994. Information not known.

Guy Clark: *Dublin Blues*. Asylum Records 61725-2, 1995.
"Hangin' Your Life on the Wall" (with Guy Clark)

Peter, Paul and Mary: *Life Lines*. Warner Bros. WB 45851-2, 1995.
"Deportee (Plane Wreck at Los Gatos)"

Rick Robbins: *Walkin' Down the Line*. Seeds of Man Records RR 00197, 1997.
"Desperados Waiting for a Train" (with Rick Robbins)

Rob McNurlin: *Cowboy Boot Heel*. Buffalo Skinner Recordings CD 3072, 2000.
"I Dreamed I Saw Woody Guthrie" (with Rob McNurlin)

Garrick Rawlings: *Million Miles*. 2003.
"Dollars to Dust" (with Garrick Rawlings)

Bob Dylan: *Rolling Thunder Revue—The Bootleg Series Vol. 5*. Columbia/ Legacy C2K 87047, 2002.
"Knockin' on Heaven's Door" (with Bob Dylan, Roger McGuinn, and Joni Mitchell)

Tim Grimm: *Coyote's Dream*. Vault Records VR 006, 2003.
"Buffalo Skinners" (with Tim Grimm)

Corb Lund: *Hair in My Eyes Like a Highland Steer*. Stony Plain Records 1309, 2005. The album was also released on vinyl as Stony Plain Records 1309 (12" LP).
"The Truck Got Stuck Talkin' Blues"

Tom Russell: *Hot Walker*. Hightone Records HCD-8177, 2005.
Bob Dylan: *No Direction Home: The Soundtrack—The Bootleg Series Vol. 7*. Columbia/Legacy C2K 93937, 2005.
"Mr. Tambourine Man" (with Bob Dylan)

Wizz Jones: *Lucky the Man*. Hux Records HUX 094, 2007.
"Sugar for Sugar" (with Wizz Jones)

Various Artists: *I'm Not There: Original Soundtrack*. Columbia/Sony 88697 12038 2, 2007.
"Just Like Tom Thumb's Blues"

Bibliography

Adams, Derroll. Notes to *Derroll Adams—65th Birthday Concert*. Waste Productions WP 9101, 1991.

Adams, Paul. "Denis Preston and the Record Supervision Story." Sing Song Entertainment Publicity. www.singsongpr.biz/news/lake3.htm (accessed 26 September 2007).

Ahlgren, Calvin. "'60s Folk Singer Ramblin' Jack Still Round and About—Elliott Logs Miles, Spins Yarns." *San Francisco Chronicle*. 7 May 1989, Sec. Sunday Datebook, 44.

Alarik, Scott. "Folk Foursome Throws Sculler's Pickin' Party." *Boston Globe*. 24 April 1998, D8.

Amaral, Anthony. *Will James, the Gilt Edged Cowboy*. Los Angeles: Westernlore Press, 1967.

———. *Will James, the Last Cowboy Legend*. Reno: University of Nevada Press, 1980.

Anderson, Ian. "Ramblin' Jack Elliott, Spider John Koerner, U. Utah Phillips, Legends of Folk, Red House RHR CD 31." *Folk Roots*. No. 85, July 1990, 43.

———. "Ramblin' Jack Elliott, Hard Travelin': Songs by Woody Guthrie and Other, Big Beat CDWIK 952." *Folk Roots*. No. 90, December 1990, 37.

———. "Ramblin' Jack Elliott, Half Moon, Putney, London." *Folk Roots*. No. 99, September 1991, 51.

Arthur, Dave. "Soho—Needless to Say: A Life of Russell Quaye." *English Dance and Song*. Vol. 46, No. 3, Autumn/Winter 1984, 2–5.

Atkinson, Bob. "Ramblin' with Jack Elliott." *Sing Out!* Vol. 19, No. 5, March/April 1970, 2–10.

Baggelaar, Kristin, and Donald Milton. *Folk Music—More Than a Song*. New York: Thomas Y. Crowell, 1976.

Bauldie, John. "A Conversation with . . . John Hammond." *The Telegraph*. No. 44, Winter 1992, 64–75.

Beck, John. "Legendary Musician Has Seen and Done It All and Still Has a Twinkle in His Eye." *Santa Rosa Press Democrat*, 5 April 2008.

Beckley, Fred. "An Evening of Just Plain Folk." *Philadelphia Inquirer*. 26 April 1998.

Beitiks, Edvins. "Jack of Hearts." *San Francisco Examiner Sunday Magazine*. 4 August 1996, 10.

———. "On the Road." *San Francisco Examiner Sunday Magazine*. 4 August 1996, MAG 24.

Bernstein, Maury. "Folksinger Jack Elliott to Appear at Union Saturday." *Minnesota Daily*. 26 February 1965, 10–11.

Bird, Brian. *Skiffle: The Story of Folk-Song with a Jazz Beat*. London: Robert Hale, 1958.

Blank, Mitchell. "I Read a Book Today, Oh Boy . . ." *The Telegraph*. No. 45, Spring 1993, 77–81.

Blue, Buddy. "Ramblin' Jack Elliott: The Rodeo Made Him Do It." *San Diego Union-Tribune*. 12 May 2005, Sec. Night & Day, 20.

Boatfield, Graham. "Record Reviews—Jack Elliott." *Jazz Journal*. January 1957.

———. "Jack Elliott—Vol. 2." *Jazz Journal*. June 1958, 16–17.

Boisson, Steve. "Hard Traveling." *Acoustic Guitar*. No. 35, November 1995, 62–69.

Booth, Stanley. "The Playboy Interview: Keith Richards." *Playboy*. Vol. 36, No. 10, October 1989, 59–68, 114–115, 143.

Boyd, Joe. "The 150 Best Recordings of American Folk Music." *Hootenanny*. May 1964, 52–53, 56.

———. Notes to *Roll on Buddy: The Jack Elliott and Derroll Adams Story, Vol. 1*. Bounty BY 6036, 1967.

Brakefield, Jay F. "Wish He'd Ramble This Way More Often—Folk Singer's Web of Tales Holds His Fans Enthralled." *Dallas Morning News*. 29 June 1996, Sec. Overnight, 39A.

Brand, Oscar. *The Ballad Mongers*. New York: Funk and Wagnalls, 1962.

Braudy, Susan. "As Arlo Guthrie Sees It . . . Kids Are Groovy. Adults Aren't." *New York Times Magazine*. 27 April 1969, SM56.

Bream, Jon. "Rock Hall of Fame Induction, Program Provided Contrast in Good, Bad Vibes." *Star-Tribune*. 21 January 1988, Sec. Variety, 16E.

———. "Legends about Ramblin' Jack Amaze Him as Much as Public." *Star-Tribune*. 23 April 1989, Sec. Entertainment, 01F.

———. "Red House Records Grab a Grammy." *Star-Tribune*. 29 February, 1996, Sec. News, 04B.

Brookes, Tim. *Guitar: An American Life*. New York: Grove Press, 2006.

Brooks, Michael. "Woody & Arlo." *Guitar Player*. Vol. 5, No. 5, August 1971, 26–29, 34–35.

Brown, G. "Asked and Answered: John Prine." *Denver Music Examiner*. www.examiner.com/x-363-Denver-Music-Examiner~y2008m6d5-Asked-and-answered-John-Prine (accessed 10 June 2008).

Brown, Hannah. "Ramblin' on Jack." *New York Post.* 16 August 2000, 64.

Brown, Jim, Harold Leventhal, and Ginger Turek (prod.). *Woody Guthrie: Hard Travelin'* (Motion Picture), 1984.

Brown, Peter. "First of the Brooklyn Cowboys, Last of the Real Folksingers." *Welcomat.* 6 October 1993, 42.

Bull, Roger. "Ramblin' Jack Elliott Wandering This Way." *Florida Times-Union.* 18 May 2004, Sec. Lifestyle, C1.

Cable, Paul. *Bob Dylan: His Unreleased Recordings.* New York: Schirmer Books, 1978.

Caltagirone, Francesco. "Ramblin' Jack Elliott, epopea del Wild West." *Buscadero.* No. 143, 1993, 23–24.

Campbell, Alex. *Frae Glesga Toon.* Woodham Walter, Essex, England: Folk Scene Publications, 1964.

Capaldi, Jim. "Conversation with Mr. Folkways: Moses Asch." *Folk Scene.* Vol. 6, No. 3, May 1978, 14–20.

———. "Conversation with Mr. Folkways: Moses Asch (Part Two)." *Folk Scene.* Vol. 6, No. 4, June 1978, 2–4.

Carr, Patrick. "Creaky Beauty." *Village Voice.* 7 April 1998, 81, 85.

Carter, Sydney. "Folk Song." *The Gramophone.* Vol. 43, No. 515, 525.

Catalano, Jim. "Elliott Brings 50 Years on the Road to Ithaca." *Ithaca Journal.* 11 September 2003. www.theithacajournal.com/entertainment/stories/20030911/culturalevents/232881.html (accessed 29 January 2005).

Catlin, Roger. "Ramblin' Jack Elliott at Home on the Road, the Motor Runnin'." *Hartford Courant.* 17 July 1992, Sec. CT Living, E1.

Chanel, Richard. "Ram-Ram-Ramblin' Jack." *CooP/Fast Folk Magazine.* September 1982, 25.

Chilton, Charles. Notes to *Ramblin' Jack in London.* Columbia 33SX 1166, 1959.

Christgau, Robert. "The Sound of the City: Men without Women." *Village Voice.* Vol. 43, 5 May 1998, 72.

Chun, Kimberly. "Ramblin' Man." *San Francisco Bay Guardian.* http://cgi.sfbg.com/printable_entry.php?entry_id=1209 (accessed 23 November 2007).

Clad, Noel, and George Pickow. "Greenwich Village—1955." *Cosmopolitan.* April 1955, 87.

Clark, Tom. *Jack Kerouac.* San Diego: Harcourt, Brace Jovanovich, 1984.

Cloves, Jeff. "Ramblin' Jack at the Roundhouse." *Zig Zag.* No. 17, December 1971, 9–12.

Coburn, Randy Sue. "On the Trail of Ramblin' Jack Elliott." *Esquire.* April 1984, 80–82, 84–85.

Cohen, John. "Interview with Roger (Jim) McGuinn of the Byrds." *Sing Out!* Vol. 18, No. 5, December 1968/January 1969.

Cohen, Ronald D. *Rainbow Quest—The Folk Music Revival & American Society 1940–1970.* Amherst and Boston: University of Massachusetts Press, 2002.

———. *A History of Folk Music Festivals in the United States.* Lanham, MD: Scarecrow Press, 2008.

Collins, Monica. "Ramblin' Man—Emmy [sic] Winning Cowboy Folk Singer Regales with Tales of Travels." *Boston Herald*. 14 July 1998, Sec. Arts, 33.

Condon, Eddie. "Pro and Condon." Great Britain: Publication unknown. 30 January 1958.

Condran, Ed. "Weary Jack Elliott Not the Ramblin' Man He Used to Be." *Bucks County Courier Times*. 10 May 2001. http://phillyburbs.com/c...retimes/news/news_archive/0510elliott.htm (accessed 4 July 2001).

Cooney, Michael. "Record Reviews—The Woody Guthrie Tribute: Another View." *Sing Out!* Vol. 22, No. 2, March/April 1973, 43.

Cray, Ed. *Ramblin' Man—The Life and Times of Woody Guthrie*. New York: W. W. Norton, 2004.

Cristiano, Nick. "Ramblin' Jack and the Monsters of Folk Tour." *Philadelphia Inquirer*. 17 April 1998.

Cromelin, Richard. "Jack Elliott Rambles Back." *Los Angeles Times*. 1 February 1973, H15.

———. "Gamblin' Gambol with Ramblin' Jack." *Los Angeles Times*, 14 February 1977, D12.

———. "Regular Folk, Yet Not." *Los Angeles Times*. 7 July 2006, E39.

"Dale." "Ashrove, L.A." *Variety*. No. 224, 1 November 1961, 76.

Dallas, Karl. "Elliott Adnopoz—The Brooklyn Cowboy." *Melody Maker*. 28 September 1963, 10.

———. "New Folk Albums: So Sad about Jack." *Melody Maker*. 27 June 1970, 32.

Dane, Barbara. "Lone Cat Jesse Fuller." *Sing Out!* February/March 1966, 5–11.

Darlington, Stan. "Jack Elliott and Derroll Adams." *Jazz Music*. September/October 1957, Vol. 8, No. 5, 7–9.

Dawson, Angela. "Documentarian [sic] Catches Up with Ramblin' Dad." *Star-Ledger*. 1 September 2000, 18.

Dellow, Nick. "John R.T. Davies: The Ultimate Preservationist." *VJM's Jazz and Blues Mart*. www.vjm.biz/articles9.htm (accessed 10 April 2008).

Dewe, Michael. *The Skiffle Craze*. Aberystwyth, Wales: Planet, 1988.

Dunaway, David King. *How Can I Keep from Singing: Pete Seeger*. New York: McGraw-Hill, 1981.

Dunson, Josh. "Off the Record: The Restless Art of Ramblin' Jack." *Mainstream*. Vol. 16, No. 8, August 1963, 62–63.

———. *Freedom in the Air: Song Movements of the 60s*. New York: International Publishers, 1965.

———. "A Far Country Come Nearer." *Sing Out!* Vol. 19, No. 1, April/May 1969, 33.

Dylan, Bob. *Chronicles—Volume One*. New York: Simon and Schuster, 2004.

Ebert, Roger. "Rambling Jack Rambles Here, Leaves Folk Songs, Anecdotes." *UI Daily Illini*. 21 November 1962.

———. "Elliott Concert." *Autoharp*. Vol. 3, No. 2, 30 November 1962.

———. "Ramblin' Man: Documentary Can't Pin Down Jack Elliott's Life." *Chicago Sun-Times*. 8 September 2000, Sec. Weekend Plus, 32.

Elliot, Marc. *Death of a Rebel: Starring Phil Ochs and a Small Circle of Friends*. Garden City, NY: Doubleday, 1979.

Elliott, Aiyana, Paul Mezey, Dan Partland, and Dick Dahl (prod.). *The Ballad of Ramblin' Jack* (Motion Picture). Lot 47 Films/Winstar Video, 2000.

Elliott, Jack. "Mailbag" (Letter to Editor). *Sing*. June/July 1957, Vol. 4, No. 2, 27.

———. "This Record Made Me Cry, Says Jack Elliott." *Melody Maker*. 13 December 1958, 15.

———. "Book Review: Woody Guthrie Revisited." *Sing Out!* Vol. 15, No. 6, January 1966, 79, 81.

———. Notes to *Ramblin' Jack Elliott—Live in Japan*. King Bellwood Records OFM 1002, 1977.

———. Notes to *Kerouac's Last Dream*. FolkFreak FF 4005, 1981.

Ellis, Bill. "Ramblin' Jack Elliott Earned His Nickname by His Mouth." *Memphis Commercial Appeal*. 31 March 2000, Sec. Playbook, G2.

English, Logan. "For the Good He Taught, and the Dignity He Gave Us." *Folk Music*. August 1964, 4, 52–53.

Ensminger, David. "Interview—Ramblin' Jack Elliott." *Thirsty Ear Magazine On-Line*. 9 August 2002. www.thirstyearfestival.com/interviews/elliot.html (accessed 29 January 2005).

Faier, Billy. "Disk Reviews—Collections: Come for to Sing." *Hootenanny*. March 1963, 20–21.

Fair View (Stephen Pickering, ed.). "Ramblin' Reminiscences of Ramblin' Jack Elliott." *Praxis One: Existence, Men and Realities*. Berkeley, CA: No Limit Publications, 1972.

Farber, Jim. "The Ballad of a Runaway Ramblin' Man." *New York Daily News*. 30 July 2000, Sec. Showtime, 14–15.

Farinella, David John. "Ramblin' Duets." Unknown. San Francisco, 1996.

Farr, Joey. "Ramblin' on: Listening to the Legendary Singer Is Like Taking a Ride Through America's Backroads." *Press-Enterprise* (Riverside, CA). 24 September, 1999, Sec. Guide, AA14.

Felty, Catherine. "Jack of All Trades." *iF Magazine*. 25 August 2000. www .ifmagazine.ifctv.com/common/article.asp?articleID=788 (accessed 4 July 2001).

Flisher, Chris. "Living Legend—Ramblin' Jack Elliott Keeps Folk Standards High." *Worcester Phoenix*. 2–9 May 1997. www.worcesterphoe.../05/02/JACK _ELLIOTT.html (accessed 18 July 1997).

Fournier, Alain. "Macadam Cowboys." *Big Beat* (France). May 1980, 36–38.

———. "Ramblin' Jack Elliott en concert a Paris." *Le Cri du Coyote* (France). 1991, 1.

———. "Ramblin' Jack Elliott—Le Cowboy De Brooklyn." *Round-Up* (France). July 1997.

———. "Le Dernier Cowboy De Brooklyn." *Le Cri du Coyote* (France). No. 37, 1997, 7–8.

———. "Ramblin' Jack Elliott – Friends of Mine." *Le Cri du Coyote* (France). No. 51, 1998, 21.

Fournier, Anne. "Ramblin' Jack Elliott—The Long Ride." *Le Cri du Coyote* (France). February 2000.

Fox, Charles. "Folk Song." *The Gramophone*. Vol. 38, No. 455, April 1961, 557.

———. "Folk-Music." *The Gramophone*. Vol. 42, No. 496, September 1964, 156.

———. "Folk-Song." *The Gramophone*. Vol. 42, No. 503, April 1965, 503.

Fuchs, Frankie. Notes to *Daddy-O Daddy: Rare Family Songs of Woody Guthrie*. Rounder Records 11661-8087-2, 2001.

Gahr, David, and Robert Shelton. *The Face of Folk Music*. New York: Citadel Press, 1968.

Gallagher, Peter B. "Hippy Trails—We're All Ramblin' Jack Imposters." *Weekly Planet*. 13 May 2004. www.weeklyplanet.com/2004-05-13/music feature2 .html (accessed 29 January 2005).

Gardner, Mark. Notes to *Brothers and Other Mothers with Stan Getz, Al Cohn, Serge Chaloff, Brew Moore, Allen Eager: The Savoy Sessions*. Savoy SJL 2210, 1976.

George-Warren, Holly. *Public Cowboy No. 1: The Life of Gene Autry*. Oxford, NY: Oxford University Press, 2007.

Gewertz, Daniel. "Jack's Still Ramblin'—In More Ways Than One." *Boston Herald*. 10 July 2004.

Gifford, Barry. "Young Brigham." *Rolling Stone*. Vol. 1, No. 7, 9 March 1968, 20.

———. "A Friendly Tribute for Ramblin' Charles Adnopoz." *Rolling Stone*. Vol. 2, No. 3, 20 July 1968, 6, 22.

Gilbert, Douglas R. *Forever Young: Photographs of Bob Dylan*. Cambridge, MA: DaCapo Press, 2005.

Gilchrist, Jim. "Woody, Bob and Me." *The Scotsman*. 12 February 2005, 22. http://news.scotsman.com/features.cfm?id=161122005 (accessed 16 February 2005).

Ginsberg, Allen, and Pierre Cotrell. "It's Not Rational but It's Logical—Allen Ginsberg Interviews Bob Dylan." *The Telegraph*. No. 33, Summer 1989, 6–33.

Gleason, Bob, and Sidsel. "Letters to the Editors." *Little Sandy Review*. No. 5, July 1960, 37–38.

Gleason, Matt. "Honoring a Legend." *Tulsa World*. 14 July 2003, Sec. Entertainment, D3.

Gleason, Ralph J. "Perspectives: Kristofferson's Fine Flick." *Rolling Stone*. 13 April 1972, 38.

Goddard, J. R. "Records: Bobby Dylan." *Village Voice*. 26 April 1962, 7.

Goldberg, Michael. "Ramblin' Jack Elliott Sings the Same Old 25 Songs." *San Francisco Examiner*. 15 July 1979.

Goldsmith, Peter. *Making People's Music: Moses Asch and Folkways Records.* Washington, DC: Smithsonian Institution Press, 1998.

Goodfellow, Kris. "What Is a Grammy Worth?" *New York Times.* 24 February 1997, D9.

Goodwin, Keith. "Jack Elliott." *Jazz Journal.* June 1958, 16–17.

"Gorm." "New Acts." *Variety.* No. 225, 31 January 1961, 60.

Gould, Jack. "TV: Pete Seeger Makes Belated Debut." *New York Times.* 15 November 1965, 75.

Gould, Ron. "The Legend of Ramblin' Jack." *Acoustic Music.* No. 29, September 1980, 14.

Graff, Gary. "Great Music, Strange Words at Rock Induction." *Detroit Free-Press.* 22 January 1988, Sec. FTR, 5C.

Graham, Eugene. "Tonder 2002: Old and New Celtic and Danish Music." *Folk World.* www.folkworld.de/23/e/tonder.htm (accessed 1 March 2009).

Green, Archie. "Folksong on Records." *Western Folklore.* Vol. 27, No. 1, January 1968, 74–75.

Green, David. *Folk Artists '69.* Providence, RI: C. Nigro Publishing, 1969.

Greenberg, Mark. "Ramblin' Jack: No Address, No Phone." *Frets.* Vol. 10, December 1988, 20–21.

Greenway, John. Notes to *Ramblin' Jack Elliott Sings the Songs of Woody Guthrie.* Prestige-International 13016, 1961.

———. "Folk Song Discography." *Western Folklore.* Vol. 20, No. 2, April 1961, 150–151.

———. Notes to *Ramblin' Jack Elliott.* Prestige-International 13033, 1961.

———. Notes to *Country Style.* Prestige-International 13045, 1962.

———. "Folk Song Discography." *Western Folklore.* Vol. 21, No. 2, April 1962, 150.

———. "Woodrow Wilson Guthrie (1912–1967)." *Journal of American Folklore.* January/March 1968, 62–64.

Greer, Herb. *The Trip.* London: Hutchinson, 1963.

Gregory, Hugh. "Ramblin' Jack Elliott." In *1000 Great Guitarists.* San Francisco: GPI Books, 1994.

Griffiths, James. "Ramblin' Jack Elliott—New Roscoe, Leeds." *Guardian Unlimited.* 19 February 2005. www.guardian.co.uk/arts/reviews/story/0,11712,1417159,00 .html (accessed 19 February 2005).

Griwkowsky, Fish. "Ramblin' Jack, Well, Rambles." *Edmonton Sun.* 12 March 2004. www.canoe.ca/NewsStand/EdmontonSun/Entertainment/2004/03/12/ pf-379355.html (accessed 29 January 2005).

Guest, Roy. "British Isles Folk Scene." *Caravan.* August/September 1959, 45.

Gulla, Bob. "Ramblin' Man—Jack Elliott Rides into Providence." *Providence Phoenix.* 11–18 May 2000. www.bostonphoenix.com/archive/music/00/05/11/ LOCAL.html (accessed 29 January 2005).

Guthrie, Arlo (ed. Happy Traum). *This Is the Arlo Guthrie Book*. New York: Amsco Music Publishing, 1969.

——. Notes to *Bull Durham Sacks & Railroad Tracks*. Reprise 6387, 1970.

——. "House of the Rising Son." *Esquire*. September 1984, 80–82.

——. Notes to *Son of the Wind*. Rising Son Records RSR 0003, 1991.

Guthrie, Woody. *American Folksong*. New York: Oak Publications, 1961.

——. "Belle Starr." *Sing Out!* Vol. 15, No. 5, November 1965, 22–23.

——. (ed. Robert Shelton). *Born to Win*. New York: Macmillan Company, 1965.

Guthrie, Woody, Millard Lampell, and Hally Wood. *A Tribute to Woody Guthrie*. New York: TRO Ludlow Music/Woody Guthrie Publications, 1972.

Hall, Michael. "Running with Friends of the Devil—Ramblin' Jack Elliott." *Pulse!* April 1995, 20.

Harding, John Wesley. "The Wanted Man Interview—Ramblin' Jack Elliott." *The Telegraph*. No. 50, Winter 1994, 10–32.

——. "No Exit: Talkin' Bob Dylan Blues with Ramblin' Jack Elliott." *BAM*. 2 June 1995, 41–42.

Hardy, Phil, and Dave Laing. *Encyclopedia of Rock*. New York: Schirmer Books, 1988.

Harris, Craig. "Ramblin' Jack Elliott, a Mosaic of Stories." *Dirty Linen*. April/May 1996, 15–17, 119.

Harris, Dana. "Lot 47 Buys 'Jack' Rights—Docu Chronicles Life of Folk Music Icon Elliott." *Variety*. www.variety.com/article/VR1117779087.html (accessed 22 November 2007).

Harris, Sheldon. *Blues Who's Who*. New York: DaCapo Press, 1979.

Hasted, John. "Don't Scoff at Skiffle!" *Sing Out!* Vol. 7, No. 1, Spring 1957, 28–30.

Hawes, Bess Lomax. "Butch Hawes 1919–1971." *Sing Out!* Vol. 21, No. 2, January/February 1972, 19–20.

——. *Sing It Pretty: A Memoir*. Urbana and Chicago: University of Illinois Press, 2008.

Heber, Shelly. "Talent in Action: Cat Stevens/Ramblin' Jack Elliott." *Billboard*. No. 84, 4 November 1972, 40.

Hentoff, Nat. "The Future of the Folk Renascence." In *The American Folk Scene: Dimensions of the Folksong Revival*, edited by David A. DeTurk and A. Poulin, Jr. New York: Dell Publishing, 1967, 326–331.

——. "Woody Guthrie Still Prowls Our Memories." *New York Times*. 16 April 1972, D28.

Herman, Lew. "Ramblin Man." *Sounds*. http://web.cln.com/archives/charlotte/newsstand/c100999/sounds.htm (accessed 4 July 2001).

Heylin, Clinton. *Bob Dylan: Behind the Shades*. New York: Summit Books, 1991.

Hilburn, Robert. "Ramblin' Jack Elliott on Stage at Ash Grove." *Los Angeles Times*. 14 March 1969, H18.

———. "Folk Music Mixes Social, Political." *Los Angeles Times*. 20 April 1970, F9.

———. "Cat Stevens Celebration at the Shrine." *Los Angeles Times*. 3 October 1972, D8.

———. "How to Write Songs and Influence People." *Guitar World Acoustic*. February 2006, 26–30, 32, 78–79.

Hinckley, David. "Art D' Lugoff." *On the Tracks*. No. 2, Fall/Winter 1993, 45.

———. "Rambling Jack Is Back: Pedigreed Folkie Giving First New York Show in a Decade." *New York Daily News*. 12 June 1996, Sec. Now, 40.

Hitchcock, H. Wiley, and Stanley Sadie, eds. *The New Grove Dictionary of American Music*. London: Macmillan Press, 1986.

Hoberman, J. "Mutiple Maniacs." *Village Voice*. 22 August 2000, 129.

Hoekstra, Dave. "Jack Elliott Rambles into Town." *Chicago Sun-Times*. 8 June 1985, 21.

———. "A Folkie's Land—Woody Guthrie Tribute Reveals Full Depth of Singer's Legacy." *Chicago Sun-Times*. 6 October 1996, Sec. Showcase, 21.

Hogg, Brian. "Bleecker & MacDougal." *Strange Things Are Happening*. Vol. 1, No. 7, Spring 1990, 20–23.

Holden, Stephen. "A Down-Home Ramblin' Persona from Brooklyn." *New York Times*. 16 August 2000, E5.

Horner, Marianne. "Ramblin' Jack Elliott—The Road Less Traveled." *Country Song Roundup*. Vol. 50, No. 445, 1998, 64.

Houlihan, Mary. "A Side She Never Saw." *Chicago Sun-Times*. 6 September 2000, Sec. 2, 44.

Houston Chronicle News Services. "Elliott Among 21 Recipients of Arts, Humanities Medals." *Houston Chronicle*. 7 November 1998, Sec. Houston, 9.

Hubbard, Zonweise, and Page Stegner. "Message from the West." *Caravan*. June/July 1959, 18.

Huehner, Dave. "A Jack Elliott Discography." *Autoharp*. Vol. 2, No. 6, 4 May 1962.

Hurlock, Frank. "Jack Elliott—Woodie Guthrie's Blues." *Jazz Music*. Vol. 8, No. 5, September/October 1957, 33.

Irvine, Andy. Notes to Woody Guthrie's "Seamen Three." *Folk Friends 2*. Folk-Freak FF 3003/4, 1981.

Irwin, Colin. "Living Legend." *Melody Maker*. 16 August 1980, 39, 42.

———. "Ramblin' Jack Elliott, South Coast, Red House Records RHR CD59." *Folk Roots*. No. 146–147, August/September 1995, 73.

Jahn, Mike. "Jack Elliott Sings Dylan and Guthrie in Return to City." *New York Times*. 15 November 1969, 44.

Jarvey, Paul. "Ramblin' Jack Elliott Wanted to Be a Cowboy." *Worcester Telegram & Gazette*. 10 October 1993, Sec. Datebook, 9.

Jay, Chris. "Jack of All Trades—Folk Legend Jack Elliott Still Rambles on." *Ventura County Reporter.* 5 May 2007. www.vcreporter.com/article .php?id=4609&IssueNum=122 (accessed 13 June 2007).

"J.D.K." "Ramblin' Jack Elliott—South Coast." *Living Blues.* No. 123, Vol. 26, No. 5, September/October 1995, 103.

Jinkins, Shirley. "Ramble on—Ramblin' Jack Elliott Lives Up to His Name." *Fort Worth Star-Telegram.* 29 March 1997, Sec. News, 4.

"J.M." "Folk Success." *Melody Maker.* 28 September 1963, 10.

"J.N.S." "Jack Elliott at His best." *Melody Maker.* 10 May 1958, 15.

Joex. "Ice House, Pasadena." *Variety.* No. 242, 13 April 1966, 67.

Johnson, Arne. "Interview with Ramblin' Jack Elliott." *Wander.* www.ventnatormag .com/oct/ramblingjack.htm (accessed 23 February 2002).

Jones, Max. "Dylan, Me, and the Legend of Woody Guthrie." *Melody Maker.* 29 May 1965, 6.

Jones, Max, and Sinclair Trail, eds. "Rosy View of Skiffle." *Melody Maker.* 6 April 1957, 5.

Jones, Wizz. "The Best of Ramblin' Jack Elliott—Talking Dustbowl, Big Beat WIK 86." *Folk Roots.* No. 74, August 1989, 42–43.

Jorgensen, Chris. "An Interview with Ramblin' Jack Elliott." *DISCcoveries.* Vol. 3, No. 10, October 1990, 98–99.

Joyce, Mike. "Gibson and Elliott." *Washington Post,* 17 September 1979.

Kagan, Shel. Notes to *Jack Elliott at the Second Fret—Recorded Live.* Prestige-International 13065, 1963.

Kahn, Ed. "Folk Song Discography." *Western Folklore.* Vol. 22, No. 4, October 1963, 297.

———. "Folk Song Discography." *Western Folklore.* Vol. 23, No. 3, July 1964, 224.

Karman, Pete. "Riverside Radio Broadcasts All-Day Folk Music Program. *New York Mirror.* 6 August 1961.

Kerouac, Jack. *Selected Letters, 1940–1956,* edited by Ann B. Charters. New York: Viking Press, 1995.

Kerrigan, Mike. "Cat Stevens." *Melody Maker.* 11 November 1972, 53.

Keyes, Bob. "Jack Elliott Rambles on about Life, Travels." *Argus Leader.* 17 November 1995.

King, Loren. "Candid View of Folk Legend, Flaws and All." *Boston Globe.* 25 August 2000, Sec. Living, C5.

Kishter, Lindsay. "Jack Elliott Shares Tales of Folk Music." *Carroll County Times.* 11 July 2004. www.carrollcounty.com/articles/2004/07/11/news/local_news/ news1.txt (accessed 17 July 2004).

Kivak, Joe. "Abandoned Love," in *Encounters with Bob Dylan,* edited by Tracey Johnson. San Francisco: Humble Press, 2000, 90–91.

Klein, Joe. *Woody Guthrie: A Life.* New York: Alfred A. Knopf, 1980.

Knemeyer, George. "Ramblin' Jack Elliott, Quiet Knight, Chicago." *Billboard.* No. 82, 2 May 1970, 28.

Korner, Alexis. "Skiffle or Piffle." *Melody Maker.* 28 July 1956, 5.

———. Notes to *Jack Elliot Sings.* 77 Records, 77 LP/1, 1957.

———. Notes to Kid Stuff: *Ramblin' Jack Elliott Sings Children's Songs by Woody Guthrie.* Columbia Records/Segment 8046, 1960.

———. "Folksong." *The Gramophone.* Vol. 37, No. 443, April 1960, 550.

———. "Folksong." *The Gramophone.* Vol. 39, No. 460, September 1961, 182.

Krogsgaard, Michael. *Positively Bob Dylan.* Ann Arbor: Popular Culture, Ink., 1991.

La Briola, John. "Ramblin' Man: Human Tumbleweed Ramblin' Jack Elliott Keeps on Rollin'." *Denver Westword.* www.westword.com/2005-06-02/music/ramblin-man/print (accessed 29 July 2007).

Laffler, William. "American Music." *Dallas Morning News.* 10 July 1976, Sec. F, 5.

Lang, Mamie. "A Bow to the West." *Tartan Umbrella.* www.tartan-umbrella .com/features_copy.asp?ID=a%20bow%20to%20the%20west (accessed 28 February 2005).

Lawless, Ray McKinley. *Folksingers & Folksongs in America.* New York: Duell, Sloane and Pearce, 1965.

Lehndorff, John. "Tales Told about an American Troubadour." *Daily Camera.* 2 December 1988.

Leichtling, Jerry. "Buddy Holly, Can You Spare a Dime?" *Village Voice.* 14 July 1975, 94.

Leitch, Donovan. *The Autobiography of Donovan: The Hurdy Gurdy Man.* New York: St. Martin's Press, 2005.

Liberatore, Paul. "Ramble on: Marin's Ramblin' Jack Elliott, a Folk Legend, Turns 75—and Has a New Album. *Marin Independent Journal.* www.marinij .com/portlet/article/html/fragments/print_article.jsp?articleId=4282404&siteI D=234 (accessed 22 February 2007).

Linde, Carsten. Notes to *Folk Friends 2.* FolkFreak 3003/04, 1981.

Lioce, Tony. "Jack's Had It—Ramblin' Jack Is 'Burned Out' from 30 Years of Folksinging." *Providence Journal-Bulletin.* 24 February 1984, Sec. Weekend, 1.

Littlewood, Joan. *Joan's Book: Joan Littlewood's Peculiar History as She Tells It.* London: Methuen, 1994.

Loftis, Jack. "Elliott Takes His Crowd through Variety of Tales." *Houston Chronicle.* 30 March 2000, Sec. Houston, 3.

Logsdon, Guy. Notes to *Woody Guthrie: Long Ways to Travel 1944–1949: The Unreleased Masters.* Smithsonian/Folkways Recordings, SF 40046, 1994.

———. *Woody Guthrie: A Biblio-Discography.* Self published, revised 6 December 1999 edition.

Lomax, Alan. "Skiffle: Why So Popular?" *Melody Maker.* 31 August 1957, 3.

———. "Skiffle: Where Is It Going?" *Melody Maker.* 7 September 1957, 5.

Lombardi, John. "The Truth Will Never Die!" *Rolling Stone.* 30 April 1970, 10.

Lonnigan, Donny. "Hylda Sims and the City Ramblers." *Skiffle Party.* No. 3, 9–13.

Lozaw, Tristram. "Travelin' Man Ramblin' Jack Elliott." *Boston Phoenix.* 20–27 July 2000. www.bostonphoenix.com/archive/music/00/07/20/JACK _ELLIOTT.html (accessed 29 January 2005).

———. "Ramblin' Man: Woody Guthrie Lives On." Guitar.com. 20 September 2001. http://ramblinjack.com/sk_092001.html (accessed 15 May 2008).

Lydon, Michael. "Sing Your Own Blues." *New York Times.* 19 April 1970, 101.

MacColl, Ewan. "Symposium: Topical Songs and Folksinging, 1965." *Sing Out!* Vol. 15, No. 4, September 1965, 12–13.

MacInnis, Craig. "Ramblin' Days Are Numbered for Jack Elliott." *Toronto Star.* 21 September 1988, Sec. Entertainment, D1.

Makin, Robert. "Good Times with Ramblin' Jack Elliott." *Courier-News.* 16 April 1998, E-9.

Mansfield, Brian. *Ring of Fire: A Tribute to Johnny Cash.* Nashville: Rutledge Hill Press, 2003.

Margolin, George. "Sidewalk Hootenanny." *People's Songs.* Vol. 2, No. 1–2, February/March 1947, 6.

Martin, Douglas. "Michael Stillman, 87, Founder of Innovative Record Company." *New York Times.* 27 April 2003, N48.

May, John. "Woody, Bob and Me." *Daily Telegraph.* 19 February 2005, Sec. Arts, 7.

Mayer, Ira. "Jack Elliott's Still Ramblin' On." *New York Post.* 17 May 1979, 34.

McConahey, Meg. "Travelin' Troubadour's Tales." *Santa Rosa Press Democrat.* 7 February, 1999, Sec. Q, 15.

McDevitt, Chas. *Skiffle: The Definitive Inside Story.* London: Robson Books, 1997.

McGlynn, Cindy. "Ramblin' Jack Talks Our Ear Off." *Eye.* 25 April 1996. www .eye.net/Arts/. . . ws/Live/1996/lv0425c.html (accessed 23 March 1997).

McGonigal, Mike. "Film—Aiyana Elliott." *New York Press.* Vol. 13, No. 33, 16–22 August 2000, 36, 38.

McGregor, Craig. "Pop: I'm Nobody's Best Friend." *New York Times.* 26 July 1970, 68.

McLaughlin, Jeff. "Gracenotes: The End of an Era at the Idler in Cambridge." *Boston Globe.* 27 September 1982, Sec. Arts/Films.

———. "After 16 Years, Folk Festivals and Crowd Return to Newport." *Boston Globe.* 4 August 1985, Sec. Metro, 67.

Meyer, Ira. "Record Reviews: A Tribute to Woody Guthrie." *Sing Out!* Vol. 21, No. 4, May/June 1972, 41.

Michaels, Mark. "The Ramblin's of Ramblin' Jack." *Off the Record.* 19 October 1988.

———. "Packed House Sees Ramblin' Man Put on Quite a Show." *Off the Record.* 26 October 1988.

Mischke, T. D. "U. Utah Phillips, Spider John Koerner, Ramblin' Jack Elliott—World Theatre, St. Paul, MN USA." *Folk Roots.* No. 74, August 1989, 57–60.

Mitchell, Rick. "Ramblin' Jack Still Rustles up Gems." *Houston Chronicle.* 8 April 1998, Sec. Houston, 1.

Mitgang, Herbert. "Some with Music." *New York Times.* 28 January 1962, 97.

Myrus, Donald. *Ballads, Blues and the Big Beat.* New York: Macmillan, 1966.

Nash, Alanna. "Ramblin' Jack Elliott, South Coast." *Stereo Review.* September 1995, 93.

Nelson, Paul, and Jon Pankake. "What's Happened to Jack Elliott?" *Sing.* October 1963, 77.

New York Times News Service. "Musician's to Remember Woody Guthrie." *Tulsa World*, 9 July 1992, Sec. Today, 5C.

Nichols, Brian. "A Breath of the Real Thing." *Jazz Journal.* No. 8, November 1955, 25.

Nicosia, Gerald. *Memory Babe: A Critical Biography of Jack Kerouac.* New York: Grove Press, 1983.

Ochs, Phil. "The Guthrie Legacy." *Mainstream.* Vol. 16, No. 8, August 1963, 35–39.

Okun, Milt, ed. *Something to Sing About.* New York: Macmillan, 1968, 83.

Oliver, Paul H. "Rambling Blues: The Saga of Derroll Adams and Jack Elliott." *Music Mirror.* Vol. 4, No. 5, 1957, 20–21.

———. "Hard Traveling—Continuing the Story of Jack Elliott and Derroll Adams." *Music Mirror.* Vol. 4, No. 6, 16–17.

Orsborne, Dod. "The Secret Adventures of Laundry Mark 45." *LIFE.* Vol. 25, No. 22, 29 November 1948, 104–120.

———. "The Phantom Islands." *LIFE.* Vol. 25, No. 23, 6 December 1948, 105–110.

Orshoski, Wes. "Renewed Fame for Folk Interpreter—Documentary, Medal, New Album Shed Light on Ramblin' Jack." *Billboard.* 25 November 2000.

Osborne, Hoyle. "Record Reviews." *Sing Out!* Vol. 19, No. 6, June/July 1970, 35–36.

Packer, Len. "Our Man in Philadelphia." *Hootenanny.* May 1964, 60.

Palmer, Robert. "The Pop Life—Friends of Phil Ochs Sing a Tribute to Him Tonight at Felt Forum." *New York Times.* 28 May 1976, 59.

———. "Friends Perform in Ochs Concert." *New York Times.* 30 May 1976, 41.

———. "Ramblin' Jack to the Rescue." *New York Times.* 9 August 1977, 28.

Pankake, Jon. "Country Music." *Sing Out!* Vol. 15, No. 4, September 1965, 90.

———. "Jon Pankake." In *Wasn't That a Time! Firsthand Accounts of the Folk Music Revival*, edited by Ronald D. Cohen. Metuchen/London: Scarecrow Press, 1995.

Pankake, Jon, and Paul Nelson. "Record Reviews: Jack Elliott: Ramblin' Jack Elliott in London." *Little Sandy Review*. No. 4, April 1960, 7–8.

———. "Record Reviews" (*Jack Takes the Floor, Woody Guthrie's Blues, and the Rambling Boys*). *Little Sandy Review*. No. 2, 1960, 12–16.

———. "Record Reviews: Ramblin' Jack Elliott Sings Songs by Woody Guthrie and Jimmie Rodgers." *Little Sandy Review*. No. 13, 37–39.

———. "Record Reviews: Jack Elliott Sings the Songs of Woody Guthrie." *Little Sandy Review*. No. 16, 29–33.

———. "A Lot of Jack." *Little Sandy Review*. No. 28, 26–27.

Pareles, Jon. "Woody Guthrie: Hard Travelin'." *New York Times*. 7 March 1984, C22.

Patterson, Rob. "Guthrie Imitator Jack Elliott Has Grown into an American Original—and One of the . . . Monsters." *Austin-American Statesman*. 9 April 1998, Sec. 40, 10.

———. "Reason to Roam—at 67, Ramblin' Jack Elliott Reclaims—Temporarily—the Urge to Wander." *Houston Press*. 9 April 1998.

Peabody, Dave. "The Banjo Man." *Folk Roots*. December 1990, 16–21.

Pellecchia, Michael. "Paris on the Trinity—Ministers from Many Worlds Drop in at the Dog." *Fort Worth Weekly*. 12 May 2004. www.fwweekly/content .asp?article=1151 (accessed 16 October 2007).

Peralta, Eyder. "Folk Singer Elliot Burns, Sometimes." *Florida Times-Union*. 21 May 2004. http://jacksonville.com/tu-online/stories/052104/met_15664841 .shtml (accessed 25 May 2004).

Perry, Mike. "On the Road—Ramblin' Jack Elliott Lives Up to His Nickname—Except When the Conversation Turns to Music." *No Depression*. No. 14, March/April 1998, 58–63.

Peterson, Susan. "Ramblin' Jack Elliott/Kajsa Ohman, McCabes Guitar Shop, Santa Monica, Calif." *Billboard*. Vol. 89, 26 February 1977, 39–44.

Phine, Ken. "For the Record." *Sing*. Vol. 6, No. 2, October 1961, 16.

Piccoli, Sean. "Daughter Documents the Life of Folk-Singer Father." *Sun-Sentinel*. 29 September 2000, 7.

Pilgrim, John. "Derroll Adams." *Independent*. 22 March 2000, 51.

"Pine." "Village Gaslight, N.Y." *Variety*. No. 256, 12 November 1969, 75.

Poe, Randy. "Ramblin' Jack Elliott: An American Minstrel." *Sing Out!* Fall 2001, 34–43.

poet, j. "A Ramblin' Kinda Guy." *San Francisco Chronicle*. 1 October, 2006, PK-46.

Preston, Denis. "Oh, Those Intellectuals!" *Melody Maker*. 21 May 1960, 8.

Preston, Dennis Lee. "Echos of Past Will Fill the Air at Folk Festival." *Philadelphia Inquirer*. 24 August 1984, F18.

"Random Notes." *Rolling Stone*. No. 132, 12 April 1973, 5.

———. *Rolling Stone*. No. 138, 5 July 1973, 5.

———. *Rolling Stone*. No. 162, 6 June 1974, 28.

————. *Rolling Stone*. No. 267, 15 June 1978, 61–62.

Reed, James. "Elliott Isn't Done with His Ramblin'." *Boston Globe*. 11 May 2006, Sec. Style/Arts, E8.

————. "Ramblin' Jack Elliott, Aged to Perfection: 'I Stand Alone' Stands with Folk Legend's Best." *Boston Globe*. 9 July 2006, Sec. Arts/Entertainment, N5.

Reimer, R. E. "Ramblin' Jack Empties Weathered Bag of Classics." *Newport (R.I.) Daily News*. 10 December 1984, 6.

Reineke, Hank. "Ramblin' Jack Elliott: See How All Those Stories Get Twisted?" *Aquarian Arts Weekly*. 17 April 1985, 10–11.

————. "America's Love Affair with Fascism and What It Did to Our Poets and Singers—From the 50s On (Part One)." *Soho Arts Weekly*. 9 October 1985, 32–36.

————. "America's Love Affair with Fascism and What It Did to Our Poets and Singers—From the 50s On (Part Two)." *Soho Arts Weekly*. 16 October 1985, 34–37.

————. "Dave Van Ronk: From the '50s and the Beats, to the '60s and Dylan and Ochs, Until Now." *Downtown*. No. 220, 28 November 1990, 1, 35–38.

Remz, Jeffery B. "Jack Rambles on." *Country Standard Time*. 11 May 1996.

Renbourn, John. "Born of Skiffle and Blues." *Frets*. Vol. 10, No. 6, June 1988, 50–52.

Robbin, Ed. *Woody Guthrie and Me*. Berkeley, CA: Lancaster-Miller Publishers, 1979.

Robinson, Bruce. "Telling Tall Tales—Ramblin' Jack Elliott's Awfully Big Adventures." *Sonoma Independent*. 5–11 December 1996. www.metroactive .c...12.05.96/music-9649.html (accessed 2 May 1997).

Rockwell, John. "Jack Elliott Dips Anew into Woody Guthrie Era." *New York Times*. 1 October 1973, 45.

————. "Jack Elliott Sings Winningly at Club." *New York Times*. 26 September 1975, 23.

————. "Bob Dylan Tour Lands on Plymouth Rock First." *New York Times*. 1 November 1975, 60.

————. "Folk-Rock Stars Give a Concert at Jersey Prison." *New York Times*. 8 December 1975, 35.

Rogovoy, Seth. "The Legend of Ramblin' Jack." *Berkshire Eagle*. 11 September 2003. www.berkshiresweek.com/091103/?id=article05 (accessed 29 January 2005).

Rolland, David. "Ramblin' Jack Elliott of Marshall Wins Grammy." *The Light*. 7 March 1996. http://pomo.nbn.com/prl/stories/mar7/jack.html (accessed 2 March 1997).

Rose, Fred. "Back Pages: New York. Dylan: Knocking on Hurricane's Cell." *Circus*. No. 128, 2 March 1976, 52.

Ross, Joe. "Ramblin' with Jack." *Folk Roots*. January/February 1993, 40–41, 43.

———. "Ramblin' with Jack Elliott." *Acoustic Musician.* Vol. 2, No. 12, March/ April 1996, 26–28.

Ross, Stuart. "Recordings Go A-Ramblin'." *The Living Tradition.* No. 61, March/ April 2005, 24–26.

Rothgery, Jim. "Ramblin' Jack Elliott/Bruce Pratt, Wilbert's, April 24." *Scene.* Undated.

Rotolo, Suze. *A Freewheelin' Time: A Memoir of Greenwich Village in the Sixties.* New York: Broadway, 2008.

Roxon, Lillian. *Lillian Roxon's Rock Encyclopedia.* New York: Grossett & Dunlap, 1969.

———. "The Guthrie Concert." *Sydney Morning Herald* in *Bob Dylan: A Retrospective,* edited by Craig McGregor. New York: William Morrow, 1972.

Rubin, Sylvia. "Rising Stars: Six Lesser-Known Bay Area Artists in the Spotlight with Grammy Nominations." *San Francisco Chronicle.* 25 February 1996, Sec. Sunday Datebook, 28.

———. "Reluctant Ramblin' Jack Went Back into the Studio: Best Traditional Folk Album 'South Coast.'" *San Francisco Chronicle.* 25 February 1996, Sec. Sunday Datebook, 28.

Ryan, Tim. "Ramblin' Through Town." *Honolulu Star-Bulletin.* 6 June 1996. http://starbulletin.com/. . . /06/features/story1.html (accessed 2 March 1997).

Samson, Chris. "Ramblin' Along with a Little Help from His Friends." *Petaluma Argus-Courier.* 3 April 1998. http://home.comcast.net/~2samsons/Chris/Writing/ Musicians/elliott.html (accessed 26 December 2005).

Sandberg, Larry, and Dick Weissman. *The Folk Music Sourcebook.* New York: Alfred A. Knopf, 1976.

Santelli, Robert, and Emily Davidson, eds. *Hard Travelin'—The Life and Legacy of Woody Guthrie.* Hanover, NH and London: Wesleyan University Press, 1999.

Santosuosso, Ernie. "Weekend: City Eyes Two Sites for Summer Concerts." *Boston Globe.* 17 February 1984, Sec. Arts/Films.

———. "Newport Folk and Jazz Lineups Announced." *Boston Globe.* 19 June 1985, Sec. Arts/Films, 65.

Sarlin, Bob. *Turn It Up! I Can't Hear the Words; The Best of the New Singer-Songwriters.* New York: Simon and Schuster, 1973.

Scaduto, Anthony. *Bob Dylan: An Intimate Biography.* New York: Grosset and Dunlap, 1971.

Scanlan, Larry. "Ramblin' Jack—The Performer Peaks." Unknown. 24 December 1979.

Schumacher, Michael. *There but for Fortune: The Life of Phil Ochs.* New York: Hyperion Books, 1996.

Seeger, Pete. "Johnny Appleseed, Jr." *Sing Out!* Vol. 9, No. 3, Winter 1959/1960, 48–49.

———. "Johnny Appleseed, Jr." *Sing Out!* Vol. 14, No. 1, February/March 1964, 71.

Seigal, Buddy. "Return Ticket: Folk Star Ramblin' Jack Elliott Has the Words and the Tunes." *San Diego Union-Tribune.* 13 April 2000, Sec. Night & Day, 31.

———. "Yakkity Yak—Ramblin' Jack Talks Back." *OC Weekly.* 9–15 March 2001. www.ocweekly.com/printme.php?&eid=22993 (accessed 29 January 2005).

Shapiro, Harry. *Alexis Korner: The Biography.* London: Bloomsbury, 1996.

Shelley, June. *Even When It Was Bad . . . It Was Good.* Xlibris Corporation, 2000.

Shelton, Robert. "Wandering Minstrel Is in Town." *New York Times.* 25 July 1961, 19.

———. "Folk Music Heard on 12-Hour Show." *New York Times.* 31 July 1961, 15.

———. (Uncredited). "Real Hung Up." *Newsweek.* 14 August 1961, 47.

———. "Hootenanny Held at Carnegie Hall." *New York Times.* 18 September 1961, 35.

———. "Americana for the Tyro." *New York Times.* 1 October 1961, X16.

———. "Bluegrass Music by Earl Scruggs." *New York Times.* 4 December 1961, 49.

———. "Hyannis Welcomes Folk Music." *New York Times.* 28 July 1962, 11.

———. "Queens College Folk Festival Begins on an Authentic Note." *New York Times.* 7 April 1963, 83.

———. "Fad to Staple—Disks Reflect 'Arrival' of Folk Music as Part of Country's Popular Arts." *New York Times.* 28 April 1963, 144.

———. "Fused Folk Arts." *New York Times.* 27 October, 1963, 130.

———. "First Edition of 'Singing Paper' Is Issued Hot Off the Guitars." *New York Times.* 2 November 1964, 59.

———. "Guthrie Honored by Folk Concert." *New York Times.* 19 April 1965, 38.

———. "Folk Bill Given by Jack Elliott." *New York Times.* 1 May 1965, 18.

———. "Newport Starts Its Festival Season." *New York Times,* 22 July, 1966, 20.

———. "Tribute to the Life and Legend of Woody Guthrie." *New York Times.* 22 January 1968, 31.

———. "Separating Pop from Pap." *New York Times.* 26 May 1968, D36.

———. "Eighth Folk Fete Opens in Newport." *New York Times.* 25 July 1968, 29.

———. *No Direction Home—The Life and Music of Bob Dylan.* New York: Beech Tree Books, 1986.

———. (Ian Woodward, ed.) "The Robert Shelton Minnesota Transcripts—Jon Pankake." *ISIS.* No. 88, December 1999/January 2000, 21–23.

———. (Ian Woodward, ed.) "The Robert Shelton Minnesota Transcripts—Paul Nelson Part One." *ISIS.* No. 90, April/May 2000, 21–23.

———. (Ian Woodward, ed.) "The Robert Shelton Minnesota Transcripts—Paul Nelson Part Two." *ISIS*. No. 91, June/July 2000, 23–25.

Shelton, Robert, and Earl Robinson. *Young Folk Song Book*. New York: Simon and Schuster, 1963.

Shepard, Sam. *Rolling Thunder Logbook*. New York: Penguin Books, 1978.

Sheridan, Alan. "Ramblin' Jack Has His Audience in Raptures." *Jersey Evening Post*. 14 August 1981, 13.

Sherman, Michael. "Ramblin' Jack Elliott on Ash Grove Stage." *Los Angeles Times*. 26 February 1970, C20.

Sia, Joseph. "Eric Von Schmidt—An Exclusive 'On the Tracks' Interview." *On the Tracks*. No. 4, Fall 1994, 20–25.

Silber, Irwin. "They're All Talking about the Little Sandy Review." *Sing Out!* October/November 1960, 26–27.

———. "Ewan MacColl: Folksinger of the Industrial Age." *Sing Out!* Vol. 9, No. 3, Winter 1959/1960, 7–9.

Silberman, Steve. "An Egg Thief in Cyberspace: An Interview with David Crosby." *Goldmine*. Vol. 21, No. 14, 7 July 1995.

Silverstein, Shel. Notes to *Jack Elliott*. Vanguard VRS-9151, 1964.

Simmons, Michael John. "Ramblin' Jack Elliott: American Folk Troubadour's Early Recordings Unearthed across the Pond." *Acoustic Guitar*. Vol. 15, May 2005, 18.

Sloman, Larry. *On the Road with Bob Dylan*. New York: Bantam Books, 1978.

Smith, Hazel. "Jack's Friends." *Country Music*. July/August 1998, 7.

Smith, Jay. "City Folk." *Sing Out!* January 1964, 87–89.

———. "Records in Review." *Sing Out!* Vol. 15, No. 3, July 1965, 79, 81.

Smith, Jeff. "For Folk Fans." *Melody Maker*. 14 January 1961.

Smith, Richard C. "Woody Guthrie Today." *Melody Maker*. 11 June 1960, 5.

———. "Woody Guthrie Today" (Part 2). *Melody Maker*. 18 June 1960, 4.

Sounes, Howard. *Down the Highway—The Life of Bob Dylan*. New York: Grove Press, 2001.

Spencer, Peter. "Folk Legend Elliott Really Does Ramble." *Star-Ledger*. 27 October 2000, 18.

Spitz, Bob. *Dylan—A Biography*. New York: McGraw-Hill, 1989.

"S.T." "Record Reviews—Jack Elliott (8in. LP)." *Jazz Journal*. December 1956, 26.

Stambler, Irwin, and Grelun Landon. *The Encyclopedia of Folk, Country & Western Music*. New York: St. Martin's Press, 1984.

Stanton, C. P. "Special Report: British Record Scene, No. 1 The Topic Label." *Caravan*. October/November 1958, 11–12, 14.

Stark, Jeff. "Hard Travelin'—Ramblin' Jack Elliott Has a Few More Stories to Tell." *Dallas Observer*. 9–15 April 1998.

Sterling, Guy. "How Friends and Music Eased a Folk Legend's Pain." *Sunday Star Ledger*. 24 July 2005, Sec. Four, 1, 8.

Stewart, Perry. "Ramblin' to Denton—Music Icon Jack Elliott Defies Catego-
ries—and Hyphenation." *Fort Worth Star-Telegram*. 20 February 2004, 19S.

Stolder, Steven. "Traveling Back with Ramblin' Jack Elliott—The Myth and
Reality of an American Folk Legend." *NARAS Inforum*. 1996. www.grammy
.com/features/jackelliot.html (accessed 22 May 1997).

Streissguth, Michael. *Johnny Cash—The Biography*. Cambridge, MA: DaCapo
Press, 2006.

Sullivan, Denise. "Ramblin' Jack Elliott's the Long Ride." *San Francisco Chronicle*.
15 September 1999. www.sfweekly.com/issues/1999-09-15/record2html (accessed 4 July 2001).

———. *Rip It Up! Rock & Roll Rulebreakers*. San Francisco: Backbeat Books,
2001.

Sullivan, James. "Ramblin' Jack's Friends Join Him on CD." *San Francisco Chronicle*. 15–21 March 1998, Sec. Datebook, 44.

———. "A Daughter's Devotion." *San Francisco Chronicle*. 29 August 2000, Sec.
Daily Datebook, C1.

Surowicz, Tom. "Return of Troubadour Ramblin' Jack Elliott—Hard Travelin'."
Twin Cities Reader. 26 April/2 May 1989.

Swain, Greg. "Derroll Adams, 65th Birthday Concert, Kotrijk, Belgium." *Folk
Roots*. No. 90, December 1990, 47–48.

Sylvester, Bruce. "Talk Talk: Ramblin' Jack Elliott." *Goldmine*. Vol. 23, No. 14,
Issue No. 442, 4 July 1997, 14–15.

Szilagyi, Pete. "Candles to Cheer a Cowboy—Jerry Jeff Walker Blows Them
Out at Rambling Concert." *Austin-American Statesman*. 18 March 1990, Sec.
City/State, B2.

Theesssink, Hans. "The Making of the CD." In *Banjoman: A Tribute to Derroll
Adams*. Rising Son Records RSR 2102-2, 2002.

Thornton, Stuart. "Jacked Up—The Ramblin' Grammy Winner Is Eager to Make
Another Pilgrimage to Big Sur." *Monterey County Weekly*. 25 September 2008.
www.montereycountyweekly.com/archives/2008/2008-Sep-25/the-ramblin-
grammy-. . . (accessed 25 September 2008).

Throckmorton, Peter. "Thirty-Three Centuries Under the Sea." *National Geographic*. Vol. 117, No. 5, May 1960, 682–703.

Thurston, Dwight. "Grammy Winner Ramblin' Jack Elliott to Perform at Roar-
ing Brook Nature Center." *Canton Voice*. 2–16 May 1996.

Tilling, Robert. *Oh, What a Beautiful City: A Tribute to the Reverend Gary Davis
1896–1972*. Jersey Islands, UK: Paul Mill Press, 1992.

Tompkins, J. H. "Dreaming Dreams, Talkin' Blues—Folk Legend Ramblin' Jack
Elliott Has Some Stories to Tell." *San Francisco Bay Guardian*. 22 August 2001,
39.

Traum, Artie. "When Legends Meet: Rambling Jack and the Master of Meditation." *Oak Report: A Quarterly Journal on Music & Musicians*. Vol. 2, No. 1,
1981.

Turner, Steve. *The Man Called Cash—The Life, Love and Faith of an American Legend*. Nashville: W Publishing Group, 2004.

Ulrichs, Wieland. "Dinsaurier des Folksongs? Ramblin' Jack uber Gott, Woody & Die Welt." *Musikblatt* (Germany). June 1991, 26–27.

Uncredited. "Theatre Royal, Stratford—The Big Rock Candy Mountain by Alan Lomax." *Times* (London). 28 December 1955, 5.

———. "Capsule Reviews." *Melody Maker*. 5 March 1958, 15.

———. "Gospel and Folk." *Melody Maker: Spring 1958 LP Supplement*. 5 April 1958, ii.

———. "Discussion—Titles from Topic." *Sing*. October 1958, 73.

———. "Blues and Folksong." *Melody Maker Supplement*. 29 August 1959, III.

———. "What's On and Who's Singing." *Sing*. Vol. 5, No. 1, September 1959, 7.

———. "Josh White—Spellbinder." *Melody Maker*. 16 April 1960, 10.

———. "Folk and Blues." *Melody Maker*. 4 February 1961.

———. "Jack Elliot Joins Ranks of 'Hoot' & Holler Boys in Ban on ABC-TV Show." *Variety*. 24 April 1963, 26.

———. "Jack Elliott, the Greenbriar Boys, Judy Roderick in Concert, Town Hall, January 25, 1964." *Tune Up*. Vol. 2, No. 2, December 1963.

———. "Ramblin' Jack in Fine Form—and Dylan in Disguise." *Melody Maker*. 17 July 1965, 11.

———. "From the Record Review Editor: Woody Guthrie." *Journal of American Folklore*. April/June 1967, 204.

———. "Bull Durham Sacks and Railroad Tracks." *Rolling Stone*. No. 60, 11 June 1970, 50.

———. "Pro's Reply." *Guitar Player*. Vol. 8, No. 10, October 1974, 6.

———. "Nights at the End." *New Yorker*. No. 51, 28 July 1975, 19–20.

———. "Dylan, Baez Open Tour." *Dallas Morning News*. 4 November 1975, Sec. A, 10.

———. "Ramblin' Jack Elliott." *Daily Times* (Anchorage, AK). 11 January 1981.

———. "Newport Folk Festival Returns after 16 Year Absence." *Atlanta Journal-Constitution*. 4 August 1985, A23.

———. "Benefit Concert to Aid Indians." *San Francisco Chronicle*. 5 October 1985, 36.

———. "Rock Hall of Fame Ceremonies Fail to Unite Beatles." *Star Tribune*. 21 January 1988, Sec. News, 07A.

———. "Rock and Roll Hall of Fame." *Rolling Stone*. No. 521, 10 March 1988, 8–17, 97.

———. "Ramblin' Jack Elliott, South Coast, Red House RHR CD 59." *Living Blues*. September/October 1995.

———. "Isaak Steals the Show at Bammies: He Wins Five Awards, including Top Musician." *San Jose Mercury News*, 10 March 1996, 11.

———. "Talking With . . . Ramblin' Jack Elliott: Just the Two of Us." *People Weekly.* Vol. 49, No. 12, 30 March 1998, 28.

Unterberger, Richie. *Turn! Turn! Turn! The 60s Folk-Rock Revolution.* San Francisco: Backbeat Books, 2002.

Van Matre, Lynn. "Music: Legendary Rambler." *Chicago Tribune.* 10 April 1970, C16.

———. "A Joyous Celebration." *Chicago Tribune.* 16 October 1972, B18.

Van Schaeren, Bart. "Bluegrass from Across the Pond: American Music Made in Europe." *Pickin'.* July 1976, 50–52.

Vassal, Jacques. *Electric Children.* New York: Taplinger Publishing Company, 1976.

Vites, Pablo. "Joe Henry Goes Electric." *Buscadero.* No. 143, 1993, 16.

———. "Ramblin' Jack Elliott." *On the Tracks.* Spring 1995, 27–29.

Von Schmidt, Eric, and Jim Rooney. *Baby, Let Me Follow You Down: The Illustrated Story of the Cambridge Folk Years.* Amherst: University of Massachusetts Press, 1995.

Walker, Jerry Jeff. *Gypsy Songman.* Emeryville, CA: Woodford Press, 1999.

Wearing, J. P. *The London Stage, 1950–1959, A Calendar of Plays and Players, Vol. 1, 1950–1957.* Metuchen, NJ and London: Scarecrow Press, 1993.

Weideman, Paul. "At Thirsty Ear—Ramblin' Jack." *Santa Fe New Mexican.* 30 August 2002, P42.

Weiner, Milt. "Milt's Meandering: Where Is Ramblin' Jack?" *Marin Scope.* 11–17 October 1988.

Weintraub, Boris. "Jack Elliot, for 25 Years A-Ramblin'." *Washington Star.* 17 September 1979.

Weitzman, Elizabeth. "Tryin' to Catch Dad's Drift: 'Ballad' Director Hit the Road to Get to Know Her Folkie Father." *New York Daily News.* 16 August 2000, 44.

West, Hollie I. "Preview: Boboquivari." *Washington Post.* 4 August 1971, B6.

Wickham, Andy. "About Our Talky Cowboy Friend, Ramblin' Jack Elliott."

———. (Uncredited). "Rambling Jack Elliott: The Man Who Ran from the City." *Country-Western Stars.* Vol. 1, No. 4, July 1970, 46–49.

Wilgus, D. K. "Record Reviews." *Journal of American Folklore.* April/June 1962, 181–182.

———. "Record Reviews." *Journal of American Folklore.* Vol. 77, No. 306, October/December 1964, 370–371.

———. "Records in Review." *Journal of American Folklore.* October/December 1966, 634.

Wilson, Sue. "Ramblin' Jack Elliott—Pleasance Cabaret Bar, Edinburgh." *The Scotsman.* 18 February 2005. http://news.scotsman.com/features.cfm?id=185072005 (accessed 19 February 2005).

Winfrey, Lee. "In Woody's Image . . . and Beyond." *Miami Herald Sunday Magazine.* 18 April 1965, 52.

Winter, Eric. "DISCussion." *Sing.* Vol. 6, No. 4, December 1961, 39.
———. "Focus on Folk." *Melody Maker.* 31 August 1963, 16.
———. "Talking Woody Guthrie" (Record Review). *Sing.* November/December 1963, 93.
Wire Reports. "Newport Folk Festival Returns after 16-Year Absence." *Atlanta Journal and Atlanta Constitution.* 4 August 1985, A23.
Woerner, Gail. *Fearless Funnymen: The History of the Rodeo Clown.* Austin: Eakin Press, 1993.
Wolfe, Charles, and Kip Lornell. *The Life & Legend of Leadbelly.* New York: HarperCollins, 1992.
Woliver, Robbie. *Bringing It All Back Home.* New York: Pantheon Books, 1986.
Woods, George A. "Children's Fare." *New York Times.* 17 November 1963, X25.
Woodward, Ian. "The Wicked Messenger #3743." *ISIS.* No. 74, August 1997, 15.
———. "The Robert Shelton Minnesota Transcripts: Part 6—Commentary and Interlude." *ISIS.* No. 93, October/November 2000, 23–24.
Yaryan, Bill. "Jack Elliott." *Folk Scene.* No. 10, August 1965, 3–4.
———. "Ramblin' Jack Elliott." *Sing Out!* Vol. 15, No. 5, November 1965, 24–28.
———. "Derroll Adams: Banjo Pickin' Expatriate." *Sing Out!* December/January 1967, 29–33.
———. Notes to *Derroll Adams: Portland Town.* Ace of Clubs SCL 1227, 1967.
Yates, Janelle. *Woody Guthrie—American Balladeer.* Staten Island, NY: Ward Hill Press, 1995.
Young, Israel G. "Frets and Frails." *Sing Out!* Winter 1959/1960, 34.
———. "Frets and Frails." *Sing Out!* February/March 1961, 84, 86.
———. "Frets and Frails." *Sing Out!* April/May 1961, 47.
———. "Frets and Frails." *Sing Out!* October/November 1961, 51.
———. "Frets and Frails." *Sing Out!* February/March 1962, 53.
———. "Frets and Frails." *Sing Out!* April/May 1962, 45, 47.
———. "Frets and Frails." *Sing Out!* April/May 1963, 59.
———. "Frets and Frails." *Sing Out!* October/November 1963, 63.
———. "Frets and Frails." *Sing Out!* May 1965, 77.
———. "Frets and Frails." *Sing Out!* July 1965, 73–75.
———. "Israel Young's Notebook." *Sing Out!* Vol. 18, No. 2, June/July 1968, 47.
———. "Israel Young's Notebook." *Sing Out!* Vol. 18, No. 3, August/September 1968, 11–12.
———. (Josh Dunson, ed.) "Moses Asch: Twentieth Century Man, Part II." *Sing Out!* Vol. 26, No. 2, 1977, 25–26.
Young, Izzy. "The Izzy Young Notebooks." *The Telegraph.* No. 56, Winter 1997, 59–70.

Yurchenco, Henrietta. "Survey of Children's Songs." *Sing Out!* Summer 1963, 55.

———. *A Mighty Hard Road—The Woody Guthrie Story.* New York: McGraw-Hill, 1970.

Index

About the Author

Hank Reineke has written about folk, blues, and country music for such publications as the *Aquarian Arts Weekly*, *Soho Arts Weekly*, *Downtown*, *East Coast Rocker*, *Blues Revue*, *On the Tracks*, *ISIS*, and *The Bridge*. He was a research consultant on Aiyana Elliott's award-winning documentary film *The Ballad of Ramblin' Jack*. Hank resides in New Jersey with his wife, Christa, and their two daughters, Emily and Sara. This is his first book.

0 1341 1273782 7